KT-231-854

Fundamentals of Cognition

MARK H. ASHCRAFT

Cleveland State University

FUNDAMENTALS OF COGNITION

An imprint of Addison Wesley Longman, Inc.

New York • Reading, Massachusetts • Menlo Park, California • Harlow, England
Don Mills, Ontario • Sydney • Mexico City • Madrid • Amsterdam

Editor-in-Chief: Priscilla McGeehon
Acquisitions Editor: Eric Stano
Associate Editor: Heide Chavez
Supplements Editor: Cyndy Taylor
Marketing Manager: Jay O'Callaghan
Project Editors: Ann P. Kearns and Donna DeBenedictis
Text Designer: A Good Thing, Inc.
Cover Designer: Kay Petronio
Cover Illustration: Photo Disc, Inc.
Design Manager: Heather Peres
Art Studio: A Good Thing, Inc.
Photo Researcher: Mira Schachne
Production Manager: Alexandra Odulak
Desktop Coordinator: Joanne Del Ben
Manufacturing Manager: Hilda Koparanian
Electronic Page Makeup: A Good Thing, Inc.
Printer and Binder: The Maple-Vail Book Manufacturing Group
Cover Printer: Phoenix Color Corp.

Library of Congress Cataloging-in-Publication Data
Ashcraft, Mark H.
Fundamentals of cognition / Mark H. Ashcraft.
p. cm.
Includes bibliographical references (p. 433) and index.
ISBN 0-321-01207-0
(hardcover)
1. Cognition. I. Title.
BF311.A727 1998
153—dc21 97-29458
CIP

Please visit our website at http://longman.awl.com

ISBN 0-321-01207-0

3 4 5 6 7 8 9 10—MA—00 99

To the three who make it all worthwhile:

Mary Helen Homerin Ashcraft

Jordan Mark Ashcraft

Laura Catherine Ashcraft

Brief Contents

Detailed Contents

PREFACE

To the Student

I've tried to write a book that you'll read. That's a strange way to start a preface, isn't it? Of course you'll read the book, you think to yourself—after all, it's assigned for the course you're taking, whether it's called Cognitive Psychology, Memory and Cognition, The Psychology of Thought, or some other similar title. But you also have to admit that you've tried to read books that don't appeal to you, books that dwell on seemingly trivial detail, books that don't engage your interest—books that put you to sleep, in other words. However scholarly and informative such books may be, the fact that you have to force yourself to read them defeats the whole purpose. You won't learn as much, and you may decide that the entire topic is one you'd rather avoid than explore further.

I truly hope you won't have that kind of problem with this book. I'm hoping that you'll be able to return to the book chapter after chapter with the same enthusiasm you started with—or even more. And I'd like you to finish the book as enthusiastic about memory and cognition as professionals in the field are—after all, what could be more interesting than studying how people think, how the mind works?

I've incorporated several features in the book that should help you study and learn the material.

- Each major section of a chapter begins with a Preview, which lists important ideas and topics, and ends with a numbered Summary of the main points. Try to get in the habit of using these Previews and Summaries as a way of monitoring your understanding.
- Throughout each chapter, the important terms are printed in boldface, all of which appear in the Glossary in the back. I sometimes think that books only have glossaries so that professors will select the book for their classes—in other words, that students never use the glossary. You should, however. For instance, my students tell me that an

excellent way to study for the final exam is to go through the glossary, testing each other on definitions, then remembering the context and main points related to the term, and if possible naming a researcher or two who has worked on that topic.

- Suggested Readings also appear at the end of each chapter. Use these to follow up on topics you read about in that chapter, or to begin the library work for a term paper or project in the course.
- Symbols appear throughout the book, in pairs, to help you find the figure, table, or supplementary material that goes along with the text. Equally important, I think, is looking at a figure or table and being able to find the place in the text that discusses the figure. So next to the relevant sentence you'll see a symbol like the one in the margin. The figure, table, photo, or supplementary "box" that accompanies the text has the same symbol on it.

★

WHAT'S THIS WWW STUFF ANYWAY

WWW stands for World Wide Web, the massive collection of information that "lives" on the Internet, the network of interconnected computers across the world. You access the Web through a special computer account, with special software. Once you're on it, you use a program such as Netscape Navigator® or Internet Explorer® to "surf" or "go to" different places on the Web. "Places" can be an individual home page, a university, a library, a business, an art museum, and so forth. If you know the exact place you want to go, "Open" that place by typing in its URL address (Open is one of the video buttons at the top of your screen). If you just want to find out what information is on the Web about a particular topic, or you don't know the specific address, click on Network Search, type in the topic, and then sit back while the software magically compiles a list of places that match your search word. Be careful! A general word like "psychology" will match thousands and thousands of places, and you'll spend all day sifting through the listings. Make your search words as specific as possible. Try "human memory," "neuroanatomy," and "cognitive science," just for starters.

Almost every page you read on the WWW will have one or more "links," words or phrases that appear in a different color on your screen. Click on one of these and you "go" to the WWW address stored with that link. The amazing thing about the Web is that distance and location don't really matter—you can be on a publisher's home page (e.g., http://longman.awl.com), which is somewhat like being "at" the publishing house (in the virtual sense!). Then you can click on a link that puts you in Paris, and from there a link to Sydney, and from there to Fargo. To get going in finding links to everything in the whole wide world, try a standard search engine like Lycos, or a standard "starting point" (something like the WWWhole Earth Catalog) like http://www.yahoo.com.

It is one of my goals to have a WWW home page for the book, a place you can go on the Internet to find additional information about cognition. Please visit http://longman.awl.com for the latest news on this book and any related Web site. There's a phenomenal amount of information on the World Wide Web, easily accessible from your Internet account. If your school provides you with access to the Net, get on and surf! If it doesn't, contact your Computer Center or a commercial provider to find out how to gain access to this incredible source. You'll find a lot of information on the Net that's useful to you for this class, and for other purposes too. Descriptions of graduate programs, visual illusions, medical images of the brain, sightseeing tours of Paris—all of these and more are at your fingertips.

Finally, I'd be delighted to receive your comments and suggestions, both about the book and about the information you find on the WWW. Write to me at one of the addresses listed at the end of this preface.

To the Instructor

This book is directed primarily toward undergraduates at the junior/senior level who are probably taking their first basic course in memory and cognition, or any other student who needs an introduction to the major areas of research on this topic. The book is deliberately briefer than many current texts in cognition, my own Human Memory and Cognition included. The reason for this is that while large, comprehensive treatments of memory and cognition have a definite place in the college (and graduate) curriculum, so do less encyclopedic, more approachable texts that provide a solid foundation in the area. As the area of cognition becomes larger and larger, we need to do a better job of capturing our students' interest in the whole field before we start teaching them the intricacies of subspecialties. And we can't expect our students to become interested in one or another subspecialty until they're interested in the field as a whole.

Many instructors will want supplementary information, including in-class demonstrations, ideas for discussions, and test items, to help them teach the course. An Instructor's Manual/Test Bank accompanies this text, and includes something I find invaluable when I teach the course—a clear, full-size copy of figures and illustrations, suitable for photocopying onto overhead transparencies. When students focus their attention on the overhead display, rather than toward their individual copies of the text, they remain engaged in the ongoing class activity. And for those students who still struggle to interpret graphic displays, nothing works as well as showing the graph on the overhead projector and talking them through it (see also the in-depth tutorial on understanding graphs in Chapter 1).

Although new material and new treatments have been included in the present book, many sections are reworkings of material in my Human Memory and Cognition (2/e, 1994), available through your local Addison Wesley Longman representative. For instructors new to the area of memory and cognition, that larger book (or any of several comprehensive texts now on the market) will have more detailed explanations and broader coverage of areas that can be consulted for additional information. Those who have taught the course several times usually have their own set of preferred topics, and may simply want a book that provides foundation information to prepare students for more advanced topics. I believe that the relatively standard organization of this book should facilitate that kind of use.

It's my hope that your students—and you—will enjoy reading this book, making it easier for the students to learn, and more enjoyable for you to teach. I'm always grateful for feedback concerning the book, both positive and negative, and questions that you or your students might have. You can reach me at the addresses shown below.

Acknowledgments

Although there's only one name on the cover of this book, it was—as all books are—a collaborative effort. Work began under the direction of Catherine Woods at HarperCollins Publishers and continued smoothly during the corporate transition to Addison Wesley Longman. Heide Chavez, patient and even-tempered, became the primary editor for the project, backed up by Eric Stano and Priscilla McGeehon, who provided important supervision and advice, and Ann Kearns, who guided the book through production. Special mention also goes to Mira Schachne, who masterfully translated my many vague ideas for accompanying illustrations into photographic reality.

I received substantial professional assistance from many people, in the form of reviews, suggestions, and feedback of various sorts. The manuscript was reviewed carefully and helpfully by

Lt. Colonel Robert Burger, United States Air Force Academy
Darlene DeMarie-Dreblow, Muskingum College
Myra Heinrich, Mesa State College
Steven K. Jones, United States Air Force Academy
James Juola, The University of Kansas
Roger Kruez, University of Memphis
T. Darin Matthews, The Citadel
H. Nicholas Nagel, Boston College
Helga Noice, Augustana College
David B. Porter, United States Air Force Academy

to whom I express my gratitude. Colleagues who provided sound advice, important ideas, and encouragement include Tom Carr, Steve Christman, Dave Geary, Morton Gernsbacher, Fred Smith, John Whalen, and Jane Zbrodoff. Locally, several of my students have assisted me at critical times during the writing process, sometimes by reading and critiquing drafts, finding references, and generating ideas and examples—and sometimes by knowing when to postpone their own questions until I got over one or another temporary obstacle. In particular, I thank Elizabeth Kirk, Richard Falk, Jim Gute, and Dave Copeland for graciously coping with their absentee adviser. And finally, I dedicate this book to my wife and children, all three of whom are now seasoned veterans in this process of getting a book written.

Mark H. Ashcraft
Department of Psychology
Cleveland State University
Cleveland, OH 44115 USA
Email: M.Ashcraft@csuohio.edu

About the Author

Mark H. Ashcraft is Professor of Psychology at Cleveland State University, Cleveland, Ohio. He earned his B.A. at Grinnell College, Grinnell, Iowa, and his M.A. and Ph.D. at the University of Kansas, Lawrence, Kansas. He has written a previous textbook, *Human Memory and Cognition* (Second Edition), and authored or co-authored nearly 40 articles and book chapters on human memory and cognition, many on topics related to mathematical cognition, published in journals such as *Journal of Experimental Psychology: Learning, Memory, and Cognition; Mathematical Cognition;* and *Memory & Cognition*. His hobbies include swimming, choral and keyboard music, surfing the net, and restoring his 80-year-old home in Cleveland Heights.

SECTION

ONE

FOUNDATIONS

CHAPTER ONE

INTRODUCTION

Hi. Welcome to the psychology of memory and cognition, and to *Fundamentals of Cognition*. This is probably your first serious exposure to the topic of human memory and cognitive processes, after a rapid introduction to the area in your introductory psychology course. My main purpose in this book is to give you a foundation in one of the most interesting areas in modern psychology, the study of human memory and cognition. I want to introduce you to the major subareas in this field, from studies of perception and pattern recognition through the varieties of human memory, and on up to problem solving and reasoning.

You'll read about questions that psychologists are pursuing in this field, such as

- Can memories be repressed and then recovered years later? Do people ever "remember" things that didn't happen?
- Where are different memories located and where do mental processes "happen" in the brain? Does each memory have its own special "place"?

Some of you will take further coursework on related topics, and a few may even decide to specialize in cognitive psychology or cognitive science at the graduate school level. But even if you don't pursue it any further than this book and this course, you're sure to run into questions about human memory and thought that you'd like to answer, questions like

- Why is it so hard to remember people's names?
- Why can't we remember anything from our infancy?
- How can I improve my memory?

This book should provide you with essential background, or at least a good starting place, to begin answering questions such as these. You'll gain specific knowledge about some questions, and some insights and new perspectives on others. Bear in mind, however, that cognitive psychology is truly a "work in progress"—it's an ongoing scientific enterprise, with many more good questions than solid answers. That's a big part of the fun of it—finding the good questions, and seeking the answers.

Defining the Topic

Preview: definitions of *memory* and *cognition;* some intuitive examples to start you thinking—2×3, robins and trucks, and Aristotle

Now let's get to the substance of the chapter, an introduction to your study of human memory and cognitive processes.

MEMORY

Our everyday understanding of memory is that it's something like a file cabinet—an analogy we'll explore in a moment. But let's start with a more formal definition of the term.

- **Memory:** The mental processes of acquiring and retaining information for later retrieval, and the mental storage system in which these processes operate.

Memory is your mental file cabinet, the mental storage system where a lifetime of experience and knowledge is stored. The term also refers to the processes that operate in this file cabinet—you put things into the cabinet to save them, you search through the cabinet to find some particular piece of information, and once you've found it, you use the retrieved information.

As you'll discover in Section II, "Varieties of Memory," there are also some misleading aspects of the file cabinet metaphor. For instance, a real file cabinet will hold only so much information, a finite number of files. You have to pay careful attention to the organization of those files or you'll never find the particular one you're looking for. Human memory, on the other hand, has an infinite capacity—you can never fill up your long-term memory. And although organization is important in human memory, the organizing and searching principles seem to differ from those of a file cabinet. For example, you don't have to make a deliberate decision about *where* to store information in your memory, although in most cases you do have to decide *that* you're going to store it (but see the topic of implicit versus explicit memory, later on).

Furthermore, unlike the file cabinet system, there's a lot of cross-referencing in memory—it's as if the contents of one memory file connect to contents of other files. In this respect, memory is much like the World Wide Web, with links connecting to other bodies of information, and those linked in turn to yet more information (see the Preface for Students for more information on this). Try the demonstration to see how interconnected  your web of information is in long-term memory.

COGNITION

We also need a formal definition of the term *cognition*. An easy way to remember that cognition refers to thought and mental processing is to notice all the other "thinking" words derived from the same base—we *recognize*, we can be *cognizant* about topics—these derive from the Latin base *cognitio* (*co* + *gnoscere*, "together" + "know"). A formal definition is

> Free-associate to the concept YELLOW for a moment, writing down the ideas that come to mind. Now, reflect on the variety of concepts you encountered during this search through long-term memory—I come up with bananas, canaries, daisies, school buses, traffic lights, and so forth. Somehow, the concept YELLOW is represented in memory with all of those concepts you encountered, linked to them and therefore linking those concepts together. Any one of them, furthermore, can trigger another cycle of retrieval—banana could lead to fruit, then to fruit trees, then to the aroma of blossoms on the trees, then . . . You get the point—memory is an interconnected web of concepts and pathways that link those concepts together.

- **Cognition:** The collection of mental processes and activities used in perceiving, learning, remembering, thinking, and understanding, and the act of using those processes.

Cognition is thought, the collection of all the mental processes we use as we perceive and recognize objects, as we learn and remember concepts and ideas, as we comprehend and use language, and as we think and reason.

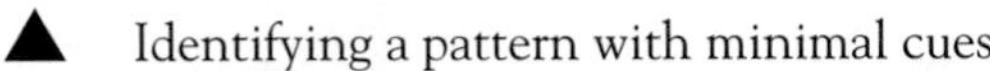

Identifying a pattern with minimal cues.

- Our perception and recognition are stunning—sometimes we need only the slightest of clues to identify a pattern. These basic processes, presented in Section I, are richly complex, and in some cases, not well understood at all.
- Memory (technically, I should say "memories," for we have several) is equally stunning, despite all of those situations that reveal how fallible memory can be. As you'll see in Section II, we store an unbelievable amount of information in long-term memory, probably permanently, and we usually have extremely rapid access to it.
- The richness of our long-term memories is most apparent when we consider language, language-based cognition, and the influence of meaning on memory, in Section III. The rapid, on-line nature of language, and the thought behind it, makes this an especially important and intriguing focus for cognitive psychology.
- Considerable evidence is now being accumulated on the neurological basis of cognition, a topic I call *neurocognition*. Section IV presents current information on this rapidly expanding field of study. In particular, you'll read what is known about brain structures and processes when we pay attention to something, when we form long-term memories, when we produce and comprehend language, and so forth.
- And finally, we think and reason based on the contents of memory, our experiences as well as our general knowledge. Especially interesting here are situations in which our reasoning and decisions are faulty, influenced by the wording of a question, by gaps in our own knowledge, or by illogical reasoning processes and tendencies. Section V covers such issues.

INTUITIVE EXAMPLES

Let's take some examples, to flesh out what the terms *memory* and *cognition* mean in cognitive psychology. We're taking an intuitive, introspective approach here, but not because those are the methods cognitive psychology relies on (you'll see why in the history section that follows). Instead, we're taking that approach here so you can begin developing a framework for your knowledge about memory and cognition, learn some key terms, and think about some fundamental issues. We'll start with a very simple act of memory retrieval.

What's 2×3?

We use the term **on-line** a lot, so it deserves a definition. Those of you who work with computers know what I mean, of course. If you're "on-line," you're working *right now*—you're connected to the Internet, for example. So we use *on-line* to refer to human mental processing too. For instance, in research on reading and comprehension, "on-line" measures keep track of where your eyes are focusing, and for how long you focus, *as you read,* during the actual reading process. That's "on-line." And we're even beginning to use the term metaphorically. "I'm on-line" becomes a metaphor for "I'm paying attention and thinking," and "I'm off-line" means "I'm goofing around, daydreaming, *not* doing what I should be doing."

Oliver Sacks, a now-famous neurologist (he wrote the book that became the film *Awakenings*), has written a collection of fascinating case histories of people with serious disruptions of thought and memory due to brain injury or disease. The book *The Man Who Mistook His Wife for a Hat* (Sacks, 1970) takes its name from the first case history in the book. It describes an elderly gentleman who was progressively losing the ability to recognize things visually, especially faces—even those as familiar to him as that of his wife. The most intriguing aspect of this case was the *selectivity* of his disruption. His ability to recognize sounds, including music and people's voices, was preserved, as were his memory and—amazingly enough—his ability to recognize parts of objects visually, like the pieces on a chessboard or an especially prominent facial feature. Question: How could our mental processes and abilities be structured so that one set of processes could become so damaged while similar processes remain intact?

Generally, when this sort of question is asked in the lab, people respond by saying "six" in about seven-tenths of a second (Campbell & Graham, 1985). Cognitive psychology typically calls such short time intervals **reaction times (RTs),** and measures them in milliseconds (abbreviated "msec"); a millisecond is *one-thousandth of a second*. So, it takes about 700 milliseconds (700-thousandths of a second) for the average college student to say "six" to the problem 2×3.

What goes into that 700 milliseconds? Well, it takes some amount of time to perceive the problem visually and register it in the mental system—this is the process of **encoding,** *bringing external information from the environment into the mental system*. Several lines of evidence suggest that we can pick up most of the necessary visual information from such a simple stimulus within about 50 to 100 milliseconds (e.g., Rayner, Inhoff, Morrison, Slowiaczek, & Bertera, 1981; Sperling, 1960). Likewise, it takes some amount of time to articulate the response: the time for the brain to send the message out and the speech mechanism to operate. A decent estimate for this is 200 milliseconds, a value close to *base reaction time*, the amount of time it takes to make a simple response to a signal.

So, after taking encoding and articulation time into account, let's call what's left—for our intuitive purposes right now—"mental time." What happens during that mental time? You retrieve the answer "six" from memory during mental time—but the term **retrieval** covers a lot of ground here. Somehow, despite the vast amount of information stored in memory, you can home in on just the relevant part of your mental file cabinet and access the particular information you need. You locate the specific concept you're searching for, possibly check to make sure you've retrieved the correct fact, and then "send" a copy of it to the speech center of the brain, which relays it to your vocal apparatus.

That's a sizable collection of mental proceses, all seeming to happen "in a flash." As you'll read a little later in this section, those processes act more slowly for a problem like 6×9 (or possibly a somewhat different set of processes is used; see LeFevre et al., 1996). In Campbell and Graham's (1985) data, 6×9 took college students an average of 1016 milliseconds, slightly over 1 second, and a full 300 milliseconds slower than 2×3; see

★ **FIGURE 1.1**

Vocal RTs (reaction times) to multiplication problems. (Data from Campbell & Graham, 1985.)

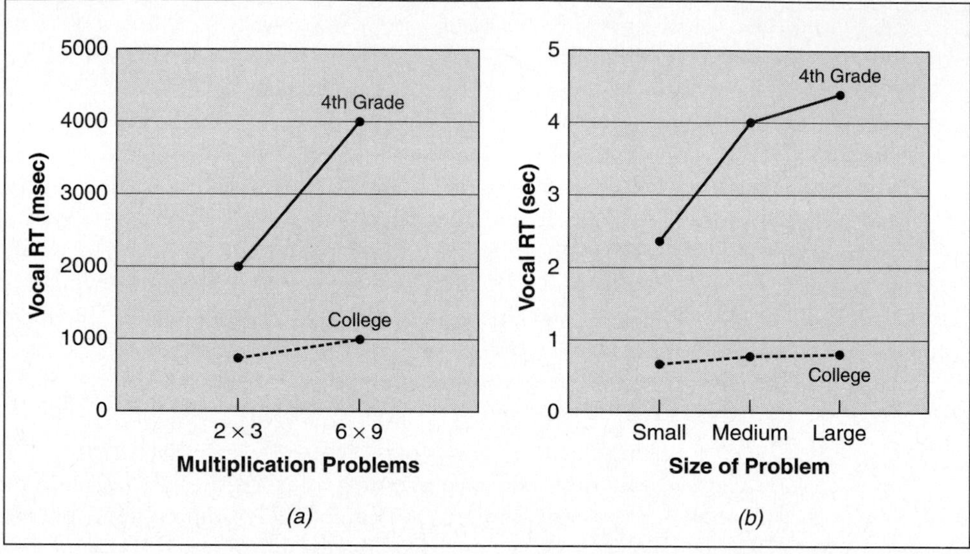

★ Figure 1.1 and the box that explains the data. The more general point here is that these mental processes *do not* occur instantly, "in a flash." Instead, they take time, measurable amounts of time. It's no surprise then that an overwhelmingly common way to investigate memory and cognition is by measuring the time it takes to respond to a stimulus ▲ like 2 × 3.

Now consider these questions.

Does a robin have feathers? Lungs?
Does a truck have wheels? A battery?

The questions about feathers and wheels are intended to be similar to the 2 × 3 example above—you've probably learned about these characteristics of robins and trucks in some direct fashion. You've seen robins flying, you've seen the wheels on trucks, so you likely have that information stored directly in your long-term memory. But did you ever learn that robins have lungs, the way you learned 2 × 3? Or that trucks have a battery? Probably not—in fact, you've probably never even seen a robin's lungs or a truck's battery. So these questions differ somewhat from the others. You're probably inferring, based on general knowledge, that robins are living things; therefore, they must have lungs—and that any motorized vehicle like a car or a truck must carry a battery to start the engine.

Now we've introduced a new wrinkle into our intuitive analysis. There's relatively straightforward memory retrieval, but there's also *inference*, an important memory process in which you apply general knowledge about birds or vehicles to specific concepts like robins and trucks. Inference has to be one of the more powerful mental processes we have, since it enables us to know things we've never learned, in other words, to deduce, reason, and think.

If you're good at interpreting data presented in graphs, don't bother with the rest of this box, just study the figures. But my impression is that students often struggle with graphed material, not understanding what's being shown nearly as well as their professors think. Because there are lots of graphs in this book that you'll need to understand, let's spend a moment going through a simple graph, showing you how it's put together and what to pay attention to as you interpret the data.

Figure 1.1 is a fairly simple graph of *reaction time* data, the time it takes to react to a stimulus by making a particular response; we almost always abbreviate reaction time as "RT," and it's usually measured in milliseconds (msec). In the figure, the label on the Y-axis reads "Vocal RT"—in other words, these subjects were making vocal responses, and the researchers measured the time between showing a simple multiplication problem and the participant's vocal response of the answer. The numbers on the Y-axis show you the range of RTs that were observed. The dependent variable is always the measure of performance that we collect in the experiment—here it's vocal RT—and it always goes on the Y-axis.

The X-axis in Figure 1.1(a) is labeled "Multiplication Problems," and I've plotted just the two problems discussed in the text, 2 × 3 and 6 × 9. It is more customary to show something more general than particular stimuli on the X-axis, as I've done in Figure 1.1(b). There I've grouped a whole set of small multiplication problems, from 2 × 3 up to 4 × 5; a set of medium-size problems, like 2 × 7 or 8 × 3; and a set of large problems, such as 6 × 8 and 9 × 7. So the X-axis label in Figure 1.1(b) reads "Size of Problem." A general rule for the proportions of a graph is that the length of the X-axis is slightly shorter than the height of the Y-axis; a 3 to 4 (or maybe a 4 to 5) ratio is about right, so that if the height of the Y-axis were 4 inches, the X-axis should be about 3 inches wide. Notice that the Y-axis is now in whole seconds, to save some space and preserve the graph's proportions.

Now the data. The points we plot in the graph are almost always the *mean* or average of the dependent variable—RT, in this case. Both panels of the graphs show two curves or lines each, one labeled C for College students, the other labeled 4 for fourth graders. (Campbell and Graham, 1985, tested fourth graders and college students on the simple multiplication problems.) Notice first that the curves for fourth graders are much higher. If you read across to the Y-axis in Figure 1.1(a), the average fourth grader took 1940 milliseconds to answer "six" to the problem 2 × 3, compared to 737 milliseconds for the average college student. In Figure 1.1(b), the average fourth grader took about 2400 milliseconds to respond to small problems, 4100 to medium, and 4550 to large. Compare this much stronger *increase* in RT as the problems got larger to the pattern for college students—there was still an increase, but only from 730 milliseconds to almost 900 milliseconds.

Why did Campbell and Graham find slower performance for fourth graders? The effect was no doubt that college students have had far more practice in doing simple multiplication problems than fourth graders. In other words, college students *know* multiplication better, have the facts stored more strongly in long-term memory, and so can access and retrieve the facts more rapidly. It's a perfectly sensible, cognitive effect, that the strength of information in memory influences the speed of your retrieval. And it's easily grasped by looking at and understanding the graphed results.

Here's my favorite example of **inference** and the processes beyond it—a question that elicits overwhelmingly similar trains of thought every time I use it.

How many hands did Aristotle have?

For such a ridiculously easy question, we're of course not particularly interested in the correct answer, "two." We are tremendously interested, however, in the thoughts you had as you considered the question. Most students I've tried this demonstration with report a train of thought something like this: "Dumb question. Of course he had two hands. Wait a minute—why would a professor ask such an obvious question? Maybe Aristotle had only one hand. Nah, I would have heard of it if he only had one hand—he must have had two."

Let's do one final intuitive analysis here, to uncover as many of the different cognitive processes as we can. First of all, a host of perceptual processes occurred as you read the question, though you were no doubt totally unaware of them. Highly overlearned visual processes focused your eyes on the printed line, then moved your focus across the line bit by bit, registering the printed material into some kind of memory system. Smoothly and rapidly, another set of processes "looked up" the encoded material in memory and identifed the letters and words. Few adults, of course, need to pay conscious attention to the nuts and bolts of perceiving and identifying words, unless the vocabulary is unfamiliar or the printing is faint. Yet your lack of awareness of these stages doesn't mean they didn't happen—ask a first-grade teacher about the difficulties children have in learning to identify letters and their sounds, and in putting these components together into words.

So, as we learned with 2×3 and with "robins have feathers," mental processes can occur with hardly any conscious awareness at all. This is **automaticity,** especially (or maybe only) true of processes that have received a great deal of practice—for example, reading skills. Second, even though these processes can operate very quickly, they are nonetheless quite complex, involving difficult motor, perceptual, and mental acts. Their complexity makes it even more amazing how efficient, rapid, and seemingly automatic they are.

As you identified the words in the question, you were also *accessing* or retrieving their meanings, and fitting those meanings together to understand the question. Much of this is also automatic: even though you weren't consciously aware of looking up the meaning of the word *hands* in your mental dictionary, you did—you found it stored with all your other general knowledge about the human body.

Likewise, you looked up *Aristotle* in memory. A few students insist that they wondered whether the question might refer to a different Aristotle—maybe Aristotle Onassis?—since a question about the philosopher Aristotle's hands seems so odd. Now it really starts to get interesting. With little effort, we retrieve the information from memory that the word *Aristotle* refers to a human being, a historical figure from the distant past. Many people know little else about Aristotle (what a shame) beyond the fact that he was a Greek philosopher. Yet this seems to be enough, combined with what we know to be true of people in general, to decide that he was probably just like everyone else—he had two hands. (How would you have reacted if the question asked, "How many hands *does* Aristotle have?")

And finally, people report a set of thoughts and judgments that involve the "reasonableness" of the question, similar in many respects to how we interpret remarks in a conversation. In general, people don't ask obvious questions, at least not to other adults. But if they *do* ask an obvious question, it's often for another reason—a trick question, for instance, or sarcasm. Consequently, students report that for a time they considered the possibility that the question wasn't so obvious after all—something like "Do I have any special knowledge about Aristotle that pertains to his hands?" I find the next step truly fascinating—so illogical, so human. Most students report that they thought to themselves "Nah. I would have heard about it if Aristotle only had one hand," and they decide that indeed it was an obvious question after all.

What? You think to yourself, "I've never heard of *x*, therefore *x* must not be true." But since when is not knowing something the same as evidence that it isn't true? This type of reasoning is called "reasoning from incomplete knowledge." It's fascinating first because it's so illogical and second because it's probably very common—so much of our everyday reasoning has to be done without benefit of complete knowledge, because we so seldom have complete knowledge of a topic.

In an interesting variation, I have asked students, "How many hands did Beethoven have?" Knowing that Beethoven was a pianist typically suggests to people "he couldn't possibly have been a very successful pianist with only one hand, therefore he must have had two." An occasional student answers, "Two—but he did go deaf before he died."

Now that's interesting, finding a connection between the physical handicap implied by "How many hands?" and a related shred of evidence in memory, Beethoven's deafness. Such an answer shows how people can also consider implications, inferences, and other unstated connections as they reason and make decisions; it shows what a great deal of knowledge can be considered even for a relatively simple question. The answer also illustrates the role of prior knowledge in such reasoning, where the richer body of information about Beethoven can lead to a more specific inference than was possible for the Aristotle question. And of course, it's another demonstration of the interconnectedness of our long-term memories.

Summary

1. *Memory* refers to the mental system where information is stored, and the encoding, retention, and retrieval processes that operate on the information.

I do the same thing—and you probably do too, for topics you know a lot about. A student asks if this or that idea has ever been tested in an experiment. If it's an area of research I don't have special expertise in, I'll hedge and indicate that I probably wouldn't know. But if it's a topic in my own area of research, and I don't remember any such study, I'll say, "No, it hasn't," because I'm fairly certain I would have read it or heard about it if the study *had* been done. Does my expertise in that area make my answer any more logical? Here's an interesting discussion topic—maybe expertise reduces the uncertainty of the answer, or increases the probability that the answer is correct, without making the answer or the process of arriving at it any less illogical.

2. *Cognition* refers to all our mental processes, from perception and recognition up through reasoning and inference.
3. Many cognitive processes, especially those that are highly overlearned and practiced, occur very rapidly and without conscious awareness of them—they're said to be automatic. Others are quite conscious, slow and deliberate, and open to our awareness.
4. Knowledge in long-term memory is interconnected—each piece of information is linked to many others. Sometimes these links enable us to draw inferences—robins have lungs. Sometimes our inferences are based on informal rules, like "Don't state or ask the obvious," or even on very flimsy evidence, like "reasoning from incomplete knowledge."

A Brief History of Cognitive Science

Preview: Aristotle's empiricism and associationism; Descartes's rationalist "I think, therefore I am"; the scientific revolution; the founding of psychology in 1879; behaviorism; the cognitive revolution of the late 1950s

A thorough course in the history of psychology can easily spend the entire term on philosophical viewpoints and positions that are important underpinnings of psychology—and you should take such a course. But *this* is a history of cognitive psychology, and an abbreviated one at that. So we'll have to content ourselves with three brief highlights from philosophy and history that are particularly relevant, then turn to the history of psychology's interests in cognition.

PHILOSOPHY AND THE SCIENTIFIC REVOLUTION

Aristotle

The first highlight brings us back to Aristotle, this time to acknowledge the important role he played in the development of all the sciences, ours included. Aristotle (385–322 B.C.) was the first *empiricist*. That is, he claimed that in order to know about something—human thought, for example—the thing had to be *observed*, as carefully and objectively as possible, with conclusions based on induction from those observations. This is a fundamental tenet in science, and it defines **empiricism;** *phenomena are investigated by careful, objective observation*. Contrast this with the **rationalist** position, that *phenomena can be understood by careful thought and logical proof*. Thus, for example, a rationalist might feel that human language, to pick just one example, can be understood by careful thinking, by devising theories based on rational, deductive thought—an approach used by linguists such as Chomsky. An empiricist, on the other hand, argues that language, or indeed any phenomenon in the real world, can only be understood by going out and doing research on it, by collecting observations or data.

Aristotle's empiricism led him to a true philosophy of the mind and its contents. He advanced the notion of the **tabula rasa,** often translated as the "blank slate" or the "blank wax tablet." His idea was that the mind—indeed everything that makes us who we are—was the product of experience. We are born as blank as the tabula rasa, and experience "writes" a record onto the slate. We do not have some formalized, inborn "idea" of things (essentially the position that Plato took). Instead, our "idea" of things is based on our experience. Notice how the role of experience was tailored to Aristotle's empiricism—our experiences account for who we are, and those experiences, and our behavior based on them, are open to observation and measurement.

Aristotle was particularly interested in memory, largely because memory contains the record of those all-important experiences—memory was the originally blank slate, now filled with the "writings" left by a person's experiences. Aristotle's conclusions about memory, described in his treatise *De memoria et reminiscentia* (Concerning Memory and Reminiscence), constituted history's first recorded theory of human memory and cognition. His basic claim was that the process of association underlies all memories—we tend to associate things that are similar to one another (horses and cows), things that contrast with one another (black and white), and things that occur together closely in time or space (thunder and lightning). He also noted the importance of *frequency*, that we remember experiences better if they are repeated more frequently. These have turned out to be absolutely vital observations throughout the history of investigations on memory and cognition.

Descartes

The second highlight, almost exactly 2000 years later, was an idea expressed by René Descartes (1596–1650), the French philosopher (he contributed more than just philosophy, however—for instance, he invented analytical geometry). What is truth? What is reality? Is there an objective reality, or could all of our awareness and knowledge of the world be imagined, a fantasy or a delusion? Descartes—rationalist that he was—reasoned this out. It could be, he decided ultimately, that all our knowledge is imagined instead of real; all our experiences and memories of events, mere illusions. If this is so, he continued, then there might be no objective reality at all. But—and here's the highlight we're look-

Aristotle may have "gotten there first" with his theory of memory, but he was by no means the first thinker to wonder about memory and cognition. The ancient Greek tradition of literature, for example, was the oral tradition, in which the orator would memorize a lengthy work—for instance, *The Iliad*—then entertain an audience by performing the work from memory. In an interesting passage in Plato's *Phaedrus,* Socrates worried that the invention of written language would weaken reliance on memory and understanding. This isn't very different from modern parents' worry that calculators will weaken the learning of math, professors' worries that the spell-checker function in your word processor will eliminate the need to learn to spell, or the general worry that sales clerks can't make change anymore unless the cash register computes it for them.

ing for—even if there is no reality, there is at least a being, an entity who is doing the imagining or hallucinating. In short, while there may be no external reality whatsoever, it is undeniable that *someone* is here, thinking of the possibility that there is no external reality. Descartes's (1637/1972) classic pronouncement was "Cogito, ergo sum" (I think, therefore I am).

This is fundamental to cognitive psychology—but in somewhat the reverse direction. Descartes reasoned from the premise, which was to him the undeniable *fact* of thought and awareness, to the conclusion: the reality of his own existence. But we needed to go the other way, from existence *back* to the conclusion that thought exists. As you'll read in a few moments, the struggle around the mid-1950s was in proving that thought exists, or more accurately, that thought and mental processes were phenomena that could be investigated scientifically and empirically, as a bona fide part of the science of psychology. We, especially in the United States, had a hard time making that argument.

The Scientific Revolution

The third highlight isn't attributable to a single person, but instead to the collection of philosophical and empirical developments that we call the scientific revolution. During this period, from about 1550 to 1700, empiricism flowered and took command. Histories of science refer to the Copernican revolution, the major upheaval in thinking about the universe that was brought about by Copernicus's claim, in 1543, that the sun was the center of the solar system rather than the earth. This claim was later upheld by Galileo, and then Newton, in his *Principia mathematica*, published in 1687.

The revolution here was one of ultimate authority. Galileo (1564–1642) took advantage of the newly invented device called the telescope, and in 1609 observed four new "planets," the moons of Jupiter—"wondrous sights," as he put it (Hothersall, 1990). He correctly interpreted these data as showing that all the planets, Earth included, rotated around the Sun, and said so a year later in his *Sidereus nuncius* (Message from the Stars). The Catholic Church, however, was the ultimate authority in that dispute. Galileo was forced to recant his conclusions, because they were deemed heresies to the doctrine of the Church.

By the time of Newton's laws of motion in 1687, however, the authority had changed—now it was science, based on observation, that was the ultimate authority, not religious dogma. Success after success was achieved through scientific observation during this time, such that the ultimate authority for truth, and the ultimate method for answering all substantive questions, became science and the scientific method. ★

THE FOUNDING OF PSYCHOLOGY—1879

The 1700s and 1800s saw an explosion of scientific discoveries and developments—the scientific method was turned to all sorts of phenomena, and tremendous progress was made. Several advances from the 1800s were particularly important for psychology.

The most influential philosophy from the era 1700–1800 was the school of philosophy known as *British associationism*. The common thread that bound men like John Locke, David Hume, and John Stuart Mill into this school was their emphasis on *empiricism* and its primary implication, the supremacy of experience over innate factors. Experience was the driving force in molding human behavior and the mind, especially as it was

★

Another example, from biology, captures the influence that the scientific revolution had on the world and our understanding of it. Existing belief up until the 1600s was that the human body consumes the blood supply, and that the heart therefore must manufacture or "concoct" blood (blood was also believed to contain animistic and supernatural spirits; R. I. Watson, 1968).

William Harvey (1578–1657) approached the question scientifically, by measuring the amount of blood in the body and the rate of blood flow. He discovered that even in half an hour, the heart pumps more blood than the total amount of blood in the body. From this he concluded that the heart couldn't possibly manufacture blood—how could 4000 gallons of blood a day be manufactured and consumed by the body? Instead, he concluded, the heart circulates the blood over and over through the body. Discovering objective truth—not by "thinking out the answer," but by collecting observations—was the heart of the scientific revolution.

Source: Based on R. I. Watson (1968).

analyzed through the concept of **association**—*the linking together of two events, objects, or ideas because they tend to occur together in experience.* The most remarkable, and ultimately persuasive, testimony to the importance of experience and the environment was the theory of evolution (e.g., Darwin, 1859/1959), which showed the absolute centrality of experience and the environment to the very existence and survival of organisms and species of the natural world. For cognitive psychology, the most influential thinking was probably that of John Stuart Mill, who claimed that sensations of objects and experiences in the real world became the "contents" of the conscious mind, and also led to ideas and, ultimately, thought.

Two other lines of evidence from the mid-1800s also had a psychological ring to them. In the 1850s, a German physiologist named Hermann von Helmholtz (1821–1894) began a series of brilliant investigations into the nervous system, by measuring the speed of the neural impulse. What was previously believed to be instantaneous, if not downright magical, turned out to be entirely understandable in scientific terms: the neural impulse is  electrical and travels at a measurable rate.

▲

Helmholtz's important work was only possible because of technological developments—measuring the speed of the neural impulse requires rather precise instruments and timing devices. Knowing the length of the neural fiber he was working with (60 mm), the exact time at which it was stimulated, and the exact time at which the attached muscle contracted, he was able to calculate that the impulse had taken only .0014 seconds, yielding a rate of 43 meters per second. For a modern-day analog to the influence that technological development has on research, read about brain imaging techniques in Chapter 10.

Helmholtz's work was part of the growing understanding of the nervous system, and its influence on behavior, which advanced tremendously in the 1860s (Hothersall, 1990). Part of that advancement occurred in 1861, when the French scientist Paul Broca (1824–1880) delivered a paper at the French Anthropological Society. Broca delivered a report based on autopsy results of a man who had lost the ability to speak fluently. Broca's paper reported clear evidence that the man's disruption in language ability was the result of damage to the left frontal region of the brain, prompting his now-famous line "Nous parlons avec l'hémisphère gauche" (We speak with the left hemisphere). The specific importance of this to our understanding of language is discussed in Chapter 10. For now, notice that Broca's evidence tied a specific brain location with a specific cognitive function, language, and paved the way for new efforts at understanding the brain and its functioning (e.g., Kolb & Whishaw, 1996).

Wundt

Given all these developments, the time was ripe for a scientific approach to the mind and human behavior, and a formal discipline to pursue it. So in 1879 the German scientist Wilhelm Wundt (1832–1920) established a laboratory for psychological research at the University of Leipzig. Wundt's interests were in questions about consciousness—What are the processes and elements that make up our conscious experience? As Hothersall (1990) notes, "Wundt was self-consciously trying to stake out a new area of science" (p. 98) in this work, a science of the conscious processes of the mind.

A genuine *Who's Who* of early psychologists studied with Wundt at Leipzig—James McKeen Cattell, Edward Titchener, G. Stanley Hall. For the most part, they were all trained in Wundt's method of introspection, his method of *having trained subjects "look inward" (introspect) and report their inner sensations and experiences*. As Hothersall (1990) de-

Wilhelm Wundt

scribes it, the method was intended to be a rigorous, controlled procedure for discovering the sensations and feelings we experience consciously. Importantly, though we often overlook it, the method of introspection was routinely augmented with other measures of performance, such as reaction times and word associations.

Titchener

Of all of Wundt's students, Edward Titchener (1867–1927) had probably the most immediate influence on the course of American psychology. Titchener came to the United States in 1892, after earning his degree with Wundt. Titchener became more and more convinced that the method of introspection was the only appropriate procedure for psychology. Across the years, his psychology became increasingly "pure," restricted to introspection, and advancing what he called structuralism, "the study of the structure of the conscious mind" (Hothersall, 1990, p. 101). He also became quite dismissive of other methods and interests. For instance, he was delighted that critics complained about psychology's inability to help solve practical problems like personality disorders (Hothersall, 1990)—in Titchener's opinion, such practicalities did not belong in psychology in the first place!

But Titchener's dogmatic insistence on the introspective method led to some serious difficulties, because of the inherent *subjectivity* of the method. That is, interpretations of subjects' introspections were ultimately the responsibility of Titchener—"Certain introspections were defined as correct and certain others as erroneous, with the final authority being Titchener himself" (Hothersall, 1990, p. 118). Thus, Titchener dismissed **attention,** for example, as not being an elementary mental process. Instead, he said, attention is merely a verbal label we "attribute" to our experiences, but is not something we ever experience directly. The opposite claim by rival psychologists in Wurzburg, Germany—that they had introspective evidence to support the process of attention—was dismissed by Titchener merely as a matter of "incorrect" introspections.

James

William James (1842–1910) deserves at least brief mention here, partly because he was the earliest American to achieve prominence in the new field of psychology—his book *Principles of Psychology* (1890/1983) was and is considered a classic. This is especially the case for cognitive psychology, because James had such significant insights and intuitions about the human mental system. He wrote intriguingly about attention and consciousness, and single-handedly introduced the distinction between what we now call short-term and long-term memory—indeed, he had strikingly useful observations on many of the topics you'll be reading about throughout this book. Importantly, however, James's writings were not accompanied by empirical research of his own—he had a personal distaste for experimentation, preferring his own rather informal style of analysis. Nonetheless, his influence on the whole of psychology was ultimately far greater than that of the overly narrow Titchener.

The Behaviorist Revolution

The unresolvable disputes among Titchener and his rivals in Germany set the stage for what eventually became a wholesale rejection of introspection. In the process, unfortu-

William James

nately, the content matter that introspection had been used to investigate—mental events and processes—was also rejected. Early in the 1900s, word began to spread about Pavlov's new, exciting, and successful research on the conditioning of reflex responses. Notable progress was also being made by psychologists interested purely in behavior—for instance, in how rats learned various simple behaviors (e.g., J. B. Watson, 1903). In con-

Watson's manifesto was reprinted in part in 1994, making it more accessible to modern students (J. B. Watson, 1913/1994, pp. 248–253). Read it for a classic example of forthright, even blunt, opinion—and as you do, reflect on the adjective most commonly used to describe John B. Watson: *antimentalistic.* Here are a few examples:

- *Psychology as the behaviorist views it is a purely objective experimental branch of natural science. . . . Introspection forms no essential part of its methods, nor is the scientific value of its data dependent upon the readiness with which they lend themselves to interpretation in terms of consciousness.* (p. 248)
- *The time seems to have come when psychology must discard all reference to consciousness; when it need no longer delude itself into thinking that it is making mental states the object of observation.* (p. 249)
- *I believe we can write a psychology . . . [and] never use the terms consciousness, mental states, mind, content, introspectively verifiable, imagery, and the like. . . . It can be done in terms of stimulus and response, in terms of habit formation, habit integrations and the like.* (p. 250)

trast, no such progress flowed from the introspectionists' laboratories. There were no triumphs to capture psychologists' enthusiasm, merely more unresolvable controversy.

In the midst of this, and as a general "call to arms," John B. Watson (1878–1958) published an article in the *Psychological Review*, a paper now commonly referred to as the "behaviorist manifesto." In the paper, titled "Psychology As the Behaviorist Views It," Watson completely rejected consciousness and introspection as appropriate domains and methods for psychology. He redefined psychology to be the "science of behavior"—observable, quantifiable, overt behavior—and called on others to join him in this "worth while" effort at devising such a science.

Watson's paper was published in 1913 (reprinted by *Psychological Review* in 1994). It supplies us with a convenient date to use as the starting point for the behaviorist era in American psychology. Between 1913 and the 1950s, behaviorism dominated academic, research-oriented psychology much as Wundt's introspection and Titchener's structuralism had dominated until then. Various forms of behaviorism, including the so-called *neobehaviorism* of researchers like Hull (e.g., 1943) and the *radical behaviorism* of B. F. Skinner (e.g., 1938, 1957), existed during this time.

But they all had one particular feature that made them relevant to the history of cognitive psychology—they rejected the notion that mental processes, mental events, and states of mind could be investigated scientifically, because they were not observable behaviors. Thus, the behaviorist era, at least from our perspective, was a period of marking time—little if any progress was made on truly cognitive topics, at least in the United States, and it would seem, little if any tolerance was shown for concerns or questions

"Stimulus, response! Stimulus, response! Don't you ever *think*?"

about mental events. At least in the United States, if you were interested in attention, or imagery, or thought, you were out of step with the times, and out of luck.

Winds of Change: 1940–1960

Phenomenal progress was made during the behaviorist era—no doubt about it. A careful, empirical understanding of the *principle of reinforcement,* supplied by the behaviorist tradition, is invaluable—for example, consider how many behavior modification and behavioral therapy programs there are, not to mention the many other applications, all inspired by the successes of behaviorists.

World War II And yet, beginning during the World War II years of 1939–1945, and continuing for some 15 years afterward, psychology became increasingly dissatisfied with the behaviorist approach as an answer to everything. What had begun as the opening of a new avenue of research—studying overt behavior and the laws that governed it—had become traditional, the status quo, "normal science," to use Kuhn's (1962) term, and many chafed under the restrictiveness of the approach.

Lachman, Lachman, and Butterfield (1979), in their persuasive account, note that American psychologists were pressed into service during World War II (as they had been in the previous world war) in order to solve various practical problems encountered by the military. One particularly interesting problem involved sonar and radar operators. These individuals had to monitor the sonar or radar screen for long periods of time, making judgments and decisions about whether a burst on the screen was or was not an enemy airplane or ship. At an intuitive level, it became clear that the problems these operators had were *cognitive* problems: their performance flagged after a time, due to fatigue and the demands of prolonged vigilance; they had to make decisions, based on criteria like "don't

sound the alarm unless you're *sure* it is an enemy plane"; the conditions they worked under were often less than ideal. It seemed clear, in Lachman et al.'s (1979) retelling of the story, that behaviorists had little or nothing to say about such situations, and had little in the way of practical advice to give the military when confronted with problems such as these. After all, their psychology had rigorously excluded questions about attention, vigilance, decision making, and the like—and had even boasted about it!

Technology Technological developments also had a large impact on postwar psychology. In particular, communications engineering introduced the interesting new viewpoint that any communication device has a limited capacity—a telephone line can only transmit a limited number of messages simultaneously. Someone noticed the similarity between such devices and human beings—we humans can only do a limited number of things simultaneously, so maybe we are similar in important respects to communication devices. As Broadbent (1958) and others noted, such insights could never have been achieved by sticking to traditional behaviorist approaches.

The Computer But the biggest, most astounding development was the invention of the computer, the electrical (and now electronic) "thinking machine." Here was a mechanism—wires and switches (nowadays chips and circuits)—that did something remarkably similar to *mental processing*. By virtually all accounts, this **computer analogy**—this similarity between the unseen electrical events in the computer and the unseen mental events in the mind—gave psychology a new way of conceptualizing the mind, a new analogy. Probably just as important, it gave psychologists a defense against the criticisms of behaviorism. Imagine the new convert to the cognitive point of view, arguing against an audience of entrenched behaviorists: "How can you behaviorists doubt the reality of mental

Given the history of digital computers, this borders on circular logic. That is, the standard design of modern computers was worked out in the 1940s by John von Neumann (1903–1957). This so-called architecture was inspired by "people's (naive) view of how the mind operated" (Norman, 1986, p. 534). That is, computer architecture dictates that one operation be carried out at a time, and that the data being operated on are different from the procedures used in the operations, at least partly because those characteristics were thought to be true of the human mind at that time.

Current evidence indicates that both of these assumptions are very probably wrong—for example, the brain routinely does several things simultaneously rather than one at a time. Interestingly, the newest computer-modeling techniques in cognitive psychology depend completely on the notion of such parallel (simultaneous) processing, techniques that are rather awkwardly handled by serial-processing, von Neumann–style computers. For an interesting discussion of these issues, and the relationships between neurology and these modeling techniques, see Chapter 2 in Kosslyn and Koenig's (1992) book *Wet Mind: The New Cognitive Neuroscience.*

events when we now have a *machine* that does exactly the same kind of thing? Simply because thought is unobservable doesn't mean it can't be studied—after all, you can't see the inner workings of the computer, and yet we know exactly what is happening inside the computer."

THE COGNITIVE REVOLUTION

There were

- Dissatisfactions with the rigid and narrow restrictions of behaviorism, restrictions on the questions that were deemed "appropriate" for the science of psychology;
- Problems during World War II that couldn't be solved with behaviorist techniques—that couldn't even be addressed, much less answered; and
- Developments in communications and the invention of the computer, which seemed to be a "thinking machine."

These factors, along with tantalizing hints of where this "new" approach might take us, led to what is termed the *cognitive revolution* (e.g., Lachman et al., 1979). There was a widespread turning away from behaviorism as the dominant "way of doing business." Researchers turned toward *cognitivism*, toward a reinstatement of mental processes as the focus of psychology.

An important milestone in this cognitive revolution was a paper by the linguist Noam Chomsky (1928–), in which he reviewed Skinner's (1957) book *Verbal Behavior;* the Chomsky review (Chomsky, 1959) is now fondly called the "cognitive manifesto." In the paper, Chomsky argued not only that the behaviorist account of language was seriously wrong and misguided, but that behaviorism was unable in principle to provide a useful, scientific analysis of language. The reason for this was rules—language acquisition and use involves rules, Chomsky argued, mental rules that govern our speech and comprehension. Such mental constructs, of course, had been excluded from behaviorism, because they were unobservable. This rendered behaviorist accounts of language "gross and superficial" (p. 28), in Chomsky's view, and "of no conceivable interest" (p. 38).

On the other hand, new research on mental processes was being published—research on attention (Broadbent, 1958), on the limited capacity of immediate or short-term memory (Miller, 1956), and on computer simulations of problem solving (Newell, Shaw, & Simon, 1958). This new research focused on decidedly *mental* topics, but with *objective* measures rather than introspective techniques. In a way, psychology finally got back on track, reintroducing its earliest topics of research—attention, decision making, and the like—but with a scientific objectivity that the approaches of Wundt and Titchener lacked.

The 1950s were the years in which a new generation of experimental psychologists started trying this new cognitive approach—people like George Miller, Herbert Simon, and Jerome Bruner. It was also the decade during which some of the established figures of behaviorism started to fight the change (Skinner, for one, continued the fight; e.g., Skinner, 1984, 1990). But we need a date to pin to the cognitive revolution—if indeed there was a cognitive revolution in Kuhn's (1962) sense of "scientific revolutions" (see Leahey, 1992b, for the counterargument).

Consider the decade of the 1950s as comparable to the decade prior to Watson's behaviorist manifesto in 1913. New and exciting research on mental events was being done, and attracting enthusiasm. All of this new effort seems to have culminated between 1955 and 1960—let's be somewhat arbitrary and pick 1960 as the "official" beginning of cognitive psychology. As you'll read in the next chapter, an important article about the very first stages of visual cognition appeared in 1960: Sperling's account of visual sensory memory. A provocative book on plans and human problem solving—thoroughly cognitive ★ topics—appeared in 1960, by Miller, Galanter, and Pribram. And, also in 1960, Miller and Bruner were able to persuade officials at Harvard University to establish the Center for Cognitive Studies there (Gardner, 1985).

Summary

1. Philosophical traditions, especially Aristotle's empiricism, Descartes's "I think, therefore I am," and the scientific revolution of the 1600s, led to the formation of psychology. The first psychology research lab was Wundt's, established in 1879.
2. Wundt's method of introspection became Titchener's dogma, an overly subjective method that was attacked forcefully by Watson, ushering in the behaviorist era from 1913 to the 1950s.
3. Dissatisfaction of various sorts, and significant developments like the invention of the computer, culminated in the 1950s with a shift away from behaviorism and toward a new approach. The new direction was cognitive psychology.

★

Gardner's (1985) important book *The Mind's New Science: A History of the Cognitive Revolution* tells a wonderful story about The Day Cognitive Psychology Was Born. There was a three-day conference at MIT in 1956, the Symposium on Information Theory, at which a stellar group of professionals gave presentations. In particular, on the second day of the conference, September 11, 1956, Noam Chomsky presented his theory of language, Alan Newell and Herbert Simon presented their work on the Logic Theory Machine, and George Miller presented his work on the capacity of short-term memory. Miller later claimed that all of them were working toward a "cognitive science," even though at the time they had no idea what to call it. This second day of the conference was apparently so stunning that the participants left with a profound awareness that what they had heard was not only new but groundbreaking. They had, by consensus and shared concerns, invented a new science.

The Cognitive Approach and Its Assumptions

Preview: the beginning of the cognitive era; basic assumptions; an overview model of memory; seven cognitive themes

In 1960, or somewhat more accurately, during the five-year period ending in 1960, *cognitive psychology* began. What had concerned psychology at its inception in 1879 was once again on the front burner: thought and mental processes. A classic statement of this commitment was offered in 1967, when Neisser published the first modern text in the area, titled simply *Cognitive Psychology:* "The basic reason for studying the cognitive processes has become as clear as the reason for studying anything else: because they are there" (Neisser, 1967, p. 5.).

ASSUMPTIONS

This is in fact the most basic assumption in cognitive psychology, the most fundamental statement of what we're all about: *Mental processes exist.* And there's an important elaboration of that assumption, the kind of elaboration that any and all scientific enterprises make, which is as follows—*Mental processes exist, and can be studied scientifically.*

Measuring Cognition

The question is, How? How do we study those processes? The modern cognitive psychology did not simply reintroduce the psychology of Wundt and Titchener. No—we learned the lessons about objectivity that the behaviorist revolution taught. The overly subjective method of introspection had led to a dead end, and had introduced nearly 50 years of neglect of cognitive topics, and so was not resurrected by modern cognitive psychology. Instead, the new cognitive psychology needed to maintain a firm commitment to objective, observational methods, the spirit of scientific evidence. This can be somewhat of a trick when studying cognition, since mental events are, after all, internal, hidden from direct observation.

Thus, we followed the example set by Ebbinghaus (see Chapter 5) and successive generations in **verbal learning,** which used measures of accuracy in learning and memory tasks. We also incorporated other measures, such as *reaction time* (which Cattell and even Wundt had used)—*how quickly a subject can respond to a stimulus.* To a limited extent, and using rather different methods, there is even a place in modern cognitive science for **verbal reports,** statements made by our subjects about their thoughts, ideas, and strategies during cognitive processing (but as you'll see in Chapter 12, the methodology of verbal reports is still somewhat controversial).

There is an especially distinguishing feature of the current **cognitive science,** *the multidisciplinary study of cognition that includes cognitive psychology, artificial intelligence and computer science, and the neurosciences.* This feature is an increasing reliance on the technology of *brain imaging.* We are seeing evidence from PET scans, functional MRIs, and ERPs (see especially Chapter 10 for descriptions and explanations of these techniques), and also reports of the disruption of cognitive function due to brain damage, all of which are important to our study of cognition.

AN OVERVIEW OF THE HUMAN INFORMATION-PROCESSING SYSTEM

While the rest of this book provides the detail and the refinements of the cognitive system, you need a place to start, a general picture of that system. Figure 1.2 shows an overview of this cognitive system, routinely also called the "human information-processing system." In this model,

- Information from the outside world comes into the system through **sensory memory,** which is actually a bank of very brief memories, one for every sensory input system. These sensory memories *encode* the information, and hold it briefly for further processing.
- **Attention** is the mental process that transfers these very brief memories into **short-term memory.** Roughly speaking, short-term memory is equivalent to awareness, to the perceptions and ideas you are currently processing in the mental system. A synonym is **working memory**—it's the mental workbench where mental activities "happen," where mental work gets done.
- Beyond short-term memory, there's a huge, subdivided **long-term memory** system, the mental file cabinet discussed earlier. Processes operating on long-term memory access its information—that's the process of *retrieval*—and bring some of it to awareness (what's your home phone number?). Knowledge, facts, and experiences are not the only types of information stored in long-term memory, however. We also have procedures—rules and strategies and "how-to" information—stored there.

FIGURE 1.2

An overview of the human information-processing system.

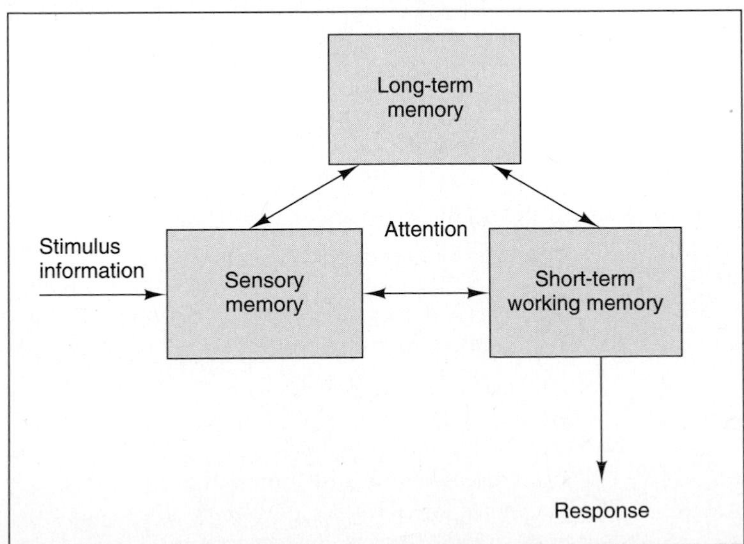

Seven Themes of Cognition

Throughout the book, you'll notice that certain themes occur again and again as you study different topics. Some of these themes are questions that cognitive science is still grappling with, some are phenomena of widespread importance, and some are ways of viewing cognition. All of them are important issues to the study of cognition. As a quick self-test on your understanding of this introductory chapter, read the list and see if you can tell which themes I've mentioned or discussed in this chapter. Then be on the lookout for them as you continue studying the most interesting question of all times: How do we think?

1. **Attention.** This is the all-important, but poorly understood mental process. It's limited in quantity, essential to most processing, but only partially under our control. Is it a mechanism? A limited pool of mental resources?
2. **Automatic versus conscious processing.** Some mental processes occur quite automatically, whereas others are slow and deliberate, quite conscious, and require lots of attention. Can *any* mental process become automatic?
3. **Data-driven versus conceptually driven processing.** Some processing relies heavily on the information we get from the environment—data-driven processing. Other processes rely heavily on our existing knowledge—conceptually driven processing. Conceptually driven processing can be so powerful that we often make errors, from mistakes in perception up through mistakes in reasoning.
4. **Representation.** How is information represented in memory? Can the variety of knowledge we have in memory all be formatted in the same mental code, or are there separate codes for the different types of knowledge?
5. **Implicit versus explicit memory.** We have direct and explicit awareness of certain types of memories—you remember the experience of buying this textbook, for example. But some memories or memory processes are implicit—they're there, but not necessarily with conscious awareness. This raises all sorts of interesting issues regarding the unconscious and its role in cognition; for instance, can an unconscious process affect your behavior and thinking?
6. **Metacognition.** This is awareness of our own cognitive systems, and knowledge and insight into its workings. It is the awareness that prompts us to write reminders to ourselves to avoid forgetting something. But is this awareness and knowledge completely accurate? Does it sometimes mislead us?
7. **Brain.** Far more than the cognitive psychology of the 1960s and 1970s, brain-cognition relationships and questions concern us now. How and where a fact is stored *in the brain* is a very different question from how and where the fact is stored *in memory*, with radically different answers appropriate to each question. And yet the neuro- and cognitive sciences are becoming more and more mutually relevant and influential.

Summary

1. The cognitive era began around 1960, with renewed interest in a scientific study of mental processes and events. The most basic assumption of cognitive psychology is that mental processes exist and can be studied scientifically.

2. Introspectionism was not part of the new cognitive psychology. Instead, our evidence consists of measures of accuracy, of reaction time, occasionally of verbal reports, and, increasingly, of brain images.
3. Seven recurring themes and issues in cognition are identified: attention, automatic versus conscious processing, data-driven versus conceptually driven processing, representation of knowledge, implicit versus explicit memory, metacognition, and brain.

Important Terms

Definitions are found in the Glossary.

association
attention
automatic versus conscious processing
automaticity
cognition
cognitive science
computer analogy
data-driven versus conceptually driven processing
empiricism versus rationalism
encoding
implicit versus explicit memory
inference
introspection
long-term memory
memory
metacognition
on-line
reaction time (RT)
representation
retrieval
sensory memory
short-term memory
tabula rasa
verbal learning
verbal reports
working memory

Suggested Readings

For the entire, fascinating story of the cognitive revolution, including the philosophical underpinnings and the current status, read Gardner's (1985) excellent *The Mind's New Science: A History of the Cognitive Revolution;* another source is Baars (1986). Leahey (1992a) and Hothersall (1990) provide thorough treatments of the history of psychology; Hothersall, especially, is useful for selective reading on different philosophers, the events of the scientific revolution, and the lives and work of early psychologists. See also the entire February 1992 issue of the journal *American Psychologist*, commemorating the 100th anniversary of the American Psychological Association. For shorter, more focused papers, see

Schonpflug (1994) on the Munsterberg's "road taken much later," cognitive science;

Sperry (1993) on the promise of the cognitive revolution;

Scarr (1993) on an application of the theory of evolution to developmental psychology;

Hulse's (1993) "The Present Status of Animal Cognition"; and

Thompson's (1994) "Behaviorism and Neuroscience," claiming that classical behaviorism's "views of thinking, that is, as reflex chains, have been largely discounted by developments in neuroscience" (p. 259).

CHAPTER TWO

PERCEPTION AND PATTERN RECOGNITION

It's a wonder we can see anything at all—or hear anything, for that matter. The structure of the eye is so implausible, even backward, and the ear so jury-rigged, so indirect, that our impressive sensory powers are all the more amazing. We can see the flame of a single candle, on a dark night, from a distance of 20 miles. We can hear the sound of a watch ticking 20 feet away, in a rather large but quiet room (Galanter, 1962).

And these acts of sensation are just the beginning of the process. **Sensation** is defined as receiving physical stimulation and encoding it into the nervous system. **Perception** is the process of interpreting and recognizing sensory information, the act of understanding what the sensation *was*. Perception of most visual and auditory patterns seems instantaneous to us—but, of course, it's not. The processes are very rapid and usually quite effortless, however, making it even harder to imagine how complex perception really is (e.g., Treisman, 1988).

This chapter is about these initial stages of cognition, the sensation and perception of stimuli in the environment, and our recognition of what those stimuli are. We'll talk about the structure of the eye and ear, and the processes by which they operate. We'll consider how humans recognize the huge variety of patterns they encounter, how we deal with the incredible variability of the environment around us. And we'll give you a first glimpse at a **connectionist model,** a modern, computer-based model of perception and the human mind.

Visual Perception

Preview: the anatomy of the eye—rods and cones; visual persistence; visual sensory memory; fading and interference; the first 50 milliseconds of a fixation

BASICS

★ Figure 2.1 illustrates the basic sensory equipment involved in human vision. Light waves enter the eye, are focused and inverted by the lens, and are projected onto the **retina.** The retina is composed of three basic layers of neurons:

- *rods and cones*, which start the process of vision,
- *bipolar cells*, the "relay stations" that receive messages from the rods and cones and send them on to
- *ganglion cells*, which merge together to form the optic nerve.

The rods and cones form the back layer of neurons on the retina, and are the neurons that are first stimulated by light, so they begin the process of vision. This is the implausibility of the eye's structure, by the way—the light has to pass through two layers of neurons, the bipolar and ganglion cells (plus blood vessels), before it can hit the rods and cones and trigger them to start the process of vision.

Once the rods and cones have become activated, they forward their messages to the second layer of neurons, the bipolar cells. These cells collect the messages and then relay them along to the third layer, the ganglion cells. The long extended axons of the ganglia converge and then exit at the rear of the eye, forming the *optic nerve*. This nerve exits the eye and threads its way back through the brain to terminate in the **occipital lobe,** where the visual cortex of the brain is located.

Our especially precise—*acute*—vision is the responsibility of the *cones*. Essentially all of the cones—some 7 million in each eye—occupy a central location on the retina called the **fovea** (see Figure 2.1, which also shows a few cones near the optic nerve). Because the cones are for precise vision, you focus so that visual stimuli—the words you're reading right now, for instance—are projected there, on the fovea. Much of the fovea's precision is due to an important fact of the eye's anatomy: With few exceptions, each cone has its own private bipolar cell for sending information into the visual system of the brain. In contrast, the rods are almost all in the periphery of the retina, away from the fovea. And, importantly, rods don't have the one-to-one connections of the cones to bipolar cells (and sometimes to ganglia too). Instead, groups of tens or even hundreds of rods *converge* into single bipolar cells. The result: not nearly enough precision for reading, but enough that a sudden stimulus in peripheral vision will attract your attention.

Sensitivity of Rods and Cones

One other interesting fact about rods and cones is their sensitivity. Cones require substantial light to function properly. Since the cones are responsible for color vision, it's no surprise that accurate color perception requires adequate illumination—you can't really tell what color a car is on a dark highway until you're close enough that your own headlights provide the illumination. Peripheral vision, based on the rods, can function with only low illumination—but, of course, that's not color vision, since the rods do not respond to color. So, to see a star on a dark night, you have to focus off to the side of the star, so its image is projected onto the rods, in the periphery of the retina. Focus the star onto the fovea and you won't see it very well—there isn't enough illumination for the cones to function correctly.

★ **FIGURE 2.1**

Anatomy of the eye. (a) The structure of the human eye, foveal pit, the optic nerve, and other structures. (b) The retina, rods and cones, bipolar cells, and ganglion cells. (From Hothersall, 1985.)

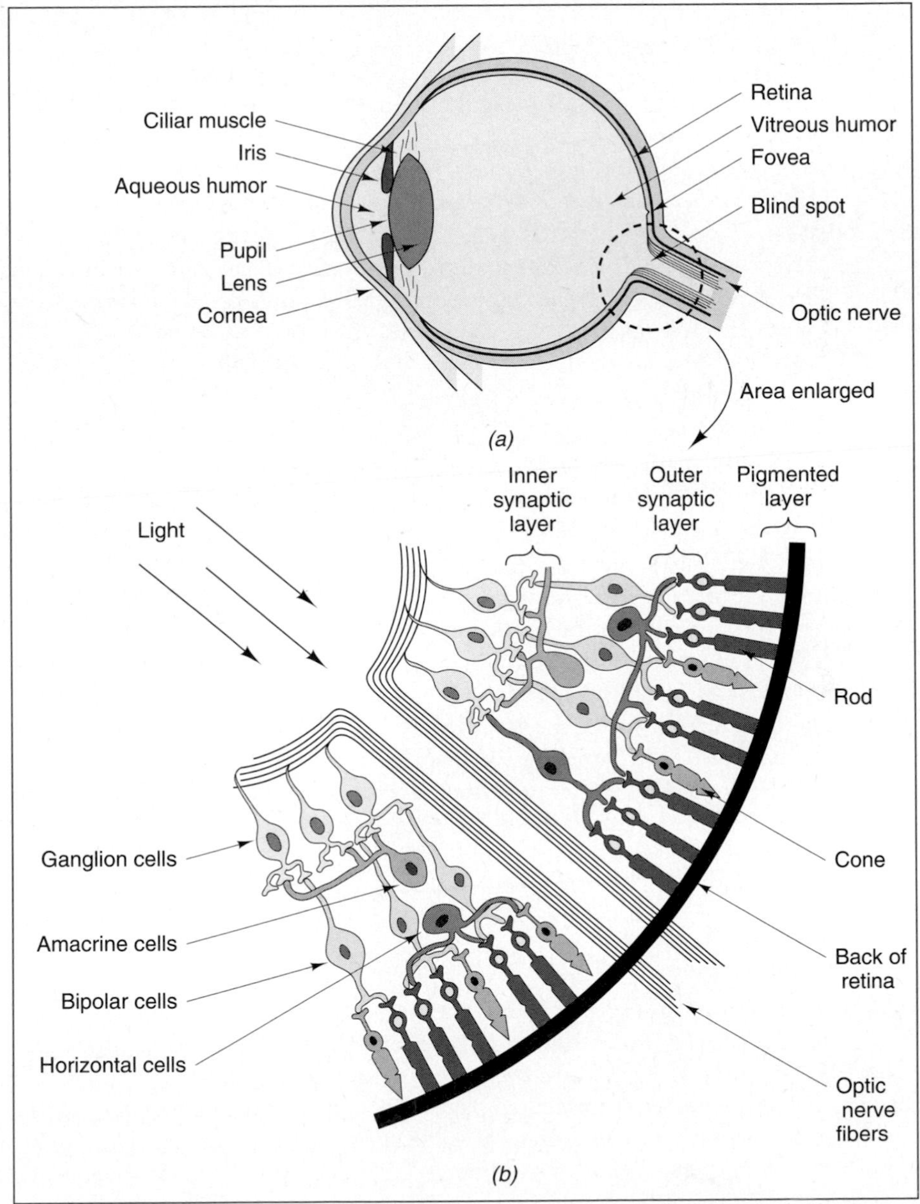

We've been talking about visual sensation, receiving stimulation from the environment and encoding it into the nervous system. But what happens next? What do we *do* with this encoded information once the optic nerve has transmitted it to the visual cortex? In other words, we want to understand visual perception, the process of interpreting and understanding sensory information. In Levine and Schefner's (1981) words, "we *sense* the presence of a stimulus, but we *perceive* what it is" (p. 1, emphasis added).

We begin by asking how the eye gathers information from the environment, then turn to the visual memory system that holds the gathered information.

HOW THE EYE GATHERS VISUAL INFORMATION

It is easy—and naive—to believe that we take in visual information in a smooth and continuous fashion whenever our eyes are open. After all, our visual experience is of a connected, coherent, continuous visual world, which can be scanned and examined at will. This is largely an illusion, however, one that you can easily disconfirm by a simple observation. Have someone watch your eyes as you read. Your friend will tell you that your eyes do not sweep smoothly across a line of print. Instead, they jerk across the line, bit by bit, with pauses between the successive movements—and the same is true for all vision, not just when you're reading.

Eye Movements

Here are the facts. The eye sweeps from one point to another in fast movements called **saccades** (French for "jerk," pronounced "suh-KAHD"); these movements are interrupted  by pauses called **fixations,** as shown in Figure 2.2. The saccade itself is quite rapid, taking anywhere from 25 milliseconds to about 100 milliseconds (e.g., Irwin & Carlson-Radvansky, 1996), depending on how far away the next fixation is. And it takes about 200 milliseconds to trigger the movement (Haber & Hershenson, 1973). During the saccade, there is suppression of the normal visual processes. Thus, for the most part, the eye takes in visual information *only* during the 200 milliseconds when we fixate on a stimulus. It's almost as if we are blind during the actual sweeping saccade movement. (If the eye did encode information during the saccade, we'd see a blur.)

Assume something in the range of 250 to 300 milliseconds for an entire cycle of fixation-then-saccade. At that rate, there is enough time for about three or four complete visual cycles per second. Each cycle registers a distinct and separate visual scene, although only a radical shift in gaze would make one cycle's input completely different from the previous one.

Visual Attention

A final important detail concerns the triggering of saccades themselves and, more generally, the engagement of visual attention. As Allport (1989) noted, there is a competition-like situation in visual attention. On the one hand, attention must be "interruptible." That is, we need to be prepared to react quickly to the unexpected—for example, when sudden movement alerts us to possible danger (a car running a red light as you drive through the intersection, a tree branch falling in a storm). So to some degree, even when you are focusing visual attention on one stimulus, the visual system must be able to process other visual inputs, those outside the focus of visual attention. Much of this low-level processing appears to occur in parallel (simultaneously) with other visual processing and involves detection of simple visual features (e.g., Treisman & Gelade, 1980).

On the other hand, visual attention should not be too interruptible. Constant switching from one input to another—from the words in this sentence to your desk lamp

FIGURE 2.2

Saccade and fixation paths of a participant looking at the photograph in the upper left. The traces show fixations and paths when the participant: Trace 1: merely viewed the photograph; Trace 2: had to estimate the economic status of the family in the photograph; Trace 3: judged the ages of the family members; Trace 4: guessed what the family had been doing before the visitor arrived; Trace 5: had to remember their clothing; Trace 6: had to remember the locations of the family members and objects; Trace 7: estimated how long the visitor had been away from the family. (From Yarbus, 1967; adapted from Solso, 1995.)

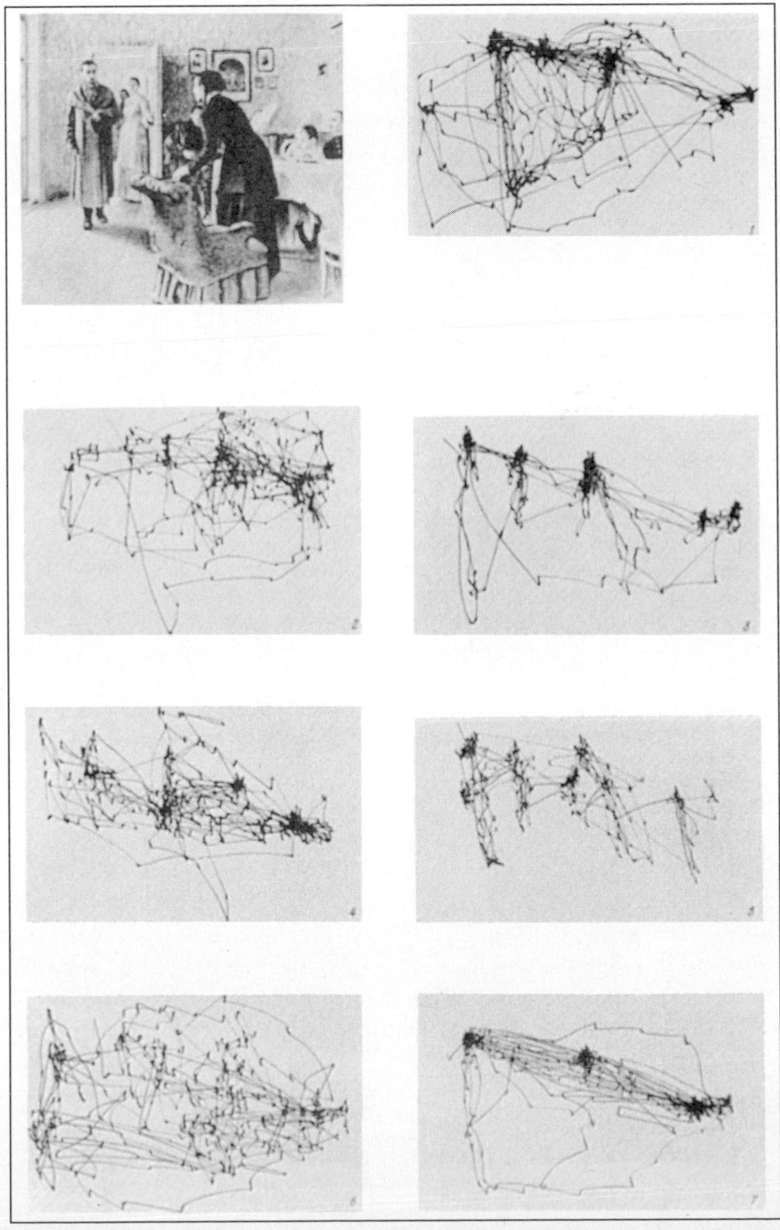

to the scene outside your window to the color of the wall—would destroy visual (and mental) continuity. Balancing these competing tendencies, then, is an ongoing process of monitoring: we evaluate the importance of current activity, of maintaining visual attention, and we monitor the importance or urgency of stimuli outside of the current attentional focus. There's even some evidence that these two functions—maintaining attention versus interrupting ongoing activity—depend on different hemispheres in the brain, the left for maintaining attention, the right for interrupting (e.g., Tucker & Williamson, 1984).

VISUAL SENSORY MEMORY—WHERE THE VISUAL INFORMATION GOES

When your saccade ends, and your eyes fixate on something, you are encoding that "something" into the visual system. So where does it go? To **visual sensory memory,** the memory system that receives visual input from the eyes and holds it for a brief amount of time. Since this memory system is so very brief, we generally have few useful intuitions about its operation. Unusual circumstances, however, can give us some clues.

Two Examples

- Swing a flashlight in a circle in a darkened room. What do you see? A circle of light—the circular path of the flashlight. It's like an on-line version of a time-lapse photograph, isn't it?

- Time-lapse photograph, showing paths of car headlights.

Something in the cognitive system is recording visual events across a brief span of time, and then holding or storing that record mentally. The "something" is visual sensory memory.

Take another example. Everyone has seen a flash of lightning during a thunderstorm—say while looking out the kitchen window into your backyard. Think about that for a moment, then guess how long you see the backyard (or other visual scene) when a bolt of lightning strikes. Most people guess that the flash of light lasts a half second or so, maybe even closer to a whole second sometimes. If this was your estimate, then it's reasonable—but not as an estimate of the physical duration of the lightning.

A bolt of lightning is actually three or four separate bolts. Each bolt lasts about 1 millisecond, with about 50 milliseconds of darkness between each bolt. The entire lightning strike lasts no more than about 200 milliseconds—two-tenths of a second—and is composed of three to four individual flashes. (Trigg & Lerner's *Encyclopedia of Physics*, 1981, is full of interesting tidbits!)

But what do you *perceive?* You perceive a flash of light that extends across time. This phenomenon is called **visual persistence,** the apparent persistence of a visual stimulus beyond its physical duration. This phenomenon usually includes the subjective feeling that you can "look around" the scene, and that the scene "fades away" rather than "switches off." Now, the eye itself does not continue to send "lightning" messages into the visual system after the flash is over (unless a retinal afterimage is involved). Therefore, your perception of the lightning is a *mental event*, one that reflects visual persistence. And—this is important—since any persistence of information beyond its physical duration defines the term *memory*, the processes of visual perception must begin with a visual memory system. There must be some sort of temporary visual buffer that holds visual information for brief periods of time. This memory is termed *visual sensory memory*. Neisser's (1967) term **iconic memory** is entirely equivalent.

Our perception of lightning is a mental event that reflects visual persistence.

◆ A tachistoscope in use.

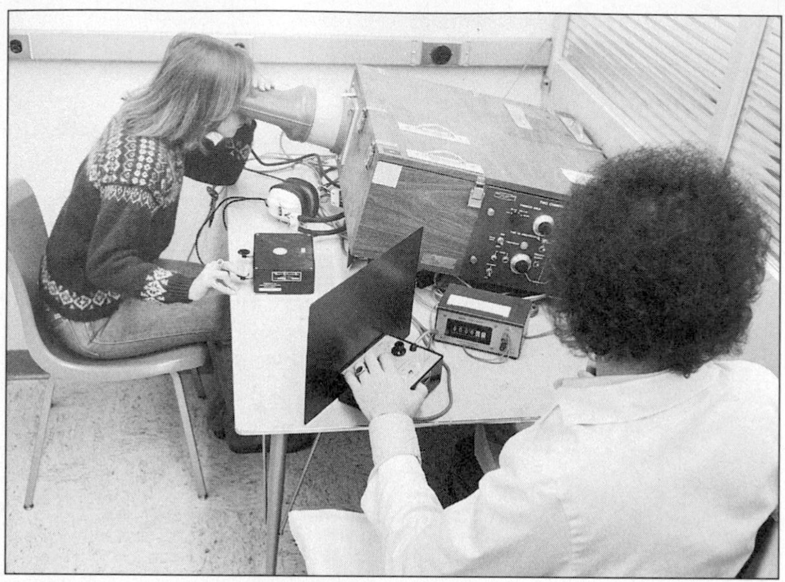

Amount and Duration of Storage

The classic cognitive research on the characteristics and processes of visual sensory memory was that reported by Sperling and his co-workers (Sperling, 1960; Averbach & Sperling, 1961). Sperling used a special apparatus for presenting visual stimuli, the **tachistoscope,** commonly known (and more easily pronounced) as a *T-scope*. This machine lets the investigator present a visual stimulus for a carefully controlled period of time, usually on the order of milliseconds, and in a carefully controlled position, usually so that the stimulus is projected on the subject's fovea. The T-scope also permits the experimenter to control what is seen before and after the stimulus, the *preexposure* and *postexposure* fields. As investigators before him had, Sperling wondered about "the information available in brief visual presentations," the title of his important monograph (1960).

In this research, Sperling presented arrays of letters and digits to participants on a T-scope for very brief durations. In all cases, the task was to report what was remembered from the display. For example, participants would be shown a series of trials, each with a 3 × 4 array of letters (three rows, four letters per row). The array was shown for 50 milliseconds and was followed by a blank postexposure field. Finally, a signal was given to report the letters from the display. See Figure 2.3 for a schematic diagram of a typical trial (but, of course, each "cube" in the figure shows the successive displays you'd see in the same place on the T-scope's display screen).

Whole-Report Condition Sperling (1960) found that the participants generally reported no more than four or five items correctly in this kind of test—when more than five were shown, they averaged about 4.5 letters correct. For a display of 12 letters, this is 37 percent accuracy. Furthermore, he found that this level of accuracy remained essentially the same for exposures as long as 500 milliseconds, and even as short as 5 milliseconds (Sperling, 1963). It appears that the average of 4.5 items correct reflected a kind of "default" strategy. That is, the participants realized they couldn't possibly remember all 12 letters in the **whole-report condition,** because the display seemed to fade from view too rapidly. So they tried to maximize their performance on at least part of the display, by concentrating on just one or two of the rows. Their level of performance, about 4 or 5 items, was what would be expected based on the **span of apprehension,** the number of individual items recallable after any short display (also known as the *span of attention* or the *span of immediate memory*; see Chapter 4).

★ **FIGURE 2.3**

A schematic diagram of a typical trial in Sperling's (1960) experiments. After a fixation point appears for 500 msec, the letter array is displayed. The visual field after the display is blank. The tone cue can occur at the same time as the postfield, or it can be delayed up to 5 sec. (Data from Sperling, 1960.)

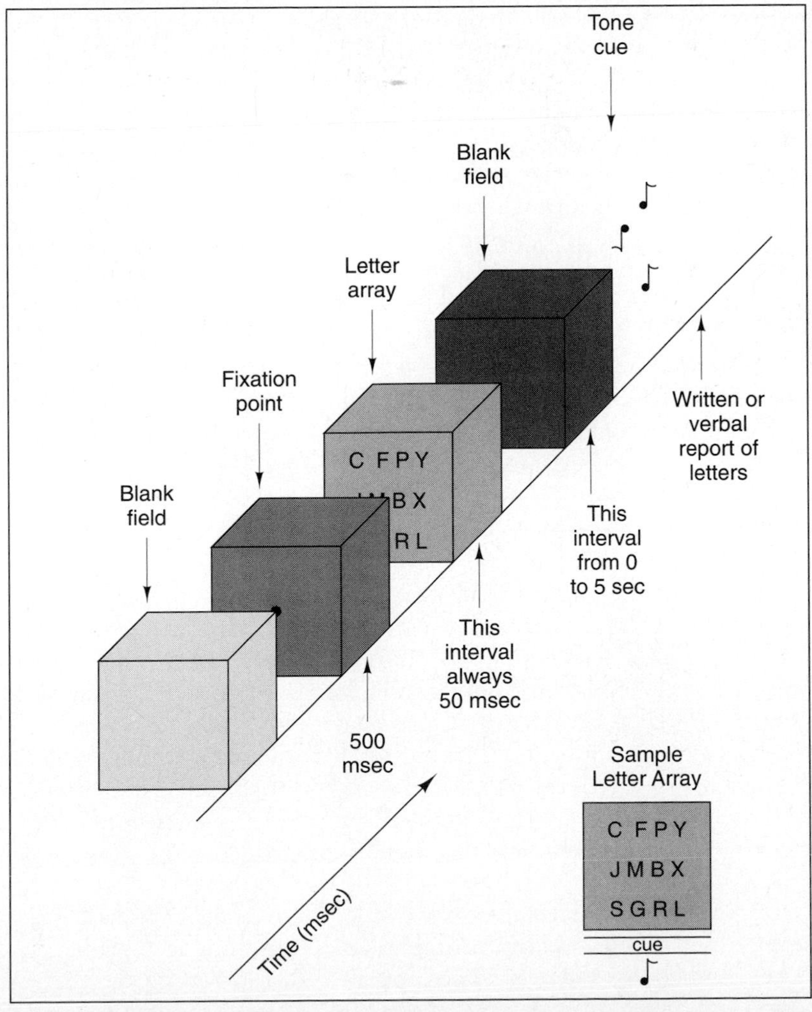

Partial-Report Condition Sperling devised an ingenious condition to contrast with these results. Rather than ask people to report the whole display, he devised a **partial-report condition,** where they had to report only a designated part of the display. The logic of this comparison was absolutely elegant.

Sperling reasoned that *all* the letters of the display might be available initially, but then would fade more rapidly than people could report them—just as "all" of the backyard is visible briefly after the flash of lightning, but then fades. If this is true, then subjects might be highly accurate on any *one* of the rows that the experimenter might choose at random, if they are told which row to report before too much fading has taken place.

So in the partial-report condition, Sperling prearranged a special signal for the participants. If a high tone was sounded right after the display went off, this cued them to report the top row. Likewise, a medium tone cued the middle row, and a low tone cued the bottom row. The crucial ingredient here is that the tone cues were presented *after* the display went off. The participants had no way of knowing ahead of time which row they would be responsible for, so they had to be prepared to report *any* of them.

Say that on a particular trial the low tone sounded right after the display went off. Given that the array should still be visible to the subject, because of visual persistence, the person should be able to focus mental attention on the bottom row and read out those letters accurately while they are still visible. Sperling found that this was exactly what happened. When the tone followed the display immediately, subjects' performance was 76 percent correct—76 percent of the cued row (about three of the four items) could be reported accurately. By logical extension, if performance was 76 percent on any randomly selected row, then their visual memory of the *entire* display must also be around 76 percent. (Professors use the same logic. If you score 76 percent on a Chapter 2 pop quiz, they infer that you'd probably get about 76 percent correct on a quiz over any other assigned chapter.)

This rather startling result suggested that immediately after a visual stimulus is displayed, a great deal of the stimulus information is available in visual sensory memory—much more than could be reported aloud. But the *icon*, the visual record of the letter array, doesn't last very long. Accuracy in partial report began to decline as the information in iconic memory began to fade, dwindling to about 36 percent if a whole second passed before the tone cue was given. Of course, this was almost exactly the accuracy level in the whole-report condition (Sperling, 1960).

▲ Figure 2.4 shows similar results, from a study that presented 18 letters in the letter display. See how the accuracy curve zoomed down within half a second when the pre- and postexposure fields were light. In Sperling's (1963) own words, "The explanation for these results is that the visual image of the stimulus persists for a short time after the stimulus has been turned off, and that the subjects can utilize this rapidly fading image. In fact, naive subjects typically believe that the physical stimulus fades out slowly" (p. 22). This is our naive impression of the flash of lightning too. As the fading continues, however, less and less of the original display is still visible in iconic memory, until by 1 second the only reportable items are those few that were transferred into the more durable short-term memory store.

Compare this rapid fading with the other curve in Figure 2.4, when the pre- and postexposure fields were dark. In this condition, fading of the icon was much slower; for instance, accuracy was still over 50 percent even after a 2-second delay (Averbach & Sper-

FIGURE 2.4

One subject's results on the number of letters available for report, as revealed by the partial-report condition. The number of reportable letters drops sharply within 0.25 sec. when the postexposure field is light; the information persists considerably longer when the postexposure field is dark. The vertical bars on the *x*-axis show the number of letters reported under whole report. (From Averbach & Sperling, 1961.)

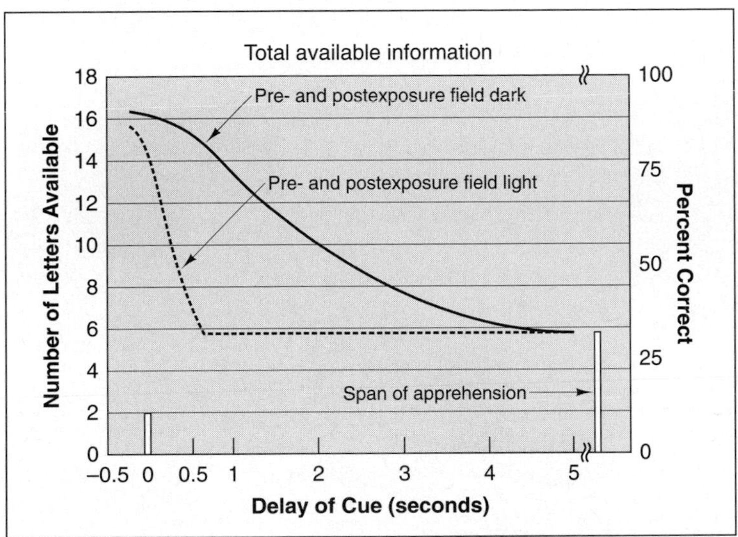

ling, 1961). In other words, dark pre- and postexposure fields lengthened the useful life of iconic information—just as a lightning bolt is more visible in a nighttime storm than a daytime storm, because of the contrast with the background illumination.

Erasure of Visual Information—Interference

A related series of experiments by Sperling and others explored a different reason for the loss of information—forgetting—from iconic memory. Sperling's original work suggested that the icon fades across time, and implied that time-based **decay** was the reason for forgetting. In the follow-up research, Sperling and his colleagues asked, What happens to iconic memory when a second stimulus is presented, when one visual scene is immediately followed by another? Their answer was **interference,** the second reason for forgetting from visual sensory memory.

In the follow-up studies (Averbach & Coriell, 1961/1973), two rows of letters, with eight letters per row, were shown for 50 milliseconds. A blank white postexposure field, varying in duration, followed the display, and was then itself followed by a partial-report cue. But Averbach and Coriell used a *visual* cue rather than a tone. The participants saw either a vertical bar marker or a circle marker. The bar marker was positioned just above (or below) the position of the to-be-reported letter, while the circle marker surrounded the position where the to-be-reported letter had just disappeared, as shown in Figure 2.5 (p. 40). As before, participants did not know ahead of time what letters would appear in the display or which letter they would have to report.

FIGURE 2.5

Stimuli and cues used by Averbach and Corriell (1961/1973). (From Averbach & Coriell, 1961/1973. "Short-term memory in vision," from *Bell System Technical Journal,* 1961, *40*, pp. 309–328. Copyright 1961, American Telephone and Telegraph Company.)

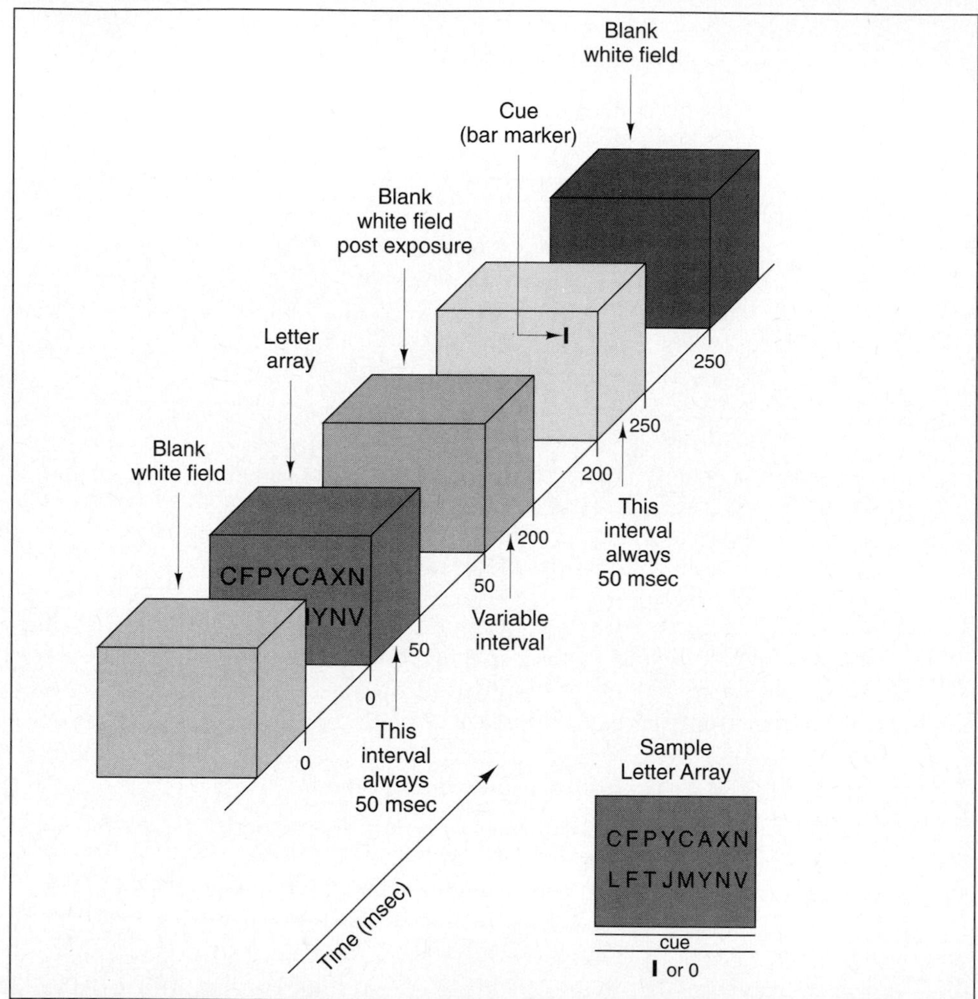

The bar marker study yielded very similar results to Sperling's earlier results—performance was high with short delays of the cues, got worse with longer delays, and showed a duration of about one quarter of a second. But the circle marker results were somewhat different. When the circle marker cued the position to be reported, subjects were considerably less accurate than they were with the bar marker. In a second study, the circle marker was filled with grid lines, and produced an even more dramatic decline in performance.

These results suggested strongly that the identical positioning of the circle had in some way "erased" the memory trace for the letter in that position. Now *that's* interesting—*"a later visual stimulus can drastically affect the perception of an earlier one"* (Averbach & Coriell, 1961/1973, p. 16, emphasis added). The effect is called **backward masking.** The masking stimulus, if it occurs soon enough after the letter display, interferes with the perception of the earlier stimulus presented at the same position. (Data on this go back as far as Werner, 1935; see Kahneman, 1968, for a review.) In general, then, when the contents of visual sensory memory are degraded by subsequent visual stimuli, the loss of the original information is termed **erasure,** a specific kind of interference.

THE DISPUTE ABOUT ICONIC MEMORY

Because of the evidence collected by Sperling, Averbach, and others, cognitive psychology proposed that iconic memory was the initial step in visual information processing, the first phase of visual perception (e.g., Neisser, 1967). Theories of visual perception therefore included iconic storage as an integral part of visual perception.

An alternate view, however, was expressed most strongly by Haber (1983) in his paper titled "The Impending Demise of the Icon." Haber did not doubt the evidence on visual persistence, nor did he quibble with the term **icon** as a label for the mental image or "snapshot" preserved by visual persistence. What he claimed, however, was that this static icon is quite irrelevant to an understanding of normal visual perception. As he put it, only somewhat facetiously, "The notion of an icon as a brief storage of information persisting after stimulus termination cannot possibly be useful in any typical visual information-processing task except reading in a lightning storm" (p. 1).

Ecological Validity

The logic behind Haber's conclusion was based in part on the concept of **ecological validity,** that the research setting and task need to resemble situations in the real world—the ecology of vision, for example. Haber pointed out that no ordinary visual experience is even remotely similar to lab tasks using the T-scope. We do not normally see only brief flashes of visual stimuli in our environment, followed by a blank field. The only real-world circumstance that even comes close to resembling this is the brief illumination provided by a bolt of lightning.

Instead, Haber argued, the visual environment remains in view as long as we fixate our eyes on it. We have continuous, rather than momentary, exposure to visual scenes, and we can extract information from those scenes across as much time as we care to devote to them. In short, Haber argued that while iconic memory and visual persistence are real, they are irrelevant to the normal task of perceiving continuous visual information.

Haber's paper was followed by a string of replies, some in favor of his conclusion, some opposed (e.g., G. R. Loftus, 1983)—fans of academic debates should read several of these. Several of these argued that, paradoxically, it may be rather irrelevant that we have continuous exposure to the visual world, and rather unimportant that the environment is continuously present. That is, despite the fact that we can sample the visual world continuously, it seems we don't.

The First 50 Milliseconds of Fixation

Powerful support for this conclusion was reported by Rayner, Inhoff, Morrison, Slowiaczek, and Bertera (1981), who examined performance during a text-reading task. After participants had fixated a word for 50 milliseconds, the word was *replaced* with a completely irrelevant stimulus, which remained in view for another 175 milliseconds in order to "fill up" the rest of the fixation time. Surprisingly, this replacement did not affect reading performance at all—the participants still reported the word they saw, and were apparently unaware that the word had changed while they were looking at it. In Coltheart's (1983) words, "Once the text has been fixated for 50 milliseconds or so, its presence during the remainder of the fixation is *irrelevant* and makes *no* contribution to reading" (p. 18, emphasis added). Thus, Haber's (1983) point about the environment—that we can continuously sample information from it—may in fact be irrelevant to the way the eye actually extracts visual information.

Second, consider Haber's point that the static "snapshot" character of the icon seems irrelevant to the issues of how people perceive movement, and how perception functions when our eyes, heads, and bodies move in relation to the visual environment. Several investigators have found evidence for "dynamic icons," iconic images that contain movement. For instance, Treisman, Russell, and Green (1975) presented a brief (100 msec) display of six moving dots to their experimental subjects and asked them to report the direction of movement. Partial-report performance was superior to whole-report performance, and accuracy under partial report declined across time. In short, the moving images of the dots were decaying just as the static letter grid had in Sperling's procedures (see also Finke & Freyd, 1985; Irwin, 1991, 1992; Loftus & Hanna, 1989).

Thus, visual perception is not a process of flipping through successive "snapshots," with three or four snapshots per second. Instead, it may be more accurately described as a process of focusing on the visually attended elements of successive fixations, where each fixation encodes a dynamic segment of the visual environment. As Irwin (1991) put it, our "perceptual representation of the environment is built up via the integration of information across [several] saccadic eye movements" (p. 420).

PULLING VISUAL SENSORY MEMORY TOGETHER

How do all of these different results make sense? How do they fit together? Consider the following integration.

Under normal viewing conditions, one moment's visual input replaces the just-previous visual input, by means of erasure or "writing over." Under unusual circumstances, say, the single brief glimpse afforded by a T-scope, even the shortest of stimulus displays will seem to last about one-fourth of a second (250 milliseconds) due to visual persistence, the duration of a normal iconic memory. With a blank postexposure field, which artificially prevents any subsequent stimulus at all, the perceptual fading of the icon is even visible.

The continuous stream of successive glimpses in normal vision, however, serves as the eraser under more normal viewing conditions. Under these circumstances, we're not aware of any fading. Notice here that the rapid extraction of information during the first 50 or so milliseconds of exposure appears to be critical to vision. Indeed, it may be that information extracted during the first 50 milliseconds or so is all that's needed to encode the stimulus into visual sensory memory. During the remaining time, we *attend* to the information—pay attention to it—and begin to replace that icon with new information from the next fixation.

Focal attention was Neisser's (1967) term for this mental process of visual attention—for instance, the mental redirection of attention when the partial-report cue is presented. It would seem that focal attention, now more commonly referred to simply as **visual attention,** might be the "bridge" between successive scenes registered by visual sensory memory. This bridging process prevents us from sensing the blank space of time occupied by the eye's saccades, by directing focal attention instead to elements of the icon. While we *sense* a great deal of visual information, what we *perceive* is just that part of a visual scene selected for focal, visual attention.

Summary

1. Rods and cones, on the back of the retina, begin the process of vision, sending messages to bipolar cells, which transmit to the ganglia that transmit through the optic nerve into the brain.
2. Visual information persists beyond the physical duration of the event, giving evidence for visual sensory memory.
3. Information endures in visual sensory memory for one-fourth to one-half of a second, after which it fades away. In normal vision, subsequent visual information erases information in the previous icon.
4. We apparently extract most of our visual information within the first 50 milliseconds of fixation. This information even includes movement and other dynamic aspects of the visual world.

Visual Pattern Recognition

Preview: template matching, recognition by components, feature detection, and top-down theories of visual pattern recognition; a connectionist model of word recognition

What are those things in Figure 2.6 (p. 44)? How did you come to interpret those patterns as drawings of triangles, circles, penguins, and flashlights? What set of mental processes enables us to take complex visual stimuli like the written samples in Figure 2.7 (p. 45) and read the words? As this figure shows, the visual world is amazingly variable—visual patterns with seemingly infinite variations flood into visual sensory memory, and yet we can easily and rapidly decide what those patterns are. Now that you've studied how the visual stimulus gets "into" the cognitive system, let's discuss the next step, how the system classifies and identifies the pattern. In other words, let's turn to the process of **pattern recognition.**

THEORIES OF PATTERN RECOGNITION

We'll discuss several specific approaches and theories about visual pattern recognition. A lot of serious effort toward understanding letter and word recognition has been exerted across the years, as much of our discussion here indicates. But there has also been concern with recognition of real-world objects, and how the visual system accomplishes this feat—we'll cover this too. As you'll see, all of this work leads us to an important fact

FIGURE 2.6

Triangles, circles, penguins, and flashlights. (Adapted from Biederman, 1990.)

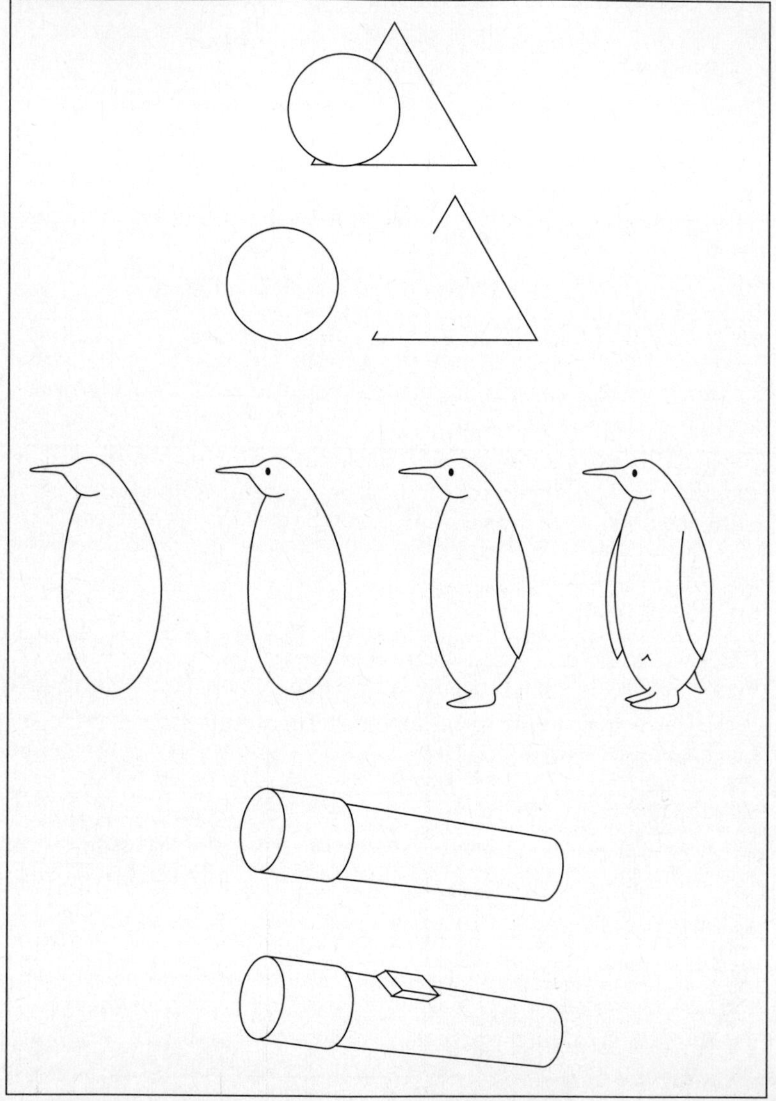

about human pattern recognition, and indeed about all of human cognition. To a much larger extent than we realize, pattern recognition is affected by our existing knowledge, by our expectations, and by the context of the stimulus. It isn't just a matter of deciphering what the visual stimulus is; it's also a matter of what you know, what you think, and what the surrounding environment suggests. This, of course, is the theme of **top-down, conceptually driven processing.**

★ **FIGURE 2.7**

Variations of written-word patterns that are easily read.

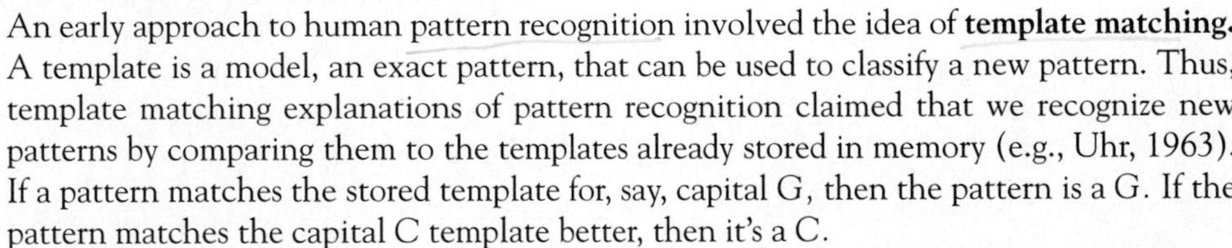

The Template-Matching Approach

An early approach to human pattern recognition involved the idea of **template matching.** A template is a model, an exact pattern, that can be used to classify a new pattern. Thus, template matching explanations of pattern recognition claimed that we recognize new patterns by comparing them to the templates already stored in memory (e.g., Uhr, 1963). If a pattern matches the stored template for, say, capital G, then the pattern is a G. If the pattern matches the capital C template better, then it's a C.

We're surrounded these days by modern-day machines that recognize patterns by exactly this process, comparing input patterns to a stored set of templates and trying to match them up. For example, the computer at your bank reads and recognizes your account number by comparing the symbols at the bottom of your checks to stored templates. The templates that the computer can read are the set of OCR (Optical Character Recognition) numbers (the last line of Figure 2.7 uses the OCR letter symbols). Bar codes printed on the products you purchase (there's one on the back of this book), on the luggage you check for an airline flight, and so forth, are "read" by a scanning device and recognized in similar fashion, because the exact pattern of lines and spaces on the printed bar code is stored in the computer's memory.

While template matching works reasonably well for certain limited settings (checking-account numbers, etc.) it has at least three serious, even fatal, drawbacks as a psychological theory of pattern recognition.

- If we recognize patterns by template matching, we would have to have learned and stored a huge number of templates in memory at some time or another. But this is most implausible. After all, while the size of memory is vast, it's certainly not that vast, not large enough to store an infinite number of templates!

Computer-generated "Lincoln"

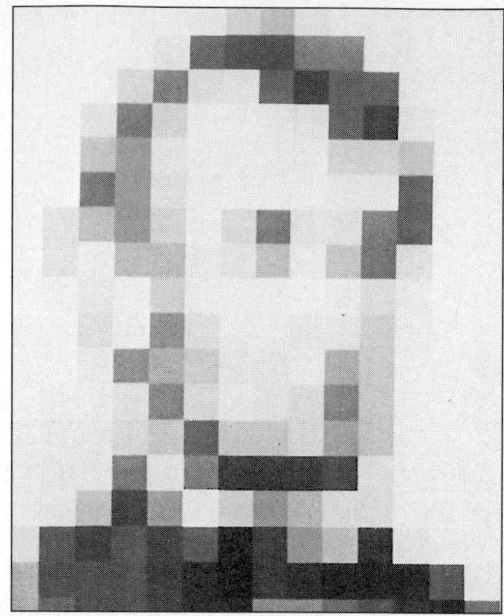

- Each different template would have to be learned before its pattern could be recognized. But how could this be true? Given the diversity of patterns, even if we just consider handwriting, it's impossible to believe that you have already learned all possible patterns at some point in your past.
- As if those difficulties aren't enough, we can easily recognize patterns that are slightly fuzzy, out of focus, sideways, or otherwise visually degraded. But template matching is a rigid process in which the pattern needs to match the template nearly perfectly. Any discrepancies make recognition very erratic or impossible—for machines anyway, but generally not for humans.

Components and Features

If we don't store an exact copy of every visual stimulus we can recognize, then how do we recognize patterns? An important idea is that we break patterns down into their constituents, that every pattern is composed of pieces—components, features. If we can identify the underlying components of a pattern, then we can compare the components to a list or index stored in memory. Thus, "rectangular object" would match the memory representation for "brick" or "box," "rectangular object with curved component on top" would match the index for briefcase or suitcase, and "cylinder with handle on the side" would match the listing for coffee mug.

Recognition by Components

This is almost exactly the approach taken by Biederman (Biederman, 1987; Biederman & Blickle, 1985) in his theory of object recognition. Biederman calls his model the **Recognition by Components (RBC) model.** He argues that all three-dimensional objects in the world are composed of simple components, which he calls **geons** (for *geometrical ions*). You remember *ion* from chemistry, right? Roughly, it's a basic building block of matter, an atom. So Biederman is saying that when we recognize objects, we are breaking them down (*parsing* is the technical term) into their components. We identify the object based on two kinds of information: first, which particular components are detected in an object, and second, the places where the components join together.

In this scheme, the recognition process starts by examining two aspects of the pattern.

- First, we find the edges of objects. This enables us to determine which edges maintain the same relationships to one another regardless of viewing orientation—however you look at a brick, those three long edges remain parallel to one another, as shown in Figure 2.8.
- Second, we carefully scan regions of the pattern where the lines intersect, usually places where deep concave angles are formed. Look at the deep "concave" angles on the last "brick," where the curved component joins the rectangle. Examining the edges and the areas of intersection enables us to determine which basic components are present in the pattern—rectangular solid joined on the upper surface by a curved segment. Then we compare this list to our stored knowledge, a mental representation of objects that contains their descriptions—something like "briefcase/suitcase: rectangular solid joined on the upper surface by a curved segment." When we find a

FIGURE 2.8

Various bricks. The last one has a handle. (Adapted from Biederman, 1990.)

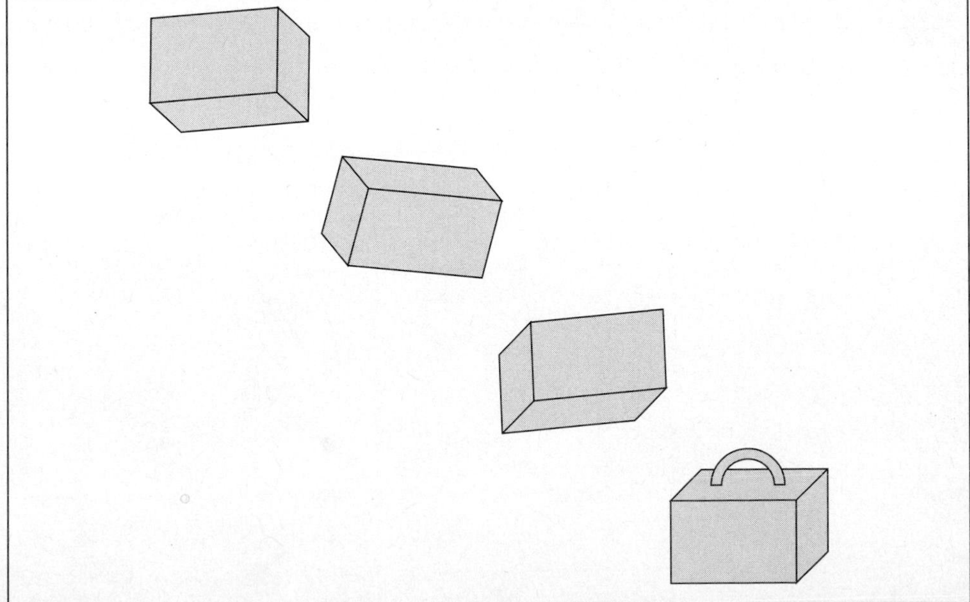

match between the identified components and the stored representation, we have recognized the pattern.

Combining Components Interestingly, Biederman (1987) suggests that there are only 36 basic components, 36 geons, in the pattern recognition system. In other words, he claims that all physical objects can be constructed out of 36 basic, primitive components. While that may not sound like enough, you'd be surprised at the variety of objects that can be constructed out of just a handful of components, as shown in Figure 2.9. Even if we restrict ourselves to objects with only three components, this translates into 154 million possible objects. This is well beyond our estimates of how many objects people actually know and can recognize. (Biederman's own estimate is 30,000 objects.)

Evidence for RBC In some fascinating research based on this model, Biederman has discovered several important facts about the object recognition process. For one, the model's emphasis on the importance of intersection or the "junction points" turns out to be critical. If a pattern is degraded, it matters a great deal where it was degraded. If segments of the smooth, continuous edges are missing, it's reasonably easy to "fill in" the missing parts from memory, and so be able to recognize the pattern. On the other hand, if the parts that are missing are those important locations where components join together, recognition is much more difficult, or even impossible.

Figure 2.10 shows several "nonrecoverable" objects, that is, drawings where people generally cannot recover from the deletions. Look at these carefully now, and try to figure out what the objects are. It's so difficult because those important intersection or junction locations have been deleted. Now look at Figure 2.11 (p. 50). Here you see "recoverable" versions of the drawings, in which parts of the continuous edges have been deleted but the intersections remain visible. It's no surprise here that it's relatively easy to identify the original objects (you *can* identify them, can't you?). In Biederman's data (Biederman & Blickle, 1985), participants never did worse than 30 percent errors in identifying recover-

FIGURE 2.9

Geons (components) and the objects they make. (From Biederman, 1990.)

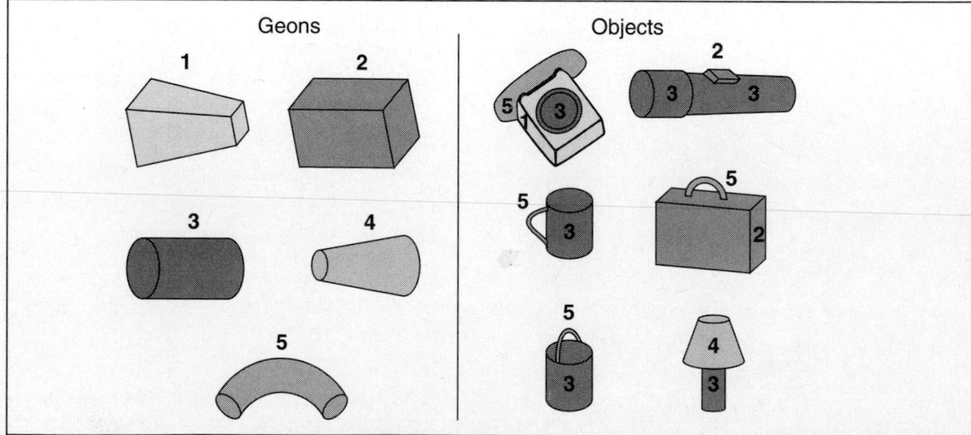

FIGURE 2.10

"Nonrecoverable" objects. (From Biederman, 1987.)

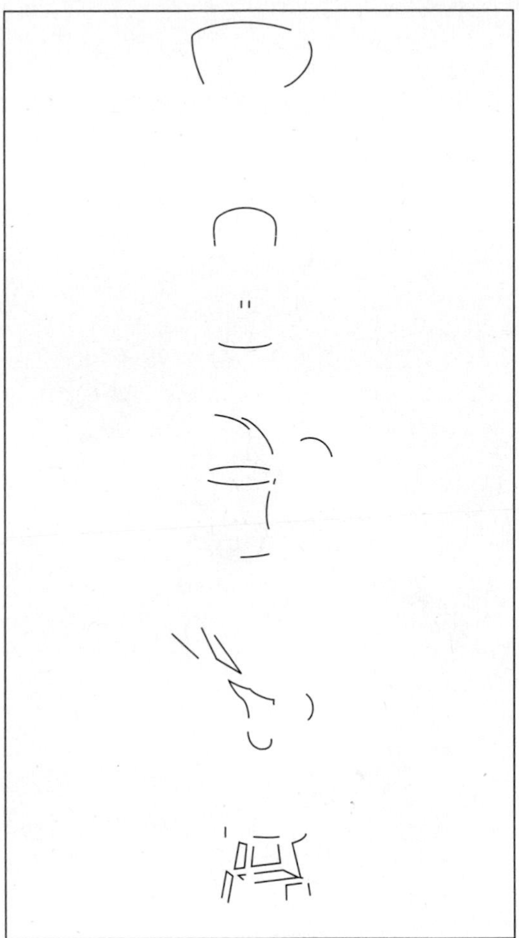

able patterns, even when 65 percent of the continuous line contours were deleted and the pattern was only shown for 100 milliseconds. But when the same percentage of the junctions or intersections were deleted, as in Figure 2.10, participants made errors in the 100-milliseconds condition almost 55 percent of the time.

Feature Detection

When we turn to letter and word recognition, we find a similar improvement over the idea of template matching. This is the **feature detection** approach, similar in many respects to the recognition-by-component position. Feature detection claims that the letter and word patterns we encounter while reading are first broken down into simple, elementary **features,** and that we recognize patterns by knowing which combinations of features signify which patterns. A feature, therefore, is a simple, elementary pattern that appears in combinations with other features.

★ **FIGURE 2.11**

"Recoverable" objects. (From Biederman, 1987.)

In this approach, our capital G would not be recognized as a whole, indivisible pattern. Instead, the pattern would be broken down into its component features: a curved line segment, open to the right, with a horizontal line at the bottom of the opening. In memory, the patterns we've learned for letters would be stored in the same way: in terms of their constituent features. So, a feature detection model (e.g., Gibson, 1969) would claim that we have feature lists or configurations stored in memory. The "entry" in that list that contains "curved line, open to the right, horizontal bar" would then be associated with the pattern name "capital G," and so forth for all other letters.

One of the main advantages of this approach is that the number of basic features is relatively small. This avoids a serious problem with template-matching models, having to ▲ learn a myriad of patterns. As an example, Gibson's (1969) "catalog" contained only 12 features for written and printed letters. In such an approach, there is an economy of basic patterns or features, but the flexibility to combine them (or their absence) into a great many distinct patterns.

David H. Hubel and Torsten N. Wiesel won the Nobel prize in 1981 for their innovative research on the visual centers of the brain (e.g., Hubel & Wiesel, 1962). They implanted microelectrodes into the visual cortex of cats' brains, and recorded how individual brain cells responded to different kinds of visual stimuli. Their results suggested strongly that different brain cells respond to different *features*. For example, different sets of neurons in the visual cortex responded to horizontal, vertical, and diagonal lines. One cluster of cells responded to movement from left to right, but a different cluster responded to top-to-bottom movement. A conclusion from this work is that the human visual cortex is similar to the cat's, and also relies on such neurological feature detectors for pattern recognition.

Pandemonium In any feature detection model, the relationships among the features are just as important as the features themselves—after all, if your recognition system didn't notice where the curved line segment was in relation to the vertical line, you couldn't tell a *b* from a *d*. A clever way of illustrating these relationships, and how they're registered in the recognition system, was an early model of the feature detection process, a model by Selfridge (1959). Selfridge conceived of pattern recognition as a four-stage process, where each stage performed its one specific task and then forwarded its result on to the next stage.

Demons To liven it up a bit, Selfridge (1959) described the whole system in a deliberately humorous—and memorable!—fashion. Imagine a large, noisy room, with hundreds of people shouting all at once. How would you describe this room? *Pandemonium!* And who are the people doing the shouting? In Selfridge's whimsical analogy, they are *demons*, as shown in Figure 2.12 (p. 52).

Selfridge claimed that there are four different stages of the recognition process, so four different kinds of demons. In the first stage, the *image demons* encode the pattern and pass the encoded image along to the next level, the *feature demons*. There is one feature demon for each simple feature that can be contained in a letter—one for a horizontal bar, one for a vertical line, one for an open circle, and so on. Each feature demon compares itself to the image that was forwarded to it. If it matches, if it detects itself in the pattern, then that feature demon starts shouting—something like "Me! Me! That pattern contains *me!*" Feature demons that match only partially also shout, but not as loudly.

Listening to all of this shouting is the third level of demons, the *cognitive demons*. Here, there is one demon for every pattern to be recognized—one cognitive demon for capital G, one for capital C, and so forth. And because each cognitive demon has just one pattern to be responsible for, it knows which of the feature demons to listen for. So the capital G demon knows to listen for two features, "curved line open to the right," and "horizontal bar at the bottom opening." If just those feature demons are shouting the loudest, then the capital G cognitive demon begins shouting too, because the evidence suggests that the pattern was indeed a capital G. Usually, this demon will be shouting louder than, say, the capital C demon, which matches two features but lacks the horizontal bar.

FIGURE 2.12

Selfridge's (1959) Pandemonium model. The image demons encode the visual pattern. The feature demons try to match the simple features present in the pattern. Cognitive demons represent the combination of features that are present in different letters of the alphabet; each tries to match the several computational demons that match the stimulus input. Finally, the decision demon identifies the pattern by selecting the loudest cognitive demon, the one whose features most nearly match the pattern being presented. (Adapted from Selfridge, 1959.)

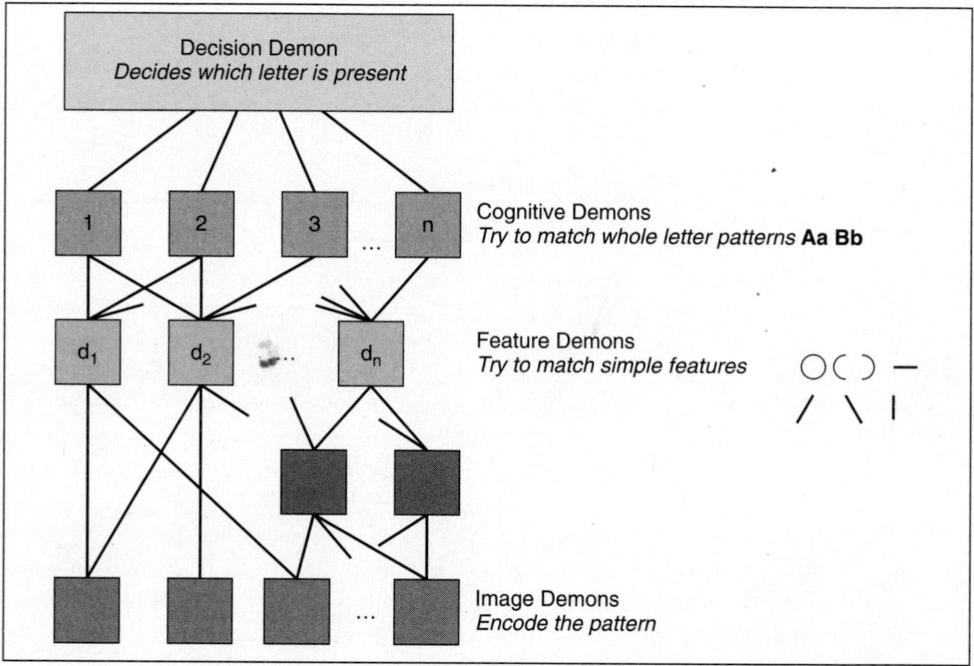

Sitting at the top of the heap is the *decision demon*, who listens to the shouting of the cognitive demons. The decision demon hears which cognitive demon is shouting the loudest, and decides that that one "is" the pattern that was presented. Thus, the decision demon recognizes the capital G, based on the evidence it "heard" passed from the lower to the higher levels.

Thus, in Pandemonium, the feature-matching process is a shouting match. The evidence filters up through the levels of demons, with the strongest evidence leading to recognition of the pattern.

BEYOND FEATURES: CONCEPTUALLY DRIVEN PATTERN RECOGNITION

Even Selfridge (1959) knew that the Pandemonium model was missing an important ingredient. Basically, Pandemonium was a completely **bottom-up processing** system, that is, completely **data driven**—the "data," patterns to be recognized, come in to the image demons, and eventually the decision demon recognizes the pattern, based totally on processes performed by the lower-level demons.

FIGURE 2.13

Top-down effects in pattern recognition. (a) The effect of context on letter recognition (adapted from Selfridge, 1959). (b) The effect of context on pattern recognition. The *B* and the *13* are identical figures (from Coren & Ward, 1989).

TAE CAT

(a)

A, B, C, D, E, F

10, 11, 12, 13, 14

(b)

But Selfridge presented examples like the one in Figure 2.13. How are the demons going to recognize the middle pattern in the two words? By rights, the shouting match should output the same result, because they are identical patterns. But of course *you* recognized them as different patterns, capital *H* and capital *A*. The bottom half of the figure shows another example—look back at the figure now, and notice that the capital *B* is in fact exactly the same pattern as the *13*. Why do you recognize these as being different? The answer is, Because of context, because of your knowledge that *THE* is a word but *TAE* is not, that *B* goes with *A, B, C* but *13* goes with *12, 13, 14*. This effect of context and knowledge is known as **conceptually driven processing,** also called **top-down processing.**

A classic demonstration of the role of conceptually driven processing in visual perception is a study by Neisser (1964). Neisser showed his participants lists of letters, and timed them as they performed different kinds of searches. For instance, in Figure 2.14, search list A for the letter *K*. Now search list B for the line without a *Q*. With sufficient practice—about two weeks of daily sessions—Neisser's subjects searched through displays like list A at a rate of about ten lines per second. For list B searches, finding the line that doesn't have a *Q*, performance never got faster than four to five lines per second.

More interestingly, searching for the *Z* in list C was considerably faster than searching for the *Z* in list D. Why? Because list C is composed mostly of curved letters. Searching for the angular *Z* here was fairly simple—the participants could "turn off" their detectors for circular features. But in list D, the angular *Z* is embedded in other angular letters, so merely searching for angles wouldn't distinguish *Z* from *M* or *V* or *X*—the search was therefore slower. (Similar evidence has been reported by Duncan & Humphreys, 1989.)

★ **FIGURE 2.14**

Neisser's (1964) search lists. In list A, the target is the letter *K*; in list B, the target is the line without the letter *Q*; in lists C and D, the target is the letter *Z*.

A. SEARCH FOR *K*	B. SEARCH FOR LINE WITHOUT *Q*	C. SEARCH FOR *Z*	D. SEARCH FOR *Z*
EHYP	ZVMLBQ	ODUGQR	IVMXEW
SWIQ	HSQJMF	QCDUGO	EWVMIX
UFCJ	ZTJVQR	CQOGRD	EXWMVI
WBYH	RDQTFM	QUGCDR	IXEMWV
OGTX	TQVRSX	URDGQO	VXWEMI
GWVX	MSVRQX	GRUQDO	MXVEWI
TWLN	ZHQBTL	DUZGRO	XVWMEI
XJBU	ZJTQXL	UCGROD	MWXVIE
UDXI	LHQVXM	DQRCGU	VIMEXW
HSFP	FVQHMS	QDOCGU	EXVWIM
XSCQ	MTSDQL	CGUROQ	VWMIEX
SDJU	TZDFQB	OCDURQ	VMWIEX
PODC	QLHBMZ	UOCGQD	XVWMEI
ZVBP	QMXBJD	RGQCOU	WXVEMI
PEVZ	RVZHSQ	GRUDQO	XMEWIV
SLRA	STFMQZ	GODUCQ	MXIVEW
JCEN	RVXSQM	QCURDO	VEWMIX
ZLRD	MQBJFT	DUCOQG	EMVXWI
XBOD	MVZXLQ	CGRDQU	IVWMEX
PHMU	RTBXQH	UDRCOQ	IEVMWX
ZHFK	BLQSZX	GQCORU	WVZMXE
PNJW	QSVFDJ	GOQUCD	XEMIWV
CQXT	FLDVZT	GDQUOC	WXIMEV
GHNR	BQHMDX	URDCGO	EMWIVX
IXYD	BMFDQH	GODROC	IVEMXW
QSVB	QHLJZT		
GUCH	TQSHRL		
OWBN	BMQHZJ		
BVQN	RTBJZQ		
FOAS	FQDLXH		
ITZN	XJHSVQ		
VYLD	MZRJDQ		
LRYZ	XVQRMB		
IJXE	QMXLSD		
RBOE	DSZHQR		
DVUS	FJQSMV		
BIAJ	RSBMDQ		
ESGF	LBMQFX		
QGZI	FDMVQJ		
ZWNE	HQZTXB		
QBVC	VBQSRF		
VARP	QHSVDZ		
LRPA	HVQBFL		
SGHL	HSRQZV		
MVRJ	DQVXFB		
GADB	RXJQSM		
PCME	MQZFVD		
ZODW	ZJLRTQ		
HDBR	SHMVTQ		
BVDZ	QXFBRJ		

Why are these examples considered to be demonstrations of conceptually driven processing? Consider how the subjects in the experiment searched list C. Realizing that the list is composed mostly of curved letters let them turn off or suppress their detectors for circular features. Where did the "instructions" to turn off those detectors come from? Not from the detectors themselves. Instead, the instructions must have come from somewhere "higher" in the system, some more cognitive process that was sensitive to the context provided by the *other* letters in the display. Something more deeply cognitive was influencing the lower-level feature detection process—making feature detection here driven by that cognitive, conceptual process.

The Top-Down Effect

We're claiming that visual pattern recognition—just like any other cognitive process—is jointly influenced by bottom-up and top-down processes. The bottom-up, or data-driven, part is clear—if a stimulus like the displays in Figure 2.10 is presented, then the speed and/or accuracy of performance will be influenced by the stimulus, the data in the display. When you read, the words on the page are a critically important source of information—that's obvious.

What may not be quite so obvious is the way **context** and your own knowledge also affect the process—these are the elements that give conceptually driven processes their drive. The displays from Neisser's (1964) work show clearly how context can affect performance. The cognitive system notices various aspects of the context, and then takes advantage of that by altering other mental processing. Thus, noticing that the search display is mostly composed of curved features means that your feature detection process is also being driven by that higher-level, cognitive information.

Just as influential as the context "out there" is *mental context*—in other words, your knowledge is a powerful source of conceptually driven processing. As you read, for example, you begin comprehending not only the words in a sentence but also the overall

Without context.

With context.

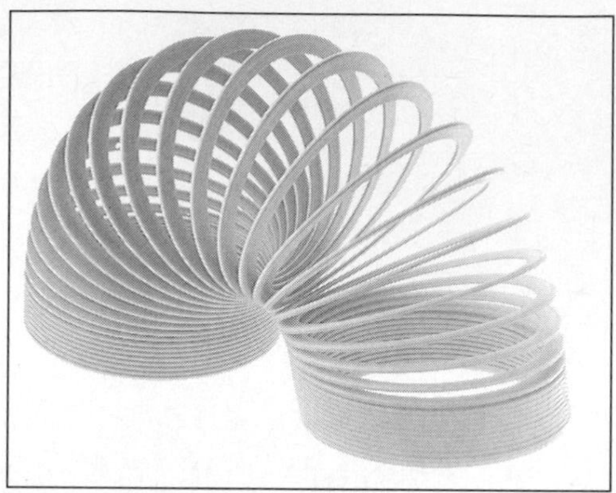

thought or idea being expressed. And in focusing more on the ideas, your cognitive system generates *expectations* about the remaining ideas in the sentence. These expectations may be so strong—you *know* the rest of the idea you're going to read about—that some lower-level processes like proofreading and noticing typograpical errors may not function as accurately as they usually do. For instance, did you notice that the word *typograpical* that you just read was misspelled? A clever demonstration of the power of conceptually driven processes is the phrase "Paris in the the spring." Because you know that familiar phrase, you can easily miss the obvious error in it, the extra *the*.

A Connectionist Model

A particularly good example of how recognition is influenced by both top-down and bottom-up processing comes from an important computerized model of word recognition, by Rumelhart and McClelland (1986). These researchers used a particular computer simulation approach known as **connectionism**—the term means the same thing as the terms **parallel distributed processing (PDP modeling)** and **neural net modeling.** The details of the approach can be rather difficult, so we'll postpone a full treatment of that until later. For now, consider the idea that "repairing" the Pandemonium model to give it top-down processing essentially turns it into a connectionist model, much like the Rumelhart and McClelland system.

Rumelhart and McClelland's Model In Rumelhart and McClelland's (1986) model, the system is trying to recognize words. The model knows—has stored in its nodes and the weights that connect the nodes—what features are present in different letters, and also what spelling patterns are common in English words. It also has a dictionary of sorts which lists possible words. The stimulus pattern given to the system is WORK, but as  shown in the bottom of Figure 2.15, parts of the letters were partially obscured—especially the final letter. Because most or all of the features for *W*, *O*, and *R* are still visible, the word-level unit in the model decides early on that the stimulus is more likely to be WORK than either FORK or WEAK. This is shown in the left panel of the figure, where the curve for WORK's level of activation begins to rise—to "win" the recognition race, in a sense—very early in the time cycles of the system.

FIGURE 2.15

A possible display that might be presented to the connectionist model of word recognition, and the resulting activations of selected letter and word units. The letter units are for the letters indicated in the fourth position of a four-letter display. (Adapted from Rumelhart & McClelland, 1986.)

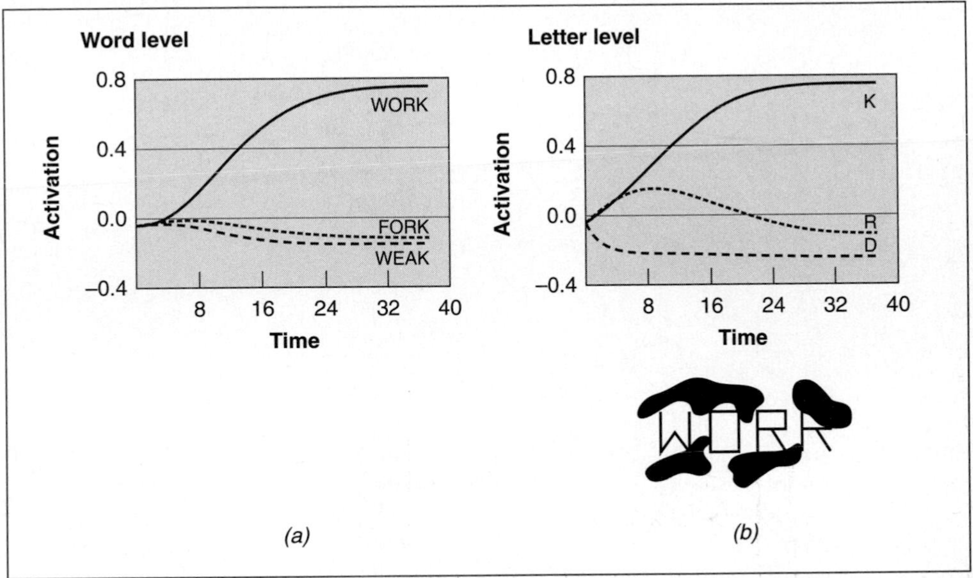

WORK is so highly activated at the word level, furthermore, that it exerts an influence on the lower level of letter recognition. So, even though much of the last letter is obscured, the system nonetheless "decides"—just like a decision demon—that the last letter is a *K*. Why doesn't the system think that last letter might be the letter *R*, you might wonder? After all, it could be, given the features that aren't obscured in the figure. The reason is that the "language user" part of the system knows that *WORR* is not a word, but *WORK* is.

This is the essence of top-down processing in a connectionist model. Knowing *WORK* is a word exerts an influence *down* toward the letter detection level, and biases the letter detectors toward recognizing a *K* instead of an *R*. Because the pattern-recognizer units have connections from the higher levels of knowledge, those higher levels influence the lower-level processes like letter detection.

Summary

1. Template-matching approaches to pattern recognition work in some limited settings, like machine/computer scanning, but cannot possibly explain human pattern recognition.
2. Feature or component detection approaches are more successful explanations of pattern recognition. Biederman's Recognition-by-Components model suggests that we recognize three-dimensional, real-world objects by detecting the elementary components they're made of; there are about 36 such components, called "geons," that the pattern recognition system identifies.

3. In work on letter recognition, Selfridge's Pandemonium model was the first serious feature detection model. Although it was successful as an explanation of bottom-up processing, Selfridge realized that it still lacked an important component.
4. The missing component was conceptually driven processing, a mechanism by which higher-level knowledge could exert an influence downward toward the pattern-recognizing mechanisms. Connectionist models provide a computer simulation format in which to model such top-down effects.

Auditory Perception and Pattern Recognition

Preview: the anatomy of the ear; auditory sensory memory; persistence, shadowing, and erasure; auditory pattern recognition; templates, feature detection, and conceptually driven processing

ANATOMY OF THE EAR

The sensory mechanism that responds to auditory stimuli—to sound waves—is an amazingly awkward combination of components. First, the sound waves are funneled into the ear, causing the tympanic membrane (the eardrum) to vibrate. This in turn causes the bones of the middle ear to move, and this movement sets in motion the fluid in the inner ear. This moving fluid then moves the tiny hair cells along the basilar membrane, which generate the neural message that is sent along the auditory nerve into the cerebral cortex (e.g., Forgus & Melamed, 1976). Thus, from the relatively unpromising elements of funnels, moving bones, and the like (see Figure 2.16) arises our sense of hearing or **audition.**

Despite all this, our hearing is amazingly sensitive. We can discriminate accurately between highly similar sounds—even infants notice the slight difference between the sounds "pah" and "bah" (e.g., Eimas, 1975). And we routinely convert the continuous stream of speech sounds into a comprehended message, with little or no apparent effort, at a rate of about two or three words per second. How does this happen? How does hearing coordinate with our knowledge of language to yield recognition and comprehension so rapidly?

AUDITORY SENSORY MEMORY

Consider Neisser's (1967) argument: "Perhaps the most fundamental fact about hearing is that sound is an intrinsically *temporal* event. Auditory information is always *spread out in time*; no single millisecond contains enough information to be very useful. If information were discarded as soon as it arrived, hearing would be all but impossible. Therefore, we must assume that some 'buffer,' some medium for temporary storage, is available in the auditory cognitive system" (pp. 199–200, emphasis added). That buffer is **auditory sensory memory,** also called **echoic memory** (Neisser, 1967). This is the brief memory system that receives auditory stimuli and preserves them for a short time—it's the auditory counterpart to visual sensory memory. Holding the sounds briefly in auditory sensory memory enables the rest of the human cognitive system to gain access to those sounds.

FIGURE 2.16

The gross structure of the human ear and a close-up of the middle and inner ear structures. (From Price, 1987.)

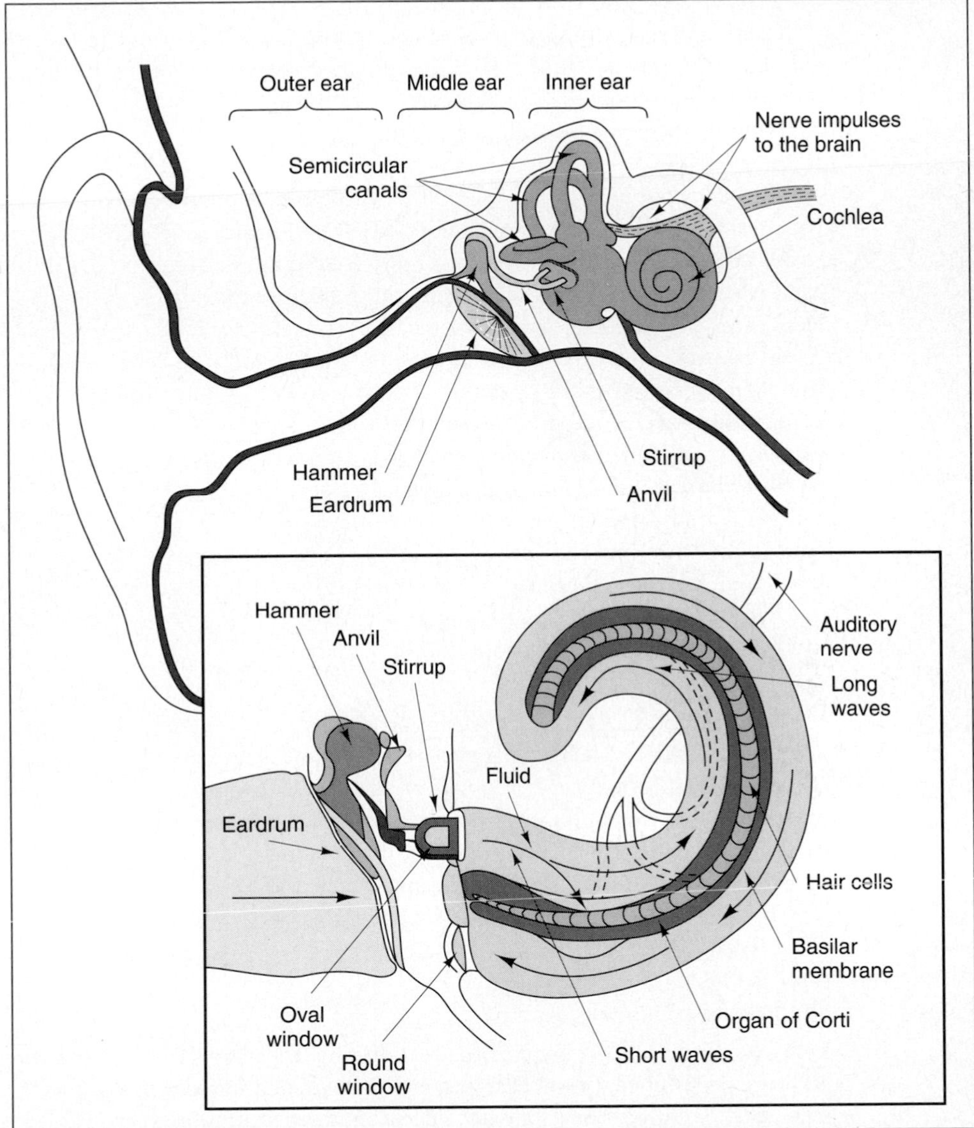

Amount and Duration of Storage

How long does encoded information reside in auditory sensory memory before it is lost? An answer to this question came from an auditory analogue to Sperling's (1960) task, called the "three-eared man" procedure. In this task (Darwin, Turvey, & Crowder, 1972; see also Moray, Bates, & Barnett, 1965), three different spoken messages came from three distinct locations. The participants heard tape-recorded letters and digits through stereo headphones, with the tape engineered so that one message was played only into the left ear, one message was played only into the right ear, and the final message was played into both ears. Of course, the message played into both ears seemed to be localized in the middle of the person's head, at the "third ear."

Each message contained three simple stimuli, say *T7C* in the left ear, *4B9* in the right ear, and *M2L* in the "third ear." Each sequence lasted one second on the tape recording, and all three sequences were presented simultaneously. Thus, in the space of 1 second, three different sequences of letter and digit combinations were played, for a total of nine separate stimuli.

As you would expect, people in the whole-report condition had to report as many of the nine items as they could remember. Their performance averaged about four items correct, as the bar shows in the inset in Figure 2.17, and was better on the third item heard in each ear, as shown in the larger portion of the figure. In the partial-report condition, they were given a visual cue, prompting recall of the left, right, or middle message. When the visual cue was presented immediately after the stimuli had been heard, performance on the cued ear was above 50 percent—nearly five items out of the original nine were still available (inset). And partial-report performance was still better than whole-report performance even when the cue was delayed 4 seconds—although performance did decline during that waiting period, as the figure shows. (Notice in the larger graph that recall of the third item in each ear was consistently higher than the first or second items—of course, the third one was the most recent). Thus, it seemed as if information in auditory sensory memory was forgotten across time, just as it is in visual sensory memory. Furthermore, forgetting was presumably due to a passive fading process—not nearly as rapidly as in visual sensory memory, but still rather quickly.

Persistence and Erasure of Auditory Information

There is also evidence showing that the duration of the auditory trace depends on how complex the information is. Darwin et al.'s (1972) estimate of 4 seconds is longer than most estimates, probably due to the simplicity of the stimuli they used (most of the studies described below used coherent spoken language). In contrast, the 4-second estimate is considerably shorter than the 10-second storage found by Eriksen and Johnson (1964)—but their subjects merely had to detect a simple tone while performing an attention-capturing task (they read novels for two hours; see also Watkins & Watkins, 1980).

Shadowing

Let's consider a well-known series of studies by Treisman (1964a, 1964b) that examined auditory persistence using a different kind of task, **shadowing.** In this task, the participant hears two messages, one in the left side of a pair of headphones, and one in the right side. The task requires the participant to repeat aloud the message heard in one ear, and ignore the other message. Because shadowing requires a great deal of effort and attention, we are reasonably certain that an influence of the ignored message will be due to its brief storage in auditory sensory memory.

Assume that Treisman's sample of participants were told to shadow the message in the right ear; call it the "attended" message. After they had begun to shadow that mes-

FIGURE 2.17

Partial-report results in the "three-eared man" procedure. The average number of items recalled correctly is shown for the first, second, and third items in the three lists, across varying delays in the presentation of the partial-report cue. The inset shows overall performance, along with the vertical bar that shows whole-report accuracy. (From Darwin et al., 1972.)

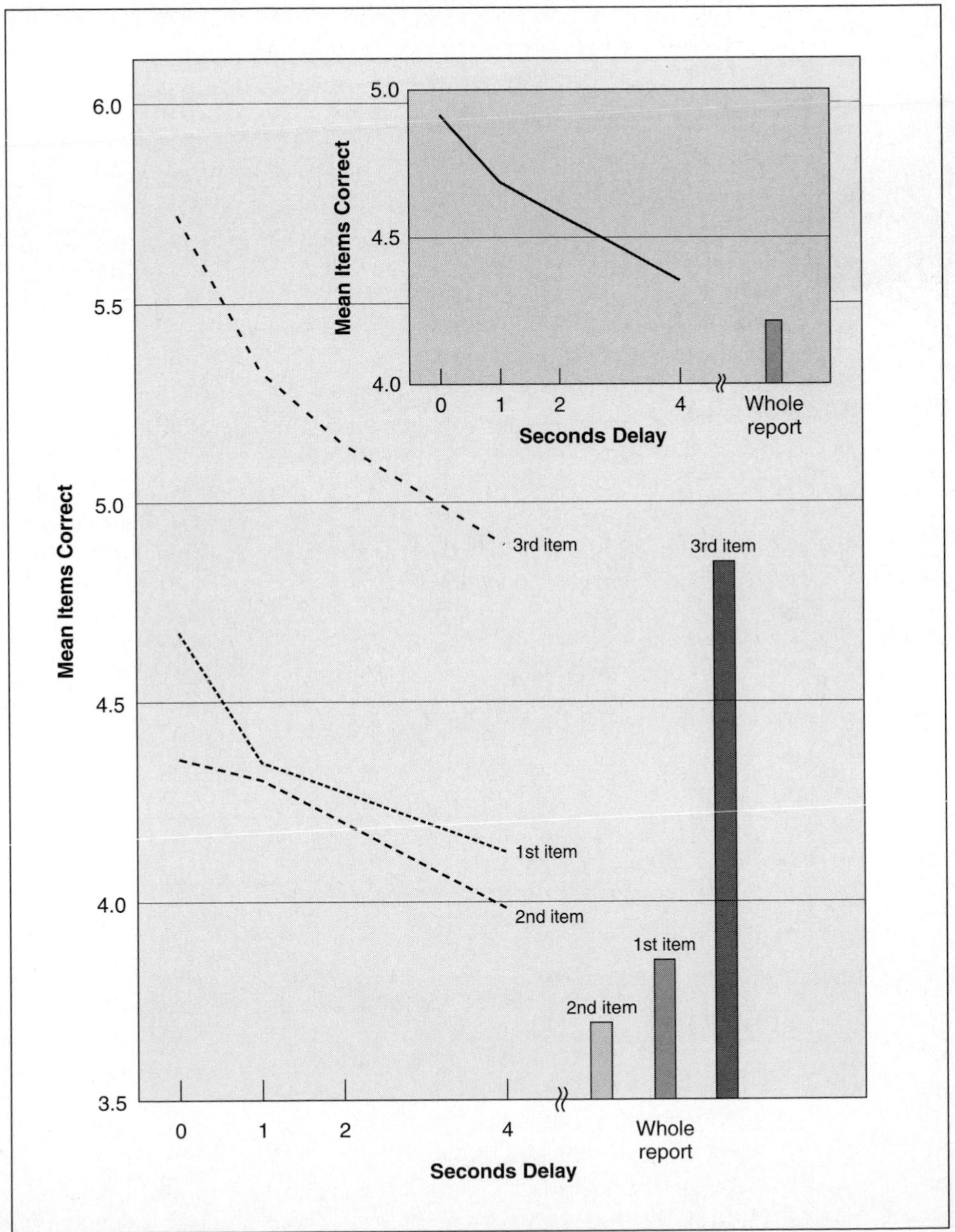

sage, Treisman then faded in an identical recording of the right-ear message *on the left-ear channel*. If the now-identical message was exactly aligned in time with the shadowed message, then of course the subjects heard the message in stereo, in both ears simultaneously. When Treisman interrupted their shadowing and asked what they remembered or noticed in the left ear, they reported correctly that it was the same message.

The two more interesting conditions involved fading in the same message to the left ear, but not in stereo. Instead, in the "message-follows" condition, the left-ear message lagged behind the right-ear message, by some variable amount of time. Notice that this is exactly like an echo which comes back to you after the original sound. In contrast, the "message-precedes" condition had the left-ear message arriving earlier than the attended message, again by an amount of time that Treisman manipulated. For lack of a better term, let's call this a "pre-echo," an echo that comes back to you before the original sound.

★ Treisman's results were fascinating, as illustrated in Figure 2.18. When the participants were asked to report what they noticed about the left ear message in the message-follows condition, they reported that it was the same message—the echo. This was only true if the echo "came back" to them soon enough, however—within 4.5 seconds on the average. This is probably due to the involvement of short-term memory. Because shadowing the right-ear message requires attention, shadowing encodes the message into short-term memory, where the "echo" is noticed.

But the message-precedes condition tested the duration of auditory sensory memory—how long did the pre-echo last in auditory sensory memory? In fact, participants noticed that the left-ear message, the pre-echo, was identical to the right-ear message only if the left-ear message came within 1.5 seconds of the attended right-ear message. If it had preceded by more than 1.5 seconds, it seemed to be lost from auditory sensory memory, because they couldn't report anything about it.

★ **FIGURE 2.18**

Treisman's results (1964a, 1964b) of shadowing. (Adapted from Treisman, 1964a.)

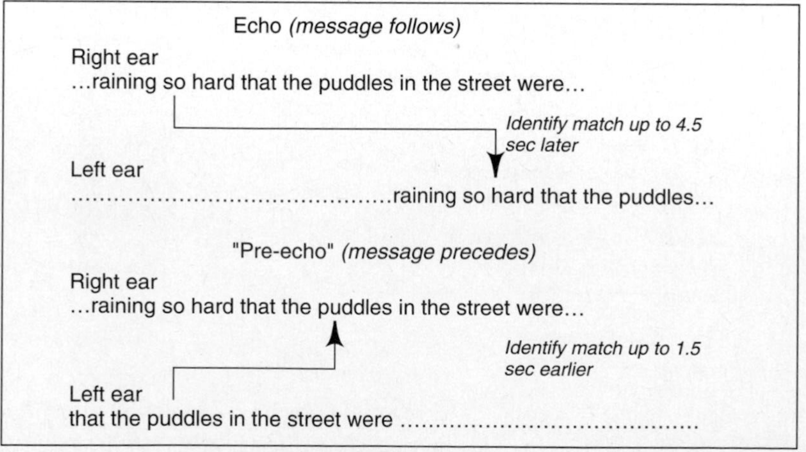

Erasure

Treisman's (1964a, 1964b) work indicated that auditory sensory memory for speech—for connected, sensible sentences—may last only about 1.5 seconds. In other words, as the tape played, the new sounds arriving in the left ear were encoded into auditory sensory memory, and this new encoding interfered with the current contents of sensory memory. This is an *erasure effect*, analogous to erasure in visual sensory memory. It's as if auditory sensory memory has a 1.5-second tape loop that continually records speech sounds, and continually records *over* the speech that occurred 1.5 seconds ago.

How do we avoid this erasure? We redirect our mental attention to the contents of auditory sensory memory. This redirection transfers the sounds into something like the short-term memory system, into awareness. Thus, just as Sperling (1960) found for vision, auditory information in sensory memory can be "read out" and attended to by means of redirected mental attention and transfer to short-term memory.

AUDITORY PATTERN RECOGNITION

We're going to postpone most of our discussion of auditory pattern recognition until later. The reason for this is that much of the research on pattern recognition in hearing is more interesting in the context of two different topics, attention, which we'll cover in the next chapter, and language, covered in Chapter 8. So here's a brief discussion of the topic, with just enough of the intriguing findings to propel you into Chapter 3 and the topic of selective and divided attention.

THEORIES OF AUDITORY PATTERN RECOGNITION

Templates

Attempts to understand how we recognize sounds, especially language sounds, have paralleled the work on visual pattern recognition. That is to say, there were some attempts at explaining auditory pattern recognition by templates, by claims that we identify incoming sounds by trying to match them to stored models or templates in memory.

These attempts were quickly abandoned, however, for an obvious reason—not only do different people produce language sounds quite differently from one another, but even the same sound produced by the same speaker varies considerably from time to time. Even more damaging to the template approach, the "same" sound varies from word to word, even when spoken by the same speaker.

This is referred to in psycholinguistics as the **problem of invariance**—the problem is that the sounds of speech are not invariant from one time to the next. Instead, any particular sound changes physically depending on what sound preceded it in a word, and what sounds are going to follow it.

Feature Detection

Parallel to the work in vision, feature detection models of auditory pattern recognition were somewhat more successful than template models. But for the most part, research on

TABLE 2.1

Warren and Warren's (1970) Sentences and Subjects' Responses

Subject hears:	*Subject reports:*
It was found that the *eel was on the axle.	wheel
It was found that the *eel was on the shoe.	heel
It was found that the *eel was on the orange.	peel
It was found that the *eel was on the table.	meal

Note: The asterisks represent a deleted sound.

feature detection leads to the same conclusion in audition as it did in vision. There's loads of evidence that context plays a decisive role—conceptually driven processing.

Conceptually Driven Processing

Let's just take two examples of research showing the effects of context, of conceptually driven processing effects. In the first, Pollack and Pickett (1964) tape-recorded the idle conversations of volunteers who were waiting to be in a research project. The tapes were then played to other volunteers, to see if words could be identified—which, of course, they could. But in the more interesting condition, individual words were spliced out of the tapes and presented in isolation. Here, only about half of all the presented words could be identified. Removing words from their normal context made it extremely difficult to recognize the patterns. By inference, then, the surrounding context plays an important role in spoken-word identification.

In the second example, Warren and Warren (1970) presented speech stimuli to their experimental subjects and asked them to report what they had heard. The tape recordings were carefully engineered so that one specific sound (the technical term is **phoneme**) was removed from a single word. Participants heard the altered sentences shown in Table 2.1, where an * indicates the sound that was removed. The word they recognized is shown at the right of each sentence. So, for instance, even though they heard "*eel," hearing the rest of the sentence—"on the axle"—was sufficient for them to perceive the word *wheel*. In fact, most never even noticed anything strange at all about what they heard—it all sounded completely natural. It's a simple but powerful demonstration: perception and identification of speech are heavily dependent on context, on top-down processing. It's also a nice reminder of the difference between sensation and perception—the physical, *sensory* nature of sensation, but the overwhelmingly *cognitive* nature of perception.

Summary

1. Sound waves are converted to auditory messages by means of vibrating membranes, moving bones and fluid, and the like. There is a brief sensory storage system for sounds, called auditory sensory memory or echoic memory.
2. Auditory and visual sensory memory are similar in that considerable information is encoded, but the information is rapidly lost. In hearing, the duration of the information is as short as 1.5 seconds, for speech, to as long as 10 seconds, for simple tones.

3. Fading is one of the two processes by which we lose information in auditory sensory memory. The other is an erasure or interference process, which occurs within 1.5 seconds for speech. Redirected mental attention within that short interval transfers the sounds to short-term memory for further processing.
4. Auditory pattern recognition—like visual—shows some elements of feature detection, but also strong effects of context, of conceptually driven processing. These effects lead to a further study of attention, and also to the topic of language.

Important Terms

audition
auditory sensory memory
backward masking
conceptually driven/top-down processing
connectionism
connectionist model
data-driven/bottom-up processing
decay
echoic memory
ecological validity
erasure
feature detection
features
fixations
focal attention
fovea
geons
iconic memory
interference
neural net modeling
occipital lobe
parallel distributed processing
pattern recognition
perception
problem of invariance
phoneme
Recognition by Components
retina
saccades
sensation
shadowing
span of apprehension
tachistoscope
template matching
visual attention
visual persistence
visual sensory memory
whole-report/partial-report condition

Suggested Readings

Many libraries still have copies of Norman's (1976) excellent book *Memory and Attention*. It contains very readable fragments from the early important papers on pattern recognition, along with his insightful commentary. The narrative leads you through the theoretical developments leading to conceptually driven models of recognition. The two articles in *Scientific American* described in this chapter, the ones by Neisser (1964) and Warren and Warren (1970), are very approachable statements of important research findings. And Neisser's book *Cognition and Reality* (1976) deals largely with perception, including the intriguing notion of the "perceptual cycle." For a fascinating look at a topic we haven't considered here—that perception and decision making might occur in short "bursts"—read Dehaene's (1993) paper "Temporal Oscillations in Human Perception."

Chapter Three

Attention

"Pay attention."

"Now, if you'll direct your attention to the blackboard, . . ."

"The lecture was so boring, I just couldn't pay attention."

Attention—one of cognitive psychology's most important and pervasive topics, one of our oldest puzzles in the study of the mind, one of the most difficult concepts to pin down and understand. What does it mean to "pay attention"? To "direct" your attention to something? To be unable to pay attention because of boredom or lack of interest? What sorts of things, whether external stimuli or internal thoughts, "grab" or attract our attention?

How much control do we have over our attention? Is it always a matter of concentration and determination when you pay attention to something? Or are some things easy to attend to, and if so, why? (By the way, "attend to" is psych-speak for "pay attention to.") I have a hard time paying attention to some things—most topics in a faculty meeting, for example. But for other topics, it seems virtually effortless—a good spy novel rivets my attention, just as a great cognition lecture rivets yours (!).

Attention, as I just said, is one of the most pervasive topics in cognitive psychology. It's also, loosely speaking, the same thing as awareness or consciousness. This means that you are aware of the process, or at least the outcome of the process, and you have some useful intuitions about it. We'll build on those intuitions throughout this chapter, as we cover the major ideas cognitive psychology has explored in its study of this most elusive but all-important cognitive process. Throughout, we'll be grappling with three interrelated ideas:

- We are constantly confronted with much more information than we can pay attention to.
- There are serious limitations in how much we can attend to at any one time.
- We can respond to some information, and perform some tasks, with little, if any, attention.

Selective Attention

> **Preview:** *attention* defined; the limited nature of attention; selective attention; filter, attenuation, pertinence, and multimode theories

ATTENTION DEFINED

Attention as a Mental Process

Let's begin with two definitions of the concept Attention, and then explore the implications of those definitions. First, let's look at attention as a mental activity.

- **Attention:** The mental process of concentrating effort on a stimulus or a mental event.

By this definition, we mean that attention is an activity that occurs within the cognitive system, a *process*. This process focuses some mental commodity—effort—on either an external stimulus or an internal event. So, when you examine a drawing like that in Figure 3.1, you focus your mental energies on an external stimulus: on the lines and edges of a standard Necker cube. If you attend to the figure for several more seconds, you'll notice that it changes its orientation—the box that was pointed up in the air is now pointed down, the classic visual illusion. Attention is the mental process that focused your eyes on the figure, and encoded the drawing into your visual system. Sustained attention then led to the reversal.

Now consider the text to the right in Figure 3.1. Read the words, then try to remember the answer to the question. If you're as familiar with that movie as most people, you know the answer—or would recognize it at better than chance level. The point for now is that most people have to work at remembering that line. It takes fairly focused, concentrated mental effort to retrieve the information from memory. It's that concentration of attention I'm trying to illustrate here: attention focused on and driving the mental event of remembering, searching for information stored in your long-term memory.

Attention as a Limited Mental Resource

Consider now a second sense of the concept Attention, in which attention is a mental resource, a kind of mental "fuel."

- **Attention:** The limited mental energy or resource that "powers" the mental system.

FIGURE 3.1

Two Aspects of Attention

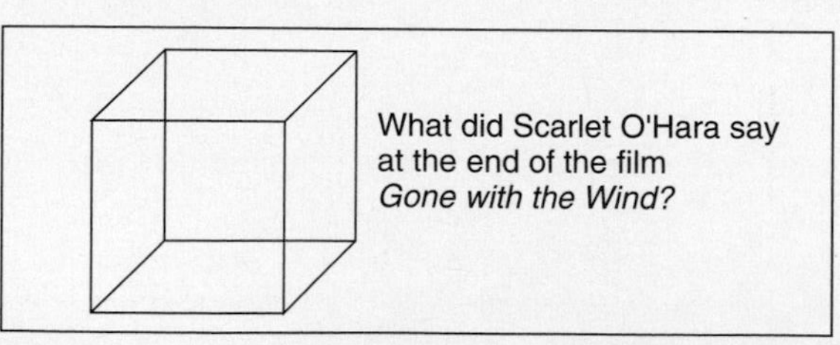

This is the other side of the coin, considering attention as a mental commodity, the "fuel" that drives our cognitions. It's this *energy* that gets focused when we pay attention—so in this sense, attention is the mental resource necessary to run the cognitive system.

A fundamentally important idea here is the notion of limitations. Attention is limited, finite. We usually state this idea by talking about **limited capacity.** Countless experiments, to say nothing of everyday experiences, show that there is a limitation in our attentional capacity. In short, there's a limit to how many different things we can attend to and do all at once.

Try this demonstration as a simple example of your limited attentional capacity. Count backward by threes, aloud and as rapidly as you can, starting with some arbitrary number (use your street address or the first three digits of your phone number, for instance). While doing this, look for words rhyming with "say" in the multiple-choice

▲

Which of these did Scarlett O'Hara say at the end of the film *Gone with the Wind?*

(a) "After all, tomorrow I'll be at Tara."

(b) "After all, tomorrow is another day."

(c) "I'll think about that tomorrow, at Tara."

(d) "I can't think about that now—I'll do it tomorrow."

The difficulty of language comprehension when working memory is overloaded.

question about Scarlett O'Hara. Even though neither of these tasks is very difficult by itself, doing them simultaneously taxes the attentional system—you probably slowed down in your backward counting, or missed some of the rhymes. You have sufficient attentional capacity to do either task alone, but it seems as if there's not enough to do them both together.

An Informal Example

Here's the kind of situation that we often face with our limited attention. You're at a party, talking to a friend, while two other conversations are taking place nearby. There's also some loud music playing on someone's stereo. And while talking with your friend, you remember a funny story about someone at the party, you're wondering why another friend is late, and you're a little worried that maybe one of those nearby conversations is about you. That's a total of seven messages—four external and three internal. How do you focus your attention?

The situation is analogous to most everyday settings. At any moment in time, we are surrounded by far more than we can attend to. When we try to focus on just one of the surrounding stimuli or events, the remaining ones are distractions that have to be eliminated or ignored. The mental process of eliminating those distractions is called **filtering** or **selecting.** Some aspect of the attention mechanism has to *filter* out the unwanted, extraneous sources of information, so we can *select* the one message we want to pay attention to. How does that mechanism work, especially when you try to focus on one message while also monitoring another one just in case it's important (That guy over there just said my name!)?

SELECTIVE ATTENTION MODELS

The term *selective attention* is used for this process of filtering out the surrounding distractions and focusing on the one important event we've chosen. In the laboratory, experiments are designed to mimic these sorts of situations by overloading the system. We do this by presenting more information than can be handled at once, and then testing accuracy for some part of the information. The point of this, of course, is to see how the filter works, to see how the attention process functions.

The Dual Task Method

This procedure for such a test is usually called a **dual task** or **dual message** procedure. Two stimuli, messages, or tasks are presented, making sure that the combination exceeds the individual's attentional capacity. Usually, a considerable portion of that attentional capacity is consumed by one of the two messages or tasks. This means that there won't be enough resources left over for conscious attention to the other information being presented. This is the rationale behind the Scarlett O'Hara demonstration you just did. In fact, it's the rationale behind virtually all research on attention, including the shadowing task you encountered in Chapter 2.

Let's discuss this research, and the development of models of selective attention. Alert readers will notice very quickly what the central question has been in all of this work: Where in the sequence of mental processes does selection—that is, selective attention—happen?

Early Shadowing Experiments

Two British psychologists, Donald Broadbent and E. Colin Cherry, performed some of the earliest research on selective attention (Broadbent, 1952/1992, 1958; Cherry, 1953; Cherry & Taylor, 1954; see also Egeth, 1992, whose introduction points out how important their contributions were both to the study of attention and to the development of

As a reminder, **shadowing** has participants listening to different messages through headphones. They must repeat aloud the message they hear in one ear, and ignore the other message.

Try the task yourself. Telephone your local recorded weather service and shadow the forecast to someone else in the room. Or have a friend read a passage aloud from a book, with you shadowing. Try not to let your shadow lag behind too much—a second or two at most—or you'll end up omitting words and paraphrasing. Reed (1996) suggests a classroom demonstration with two students reading aloud from the textbook, the class trying to pay attention to just one of the two. Read the remainder of this section of the text to see what kinds of difficulties you'll encounter in such a situation.

cognitive psychology). These researchers were interested in the basics of speech recognition and attention. Cherry (1953) characterized the research procedures, and for that matter the question being asked, as "the cocktail party problem": How do we pay attention to and recognize what one person is saying when we are surrounded by other spoken messages?

Cherry modeled this real-world situation in the laboratory by using the **shadowing** task. He recorded all sorts of different messages on both the *attended* channel, the message that was to be shadowed, and on the *unattended* channel, the message to be ignored. He found that it requires a surprising amount of attention and concentration to shadow a message accurately. On the one hand, participants were reasonably accurate in producing "shadows" and reported that the task became relatively easy. On the other hand, Cherry found that people's spoken shadows were usually produced in a monotone voice, and generally lagged behind the taped message by a second or so. Interestingly, the subjects seemed unaware of the strangeness of their spoken shadows, and usually could not remember much of the content of the shadowed message.

The especially interesting part of Cherry's research came from manipulating the nature and content of the unattended message, in order to see what kinds of information, if any, the participants noticed about that message. This is essentially asking the question, What gets into the cognitive system *without* attention? After they had shadowed for a period of time, Cherry's participants were interrupted and asked what, if anything, they could report about the unattended message in the left ear.

The answer was, Not much. Generally, the participants could report accurately on the physical characteristics of the unattended message—for example, if it was a tone or human speech, a man's or a woman's voice, whether it was fast or slow paced. But very few noticed when the unattended message was changed to reversed speech, or when it switched from English to another language. Most dramatically, they were unable to identify words or phrases that had been in the unattended message. The most well-known and amazing demonstration of this was reported by Moray (1959). He found that even a word presented 35 times in the unattended message was never recalled by the participants!

Broadbent's Early Selection/Filter Model

It appeared that virtually any physical difference between the messages permitted the subjects to distinguish between them, that is, helped them selectively attend to the target message. Because the first stage of perception involves an acoustic analysis of the message, based on its physical characteristics, it was clear that the selection process could happen very early in the attentional process. Eysenck (1982) has called this "stage 1 selection," when selection is based on physical features of the message. Cherry's evidence demonstrated stage 1 selection, based on loudness, location of the sound source, pitch, and so forth (see also Spieth, Curtis, & Webster, 1954; Egan, Carterette, & Thwing, 1954).

A model that specifically accounted for this evidence was proposed by Broadbent (1958), a model we'll call the "early selection/filter model." Broadbent proposed that attention works like a selective filter, screening out unwanted messages while selecting one target message for further processing. A diagram of this model is shown in Figure 3.2. Regardless of how many competing channels or messages are coming in—messages A through D in the figure—the filter can be tuned or switched to any one of the messages, based on characteristics such as loudness or pitch. And, importantly, it lets only that one

FIGURE 3.2

Broadbent's (1958) early selection/filter model. Four messages are presented, yet only one is selected and passed to the limited-capacity decision channel. (Adapted from Broadbent, 1958.)

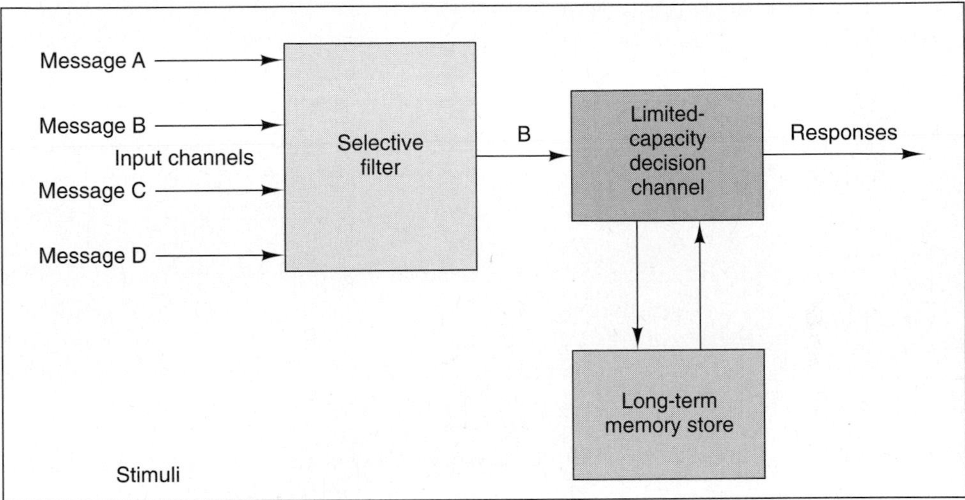

message through to the "limited-capacity decision channel," which is essentially the same as short-term memory. Because the model claimed that this is the only message that enters awareness, Broadbent's view was that it should be the only message to affect performance. (For a real-world example, notice the similarity to the channel selector on your TV.)

Difficulties for Broadbent's Model It was realized very quickly that Broadbent's (1958) filter approach had some serious shortcomings. For one, common intuition tells us that we can notice information from a message we are not attending—for instance, if your name is spoken in one of those nearby conversations at the party. Moray (1959) found this exact result in his experiment. While people did not recall a word presented 35 times to the unattended ear, a fair number noticed their own name spoken on the unattended channel, a result recently replicated with more careful methodology by Wood and Cowan (1995b). In short, if unattended information can slip past the filtering mechanism in Broadbent's theory, the theory must be wrong.

Treisman (1960, 1964a) decided to explore the filtering mechanism, the source of the "slippage," more closely. She used the standard shadowing task, but varied the nature of the unattended message across a much more subtle range of differences. The especially interesting conditions in her research eliminated the physical differences between messages—both the attended and unattended messages were tape-recorded by the same speaker, speaking in the same pitch, with the same intonation, stress, and so forth.

Treisman found that people were still able to shadow quite accurately, even in the absence of physical differences. The basis for selection here was *message content*—what the message was about rather than its physical characteristics. Eysenck (1982) called this "stage 2 selection," where grammatical and semantic features are the basis for selection (*semantic* refers to meaning). Of course, Treisman's (1960, 1964a) evidence for stage 2 selection was powerful evidence against Broadbent's model.

Treisman's Attenuation Model

To show the power of selection based on the content of the message, Treisman conducted a study now considered a true classic (Treisman, 1960); the setup for the experiment is depicted in Figure 3.3. Treisman arranged the tape recording so that the message being shadowed was unexpectedly *shifted* to the unattended channel. Quite literally, the sentence the participant was saying switched from the right to the left ear. Despite a high degree of practice in shadowing, and the high level of concentration required, participants routinely switched their attention to the left-ear message, the one that completed the meaning of the shadowed sentence. While shadowing the "wrong" ear didn't continue for very long, the fact is that when the meaningful sentence switched to the unattended ear, attention also switched. Clearly, selective attention can also be performed based on semantic characteristics. Just as clearly, more information is getting into the system than Broadbent's (1958) filter predicted (see also Lewis, 1970; Carr, McCauley, Sperber, & Parmalee, 1982, found comparable results for visually presented stimuli).

Threshold and Attenuation But how can some words on the unattended channel enter the attention mechanism while others don't? Treisman (1960) proposed the following. Assume that words have a certain threshold or criterion, a level that determines whether they will be detected or not. Words being spoken on the attended message are easy to detect; this is because the attended message is receiving considerable attention, and that boosts the word over the threshold of detection. Normally, words on the unattended message are not detected, because nothing boosts them up above their threshold.

FIGURE 3.3

Experimental setup for Treisman's (1960) shadowing research. Two messages are played simultaneously into different ears, then, at the slash, the ear of arrival is switched for the two messages. (Adapted from Lindsay & Norman, 1977.)

Right ear:
While Bill was walking through the forest/
a bank can lend you the money.
Left ear:
If you want to buy a car/
a tree fell across his path.
"through the forest, a tree fell–uh..."

This is because the unattended messages in Treisman's model were **attenuated**—their loudness and informational value were reduced.

But now, think about words on the unattended message that are *related* to the content of the message—the "tree fell in the forest" idea in Figure 3.3. Even though that message is attenuated, those words have been boosted up by the sentence being shadowed because they're related to the meaning of the forest sentence. It only takes a little boost to make them enter the attention mechanism—and the shadowed and unshadowed messages combine to give them that boost.

Thus, Treisman proposed that unattended messages receive a kind of low-level analysis or monitoring. If the information is irrelevant, it is treated as "noise" and doesn't enter awareness. But if it contains a word that's been boosted up near threshold, even the attenuated message can push it over the criterion and into consciousness.

Treisman's attenuation model can be described as a "stage 1 *or* 2 selection" model. In other words, under some circumstances, selective attention can occur at the level of physical, sensory analysis (stage 1), the way Broadbent (1958) proposed. But when physical differences are eliminated, selective attention can occur at the semantic-analysis phase, based on word meanings (stage 2). A more extreme view, proposed by Deutsch and Deutsch (1963), claimed that selection takes place only after *all* messages have been fully analyzed—in other words, just before the response stage. This "late selection" or stage 3 theory was never widely accepted, and has recently been convincingly ruled out by Wood and Cowan (1995a).

Norman's Pertinence Model

▲ Donald Norman (1968) proposed a useful modification to the Treisman scheme, depicted in Figure 3.4 (p. 76). Despite the more complex illustration, the model is rather straightforward and appealing. It claims that, at any instant in time, attention to some piece of information—some message—is determined by two factors, sensory activation and **pertinence.**

Consider sensory activation first. If the message is loud, in a distinct voice, or otherwise salient from a sensory standpoint, its sensory activation will be high—that's the message you'll pay attention to. In simple terms, if the stereo at the party is considerably louder than anything else, you'll be unable to attend to anything but the music. The figure shows that messages A, B, and C have some degree of sensory activation—maybe the music and the two nearest conversations.

Now add pertinence to the mixture. At any moment in time, certain things—ideas, words, and so forth—are highly pertinent to you, and others are low in pertinence. Pertinence can be temporary, as in Treisman's (1960) results on message content; if you're listening to a message about a forest, words like *tree* are high in pertinence. But pertinence can also be relatively permanent—your name probably stays at a high level of pertinence on a permanent basis, for instance. In either case, the higher an item is in pertinence, the higher that item is boosted toward its criterion or threshold for awareness. In the figure, items C, D, and E are highly pertinent.

Now all we have to do is add the pertinence and sensory activations together. In Norman's (1968) model, those items in memory that have the highest combination of sensory and pertinence scores are the ones that are selected for attention. Thus, selective attention in Norman's theory was a continuous process. On a moment-by-moment basis,

FIGURE 3.4

Norman's (1968) pertinence model. (Adapted from Norman, 1968.)

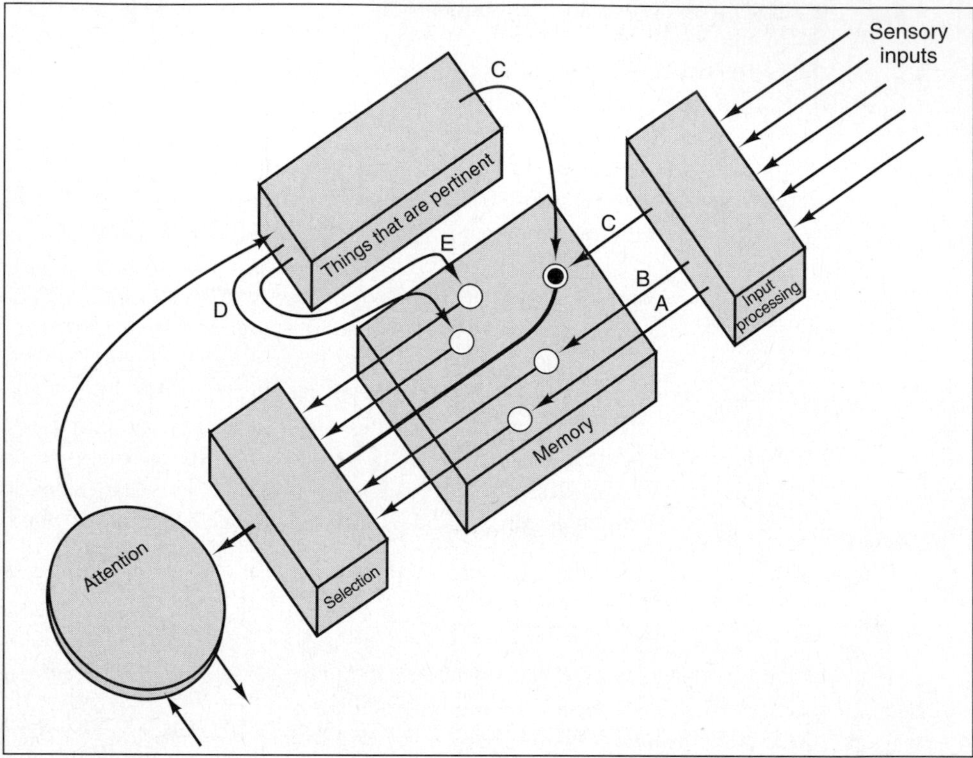

the item with the highest combination score is selected for conscious, deliberate attention. In the figure, this is represented by the darkened item C—it's pertinent *and* has substantial sensory activation (maybe it's your name, in one of those nearby conversations).

Multimode Model of Attention

Where does this leave us, you ask? It leaves us knowing two things about selective attention.

- First, selective attention can occur very early in the processing sequence, based on very low level, physical characteristics, as Broadbent proposed. It can also occur later, based on meaning or message content, as Treisman demonstrated.
- Second, it can be influenced by both permanent and temporary factors. Permanent factors would include highly important information like your name, and highly overlearned and personally important factors. Like you, I always hear my name, even when it's just a coincidence that a passerby says it. But I also always hear the word *psychology*, even when it's spoken on an "unattended" message. So names aren't the only possible items that can be permanently boosted in their pertinence. Temporary pertinence factors would include message content as well as momentary fluctuations in interests. In short, attention is *flexible*.

An important paper, by Johnston and Heinz (1978), said just that—that attention is a highly flexible process that can operate in multiple *modes*. By "modes," these authors meant the sort of factors described here as stage 1, 2, or 3 models—operating in a physical mode, a meaning-based mode, and the like. This is illustrated in Figure 3.5. Johnston and Heinz's answer to the question, Where does selective attention operate? is, Anywhere. Selective attention can operate in multiple modes—early, middle, or late.

There is an important limitation to this flexibility, however, one that involves capacity. Johnston and Heinz pointed out that while selective attention can vary from quite early to quite late, the downside of this flexibility is that later selection requires more of

FIGURE 3.5

The sequence of processes in the shadowing task, with early, middle, and late operation of the selective attention mechanism. (Adapted from Johnston & Heinz, 1978.)

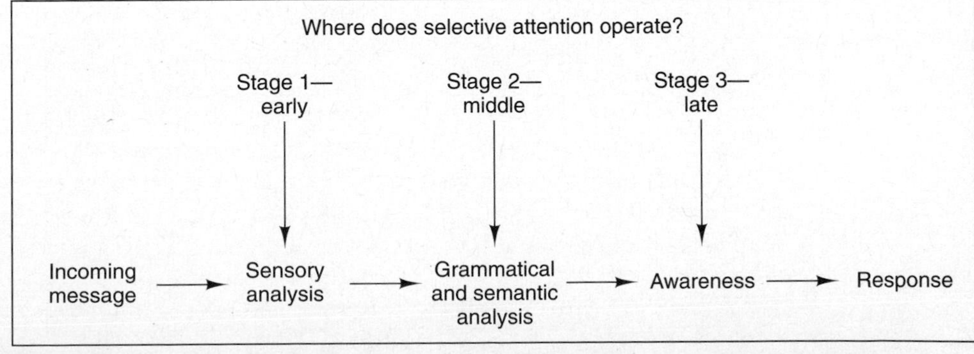

the limited attentional capacity. In other words, later selection uses up more capacity, so tends to be either slower or less accurate when it comes to remembering the information that was attended to.

Their data illustrated this trade-off quite clearly. In their experiments, the subjects listened to multiple messages, some differing physically and some differing in terms of meaning. They always had to remember information from one list—the target list—and try to ignore any other messages that were also presented. While listening to the message(s), they also had to monitor a light in front of them and press a button as soon as it came on. To make this challenging, the light came on at random, unpredictable intervals. The reasoning here was that detecting the light would be slower in those message conditions that required more attentional capacity. If selective attention is more difficult, because of similarities in the competing messages, this should slow down detection of the light.

This is exactly what happened, as illustrated in Figure 3.6. The figure shows the *costs* in performance—in other words, how much slower people were in responding to the light, compared to baseline when no message was presented. (Higher costs on the graph mean worse performance than in the baseline condition.) Having to listen to one mes-

FIGURE 3.6

Results from Johnston and Heinz's (1978) research on the multimode model of attention. (Data from Johnston & Heinz, 1978.)

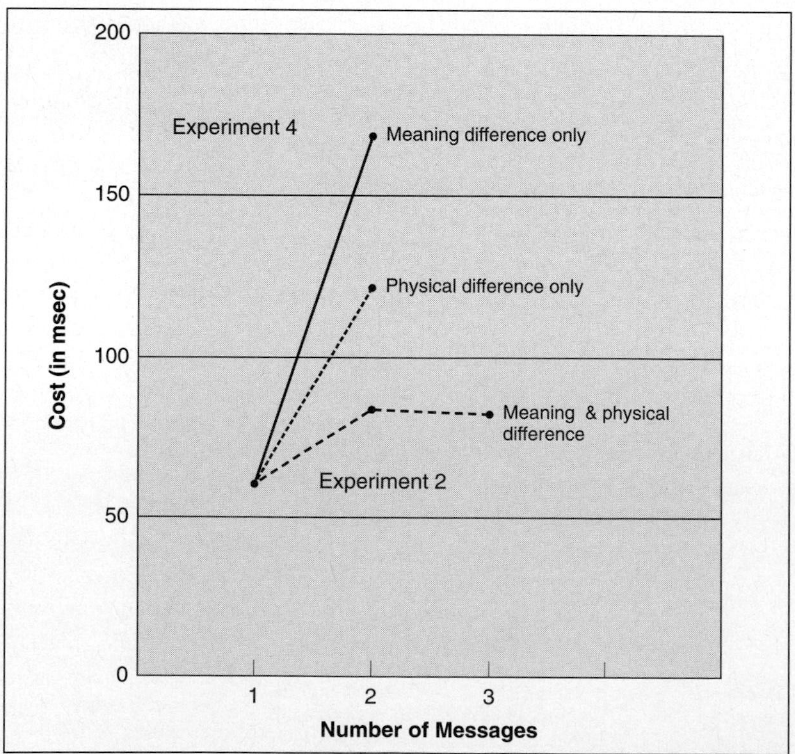

sage slowed down light detection by about 60 milliseconds; this is the first point on the graph. It shows that burdening the attentional system with the extra task, listening to the target message, used some of the available attentional capacity, thus slowing down light detection.

Johnston and Heinz then went on to show how much more attentional capacity was drained when two or more messages were presented simultaneously, as in the shadowing research described earlier. In a second experiment, the target message was presented along with either one or two extra messages, the distractor messages (for a total number of messages of either two or three). But because the distractors differed both physically and in meaning from the target, this added only another 20 milliseconds to the participants' time to detect the light; this is shown in the bottom curve in Figure 3.6. In other words, it took very little extra attention when given two types of cues—physical and meaning—to help them ignore the distractors. (It's not all that difficult to ignore one or two nearby conversations if they're about different topics.)

Their fourth experiment, however, examined the more taxing conditions for selective attention that you read about before, that is, when the extra message differs only physically from the target, or when it differs only in terms of meaning. As the middle curve in the figure shows, the "physical difference only" task added 120 milliseconds to participants' responses, showing a considerable drain on attentional capacity due to the difficulty of the listening task. This is rather like saying that stage 1 selection, based on physical differences, *costs* the attentional system an extra 120 milliseconds. And when only meaning differentiated the messages, the cost to light detection speed was a whopping 170 milliseconds.

This is the crux of Johnston and Heinz's Multimode Model. Selective attention can operate early in the sequence of processing, or it can operate late. But as it operates later and later, extra capacity is consumed by the attentional mechanism. This slows down (and makes less accurate) any other ongoing process, because it subtracts from the total pool of mental resources that are available for performance (see also Wood & Cowan, 1995a).

In short, it boils down to the issue of *capacity*. We started with the notion of limited capacity, you'll recall, and then worked through the models of selective attention. Now we run into the capacity issue again. Selective attention is flexible, but consumes some of the limited capacity of the human information-processing system. The harder it is to attend selectively to just one of several competing messages, the more capacity the selective attention process requires.

Summary

1. Attention can be defined as the mental process that concentrates effort, or as the energy or resource being focused. We're always confronted with more information than we can attend to at once, because of limitations in our attentional capacity.
2. Selective attention is usually studied within a dual-task procedure, such as the shadowing task. Cherry's early work with this task showed the ability to select based on physical differences between messages, leading to Broadbent's early selection/filter model.

What attracts attention? Notice that the combination of sensory activation and pertinence provides us with a good working answer to the question, What attracts our attention? Sensory events—a noise, a flash of light—attract attention if they are unexpected, as can their absence if the absence itself is unexpected. This is called the "orienting reflex," a built-in mechanism that literally orients you toward the stimulus—you turn your head toward the source of the stimulus (e.g., Bridgeman, 1988). Cowan (1995) has argued strongly that orienting and habituation can go a long way in explaining our ability to selectively attend (habituation is the gradual elimination of the orienting response when a stimulus is repeated). And pertinence, in Norman's (1968) sense, means a variety of things, from the temporarily pertinent content of a conversation to the permanently pertinent interests and factors you carry around in memory. Anything that's pertinent in this sense can attract your attention too.

Factor in the notion of limited capacity now. Maybe we notice minor distractions more easily if we aren't fully focused on a single message or task—aren't you more easily distracted by a stray noise or movement during a boring lecture? And haven't you ever "missed" the content of a lecture because of some ongoing train of thought, anything from an interesting daydream to a worry or anxiety (e.g., Eysenck, 1992)?

3. Treisman documented our ability to selectively attend based on the meaning of the incoming message, and proposed that unattended messages are attenuated by the attentional system.
4. Norman added the important concept of pertinence to the study of attention, so that whatever we attend to is a joint function of the stimulus itself and the moment-by-moment pertinence of different kinds of information.
5. The flexibility of attention must be considered in relation to the attentional capacity used in different settings. The more difficult it is to selectively attend, the more attentional capacity is consumed by the process.

Limited Attentional Capacity and Automaticity

Preview: limited capacity and automaticity; diagnosing automaticity and conscious processing; the role of practice and memory; trade-offs between automatic and conscious processing

Consider the following quotation from one of the early giants in American psychology, William James (1842–1910). Even though little research supported James's thinking at that time, the ideas he identified as critical to an understanding of attention are still with us, and still important.

> *If, then, by the original question, how many ideas or things can we attend to at once, be meant how many entirely disconnected systems or processes of conception can go on simultaneously, the answer is,* not easily more than one, unless the processes are very habitual; but then two, or even three, *without very much oscillation of the attention. Where, however, the processes are less automatic . . . there must be a rapid oscillation of the mind from one to the next, and no consequent gain of time.* (James, 1890/1983, p. 409)

What are the important ideas here? First, James was clearly talking about the overload of incoming information, and the process of selectively attending to only some part of that overload—literally, selectively attending to some fraction of the incoming information, then dividing attention among those that were selected. Second, there's the notion of limited capacity—"not easily more than one," he said. But the third notion is new to this chapter. It's the notion of *automaticity*; James used the term *habitual*, and then *automatic*. What does it mean for a process to be automatic, so habitual that it can occur simultaneously with other processes?

The recent history of cognitive science, dating from about the mid-1970s, attests to the importance of this issue, for an understanding of attention as well as all kinds of high-level mental processes. And cognitive science has devoted a huge amount of effort to recasting James's ideas about automaticity, and attention, into more formal, quantifiable concepts. We've spent nearly as much effort fighting over the idea too, debating whether or not the concepts of automaticity and capacity really advance our understanding of human cognition (e.g., Allport, 1980; Navon, 1984; Pashler, 1994; Posner & Snyder, 1975).

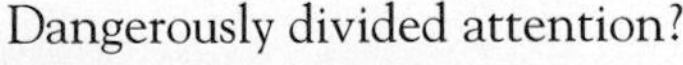

Dangerously divided attention?

LIMITED CAPACITY

It seems a given that the human information-processing system is limited in how much it can do at one time, regardless of the mental process we're considering—we cannot easily attend to more than one source of information at a time, cannot easily retrieve more than one fact from memory at a time, cannot solve more than one problem at a time. All of the research you've been reading about attests to this kind of limitation. It's obvious, isn't it? When Cherry (1953) simultaneously presented two messages to his experimental subjects, asking them to shadow just one, they were unable to remember much of anything about the other message. If our attentional capacity were extremely large, listening to two or more messages at once should be quite easy. In fact, if the human information-processing system were not limited, you could be reading this book and watching TV and talking to a friend on the phone all at the same time, with no difficulty, and with no loss of information from any of those sources.

But there is a limitation, of course. One tricky problem, however, is determining how much capacity there is in the first place. Theorists (e.g., Eysenck, 1982; Kahneman, 1973) have likened this capacity to the concept of **arousal** or alertness—an almost physiological way of conceptualizing the issue (see Chapter 10 for information on brain-based aspects of attention). Our alertness or arousal can fluctuate widely—it's very low during sleep, of course, and very high under extremely challenging conditions (public speaking, an Olympic competition). To an extent, our "normal" level of arousal responds to challenges too. Your alertness is lower during a lecture than during an important exam, it's lower when doing an easy task than a difficult one, it's lower when you're unmotivated or uninterested. The difficulty, however, is that we don't have a handy measurement of arousal or capacity, no way to gauge what our capacity is right now, or how much of it is being used by this or that task.

Our method for investigating capacity, then, is indirect—it's our old friend the dual-task procedure. By pitting two processes or tasks against one another, we can see indirectly how much capacity is "left over." When performing one task well—for instance, rapidly, with high accuracy—means that the second task cannot be done well, then we have indirect evidence of the capacity limitation. (I'm repeating this logic here because it's important—you'll run into it repeatedly, throughout this book and throughout cognitive science.)

AUTOMATIC PROCESSING

A particularly dramatic illustration of automaticity was reported by Spelke, Hirst, and Neisser (1976; see also Hirst, Spelke, Reaves, Caharack, & Neisser, 1980). They had two individuals read stories at normal rates—no big deal for literate adults, although still a task that should require a fair amount of attention. But then they also had them listen to a tape recording and copy words from the recording, as if taking dictation; in some conditions, the people were asked to categorize the words according to meaning. At first, of course, they had terrible difficulties doing the dictation task while reading. But with what can only be described as massive practice, the participants were eventually able to read stories at normal rates, and with high comprehension, while they simultaneously copied or categorized the tape-recorded words.

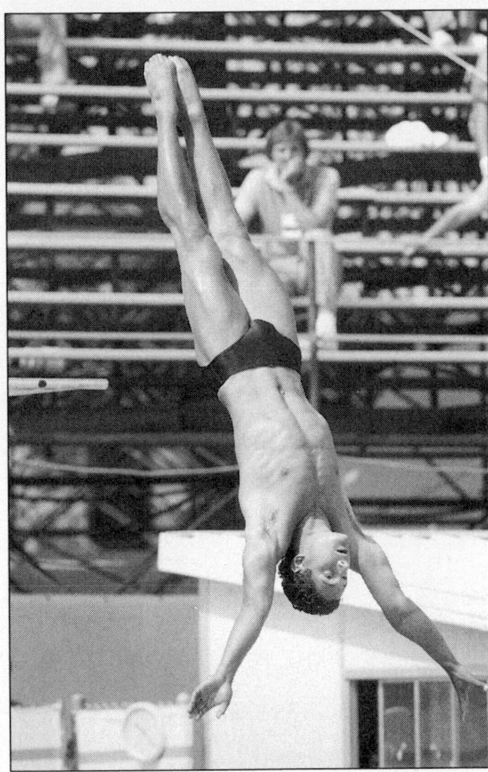

Greg Louganis: The role of practice.

What happened here? All of a sudden, there's evidence of efficient dual-task performance, of doing two things simultaneously as easily as one. What makes this combination of tasks different from other dual-task settings?

The essential ingredient was **practice.** With massive practice, dictation became very automatic, that is, much less demanding of the attentional system. As such, plenty of mental resources were left over to do the reading task at the same time.

Taking its place along with the notions of limited capacity and selective attention, there is now considerable evidence for James's third important idea. We now believe that a huge variety of perceptual and cognitive processes can be executed in an *automatic* fashion, with no necessary involvement of a conscious, limited-attention mechanism. In other words, some mental processes display what's called **automaticity,** the ability to perform some processes with little or no attentional involvement.

Two explicit theories of automaticity have been proposed, one by Posner and Snyder (1975), and one by Shiffrin and Schneider (1977; Schneider & Shiffrin, 1977). These theories differ in some of their details, but by and large are similar in their overall message.

DIAGNOSING AUTOMATIC PROCESSING

Posner and Snyder (1975) described three characteristics that are necessary for the "diagnosis" of an automatic process, for determining whether or not a process is more conscious

 or more automatic. These are listed for convenience in Table 3.1 (p. 84).

TABLE 3.1

Diagnostic Criteria for Automatic and Conscious Processing

Automatic	Conscious
1. The process occurs *without* intention, without a conscious decision.	1. The process occurs only *with* intention, with a deliberate decision.
2. The mental process is not open to conscious awareness or introspection.	2. The process is open to awareness and introspection.
3. The process consumes few if any conscious resources; that is, it consumes little if any conscious attention.	3. The process uses conscious resources; that is, it drains the pool of conscious attentional capacity.
4. (Informal) The process operates very rapidly, usually within 1 second.	4. (Informal) The process is relatively slow, taking more than a second or two for completion.

1. *Occurs without intention*. First, an automatic process occurs without intention—in other words, an automatic process occurs whether you consciously want it to or not. The classic demonstration of this is the so-called *Stroop effect*, named after the researcher who originally published the result (Stroop, 1935). It's a fail-safe demonstration, by the way, easily duplicated with some colored markers and a watch with a second hand. Individuals are shown a paper with words written in colored ink. The twist is that they have to report the ink color, not the words. This is not difficult when the words are ordinary, color-neutral words like *book* or *friend*. But when the word names a color (red) that's different from the ink color (green), people's responses are slowed considerably. They keep trying to say the word they're reading, rather than the color it's written in. An analogue of the Stroop task is shown in Figure 3.7.

How do we explain this? It's that reading the word itself is automatic, occurring even when you don't intend it to happen. Due to the years of practice you've had with reading, it's virtually impossible for you to see a printed word without reading it, without accessing its meaning in memory. The Stroop effect, thus, is an excellent demonstration of this aspect of automatic processing—the process occurs without any deliberate intention.

In Posner and Snyder's (1975) terms, accessing the meaning of the written symbol RED is automatic—it requires no intention, it happens whether you want it to or not. In the research that demonstrates automatic access to word meaning, the term we use is **priming.** A word automatically activates or primes its meaning in memory, and primes or activates meanings closely associated with it. This priming, then, makes related meanings easier to access: because of priming, they've been boosted up, given an extra advantage or head start, just as well water is pumped more easily when you "prime the pump." (See Dunbar & MacLeod, 1984, and MacLeod, 1991, for an explanation of Stroop interference based on priming.) This is quite obviously the mechanism underneath Treisman's "tree-forest" result in the shadowing task (1960; see also Lewis, 1970; Carr et al., 1982).

2. *No conscious awareness*. Second, an automatic process does not reveal itself to conscious awareness. Stated another way, you are unable to describe the mental processes of looking up the word *red* in memory. The look-up processes are automatic, and are

FIGURE 3.7

An analogue of the Stroop task. (a) For this task, begin with the upper left square and call out the number of digits in each square as rapidly as possible. Ignore the names of the digits. (b) A control condition, for which calling out the number of letters in each square is considerably easier. (Adapted from Howard, 1983.)

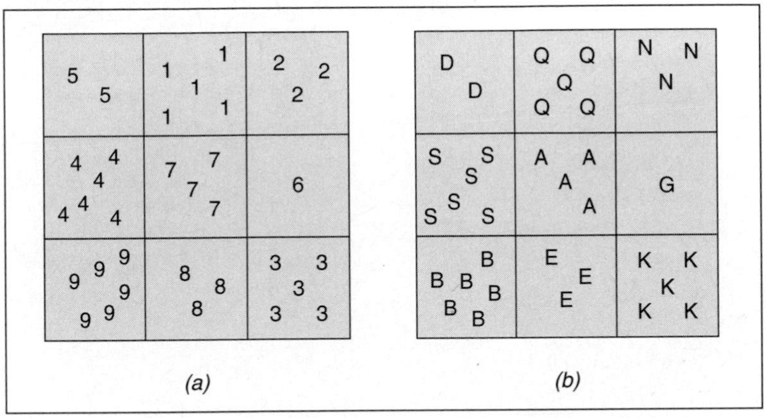

(a) (b)

not available to conscious awareness. You are not aware of the operation of automatic processes—for instance, the perceptual mechanisms of looking at the visual pattern T and recognizing what it is. In Chapter 1, you weren't aware of the operation of your memory mechanisms when you checked to see if robins have feathers.

3. *Consumes no conscious resources*. Finally, the third criterion of automaticity, according to Posner and Synder (1975), is that a fully automatic process consumes few or no conscious resources. Such a process should not interfere with other tasks, certainly not those that do use conscious resources. Walking, to take an obvious example, is so automatic for adults that it simply does not interfere with other processes—you can walk and talk at the same time. When a process becomes more and more automatic, it drains fewer and fewer resources from the system—and, of course, thereby "releases" those resources for other tasks.
4. A fourth criterion, quite informal but nonetheless useful, is that automatic processes tend to be very fast; a good rule of thumb is that a response requiring no more than 1 second is heavily automatic.

CONSCIOUS PROCESSING

Let's contrast these diagnostic criteria for automaticity with those for conscious processing (again, refer to Table 3.1).

1. *Occurs with intention*. First, conscious processes occur only with intention. They are optional, and can be deliberately performed or not performed. You don't have to intend to solve the problem 3 × 2—that retrieval is considered quite automatic (e.g., Ashcraft, 1995). But you do have to intend to solve the problem 351 ÷ 13.
2. *Open to awareness*. Second, conscious processes are open to awareness. We know that they are going on, and within limits we know what they consist of.

◆ **FIGURE 3.8**

A scheme representing dual-task performance with fixed, limited resources and automaticity.

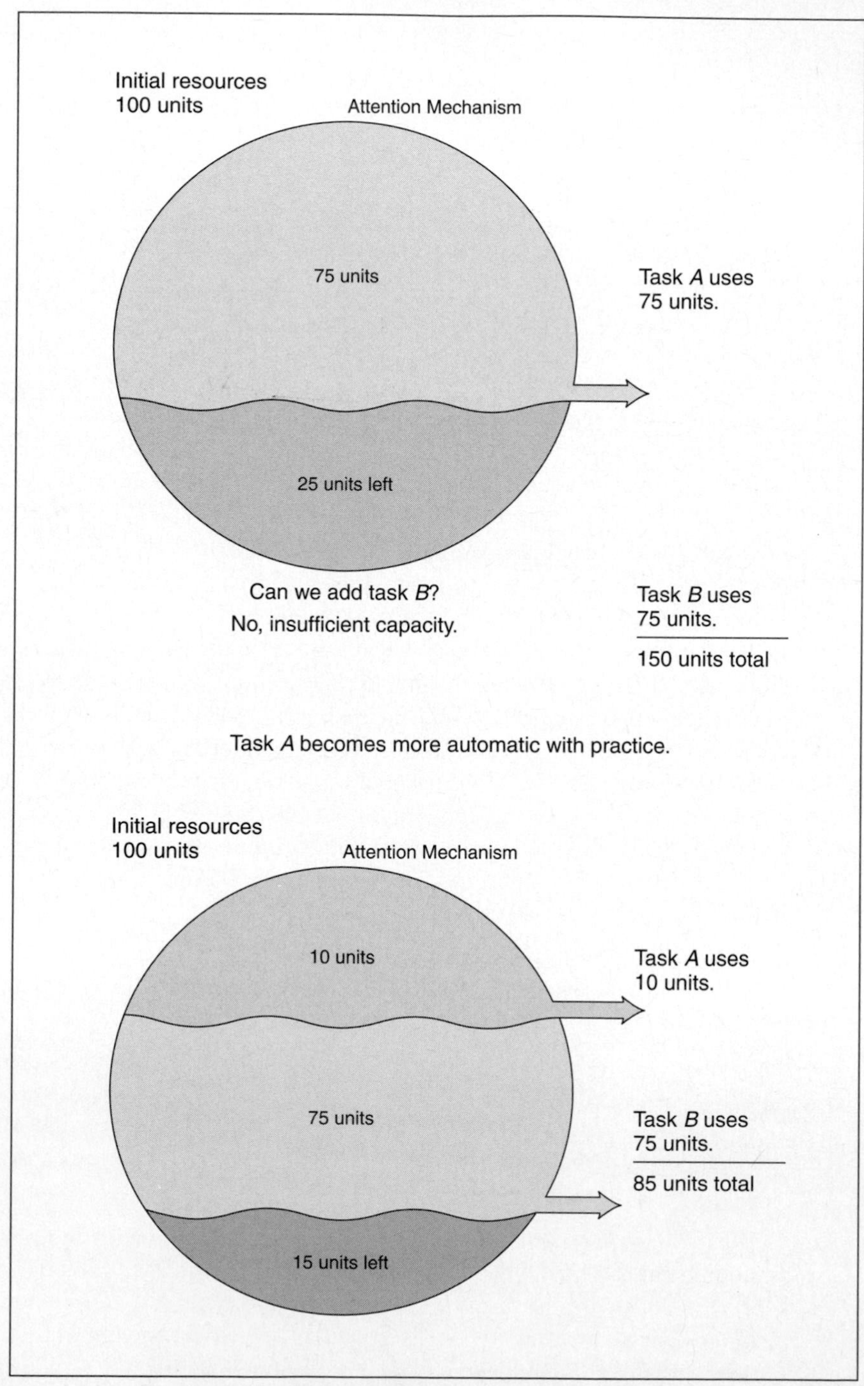

3. *Uses conscious resources*. Finally, and of greatest importance to the research, conscious processes require attention. They consume some of those limited attentional resources in the cognitive system. A demanding conscious process should leave very few resources still available for use by a second conscious process. Of course, if a second process is highly automatic, then both processes may proceed without interference. As mentioned above, you can walk and talk at the same time. Walking is so automatic that it does not interfere with any other ongoing activity (unless the terrain gets rough, of course). Contributing to a conversation, however, should require a fair amount of conscious processing, and should prevent you from simultaneously doing other attention-consuming activities (e.g., playing the piano, studying for an exam, etc.).

◆ The general scheme is sketched in Figure 3.8. In the top of the figure, both tasks A and B have to be performed at a very conscious level. Because the system is overloaded by the combination of the two tasks, something deteriorates—let's say it's performance to task B (this will depend on how heavily the instructions emphasize task A vs. task B). But in the bottom half, task A has become more automatic. It consumes very few resources after sufficient practice, so that the two tasks together do not overload the system. The consequence here is efficient performance to both tasks simultaneously. (The problem with this sketch, noted earlier, is that we have no clear-cut way of measuring available resources, or the "units" of attention required by different tasks. A Nobel prize goes to the person who devises a way to do this!)

Evidence on Automaticity and Practice

An excellent example of the role of practice in automaticity was presented by Shiffrin and Schneider (1977), along with their theory of automatic and conscious processing (actually, they used the term *controlled processing* instead of *conscious processing*). Their experiments asked participants to detect one or more target stimuli in successively presented ★ displays, as shown in Figure 3.9. For example, in Schneider and Shiffrin's (1977) experi-

★ **FIGURE 3.9**

Two examples of a positive trial in the single-frame search paradigm: varied mapping with memory set = (J, D) and consistent mapping with memory set = (4, 7, 8, 1). 1: presentation of memory set; a: fixation dot goes on for .5 sec when subject starts trial; b: two frames of masks; c: target frame; d: two postmask frames. Frame time = 160 msec for each of the five frames. (From Schneider & Shiffrin, 1977.)

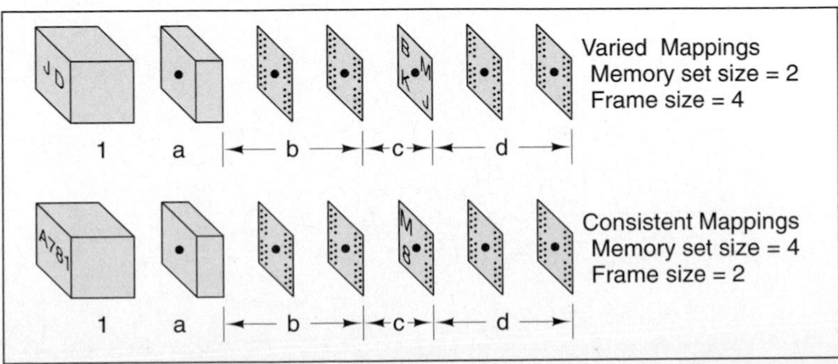

ment 1, the participant might hold the targets J and D in memory on one trial, then see a frame with one, two, or four characters (embedded in a sequence of visual masks). The subject had to respond as quickly and accurately as possible, pressing the yes button if either J or D was in the frame, or the no key if not. On the next trial, the target characters might be C and G, then B and H on the trial after that. This was called the "varied-mapping" condition, because from trial to trial, the mapping between targets and responses (saying yes or no) changed. Schneider and Shiffrin found that detection of the target character remained relatively slow across the entire experiment in this condition.

In the "Consistent-Mapping" condition, however, participants were given one set of characters as targets, and these remained the targets across the entire experiment. As the bottom of Figure 3.9 shows, the targets 4, 7, 8, and 1 in the Consistent-Mapping condition were always the targets for the participant. Schneider and Shiffrin predicted that such extensive practice with the same set of characters might lead to faster, more automatic detection of the targets.

Figure 3.10 shows the results. For the Varied-Mapping group, RT increased as the memory set grew larger, as the number of targets people were searching for grew from one to four. In the most difficult condition, searching through four characters for any one of

FIGURE 3.10

Results of Schneider and Shiffrin's (1977) consistent- and varied-mapping experiment. (From Schneider & Shiffrin, 1977.)

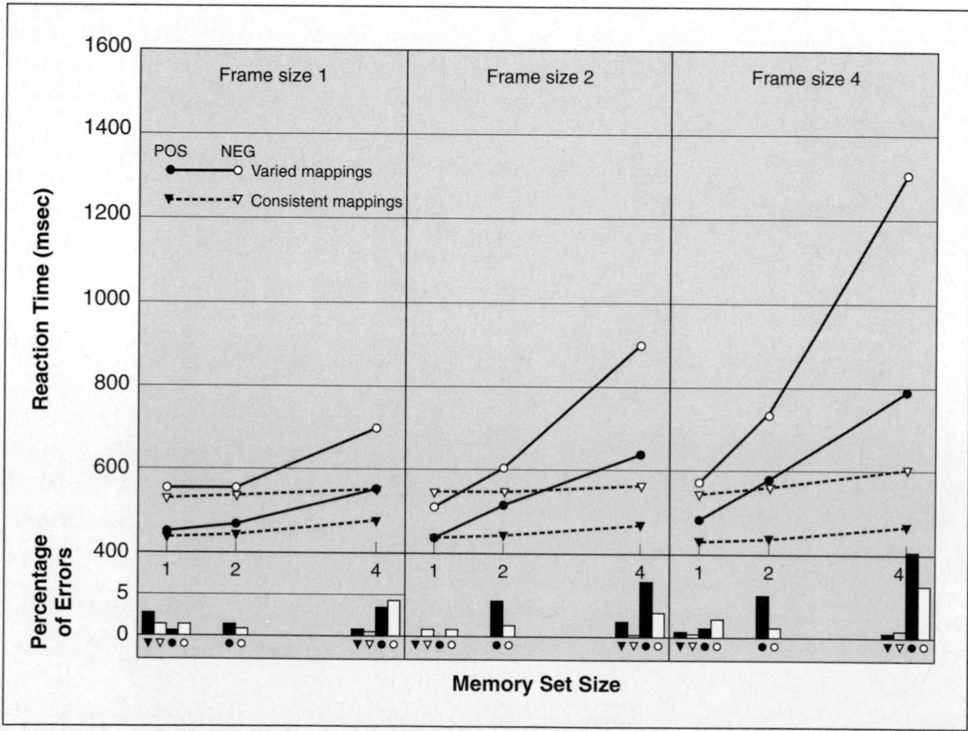

four targets took the longest amount of time: 1300 milliseconds when none of the characters was present. This search rate did not speed up appreciably across the experiment.

On the other hand, the consistent-mapping group revealed essentially no increase in RT, regardless of whether they were searching through one, two, or four characters for one, two, or four targets. On "no" trials, the search time was about 550 to 600 milliseconds; when a target was present, it took only around 450 milliseconds to detect it. The lower curves in the figure, for the consistent-mapping group, were essentially flat.

Why was this search so rapid? Because detecting the same characters over and over allowed the subjects to develop "automatic detection processes," in the authors' words. The participants in the varied-mapping search could never develop those automatic processes, because their target characters kept changing.

Several additional studies confirmed the difference between automatic detection and more difficult, "controlled" or conscious search. In one, some participants were given a total of 2100 detection trials with consistent mapping, and some had 2100 trials with varied mapping. The same result was obtained as described above. But then the targets were changed for the consistent-mapping group—what had been a target for 2100 trials was now a distractor, and vice versa. The results showed that switching the search items in this way had a huge effect. Even after another 2000 trials, those who experienced the switch had still not overcome the effects of their earlier sessions—they still made more errors after the switch than they had at a comparable position in the first half of the experiment. This, of course, is a testimony to the durability of automatic processes; once a process becomes relatively automatic, it is extremely difficult to "undo" that learning and acquire new mappings. (Skilled typists might have extreme and long-term difficulties in adapting to a new and completely rearranged keyboard.)

The generalization here is that **practice** enables a process to occur with lower and lower demands on attention, consuming fewer of those limited resources. The processes that can become automatic range from physical skills all the way up through mental operations. A beginning typist labors slowly—and with many errors—to type a passage of text, with a high degree of awareness of the process; you sit at the keyboard, wondering to yourself, "Where is the D key? Which finger do I use to type the number 6?" By the end of the typing class (if you stuck with it, and really learned touch typing), you can type much more rapidly, with only occasional lapses into conscious questioning of where a particular key is. Words that occur frequently (e.g., *the*) are typed as a unit, rather than as three separate letters, and your fingers begin moving into position in anticipation of an upcoming letter (e.g., Salthouse, 1984; see Norman, 1976, for several similar examples of learned skill and automaticity, such as playing a musical instrument and juggling).

Integration with Memory and Conceptually Driven Processes

Let's go one step further now, to integrate this explanation with an important theme in current cognitive science, the notion of **data-driven versus conceptually driven processing.** As you read in Chapter 1, certain aspects of mental processing rely heavily on the stimulus that's coming into the system. This is referred to as **data-driven processing,** where your mental activity is "driven" mostly by the stimulus itself (we also use the term **bottom-up processing** here). As an example, imagine being in a shadowing experiment where the attended message consists of unrelated words, not coherent thoughts like "While walking through the forest" but arbitrary words like "button exhaust probable tree." Recognizing and shadowing those words will be very difficult (e.g., Miller & Isard, 1963), and very data driven.

Contrast this with a shadowing task in which the attended message is a coherent phrase, like "While Bill was walking through the forest." Your knowledge of the language—that is, your highly practiced skills of hearing and interpreting language—now assist you greatly in the recognition and shadowing task. This contribution of your existing knowledge and skill is called **conceptually driven processing** or **top-down processing**—knowledge at the top of the mental system is exerting an influence down toward the lower-level perception and attention. Because of a lifetime's practice and skill in language, you can comprehend more easily.

This is a *memory* contribution, this conceptually driven processing effect. Once you have begun to understand the content of the shadowed message, then your conceptually driven processes assist you by narrowing down the possible alternatives, by "suggesting" what might come next. Saying that conceptually driven processes suggest what might come next is an informal way of referring to the important process of priming. You shadow "While Bill was walking through the forest." Your semantic analysis primes related information, and thereby "suggests" the likely content of the next clause in the sentence—it's probably about trees, and probably not about banks and cars. Your forest knowledge has been *primed* or activated in memory, and is ready to be perceived more easily. In short, automatic priming of long-term memory has exerted a top-down influence on the earliest of your cognitive processes: auditory perception and attention.

This places memory at the center of our understanding of attention and automaticity. Several investigators in fact claim that we can only understand attention and the role of automaticity by considering memory and its contributions (e.g., Cowan, 1995). Logan and Klapp (1991; see also Zbrodoff & Logan, 1986), for instance, suggest that the effect of practice is to store relevant information in memory. When it's stored there, then it can be accessed and used in an automatic fashion. And Logan and Etherton (1994) provided the final piece to this puzzle. When their participants' attention was directed to target information, the information was learned and then supported automatic processing. But when their attention was directed to only one part of the information, only that part affected their later performance. The unattended part of the stimulus was not learned, and did not lead to automatic processing later on (e.g., Mulligan & Hartman, 1996).

Summing Up

Attention, in its usual, everyday sense, is essentially equivalent to conscious mental capacity or conscious mental resources. We can devote these attentional resources to only one demanding task at a time—or to two somewhat less demanding tasks simultaneously, as long as the two together do not exceed the total capacity available. This devotion of resources means that few, if any, additional resources will be available for other demanding tasks. Alternatively, if a second task is performed largely at the automatic level, then it can occur simultaneously with the first, since it does not draw from the conscious resource pool. (Or, to change the metaphor, the automatic process has achieved a high level of skill; see Hirst & Kalmar, 1987.) The more automatically a task can be performed, the more mental resources will be available for other processes.

DISADVANTAGES OF AUTOMATICITY

We've been talking as if automaticity were a completely positive, desirable characteristic for mental processes—anything that reduces the drain on the limited available mental capacity is a good thing. This is not an entirely true picture, however. There are several situations in which achieving automaticity can lead to difficulties.

You've encountered one of these already, in a sense. Schneider and Shiffrin's (1977) participants learned automatic detection processes in the Consistent-Mapping condition—it took them no more time to search for four targets than for one after 2100 trials. But then, when the target letters were switched, it took well over an additional 2100 trials for them to overcome the automaticity they had achieved. It's hard to "undo" what has become automatic, in other words.

But does this have any practical application? Of course, the answer is yes. We are often confronted with change, with situations that differ enough from what we've become accustomed to that some relearning has to take place. Your new car has some of its controls in a different location from where they were on the older one, so you have to overcome the "habit" of reaching to the left side of the dashboard to turn on the lights. (This is why some controls, e.g., accelerator and brake pedals, do *not* change position.) If you switch to a new word processor after becoming fluent with a different system, it'll take some relearning to overcome your accumulated practice with the old system.

More critically, sometimes we *should* be consciously aware of information or processes that have become too routine and automatic. Barshi and Healy (1993) provide an excellent example, using a proofreading procedure that mimics how we use checklists. All participants in their study scanned pages of simple multiplication problems. Five mistakes, like $7 \times 8 = 63$, were embedded in the pages of problems. All participants saw the same sets of ten problems over and over. In the Fixed-Order condition, the problems were in the same order each time; while in the Varied-Order condition, the problems were in a different order each time. Those tested in the Fixed-Order condition missed significantly more of the embedded mistakes than those tested in the Varied-Order condition; an average of 23 percent missed in Fixed Order, compared to the 9 percent miss rate with Varied order. Figure 3.11 shows this across the five embedded errors. Performance did improve in the Fixed-Order condition, as more and more of the mistakes were encountered. But that first multiplication error was detected only 55 percent of the time, compared to the 90 percent detection rate for the Varied-Order group.

The fixed order of problems encouraged automatic proofreading, which disrupted accuracy at detecting errors. In fact, it took either an earlier error that was detected or a specific *alerting* signal (experiment 3) to overcome the effects of routine, automatic proofreading.

The implications for this kind of result should be clear, as Barshi and Healy pointed out. Pilots are required to go through checklist procedures—say, for landing an airplane—to ensure safety. And yet, because the items on the checklist are in a fixed order, repeated use of the list probably leads to a degree of automaticity—and, likely as not, a tendency to miss errors. This is exactly what happened in March 1983, when a plane landed in Casper, Wyoming, without its landing gear down, even though the flight crew had gone through its standard checklist procedure, and had "verified" that the wheels were down.

FIGURE 3.11

Results of Barshi and Healy's (1993) experiment showing the percentage of participants detecting the five embedded errors in proofreading multiplication problems. Problems were presented either in fixed order or varied order. (Data from Barshi & Healy, 1993.)

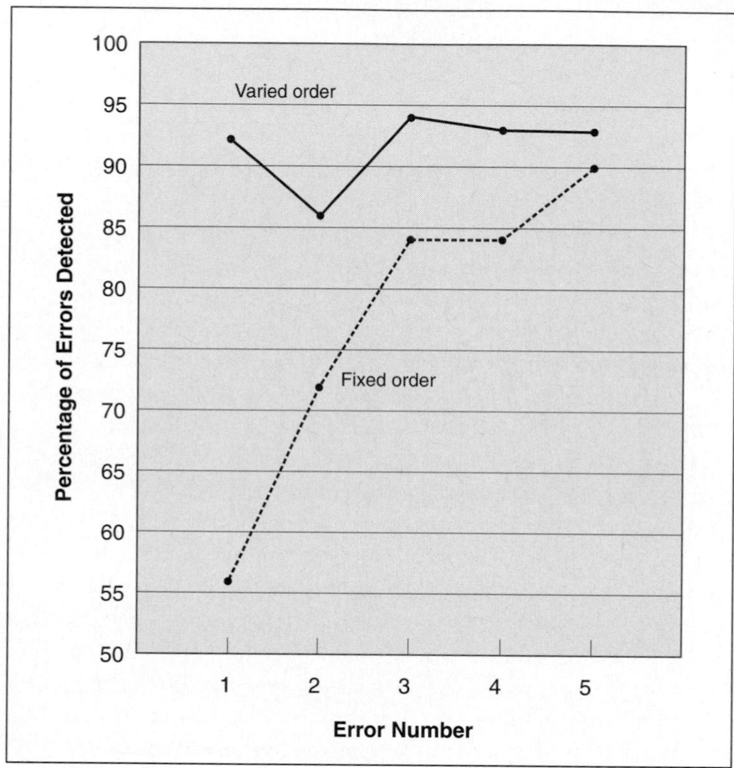

In Barshi and Healy's (1993) words, this incident "reminded the crew and the rest of the aviation community that the countless repetition of the same procedure can lead to a dangerous automatization" (p. 496).

Summary

1. The evidence strongly suggests that a variety of mental processes can become automatic; that is, they can eventually be performed without conscious attention, thus supporting James's observation of more than 100 years ago.
2. Conscious attentional capacity is limited, meaning that there is a limit to how many different tasks can be performed simultaneously. Alertness and arousal are similar concepts to attentional capacity, and we often use the term *mental resources* to refer to this capacity.
3. Automaticity provides a way of getting around the limitation in capacity. When a process becomes automatic, it occurs (a) without intention, (b) without conscious awareness, and (c) without conscious resources. The evidence suggests that ex-

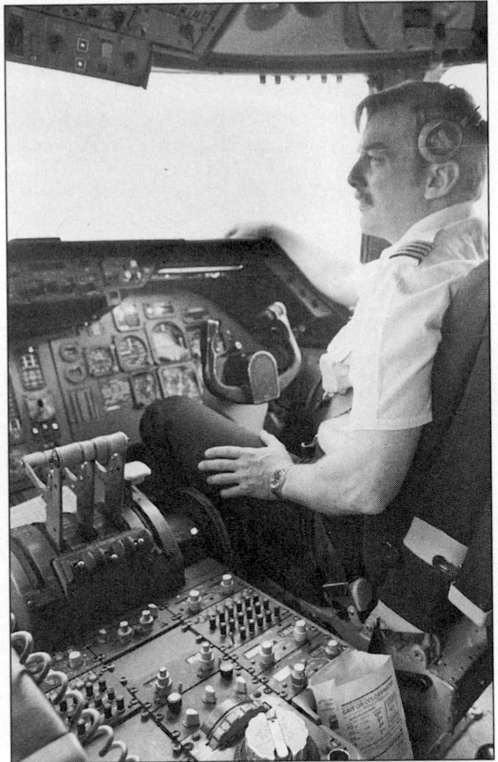

The demands on attention and memory in flying a jet airplane are enormous. The pilot must simultaneously pay conscious attention to multiple sources of information while relying on highly practiced, automatic processes and overlearned actions to respond to others.

tended practice with a relatively unchanging task is necessary for the development of automaticity.

4. Memory contributes to an understanding of attention in that it is where practice has its effect; when an item is stored in memory, it can be accessed and used in an automatic fashion, according to Logan. Priming of concepts in memory provides the top-down assistance that accounts for occasional awareness of unattended information.
5. However important automaticity is to fluent cognitive processing, there can be disadvantages. Repeated exposure and practice induce automaticity, which then makes it difficult to attend consciously to the material.

Important Terms

arousal
attention
attenuation
automaticity
data-driven/bottom-up processing versus conceptually driven/top-down processing
dual task/dual message
filtering
limited capacity
pertinence
practice
priming
selective attention
shadowing

Suggested Readings

The attention literature is rather difficult for an outsider to read and appreciate; it's highly technical and methodologically complex. Some of the more accessible papers are Posner's (1992) paper on attention as a cognitive and neural system, Pashler (1992) on attentional limits in dual-task settings, Norman's (1976) excellent, though now outdated, book, and Eysenck's (1982, 1992) books on attention, arousal, and anxiety. Read Broadbent's classic paper (1952), reprinted in 1992, along with Egeth's (1992) introduction.

SECTION

Two

VARIETIES OF MEMORY

CHAPTER FOUR

SHORT-TERM, WORKING MEMORY

An object which is recollected, in the proper sense of that term, is one which has been absent from consciousness altogether, and now revives anew. It is brought back, recalled . . . from a reservoir in which, with countless other objects, it lay buried and lost from view. But an object of primary memory is not thus brought back; it never was lost; its date was never cut off in consciousness from that of the immediately present moment. (James, 1890/1983, p. 647)

Focus on the two major ideas in this well-known quotation from James's book. First, information is recalled from long-term memory—an "object" is "recollected"—into "primary memory," which we now commonly call "short-term memory (STM)" or "working memory (WM)." And second, information in short-term memory is part of the "immediately present moment," part of our conscious experience of *right now*. You read in the last chapter that attention is the process that leads to awareness or consciousness. So now we're taking the equation one step further—the information you're attending to, what you're aware of right now, is the same as the information being held in short-term memory. When you're paying attention to *this sentence in this textbook*, it's *this* sentence that is in short-term memory—its meaning, possibly some elements of its grammar or style, maybe even some of the sounds you'd make if you said it aloud.

As you begin reading about short-term, working memory, you'll notice that many of the ideas here are already familiar to you. In particular, you'll read about the limitations of the short-term memory system. We have difficulties in doing more than one thing at a time, difficulties in holding more than some smallish amount of information—these are exactly the concepts we covered in discussing attention. But they take on greater significance in the context of short-term, working memory. Why? Because short-term, working memory is im-

★

PROVE IT

You can administer several of the short-term memory tests very easily, with minimal preparation and equipment. Use the sample lists given here as a guide to come up with your own.

1. Memory Span. Memory span, or span of apprehension, is always tested under serial recall instructions. Have at least four lists ready for each list length, using lengths from four or five to about ten items, to be sure to get enough measurements to determine memory span accurately. The classic definition of **memory span** is the particular list length that subjects recall perfectly on half the trials. So if you present four trials per length, and your subject gets all the six-item lists correct, half of the seven-item lists, and none of the eight-item lists, memory span would be 7.

(a) four to ten digits

8 7 0 3   7 1 5 0   2 8 6 4   7 2 8 3
2 8 1 4 6 3   2 8 7 4 9 1   6 9 1 3 5 2
5 2 9 1 4 6

etc.

(b) letters

t s y r   c w m x   k h q d   d t m l
l b n s b   x d w m c   j t f r z   p d r k

etc.

2. Probe Digit Task. You'll read about this task later in the chapter, but here's the setup. Read a list of random letters or digits to the subject. Try not to use any item more than twice, to avoid confusion. The last item in the list is a repetition of an earlier item. When the subject hears that last item, the *probe,* it's a prompt to recall the item that followed the probe in the list. For example,

x d w c r k b v c

The probe letter is *c,* and *r* is the correct response.

7 1 9 6 4 2 7 5 8 3 9

The probe number is 9, and 6 is the correct response.

3. Release from PI. This is another task you'll read about later. For now, have five lists prepared, each containing three words. For the first four lists, use words from one category (e.g., professions), and for the fifth list use words from a different category.

Give your subjects some practice in the distractor task of counting backward by threes; to be really effective, have them count backward at a fairly rapid rate, like one count per second. Once they've practiced, present a list and then the count number; have them count for 20 seconds, then recall the words. Do this for each of the five lists, recording their word recall on each one. You'll probably see noticeable decline across the four similar lists, then a big increase in recall on list 5.

4. Nonverbal STM. This is a nonverbal analogue to a memory span task, sometimes used in neuropsychological testing for patients who are unable to speak. The stimulus lists are sequences of "taps" on a visual array of four locations. You tap out a sequence of length 7, for instance, and then the subject "recalls" by tapping the sequence back to you.

Draw four squares in a row on a piece of paper. Present the lists of "items" to the subject by tapping the squares in a predetermined random sequence. Make several lists of different lengths (e.g., from four to ten items), using the digits 1 through 4 in random order (e.g., 1 4 3 4 2 1 3). Tap the squares in those orders as if the leftmost square were 1, the next square

PROVE IT *(continued)*

were 2, and so on. Obviously, don't tell your subject the square numbers, and don't suggest that the sequences can be recoded into numbers. Just as you did for the regular memory span task, the list length at which the subject gets half of the sequences correct will be the subject's nonverbal short-term memory span.

plicated in a huge variety of mental processes and abilities—reading and comprehending (e.g., Daneman & Carpenter, 1980; Engle, Cantor, & Carullo, 1992), problem solving and reasoning (e.g., Anderson, Reder, & Lebiere, 1996; Salthouse, 1992), even things like daydreaming and self-control of mental activity (e.g., Teasdale et al., 1995; Wegner, 1994).

Prove these limitations, and the importance of short-term memory, to yourself *now,* ★ before reading any further. Work through the demonstrations with a friend, or as part of a class exercise. This, along with the metacognitive awareness you already possess about short-term memory, will give you a base of intuitive understanding to refer to as you read the rest of this chapter. Notice, however, that while you're aware of the contents of your short-term memory, you are not necessarily aware of the processes that occur in short-term memory—precisely the reason you need to study the material in this chapter!

One final preparatory remark is called for here. Toward the end of the chapter, we'll switch from the term **short-term memory** to the newer term, **working memory.** I'm using both terms here rather than just one, partly for historical reasons. That is, **short-term memory** is the older of the two terms, and carries a somewhat simpler, less elaborate sense to it. We use it when the focus is on the input and storage of new information. When a rapidly presented string of digits is tested for immediate recall, for example, we generally refer to short-term memory and imply a simple "recycling" kind of mental activity as an ▲ explanation of recall. An early portrayal of this recycling notion is shown in Figure 4.1 (p. 100), from Waugh and Norman (1965). Likewise, when we focus on the role of rehearsal, we are examining how short-term memory assists in the memorization of new information, highlighting various "control processes" or strategies (Atkinson & Shiffrin, 1971) used for memorization.

The term **working memory,** on the other hand, is the newer term for this "short" component of the memory system, and has been the subject of intense interest over the past 25 years or so. The term generally has the connotation of a mental workbench, the place where conscious, attention-consuming mental effort is applied (Baddeley, 1992a; Baddeley & Hitch, 1974). One advantage of the term *working memory* is that it emphasizes the activity, the mental work, that's being done, and the limitations we run into when we ask the system to do too many things at once. So bear in mind the differences—"short-term memory" emphasizes the size of this limited system, whereas "working memory" emphasizes the work being done.

FIGURE 4.1

Waugh and Norman's (1965) model of primary memory. All verbal items enter primary memory, where they are either rehearsed or forgotten. Rehearsed items may enter secondary memory. (From Waugh & Norman, 1965.)

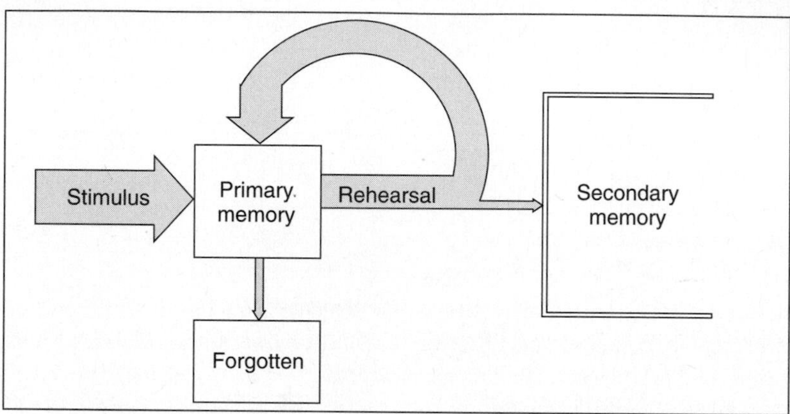

Short-term Memory—The Limited-Capacity "Bottleneck"

Preview: short-term memory defined; the limited-capacity bottleneck; recoding; decay and interference explanations of forgetting

Three important characteristics of short-term memory are highlighted in the following definition.

- **Short-term memory:** The limited-capacity memory component for temporary information storage and manipulation.

Consider this predicament. You've gone into a phone booth to dial a familiar number, but a recording tells you the number has been changed. As you search frantically for a pencil, the recording starts giving you the new number. What do you do? You repeat the number, either aloud or silently to yourself, so you can remember it long enough to dial the number.

It's an almost perfect example to illustrate the three characteristics of short-term memory. First, recycling the phone number, by repeating or rehearsing it, is the mental manipulation or process for maintaining the information in short-term memory. Second, the simple recycling process illustrates a decision you've made—you only intend to remember the phone number long enough to dial it, so you aren't memorizing it with some elaborate strategy. Once you've dialed the new number and begun speaking, the temporarily stored number will be gone, forgotten from short-term memory.

Finally, the phone number is not a great quantity of information—the limited capacity of short-term memory is sufficient for seven-digit (in North America) or eight-digit (in much of Europe) phone numbers. But for situations involving longer sequences, the limitation is serious. For instance, if you hear a string of about ten single digits, read at a constant and fairly rapid rate, and then are asked to reproduce the string, you generally cannot recall more than about seven or eight of the digits. This is roughly the amount you can say aloud within about 2 seconds (Baddeley, Thomson, & Buchanan, 1975). Likewise, you can reproduce only about seven unrelated words, presented in a comparable fashion (you discovered this a few moments ago in the "Prove It" box). This is commonly called the **memory span,** the number of items that can be recalled immediately, in order, after brief presentation (you'll also see it called the *span of apprehension*).

THE MAGICAL NUMBER SEVEN, PLUS OR MINUS TWO

Figure 4.2 shows an idealized graph of memory span data. When the lists are short, people get 100 percent of the items correct (e.g., Oberly, 1928). Beginning with lists about four or five items long, the function starts to depart from perfect performance, and it essentially levels out at around seven items. In some such studies, using different stimulus types or tasks, the estimates of memory span (for adults) are as low as 5, and for some the estimates are closer to 9. So overall, memory span averages about 7 ± 2.

George Miller reviewed such data, and summarized this finding in his classic review article (1956), titled "The Magical Number Seven, Plus or Minus Two: Some Limits on Our Capacity for Processing Information." As he put it, "Everybody knows that there is a finite span of immediate memory and that for a lot of different kinds of test materials this span is about seven items in length" (p. 91). In other words, immediate memory cannot encode

FIGURE 4.2

Idealized memory span results.

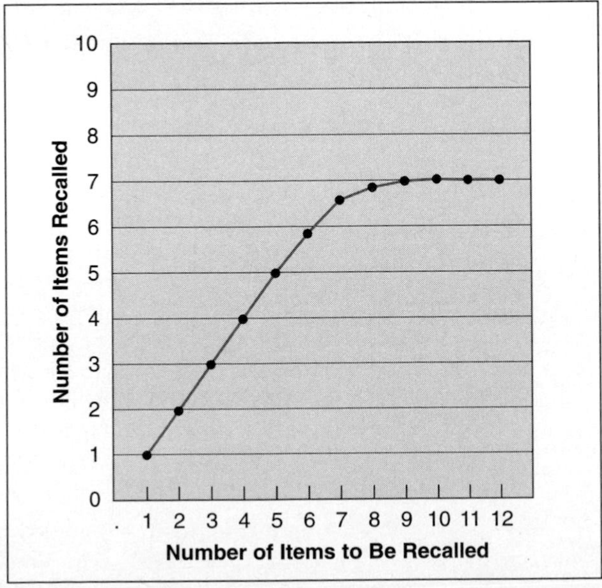

vast quantities of new information and hold that information accurately. Instead, there is a rather severe limit on how much can be encoded, held, and reported immediately.

To be sure, we can take in large amounts of stimulation into the sensory memories, and we can hold truly vast quantities of information in a permanent long-term memory system. But the transfer of information between sensory and long-term memory is troublesome. Immediate or short-term memory is like the the four-lane bridge between sensory and long-term memory, with only one tollgate open. It's the "bottleneck," in Miller's description, that imposes "severe limitations on the amount of information that we are able to receive, process, and remember" (p. 95).

Overcoming the Bottleneck—Recoding

But, Miller (1956) continued, there is a way to overcome this bottleneck. If the seven items we are trying to remember are richer and more complex than seven single digits, if the items are grouped in some fashion, then we can easily exceed the 7 ± 2 capacity by remembering the groups or **chunks** of information—the 3-4 grouping of a telephone number or the 3-2-4 grouping of a social security number makes these sequences much easier to remember. According to Miller, the richer, more complex item is properly referred to as a chunk of information, a unit that can hold more information than a single digit or letter. By chunking several items into a group, we can overcome this limitation and "break (or at least stretch) this informational bottleneck" (p. 95). As a demonstration, go back to the "Prove It" box and attempt the longest lists of digits again, but this time group them as double-digit numbers (28, 14, 63, etc.).

Miller's central point was that our short-term memories are inherently limited in the total amount of information that can be held at any one time. The limit seems to be seven units or chunks, plus or minus two. Any quantity greater than this, if it is to be retained successfully, must be grouped or chunked, again with a limit of about seven of these enriched chunks. We call this the process of **recoding,** grouping items together, then remembering the newly formed groups. (In fact, Brooks & Watkins, 1990, suggest that there is already a subgrouping effect in the memory span, with the first half of the span enjoying somewhat of an advantage over the second half.)

Notice a vitally important point about recoding: It requires the active involvement of the person to recode the items into richer groups and then maintain those groups in short-term memory. The bottleneck in the system can be overcome by chunking or recoding, but only under either of two conditions, it seems.

- First, we can recode if there is sufficient time to apply the recoding scheme, or if there are sufficient mental resources such as attention still available to do the recoding.
- Second, we can recode successfully if the recoding scheme is highly overlearned.

Long-term Memory Involvement in Recoding

Think about that again—we can recode if the recoding scheme is highly overlearned, that is, highly practiced. Morse code is an example—the trained Morse code operator can easily recode individual dots and dashes into familiar groups, but only because the recoding scheme is stored in long-term memory. In a stunning example of this, Chase and Ericsson (1982) described a man who was able to recall 82 digits *in order* by recoding the digits into groups on the basis of a personally meaningful scheme. (The man was a runner, so he remembered the digits by relating them to known facts about running; e.g., 351 recoded as "3:51 was the former world record time for running the mile".) Thus, his specialized long-term memory knowledge enabled recoding of the digits, and in turn helped overcome the limitations of short-term memory.

Recoding Based on Language One of Miller's (1956) most profound observations involved language and its role in short-term memory: "In my opinion, the most customary kind of recoding that we do all the time is to translate into a verbal code. When there is a story or an argument or an idea that we want to remember, we usually try to rephrase it 'in our own words' " (p. 95). In other words, rephrasing is an excellent, flexible, and overlearned recoding scheme that helps overcome the limited capacity of short-term memory. Notice that this places short-term memory squarely into the business of language comprehension, an important and far-reaching insight we'll return to later in this chapter.

DECAY AND INTERFERENCE AS CAUSES OF FORGETTING

But what about situations when you don't remember information stored in short-term memory? We've all had the experience of losing our train of thought during a conversation (or during a lecture!), of being momentarily distracted and then forgetting what we were just doing ("Why did I start looking through this book?" "Why did I go downstairs?"). What explains this forgetting of information in short-term memory?

The Brown-Peterson Task—Decay from Short-term Memory

Under some circumstances, it turns out that we can't even hold half the items in short-term memory that would be expected based on memory span. In the late 1950s, at the very dawning of cognitive psychology, J. A. Brown (1958) and Peterson and Peterson (1959) published compelling demonstrations of this surprising effect, in research that is still viewed as trendsetting. Their topic: What causes forgetting in short-term memory?

The basic idea in the Brown and the Peterson and Peterson papers was that forgetting might be due simply to the passage of time before testing. This would be a case of forgetting caused by **decay,** the fading or forgetting of a memory trace across time. This is a very simple hypothesis about forgetting in short-term memory, of course, because it claims that time alone is the important variable in how much we forget.

Brown (1958) and Peterson and Peterson (1959) independently devised a rather simple task to test this idea; cognitive psychology still refers to the task as the **Brown-Peterson task.** On each of many individual trials, a simple three-letter stimulus is presented to the participants (e.g., CHJ), followed by a three-digit number (e.g., 506). They are instructed first to attend to the stimulus, then to begin counting backward by threes, starting with the presented number. Counting has to be done aloud, in rhythm with a metronome clicking twice per second. The participants are interrupted after an interval of 3 to 18 seconds, and are asked to report the three letters. (In Brown's version, the people merely read numbers aloud for the distractor task.)

◆ The results, shown in Figure 4.3, were amazing. After merely 6 seconds of backward counting, accuracy in recalling the three letters had dropped to about 40 percent—and

◆ **FIGURE 4.3**

Peterson and Peterson's (1959) results, showing the decline in accuracy across retention intervals of different lengths. (From Peterson & Peterson, 1959.)

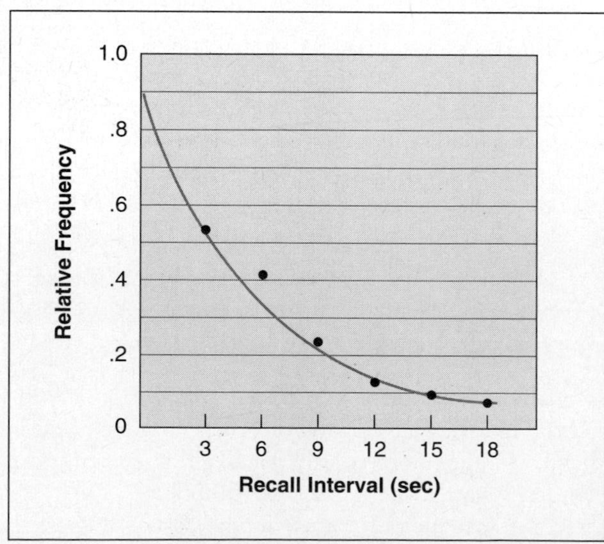

was below 20 percent after 12 seconds. Imagine, you only have to remember three letters, and yet the more time you spend counting, the lower your recall. The effect seemed clear at the time—the longer the information stayed in short-term memory, the more it was forgotten.

The essential ingredient in this finding, as you'd expect, was the distractor task, the backward counting. The Petersons included it to prevent rehearsal, reasoning that numbers are different enough from the stimulus letters that there should be little interference between the two. Thus, the distractor task required a great deal of attention, and consequently prevented rehearsal.

Interference Versus Decay in Short-term Memory

But was it true that the distractor task, counting backward by threes, really did not interfere? Had the Brown-Peterson task really demonstrated simple decay? Later research questioned this assumption, and in fact showed that the distractor task was a source of interference, of competition or disruption. Waugh and Norman (1965), in particular, demonstrated that the Brown-Peterson result was due to interference rather than simple decay.

Waugh and Norman began by pointing out an alternative interpretation for the Peterson and Peterson (1959) result. They noted that if the numbers spoken by the subjects during backward counting had interfered with the short-term memory trace, then longer counting intervals would have provided more opportunity for interference, since the subjects would have produced more numbers during the longer interval. As such, it could just as well be that the additional numbers were the reason for forgetting, instead of the additional time with longer counting intervals.

These suspicions were confirmed in what they called a "probe digit task." Participants heard a list of 16 digits, read at a rate of either 1 digit or 4 digits per second. The final item
★ in each list was a repeat of an earlier item, and it served as the probe or cue to write down the digit that had followed the probe in the original list. Study the illustration to make sure you understand the task.

For the issue of decay versus interference, the important part of the experiment was the time it took to present the 16 digits. Presentation of the entire list took 16 seconds for one group, but only 4 seconds for the other group. If forgetting were due to decay from short-term memory, then the groups should have differed markedly in their recall, since so
▲ much more time had elapsed in the 16-second group. Yet as Figure 4.4 (p. 106) shows, the two groups barely differed at all in their recall accuracy.

Waugh and Norman's (1965) results demonstrated, in short, that forgetting from short-term memory was influenced by the number of intervening items between the critical digit and the recall test, and not merely by the passage of time. In other words, forgetting from short-term memory was caused by interference, not simple decay. Other research went on to show that the particular nature of the distractor task had an effect too. For example, Talland (1967) used two different distractor tasks with the Brown-Peterson task—one group did subtraction during the retention interval, the other group merely read the same numbers they would have spoken if doing subtraction. Not surprisingly, the group that actually had to do subtraction performed worse on recall than the group that read (see also Dillon & Reid, 1969; Peterson, Peterson, & Miller, 1961).

WAUGH AND NORMAN'S (1965) "PROBE DIGIT TASK"

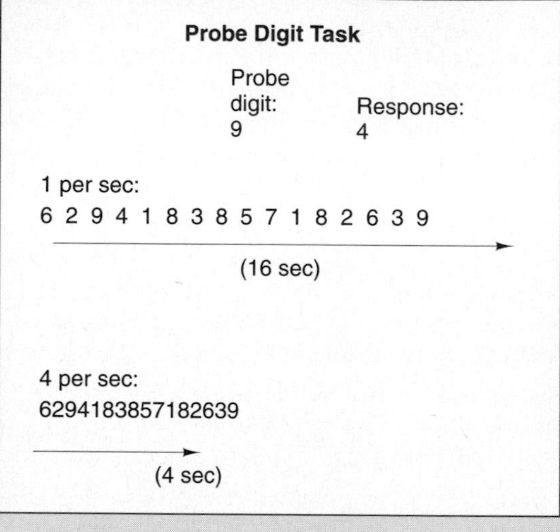

Source: Based on Waugh & Norman (1965).

FIGURE 4.4

Relative accuracy in the Waugh and Norman (1965) probe digit task as a function of the number of interfering items spoken between the target item and the cue to recall; rate of presentation was either 1 or 4 digits/sec. (Adapted from Waugh & Norman, 1965.)

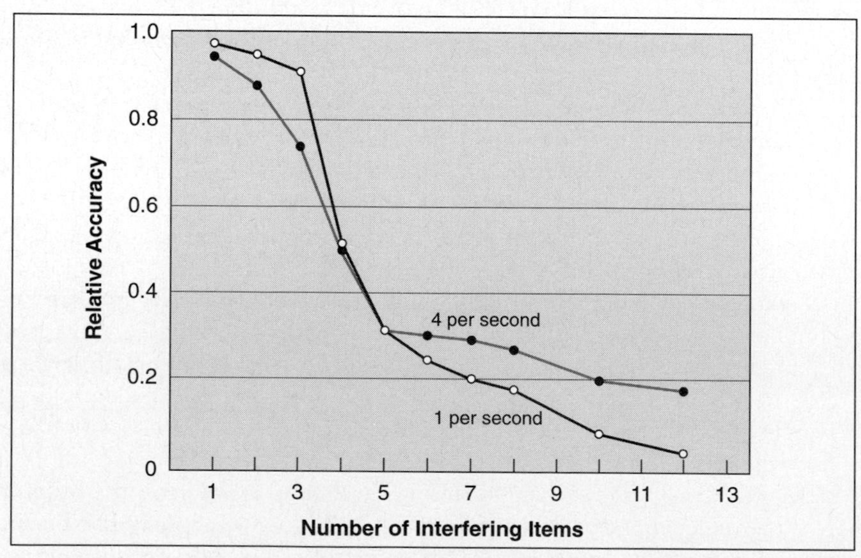

Release from PI

Very shortly after the Peterson and Peterson (1959) report, Keppel and Underwood (1962) challenged another part of Peterson and Peterson's results. It seems that the participants forgot at the dramatic rate reported by the Petersons only when they had been tested on several trials in the short-term memory task. On the first trial, memory for the three-letter stimulus was virtually perfect. But as more trials took place, more and more forgetting was observed. Keppel and Underwood pointed out the likely reason for this result. As you experience more and more trials in the Brown-Peterson task, recalling the stimulus becomes more difficult because the previous trials are generating interference. This form of interference is called **proactive interference (PI),** when older material interferes forward in time with your recollection of the current stimulus. This is the opposite of **retroactive interference (RI),** in which newer material interferes backward in time with your memory for older items. The loss of information in the Brown-Peterson task, according to Keppel and Underwood, was due to proactive interference.

In an important series of studies, Wickens and his co-workers (Wickens, 1972; also Wickens, Born, & Allen, 1963) used this effect of proactive interference to establish several other points about short-term memory. He reasoned that proactive interference from earlier trials was probably due to the similarity of the three-letter combinations the participants were asked to remember. In other words, after seeing CHJ, then BZR, then MHQ, and so on, recalling yet another letter combination becomes very difficult—participants often end up remembering letters from an earlier trial, the proactive interference effect. As such, Wickens reasoned that a change in the stimuli might eliminate the interference. This is referred to as **release from PI,** when the proactive interference is reduced or eliminated due to a change in the stimuli.

This is exactly what Wickens (e.g., 1972) found. Participants in his study were given triads of names in categories for three trials. Group 1 saw profession names; group 2, flower names; group 3, vegetable names; and group 4, fruit names. All four groups had a 20-second period of backward counting after each trial. Then, on trial 4, all four groups got a triad of fruit names. For the control group (group 4), this was just another trial of fruit names. Because there was no switch in the lists, their performance remained low. But the other groups experienced a switch in the words, so they experienced different degrees of release from PI. The dissimilarity of the vegetable, flower, and profession names to the fruit names they studied on trial 4 produced release from PI, as shown in Figure 4.5 (p. 108).

The interference interpretation here is very clear. Performance deteriorates across trials because of the buildup of proactive interference; the buildup is due to the similarity of the successive lists. If the to-be-remembered stimulus changes, however, then you are "released" from the interference. Your performance is no longer depressed by the growing amount of interference, so you once again recall with high accuracy. Wickens's research showed the release-from-PI effect across a large array of changes—for instance, changing the stimulus lists from one category to another, as shown in Figure 4.5, from "masculine" words like *butler* and *tuxedo* to "feminine" concepts like *queen* and *blouse,* even changing from frequent to rare words in the language. All of this work, summarized in Wickens (1972), demonstrated conclusively the buildup of proactive interference with similar lists, and then the release from PI when a dissimilar list was presented.

FIGURE 4.5

Recall accuracy in a release-from-PI experiment reported in Wickens (1972). All subjects received word triads from the fruit category on trial 4. On trials 1 to 3, different groups received triads from the categories fruits, vegetables, flowers, and professions. (From Wickens, 1972.)

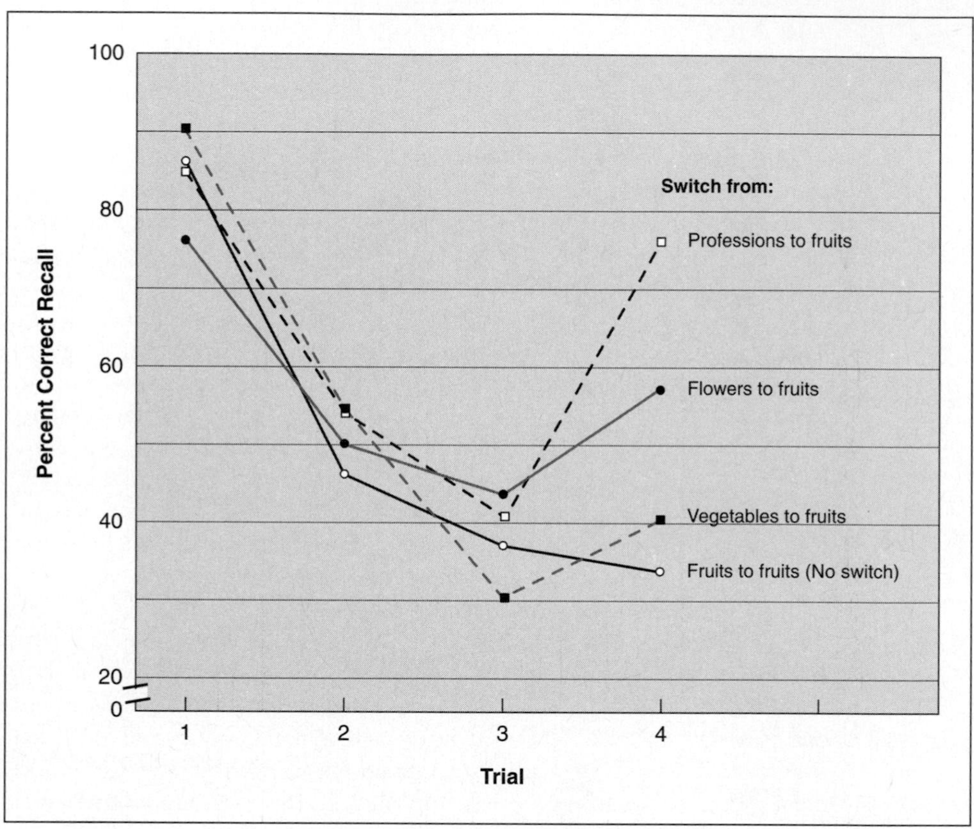

Summary

1. Short-term memory is a limited-capacity system for holding and manipulating information temporarily. It is loosely the same thing as consciousness, in the sense that the material we are aware of at any moment is the material currently stored in short-term memory.
2. Under most situations, no more than about seven units of information, plus or minus two, can be held in short-term memory. Recoding is the general process by which this limitation can be overcome, by chunking separate items into groups, or even by paraphrasing language as it is being understood.
3. Early demonstrations, especially using the Brown-Peterson task, suggested that forgetting from short-term memory is due to decay, the passage of time. Later research showed that interference provides a more adequate explanation of forgetting.

4. The more similar intervening information is to the material being held in short-term memory, the more interference leads to forgetting. Further, forgetting is also influenced by the attention paid to a distractor task.

Rehearsal and Retrieval in Short-term Memory

Preview: recall tasks; two functions of rehearsal, recycling and transfer to long-term memory; retrieval from short-term memory

When information in short-term memory goes unrehearsed—say, because of some intervening activity—what happens? It's forgotten from the short-term store, usually because of interference. Let's turn now from the topic of forgetting and instead look at the other side of the coin: remembering. How do we use short-term memory to remember information, either for a short period of time or more permanently? This is the study of **rehearsal,** the deliberate mental repetition or practicing of to-be-learned material. To understand rehearsal, you first need to understand something about the tasks and terms used to investigate it.

RECALL TASKS

We've already covered one of the most straightforward tasks for investigating short-term memory: recall. When people perform in a memory span task, they recall the list items, usually orally but sometimes in written form. This is one version of the recall task, called **serial recall,** in which the items must be recalled in their order of presentation. Memory span is always tested under serial-recall instructions. Contrast this with **free recall,** in which the items may be recalled in any order. Both versions of the recall tasks can be used for studying characteristics of short-term memory (and long-term memory too, as you'll read in the next chapter).

When we examine recall accuracy, it's useful to know more than simply the percent correct for the total list. In particular, we often look at accuracy in terms of where an item appeared in the list. This kind of graph is known as a **serial-position curve,** simply a graph showing recall accuracy as a function of an item's original position in a list. Two ◆ good examples of such graphs are shown in Figure 4.6 (p. 110). In Figure 4.6(a), from a study by Murdock (1962), participants saw lists of 20, 30, or 40 items, at a rate of 1 item per second. The slightly elevated first part of the curve is called the **primacy effect,** recall of the early list items ("primacy" refers to the "first" items). The end portion of the curve is called the **recency effect,** recall of the last few items (i.e., the most recently seen items).

Murdock's data, collected under free-recall instructions, are telling us two important things about rehearsal and short-term memory. First, notice that the recency effect is quite pronounced at all three list lengths. This high accuracy—the recency effect—was due to the free recall instructions. That is, because they could name the items in any order, subjects began by recalling the last few items first, the items they had seen most recently. These last items had just been stored in short-term memory so were easy to recall, easy to "spew out," so to speak, without further rehearsal. In other words,

- With no intervening distractor task, items in short-term memory can be immediately recalled with very high accuracy.

FIGURE 4.6

Murdock's (1962) and Glanzer and Cunitz's (1966) serial-position results. (a) Serial-position curves, showing recall accuracy across the original positions in the learned list. Rate of presentation was one item per second. (b) Serial-position curves, showing the decrease in recency when either 10 or 30 sec of backward counting is interpolated between study and recall. (c) Three different rates of presentation: 3 sec, 6 sec, and 9 sec (Data from Murdock, 1962, and Glanzer & Cunitz, 1966.)

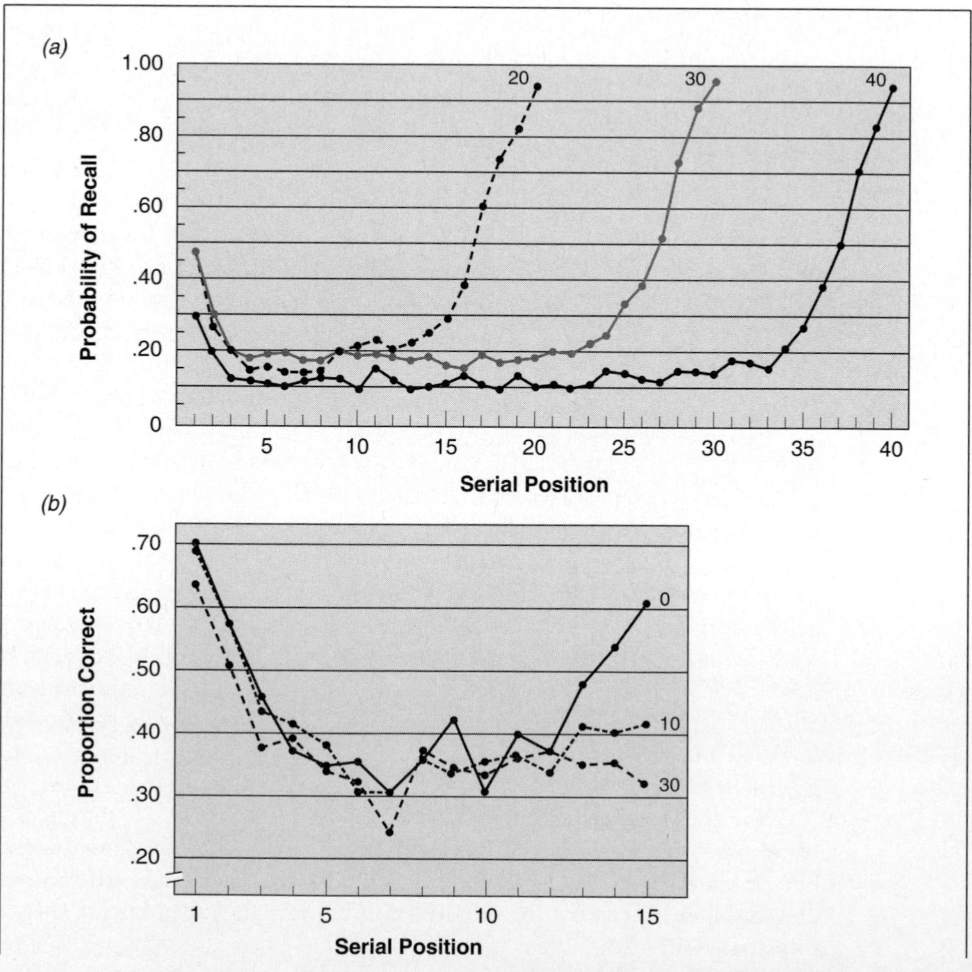

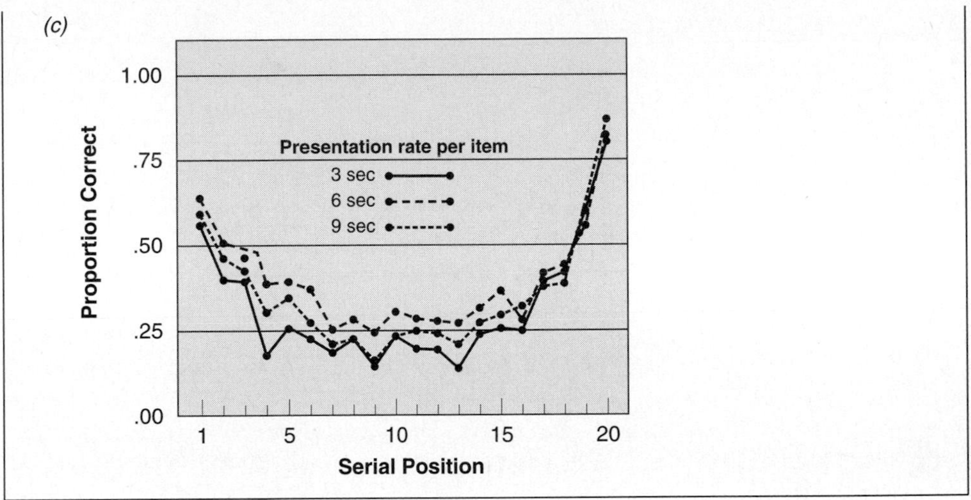

Confirmation of this point was provided by Glanzer and Cunitz (1966), whose results are shown in Figure 4.6(b). Participants who had a 0-second delay before recall showed high recency, whereas those who had either 10 or 30 seconds of a distractor task (counting forward by ones) showed markedly lower recency.

The second important aspect concerned rehearsal time. Murdock (1962) used a very rapid presentation rate, one item per second. This was so rapid in fact that it seemed to prevent people from engaging in rehearsal—the items kept coming and coming, without enough time left over to use a rehearsal strategy to prevent forgetting. Except for the very first items, when the load on memory had not yet built up, recall was very low for all but the last four or five list positions. In other words, there was only a small primacy effect. In effect,

- With insufficient time for rehearsal, no lasting record of the information remains in short-term memory, and little if any can be recalled from long-term memory.

Figure 4.6(c) also confirms this point—the primacy portions of these curves were much higher than those shown in Figure 4.6(a), no doubt because Glanzer and Cunitz (1966) used a much slower presentation rate, one item per 3 seconds. In fact, another experiment by these authors supported this conclusion exactly. In this study, the primacy effect was lower for groups given 3 seconds per item than for groups given either 6 or 9 seconds per item; this is shown in Figure 4.6(c). The additional input time permitted additional rehearsal, and therefore additional transfer of the items into long-term memory.

THE REHEARSAL BUFFER

The experiments just described focused on short-term memory as the memory component where rehearsal takes place. This was exactly the point of the Waugh and Norman (1965) model of primary memory shown in Figure 4.1—short-term memory as the place where recycling happens. A more thorough treatment of the rehearsal function of short-term memory appeared in the classic papers by Atkinson and Shiffrin (1968, 1971); their well-known illustration appears in Figure 4.7 (p. 112).

★ **FIGURE 4.7**

The Atkinson and Shiffrin (1971) model of information flow through the memory system. (From Atkinson & Shiffrin, 1971.)

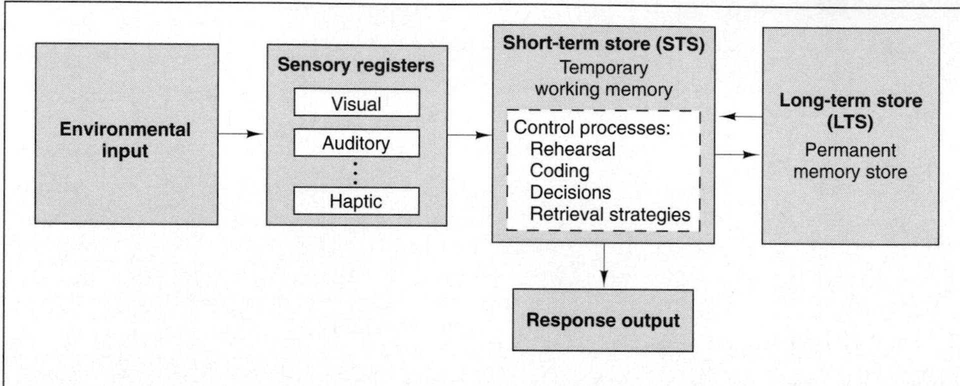

Information Flow through the memory system is conceived of as beginning with the processing of environmental inputs in sensory registers (receptors plus internal elements) and entry into the short-term store (STS). While it remains there the information may be copied into the long-term store (LTS), and associated information that is in the long-term store may be activated and entered into the short-term store. If a triangle is seen, for example, the name "triangle" may be called up. Control processes in the short-term store affect these transfers into and out of the long-term store and govern learning, retrieval of information, and forgetting.

As you'll notice, short-term memory in this model was considerably more elaborate than the simple recycling model in Waugh and Norman (1965). Here, Atkinson and Shiffrin (1971) proposed that short-term memory has multiple characteristics and does many different things. Foremost among these were the functions listed as "control processes." Included here were the various strategies and procedures we have for holding and manipulating information—in other words, rehearsal strategies. But further, short-term memory was the component responsible for making decisions, for retrieving information (say, from long-term memory), and for communicating to the outside world by making a response.

Two Functions of Rehearsal

Consider recycling again, a low-level repetition of information that continues until the information can be recalled. Atkinson and Shiffrin (1968) argued that the final recency portion of a serial-position curve, like that shown in Figure 4.6(a), illustrates the effects of this kind of repetitive rehearsal. Without much effort, a few items will stay in short-term memory and can be immediately recalled unless there's some distraction. This strategy works in a free-recall task, because the last few items are still in short-term memory and can be named first. Thus,

- The first function of rehearsal is maintaining information in short-term memory by simple repetition or recycling.

But you clearly cannot capitalize on recency in a serial-recall task; you must start your recall with the first item in the list. Since you cannot rely on immediate recall for any of the items in serial recall, you must rehearse them as they are shown, in order to store them in a more enduring form. Thus,

- The second function of rehearsal is transferring information into long-term memory.

We'll discuss this second function of rehearsal thoroughly in the next chapter. At that time, we will take up the distinction between maintenance rehearsal and elaborative rehearsal (Craik & Lockhart, 1972). As the names imply, "maintenance" corresponds to the first function of rehearsal, the recycling idea, and "elaborative" corresponds to the kind of rehearsal that transfers information into long-term memory.

For now, notice that this research established that rehearsal is a short-term memory process, a characteristic *activity* of the short-term memory system. Rehearsal was said to be an optional control process, which could do two things, either maintain information in the short-term store or transfer it to long-term memory by a more elaborate, strategy-controlled rehearsal process. The results revealed by serial-position curves are in agreement with these ideas, with "recycling" rehearsal responsible for the recency effect and "transferring" rehearsal responsible for the primacy effect.

RETRIEVAL FROM SHORT-TERM MEMORY

Our focus so far has been on rehearsal and its effects, especially how we maintain information in short-term memory and how we transfer it to long-term memory. We turn now to a rather different question: How do we access or retrieve the contents of short-term memory itself?

Think of this question as the short-term memory equivalent of a question that seems more sensible to our introspections: How do we access or retrieve information from long-term memory? We would all agree that some long-term memory information is difficult and slow to retrieve, and that we're sometimes aware of this difficulty (e.g., what was your second-grade teacher's name?). But it's equally valid to ask how retrieval takes place, whether from short- or long-term memory, when it's extremely rapid and out of conscious awareness (e.g., does a robin have feathers?). That's the focus of this section, how the rapid process of retrieval happens in short-term memory. To answer this question, we turn to a second kind of memory task, recognition.

Recognition Tasks

All students are familiar with a common version of a recognition task, multiple-choice tests. In this format, you select the one alternative that's correct, and in the process you reject the others as being incorrect. From the standpoint of cognitive processes, you've said Yes to the correct alternative, essentially the same as saying, "Yes, I recognize that as the information I studied for the test." Similarly, deciding that an alternative is wrong is the same as deciding, "No. That choice is 'new.' I didn't study it." Clearly, making these decisions requires you to access some stored knowledge, then compare the alternatives to that knowledge. When one of the alternatives "matches" your knowledge, then you can respond, "Yes, that's the correct alternative."

The important wrinkle in cognitive science is that we often time people as they make their yes/no recognition decisions, and then try to infer the underlying mental processes used in the task on the basis of how long they took. This is standard procedure in cognitive research—you read about it in Chapter 1, in the section called "Measuring Cognition." The measure is reaction time, abbreviated "RT," usually measured in thousandths of a second, or milliseconds. It was exactly this methodology, and the question of how we access information in short-term memory, that Saul Sternberg (1966, 1969, 1975) attempted to answer in his groundbreaking research on short-term memory scanning.

SHORT-TERM MEMORY SCANNING: THE STERNBERG TASK PARADIGM

Sternberg (1966, 1969, 1975) began his work by noting that the use of RT tasks to infer mental processes had a venerable history, dating back at least to Donders's work in the 1800s (1969/1868). Donders had proposed a general method called the "subtractive method" for determining the time necessary for simple mental events. For example, if your primary task involves processes A, B, and C, you devise a comparison task that has only processes A and C in it. After administering both tasks, you then subtract the A + C time from the A + B + C time. The difference should be a measure of the duration of process B, since it's the process that was "subtracted" from the primary task.

Sternberg (1969) pointed out a major difficulty in applying Donders's subtractive method. It is virtually impossible to make sure that the comparison task, the A + C task, truly contains exactly the same A and C processes as they occur in the primary task. There is always the possibility, Sternberg reasoned, that you may inadvertently simplify the A and C components when you eliminate process B. If so, then subtracting one from the other can't be justified.

Sternberg's solution to this knotty problem was a genuine innovation. Rather than try to eliminate one process from the primary task, he arranged his experiments so that the critical process would have to repeat some number of times during a single trial. Across an entire experiment there would be many trials on which process B had occurred only once, many on which it occurred two times, three times, and so forth. He then examined the RTs for these successive conditions and inferred the nature of process B by determining how much time was added to people's responses for each repetition of process B.

TABLE 4.1

Sample Trials in the Sternberg Task

Trial	*Memory Set Items*	*Probe Items*	*Correct Response*
1	R	R	Yes
2	LG	L	Yes
3	SN	N	Yes
4	BKVJ	M	No
5	LSCY	C	Yes

Source: Based on Sternberg (1969).

The Sternberg Task

The task Sternberg (1966, 1969) devised was a short-term memory-scanning task, now simply called a **Sternberg task.** Participants first stored a short list of letters, referred to as the *memory set,* in short-term memory. They then saw a single letter, the *probe item,* and responded yes or no depending on whether the probe item was among the letters in the memory set. So, for example, if you stored the set LRDC in short-term memory, and then saw the letter D, you'd respond yes. If the probe item were M, however, you'd respond by pressing the no button.

In a typical experiment, Sternberg's groups were shown several hundred trials, each consisting of these two parts—memory set, then probe item—as shown in Table 4.1. Memory sets were from one to six letters (or digits, in some experiments) long, well within the span of short-term memory, and they changed on every trial. Probe items changed on every trial too, and were selected so that on half of the trials the correct response was yes and on half, no. More importantly for his logic, when the probe item did match one of the letters in the memory set, it matched each position in the set equally frequently. This is illustrated by trials 2 and 3 in Table 4.1. Take a moment to try several of these trials, covering the probe item until you've stored the memory set in short-term memory, then covering the memory set and uncovering the probe, and making your yes/no judgment. For a better demonstration, have someone read aloud the memory sets and probe items to you.

Figure 4.8 illustrates the four-stage process model that Sternberg (1969) proposed for this task, simply a flowchart of the four separate mental processes that occurred during timing on every trial. At the point marked "Timer starts running here," the individual begins to encode the probe item. Once this process is finished, the search or scan through short-term memory could begin. That is, the mentally encoded probe could then be compared to the items held in memory, to see if there were a match or not. A simple yes/no decision could then be made, after which the person could make the physical response—pressing the button—that stopped the timer.

FIGURE 4.8

Sternberg's (1969) four-stage process model for short-term memory scanning. (Adapted from Sternberg, 1969.)

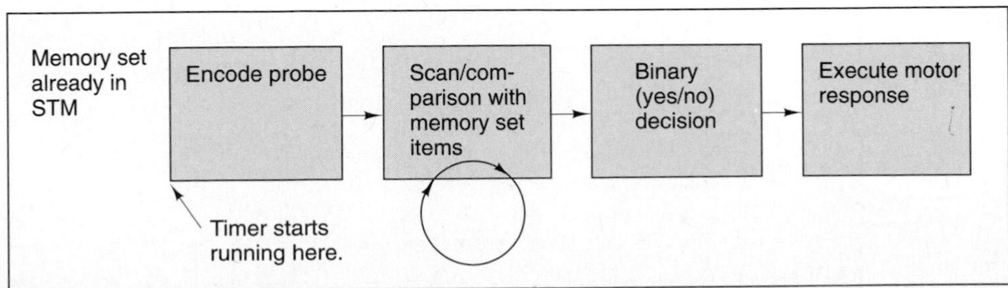

In terms we used above, it was the search process, the scan through the contents of short-term memory, that was of particular interest. Notice—this is critical—that it was this process that repeated different numbers of times, depending on the size of the memory set. That is to say, when two items were stored in short-term memory, the scan/comparison process would have to occur twice, once for the item in position 1, once for the item in position 2. If five items were stored, likewise, the probe would have to be compared to each of the five.

Thus, by manipulating the size of the memory set, Sternberg influenced the number of cycles through the scan/comparison process. And by examining the slope of the RT results, he could determine how much additional time was necessary for each cycle through the scanning process.

Sternberg's Results

Figure 4.9 shows Sternberg's (1969) results. There was a linear increase in RT as the memory set got larger and larger, and this increase was nearly the same for both yes and no trials. The equation at the top of the figure shows that the y-intercept of this RT function was 397.2 milliseconds. Roughly speaking, this would be the combined time for the encoding, decision, and response stages, the stages that occur only once per trial (refer back to Figure 4.8). The slope of the equation was 37.9 milliseconds, which means that for each additional position in the memory set, the mental scanning process took an additional 37.9 milliseconds. Putting it slightly differently, the results indicated that the

FIGURE 4.9

Sternberg's (1969) results on the memory scanning task. (Data from Sternberg, 1969.)

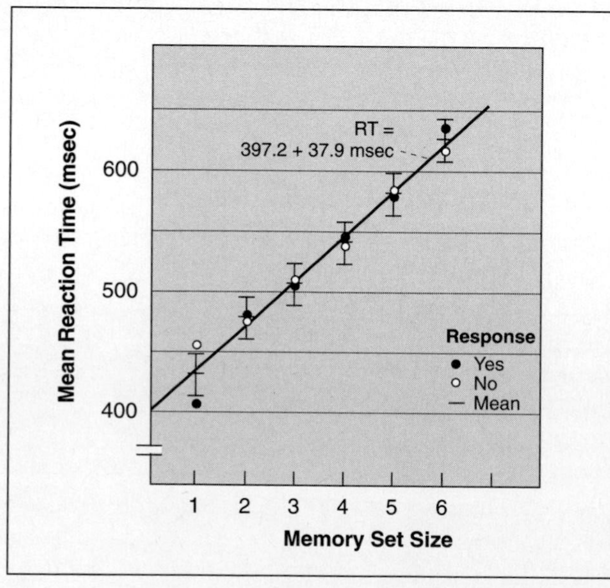

search rate through short-term memory is approximately 38 milliseconds per item. (In case you hadn't noticed, this is *very* fast—less than one-twentieth of a second!)

But a major goal of Sternberg's research was to determine how the contents of short-term memory are searched, that is, to investigate the nature of the **memory search** process. He considered three theoretical possibilities.

The most intuitively appealing possibility was called "serial self-terminating search," in which the positions in short-term memory are scanned one by one, and the scan stops when a match is found; this is, of course, exactly how you search for your lost car keys. This kind of search predicts that, on the average, the slope of the RT curve for yes responses should be shallower than the slope for no responses. That is, on no trials, all positions have to be searched, but on yes trials you encounter matches at all positions in the memory set, sometimes early, sometimes late, with equal frequencies at all positions. But the data showed the same slope for both kinds of trials, so this type of search was rejected.

In a *parallel search*, each position in the memory set would be scanned simultaneously—that's the meaning of a parallel process, that is, processes occurring at the same time. If short-term memory were scanned in parallel, in Sternberg's reasoning, then there should be no increase in RT at all—if all the positions can be scanned simultaneously, it shouldn't take any longer to scan six items than three, for example. But again, the data did not match this prediction, so parallel search was also rejected.

Sternberg inferred, instead, that short-term memory is searched in a *serial-exhaustive* fashion. That is, the memory set is scanned one item at a time, and the entire set is scanned on every trial, whether or not a match is found. Notice that this would have to be the type of search used on no trials, because all positions have to be scanned before you can confidently make a no decision. The similarity of the yes and no curves in Figure 4.9 therefore argues strongly that both reflect the same mental process, serial-exhaustive search through short-term memory (Sternberg, 1969, 1975). How quickly can the contents of short-term memory be scanned? Apparently, based on Sternberg's classic results, the contents can be scanned at a rate of about 38 milliseconds per item. And how do we  search short-term memory? By means of a serial-exhaustive search.

Summary

1. Serial-recall and free-recall tasks are commonly used for testing short-term memory. Accuracy on the early serial positions is referred to as the primacy effect, and accuracy on the end of the list is called the recency effect.
2. The recency effect in free recall shows the simple recycling or maintenance aspect of rehearsal, in which items can be maintained for immediate recall. The primacy effect varies with the amount of rehearsal possible during learning, and so represents the other aspect of rehearsal, transfer of information into long-term memory.
3. Retrieval from short-term memory has been extensively investigated with a timed recognition task referred to as the Sternberg task. When a set of items is held in short-term memory and then scanned, the scan process occurs at about 38 milliseconds per item. Sternberg concluded in favor of a serial-exhaustive search process in short-term memory.

★

THE PLAUSIBILITY OF SERIAL-EXHAUSTIVE SEARCH

Sternberg argued that serial-exhaustive search might be more efficient than the intuitively plausible serial self-terminating search. Consider first the very rapid search rate of 38 milliseconds per item, less than one-twentieth of a second. Sternberg (1969) suggested that such a rapid search process might be impossible to stop once it begins. In other words, once the high-speed scanning process is triggered, maybe it "runs to completion" more or less automatically and cannot be voluntarily stopped (as Zbrodoff & Logan, 1986, have described an "autonomous" mental process). Further, under serial-exhaustive search, you scan short-term memory, then merely make one yes/no decision at the completion of scanning. In contrast, if you searched in a self-terminating fashion, you'd have to switch repeatedly between scanning a position and deciding if the probe matched or not. In the end, you will have made many extra decisions that could have been avoided just by postponing the decision stage until your search was completed.

On the other hand, several researchers criticized Sternberg's (1975) conclusions on the grounds that other search models were also consistent with his results. For example, it could be that multiple scans were occurring simultaneously, each at a slower rate. This would be a parallel search that still showed an increase in RT across memory set size (e.g., Baddeley, 1976). Others disagreed with the idea that the four stages operate one by one, with no overlap; McClelland (1979), for example, suggested that the stages might overlap partially, resulting in a kind of cascading progression through the stages. Despite these disagreements, most would agree that Sternberg's careful and innovative research represented a genuine advance for cognitive psychology. He set an example of asking more sophisticated questions about mental processes than others had asked, and showed a way to investigate those questions with greater precision and insight.

Working Memory—Multiple Codes, Multiple Components

Preview: verbal, semantic, and visual codes in short-term memory; Baddeley's three-component working-memory model; dual-task evidence for working memory

We turn now to a somewhat different question about short-term memory: How is information represented in short-term memory? What is the form of the stored information, and what kinds of codes can be maintained and manipulated there? Research on this topic, and also some interesting evidence from brain-damaged patients, leads to our current view of the working-memory system in human cognition.

CODES IN WORKING MEMORY

Several different types of working memory codes have been proposed and investigated. We'll discuss three types here: verbal, semantic, and visual codes.

Verbal Codes

The research you've been reading about has almost universally used verbal materials—usually letters or digits—as the information to be stored, maintained, and retrieved from short-term memory. And the tasks almost always have had people recall the stored information orally. In other words, most tests of short-term memory have been, almost by default, tests of verbal short-term memory.

No one would deny that short-term memory uses the verbal code for information storage, and is even specialized for doing so. Early work in cognitive psychology documented the verbal-based, even acoustic nature of the short-term memory system quite extensively.

Two examples will illustrate this work. R. Conrad (1964) presented a string of letters visually to his subjects, and then recorded their errors in immediate recall. He found that when they made mistakes, they were quite likely to "recall" a letter that *sounded* like the correct one, substituting *D* for *E*, for example. Visual confusions, such as substituting *F* for *E*, were rare. So even though the letters were presented visually, participants apparently stored them in short-term memory in an acoustic, sound-based fashion. In a similar study, Wickelgren (1965) presented four letters to his participants, distracted them by having them copy down eight different letters, then had them try to recall the original four letters. Participants did poorly when the eight copied letters rhymed with the four target letters, a clear case of verbal or auditory interference.

This verbal form of short-term memory storage is usually referred to as an **acoustic-articulatory code,** since either the actual sound (acoustic code) or the pronunciation (articulatory code) could be important. But other research, especially from the 1970s on, has shown that this is not the only format for storage in short-term memory.

Semantic Codes

You've already read about evidence for semantic codes in short-term memory, in the earlier section on release from PI. Recall that Wickens (1972) used a Brown-Peterson task, with words from different categories as the list items. After presenting several lists from one category (e.g., professions), the list switched to a different category (fruit). This switch led to a big increase in recall, which is called release from proactive interference (go back and look at Figure 4.5 again). The fact that a semantic switch, a switch in meaning-based categories, produced release from PI is evidence that short-term memory is sensitive to meaning. In other words, elements of the words' meanings must have been encoded in short-term memory, because changing the meanings led to a change in performance. Thus, semantic codes are also part of the short-term memory representation of information.

Visual Codes

What about nonverbalizable information, like visual patterns? Can this kind of information be stored in short-term memory too? A variety of experiments suggest the answer is yes. Critically, these studies begin to suggest why cognitive psychology started broadening its view from traditional ideas about short-term memory to more current notions of working memory.

MOVEMENT-BASED CODES IN SHORT-TERM MEMORY

Shand (1982) considered an interesting question: What kind of short-term memory code might be used by individuals who are congenitally deaf, people with no acoustic or articulatory experience? To answer this question, he presented five-item lists for serial recall. One type of list contained English words that were phonologically similar (*shoe, through, new*), and one contained words that are similar to one another in American Sign Language (ASL), that is, similar in the hand movements necessary to form the sign (e.g., wrist rotation in the vicinity of the signer's face). Confusions in recall showed interference based on similarity of signs in ASL, and no interference based on the word sounds. Shand's deaf subjects were recoding the written words into an ASL-based code in short-term memory, then basing their performance on that code. It would appear that short-term memory can recode information in any format that can be sensed or used by the mental system, including movement.

Although several lines of research could be described here (e.g., Brooks, 1968; Segal & Fusella, 1970), the most dramatic evidence of visual codes in short-term memory came from studies of *mental rotation*, by Shepard and associates (Shepard & Metzler, 1971; Cooper & Shepard, 1973). In the Shepard and Metzler research, people were shown two complex perspective drawings, one at a time, and had to judge whether the second was the same shape as the first. The critical factor here was that the second drawing was depicted as if it had been rotated from the orientation of the first drawing. To make accurate judgments, the subjects had to perform some transformation on the second drawing, mentally rotating it into the same orientation as the first so they could compare it to the pattern stored in short-term memory.

Figure 4.10 displays several such pairs of drawings and the basic findings of the Shepard and Metzler (1971) study. Overall, people took longer to make their yes/no judgments as the angular rotation needed for the second drawing increased. In other words, a figure that needed to be rotated 120 degrees to bring it back to the orientation of the first drawing took longer to judge than one needing only 60 degrees of rotation. In the Cooper and Shepard (1973) report, participants were shown the first figure and were told how much rotation to expect in the second figure. This advance information on the degree of rotation permitted them to do the mental rotation ahead of time, so that it took very little extra time to make their decisions once the second figure was shown.

Notice in both of these studies that people were performing a complex, visually based mental task—holding a mental image in short-term memory, then doing difficult, attention-consuming mental work on that image. It is almost inconceivable, especially for the shapes shown in Figure 4.10, that such performance could be achieved if short-term memory has only acoustic or verbal-based codes. And furthermore, how can we apply the notion of short-term memory as a limited-capacity system to this task? Saying that short-term memory can hold seven chunks of information, plus or minus two, seems completely irrelevant to visual images like those in the figure.

FIGURE 4.10

A mental rotation experiment. (a) Three pairs of drawings are shown. For each, rotate the second drawing and decide if it is the same figure as the first drawing. The patterns in pair 1 differ by an 80-degree rotation in the picture plane, and those in pair 2 differ by 80 degrees in depth; the patterns in pair 3 do not match. (b) The RTs to judge "same" are shown as a function of the degrees of rotation necessary to bring the second pattern into the same orientation as the first. Reaction time is a linear function of the degree of rotation. (From Shepard & Metzler, 1971.)

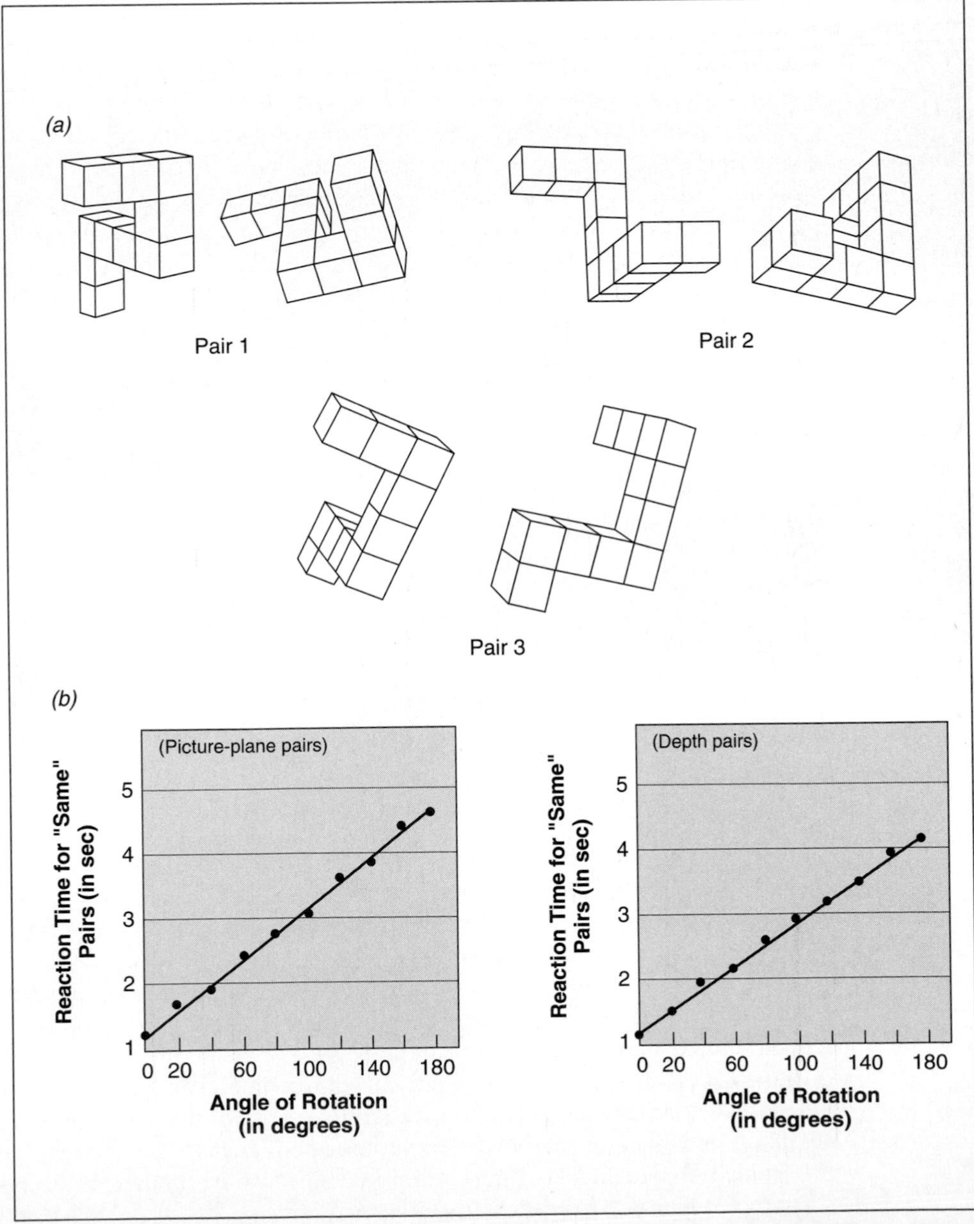

Instead, the mental image and rotation studies demonstrated rather conclusively that when we give people the chance, they can generate and use visual codes in short-term working memory. And, considering the kind of mental processing required, it certainly seems more natural to refer to the memory component for this rotation process as working memory.

BADDELEY'S WORKING-MEMORY MODEL

So what kind of system should replace traditional conceptions of short-term memory? Adding semantic, visual, and other kinds of codes is a step in the right direction, but still seems inadequate. We need a theory that conceives of short-term storage and mental processing in a much more flexible way. The most clearly described system that matches this description is the model of working memory developed by Alan Baddeley and his associates (e.g., Baddeley, 1986, 1992a, 1992b; Baddeley & Hitch, 1974).

Baddeley pointed out that there are other reasons, aside from the need for flexibility, for revising our ideas about short-term memory. Baddeley and Hitch (1974) described a particularly dramatic case study, reported originally by Warrington and Shallice (1969; see also Shallice & Warrington, 1970; Warrington & Weiskrantz, 1970). These authors had found a brain-damaged patient with seriously disrupted short-term memory performance—he was quite impaired on the Brown-Peterson task, and his memory span was only two items. And yet, with further testing they discovered that his learning, transfer of information to long-term memory, and comprehension were all quite normal.

Baddeley and Hitch (1974) posed the obvious question: How can working memory and short-term memory be the same thing when a patient with grossly defective STM performance exhibits no memory deficiencies in other tasks attributed to STM? Their answer, to paraphrase, was that the problem lies with the theory of an undifferentiated short-term memory system. In Baddeley's view, traditionally defined STM is but one component of a larger, more elaborate system, **working memory.**

THREE COMPONENTS OF WORKING MEMORY

Baddeley and his associates (Baddeley, 1986, 1992a; Baddeley & Hitch, 1974) proposed a three-component, overall working-memory system to replace the simple 7 ± 2 short-term memory that went before. He suggested that working memory should be thought of as a mental workbench, a system in which some finite amount of mental work can be performed. An informal illustration of the system is shown in Figure 4.11. A more detailed version (minus the memorable images) is shown in Figure 4.12 (p. 124).

At the heart of this system was the *central executive*, the overall controller in the model. The central executive was thought to be the primary workbench area of the system, the place where mental work of all sorts is done. It initiates a variety of mental processes, such as decision making, retrieval of information from long-term memory, and rehearsal for transferring new information into long-term memory. Importantly, it is also the place in working memory where reasoning and language comprehension take place. Notice that in many respects, the central executive can be thought of as a pool of mental

FIGURE 4.11

Informal representation of Baddeley's working-memory system.

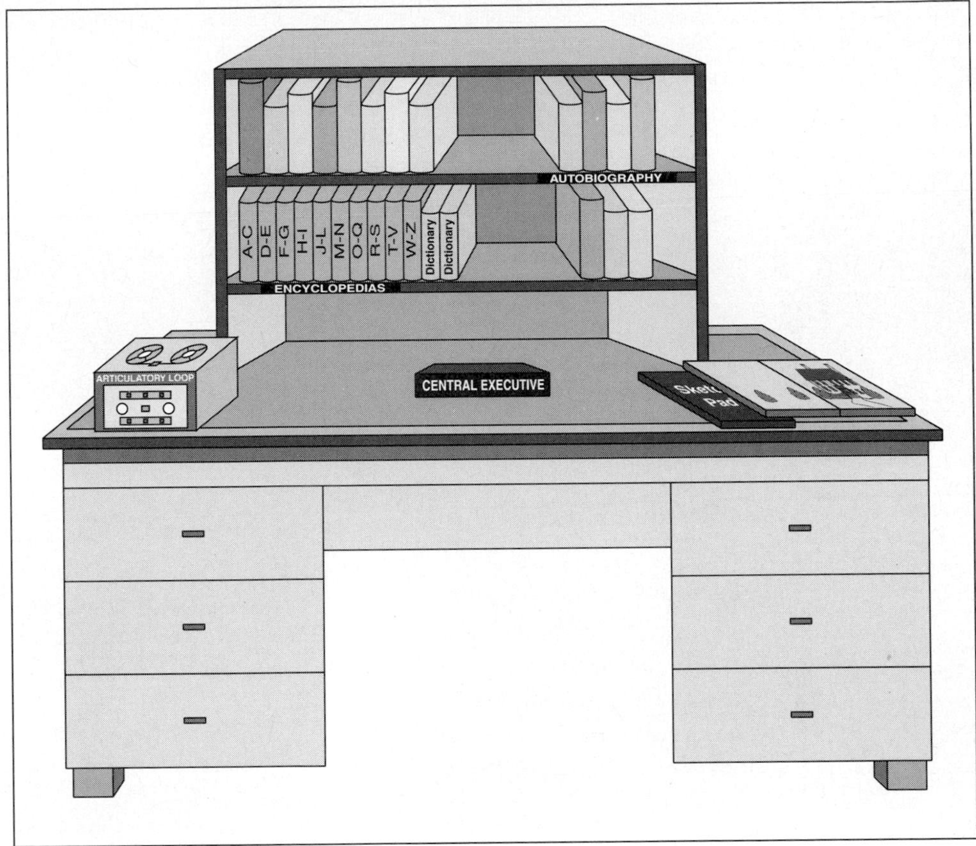

resources, available for any of several different tasks but limited in overall quantity; this is, of course, the idea you encountered as a description of attention in the last chapter. According to this idea, the central executive can perform any of several demanding activities, but because of the limited resources, it generally cannot do more than one demanding thing at a time.

For certain specialized types of information, however, the central executive has two distinct subsystems at its disposal, termed *slave systems*. First, for the kind of maintenance rehearsal we discussed earlier, there is an **articulatory rehearsal loop,** a sound-based system that can hold and recycle small quantities of information. This component corresponds almost exactly to the older notion of a short-term rehearsal buffer. Second, there is a **visuo-spatial sketchpad,** a specialized slave system that holds visual and/or spatial codes for short periods of time (Baddeley & Lieberman, 1980). This would be the system responsible for holding and rotating the mental images in Shepard and Metzler's (1971) research, for example.

★ **FIGURE 4.12**

Formal version of Baddeley's working-memory system. The executive control system supports reasoning, language comprehension, and other such tasks by using resources from the central pool. Both the articulatory rehearsal loop and the visuo-spatial sketchpad have their own mental resources, but these are insufficient for especially demanding tasks. When necessary, each of these can drain resources from the central pool in the executive control system.

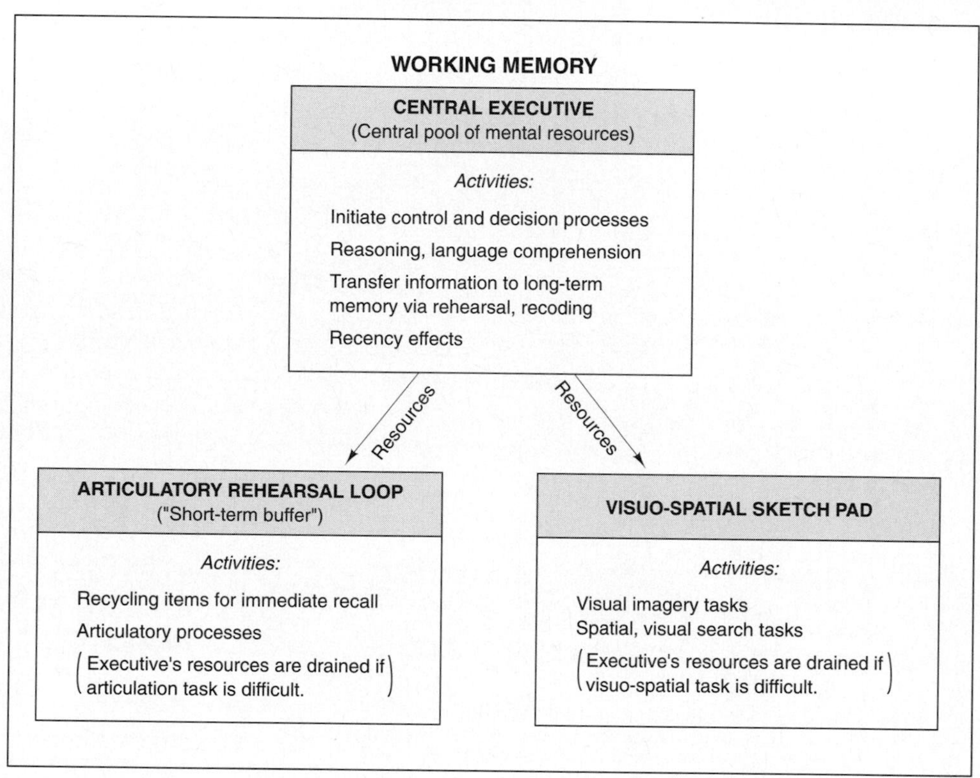

An extremely important aspect of the working-memory system involves the mental resources available for processing. As noted, the central executive has a limited pool of resources for its own activities. Each of the two slave systems also has a limited pool of resources. The arrows connecting the components, however, reflect how the resources are shared. In particular, Baddeley (1986) proposed that resources are shared downward only, from the central executive down to either the articulatory rehearsal loop or the visuo-spatial sketchpad. This happens when either one of the slave systems becomes overburdened, and needs extra resources.

When might that happen? When we give one of the slave systems an overly demanding task—for instance, a six- or seven-item list of digits to recycle, or a particularly complex drawing to be mentally rotated. The consequence of this kind of resource sharing is especially important to notice—when the central executive shares its resources, it often ends up having insufficient capacity to do its own work.

Dual-Task Investigations of Working Memory

This kind of thinking is old hat to you by now—it's the dual-task setting again. The general outlines of the research are clear. Have the central executive perform some mental task, then give a second task to one of the slave systems. As the tasks become more and more demanding, we should start seeing interference effects, usually a slowing down of performance or an increase in errors. By investigating a variety of tasks in this framework, we can determine the specific activities and functions of the different components.

The Articulatory Rehearsal Loop

Let's consider how dual-task studies have been used to understand working memory processes for verbal and verbally based information—in particular, how reasoning and language comprehension depend on working memory.

Working Memory and Reasoning In one of Baddeley and Hitch's (1974) earliest experiments, experimental participants were asked to hold six randomly chosen letters or digits in the short-term "buffer" (i.e., the articulatory rehearsal loop responsible for memory

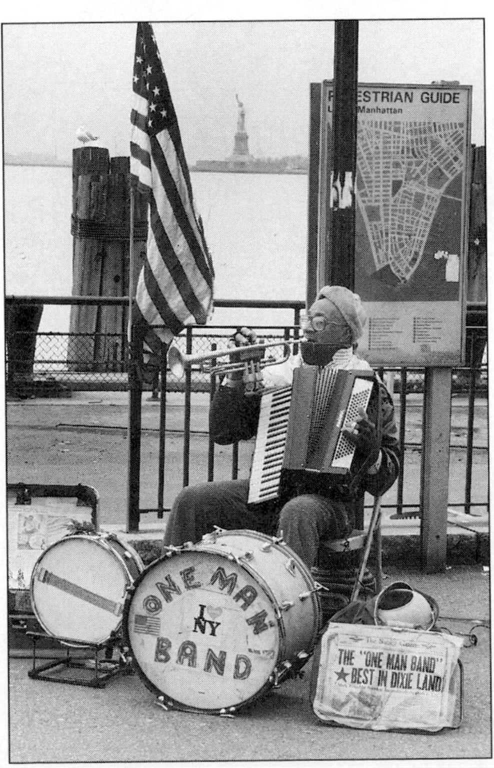

span). Naturally, their recall for those items was always tested. The other activity in the dual-task procedure was a concurrent (simultaneous) language-based reasoning task. That is, while the several items were being held in short-term memory, participants also had to do a mental reasoning procedure. Stimuli such as AB were presented, and the participants had to respond true or false to an accompanying sentence. For a stimulus like AB, true sentences might be a declarative "A precedes B," a passive-voice "B is preceded by A," a negative "B does not precede A," or a passive negative "A is not preceded by B."

As you would expect, the time it took to make the true/false judgments increased as the test sentence became more complex. The slowest and most difficult sentence type to judge was the passive negative type. This is represented by the control RT curve in Figure 4.13.

Now comes the good part. While still doing the reasoning task, the participants were given different articulation tasks in three other conditions, repeating "the the the" during

FIGURE 4.13

Results from Baddeley and Hitch's (1974) reasoning experiment. Average reasoning time is shown as a function of two variables: the grammatical form of the reasoning problem and the type of articulatory suppression task that was performed simultaneously with reasoning. In the "random digits" condition, a randomly ordered set of six digits had to be repeated aloud during reasoning; in the other two suppression tasks, either "the the the" or "one two three four five six" had to be repeated aloud during reasoning. (Adapted from Baddeley & Hitch, 1974.)

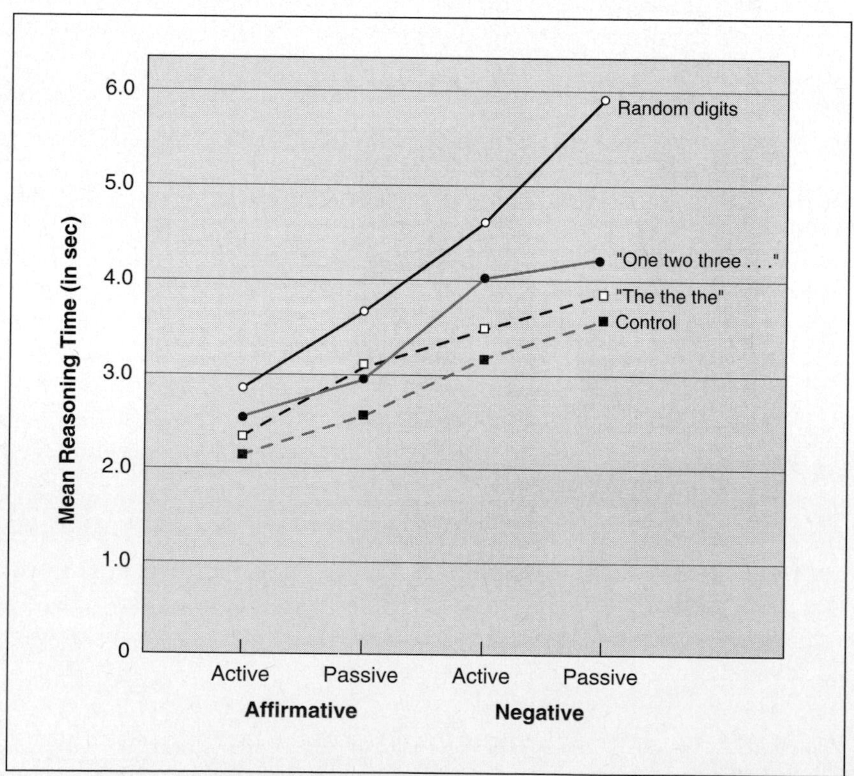

the reasoning period, repeating the numbers one through six, or remembering a six-digit list of random numbers, the most taxing articulating task.

Now, repeating "the the the" or "one two three four five six" should not be particularly difficult for the articulatory rehearsal loop, so we wouldn't expect much interference from these tasks. This prediction was upheld, as shown in the middle two curves in Figure 4.13.

But the genuine memory load condition, random digits, apparently overloaded the capacity of the articulatory rehearsal loop and so caused a drain on the central executive. Evidence for this was that the random-digits condition prompted a sharp increase in reasoning time, especially on the most difficult reasoning problems, passive-negative statements "(A is not preceded by B)". In Baddeley and Hitch's interpretation, the articulatory rehearsal loop swiped resources from the central executive for its own purposes, maintaining the random digits. This deprived the central executive of enough resources for reasoning, so the reasoning process slowed down.

Language Comprehension Baddeley and Hitch (1974) found comparable results when they used a language comprehension task: holding six digits in memory significantly disrupted language comprehension scores, and also significantly impaired memory span performance. In companion experiments, reasoning and comprehension speed were tested when the stimulus sentences were phonetically similar ("B precedes P"; "Redheaded Ned said Ted fed in bed") versus dissimilar ("M precedes C"; "Dark-skinned Ian thought Harry ate in bed"). Of course, the fact that the articulatory rehearsal loop relies on a sound-based code means that phonetically similar items should be more difficult to process (recall the acoustic confusion results described earlier). This was exactly what happened.

The Visuo-Spatial Sketchpad

Similar research has also been reported on the existence of a specialized visual and/or spatial system of working memory, the visuo-spatial sketchpad. A representative report by Logie, Zucco, and Baddeley (1990) will illustrate.

In this study, people were given a visual memory span task. On each trial, they saw a grid of squares, with a random half of the squares filled. The pattern disappeared, and then a changed pattern appeared, where one of the previously filled squares was now empty. The participants merely had to point to the square that changed, based on their memory of the earlier pattern.

For the secondary activity, Logie et al. selected two tasks, a mental addition task thought to be irrelevant to the visuo-spatial system, and an imaging task thought to use the visuo-spatial system. The results of these manipulations are shown in the left half of Figure 4.14 (p. 128). Notice that the graph shows the percentage *drop* in dual-task performance as compared to baseline. So, for instance, the value 15 percent means that dual-task performance was at 85 percent of the single-task baseline—performance only dropped 15 percent from baseline. This 15 percent bar in the figure was for doing mental addition and the visual span tasks together—in other words, adding disrupted visual memory to a modest degree. But when the secondary task involved visual imagery, performance dropped 55 percent from baseline, a large interference effect.

Logie et al. also tested a letter span task, which should rely on the resources of the articulatory rehearsal loop. The pattern of disruption in this condition is shown in the right

FIGURE 4.14

Results from Logie, Zucco, and Baddeley's (1990) experiment on the visuo-spatial sketchpad. (Data from Logie, Zucco, & Baddeley, 1990.)

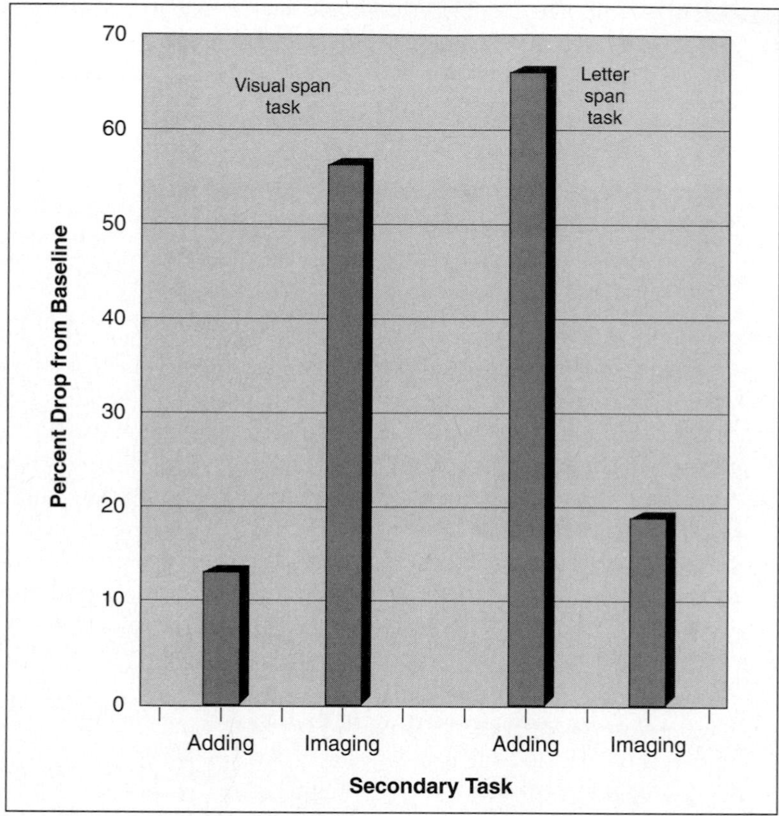

half of the figure. As expected, it was somewhat a mirror image of the first. The letter span task and the articulatory activity in mental addition interfered with one another a great deal, leading to a serious disruption in performance. But this disruption was minor when letter spans and the imaging task were performed concurrently.

Overview

The general conclusion from research by Baddeley and others is that *working memory* is a more suitable name for the attention-limited "workbench" system of memory. Working memory is responsible for the active mental effort of reasoning and language comprehension, as well as for the transfer of information into long-term memory by means of rehearsal. In addition to the central executive of working memory, there is a separate articulatory rehearsal loop component (sometimes also called the "phonological loop"), and a separate visuo-spatial component. The two slave systems are partially autonomous, in that they can recirculate a small amount of information without interfering with the central executive's performance, and without interfering with each other. When overloaded, however, they begin to drain extra mental resources from the central executive. This disrupts ongoing activity of the central executive, whether it is reasoning, comprehending, or learning. Importantly, there is an overall limitation in the mental resources available to working memory—it's a "closed" system, with only some fixed quantity of mental resources to spread around. When extra resources are drained by the slave systems, the central executive merely suffers along with insufficient resources for its own work. And, naturally, as processes become more automatic, fewer of working memory's resources will be tied down by the task (see Hirst & Kalmar, 1987, and Pashler, 1994, for an analysis and critique of the "pools of resources" metaphor).

Summary

1. The release-from-PI task, one of several that illustrates interference effects, has been used to document the fact that short-term memory can hold a variety of informational codes. The evidence suggests that short-term memory often relies on an acoustic-articulatory code, but can also hold visual information, semantic information, and even information related to physical movement.
2. Dissatisfaction with the traditional conception of short-term memory led to a broader conceptualization, that of a working-memory system. The most widely known and investigated of such models is Baddeley's working-memory system.
3. Baddeley claims that working memory is a three-component system. The central executive is the control component, in charge of decisions, retrieval from long-term memory, comprehension, and reasoning. The articulatory rehearsal loop and the visuo-spatial sketchpad are two slave systems, assistants to the central executive that are specialized for auditory and visual-spatial information.
4. Each of the three components has a limited amount of mental resources, but the two slave systems can drain resources from the central executive if their tasks become difficult. This has the effect of disrupting the activity taking place in the central executive. Research shows how selective these demands for resources can be, with auditory tasks interfering only minimally with visual-based tasks, and vice versa.

Important Terms

acoustic-articulatory code
articulatory rehearsal loop
Brown-Peterson task
central executive
chunk
decay
free recall
interference
memory search
memory span
primacy effect
proactive interference (PI)
recency effect
recoding
rehearsal
release from PI
retroactive interference (RI)
serial-position curve
serial recall
short-term memory
Sternberg task
visuo-spatial sketchpad
working memory

Suggested Readings

Atkinson and Shiffrin's (1971) article in *Scientific American* should be high on your reading list; aside from being very readable, it was one of the first contributions to that prestigious journal by cognitive psychologists (authorship of a *Scientific American* article is by invitation only). Sternberg's (1966) original paper is also interesting to read, partly because its "modesty" is an interesting contrast with the eventual high regard the paper achieved.

Baddeley's (1992a, 1992b) recent papers provide excellent and very approachable summaries of the entire program of research on working memory. In the 1992a article (the written version of his "Bartlett Lecture"), he also considers disruption of the central executive as a major consequence of Alzheimer's disease; see Hasher, Stoltzfus, Zacks, and Rypma (1991) and Salthouse (1992) for possible connections between working memory and the process of aging. For the connection between working memory and reading comprehension, see Baddeley (1992b), King and Just (1991), and Budd, Whitney, and Turley (1995). Kruley, Sciama, and Glenberg (1994) analyze the contribution of the visuo-spatial sketchpad to how we read texts with illustrations.

CHAPTER FIVE

EPISODIC LONG-TERM MEMORY

Read the first quotation in the box, if you haven't already. It's from a book titled *Memory and Its Cultivation*, published in 1900! Consider seriously for a moment the author's evocative insight into the importance of memory: without it, we're nothing. This alone is sufficient to justify our interest in memory, and to evoke questions such as, How is information stored and retrieved in long-term memory? How much can be stored there? and Why do we forget?

The quotation makes another point too, concerning the history of psychology in the twentieth century. Edridge-Green's book appeared in 1900, before the behaviorist revolution you read about in Chapter 1. But once behaviorism was under way, especially after the influence of J. B. Watson's (1913/1994) "manifesto," it excluded consciousness and other mental processes from the "natural science" of psychology, including most aspects of memory. Decades went by in which researchers wrote about the topic of learning, for example, without really mentioning where the learned behavior or information was—as if using a mentalistic term like *memory* branded an author as a heretic (or worse). Thus, even as late as the early 1960s, a respected and widely used introductory psychology text (Kimble & Garmezy, 1963) devoted only two pages to a discussion of short- and long-term memory (in a chapter titled "Retention" rather than "Memory"). It said nothing

Memory is the most important function of the brain; without it life would be a blank. Our knowledge is all based on memory. Every thought, every action, our very conception of personal identity, is based on memory. . . . Without memory, all experience would be useless. (Edridge-Green, 1900, p. 1)

We must never underestimate one of the most obvious reasons for forgetting, namely, that the information was never stored in memory in the first place. (E. F. Lofus, 1980, p. 74)

about the functions of memory, its importance to our personal identity or our understanding of experience—indeed, it virtually apologized for using the term *memory* at all.

But that's all over now. Welcome to modern cognitive psychology—we talk constantly about memory, its functions and roles, its subdivisions and types. It will take us three chapters just to deal with the most direct evidence on the nature and functioning of long-term memory. And most of the remaining topics in the book, from language to problem solving, involve heavy doses of long-term memory as well. So sit back and get ready to explore the vast storehouse of knowledge, the mental file cabinet, that is human long-term memory.

Basic Issues

Preview: distinction between episodic and semantic long-term memory; metamemory and mnemonic devices; three mnemonic principles; invented mnemonics

THE DISTINCTION BETWEEN EPISODIC AND SEMANTIC MEMORY

Endel Tulving, one of the true giants in modern cognitive psychology, proposed a two-part classification of long-term memory in his enormously influential chapter "Episodic and Semantic Memory" (Tulving, 1972). His point was that we store two broad classes of knowledge in long-term memory, one very individual, the other very general. His term for the first type was

- **Episodic memory:** A person's memory of personally experienced events or episodes—one's autobiography.

A sampling of episodic memories would include remembering your current psychology professor's name, what you had for dinner last Tuesday, and the color of your bedroom walls. Most of the traditional "verbal learning" research on memory—say, up through the mid-1960s—tested episodic memory. For example, the words you learn and recall in an experiment are stored in episodic memory. The critical aspect here is that the memories are part of your own personal history and are not generally shared by others.

Tulving's term for the second type of long-term memory was

- **Semantic memory:** A person's general world knowledge, including language, and the conceptual knowledge that relates concepts and ideas to one another—one's mental dictionary and encyclopedia combined.

For instance, you know the word *bird* and how to spell it, you know what a bird is, and you know that robins are, but penguins aren't, typical of the category. Furthermore, semantic memory enables you to know more than you ever learned specifically; recall the example from Chapter 1, in which you reasoned by inference that robins have lungs even though you probably never learned that fact directly.

Episodic and semantic memory are highly interdependent, to be sure. In fact, there is a recurring professional debate over whether or not they are truly separate types of memory (e.g., McKoon & Ratcliff, 1986; Tulving, 1989, 1993). Regardless of this debate, separating episodic from semantic memory is a useful organizational device. Thus, we will devote this chapter almost exclusively to episodic memory principles and processes, especially those you are aware of explicitly. These are the more traditional issues in the study of human memory, including phenomena such as rehearsal, recall, and forgetting. Chapter 6 is then devoted to the semantic memory system, its organization and principles of operation. Finally, we'll turn in Chapter 7 to long-term memory as it operates in natural, "real-world" settings, and the ways in which episodic and semantic memory interact.

METAMEMORY AND MNEMONIC DEVICES

One of the seven themes of cognitive psychology introduced in Chapter 1 was **metacognition,** our awareness of and knowledge about our own cognitive system. A. L. Brown (1975) referred to this as "knowing about knowing," in other words, knowing about the processes involved in knowing something. When we're talking specifically about learning and memory, this is called **metamemory,** knowledge about (*meta*) one's own memory system, how it works, and how it fails to work. Brown described this as "knowing how to know."

We all know, for example, that learning an arbitrary list of items—say, 15 or so unrelated words—will be impossible if we just rely on short-term memory. In other words, we know that knowing this list of words, remembering it for the long term, will require some deliberate mental activity or strategy to get the information into long-term memory. Adults are fairly proficient at generating these strategies for remembering, at developing methods to rehearse material they realize will be hard to learn. Further, they aren't surprised when unrehearsed material can't be remembered (you're not really surprised when you can't remember someone's name shortly after being introduced, particularly if you made no special effort to remember the name in the first place). Your metamemory processes include the awareness that things don't merely "get into" memory. You must "get them in" by performing some intentional activity.

This intentional mental activity and its effects on remembering make up the study of rehearsal. Rehearsal was the major *control process* that Atkinson and Shiffrin (1968, 1971) had in mind in their model of human memory, and not surprisingly their work prompted much of the research on rehearsal (e.g., Rundus & Atkinson, 1970). But the whole story on metacognitive awareness and rehearsal begins much earlier, with the ancient Greeks and the topic of mnemonic devices.

Mnemonic Devices

The word *mnemonic* (the first *m* is silent: ne-mahn'-ick) means "to help the memory." The term **mnemonic device,** then, always refers to an active, strategic kind of learning device or method—a rehearsal strategy, if you will. Both formal mnemonic devices, where you learn the mnemonic "scheme" and then apply it in different situations, and informal mnemonic devices, which you invent yourself, are characterized by three important mnemonic principles.

- First, the material you're trying to learn is structured and integrated into a preexisting memory framework or scheme.
- Second, the material to be remembered must be practiced repeatedly, using the scheme or device; as the old saying goes, "repetition is the key to learning."

- Finally, now that you've used the mnemonic device for storing the information, the device provides an excellent plan or scheme for retrieving the information.

Let's cover two classic mnemonic devices first, then turn to the issue of inventing new mnemonics as the need arises.

Method of Loci The first historical mention of mnemonics is in Cicero's *De oratore* (Yates, 1966), a Latin treatise on rhetoric (the art of public speaking, which in Greek and Roman days meant speaking from memory). In this work, Cicero describes a technique based on visual imagery and memorized locations, ascribed to the Greek poet Simonides (c. 500 B.C.). The mnemonic is now commonly referred to as the **method of loci** (*loci*, pronounced "LOW-sigh," is the plural of *locus*, meaning "a place").

As the story goes, Simonides was performing a lyric poem at a banquet when he was called out of the hall for a message. While he was outside, the roof of the hall caved in. The disaster was so bad that the bodies of the guests, mangled by the falling roof, were unidentifiable. Simonides, however, was able to identify the dead by visualizing the banquet table where they had been sitting, mentally looking around the table and remembering who was sitting where.

The two "active ingredients" in the method of loci are, first, the memorized physical locations and, second, the mental images of the to-be-remembered items, one per location. Decide upon a set of places or locations that can be easily recalled in order—for instance, a set of 10 or 12 locations you encounter as you walk across campus. Now, form a ▲ mental image of the first thing to be remembered in the first location (see Figure 5.1 for an illustration), then continue with the second item in the second location, and so forth. Form a *good*, distinctive, even bizarre mental image of each item in its location (Burns, 1996; McDaniel & Einstein, 1986; Kroll, Schepeler, & Angin, 1986). If possible, come up with an image that would trigger a "surprise response" (e.g., Hirshman, Whelley, & Palij, 1989) if you actually saw it (wouldn't you be surprised if you saw a giant telephone hand-

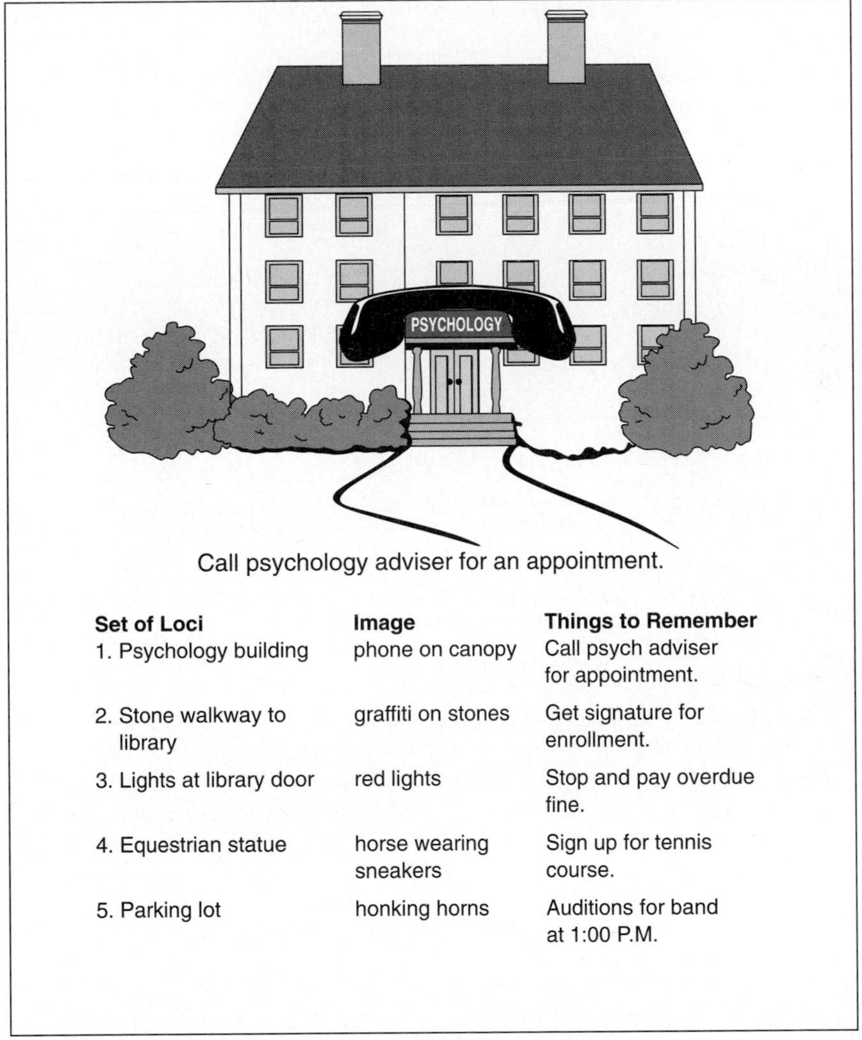
PSYCHOLOGY
Call psychology adviser for an appointment.

Set of Loci	Image	Things to Remember
1. Psychology building	phone on canopy	Call psych adviser for appointment.
2. Stone walkway to library	graffiti on stones	Get signature for enrollment.
3. Lights at library door	red lights	Stop and pay overdue fine.
4. Equestrian statue	horse wearing sneakers	Sign up for tennis course.
5. Parking lot	honking horns	Auditions for band at 1:00 P.M.

FIGURE 5.1

Depiction of a mental image formed using the method of loci.

set over the door of the Psychology Building?). Then, when it's time to recall the items, all you need to do is mentally stroll through your set of locations, "looking" at the places and "seeing" the items you have placed there.

Peg-Word Mnemonic Another mnemonic device is worth mentioning here as well, partly because it is so commonly known and easy to use. The technique is known as the **peg-word mnemonic** (e.g., Miller, Galanter, & Pribram, 1960), in which a prememorized set of words serves as a sequence of mental "pegs" onto which the to-be-remembered material can be "hung." The peg words rely on rhymes with the numbers one through ten, such as "One is a bun, two is a shoe," and so forth (see Table 5.1). The material being

TABLE 5.1

The Peg-Word Mnemonic Device

Numbered Pegs	*Word to Be Learned*	*Image*
One is a bun	Cup	Hamburger bun with smashed cup
Two is a shoe	Flag	Running shoes with flag
Three is a tree	Horse	Horse stranded in top of tree
Four is a door	Dollar	Dollar bill tacked to front door
Five is a hive	Brush	Queen bee brushing her hair
Six is sticks	Pan	Boiling a pan full of cinnamon sticks
Seven is heaven	Clock	St. Peter checking the clock at the gates of heaven
Eight is a gate	Pen	A picket fence gate with ballpoint pens as pickets
Nine is a vine	Paper	Honeysuckle vine with newspapers instead of blossoms
Ten is a hen	Shirt	A steaming baked hen on the platter wearing a flannel shirt

learned is then "hung" on the pegs, item by item, making sure that the rhyming word and the to-be-remembered word form a mental image. Work through the example in Table 5.1, coming up with the visual images (e.g., your running shoes decorated with little flags), and then test your memory for the list of words.

The evidence shows that using such mnemonic devices can be very effective in improving your memory. Bower (1970), for example, described a study by Ross and Lawrence (1968), in which participants used a set of 40 campus locations as their loci, then had to learn several 40-item lists using the method of loci. The items were presented about one every 13 seconds, and were followed by an immediate recall test (participants also returned the next day for a delayed recall test). Average performance on immediate recall, using the method of loci, was 38 out of 40, in their correct order! One day later, the average number correct was 34 items, again in order—very impressive!

Three Mnemonic Principles

You already know the conclusion to Bower's (1970) paper—it's the "three mnemonic principles" from above. What makes a mnemonic device effective?

- First, it provides a structure for learning, for acquiring the information. The structure may be relatively elaborate, as a set of 40 loci would be, or it may be simple, for example, rhyming peg words. It can even be very arbitrary if there's not a lot of material to learn. For example, the mnemonic for the names of the five Great Lakes—remembering the word *HOMES* for Huron, Ontario, Michigan, Erie, and Superior—isn't especially related to the to-be-remembered material, but it is quite simple.
- Second, because you must devise visual images, rhymes, or other kinds of associations, the mnemonic ensures a durable record of the material in memory, one that won't easily be forgotten (What's sticking out of your running shoes?). The device forces you to spend some time coming up with the associations, and time to repeat

"I forget the name of the product, but the jingle on TV goes something like 'Ya-dee-dum-dee-rah-te-dum-dee-rah-dee-dum.'"

and practice the associations. These factors make for a more durable record in memory. (For a fascinating glimpse at the most important factor, practice, leading to world-class expertise—for instance, becoming a concert pianist—see Ericsson, Krampe, & Tesch-Romer, 1993.)

- Finally, the mnemonic guides you through retrieval by providing effective cues for recalling the information. As we'll discuss later on in the chapter, this function of the mnemonic device is critically important, since much of what we casually call "forgetting" may instead be a case of retrieval difficulty.

Invented Mnemonics

Take a moment to apply this thinking to your own situation. Don't we all wish that we had better memory, that we could remember names better, that we weren't so forgetful? College students in particular face stiff demands on memory—your job as a college student is to learn and remember (and understand!) new information, often quite unfamiliar and unrelated to things you already know. How do you deal with these memory demands?

Start first with what you know about metamemory and metacognition. How aware are you of your own state of knowledge about new information? Do you spend more time studying when the material is unfamiliar, or when you judge it as more difficult to learn (e.g., Cull & Zechmeister, 1994; Nelson & Leonesio, 1988)? Do you monitor your performance as you read a text, testing your memory as you go along, or do you merely read through a chapter, treating all the information in the same, undifferentiated way? You should be able to point to something you *do* that signals your metamemory awareness—a

Try learning the seven themes I described at the end of Chapter 1, using either the following mnemonic or one of your own devising.

Amazing	Attention
Actually	Automatic versus conscious processing
Did	Data-driven versus conceptually driven processing
Remember (the)	Representation of Knowledge
Introduction (to)	Implicit versus explicit memory
Memory	Metacognition
Book	Brain

Generally, you'll remember information (and your mnemonic device) better if you invent the mnemonic yourself. The reason for this has to do with what's called the **generation effect,** improved memory performance on material that is self-generated rather than merely read or copied (e.g., McNamara & Healy, 1995; Slamecka & Graf, 1978). Thus, the actual forming of the mental image in a classic mnemonic—having to dream it up yourself, with all the mental work involved in that—will improve your retention of the image. Likewise, coming up with your own mnemonic sentence for the seven themes will be more memorable than using the one given above.

slower reading rate on unfamiliar material, more note taking on difficult lecture topics, different colors of markers for underlining, and so forth. If you can't find any behavioral way to prove your metamemory awareness, then you're probably not studying and learning as efficiently as you can.

Second, what kinds of memory "tricks" do you devise to ensure that you'll remember something? Do you ever invent your own mnemonic devices? As a lesson to yourself, pick something from this book to learn by an invented mnemonic. Try to come up with a mnemonic based on images, rhymes, or acronyms so that you can remember the list easily. The very act of inventing the mnemonic yourself will probably ensure that the material is stored strongly in memory, and the image or rhyme will help assure that it remains in memory until you test yourself. Make sure your mnemonic itself is memorable, so that it can guide you through retrieval by cuing the several items you're trying to remember.

Finally, be on the lookout for "ready-made" mnemonics, or situations in which a mnemonic association is almost built into the material. As an example, did you notice in Chapter 2 that Cherry (1953) did research on the cocktail party phenomenon, and can't you "see" that maraschino cherry in the cocktail glass? The more you notice such easily associated items, the easier it will be to come up with invented mnemonics for other material as well. [One of the most stunning descriptions of mnemonic effectiveness is a report by Ericsson & Polson, 1988, which describes "a waiter (JC) who can take up to 20 complete dinner orders without taking notes," p. 305.]

Summary

1. Episodic memory is long-term memory for personal experiences, whereas semantic memory is general, conceptual long-term memory. Traditional experimental research on learning and memory generally investigated episodic memory.
2. We have metacognitive awareness of much of our long-term memory, termed metamemory. This awareness alerts us to the need to rehearse information deliberately, using some kind of systematic plan or scheme. The classic version of such rehearsal is the mnemonic device.
3. The three mnemonic principles involve using a preexisting scheme or device, practicing or rehearsing the material repeatedly, and using the device as a guide for retrieval.
4. Invented mnemonics operate in the same fashion, and also demonstrate our metamemory awareness of the need for special efforts to learn difficult material.

Early Research on Memory—The Ebbinghaus Tradition

Preview: Hermann Ebbinghaus; relearning and nonsense syllables; memory effects; the Ebbinghaus legacy

The earliest systematic research on human learning and memory was conducted by the German psychologist Hermann Ebbinghaus and published in his 1885 book; the Eng-

Hermann von Ebbinghaus

lish translation, *Memory: A Contribution to Experimental Psychology*, appeared in 1913 and was reprinted in 1964.

In all of his experiments, Ebbinghaus used (in fact, he invented) the **relearning task,** in which lists of materials are learned to a fixed criterion of mastery, set aside for a period of time, and then relearned to the same criterion. His measure of memory and retention was a comparison of the original learning session with the second session, termed the **savings score;** how many fewer trials were necessary during relearning compared with the number necessary during original learning (or in some studies, how much less time was necessary). So the savings score represents the amount of information saved in memory, the amount that did not need to be relearned because it was still in memory. For example, if it took 10 trials to learn a list originally, but only 6 upon relearning, then 4 trials out of 10 had been saved—a savings score of 40 percent.

As is commonly known, the materials Ebbinghaus learned in these lists were *nonsense syllables*, three-letter consonant-vowel-consonant combinations that did not form words. Ebbinghaus's reason for inventing this kind of stimulus was rather straightforward: he was attempting to avoid a contamination of the results, a contamination in which preexisting meaning might influence current learning. He reasoned that because of existing knowledge and associations, using real words on the memory lists would complicate the interpretation of the data—and in fact he demonstrated much faster learning and relearning when passages of poetry were used. Rather than deal with those complications, he simply tried to eliminate them by using meaningless letter combinations.

Other features of Ebbinghaus's procedures are important to note as well. To standardize the degree of learning achieved, he used a fixed learning criterion. In some studies, this meant one perfect recitation of the list without hesitations; in other studies, two. To guard against the possibility that he might use some mnemonic device or other meaningful form of rehearsal, he presented the nonsense syllables to himself at a fixed and rapid rate, 2.5 items per second. And to obtain reliable data, he tested himself on a huge number of trials—for instance, on the famous forgetting curve you'll see next, he learned more

than 1200 lists, each consisting of 13 nonsense syllables!

MEMORY EFFECTS

So, what did Ebbinghaus discover about memory? Let's look at that famous forgetting

curve in Figure 5.2 (p. 142), showing the percent savings on relearning after seven different retention intervals, from 20 minutes to 31 days. What does the figure show? That as more time passes, savings in memory declines. The savings score was 100 percent immediately after original learning, of course, but dropped sharply after only 20 minutes. Savings continued to drop at intervals of 1, 2, 6, or 30 days, although not as sharply as at the shorter retention intervals (see also Wixted & Ebbesen, 1991). Thus, the bulk of the forgetting—the decline in savings—takes place very shortly after original learning.

Another important variable Ebbinghaus (1885/1913/1964) investigated involved the effect of repetition or overlearning, which he examined in several ways. In one experiment, he studied some lists 32 times each, approximately the number needed for one perfect recitation. This was the control condition in the study. In the overlearning condition, different lists were studied 64 times, twice the number needed for perfect performance. At relearning, overlearned lists showed twice the savings found for the con-

★

THE EBBINGHAUS ACHIEVEMENT

It's impossible to describe Ebbinghaus's (1885/1913/1964) work without marveling at the nature of his achievements—and rightly so. Ebbinghaus worked alone, not in a psychology department furnished with thought-provoking colleagues, but by himself. He tested only himself as a subject, across unbelievably large numbers of trials, lists, and days, with only everyday items like pencil and paper for equipment. There was no body of related research on memory for him to read, no collection of standard laboratory tasks to choose from, not even an accepted set of statistical analyses to use in analyzing his data. He very literally invented it all, from scratch.

What is especially amazing about this is how right he was, how insightful he was about memory issues that have turned out to be quite important, how careful he was in methodology and procedures, and how modest he was in presenting this information to the scientific community. The impressive nature of his accomplishment was apparent even at the time (Hilgard, 1964), and our appreciation of it continues. Read some recent kudos:

- from Hilgard's introduction to the 1964 reprinting of the book: "For the beginner in a new field to have done all of these things—and more—is so surprising as to baffle our understanding of how it could have happened" (p. vii).

Three authors commented on Ebbinghaus in a set of papers commemorating the 100th anniversary of his book:

- The relearning task that Ebbinghaus invented was a "radical idea that was far ahead of its time, both methodologically and conceptually" (Nelson, 1985, p. 472).
- Ebbinghaus was "the founder of our discipline" (Slamecka, 1985a); "He set out to show that an empirical science of memory was possible. . . . He succeeded admirably in this enterprise" (Slamecka, 1985b, p. 497).
- Ebbinghaus's contribution represented "a door being opened into the human mind, the realization—contrary to then established wisdom—that it is in fact possible to gain positive knowedge about human memory" (Mandler, 1985, p. 464).

trol lists—in other words, overlearning yields a much more durable effect on memory. (Remember, repetition is the key to learning.)

Ebbinghaus found the same effect when he varied the length of the list he was learning. Long lists required many more original learning trials for mastery than shorter lists—no surprise there. But upon relearning after 24 hours, the short list showed savings of only 33 percent, whereas the long list had a 58 percent savings score. In essence, while it was harder to learn a long list originally, the longer list was nonetheless remembered better because there were more opportunities—more learning trials—to overlearn it in the first place.

Finally, in one experiment, Ebbinghaus continued to relearn the same set of lists across a five-day period. The savings scores he obtained showed a trend that, if extrapolated, would eventually show perfect savings, that is, no forgetting at all. As an interesting contrast here, Ebbinghaus also reported his results on relearning passages of poetry

FIGURE 5.2

The classic forgetting curve from Ebbinghaus (1885/1913/1964). The figure shows the reduction in savings across increasing retention intervals, time between original learning and relearning. (Data from Ebbinghaus, 1885/1913/1964.)

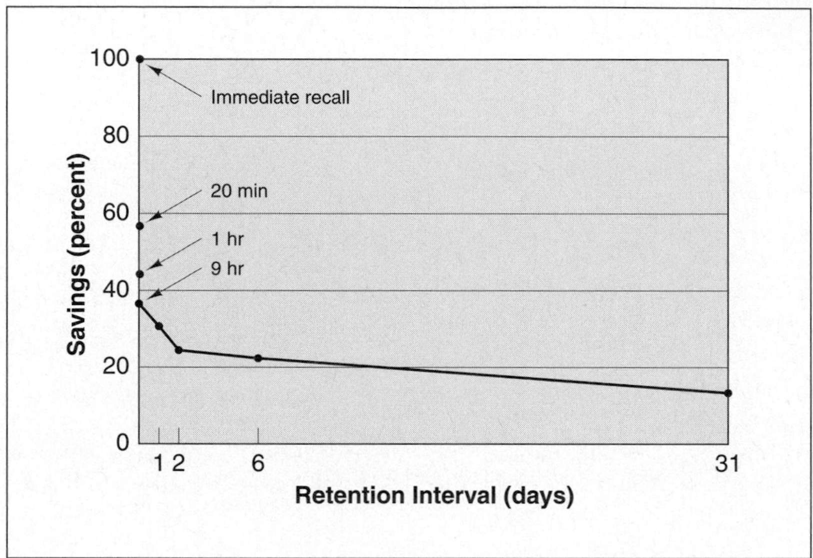

(kept at 80 syllables in length). After the fourth day of learning, savings was 100 percent. (Is it any wonder that actors overlearn their parts through multiple rehearsals?)

THE EBBINGHAUS LEGACY

For the longest time—say, up through the 1960s—the discipline that studied human memory was referred to as *verbal learning*, how people learn and remember verbal materials. As cognitive approaches to memory developed, and as we extended our interests to topics beyond "verbal" materials, the term *verbal learning* fell by the wayside—but Ebbinghaus's legacy did not. As Slamecka (1985a) pointed out, Ebbinghaus was the founder of our discipline, that is, the discipline of studying human memory and cognition, regardless of what label is attached to it. He was the first to apply rigorous scientific methods and procedures to an objective examination of human memory. The example he set for the study of human memory had a profound influence, one that is still felt today. In contrast to the largely discredited introspective methods of Wundt and Titchner (see Chapter 1), Ebbinghaus's methodological approach has endured—we still exert careful control over the stimuli to be learned, over the presentation rate of the materials, and so forth.

But some have bemoaned Ebbinghaus's influence. By inventing and using the nonsense syllable, he excluded meaning from the stimuli to be learned and remembered. This began a tradition of studying just that, the learning of nonsense syllables, a tradition that continued up through the 1960s (and even the 1970s—to some critics, this was the essence of verbal learning). The problem with nonsense syllables, it is generally con-

Why do we rehearse?

ceded, is that for the most part people will not deal with a truly meaningless stimulus. Instead, they will attempt all sorts of mediating, mnemonic, or other rehearsal strategies to render a "nonsense" syllable sensible—mentally turning BEF into BEEF, for example. Furthermore, in retrospect it seems obvious that questions about memory functioning are more profitably investigated with meaningful material—after all, since the purpose of memory is to enable us to deal with the meaningful environment, doesn't it make more sense to study memory with meaningful stimuli? Contemporary criticism of the artificiality of laboratory research (e.g., Neisser, 1978) often asserts that Ebbinghaus's example misled psychology, and inspired decades of ungeneralizable, even irrelevant, results. To quote Kintsch's (1985) evocative remark, "Instead of the simplification that Ebbinghaus had hoped for, the nonsense syllable, for generations of researchers, merely *screened* the central problems of memory from inspection with the methods that Ebbinghaus had bequeathed us" (p. 461, emphasis added).

The Ebbinghaus tradition, in short, has been understood (or misunderstood) as an admonition, as if Ebbinghaus had said that "meaning complicates matters, so eliminate it from the stimuli." A more temperate view might note that, in the absence of previous research, Ebbinghaus quite properly simplified the experimental situation so as to get interpretable results, a view that Kintsch (1985) also stated. We might further suggest that the fault lies less with Ebbinghaus than with his successors, who slavishly stuck to his methods without questioning their intent or usefulness.

Consider one final point. By carefully controlling the stimuli to eliminate meaning, and by carefully avoiding the opportunity to use mnemonic strategies, wasn't Ebbinghaus acknowledging the fact that meaning and rehearsal are important factors in memory? In fact, most of the research we turn to now demonstrates exactly those points. Meaning is critically influential in what we remember, and we have a strong tendency to be active learners, to invent mnemonic "tricks" if given the opportunity. If Ebbinghaus hadn't been mindful of these issues, why would he have taken such pains to prevent them from influencing his results?

Summary

1. Hermann Ebbinghaus literally invented research on human memory, as described in his 1885 book. He described an objective way of investigating long-term memory, using nonsense syllables for his materials, the relearning task, and the savings score as the measure of memory performance.
2. Ebbinghaus's forgetting curve showed that forgetting occurs most rapidly within a short time after original learning. His results also showed that repetition and overlearning improve savings in memory, as does using meaningful material.
3. Although some have complained that Ebbinghaus led us astray with his nonsense syllables, most agree on the overwhelmingly positive effect of his research, an influence still felt in contemporary research.

Storage of Information in Episodic Memory

Preview: rehearsal and serial-position effects; depth of processing and two kinds of rehearsal; organization; imagery

How is information stored in episodic memory, especially "new" information, so that it will be preserved until some future time when it's needed? And how can we measure this storage of information? Going beyond Ebbinghaus's evidence on repetition and relearning, what do we know about this process of storing information in long-term memory?

We'll cover three important "storage" effects here: rehearsal, organization, and imagery. Then we'll turn to the topics of retrieval and modern theorizing about forgetting.

REHEARSAL

A fundamental statement on storage was made by Atkinson and Shiffrin (1968) in their influential model of human memory. In their formulation, information that resides in short-term memory may be subjected to **rehearsal,** a deliberate recycling or practicing of the contents of the short-term store. Atkinson and Shiffrin proposed that there are two effects of rehearsal.

- First, rehearsal maintains information in the short-term store, preventing it from being lost or displaced by other information.
- Second, the longer an item is held in short-term memory by rehearsal, the greater the probability that the rehearsal will also store the item in long-term memory.

Basically, this position states that rehearsal "copies" or "transfers" the item into long-term memory, with the strength of the long-term memory trace depending on the amount of rehearsal (see also Waugh & Norman, 1965). Of course, in most experimental situations, the items being transferred are words that the person already knows (obviously not the case for nonsense syllables). Thus, the transfer function is generally taken to mean storing some "tag" or other indication that a certain word is an item in the list being learned.

What evidence is there of this transfer function for rehearsal? Aside from the classic Ebbinghaus work, many experiments have shown that rehearsal of information leads to better long-term retention. For example, Hellyer (1962) used the Brown-Peterson short-term memory task to examine the effects of rehearsal. The participants were shown a three-letter nonsense syllable, as usual, and were asked to perform an arithmetic task between study and recall, also as usual. The difference in this study was that on some trials the syllable had to be spoken aloud once, and on some trials twice, four times, or eight times. Figure 5.3 shows the results of this experiment. The more frequently rehearsed the item was, the better it was retained across the distracting period of arithmetic.

Rehearsal and Serial-Position Effects

Consider now the well-known studies performed by Rundus and his co-workers (Rundus, 1971; Rundus & Atkinson, 1970). Rundus had his participants learn 20-item lists of unrelated words, presenting them at a rate of 5 seconds per word. They were asked to rehearse

FIGURE 5.3

Hellyer's (1962) recall accuracy results, showing better recall for material that is rehearsed more. (From Hellyer, 1962.)

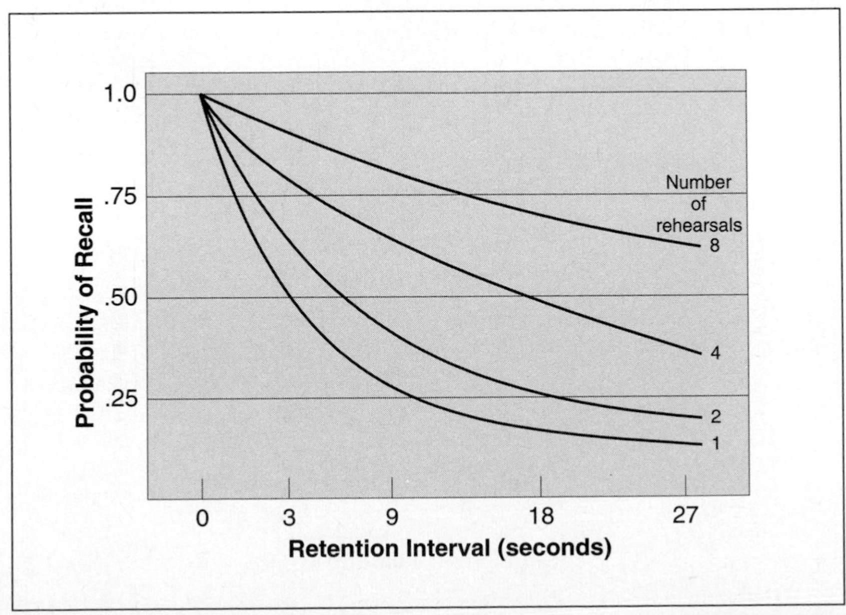

aloud as they studied the lists, repeating whatever words from the list they cared to during each 5-second presentation. Rundus then tabulated the number of times each of the words had been rehearsed, and compared this tally to the likelihood of recalling the word correctly in the free-recall task.

Figure 5.4 shows Rundus's most telling results. In the early primacy portion of the serial-position effect there was a direct and positive relationship between the frequency of rehearsal and the probability of recall. In fact, Rundus also examined a proportional measure of rehearsal and found that "for a given amount of rehearsal, items from the initial serial positions have no better recall than items from the middle of the list" (Rundus, 1971, p. 66). In other words, the *primacy effect*—higher recall of the early items—was viewed as entirely dependent on rehearsal; the early items can be rehearsed more frequently (no doubt because of the experimenter-paced task at 5 sec per item), so are then recalled better. On the other hand, recall was quite high in the recency portion of the curve showing the **recency effect,** even though there were very few rehearsals of those last list items. Thus, Rundus's research showed the direct relationship between rehearsal and recall from long-term memory, and also that short-term memory is responsible for recall of the most recently presented items.

This is, of course, in complete agreement with the work on primacy and recency you studied in the last chapter. The typical U-shaped **serial-position curve** (showing that "memory sags in the middle," as Martin and Noreen quipped in 1974) indicates two kinds

FIGURE 5.4

Rundus's (1971) results relating number of rehearsals to the probability of recall. The probability of recall, P(R), is plotted against the left axis, and the number of rehearsals afforded an item during storage is plotted against the right axis. The similar pattern of these two functions across the primacy portion of the list indicates that rehearsal is the factor responsible for primacy effects. (From Rundus, 1971.)

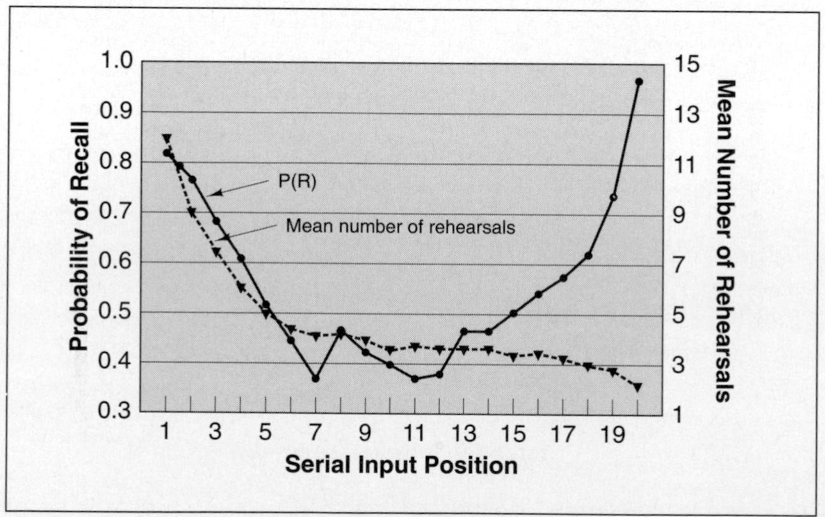

of memory performance: primacy effects due to recall from long-term memory, and recency effects due to short-term memory recall. As a logical extension, Rundus's results showed that deliberate, overt rehearsal improved the accuracy of recall in primacy, the portion of the list influenced by long-term memory. Recall for the recency items, however, was high despite the fact that they had been rehearsed very little.

Later research has focused on the rehearsal activity per se, rather than on the general issue of whether rehearsal stores information in long-term memory or not. For example, Kellas, McCauley, and McFarland (1975) found that participants who rehearsed aloud tended to rehearse and recall the items in serial order, whereas those who rehearsed silently showed greater flexibility in rehearsal and recall order. Rehearsing aloud apparently led to the rather unimaginative strategy of merely repeating the words aloud, whereas people in the silent rehearsal group were able to use more elaborate and complex kinds of rehearsal, for instance, devising sentences or images to help remember the words. Since these elaborate kinds of rehearsal couldn't be easily vocalized, they did not appear in the groups that rehearsed aloud.

DEPTH OF PROCESSING

A major theoretical position about such "elaborate kinds of rehearsal" claims that there are in fact two major kinds of rehearsal, each with different effects on storage (Craik & Lockhart, 1972). Remember from the last chapter that we used this distinction in connection with short-term memory rehearsal.

According to Craik and Lockhart's position, **maintenance rehearsal,** also called **type I rehearsal,** is a low-level, repetitive kind of information recycling. This is the kind of rehearsal you'd use to recycle a phone number to yourself until you dial it. The essential idea here is that maintenance rehearsal merely maintains information at a particular level in the memory system, without storing it more permanently or deeply.

Elaborative rehearsal (or **type II rehearsal**), on the other hand, is a more complex kind of rehearsal that uses the meaning of the information to help store and remember it. When information is rehearsed elaboratively, according to Craik and Lockhart, it is stored more deeply in the memory system, at a level that makes contact with the meaning of the information. As a consequence, material that was rehearsed elaboratively should be more permanently available for retrieval from memory—in short, it should be remembered better. Among other things, you might

- include imagery or mnemonic elaboration in your elaborative rehearsal;
- try to construct sentences from the words in a list you're trying to learn;
- impose some organization or structure on the list;
- even try to convert "nonsense syllables" like BEF into more meaningful items, like BEEF.

LEVELS OF PROCESSING

Craik and Lockhart's (1972) proposal on rehearsal also advanced a new kind of memory theory, one quite different from the customary "stage" approach of sensory, short-term, and long-term memory. They embedded their proposal of two kinds of rehearsal into a framework they termed **levels of processing** or **depth of processing,** an approach that still exerts an influence on research and theorizing (e.g., Thapar & Greene, 1994). An informal illustration of Craik and Lockhart's ideas is presented in Figure 5.5.

The essence of this framework goes as follows. Any perceived stimulus receives some amount of mental processing. Stimuli that receive only incidental attention are only processed to a very "shallow" level in memory, possibly no deeper than a sensory level (as in hearing the sound of the words without attending to their meaning, as a daydreamer might do during a lecture). Other stimuli, on the other hand, are given more intentional and meaningful processing. This deeper processing elaborates the representation of that item in memory, for example, by drawing relationships between already known information and the item currently being processed.

Thus, maintenance rehearsal is a superficial kind of processing, similar to merely recycling information in the articulatory rehearsal loop of working memory (Nairne, 1983). Meaningful processing, however, requires much more attention and effort, and corresponds to elaborative rehearsal. A key element in this framework is that the mental activities a person engages in during processing are as important for understanding memory as a determination of the "final resting place" of the information (what we've termed short- or long-term memory).

FIGURE 5.5

A schematic illustration of the depth-of-processing model.

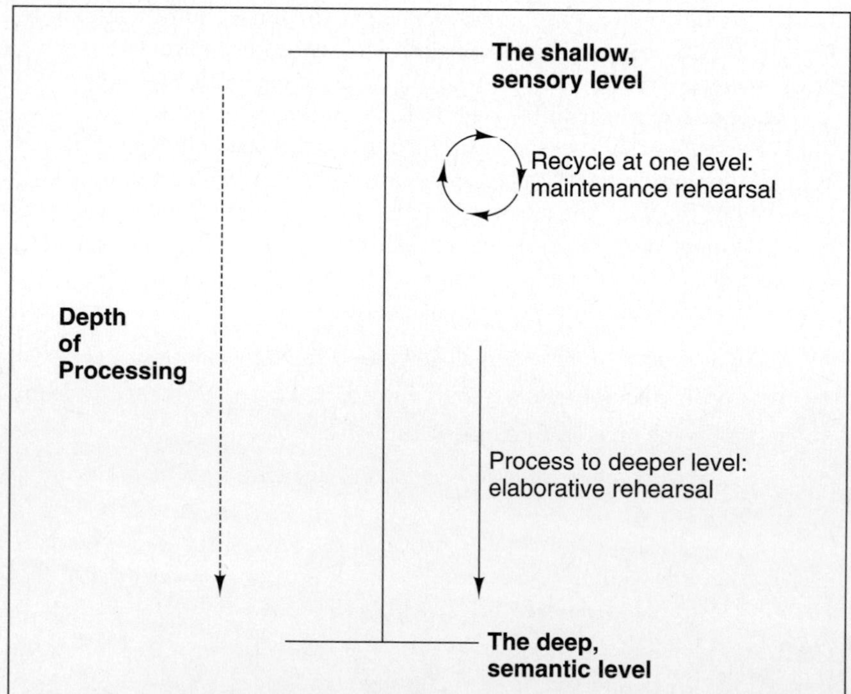

Evidence for Depth of Processing

Several experiments have confirmed the predictions derived from the depth-of-processing framework—and of course, the framework has been revised somewhat in the process. We'll cover both.

For confirmation, consider the following study. Craik and Watkins (1973) asked their subjects to monitor a long series of words on a tape recording, listening for words beginning with some critical letter, say G. When a new "G-word" was presented, they were to discard the old one and keep track of the new one, by maintenance rehearsal. At the end of several such trials, the subjects were then asked to recall any and all words they had heard in the lists. The results showed that the amount of time that items had been "maintained" made no difference in how accurately they were recalled—a G-word maintained through eight intervening words was recalled no better than one maintained through only two. Craik and Watkins concluded that "time in short-term store will only predict later long-term store performance when the subject has used the time to encode the items elaboratively" (p. 603).

Task Effects

Several investigators, on the other hand, either criticized aspects of the depth-of-processing framework (e.g., Baddeley, 1978), or showed that there are at least some relatively permanent effects of maintenance rehearsal. In particular, it turns out that Craik and Lockhart's (1972) claims about the effects of maintenance rehearsal depended critically on the memory task that was used. Typically, data from recall tasks showed that maintenance rehearsal did not improve memory. But a potential difficulty with this is that recall is not particularly sensitive to unconscious factors—you must consciously remember an item before you can recall it. It doesn't do you any good in a recall task if you have only fragments of information stored in memory, or if you are unable to remember the item consciously.

Other tasks are much less influenced by this "conscious recollection" difficulty (e.g., Ebbinghaus's relearning task). And the heavily used **recognition task,** in which you decide if you have or haven't seen the item, is also much less influenced by this difficulty. ▲ (See Table 5.2, p. 150, for a helpful summary of typical memory tasks.)

Have you figured it out by now? Craik and Lockhart's (1972) predictions about maintenance rehearsal were confirmed when a recall task was used, but not necessarily when memory was tested with a recognition task. As an example, Glenberg, Smith, and Green (1977) asked their participants to remember a four-digit number while repeating either one or three words aloud as a distractor task. Because participants were led to believe that digit recall was the important task, they presumably devoted only minimal effort to the word repetitions; that is, they probably used only maintenance rehearsal.

At the end of the 60 experimental trials, the participants were surprised with either a free-recall test on the words they had spoken during the distractor periods or a recognition task on those words. Recall showed no effect of rehearsal, but recognition scores did—words rehearsed for 18 seconds were recognized significantly better than those rehearsed for shorter intervals. In fact, the same beneficial effects of rehearsal were shown in the recognition task when the participants rehearsed nonsense syllables instead of words (Glenberg et al., 1977, experiment 3).

There are positive effects of maintenance rehearsal after all, under certain circumstances (Gardiner, Gawlik, & Richardson-Klavehn, 1994; Wixted, 1991, also discusses

TABLE 5.2

Memory Tasks

I. Relearning Task
1. Original learning: Learn list to a fixed-accuracy criterion.
2. Delay after learning list.
3. Learn list a second time.

Performance measure: savings score, how many fewer trials to learn the list a second time

II. Paired-Associate (P-A) Learning Task
1. Study trial: Study the pairs one at a time, trying to learn the correct response term for each stimulus term.
2. Test trial: Present stimulus terms one at a time, trying to recall the response term.
3. Continue to alternate between study and test until naming all response terms correctly.

Performance measure: number of study trials to achieve perfect recall of responses

III. Recall Task
1. Present the list items one at a time, for a fixed time.
2. Recall list items in:
   a. any order (free recall)
   b. order of presentation (serial recall)
   c. with cues (cued recall)

Performance measure: percentage of items recalled

IV. Recognition Task
1. Present the list items (targets) one at a time, for a fixed time.
2. Make yes/no decisions about test words, where half of the test words are targets and half are new (distractors).

Performance measure: percentage correct on targets and on distractors

the metacognitive effects of deciding which type of rehearsal to use). And Craik and Tulving (1975) demonstrated in several experiments that both recall and recognition can be influenced by the type of encoding given to information. They showed, for example, considerably higher recognition performance when participants made "deep" decisions about words ("Does the word belong to the animal category?" with 96 percent correct recognition) than when they made "shallow" decisions during encoding ("Is the word printed in uppercase letters?" with 18 percent correct recognition). ■

ORGANIZATION IN STORAGE

Another vitally important piece of the "storage puzzle" involves the role of **organization,** the structuring or restructuring of information as it is being stored in memory. Part of the importance of organization is derived from the powerful influence it exerts—well-organized material can be stored and retrieved with impressive levels of accuracy. Especially

GOOD ADVICE

Baddeley (1978) was one of the critics of the depth-of-processing viewpoint, concluding that it was valuable only at a rough, intuitive level, but not particularly as a scientific theory. While that may be true, it's hard to beat Craik and Lockhart's (1972) insights if you're looking for a way of improving your own memory—at the more everyday level, it's a very good rule of thumb. Think of maintenance rehearsal versus elaborative rehearsal as simple recycling in short-term memory versus meaningful study and transfer into long-term memory. Apply this now to your own learning. When you're introduced to someone, do you merely recycle that name for a few seconds, or do you think about it, use it in conversation, and try to find mnemonic connections to help you remember it? When you read a text, do you merely process the words at a fairly simple level of understanding, or do you actively elaborate what you're reading, searching for connections and relationships that will make the material more memorable? In other words, incorporate the depth-of-processing ideas into your own metacognition.

when the organizing strategy requires the learner's involvement, organization appears to be one of the best, all-purpose mnemonics available.

Here's a straightforward example. Bousfield (1953) gave 60-item lists—that's a lot!—to participants in a free-recall task. But the lists were composed of related words, 15 each from the categories animals, personal names, vegetables, and professions. Although the lists were presented in a randomized order, participants recalled the words by category, saying, for instance, "dog, cat, cow, . . . pea, bean, . . . John, Bob," etc. What Bousfield's participants were doing, of course, was organizing the list, taking advantage of the category structure to help them remember the words. At some point during input, they noticed that several words were drawn from the same categories. From then on, they used a grouping strategy (there's a nice metamemory effect here as well). After reorganizing the list as it was presented, by means of rehearsal, the reorganization then governed the way it was recalled—by category.

Notice that the benefits of category clustering or organization are the same as the benefits of *any* rehearsal strategy, including standard and invented mnemonics. Indeed, Mandler (e.g., 1967) suggested that "organization is a *necessary condition* for memory" (p. 328, emphasis added), and further, that "all organizations are mnemonic devices (p. 329), and likewise, that all mnemonic devices provide organization. Researchers realized that the organization in Bousfield's (1953) category lists was essentially the same as the organization we called "chunking" in our discussion of short-term memory (Miller, 1956). Thus, organization was related to the capacity of short-term memory and the formation and transfer of chunks into long-term memory. Clustering was seen as a powerful *recoding* strategy, in which "dog, cat, cow" could be grouped together into a chunk, with the category name "animal" serving as a *code* for that chunk.

How powerful? Stunningly! Bower, Clark, Lesgold, and Winzenz (1969) presented ◆ 112 words in an organized, clustered structure, as shown in Figure 5.6. In this organized condition, participants achieved 100 percent accuracy by their third learning trial, as ★ shown in Figure 5.7. Participants shown the same words in a random arrangement, however, hadn't even reached 50 percent accuracy by that stage. As Anderson (1985) and others have noted, a chapter outline can serve much the same function as the hierarchies used by Bower et al. (1969), with obvious implications for students' study strategies.

Subjective Organization

Furthermore, organization during rehearsal is not limited to lists of words that belong to obvious, known categories. In fact, some of the most provocative evidence for organization has come from research in which subjects formed their own ad hoc categories, a phenomenon known as **subjective organization.**

Consider the classic work on this topic, a study by Tulving (1962). Tulving presented a long list of unrelated words across several trials, rearranging their order on each new trial, and had his participants free-recall the words after each trial. When he analyzed the order in which the words were recalled, he discovered that the subjects had developed their own groupings of the words, recalling *dog, apple, lawyer, brush* together, for example, on the successive recall trials.

This consistency, despite the experimenter's reordering of the list items from trial to trial, suggested that the participants had formed clusters or chunks based on some idiosyncratic basis, and used those clusters to store the list items in memory. For example, one in-

◆ **FIGURE 5.6**

One of the hierarchies used by Bower et al. (1969). (From Bower, Clark, Lesgold, & Winzenz, 1969.)

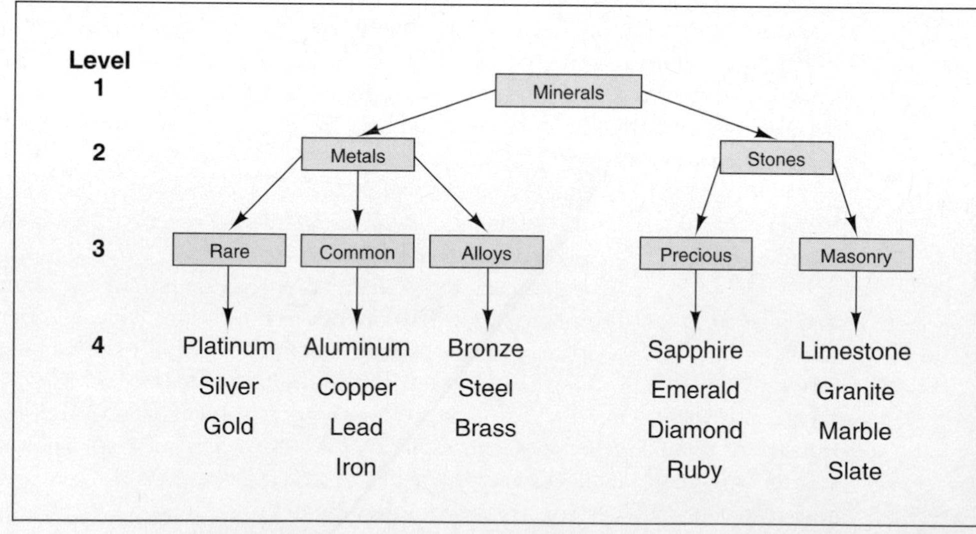

★ **FIGURE 5.7**

Recall performance for organized versus random lists. (Data from Bower et al., 1969.)

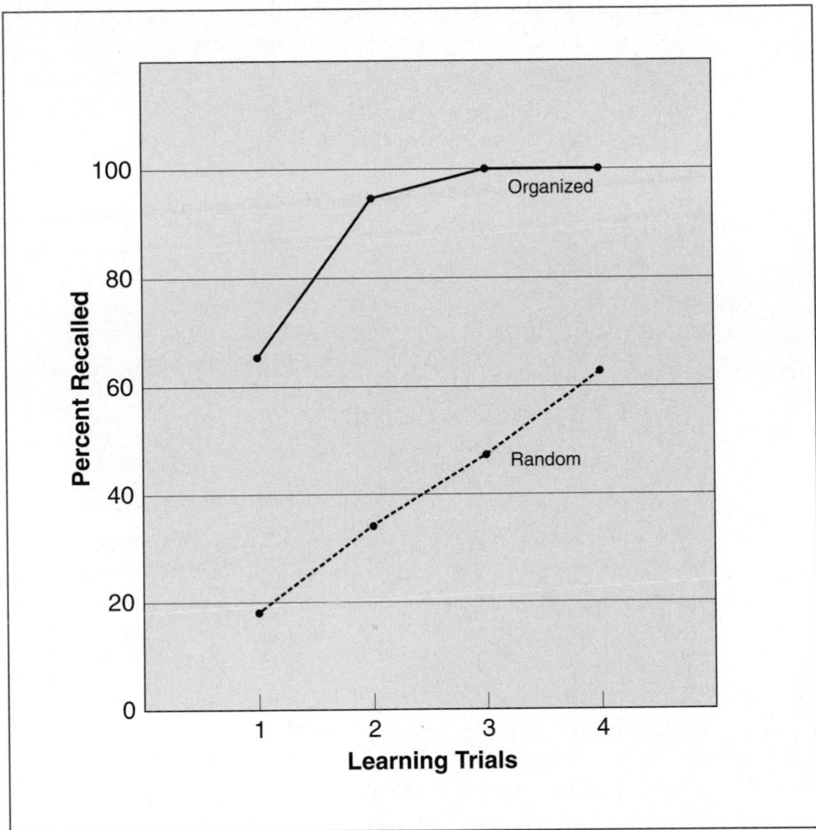

dividual might link the words together in a kind of sentence or story: "The dog brought an apple to the lawyer, who brushed his hair." Thus, these individually invented groupings served as the same kind of organized unit that "dog, cat, horse, cow" would in an experimenter-defined cluster, that is, improving both storage and recall.

IMAGERY

The last storage variable to be considered here involves **visual imagery,** the mental picturing of a stimulus that then affects later recall or recognition. Of course, we've discussed two prominent visual-imagery effects already, the mental rotation studies, which suggest a visual-imaginal code in working memory, and the imagery-based mnemonic devices. What we are focusing on now, however, is the effect that visual imagery has on the storage of information into long-term memory, the possible boost that imagery gives to material you're trying to learn.

The name most closely associated with early research on imagery is Alan Paivio. In his book, Paivio (1971) reviewed scores of studies that illustrated the generally beneficial effects of imagery on learning and retention. These beneficial effects are over and above those due to other variables, such as word- or sentence-based rehearsal, or meaningfulness (e.g., Bower, 1970; Nelson & Schreiber, 1992; Yuille & Paivio, 1967).

Paivio (1971) summarized these beneficial effects with his **dual-coding hypothesis.** This hypothesis states that words that denote concrete objects, as opposed to abstract words, can be encoded into memory twice, once in terms of their verbal attributes and once in terms of their imaginal attributes. Thus, a word like *book* enjoys an advantage in memory studies. Because it can be recorded twice in memory, once as a word and once as a visual image, there are two different ways it can be retrieved from memory, one way for each code. An item like *idea,* on the other hand, probably has only a verbal code available for it, since it does not have an obvious imaginal representation. (This is not to say that people can't eventually create an image to help remember a word like *idea,* but merely to say that the image is much more available and natural for concrete words.)

Imagery and Rehearsal

Consider a study by Watkins, Peynircioglu, and Brems (1984), which examined how imagery can be used as a rehearsal strategy. Participants saw picture-word pairs as lists. One group was given verbal rehearsal instructions for learning, and the other group was given pictorial rehearsal instructions ("Try to maintain an image of the picture in your mind's eye"). The pictures were displayed by slide projector, the words by tape recorder. Some of the picture-word items were followed by a 15-second interval of time, during which rehearsal could take place, and some were immediately followed by the next picture-word pair, thus preventing rehearsal.

After the lists had been presented, the participants were given a cued recall task, in which either a fragment of the printed word or a fragment of the picture was presented as a cue. The most important results involved the match between study and test conditions. When participants had been shown the pictures, and had been given the 15-second rehearsal interval, their test performance was better on the picture fragment test, as shown

in the top half of Figure 5.8. Likewise, those who had rehearsed verbally during the 15-second interval did better on the word fragment test, shown in the bottom half of the figure. All other performance was relatively low—for example, on items that had received no rehearsal, and in conditions where the study and test formats did not match (e.g., when word fragments were rehearsed, then picture fragments were provided as cues; see also Brandimonte, Hitch, & Bishop, 1992). Clearly, people can rehearse a visual image, and doing so improves their memory for image-based items.

Summary

1. Rehearsal strategies or mechanisms are the mental process used for storing new information in long-term memory. When the amount of rehearsal given to list items is examined, there is a direct relationship between amount of rehearsal and recall accuracy in the primacy portion of the list. Thus, rehearsal transfers information into long-term memory.

Figure 5.8

Percentage of picture and word fragments identified correctly, as a function of type of rehearsal and amount of rehearsal time. (From Watkins, Peynircioglu, & Brems, 1984.)

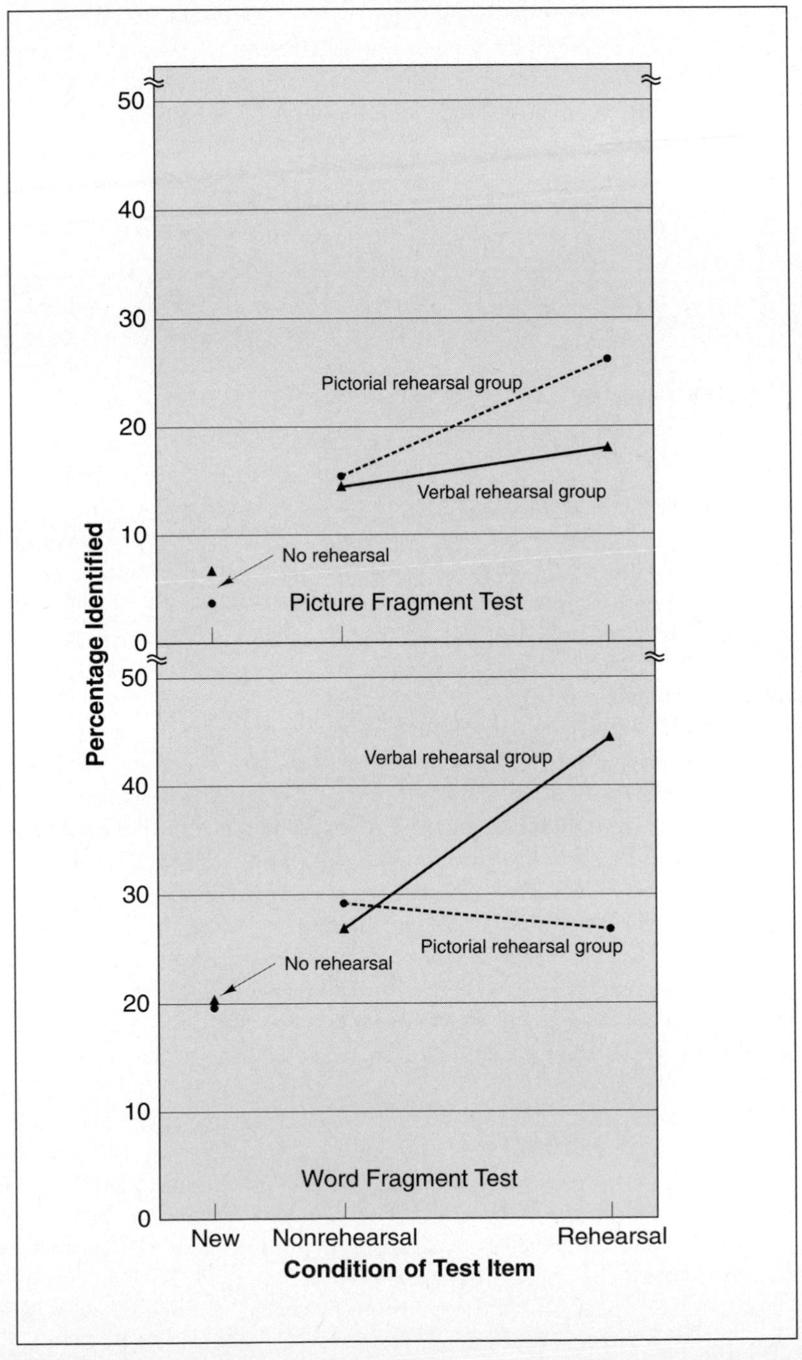

2. Craik and Lockhart, in the depth-of-processing framework, propose that maintenance rehearsal merely recycles information without storing it for long-term retention, whereas elaborative rehearsal does affect the memorability of information. Evidence suggests that this limitation of maintenance rehearsal only applies when memory is tested with the recall task.
3. Organization, whether by category or by subjectively defined groupings, improves memory performance, by providing for more effective encoding and retrieval. Organized groupings serve as "chunks" of information.
4. High imagery items are more easily remembered because they can be encoded with both imagery and verbal codes. Imagery can also serve as an effective rehearsal strategy, but only if the memory test is congruent with that rehearsal.

Retrieval of Episodic Information

Preview: decay and interference theories of forgetting; retrieval failure; encoding specificity and retrieval cues

We turn now to the other side of the coin, the retrieval of information from episodic memory. And as we do, we reencounter the two theories of forgetting that have preoccupied cognitive psychology from the very beginning: decay and interference.

DECAY

It's a bit unusual for the name of a theory to imply the content of the theory so clearly as the term **decay.** Nonetheless, that's what decay theory is all about—the older a memory trace is, the more likely that it has been forgotten, that it has decayed away, just as the print on an old newspaper fades into illegibility. Thorndike (1914) enunciated this principle in his law of disuse: Habits, and by extension memories, that are used repeatedly are strengthened, and habits not used are weakened through disuse. Thorndike's proposal was a beautiful example of a theoretical hypothesis—easily understood, and straightforward in its predictions. Unfortunately, it's wrong, at least as far as long-term memory is concerned.

Any number of examples demonstrate how an unelaborated decay theory simply can't possibly be correct. Such a theory predicts you should always remember older information more poorly than newer information. But, for example, if you remember your first-grade teacher's name but not the name of a later teacher, you've disconfirmed simple decay theory.

More persuasively, consider McGeoch's (1932) definitive criticism of decay theory. McGeoch argued from both theoretical and empirical grounds that decay theory was fundamentally wrong, that time per se is an inadequate basis for understanding or predicting loss of information. Instead, he claimed that the activities that occur during the intervening time are responsible for forgetting—in short, that those activities produce **interference.** This is very similar, of course, to the interpretations you read about short-term memory forgetting in the last chapter—it's the counting backward by threes in the Brown-Peterson task that causes forgetting of the stimulus item, not the mere passage of time.

INTERFERENCE

Interference theory is a far more acceptable theory of forgetting from long-term memory. Tests of interference effects were especially common during the days of verbal learning, especially because they were so easy to produce, especially with the paired-associate (P-A) learning task (go back to Table 5.2 for a description). As you have learned, **proactive interference,** in which older information interferes with memory for newer material, was an essential component of performance in short-term memory—remember the buildup of proactive interference, and then **release from PI?**

Likewise, **retroactive interference,** when newer information interferes with memory for older material, is also easily demonstrated. We'll use a P-A learning task as an example. First, participants in a P-A learning experiment would learn list A–B, pairings of the A terms with the B responses (e.g., tall–bone, plan–leaf; see sample lists in Table 5.3). Then they would learn another list, list A–C, in which new responses are paired with the same A stimuli. After this had been done successfully, the experimenter would then ask for one more recall of the original A–B pairings. Of course, this is now very difficult, because the newer list interferes with memory for the original pairings. The consequence here, as many experiments showed, is "massive" interference (see standard works such as Postman & Underwood, 1973; Underwood, 1957; and Klatzky's very readable summary, 1980, chapter 11).

Forgetting Defined

Here's a question, though. Was interference genuine forgetting? Or was the interfering effect more temporary—could retroactive interference merely have made it difficult to recall the pairings without genuinely causing forgetting? These questions point to an important point which we've neglected up until now: What precisely do we mean by the term *forgetting?* The word is commonly used by laypersons to mean the entire range of memory disruptions, all the way from a momentary, minor difficulty in recalling something, up to seemingly permanent, complete loss of information that was known before.

TABLE 5.3

Paired-Associate (P-A) Learning Lists

List 1 (A–B)	*List 2 (A–C)*
tall–bone	tall–safe
plan–leaf	nose–bench
nose–fight	grew–pencil
park–flea	pear–wait
grew–cook	print–student
rabbit–few	plan–window
pear–rain	park–house
mess–crowd	rabbit–card
print–kiss	mess–color
smoke–hand	smoke–flower

For psychology's purpose, we need something more precise than that. Consider **forgetting,** in the technical sense, to mean genuine loss of information from memory—what used to be there isn't any longer. We didn't quibble about this definition before because we discussed it in terms of sensory and short-term memory, memory systems we all acknowledge to be nonpermanent. But it's important to be precise when discussing long-term memory, because of the possibility that there is no true forgetting from the long-term memory system.

RETRIEVAL FAILURE

Read that last sentence again—there's a possibility that we don't forget at all in long-term memory. ("Who's he trying to kid?" you ask yourself.) In fact, research on the topic of retrieval since the mid-1960s leads to exactly that conclusion: with the exception of memory loss due to physical, organic factors (e.g., Alzheimer's, brain injury), there may be no true forgetting from long-term memory. Instead, the evidence points increasingly toward **retrieval failure,** a loss of access to stored information for some period of time. As Jenkins (1974) put it in the title of his article: "Remember that old theory of memory? Well, forget it!"

A Common Retrieval Failure—Tip of the Tongue

Everyone is familiar with retrieval failure, the classic **tip-of-the-tongue** (TOT, pronounced "tee-oh-tee") phenomenon. People are in a **TOT state** when they are momentarily unable to recall some shred of information that they know is stored in long-term memory, often a person's name. Interestingly, even though you may be unable to retrieve

You haven't really forgotten all seven names. If you need a big hint, see page 164.

a word or name during a TOT state, you usually have access to partial information about it, for instance, the sound it starts with, its approximate length, the stress or emphasis pattern in pronunciation, and so forth. (See Brown & McNeill, 1966, the classic TOT paper; also Burke, MacKay, Worthley, & Wade, 1991; Jones, 1989; Meyer & Bock, 1992. The Burke et al. paper even gives a list of questions that can be used to trigger a TOT state, in case you'd like to investigate it yourself.)

But retrieval failure, like the TOT phenomenon, is not limited to occasional lapses in remembering names or unusual words. In fact, as Tulving and his associates found, it is a fundamental aspect of long-term memory.

Research on Retrieval Failure

An early and powerful laboratory demonstration of retrieval failure was provided in a study by Tulving and Pearlstone (1966). In this study, two groups of people studied the same list of 48 items, four words from each of 12 different categories (animals, fruits, sports, etc.; other participants learned shorter lists, or lists with fewer items per category, but we'll focus only on the two most dramatic groups here). The items were preceded by the appropriate name of the category (e.g., crimes—treason, theft; professions—engineer, lawyer) but participants were told that they only had to remember the items themselves. Because both groups were treated identically until the beginning of the recall period, it's safe to assume they both acquired the same amount of information from the list, and both retained equal amounts in memory.

At recall, both groups were asked for standard free recall, but one was given the names of the categories as retrieval cues, that is, a **cued-recall** condition. The results were both predictable and profound in their implications. The free-recall group was able to recall 40 percent of the list items, while the cued-recall group named 62 percent of the items. In short, more information was encoded than could be recalled without cues—the cues provided access to "unrecallable" information. As Tulving and Pearlstone put it, "information about many words must be *available* in the storage . . . even when this information is not *accessible*" (p. 389, emphasis added) under free-recall conditions.

What was the profound implication? It was that unsuccessful retrieval—retrieval failure—might prove to be a critical component of what we normally call "forgetting." In fact, retrieval failure might be the major (or even the only) cause of forgetting—which would mean, of course, that there is no genuine forgetting at all. On this view, information stored in long-term memory remains there permanently, so is available, just as a book on the library shelf is available. Successful performance, however, depends not only on **availability,** but also on **accessibility,** the degree to which information can be retrieved from memory. Items that are not accessible are not immediately retrievable, just as the misshelved book in the library cannot be located or retrieved. This position suggests that information is not lost *from* memory, but instead is lost *in* memory, so to speak. This loss of access will persist until some effective retrieval cue is presented, some cue that "locates" the item that can't be retrieved.

RETRIEVAL CUES AND ENCODING SPECIFICITY

The principle that ties these effects together is called **encoding specificity** (e.g., Thomson & Tulving, 1970; Tulving & Thomson, 1973). By this phrase, Tulving and Thomson meant that information is not encoded into memory as a set of isolated, individual items.

Do you remember when you saw this movie? whom you saw it with? where you saw it?

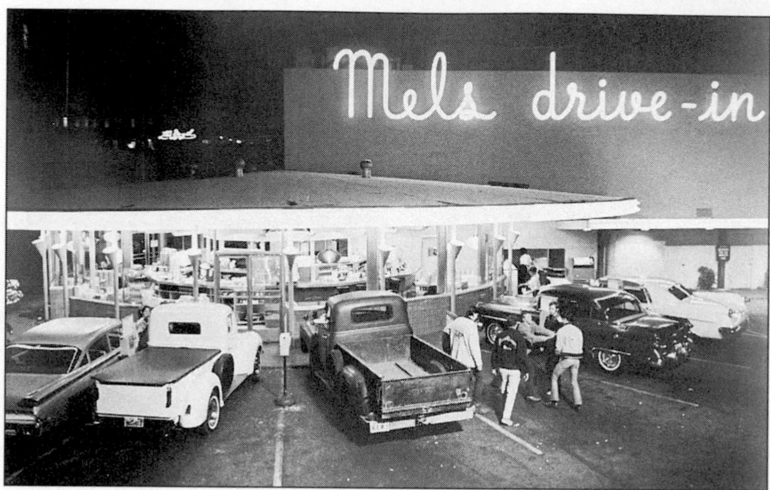

Instead, each item is encoded into a richer memory representation, one that includes any extra information about the item that was presented during encoding. So if you encounter *cat* in a list of words, you're also likely to encode related information that you know or thought about when seeing "cat," such as the concept ANIMAL. Then, at retrieval time, the additional information you encoded (ANIMAL) will provide an internal retrieval cue for remembering the target item "cat."

We're all familiar with this effect on an everyday basis. A song comes on the radio, and it "takes you back" to high school memories, not just memories of the song, but also other episodic information that was associated with the song—often very specific information, like where you were when you heard it, who you were with, and the like. The song, in other words, served as a retrieval cue for remembering those other aspects of the original situation. For a truly convincing demonstration, work through the material in

Tables 5.4 (opposite page) and 5.5 (p. 162), from Bransford and Stein (1984).

Evidence from the lab confirms the power of the encoding-specificity principle, and the notion that forgetting, in the technical sense of genuinely losing information from long-term memory, may instead be a case of retrieval failure. In one experiment, Thomson and Tulving (1970) asked people to learn a list of words for later recall. Some of the list words were accompanied by "cue words" printed in lowercase letters; participants were told they need not recall the cue words, but that the cues might be helpful in learning the items. Some of the cue words were high associates of the list items, for instance hot-COLD, and some were low associates, for instance, wind-COLD. During recall, participants were tested for their memory of the list under one of three conditions, low- or high-associate cues, or no cues at all.

The results were exactly as predicted from the encoding-specificity principle. High associates used as retrieval cues benefited recall both when the high associate had been presented during study and when no cue word had been presented. Presumably, when no cue word had been presented, the participants spontaneously retrieved the high associate

TABLE 5.4

Retrieval Cue Demonstration

This demonstration experiment illustrates the importance of retrieval cues. You'll need a blank sheet of paper and a pencil. Please follow the instructions exactly.

Instructions: Spend 3 to 5 seconds reading each of the sentences below, and read through the list only once. As soon as you are finished, cover the list and write down as many of the sentences as you can remember (you need not write "can be used" each time). Please begin now.

A brick can be used as a doorstop.
A ladder can be used as a bookshelf.
A wine bottle can be used as a candleholder.
A pan can be used as a drum.
A record can be used to serve potato chips.
A guitar can be used as a canoe paddle.
A leaf can be used as a bookmark.
An orange can be used to play catch.
A newspaper can be used to swat flies.
A TV antenna can be used as a clothes rack.
A sheet can be used as a sail.
A boat can be used as a shelter.
A bathtub can be used as a punch bowl.
A flashlight can be used to hold water.
A rock can be used as a paperweight.
A knife can be used to stir paint.
A pen can be used as an arrow.
A barrel can be used as a chair.
A rug can be used as a bedspread.
A telephone can be used as an alarm clock.
A scissors can be used to cut grass.
A board can be used as a ruler.
A balloon can be used as a pillow.
A shoe can be used to pound nails.
A dime can be used as a screwdriver.
A lampshade can be used as a hat.

Now that you've recalled as many sentences as you can, turn to Table 5.5.

Source: From Bransford and Stein (1984).

during input, and encoded it along with the list item. In contrast, when low associates had been presented during learning, only low associates functioned as effective retrieval cues. High associates used as retrieval cues were no better for these people than no cues at all. In other words, if you had studied wind-COLD, the word *hot* was not an effective retrieval cue for COLD.

★ **TABLE 5.5**

Continuation of Retrieval Cue Demonstration

Do *not* look back at the list of sentences in Table 5.4. Instead, use the following list as retrieval cues, and now write as many sentences as you can. Be sure to keep track of how many you can write down, so you can compare this to your earlier recall performance. Begin now.

flashlight	lampshade
sheet	shoe
rock	guitar
telephone	scissors
boat	leaf
dime	brick
wine bottle	knife
board	newspaper
pen	pan
balloon	barrel
ladder	rug
record	orange
TV antenna	bathtub

Source: From Bransford and Stein (1984).

More surprising than this, encoding specificity can even override the usual advantage that recognition shows over recall. A series of influential papers by Tulving (e.g., Tulving & Thomson, 1973; Watkins & Tulving, 1975) has demonstrated a paradoxical result, termed "recognition failure of recallable words." In these studies, a weakly associated cue is presented along with the target word during original learning—say, glue-CHAIR. When a recognition test is presented later, the target CHAIR is often not recognized if it appears in a very different context, for instance, in the set "desk, top, chair." In other words, participants fail to identify *CHAIR* as a word they have seen previously in the experiment, since its current context is so different from the original encoding. This is, of course, recognition failure.

Following this, however, participants are given a cued-recall test. Here they routinely do recall CHAIR when presented with "glue" as a retrieval cue. While these experiments used rather arbitrary contexts (who would spontaneously think of "glue" as a cue for CHAIR?), the similarity of the result to the earlier point about congruous study and retrieval contexts is obvious. In short, even simple recognition depends on encoding specificity.

Tulving and Thomson (1973) explained the encoding-specificity principle as follows: "Specific encoding operations performed on what is perceived determine what is stored, and what is stored determines what retrieval cues are effective in providing access to what is stored" (p. 369). Whatever information you encoded, target items as well as related information, determines what gets stored in your memory representation. In other words, a

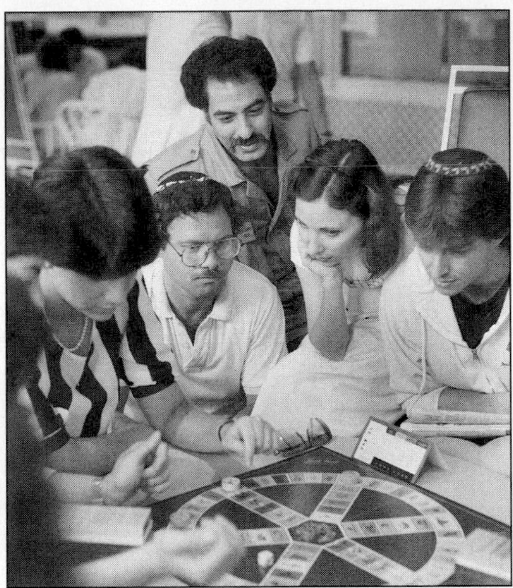

Sometimes the questions in Trivial Pursuit serve as successful retrieval clues—and sometimes not.

retrieval cue will be effective if you thought of it and encoded it spontaneously during learning, or if it was presented (and you encoded it) during the learning sequence, that is, if it came either from conceptually driven or data-driven processes (Micco & Masson, 1991). Retrieval cues that are not effective simply don't match your encoded representation of the item, because they weren't explicitly presented or spontaneously generated during learning.

Here's a final demonstration of this principle. Think of all the words you've read in this chapter, and the lists you've learned. Limiting yourself to just these words, can you remember a word that goes with the concept PATRIOTISM? If not, maybe it will be easier with a cue that you encoded specifically along with the target word. Fill in the blank with the cue "two-shoe-_______".

Summary

1. The decay theory of forgetting predicts loss of information due to the passage of time, a position shown by studies of interference to be inadequate. Interference, whether proactive or retroactive, clearly influences long-term memory performance.
2. Retrieval failure, as in a TOT state, suggests that there may be no true forgetting from long-term memory. When retrieval cues are given during free recall, people are usually able to recall more of the information they originally encoded. This shows that more information is available in memory than is usually accessible for recall.
3. The principle of encoding specificity states that we encode associated material along with target information as we acquire information. This material will serve as an effective retrieval cue, and is sometimes even more powerful than already associated information.

Important Terms

accessibility
availability
cued recall
decay
depth of processing
dual-coding hypothesis
elaborative rehearsal
encoding specificity
episodic memory
forgetting
free recall
generation effect
interference
levels of processing
maintenance rehearsal
metacognition
metamemory
method of loci
mnemonic device
organization
peg-word mnemonic
primacy effect
proactive interference
recency effect
recognition task
rehearsal
relearning task
release from PI
retrieval failure
retroactive interference
savings score
semantic memory
serial-position curve
serial recall
subjective organization
tip-of-the-tongue phenomenon
type I rehearsal
type II rehearsal
verbal learning
visual imagery

Suggested Readings

Bower's (1970) paper on mnemonic devices is excellent. Several books have dealt with mnemonics, including Lorayne and Lucas (1974) and the somewhat more focused book by Cermak (1975), *Improving Your Memory*. Norman's (1976) book also contains a chapter on mnemonics. Classics in the area include Yates's (1966) *The Art of Memory* and Luria's (1968) *The Mind of a Mnemonist*.

The special issue of the *Journal of Experimental Psychology: Learning, Memory, and Cognition* that contains the 100th anniversary papers on Ebbinghaus is the July 1985 issue (Vol. 11, No. 3, pp. 413–500). Slamecka's (1985a) delightful introductory article is followed by 12 briefer articles commenting on various aspects of the Ebbinghaus tradition, written by a *Who's Who* in cognitive psychology (see also Gorfein & Hoffman, 1987).

Finally, Tulving's (1983) *Elements of Episodic Memory* is a substantive review of memory research accompanied by his personal reflections on various topics. Since Tulving is one of the genuine leaders in the learning and memory field, his thoughtful comments and observations are often more important and provocative than others' carefully designed research and theories.

Hint for page 158: Which name is wrong? Sleepy, Sneezy, Dopey, Goofy, Happy, Bashful, Doc.

CHAPTER SIX

SEMANTIC MEMORY

This chapter is concerned with a rather different kind of long-term memory from the type we discussed in Chapter 5. Here we're concerned with *semantic memory*, literally, "memory for meaning," or to put it simply, "knowledge." **Semantic memory** is our *permanent memory store of general world knowledge*, sometimes described as a combination of dictionary, thesaurus, and encyclopedia. Semantic memory is where your knowledge of language and other conceptual information is stored. It's the permanent storehouse of information you use for all kinds of cognitive activities, most prominently activities like comprehending and producing language.

Notice the *generic* aspect of semantic memory—it's our collection of *general* world knowledge, of commonly known information. This makes it rather different from episodic memory. That is, your episodic memory differs quite a bit from mine—our autobiographies are unique. But our semantic memories are very similar, at least to the extent that we have similar cultural and language backgrounds. Thus, we all probably have very similar concepts for terms like "maiden name" and "hobby"—we all mean essentially the same thing by those terms—even though you don't know what *my* mother's maiden name is or what my hobbies are.

Because people's semantic memories are so similar, cognitive science does rather different kinds of experiments on semantic memory than on episodic memory. In the episodic tasks in Chapter 5, participants first had to learn a particular set of items before they could be asked to recall or recognize them. In semantic tasks, however, we can usually assume that our participants already have the same knowledge in memory, so we can just test them without any learning phase to the experiment. As examples, you might walk into a semantic memory experiment and be asked questions like these:

- Yes or no, MANTLE is an English word? MANTY?
- True or false, Banana is a fruit? Rhubarb?
- Is a poodle a "good" or typical member of the dog category? What about a chihuahua?
- Name three characteristics of birds; robins; mudlarks.

Now obviously, cognitive science isn't going to make much progress by simply examining how accurately people can answer such questions—the questions are too easy, at least some of them. Instead, we are more often interested in *how long* it takes a participant to respond to the question—in other words, *reaction times* (RTs) are often the data we collect

★ **FIGURE 6.1**

RTs (reaction times) to multiplication problems. (From Campbell & Graham, 1985.)

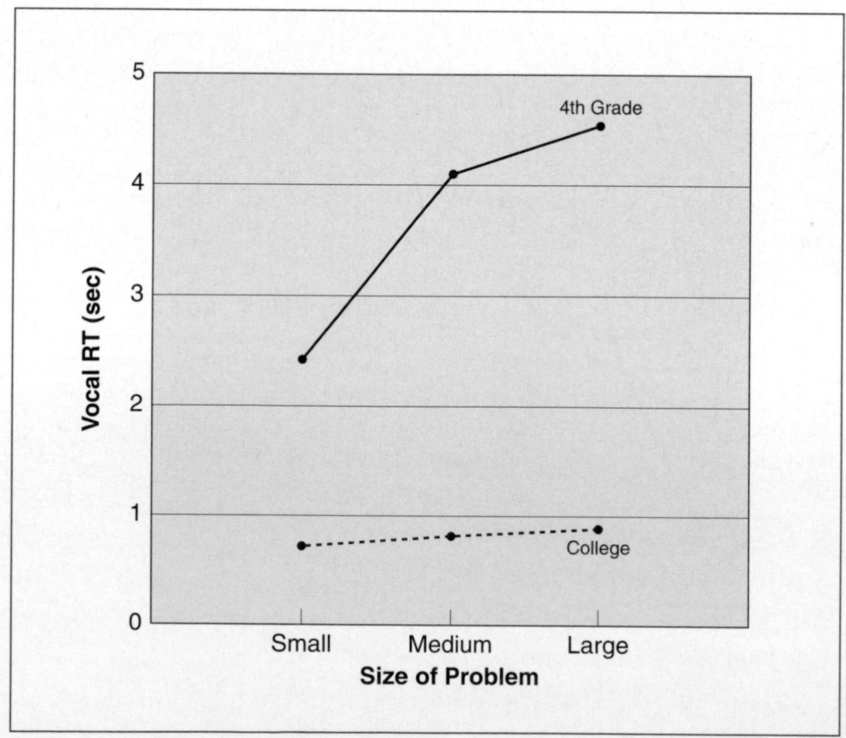

from participants. By examining RTs to the different types of stimuli, we can often draw inferences—or at least testable hypotheses—about the structure and processes of semantic memory. See Figure 6.1 and the accompanying explanation for an example of this logic.

Structure and Processes of Semantic Memory

Preview: nodes in a network; spreading activation; feature comparisons; the semantic relatedness effect

INFERENCES BASED ON REACTION TIME

An example will help you appreciate this important idea about inferences based on RTs. Let's go back to a situation you read about in Chapter 1, the time it takes fourth graders and college students to give answers to simple problems like 2 × 3 and 6 × 9. The figure you studied then is repeated here as Figure 6.1, showing that for both fourth graders and college students it takes longer to give answers to larger problems like 6 × 9 than to problems with smaller answers, like 2 × 3 (Campbell & Graham, 1985).

The interesting question is, Why? Why are larger problems harder? Or more usefully, What is it that's different between smaller and larger problems that causes the RTs to go up? Let's start by ruling out a few possibilities. For example, it shouldn't take more time to perceive and encode larger digits than smaller digits, and it probably doesn't take you any more time to start saying "fifty-four" than to start saying "six." As such, we are reasonably confident that the *increase* in RT is due to "mental time," by which we mean time spent in some kind of mental processing. But what kind of mental processing?

In fact, several different explanations have been proposed (for reviews, see Ashcraft, 1995; LeFevre et al., 1996), each digging deeper into the question, What are the mental processes of simple multiplication? Start with a strange fact—not only do we encounter smaller numbers more frequently than larger numbers (Dehaene & Mehler, 1992), elementary school textbooks present smaller problems like 2 × 3 much more frequently than larger problems like 6 × 9 (Ashcraft & Christy, 1995; Clapp, 1924). This might mean that smaller problems are stored more strongly in memory, so can be retrieved more rapidly (e.g., Ashcraft, 1995; Siegler & Jenkins, 1989). Or, larger problems might be more confusible with each other, that is, more susceptible to interference, maybe because they weren't learned as well originally (Campbell, 1987). A third possibility is that we use only retrieval on smaller problems, but use strategies or computations on larger problems—for 6 × 9, solving the easy problem 6 × 10, then subtracting 6 to get 54 (e.g., LeFevre et al., 1996).

Each of these is a specific cognitive hypothesis about what goes on during the "mental time" of simple multiplication. And each can be tested by examining RTs for answering simple multiplication problems.

The first time anyone used the term *semantic memory* was in 1966, in M. Ross Quillian's doctoral dissertation. Quillian was trying to program a computer to understand language, so it could answer questions (e.g., What does it mean to cry?) and paraphrase texts in reasonably humanlike fashion. What Quillian discovered in this work is that the computer must have a large storehouse of conceptual knowledge if it's going to understand even the simplest of questions. The implication, of course, was that if computers needed all that knowledge in order to comprehend, people must need it too. The study of that vast storehouse became the study of semantic memory.

Quillian's model of semantic memory (e.g., 1968) was called *TLC*, for Teachable Language Comprehender. It was not a genuine psychological model, but rather a computer program for understanding language. Very soon, however, Quillian began a collaboration with psychologist Allan Collins. The psychological model the two of them based on TLC became the first serious attempt in cognitive psychology to explain the structure and processes of semantic memory.

THE COLLINS AND QUILLIAN (AND LOFTUS) MODEL

The Collins and Quillian model of semantic memory (Collins & Quillian, 1972; Collins & Loftus, 1975) was an extensive theory of semantic memory, comprehension, and meaning. At the heart of the model were two fundamentally important assumptions, one about

DO WE NEED *THE VAST STOREHOUSE* TO COMPREHEND?

This is a story I tell my own classes, to illustrate the quantity of semantic knowledge that is necessary when we understand. An important point in the demonstration is the idea of *tacit knowledge,* in other words knowledge that you may not consider *consciously* when you comprehend, but knowledge that you nonetheless *must* have used in the act of comprehension.

> *Billy was excited about the invitation to his friend's birthday party. But when he went to his piggy bank and shook it, there was no noise. "Hmmm," he thought to himself, "maybe I can borrow some from Mom."*

Everyone understands Billy's dilemma in the ordinary fashion—

(a) Billy needs to take a *present* to the friend's party,

(b) Billy needs *money* to buy the *present,*

(c) Billy's piggy bank is *empty,* meaning

(d) he'll have to borrow *money* from his mother.

But of course, the story said nothing explicitly about having to take a present, and it never even mentioned the word *money.* Instead, you retrieved these ideas from semantic memory, and relied on those ideas for comprehension (I've italicized these retrieved ideas in a. through d.). The amazingly rich knowledge structure that you access is your semantic memory, absolutely essential for even the simplest acts of comprehension.

the *structure* of semantic memory, and one about the *process* of retrieving information from that structure. Because these two assumptions have been typical of many models since the early Collins and Quillian work (e.g., Anderson, 1983; Glass & Holyoak, 1975; see Chang's review, 1986), including current connectionist models (which you'll read about soon), you need a firm grasp on what they mean.

Nodes in a Network

Collins and Quillian viewed the entries in semantic memory as being nodes in a network. A **node** is a point or location in the semantic space. Each concept node in the network is linked to other nodes by **pathways,** labeled, directional associations between concepts. This entire collection—nodes connected to other nodes by pathways—is the **network,** the interrelated set of concepts, the interrelated body of knowledge. Figure 6.2 gives an illustration of one small part of such a network structure, a fragment of what you know about birds.

What kinds of information can be represented by nodes and pathways? Any kind! Collins and Quillian (1972) pointed out that it's quite easy to diagram networks like those in Figure 6.2, where the nodes are labeled with the words that name the concepts. But they also reminded us that other concepts, including those not so easily named, are also stored as nodes in the network. For example, consider your concept ROOSTER. In

FIGURE 6.2

A simplified semantic network.

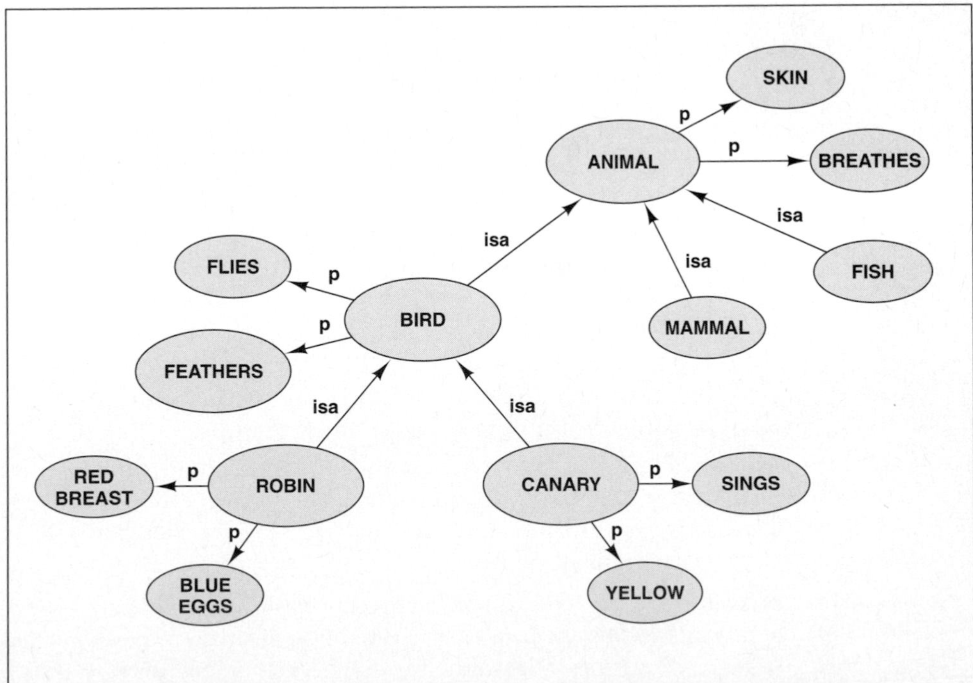

addition to other information you know about roosters, you probably have a visual image of a rooster stored in the semantic network, and an auditory image for the sound that roosters make. Most of us also have a node corresponding to a phrase that *names* that sound ("cock-a-doodle-doo" in English)—and we also know that the phrase doesn't sound exactly like the real sound (if it did, then different languages would use the same phrase).

Thus, Collins and Quillian proposed that our semantic knowledge is represented in memory as a network of interrelated concepts. The structure is very hierarchical—ROBIN and CANARY (and ROOSTER too) are members of the higher-order category BIRD, which along with MAMMAL, FISH, and so forth are members of an even higher category, ANIMAL. So, in the jargon of semantic networks (e.g., Rumelhart, Lindsay, & Norman, 1972),

- ROBIN *isa* BIRD, where *isa* is a *superordinate* relationship, and
- ROBIN *prop* RED BREAST, that is, one of the *properties* of ROBIN is RED BREAST.

Spreading Activation

According to Collins and Quillian, the major process that operates on this structure is that of **spreading activation,** the mental activity of accessing and retrieving information from the network. Concepts are usually in a relatively quiet, unactivated state—they are at a resting, baseline level. For example, at this very instant in time, as you're reading this sentence, one of the many concepts in your semantic memory that is probably not activated is MACHINE. When you read that word, however, its mental representation receives a boost in activation—MACHINE is no longer quiet and unactivated; it's active, primed, "awakened," so to speak. This activation, for Collins and Quillian, *was* the process of retrieval, the process of accessing the meaning of a concept.

There are several key features about activation that you'll want to remember.

- The most basic feature is that activation *spreads* through the network. That is, once a concept becomes activated, it begins to spread activation to all the other concepts it's linked to. These concepts in turn continue to spread activation further, to the nodes *they* are connected to. In Collins and Quillian's view, the spread of activation corresponds to a search through memory, a search that "continually widens like a harmless spreading plague" (1972, p. 326).
- It takes *time* for activation to spread. For a structure like the BIRD knowledge in Figure 6.2, this means that it would take longer for activation to get from ROBIN to ANIMAL than from ROBIN to BIRD—the interconnecting pathway is longer, so it takes activation longer to spread down the pathway.
- The further the activation spreads, the weaker and more *diffused* it becomes, to the point that it soon has little or no effect. For example, ROBIN will probably spread some activation as far as ANIMAL, but probably not back down the animal hierarchy to a concept like HORSE.
- Activation *decays* across time. Once a concept has been activated, it does not remain activated indefinitely. Instead, the activation dissipates across some brief interval of time, returning the nodes to their baseline levels of inactivity.

Intersection Search

Collins and Quillian proposed that a spread of activation is triggered each time a concept is activated in semantic memory. So when *two* concepts are activated, there are *two* simultaneous spreads of activation, one from each concept node. If the concepts are close enough, and if there's a pathway between them, there will eventually be an **intersection,** when the activation from one source encounters activation from the other source. When this happens, the pathway that connects the two concepts has been retrieved. As an exercise, do a "hand simulation" of spreading activation. Mark the nodes in Figure 6.2 that will be activated by the sentence "A robin can breathe." ROBIN activates BIRD, RED BREAST, and so on, and BREATHES activates ANIMAL, which soon would activate BIRD, MAMMAL, FISH, and so forth.

Now, if you've done it correctly, you've discovered two important properties of spreading-activation search on your own. First, you found that the activation originating with ROBIN eventually primed a node that was *also* primed or activated by BREATHES. This is the *exact* process proposed by Collins and Quillian to explain how information is retrieved from semantic memory—when one harmless spreading plague encounters the other one, then an intersection has been retrieved in semantic memory, a connecting route or set of pathways has been identified. The second principle you discovered is that many additional nodes become activated by such a search, "extra activation" in a sense. Research you'll read about in a few moments capitalizes on just this "extra" activation.

Once an intersection has been found, then a decision stage must operate to make sure that the retrieved pathway is valid, that is, that it represents the relationship specified in the sentence. In other words, the pathway you find between ROBIN and BREATHES is a valid one, unlike the activated pathway you'd find for the sentence "All animals have red breasts." In both cases, some decision mechanism has to evaluate the retrieved pathway before a decision can be reached. (Incidentally, this should sound familiar, a search stage followed by a decision stage; see Chapter 4 on the Sternberg task.)

Empirical Support for the Network Model

Collins and Quillian's (1969) earliest report tested a straightforward prediction from their model, that two concepts that are closer together in the network should require less retrieval time than two that are farther apart. Their evidence was based on the **sentence verification task,** in which simple sentences are presented to participants, who make timed yes/no decisions. The stimuli were sentences like "A robin is a bird" and "A canary is yellow," where the first is a *superordinate* sentence, and the second a *property* sentence. (Needless to say, there was also a set of false sentences, to balance out the true ones.) The stimuli included both superordinate and property sentences, and also varied the extent of the search necessary to find the relevant information. That is to say, if the sentence was a level 2 sentence like "A robin is an animal," the theory predicted that search would have to proceed up *two* levels from ROBIN to find the intersection with ANIMAL, whereas ROBIN to BIRD would only be a level 1 sentence. The same levels applied to property sentences, including level 0 types where the property is stored directly with the concept (e.g., "A robin has a red breast").

★ Figure 6.3 (p. 172) shows the results Collins and Quillian reported in this now-classic experiment. Just as the network model predicted, concepts that are stored farther apart—

★ **FIGURE 6.3**

The original Collins and Quillian (1969) results. Reaction time to superordinate (S) sentences and property (P) sentences is shown as a function of levels within the hierarchy. An S2 sentence involves a superordinate connection two levels up the hierarchy; S1 means one level up in the hierarchy; a level 0 sentence had the predicate stored at the same hierarchical level. (From Collins & Quillian, 1969.)

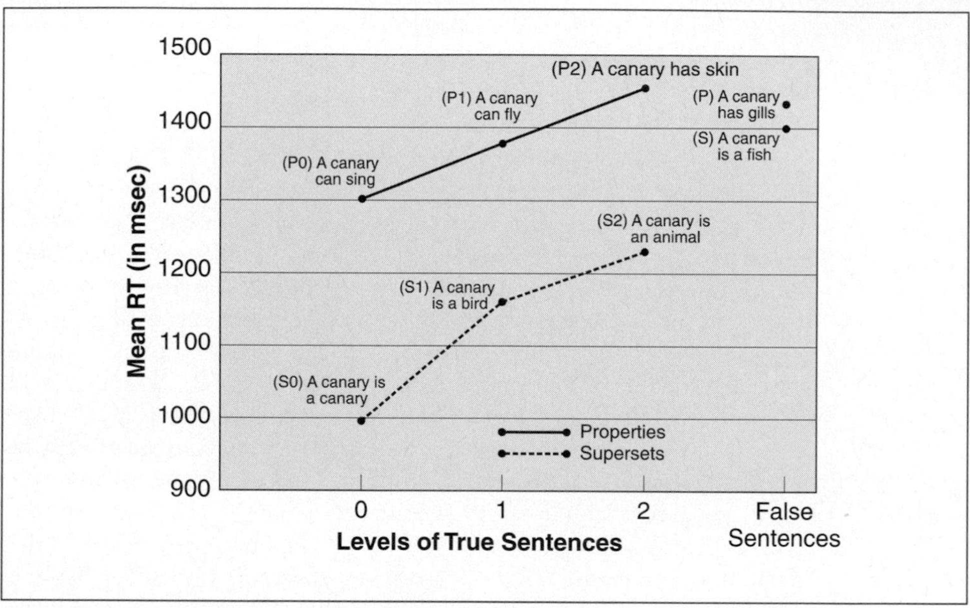

concepts with longer connecting pathways—required more time than concepts stored at closer levels in the network. And furthermore, superordinate sentences were considerably faster than property sentences, suggesting that the *isa* pathway might in fact be stronger than *property* pathways (see also Hampton, 1984).

SMITH'S FEATURE OVERLAP MODEL

Several other approaches to semantic memory appeared soon after Collins and Quillian's (1969) original work. Let's focus here on just one of those other approaches, the Smith Feature Overlap Model, since it offered a clear contrast to the Collins and Quillian model, and since it was the most successful challenger to that model. (See Chang, 1986, for a review of all the major models.)

Feature Lists

Smith's model (e.g., Smith, Rips, & Shoben, 1974) made considerably simpler assumptions about the structure of semantic memory than the Collins and Quillian network model made (but as a consequence was somewhat more elaborate in its assumptions about the process of retrieval). Its most basic structural element was the **feature list.** Rather than postulate extensive networks of concepts and pathways, Smith et al. suggested that we consider semantic memory to be a collection of lists. Each concept in semantic memory was represented as a list of **semantic features,** simple, one-element characteristics or properties of the concept. Thus, the concept ROBIN would be represented as a list of ROBIN's features, like animate, red-breasted, smallish, winged, feathered, and so forth. Figure 6.4 contrasts the way Smith's model represented concepts with the Collins and Quillian scheme.

Smith et al. suggested that feature lists were ordered in terms of a factor they called *definingness*. That is, they said that the feature lists stored in memory were ordered in a kind of priority ranking, with the most defining features for a concept toward the top of the list, and the least defining features toward the bottom. Thus, an absolutely essential feature was called a **defining feature,** like *animate* for BIRD, and would be stored near the top of the feature list. Conversely, features that are not particularly important for the concept, say that a ROBIN *perches in trees*, would be placed toward the bottom of the list. In fact, Smith et al. proposed that these lower features were more appropriately called **characteristic features** of the concept, features that are merely common or frequent, but not essential to the meaning of the concept.

Feature Comparison

The process of semantic retrieval in the Smith model was the process of comparing features; follow the sequence of processes illustrated in Figure 6.5 (p. 174) as you read. Say you were given the sentence "A robin is a bird," and had to make a timed true/false

FIGURE 6.4

Contrasting the Smith Feature Overlap Model (E. E. Smith, Rips, & Shober, 1974) and the Collins and Quillian (1972) model. Information in semantic memory is represented differently in feature list models and in hierarchical network models. In feature list models, a concept is represented as a list of simple semantic features; in hierarchical network models, concepts are represented as nodes that connect to other nodes via pathways. The Smith et al. (1974) model is a feature list model, and the Collins and Quillian (1972) model is a hierarchical network model. (Adapted from E. E. Smith, 1978.)

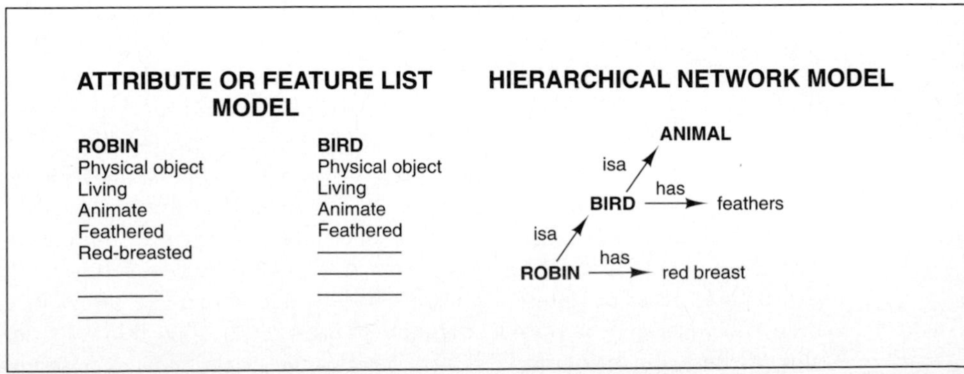

FIGURE 6.5

The comparison and decision processes in the Smith et al. (1974) model.

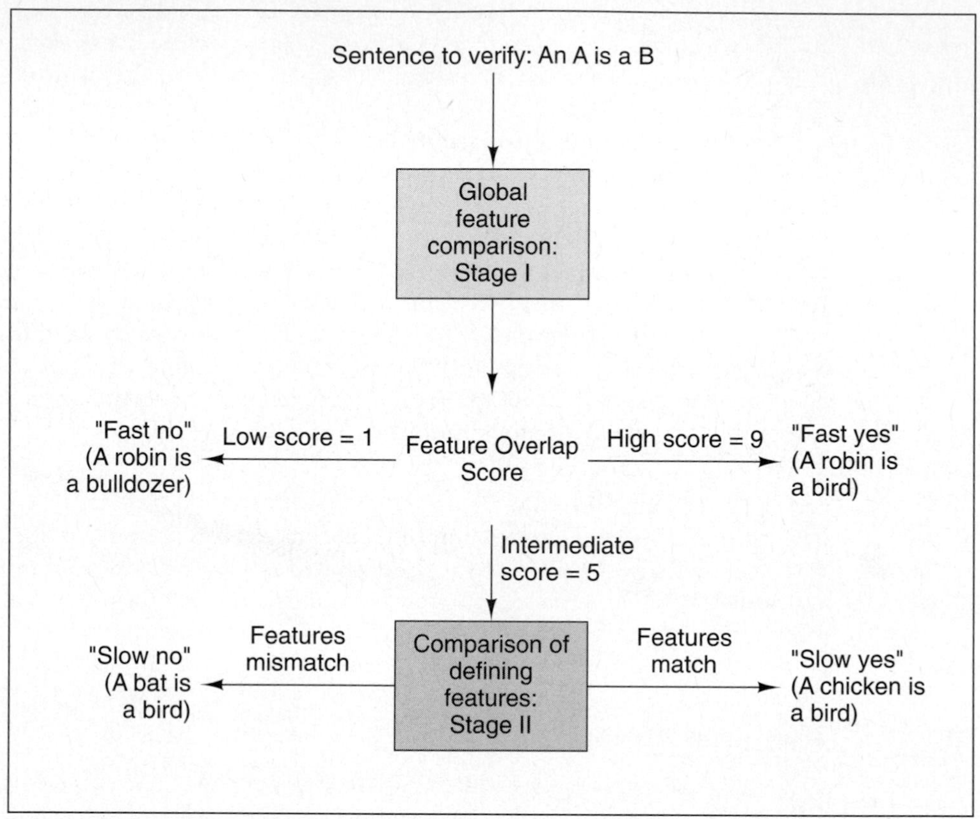

judgment. According to the model, you would access the two concepts ROBIN and BIRD in semantic memory, and then proceed to compare the features on those two lists. This *stage I* feature comparison process involved a global comparison of the features—a randomly selected subset of features on each of the two lists would be compared in order to "compute" the similarity between the two concepts. This comparison process yielded a *feature overlap score*, simply an index or measurement of the similarity of the two concepts. For illustration purposes here, assume that these scores range from 1 to 10.

Of course, for the concepts in "A robin is a bird," the feature lists should overlap a great deal, since there are hardly any ROBIN features that aren't also BIRD features. The outcome of this feature comparison process then would be a very high overlap score (e.g., 8 or 9), so high that you could confidently respond "yes" immediately on the basis of this global comparison of features. Conversely, with a sentence like "A robin is a bulldozer," there should be so little feature overlap (e.g., 1 or 2) that you could respond "no" immediately without any further processing. These "fast yes" and "fast no" responses were called

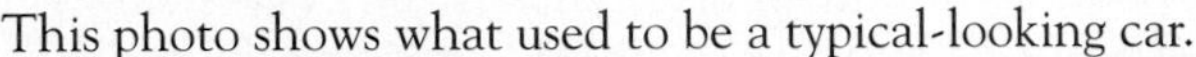
This photo shows what used to be a typical-looking car.

stage I responses by Smith et al. (1974). When overlap scores are either very high or very low, there is no need to continue the search, so a response is made immediately.

Two other kinds of sentences state relationships that aren't quite so obvious. First, consider "A chicken is a bird." As before, the process of retrieving information is the feature comparison process, now being performed on the CHICKEN and BIRD features. Most people's intuition is that chickens are a somewhat less representative example of the bird category. Compared to your average bird, chickens seem rather unusual—they don't perch or make nests in trees, they don't eat worms, they're larger, and so on. Isn't it clear, then, that the stage I comparison process should find only an intermediate degree of overlap between CHICKEN and BIRD?

Smith et al. claimed that when the overlap scores indicated only moderate similarity (say between 4 and 6), a second comparison was necessary, a *stage II comparison*. Unlike the fast, global stage I process, the stage II comparison was a careful and rather slow one, and it used *only* the defining features to compute its evidence. Thus, for the CHICKEN-BIRD sentence, only the defining features of the two concepts would be compared in stage II. Since it is in fact true that chickens are birds, presumably there would be a match on all the tested features in this stage, yielding a "slow yes" response; the response would be "slow" because it involved stage II comparison, and "yes" because all of the defining features from CHICKEN would match those from BIRD.

On the other hand, consider a sentence like "A bat is a bird." This would also yield only a moderate overlap score during stage I, thus necessitating a stage II comparison. During stage II, however, there will be several important *mismatches*, because stage II only considers the defining features of concepts. It would seem that only the characteristic features of bats make them similar to birds. Their defining features (mammal, furry, teeth, etc.) give convincing evidence that the sentence is false. This would produce a "slow no" response, "slow" because it required stage II processing, and "no" because of mismatches on the defining features.

Empirical Support for the Feature Comparison Model

The early empirical support for the Smith et al. (1974) model involved just this idea of fast versus slow responses. Smith et al. isolated a variable that clearly influenced performance, in exactly the way predicted by their model. The effect came to be known as the **typicality effect,** and showed, simply, that typical members could be judged as belonging to the category more rapidly than atypical members—you're faster to decide that "robin is a bird" than to decide that "chicken is a bird." Figure 6.6 illustrates this effect across several different categories (see also Casey, 1992; Larochelle & Pineau, 1994).

Especially dramatic in this clash between the network and the feature comparison models was the fact that Collins and Quillian (1972) had not devoted much attention to variables like typicality, either in the theory or in their empirical results. This meant that

FIGURE 6.6

Mean RTs to members of categories that are high, medium, or low in typicality. The RTs are considerably faster than in comparable studies because the category names were given at the beginning of a block of trials and did not change within the block. Thus, each trial consisted of only the target word, and subjects judged if it belonged to the given category name. (From Smith et al., 1974.)

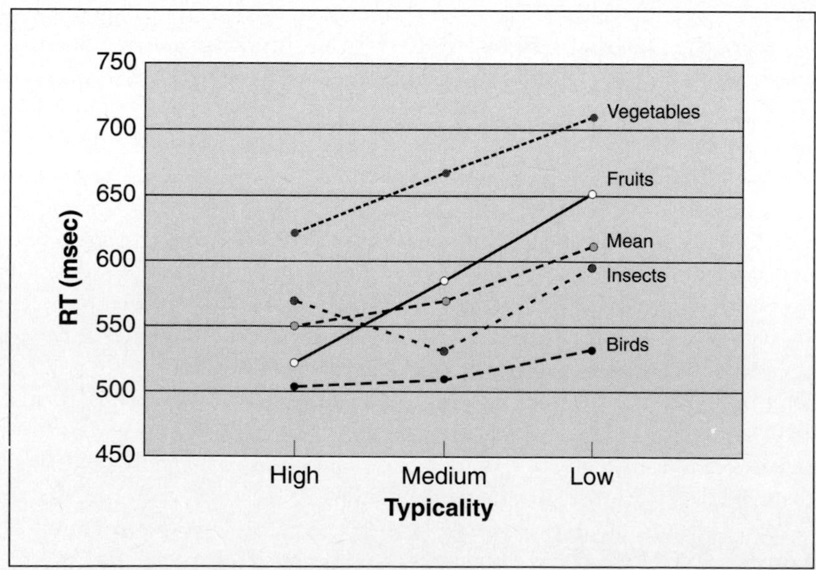

the Smith et al. (1974) demonstration was a bit of an embarrassment to the Collins and Quillian model, especially as the theoretical understanding of typicality, and of category prototypes (e.g., Rosch, 1975), grew.

RESOLVING THE CLASH BETWEEN MODELS

On the other hand, as more research on semantic memory became available, several other issues were raised that tipped the scale back toward the network model. We'll cover two of these now, concerning the principle of cognitive economy and the verification of property statements. But we need to spend considerable time on a third issue, the issue of priming, since it's absolutely key to an understanding of semantic processing. We'll devote the entire next section to it, and then return to it repeatedly throughout the rest of the book.

Cognitive Economy

Quillian's (1968) original TLC model was absolutely clear on one point, that redundant information is *not* stored in semantic memory. As he put it, "The sheer quantity of information . . . argues strongly that both the human subject's memory and our model thereof contain as little redundancy as possible and that it [should] contain stored facts only when these cannot otherwise be generated or inferred" (p. 228). This position has been given the name **cognitive economy:** To economize in the number of concepts that must be stored, only nonredundant facts will be stored in memory.

If you'll look back at Figure 6.2, you'll see this illustrated—FLIES *could* be stored as a property of ROBIN, CANARY, MUDLARK, and so on, but it's not. Instead, the principle of cognitive economy dictated that FLIES is stored only once, at its highest level of generality. Quillian's model claimed this principle for two reasons. First was his point about inference—properties like FLIES can be *inferred* from the superordinate category, so it would be needlessly repetitive to store them for every single bird in semantic memory. Second, notice that Quillian was programming a computer in the 1960s, when computer memory was severely limited. From this very practical standpoint, it made sense for Quillian to limit storage to just the information that could not be inferred or otherwise generated.

There is clearly a grain or two of truth to the cognitive economy idea. After all, it strains the imagination to suppose that we fill memory with such facts as "the philosopher Aristotle had two hands," that we would waste mental effort and space in such a colossal fashion (although no one claims that there is some finite limit on the amount that can be stored in human memory). On the other hand, doesn't the principle of cognitive economy imply that once you learn a general property you'd have to "erase" or forget that fact about specific concepts? Wouldn't you have to delete the ROBIN-FLIES connection from memory once you learn the more general connection between BIRD and FLIES? Such erasure or forgetting is a rather difficult position for psychologists to swallow, given what we know about forgetting from long-term memory.

Indeed, evidence was soon reported that showed the flaws in the strict cognitive economy principle. For example, C. Conrad (1972) asked a sample of college students to write down properties of a variety of concepts (like "robin," "banjo," "onion," etc.). She then tabulated the frequency with which different properties occurred in these written listings, and found that this frequency was a better explanation of RT results than the hierarchical levels originally tested in Collins and Quillian (1969). In other words, referring back to Figure 6.3, a sentence like "A canary has skin" was slower than "A canary can fly" because SKIN is simply stored more weakly with CANARY than FLIES is—no need to presume that SKIN has to be inferred from two levels up in the hierarchy. More generally, Conrad found that there was very little evidence for the economical scheme implied by cognitive economy—properties at various levels in the hierarchy seemed to be stored *repeatedly*, not in the overly tidy, nonredundant fashion implied by Quillian (see also Ashcraft, 1978), but in a redundant, messy, cluttered semantic network instead.

Property Statements

While Conrad's (1972) research was "bad news" for the Collins and Quillian model, it, along with several other studies, was also "bad news" for the Smith et al. (1974) feature model. Did you notice that the Smith et al. feature comparison model focused exclusively on superordinate statements, the *X is a Y* kind of statement? But Conrad and others began testing property statements, in which the sentence *asserts that some concept, X, has a certain property or characteristic, Y*—A robin *has* wings, *is* small, and so forth. How did the Smith et al. model cope with this slight change in methodology?

The answer was, Not too well. Consider "A robin has wings." The normal Smith et al. comparison process, you'll recall, was to access the feature lists for both concepts, then do a global stage I comparison on these lists, followed by a stage II evaluation if necessary. To be consistent, the model had to make the same predictions for property statements too. Thus, the model claimed that you access the feature lists for both concepts, your concept of ROBIN and your concept of THINGS WITH WINGS. You would then conduct the regular feature-overlap comparison process on these two feature lists.

Several aspects of this explanation were problematic, it turned out. One peculiarity involved categories like THINGS WITH WINGS, or to use a Smith et al. example, BROWN THINGS (as in "An ostrich is brown"). It seems a bit far-fetched that we actually have concepts or categories in semantic memory corresponding to THINGS WITH WINGS or BROWN THINGS, each with its own feature list. And if we did, what features would be on such lists? Aside from *is brown*, what other features might be on the BROWN THINGS list? A third difficulty was also offered: If WINGS is already on the feature list for ROBIN, why would the feature comparison process even be necessary? Aside from the fact that feature comparison was the fundamental process hypothesized by the Smith et al. model, it didn't really seem necessary for properties like WINGS. All in all, it seemed that the Smith et al. model had been so narrowly focused on superordinate statements that it simply didn't generalize satisfactorily even to slightly different sentences like property statements.

In contrast, network models contained both property and superordinate pathways, so had no difficulty in explaining how people verify property statements—the same intersection search process applies to both. Furthermore, the troublesome distinction between defining and characteristic properties was not in Collins and Quillian's network model, whereas Smith et al. had some difficulties in convincing researchers that such a distinction even existed, much less that it was as central to semantic memory processes as they had proposed (but see Malt, 1990, for the influence of subjects' *beliefs* that there are defining features for some categories). And finally, Collins and Loftus (1975) suggested that it seemed quite arbitrary—and probably wrong—that the Smith et al. model stored any and all features about a concept *except* for that concept's superordinate, that is, the important information about which category it belongs to. If semantic memory is as untidy and redundant as the research was showing, they reasoned, why not accept as fact that people *do* store category membership along with all sorts of other information?

The Revised Network Model—Semantic Relatedness

★ Figure 6.7 shows some of the ways the original network model proposed by Collins and Quillian (1969; 1972) changed in response to accumulating research—the figure is sim-

★ **FIGURE 6.7**

A revised semantic network.

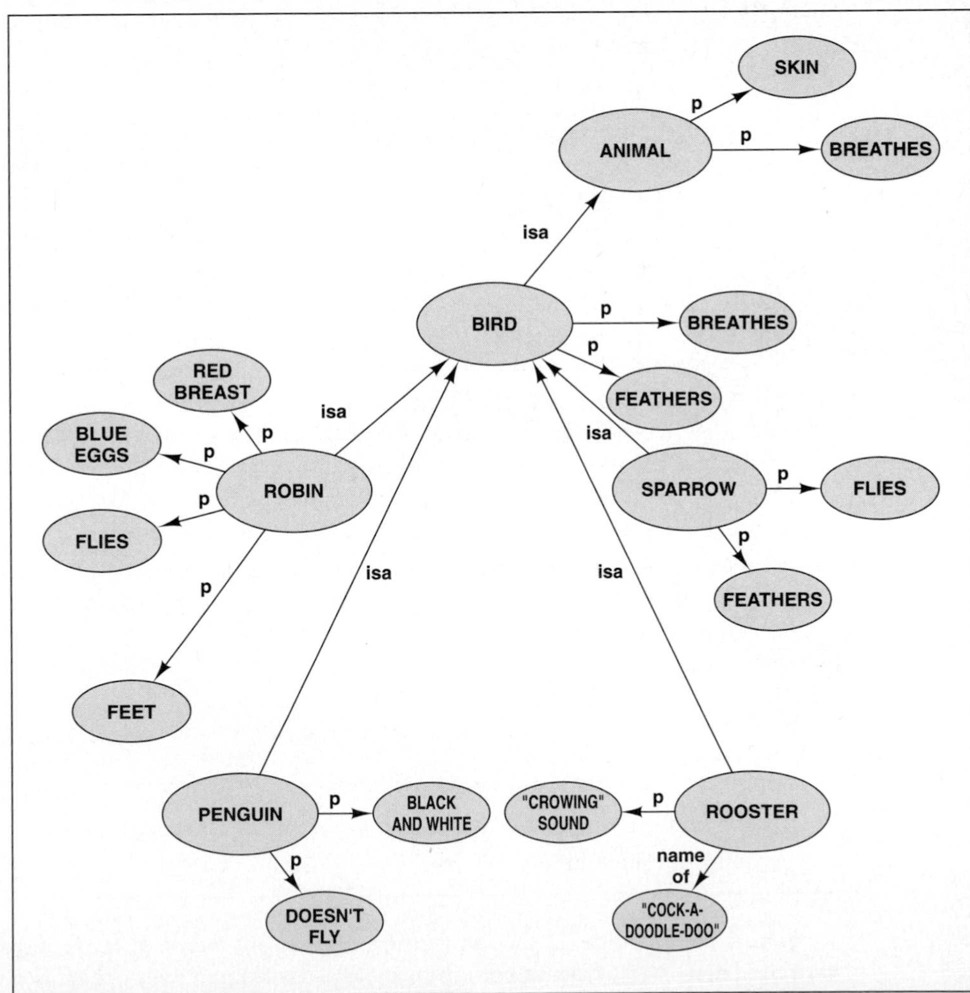

plified in other respects, to highlight the changes. The biggest two changes involved *typicality* and *cognitive economy*. In the revised network model (Collins & Loftus, 1975), the lengths of the pathways now clearly reflect how strongly or weakly two concepts are related—short paths indicate a close relationship, and long paths a weak one. Thus, ROBIN and SPARROW are particularly typical members of the BIRD category, illustrated with short pathways, whereas PENGUIN and ROOSTER are very *atypical*, as shown by the long paths. Second, notice that several redundant properties are shown in the figure—FLIES is stored with ROBIN and SPARROW as well as BIRD, and so forth.

While diagrams of such structures become very cluttered, the advantages to semantic theory are considerable. In particular, the network now captures the most important principle identified so far in the research on semantic memory, the principle of **semantic relatedness.** This principle, that related concepts are stored closely together in the network, with strong connecting pathways, summarizes the results reported in the literature. That is, when two concepts are being compared, or when a connection between the concepts is being retrieved, the underlying mental processes are heavily affected by the degree of semantic relationship between the concepts.

Summary

1. The earliest proposal for human semantic memory was the Collins and Quillian network model. Semantic memory was hypothesized to be a network of semantic nodes, with the relationships among concepts coded as pathways between the nodes. The major mental process in the network was one of spreading activation and intersection search.
2. Collins and Quillian's model had a competitor in Smith et al.'s feature comparison model. Smith proposed that concepts in semantic memory can be represented as lists of features, and that decisions were based on a two-stage feature comparison process.
3. Early research suggested that human semantic memory does not follow the principle of cognitive economy, and that varying degrees of typicality within categories needed to be explicitly acknowledged. Collins and Loftus revised the model to account for these effects. Conversely, the necessary revision of Smith et al.'s model to accommodate property statements was not persuasive to most researchers.
4. Semantic memory is now generally assumed to reflect the important effect of semantic relatedness, that the structure of the semantic network reflects the semantic relationships among concepts.

Priming in Semantic Memory

Preview: the terminology of priming; basic priming effects; priming across tasks; priming and automaticity

Think back a bit to the section on the all-important mental process of spreading activation. There were four important principles associated with this idea—activation spreads, the spreading takes time, activation becomes diffused as it spreads farther out from the origin, and the activation decays across time. Researchers immediately began testing these ideas, especially as they related to the principle of semantic relatedness. That is, if semantic relatedness is the organizing principle for semantic memory, then relatedness should determine a great deal about the spread of activation through that structure. Researchers wondered exactly how far out into the network activation spreads, and how long-lasting the effect of activation would be? Does more activation spread to highly related concepts? Does it decay faster for less related concepts?

Why all this interest in the process of spreading activation, the mental **priming** of concepts? The reason is straightforward—priming is very possibly the most fundamental process of retrieval from semantic memory. It has become one of the most frequently tested—and argued about (e.g., McNamara, 1992; Ratcliff & McKoon, 1988)—effects in the study of long-term memory, with dozens of articles appearing yearly. It's absolutely key to an understanding of semantic processing—we'll return to it repeatedly throughout the entire book. So you need to understand priming, how it affects basic semantic memory processing, and how it has been studied.

PRIMING TASKS

Nuts and Bolts of a Priming Task

In Chapter 3, priming was defined as the activation of a word and its meaning. It was part of the automatic process of word access observed in the Stroop task (remember? name the color of ink). But priming is a bit more general than that, in that it refers to activation of any concept in memory, whether that concept is named by a word or not.

▲ Let's introduce some precise vocabulary for priming, to facilitate the explanation that follows; Figure 6.8 (p. 182) gives an illustration. To begin with, we have the

- **Prime:** Any stimulus that is presented first, to see if it influences some later process. This is simple enough, you'll agree. The term is also used as a verb, as when we say that a stimulus *primes* some later information.

Next is the

- **Target:** The stimulus that follows the prime; the target *is* that later information. It is the presumed *destination* of the activation or priming process, the concept we believe may be affected by the prime. So, primes precede the targets, and targets are primed, i.e., are influenced by the primes.

When this influence is beneficial, for instance when the target is easier or faster to process because it was primed, this positive influence on processing is referred to as **facilitation;** sometimes we simply call this **benefits.** Facilitation is almost always a speedup of RTs (i.e., lower RT), compared to performance in a baseline condition. Occasionally, the influence is negative, as when a prime is unrelated to the target, and therefore is misleading or irrelevant. When the prime slows down RT performance to the target, the negative influence on processing is called **inhibition;** in this case, we also say that there were **costs** associated with the prime.

FIGURE 6.8

A depiction of two types of priming tasks.

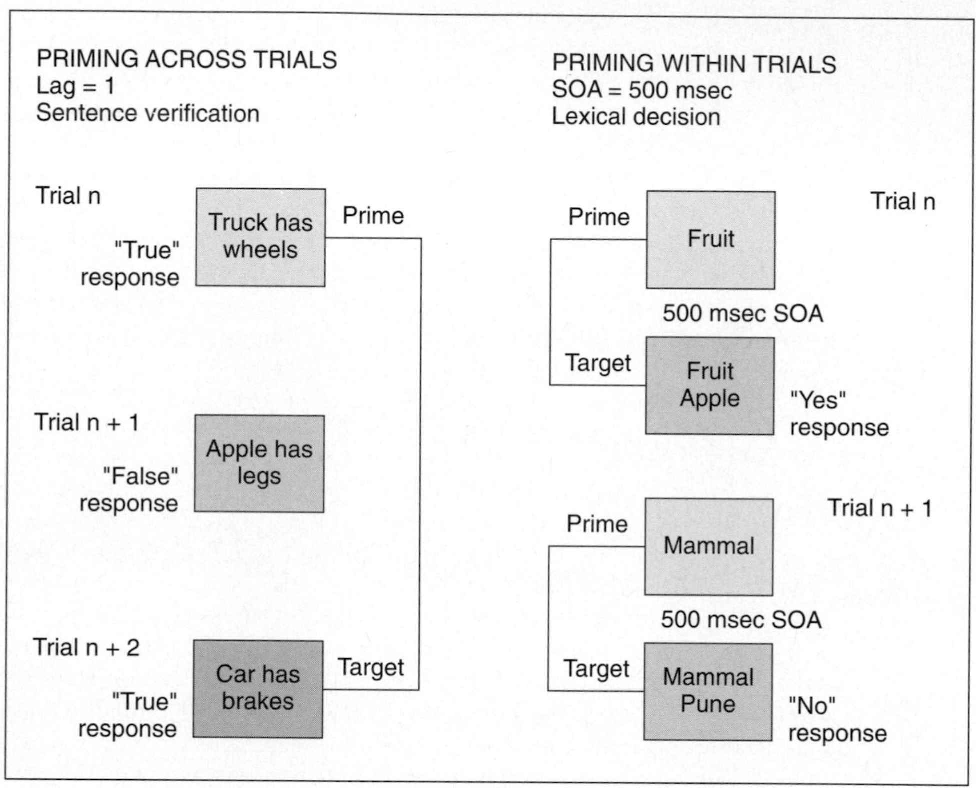

Priming Across Trials Finally, since we're interested in how long activation takes to dissipate, we often need to keep track of the period of time that intervenes between the prime and the target. In some studies, this period of time is filled with other stimuli or trials. In this case, the **lag** between prime and target, usually the number of intervening stimuli, is our index of the separation between prime and target. So for example, lag 2 would simply mean that two trials came between the prime and the target.

Priming Within Trials In other kinds of priming studies, the prime and target are presented within the same trial. In these studies, the time interval between the prime and the target is of interest. This period of time is called the **SOA,** the **stimulus onset asynchrony.** If you consider the prime and target to be the two halves of a complete stimulus, then the onset or beginning of the two halves occurs *asynchronously*, at different times. Thus, we might present a prime, and then 500 milliseconds later present the target. This would correspond to an SOA interval of 500 milliseconds. So the definition of SOA is the length of time between the onset of the prime and the onset of the target.

PROVE IT

If you believe that you *can* rapidly activate words based on a letter prime, try the following demonstration. Check your watch, then give yourself 10 seconds to name as many words as you can that begin with *D*. You'll be surprised at how few you can name. Now, contrast that with naming members of a semantic category for 10 seconds—say, fruits or trees.

Empirical Demonstrations of Priming

Let's consider a pair of experiments on word naming, an early report by Freedman and Loftus (1971), and one by Loftus and Loftus (1974) that built on the earlier result. Both were studies of priming within semantic memory.

Freedman and Loftus (1971) were interested in the process of word naming and retrieval, and how that process was affected by priming. They asked their participants to name a member of a category that either began with a certain letter or was described by a certain adjective; for example, "name a *fruit* beginning with *P*," or "name a red flower." On half of the trials, participants saw either the letter or the adjective as a prime, and then the category name as the target. In the other half of the trials, the reverse order was used—the category name was the prime, and the letter or adjective was the target.

Freedman and Loftus found clear evidence that the category name is an effective prime. In their data, performance was significantly faster for trials like "fruit–P" than trials when the letter or adjective served as the prime ("P–fruit" or "red–fruit"). This suggested that the category name activated its semantic representation, and that this activation then spread to the members of the category. When the letter or adjective was presented, a relevant member of the category such as Plum or Apple had already been primed, so was faster to retrieve from semantic memory. Conversely, letter or adjective primes had very little effect—which is another way of saying that there is no "category" in semantic memory corresponding to "words beginning with *P*" or "red things."

A Demonstration of Priming Across and Within Trials Loftus and Loftus (1974) used this word-naming task again, but with two twists. Often during the experiment, a trial like "fruit–P" was followed by *another* "fruit" trial—the first "fruit" trial was the prime, and the second was the target. (Don't get confused here. Not only was one trial the prime for a target trial, but within a trial there was also a prime and a target, for example "fruit–P," just as in the earlier experiment.) Sometimes the target trial followed immediately, at a lag of 0, and sometimes at a lag of 2, when two unrelated trials intervened. The results are shown in panel A of Figure 6.9 (p. 184).

Notice three things about the results. First, seeing the category name as a prime (seeing it first) always yielded faster performance than seeing letters as primes—the dashed line is at least 100 milliseconds lower at every point on the graph. This is exactly what Freedman and Loftus (1971) found. Second, the points shown at lag 0 are considerably

FIGURE 6.9

Priming results from Loftus and Loftus (1974). Reaction time in seconds is shown for simultaneous presentation of the prime and target (panel A) and an SOA of 2.5 seconds (panel B). In both panels, the curves show RT to the prime ("initial") and the targets at lags 0 and 2. (From Loftus & Loftus, 1974.)

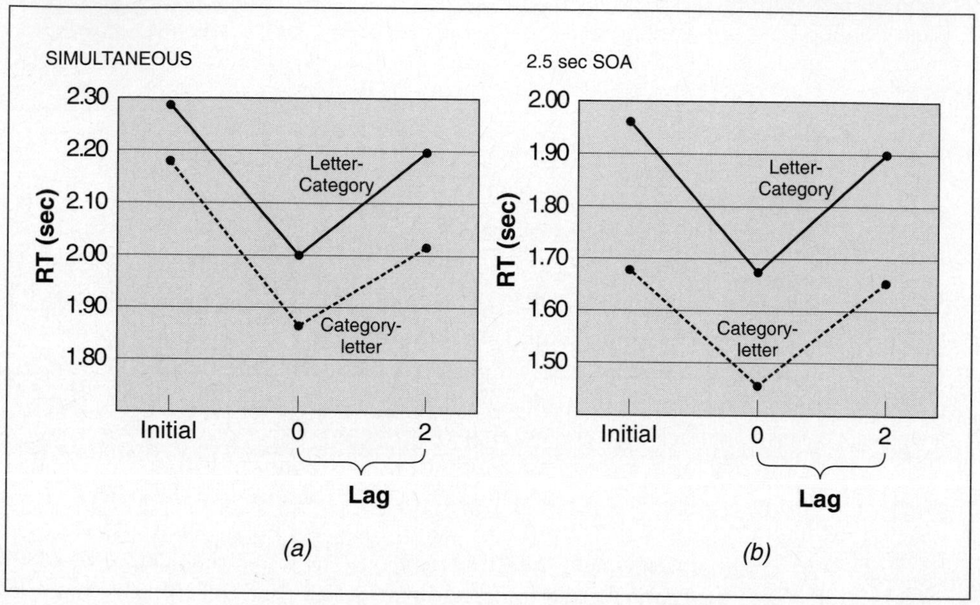

faster than the RTs for the initial prime trial. In other words, if you had just seen a "fruit–P" trial, then seeing another one ("fruit–A") immediately reduced the necessary processing time for the second trial, by at least 300 milliseconds. *That's* priming across trials. And third, notice that the priming effect at lag 2 isn't as strong as the effect at lag 0—performance was still faster than baseline, but not as fast as in the immediate priming condition. In other words, the priming from the initial trial had dissipated or decayed somewhat at lag 2—there was still a benefit; it just wasn't as strong.

The second twist in the Loftus and Loftus (1974) study is shown in panel B of the figure—priming *within* trials was also examined when the prime and target were separated in time. This part of the experiment was nearly the same as the first part, except that the prime (the category name or letter) appeared by itself for 2.5 seconds on every trial, and was then followed by the target. This was a manipulation of SOA, of course, the time between the two parts of a stimulus. So panel A shows what happened with simultaneous presentation, and panel B displays the results with a 2.5-second SOA.

What does panel B tell us? All of the curves there are lower than the equivalent curves in panel A. In other words, when participants saw the prime for 2.5 seconds, they could name a word that fit the letter restriction of the target more rapidly than when prime and target were simultaneous. There was more priming, a greater spread of activation, with the additional time—with more time, more of the members of the primed category became activated. This is exactly what the network model predicted about the spread of activation across time. Just as interesting, the priming also seemed to have decayed or dissipated across intervening trials, because lag 2 responses were slower than lag 1 responses.

Priming in Other Tasks

Similar outcomes have also been reported in several other tasks. For example, priming across trials has been reported using the sentence verification task (e.g., Ashcraft, 1976)—a sentence like "A sparrow has feathers" facilitated another sentence about the same category, for example, "A robin can fly," but only if the target sentence concerned a high frequent or important property.

Similarly, Rosch (1975) found significant priming within semantic categories, especially if the targets were typical members of the category. She used a matching task, in which pairs of words are presented and participants must say "yes" if both words belong to the same category. The primes for these word pairs were either the name of the category or, for the neutral prime condition, the word *blank*. With a 2-second SOA, word pairs that had been primed with the correct category name were significantly faster than those primed with *blank*. Of particular interest were the results for the other variable Rosch investigated, typicality. She found that priming was especially strong when the pair of words were typical members of the category (e.g., BIRD; robin sparrow). Priming of atypical members was significant, yet not nearly as strong.

Priming and the Lexical Decision Task

A very popular task in cognitive science, and one that has been used extensively to investigate priming, is the **lexical decision task.** You ran into a brief example of this at the beginning of this chapter—remember "Yes or no, MANTLE is a word? MANTY?" In this task, participants judge whether a string of letters is a word, and are (of course) timed as they make their decisions. The name of the task comes from the word *lexicon*, meaning a dictionary or a list of words. So in a sense, the lexical decision task asks you whether the string of letters is a genuine entry in your mental lexicon, your mental dictionary.

A huge range of topics has been investigated with the lexical decision task, including the priming and semantic relatedness effects we're interested in now. The task has also shown the intimate and unavoidable relationship between our semantic concepts and the words we use to name them—in other words, the relationship between the semantic and the *lexical* entries in memory.

The groundbreaking work on this task was reported by Meyer and co-workers (Meyer & Schvaneveldt, 1971; also Meyer, Schvaneveldt, & Ruddy, 1975). These investigators presented two letter strings at a time, and told their participants to make a "yes" decision only if *both* were words. In addition to trials with unrelated words like TRUCK PAPER, they included trials with related words like BREAD BUTTER (and of course, "yes" trials were matched with an equal number of "no" trials, on which at least one of the letter strings was not a word, e.g., CHAIR ZOOPLE).

The related condition yielded the most dramatic result in this study; two related words such as BREAD BUTTER are judged more quickly as "words" than two unrelated

TABLE 6.1

Priming in the Lexical Decision Task

Type of Stimulus Pair					
Top String	*Bottom String*	*Correct Response*	*Sample Stimuli*	*Mean RT (msec)*	*Mean Percent Errors*
Word	Associated word	Yes	Nurse-doctor	855	6.3
Word	Unassociated word	Yes	Bread-doctor	940	8.7
Word	Nonword	No	Book-marb	1087	27.6
Nonword	Word	No	Valt-butter	904	7.8
Nonword	Nonword	No	Cabe-manty	884	2.6

Source: From Meyer and Schvaneveldt (1971).

words, such as NURSE BUTTER. Table 6.1 displays Meyer and Schvaneveldt's (1971) results, and shows this priming effect quite clearly. Related words were judged in 855 milliseconds, compared to 940 milliseconds for unassociated words.

One particularly interesting aspect of these results—in fact of *all* results with the lexical decision task—is the following. It is not logically necessary for participants to access the *meanings* of words in the lexical decision task. Technically, they need only "look up" the words in the mental lexicon, to determine if the word is there or not. Yet, the results repeatedly show the influence of the meanings of the words—it is the *meaningful* connection between BREAD and BUTTER that facilitates this decision, rather than some lexical connection (you might think since both begin with *B* that there is a lexical basis for the facilitation, but the same benefits are found with word pairs that are quite dissimilar in spelling, for instance NURSE DOCTOR). It seems as if we cannot look up the lexical entry for a word without also accessing the word's meaning.

Priming Is Automatic

Interestingly, this facilitation appears to be quite automatic; that is, it happens extremely rapidly, and with no deliberate intention on your part. In fact, it's exactly the same effect that Stroop (1935) found with his color words (see Chapter 3). When you see a word, you access the word's meaning automatically, even though you aren't required to by the task.

Here's an example. Neely and associates (Neely, 1976, 1977; Neely, Keefe, & Ross, 1989) selected word pairs so that one of the members was the primary associate to the other at least 40 percent of the time (based on free-association norms). These related pairs were contrasted with unrelated word pairs, and also with a condition in which the neutral letter X was paired with a word. For all trials in the experiment, subjects had to judge whether the target string, the second member of each pair, was an English word—the standard lexical decision task. As Figure 6.10 shows, the processes involved in making these lexical decisions were greatly facilitated when the prime was a related, associated word. Benefits of priming grew from 17 milliseconds at the shortest SOA, to 56 milliseconds with a 2000-millisecond (2-sec) SOA. And inhibition was observed for the unre-

FIGURE 6.10

Priming effects across SOAs. The numbers in parentheses are the error rates in each condition. (From Neely, 1976.)

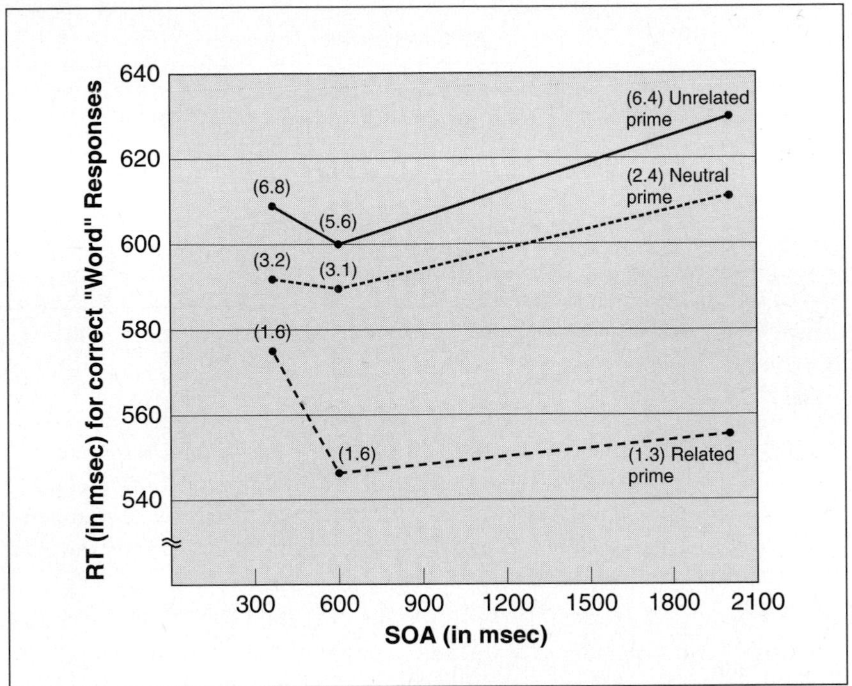

lated word pairs; there was a relatively constant 16-millisecond cost of receiving an unrelated word as a prime.

But how do we know this priming is automatic? In a more thorough examination of priming, Neely (1977) tested not only the effects of semantic relatedness on performance in the lexical decision task, but also the effects of SOA. The thinking here is that *expecting* to see a related word probably reflects a very conscious process, one that takes place rather slowly. But responding more quickly to a related word when you've had very little time to prepare or develop an expectancy should be evidence of automatic priming, literally automatic spread of activation.

Neely (1977) tested these ideas using—you guessed it—the lexical decision task. On each trial, participants saw a letter string and had to make a standard lexical decision. Each letter string was preceded by a prime, either a related word, an unrelated word, or a neutral prime, the baseline condition. Table 6.2 (p. 188) summarizes the experiment and shows sample stimuli. Because the results are a bit complicated, we'll take them in stages.

- First, Neely found standard semantic priming in his experiment. For prime-target trials like BIRD-robin, there was significant facilitation, as shown in panel A of Figure 6.11 (p. 189) (notice that any point above the dashed baseline indicates facilitation,

TABLE 6.2

Conditions and Stimuli for Neely's (1977) Study

Condition	*Sample Stimulus*[a]
	No Category Shift Expected
No shift	BIRD–robin
Shift	BIRD–arm
Category Shift Expected from Building to "Body Part"; from Body to "Part of a Building"	
No shift	BODY–heart, BUILDING–window
Shift to expected category	BODY–door, BUILDING–leg
Shift to unexpected category	BODY–sparrow

[a]Prime is in capital letters.

and any point below baseline indicates inhibition). Because he found this speedup even at very short SOAs, the conclusion is that normal semantic priming is automatic—the spread of activation happens very rapidly. Notice also that this curve showed more facilitation as the SOA got longer. This suggests that with more and more time to prepare for the letter string, priming grew stronger due to the additional effect of conscious factors.

- Second, he found significant inhibition, a slowing down of RT, when the prime was unrelated to the target. If you had seen BIRD as a prime, you were then slower than baseline to decide that *arm* was a word. Not surprisingly, this inhibition effect grew stronger across longer and longer SOAs—again, the conscious preparation for a member of the bird category worked against you when you saw *arm* as the target.

The truly impressive (and complicated) part of Neely's study comes next. He told his participants that when they saw one particular prime, the category name BODY for example, they should *expect* to see a target from a different category, for instance, a part of a building like "door" or "window." Likewise, they were told that if they saw FRUIT as a prime, they should expect to see a body part like "arm" as the target. In other words, participants were essentially told "Expect a switch to a *different* category when we show you these particular primes."

What happened with these expectations?

- When the switch from one category (BODY) to a different one ("door") really happened, there was significant priming *only* at the long SOAs, as shown in the top curve on panel B of Figure 6.11. This makes perfectly good sense, if you'll stop and think about it. You see BODY. It takes you a bit of time to remember that you were told you'd probably see part of a building as a target. When you're given that time, then you're ready for "door," "window," and so forth. But notice in the figure that at the shortest SOA, there was *no* facilitation on this kind of trial—BODY–door was no faster than baseline. Clearly, at short SOAs there wasn't enough time to prepare for the category shift.

FIGURE 6.11

Results from Neely's (1977) experiment on priming and expectancy.

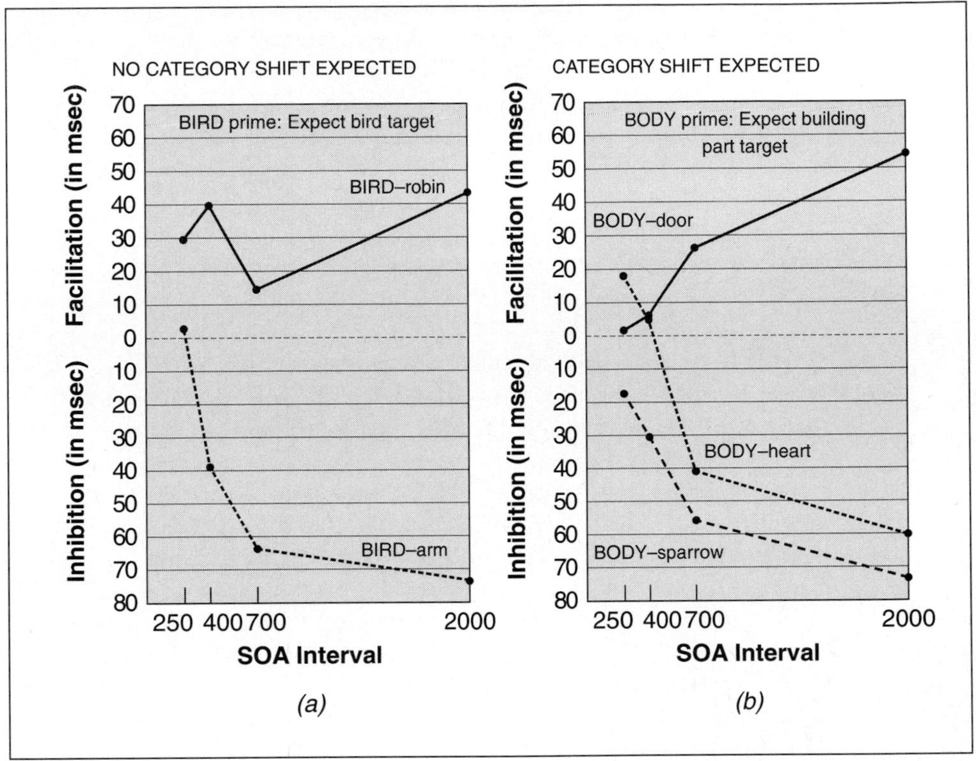

- Finally, what about that small percentage of trials when the category switch *didn't* occur, that is, when you saw BODY but then saw "heart" or "leg" as the target? The clever thing about this condition, of course, is that it should tap into normal semantic priming, since "heart" and "leg" are in the BODY category. This was exactly what Neely found, *but only at short SOAs*. When longer preparation time was given, with longer SOAs, participants could and did prepare for the category switch. Then when it *didn't* happen, they were slowed down, as shown in the bottom curve of panel B in the figure.

Priming Is an Implicit Process

Accessing a word's meaning is automatic (e.g., Friedrich, Henik, & Tzelgov, 1991). Can it occur even without conscious awareness of having seen the word? Marcel (1980, 1983) reported an impressive set of results that seem to answer "yes" to this question. Marcel examined word recognition in a lexical decision task with priming. He presented the primes in a rather different way than was typical, however—the prime was immediately followed by a scrambled visual pattern, a "visual mask." The purpose of this was to present the masking pattern so soon after the prime that subjects were not consciously aware of the prime word at all, a form of backward masking (see "Visual Sensory Memory—Where the Visual Information Goes" in Chapter 2).

The task worked. Subjects claimed they had not seen a prime at all—there was no conscious awareness of the prime. And yet, relevant primes such as CHILD facilitated lexical decisions about words such as *infant*.

These results suggest that semantic priming occurs both automatically and without any conscious awareness. In terminology introduced in Chapter 1, this is called an implicit effect—the mental process occurs without any necessary involvement of conscious awareness. Although Marcel's initial findings generated some controversy (e.g., Carr & Dagenbach, 1986; Merikle, 1982), recent evidence (e.g., Hirshman & Durante, 1992) indicates that the effect is genuine and widespread. Semantic priming, at least in the lexical decision task, can indeed occur automatically, without conscious identification of the prime.

We'll return to implicit memory effects again in the next chapter, and also in Chapter 10 when we talk about amnesia. For now, think of priming as a two-component process. As you've been reading, a significant degree of priming is obtained under very rapid conditions, for instance SOAs less than 250 milliseconds. Such a rapid effect suggests strongly that priming can operate automatically, without the need for conscious awareness or recollection. Participants in Neely's (1977) experiment showed this kind of automatic priming effect when they saw normal, straightforward primes and targets, for instance, BIRD-robin, at very rapid SOAs. This is the essence of **implicit memory.**

Explicit memory, on the other hand, refers to intentional, deliberate, and conscious mental processing, including recollection and awareness (e.g., Schacter, 1989). In Neely's (1977) "expect a switch" conditions, it took some extra amount of time for participants to switch from BODY to the expectation of "part of a building." But once they did, then there was also a priming effect, this due to more conscious processing. Because they had to deliberately remember to switch, this was an explicit memory priming effect.

It may be some time before cognitive science figures out how all the pieces fit together in this distinction between implicit and explicit memory. But even now, there seems to be agreement that priming has a clear implicit basis—there can be priming effects even in cases when the participants have lost the ability to recall information consciously, that is, in cases of amnesia (see Chapter 10).

Summary

1. Priming tasks have become important tools for understanding the process of retrieval from semantic memory. A prime is presented, followed by a target, to see if performance to the target is either facilitated or inhibited because of the prime. The prime and target can appear on the same trial, separated by a time interval called the SOA, or can appear on different trials, separated by different lags.
2. Significant priming, especially facilitation, is observed for semantic retrieval under both across-trials and within-trials conditions. A category name in particular serves as a facilitating prime for retrieval of category members, especially for highly typical members of the category.

3. The lexical decision task—deciding if a letter string forms a word—is a particularly important task for investigating priming. Evidence from this task shows how rapidly priming can operate, suggesting that priming is an automatic process, and how conscious expectation can also serve a priming function.
4. Rapid, automatic priming is taken as a clear example of an implicit memory effect, when no conscious awareness of the process is necessary. Slower effects based on expectation, and any effects that require conscious recollection of experiences, are explicit memory effects.

Context and Connectionism

Preview: the importance of networks; context effects as priming; connectionism and connectionist models in semantic memory

As mentioned earlier, the original Collins and Quillian (1972) model needed a few revisions, to account for results that accumulated shortly after its publication. But interestingly, no major revision was ever attempted for the Smith et al. (1974) model. The reason, in retrospect, was clear—nothing in the Smith et al. model, no mechanism or process, seemed able to account for the all-important effect of priming. In essence, the major contender to the network approach seemed to drop out of the running.

At about the same time, investigators in the mid- to late 1970s began to examine much more complex semantic relationships and representations than the simple semantic categories you've been reading about. Research began on the comprehension of complex sentences and paragraphs, of connected text, and of spoken conversations. People became interested in large-scale semantic representations that involved distinctly episodic as well as semantic knowledge. The (unspoken) consensus in most of this work was that network approaches, especially when coupled with the process of priming, provided a convenient, flexible, and powerful way of attacking these psychological processes. Networks had, in a sense, proved their usefulness in explaining the basics of semantic memory, so were now being expanded into more complex areas—with great success.

CONTEXT

The dictionary defines **context** as

1. the parts of a sentence, paragraph, discourse, etc., immediately next to or surrounding a specified word or passage and determining its exact meaning.
2. the whole situation, background, or environment relevant to a particular event, personality, creation, etc.

Let's take two examples. What does the word *count* mean? Well, you can't really say, can you, because it's **ambiguous,** it has more than one meaning. Maybe putting the word in a sentence will help—"We had trouble keeping track of the count." Most of us would agree that the sentence doesn't help much—you still can't tell which meaning of the word is intended.

What's missing? *Context.* With an adequate context, you'll be able to determine which sense of the word *count* I have in mind. Consider two different contexts.

My dog wasn't included in the final count.
The vampire was disguised as a handsome count.

These sentences, taken from Simpson's (1981, 1984) work on ambiguity, point out the importance of context—with adequate context, one that helps you determine the intended meaning, the correct word meaning can be retrieved from memory, even when the word is ambiguous in isolation. In fact, Simpson found that with neutral contexts, like the "We had trouble" sentence above, word meanings are activated as a simple function of their commonness—the number sense of *count* is more common, so that meaning becomes activated to a greater degree. But a context sentence that biases the interpretation one way or the other results in much stronger activation for the biased meaning—with *vampire* you activated the meaning of *count* related to royalty and Count Dracula (see also Balota & Paul, 1996; Paul, Kellas, Martin, & Clark, 1992; M. C. Smith, Besner, & Miyoshi, 1994).

Think about this again—the context sentence led to activation of one or the other meaning of the ambiguous word. Isn't that *exactly* what happens when you see a prime? Doesn't the prime BIRD activate typical members of that category in semantic memory, allowing faster retrieval of "robin" and "sparrow"? Yes—the effect of context seems to be precisely the effect of priming that you've been reading about.

★ Let's consider the second example. Read the story in Table 6.3 now.

What? Such a disjointed paragraph—what's it *talking* about? In Bransford and Johnson's (1972) study, reading this paragraph in this fashion resulted in very poor recall, and very low comprehension ratings. But a different group of participants was given the topic—Washing Clothes—before reading the paragraph. This group recalled more than twice as many idea units than the No Topic group. (You're in the Topic After group, since

★ **TABLE 6.3**

The procedure is actually quite simple. First you arrange items into different groups. Of course one pile may be sufficient depending on how much there is to do. If you have to go somewhere else due to lack of facilities that is the next step; otherwise, you are pretty well set. It is important not to overdo things. That is, it is better to do too few things at once than too many. In the short run this may not seem important but complications can easily arise. A mistake can be expensive as well. At first, the whole procedure will seem complicated. Soon, however, it will become just another facet of life. It is difficult to foresee any end to the necessity for this task in the immediate future, but then, one never can tell. After the procedure is completed one arranges the materials into different groups again. Then they can be put into their appropriate places. Eventually they will be used once more and the whole cycle will then have to be repeated. However, that is part of life.

Source: From Bransford (1979, pp. 134–135).

you got the topic only after reading the paragraph. Your recall would be quite low too, unless you go back and read it again.)

The reason for these effects was, understandably, *context*. With the topic beforehand, you're given sufficient context to interpret the ideas, and consequently can remember them much better. It's clear, in this situation, that the topic enables you to prime relevant knowledge in semantic memory, essentially your knowledge about washing clothes. And with such priming, relevant concepts are activated, guiding your comprehension and enhancing your memory. In short, what we're concluding here is that context effects serve the same function as priming, activating relevant knowledge, facilitating performance. In a real sense, context *is* priming.

CONNECTIONISM

A way to model the effect of priming in a semantic network is to use the modern computer-based approach to theorizing in cognitive science. This approach is **connectionism,** a framework in which interconnected nodes in a network, pathways, and priming can be studied. You had a small dose of this approach in Chapter 2, when we considered word recognition. You'll recall that the computer system was trying to recognize the word *WORK*, but that the final *K* was obscured. Because of connections among "letter level" and "word level" nodes, the system ended up identifying the word correctly.

At the most fundamental level, *connectionist models* (equivalent terms are *PDP models* and *neural net models*) contain a massive network of interconnected nodes. The nodes can represent virtually any kind of information, from the simple line segments and patterns Chapter 2 considered for letter recognition to the more complex features and characteristics we're discussing here, for instance "has wings," "red breast," "can fly," and so forth. Indeed, what makes connectionist models attractive is that, in principle, *any* type of knowledge can be represented by the nodes and their weighted, interconnecting pathways.

▲ Consider Figure 6.12 (p. 194), a sample connectionist network for part of the FURNITURE category (Martindale, 1991). First, you'll notice that each concept node is connected to other nodes by pathways, just as in all network models. The difference here is that each pathway has a number next to it, the *weighting* mentioned above. The weightings are the indicators of how strongly or weakly connected two nodes are; generally, the weighting scale goes from −1.0 to +1.0, with positive numbers indicating pathways that facilitate, and negatives indicating inhibition. So, for example, the weighting between FURNITURE and CHAIR is +0.8, indicating that CHAIR is an important, central member of the category; ASHTRAY, however, with its +0.1, is very weakly associated with FURNITURE.

If we present the category name FURNITURE to the model, heavily weighted members like CHAIR and SOFA will be highly activated, and the system can thus make decisions about them quite rapidly. This is exactly like the priming experiments you've been reading about—FURNITURE would prime CHAIR. But RUG might actually be slower than baseline with FURNITURE as a prime. To understand this, note first that the weighted connection from FURNITURE to RUG is quite weak. Second, because FURNITURE will prime CHAIR and SOFA a great deal, *these* nodes tend to inhibit, tend to spread "negative" activation, to RUG—see the weight of −0.8 between CHAIR and RUG. (When neighbors at the same level inhibit one another, this is called *lateral inhibition*.)

FIGURE 6.12

Part of a connectionist network for FURNITURE. (Adapted from Martindale, 1991.)

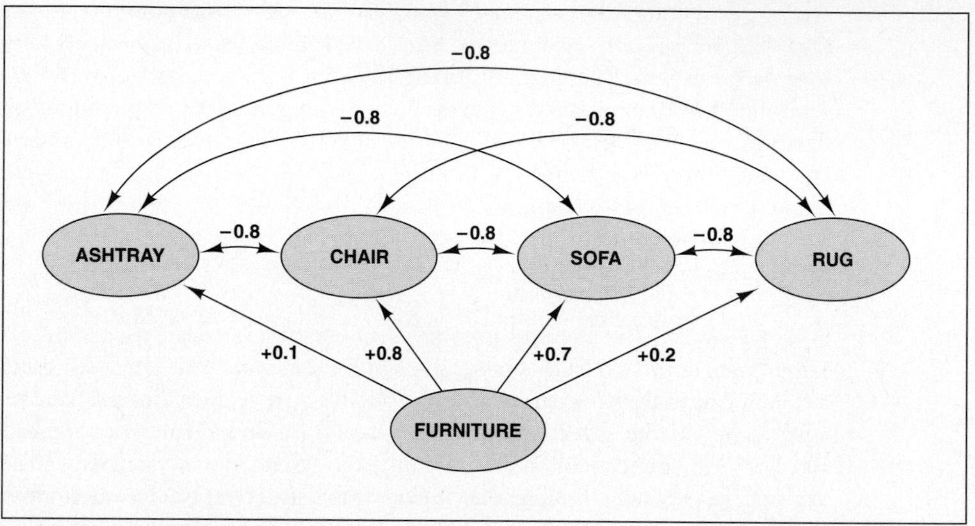

A considerable amount of effort has recently gone into building connectionist models of various cognitive structures and processes, for example, in letter identification (McClelland & Rumelhart, 1981) and word recognition (Seidenberg & McClelland, 1989). And in the area of semantic memory there is a model of semantic priming, by Masson (1995).

As Masson's discussion makes clear, the glimpse at connectionism here is rather simplified. In many respects, connectionist models make rather different assumptions—though rather similar predictions—than more typical spreading activation models, like the Collins and Loftus (1975) model. For instance, activating a node in a network model means activating that particular *point* in the network, followed by a spread of the activation to surrounding nodes. In a connectionist model (or, more precisely for Masson's approach, a distributed memory model), however, a concept is defined as a *pattern of activation* across units in the network. Priming, in this model, is explained by the similarity of activation patterns between a prime and a target—the FURNITURE concept has an overwhelmingly similar pattern of activation to the pattern for CHAIR, so the one serves as an effective prime for the other.

CONTEXT AND CONNECTIONISM

To give you a sense of the power of the connectionist approach, let's envision a connectionist model that produces semantic context effects during reading. We're going to build our model with two rather different types of "layers" or levels, to show how each layer can influence ongoing activity in the other layer (of course, a fully adequate model would need many more layers and processes than just these two). The model should give you some insight into the nature of connectionist explanations of cognition and illustrate why connectionism has attracted the interest of so many cognitive scientists.

The first layer we need involves word recognition. Let's adopt the Rumelhart and McClelland (1986) connectionist model that you studied in Chapter 2. As you recall, the model was able to recognize WORK even though the final K was partially obscured. The reason for this involved the interconnections between Letter Level Units and Word Level Units. In particular, knowledge at the Word Level—that WORK is a word but WORR is not—activated nodes in the Letter Level network, thus "helping" that level recognize the obscured letter as a K.

Now let's add a Semantic Level network of the kind we've been discussing, one in which related concepts can activate (or inhibit) others. You (or your participants in an experiment) are in the process of reading a sentence, say:

Because of all the heavy lifting, moving furniture is hard _______.

At the semantic level, concepts mentioned in the sentence are accessed or activated, and the positive and negative activation (called excitation and inhibition in these models) begins to spread throughout the semantic network. Especially because of words like "heavy" and "moving," nodes and pathways associated with concepts like SOFA should be especially activated. Conversely, concepts like ASHTRAY, which are rather atypical for the furniture category even at the outset, should become even more inhibited; this is the combined effect of the weak (+.1) weight between FURNITURE and ASHTRAY and the strong negative (–.8) weights from CHAIR and SOFA, as shown in Figure 6.12.

Have you guessed how the sample sentence finishes? The participants in your experiment have to name the final word, as rapidly as possible. The word you showed them is the partially obscured WORK. In addition to the facilitation due to the Word Level of the network, documented by Rumelhart and McClelland (1986), there is now an additional source of facilitation, the activation from the Semantic Level network. In essence, the word recognition component is now getting an extra benefit because of priming from the semantic network, a top-down influence based on meaning. Your participants—*and* the connectionist model—will be even faster at recognizing WORK because of the additional facilitation, due to the sentence context.

THE ESSENCE OF CONNECTIONISM

The connectionist approach emphasizes a rather different set of principles from earlier ways of understanding human cognition. For example, the information processing approach to cognition viewed mental processing as a sequence of independent, one-at-a-time stages, say, the sensory, short-term, and long-term memory components of the Atkinson and Shiffrin (1968) model. Connectionism, instead, emphasizes several different assumptions and principles (for complete treatments, see Martindale, 1991; Chapter 2 of Rumelhart & McClelland, 1986).

- Each network of knowledge, or "layer," consists of heavily interconnected nodes, with positive and negative connection weights coding the knowledge we possess.
- Nodes can be activated or inhibited by their weighted connections to other nodes. Learning and experience change the weights between nodes.

- Each network is heavily interconnected with the other networks, as the word recognition and semantic networks were in the FURNITURE–WORK example. These interconnections enable each network to influence activity in the other networks.
- Complex mental processes represent the combined effects of "massively parallel processing," that is, multiple levels of knowledge and activity going on simultaneously.

As you can see, what's exciting about connectionist models, despite their differences (and despite the ongoing debate about their usefulness; e.g., McCloskey, 1991; Seidenberg, 1993), is that the approach gives us a tool for understanding the richness of cognition. Connectionist models give us a working "machine" in a sense that lets us see what happens when multiple layers of knowledge influence even the simplest acts of cognition.

Summary

1. While the strictly feature comparison approach failed to predict priming, network models were quite successful at explaining how one concept influences performance to other, related concepts. As cognitive science grew more interested in larger-scale topics, like paragraph comprehension, network approaches dominated.
2. Investigations of more diverse processes, such as how ambiguous words are retrieved or how paragraphs are understood, revealed the importance of context to comprehension. Priming serves as a model for the effects of context.
3. Modern computer-based theories of cognition are often based on the principles of connectionism, where units are interconnected by weighted pathways, each capable of spreading activation through the structure. Connectionist models give us a functional tool for exploring the complexity of semantic memory.

Important Terms

ambiguity
cognitive economy
connectionism
context
defining features
facilitation/benefits
feature list
implicit/explicit memory
inhibition/costs
intersection
lag
lexical decision task
network
nodes
pathways
priming
prime/target
semantic features
semantic memory
semantic relatedness
sentence verification
stimulus onset asynchrony (SOA)
spreading activation
typicality effect

Suggested Readings

I still have not found a more useful introduction to semantic memory than the 1972 Collins and Quillian paper. It's thought-provoking, insightful, clever, and delightful to read. I would strongly encourage you to read it, to see how these authors manage to discuss generalization and discrimination, basic memory retrieval, imagery, metaphoric language, language comprehension, and computer simulation while maintaining a lively, often humorous style. It's a classic.

Beyond that paper, several reviews and summary papers on semantic memory exist; see, for instance, E. E. Smith (1978), and Kounios, Osman, and Meyer (1987), in which the hybrid model has both a network search and a feature list comparison process occurring simultaneously; the one that finishes first is the "winner," the one that determines RT to the stimulus. This approach suggests that at some deep level, network and feature list approaches are entirely compatible.

Research continues on the structure and processes of semantic memory; for example, on multiple primes that converge on a target (e.g., LION–STRIPES–TIGER; Balota & Paul, 1996), on social categories such as WORKER, EMPLOYER, and POLITICIAN (Dahlgren, 1985), and on "event categories" such as school activities and types of shopping (Rifkin, 1985). Look at a paper by L. C. Smith (1984) for a report on the "semantic satiation" effect, that after continued repetition of the same concepts, the spread of activation can actually slow down due to excessive priming. And consider how priming works in the following question: How many animals of each kind did Moses take onto the Ark? It's a "semantic illusion" (it was Noah, not Moses; see Erickson & Mattson, 1981).

CHAPTER SEVEN

MEMORY IN NATURAL SETTINGS

Before you read any further, take out two sheets of paper. On the first, write down the Billy's Dilemma story you read in the last chapter (hint: birthday party). And on the second, try to diagram the "bird portion" of the first semantic network you looked at in that chapter as completely as possible (hint: robin, sparrow, mudlark). Save these for demonstrations later in the chapter.

Leitmotif is a German word meaning "a dominant theme or underlying pattern" (*New World Dictionary*, 1980). It was originally used to describe the musical themes in Wagner's operas, but is now applied more generally to mean the dominant theme or idea in any work, musical, literary, or otherwise.

So, what's the *leitmotif* of this chapter, its dominant theme? It concerns "real" memories, memories of experiences, the kind of information we ordinarily use our long-term memories for. We're dealing with more realistic—and more complex—information than the previous two chapters. Here we're *not* asking you to learn and recall a list of 20 arbitrary words in the lab, *not* presenting simplified semantic statements like "A robin is a bird." These simple situations are important to study, of course, because they give us fundamental insights into how memory works, how knowledge is encoded, stored, and retrieved. The effects you've read about in Chapters 5 and 6 are literally the backbone of cognitive psychology (e.g., Kintsch, 1985).

But now we're ready to move beyond those simplified tasks and stimuli, and consider how long-term memory works in much broader contexts. So this chapter is about the *combination* of episodic and semantic memory, how these two different aspects of long-term memory work together, how they *integrate* our experiences. How well do we remember specific information we've learned, not a list of words in a memory experiment, but for example the math or Spanish we learned in high school? We're also interested in the distortions and failures of memory—for instance, how do two eyewitnesses come to "remember" the same event quite differently?

Schacter's (1996) eloquent book *Searching for Memory* captures the essence we're looking for—"Memory's Fragile Power." Long-term memory is awesomely powerful; at a moment's notice we can retrieve a stunningly wide variety of information, usually with little effort. And at one and the same time, our memories are easily disrupted, or *corrupted* such that we can't remember, we remember incorrectly, or we "remember" events that never happened.

Don't expect cognitive science to abandon the lab, or the insights it can furnish on complex issues like these (e.g., Banaji & Crowder, 1989; G. R. Loftus, 1983)—indeed you'll be reading about lab experiments all through this chapter. But the focus is different—how does long-term memory work when it encounters everyday, ordinary real-world experiences, when we "remember" meaningful situations and episodes in both laboratory and "natural contexts" (Neisser, 1982)?

Reconstructive Memory and Scripts

Preview: reconstructive versus reproductive memory; schemata as existing knowledge structures; scripts and script theory

BARTLETT AND RECONSTRUCTIVE MEMORY

War of the Ghosts

★ Table 7.1 contains a story called "The War of the Ghosts." The story is important not only because of the psychological points it raises, but also for historical reasons: Bartlett (1932) used it in one of the earliest research programs on remembering meaningful material. Do the demonstration in the table now, before reading any further.

Now that you have read and recalled the story, spend a moment jotting down some of the thoughts that occurred to you as you read and then tried to recall it. For example, if you remembered some specific details, comment on what made those details more memorable to you. Did you get most of the story line correct, or did you do some guessing? What was your sense of the story as you read it? You no doubt noticed what a peculiar story it was, with unfamiliar names and characters, with vague and hard-to-understand twists of the story line, and with unexplainable events. The story is a North Pacific Indian (Inuit—Eskimo) folktale, so it's not surprising that it differs so much from stories that are familiar or "normal" to you.

Once you've exhausted your intuitions, turn to Table 7.2 (p. 202) and compare your recalled version with the retellings in the table. While yours may be closer to the original, because so little time passed since you had read it, you should see several similarities to the tabled retellings.

Bartlett's Research

Bartlett (1932), not unlike Ebbinghaus (1885/1913/1964), wanted to study the processes of human memory with the methods of experimental psychology. Very much *unlike* Ebbinghaus, however, he wanted to study memory for meaningful material, so he used folktales, ordinary prose, and pictures in his investigations. Typically, his participants studied the material for a period of time, then recalled it several times, once shortly after

★ **TABLE 7.1**

Bartlett's (1932) "The War of the Ghosts"

Read the following, then attempt to reproduce the story by writing it down from memory.

One night two young men from Egulac went down to the river to hunt seals, and while they were there it became foggy and calm. Then they heard war-cries, and they thought: "Maybe this is a war-party." They escaped to the shore, and hid behind a log. Now canoes came up, and they heard the noise of paddles, and saw one canoe coming up to them. There were five men in the canoe, and they said:

"What do you think? We wish to take you along. We are going up the river to make war on the people."

One of the young men said: "I have no arrows."

"Arrows are in the canoe," they said.

"I will not go along. I might be killed. My relatives do not know where I have gone. But you," he said turning to the other, "may go with them."

So one of the young men went, but the other returned home.

And the warriors went on up the river to a town on the other side of Kalama. The people came down to the water, and they began to fight, and many were killed. But presently the young man heard one of the warriors say: "Quick, let us go home: that Indian has been hit." Now he thought: "Oh, they are ghosts." He did not feel sick, but they said he had been shot.

So the canoes went back to Egulac, and the young man went ashore to his house, and made a fire. And he told everybody and said: "Behold I accompanied the ghosts, and we went to fight. Many of our fellows were killed, and many of those who attacked us were killed. They said I was hit, and I did not feel sick."

He told it all, and then he became quiet. When the sun rose he fell down. Something black came out of his mouth. His face became contorted. The people jumped up and cried.

He was dead.

---

study and then again at later intervals. By comparing the successive attempts, Bartlett examined the progressive changes in what they remembered. (Interestingly, if you test your memory several times, with only short periods between tests, your performance often improves across tests, a phenomenon known as *hypermnesia;* e.g., Wheeler & Roediger, 1992. If substantial time intervenes between tests, however, then we see the more customary effect, greater forgetting across time.)

Bartlett's evidence suggested that memory for such meaningful material is not especially *reproductive*—that is, it does not reproduce or recall the original passage in the strict sense of those terms. Instead, memory performance seemed to be **reconstructive,** in which we construct a memory by combining elements from the original material with existing knowledge.

Two aspects of Bartlett's results led him to this conclusion. The first concerned *omissions,* information that his participants failed to recall. For the most part, subjects did not recall many details of the story, either specific names (e.g., Egulac) or specific events in

TABLE 7.2

Two Retellings of Bartlett's (1932) "The War of the Ghosts"

First recall, attempted about 15 minutes after hearing the story:

Two young men from Egulac went out to hunt seals. They thought they heard war-cries, and a little later they heard the noise of the paddling of canoes. One of these canoes, in which there were five natives, came forward towards them. One of the natives shouted out: "Come with us: we are going to make war on some natives up the river." The two young men answered: "We have no arrows." "There are arrows in our canoes," came the reply. One of the young men then said: "My folk will not know where I have gone"; but, turning to the other, he said: "But you could go." So the one returned whilst the other joined the natives.

The party went up the river as far as a town opposite Kalama, where they got on land. The natives of that part came down to the river to meet them. There was some severe fighting, and many on both sides were slain. Then one of the natives that had made the expedition up the river shouted: "Let us return: the Indian has fallen." Then they endeavored to persuade the young man to return, telling him that he was sick, but he did not feel as if he were. Then he thought he saw ghosts all round him.

When they returned, the young man told all his friends of what had happened. He described how many had been slain on both sides.

It was nearly dawn when the young man became very ill; and at sunrise a black substance rushed out of his mouth, and the natives said one to another: "He is dead."

Second recall, attempted about 4 months later:

There were two men in a boat, sailing towards an island. When they approached the island, some natives came running towards them, and informed them that there was fighting going on on the island, and invited them to join. One said to the other: "You had better go. I cannot very well, because I have relatives expecting me, and they will not know what has become of me. But you have no one to expect you." So one accompanied the natives, but the other returned.

Here there is a part I can't remember. What I don't know is how the man got to the fight. However, anyhow the man was in the midst of the fighting, and was wounded. The natives endeavored to persuade the man to return, but he assured them that he had not been wounded.

I have an idea that his fighting won the admiration of the natives.

The wounded man ultimately fell unconscious. He was taken from the fighting by the natives.

Then, I think it is, the natives describe what happened, and they seem to have imagined seeing a ghost coming out of his mouth. Really it was a kind of materialisation of his breath. I know this phrase was not in the story, but that is the idea I have. Ultimately the man died at dawn the next day.

---

the narrative (e.g., the phrase "His face became contorted"). The level of recall for the main plot and sequence of events wasn't too bad, but minor events were often omitted. As a result, the retellings of the story are considerably shorter than the original. Of course, the subjects were not asked for *verbatim* (word-for-word) recall, so rephrasing and condensing are to be expected. Nonetheless, there were significant and widespread losses of information in the recall protocols.

The second aspect of Bartlett's results is more fascinating. There was a strong tendency for the successive recalls to *normalize* the story. Basically, the retellings modernized and demystified the original, made the story more conventional—the ghost theme became less prominent across the retellings, and the "canoe paddling up the river" in the original became "a boat, sailing towards an island." Furthermore, there was an overwhelming tendency to add to and alter the story, to supply additional material that was not contained in the original and to drop unfamiliar or unusual ideas.

The critical issue here concerns the *source* of the additional material. Where did it come from, if not from the story itself? It came from the subjects' memories.

Schemata

Bartlett borrowed the term **schema** (*schemata* is the plural) to explain the source of these adjustments and additions. In his use of the term, a schema was "an active organisation of past reactions or past experiences" (1932, p. 201), essentially what we've been calling general world knowledge. More generally, a schema is a stored framework or body of knowledge about some topic. Bartlett claimed that when we encounter new material, such as the "Ghosts" story, we try to relate the material to our existing schemata. If the material does not match an existing schema, then we tend to alter the material to make it fit (similar in spirit to Piaget's concept of assimilation). As such, recall is not a true, exact recollection or reproduction of the original material. Instead, it is a reconstruction based on elements from the original story and on our existing schemata.

That's important—recall of meaningful material is not a true, exact recollection or reproduction. It is a *reconstruction*, in which parts of the original are integrated with existing knowledge. Go back to the Billy's Dilemma story on page 168 in Chapter 6, and compare it word for word, idea for idea, with your recall. Did you "remember" words that weren't in the original like *present* and *money?* Now look at that first semantic network (Figure 6.2) in Chapter 6 and compare it with what you diagrammed. You surely left out some of the concept nodes that were in Figure 6.2—maybe CANARY, FISH, MAMMAL, maybe SKIN, and so on. But did you include SPARROW and MUDLARK, because of the hint? The strong tendency here, of course, is to diagram what *you* know about BIRDS, not to limit yourself to the exact experience you had when you studied the figure (which didn't show either SPARROW or MUDLARK). And, interestingly, you probably didn't realize how your existing knowledge and the hints affected your recall.

An unimaginative way of looking at these results would be to claim that information already stored in memory is exerting an interference effect on current memory performance. We called it *proactive interference* in Chapters 4 and 5 (see also Dempster, 1985). A much more intriguing perspective is the following:

- Normal comprehension takes place within the context of an individual's entire knowledge system. As such, efforts to understand and remember meaningful material involve one's own meaning system or general knowledge of the world. In short, what we already know exerts a strong influence on what we remember about new material.

Extensions of Reconstructive Effects

Let's explore some extensions of these reconstructive memory effects, to see the importance of existing knowledge or schemata. For example, as you read in the last chapter, knowledge of the theme or topic of a passage improves your memory for the passage; this was the demonstration with the Washing Clothes paragraph (Bransford & Johnson, 1972; also Dooling & Lachman, 1971). On the other hand, providing a theme, say, by attaching a title to a story, can also distort recall or recognition in the direction of the theme.

A clever demonstration of this distortion effect was provided by Sulin and Dooling (1974). One group of participants read a paragraph about a fictitious character, which began:

> *Gerald Martin's seizure of power. Gerald Martin strove to undermine the existing government to satisfy his political ambitions. Many of the people of his country supported his efforts.* (p. 256)

A second group read the same paragraph, but the name Adolf Hitler was substituted for Gerald Martin. After a five-minute waiting period, the participants were shown a list of sentences and had to indicate whether each was exactly the same, nearly the same, or very different from one in the original story.

Preexperimental knowledge—that is, existing knowledge about Hitler—led to significant distortions in the subjects' recognition of sentences. Participants who read the Hitler paragraph rated sentences as "the same" more frequently when the sentences matched their existing knowledge about Hitler (e.g., "Hitler was obsessed by the desire to conquer the world," p. 259), even though the original passage contained no such information.

Furthermore, these **thematic effects,** as they were called, grew stronger in the group that was tested one week after reading the story. In Sulin and Dooling's second study, only 5 percent of the participants recognized, that is, said "yes," to the sentence "She was deaf, dumb, and blind," when they had read a story about Carol Harris. But 50 percent of the group that read the same story with the title *Helen Keller* recognized the sentence—and of course, no such sentence had been in either story (see also Dooling & Christiaansen, 1977). In both experiments, people responded "yes" to statements that referred to thematically consistent information, as if they were drawing inferences from their existing knowledge rather than remembering the passage on its own terms.

■ These effects are shown in Figure 7.1 (p. 205). Recognition scores were high when the recognition test occurred only five minutes after participants read the story, for both the fictitious (Carol Harris) and the famous (Helen Keller) character, even when the "foil" sentence ("deaf, dumb, and blind") was highly related to the theme. But after a one-week retention interval, recognition became very poor in that condition—this is the condition where 50 percent of the participants "recognized" the foil sentence.

Kintsch (1977) has pointed out that such results argue that recall for connected, meaningful passages shows *three* different kinds of influences,

- *reproductive* memory, in which we recall accurately certain aspects of the original passage,

FIGURE 7.1

Recognition scores. (From Sulin & Dooling, 1974.)

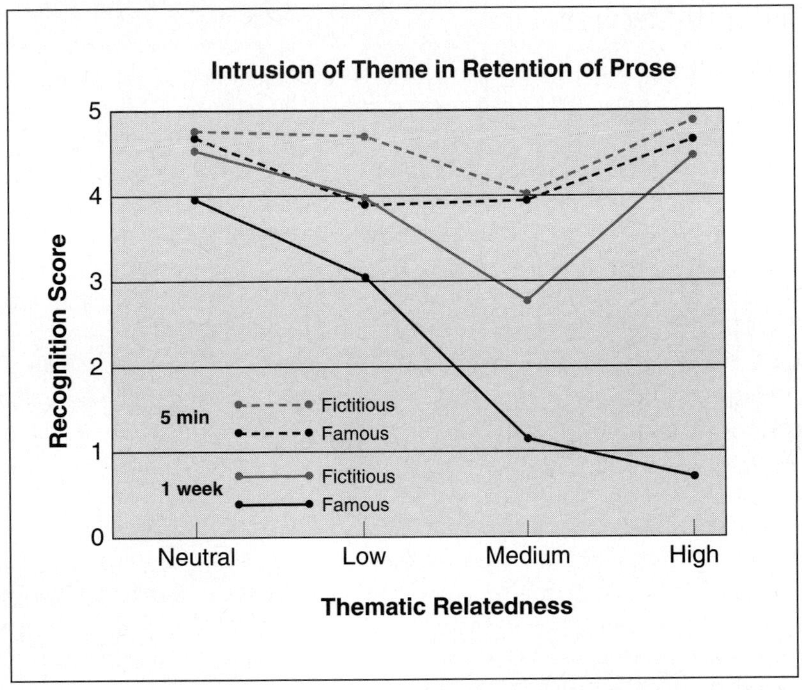

- *constructive* memory, in which the inferences we draw during comprehension become part of our memory for the passage, and
- *reconstructive* memory, in which we encorporate additional knowledge from memory after the fact, and then "recall" not the original passage but our elaborated version of it.

In general, it can be quite difficult to disentangle inferences drawn during original comprehension from those drawn during retrieval (but see Frederiksen, 1975), unless performance is tested both immediately after comprehension and then again at a later time. This of course introduces another complexity, since recalling a passage serves as rehearsal, which will influence a second recall attempt. But for now, just remember the most prominent feature of the results: *Existing knowledge can exert a tremendous influence on our memory for meaningful material.* As a normal by-product of comprehension, we relate new information to general knowledge already stored in memory. Later on, of course, our recollection is based on both of these, the information we comprehended and our general knowledge.

It is probably impossible to find a more convincing example of conceptually driven processing than this, the effect that existing knowledge has on current comprehension.

And it's a clear example of how episodic and semantic memory interact, how memory for a meaningful experience becomes integrated with existing knowledge.

SCRIPTS AS SCHEMATA

Although Bartlett (1932) used the term *schemata* to refer to the collections of existing knowledge, he expressed some dissatisfaction with the term because of the many different ways it had been used (pp. 200–201). A more modern way to refer to this knowledge is to call these knowledge structures **scripts,** large-scale semantic and episodic knowledge structures that accumulate in memory and guide interpretation and comprehension of ordinary experiences. In a very useful sense, scripts are the mental versions of true scripts. The scripts for *Hamlet* or *Phantom of the Opera* give the cast of characters, the settings, and the lines to be spoken in the play. Your *mental* scripts tell you about ordinary settings like a college class, going to a restaurant, or taking an airplane trip—who the people are, what they do, what happens, and so forth.

Scripts are considerably more detailed than the rather simple semantic memory concepts we've discussed, since people know considerably more about "real-world" concepts than the *isa* and *property* kinds of relationships of semantic memory. Think once more about the Billy's Dilemma story, and the knowledge you called up from memory in order to comprehend the story. *That*'s your "BIRTHDAY PARTY" script, your scripted knowledge of the events and characters associated with the birthday party setting.

The overall theory behind the notion of scripts is quite straightforward. People record in memory a generalized representation of events they have experienced, and this representation is *invoked* or retrieved when a new experience matches an old script. One function of a script, in either a written or spoken story, is that it provides a kind of "shorthand" for the whole event; you need not describe every element of the experience, but can merely refer to the whole event by invoking the script. More importantly, the activated script provides a framework within which new experiences can be understood, and within which a variety of inferences can be drawn to complete your understanding (Abbot, Black, & Smith, 1985; Reiser, Black, & Abelson, 1985; Seifert, Robertson, & Black, 1985).

Consider the following abbreviated stories, designed to illustrate the richness of your script knowledge (examples adapted from Schank & Abelson, 1977, pp. 38–40):

1. John was hungry. He went to a restaurant and asked for a hamburger. He paid the check and left.
2. John went to a restaurant. He asked the waiter for a hamburger. He paid the check and left.
3. John went into the restaurant. He ordered a Big Mac. He paid for it and then ate it while driving to work.

According to Schank and Abelson (1977), our understanding of stories 1 and 2 is guided by our scripted knowledge of a particular situation, going to restaurants. According to these authors, we store in memory a huge number of separate scripts, generalized knowledge structures pertaining to routine, frequently encountered situations or events. Thus the average adult, having experienced many different instances of "eating in restau-

FIGURE 7.2

A depiction of a standard restaurant script. (Adapted from Schank & Abelson, 1977.)

Script: Restaurant
Track: –
Props: Tables
Menu
Food
Check
Money

Roles: Customer
Waiter
Cook
Cashier
Owner

Entry conditions: Cust. is hungry, has money
Exit conditions: Cust. not hungry, has less money
Owner has more money

SCENE 1: Entering → Cust. into restaurant
To table
Sits down

SCENE 2: Ordering → Menu on table
or
Asks for menu → waiter brings menu
Cust. reads menu
Cust. places order
Cust. waits for food → cook prepares food

SCENE 3: Eating → Waiter gets food from cook, brings to cust.
Cust. eats food → options
Cust. returns food
Cust. orders more

SCENE 4: Exiting → Waiter brings check
Cust. pays cashier, leaves tip for waiter
Cust. leaves restaurant

rants," has a generalized script representation of this situation. Figure 7.2 depicts a standard restaurant script.

How do you know which of your many scripts is appropriate for a particular setting? In Schank and Abelson's model, early words and concepts in the story that alert you to the topic are called **headers.** These headers will "trigger" or activate the appropriate script—in other words, the headers prime the script. And because of this priming, all subsequent events in the story (or events in a real-world experience) are interpreted in terms of the activated script. So headers like HUNGRY, RESTAURANT, or WAITER will activate the restaurant script, providing access to the entire body of "restaurant knowledge."

Finally, story 3 requires a variation of the restaurant script, the "fast food" *track*, because the identifier "Big Mac" was mentioned. If this version of the restaurant script isn't retrieved, then there will be comprehension problems with the rest of the story—after all, a typical restaurant doesn't usually let you eat in your car. So the "Big Mac" header activates a particular version or track in the overall script. If you have specific knowledge of that track, you won't be surprised that John ate his lunch on the way to work. If you've never heard of a Big Mac before, you'll have some difficulty in understanding why that event took place.

Finally, consider a somewhat longer story (from Abelson, 1981):

4. John was feeling very hungry as he entered the restaurant. He settled himself at a table and noticed that the waiter was nearby. Suddenly, however, he realized that he'd forgotten his reading glasses.

While this story doesn't necessarily call up any particular track of the general restaurant script, it does illustrate some of the predictive and interpretive power that a script theory provides for explaining human comprehension. Virtually all readers (or listeners) will understand John's difficulty as "unable to read the menu." It makes little difference, actually, that the word *menu* was never mentioned. The restaurant script is activated by the headers HUNGRY and RESTAURANT, which in turn activate the whole set of **frames** (also called slots), details about specific events within the script. This prepares you to receive specific information about those frames.

When the detail comes along, for instance, "the waiter," that particular detail is stored in the appropriate frame. If the detail does *not* come along—"the menu"—it is simply inferred from the generalized script knowledge. Your comprehension can then proceed normally after "forgotten his reading glasses," since the unmentioned "thing you read in a restaurant" is supplied by the script.

In script terminology, the menu is a **default value** for the frame, the common, typical value or concept that occupies the frame. In the restaurant script, the default value MENU is the ordinary way that patrons find out what is available for dinner. Thus unmentioned details in the story are "filled in" by the default values. This means that a storyteller doesn't need to mention everything. We merely assume that the listener will supply any missing details from the stored script. In intuitive terms, the rule goes something like this:

- If no detail was mentioned, assume the normal, default values as specified by the script; if a detail was mentioned, replace the default value with the detail.

Tests of Script Theory

A rather strong prediction from script theory is that people's recall of a story will be influenced not merely by the words and ideas that were mentioned, but also by the events and details that were *inferred* based on scripted knowledge—for instance, you might "remember" that a restaurant customer left a tip for the waiter even if the story didn't mention that detail. Where does the tip come from, so to speak? It comes from your script (the same place that "sailing to the island" came from in Bartlett's work). There should be confusions, in other words, between scripted actions not present in a story and script actions which *were* in the story (e.g., Bower, Black, & Turner, 1979; Graesser, 1981; Long, Golding, Graesser, & Clark, 1990).

Furthermore, according to the *Script Pointer Plus Tag* hypothesis (Schank & Abelson, 1977; D. A. Smith & Graesser, 1981), this basic effect is joined by a second one, in which

★ **TABLE 7.3**

Going to the Movies

A young couple, Sarah and Sam, decide to spend Saturday evening at the movies. It's been a long week and they really want to go out. They look in their newspaper to see what's playing. When they arrive at the theater they get in line to buy tickets. At first, they were in the wrong line but then they got in the right one. Sam sees a woman he knows from work. The usher tears their tickets in half and gives them the stubs. A child runs through the theater and smashes head on into Sarah. Sam notices that the carpet is red and incredibly dirty and stained. Then they buy a large tub of popcorn and some diet cokes. They walk down the aisle until they spot some good seats. The theater starts the wrong movie but then they get it right. They watch the movie. Sarah mentions to Sam that the screen is the biggest she has ever seen. When the movie is over, they get up and leave.

Source: From Davidson (1994, pp. 772–773).

any unusual events or details in the story are *tagged* and added to your overall memory. In other words, you store a copy of the generic script as your main memory for the story. But you also tag onto that memory specific details that occurred in the story that are not part of the standard script. After we take guessing into account (e.g., Smith & Graesser, 1981), you might actually remember the unusual, nonscripted details better than scripted events.

Let's consider a recent study by Davidson (1994; see also Smith & Graesser, 1981) as a particularly thorough investigation of script theory. Davidson asked her sample of college students to read three passages, Going to the Movies, Getting Up in the Morning, ★ and Dining at a Restaurant; Going to the Movies is shown in Table 7.3. Each passage told a regular script story, but also contained sentences in which atypical events occurred. Interestingly, some of these events were not only unusual for the script but also quite vivid, while others were merely "pallid," atypical but not especially strange or unusual. All three groups of participants read the stories, and then, for distraction's sake, completed a decision-making task for another experiment.

One of the three groups of participants returned one hour later for the second part of the experiment, a recognition test on their memory for the stories. A second group was tested 48 hours after reading the stories, and a third group was tested one week later. Consistent with earlier research, accuracy at recognizing which sentences had and hadn't been in the stories was high for the nonscripted, atypical events that occurred in the ▲ story, and lower for the scripted, typical ones; see the left panel of Figure 7.3 (p. 210). Because a typical, scripted sentence like "The usher tears their tickets in half and gives them the stubs" is *so* typical, so predictable, people were unsure whether they had really read it or whether they had merely inferred it from their general GOING TO THE MOVIES script. The figure also shows that recognition of the Vivid sentences was more accurate than recognition for Pallid ones—it was easier to recognize "the carpet is red and incredibly dirty and stained" than "Sam sees a woman he knows from work."

FIGURE 7.3

Recognition and recall scores. (From Davidson, 1994.)

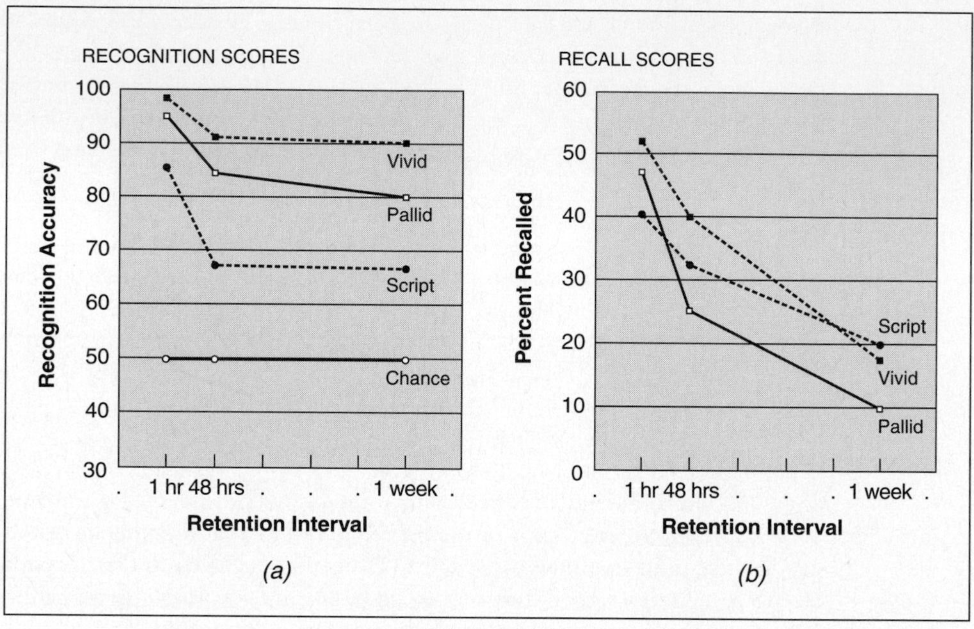

Davidson's second and third experiments were nearly identical, except that the participants returned for a *recall* rather than recognition test; the recall results are in the right panel of Figure 7.3. Here, Pallid sentences were recalled better than Script sentences only at the one-hour interval—after that, Script sentences were recalled more accurately. And after one week, even the Vivid sentences were remembered no better than Script sentences. The extra boost due to vividness disappeared in recall, in other words, and what remained about the "incredibly dirty carpet" was no better than regular scripted information.

Summary

1. Bartlett's work provided early evidence that memory for meaningful material is highly reconstructive, in which elements of the original are combined with the individual's existing knowledge.
2. Reconstructed memories often omit information, but more importantly tend to distort and normalize the material. In general, this is the thematic effect, when the remembered material is influenced by schemata, by existing knowledge structures.
3. We often use the term *scripts* now instead of *schemata*, referring to knowledge about situations and episodes stored in memory. Headers are early words or concepts in a story that activate the relevant script; typical events and details in a script are called default values.

4. Our memory of a story tends to follow the script and the default values, unless unscripted events occur within the story. Reliance on the script is another form of reconstructive memory.

Semantic Integration

Preview: integrating semantically related ideas; technical and content accuracy

Let's take a different perspective on reconstructive memory now, one that shows how accurate we can be for general information despite inaccuracy for specifics. This is the topic of **semantic integration,** the tendency for related information to be stored together in memory. We'll start with the classic studies by Bransford and Franks (e.g., 1971, 1972). As before, this important set of results will be more sensible to you if you begin with the demonstration in Table 7.4 (p. 212).

Bransford and Franks (1971) were interested in the general topic of how people acquire and remember *ideas*, not merely individual sentences but integrated, semantic ideas. They asked college students to listen to sentences like those in Table 7.4, and then (after a short distractor task) answer a simple question about each sentence. After going through this procedure for all 24 sentences and taking a five-minute break, the students were then given a second test. During this second test, the subjects had to indicate for each sentence whether it had been on the original list of 24 sentences or not, simply by deciding "yes" or "no." They also had to indicate, on a 10-point scale, how confident they were about their judgments: positive ratings (from +1 to +5) meant they were sure they had seen the sentence, negative ratings (from –1 to –5) meant they were sure they had not.

Without looking back at the original sentences, take a moment now to make these judgments about the sentences in Table 7.5 (p. 213); OLD means "Yes, I've seen it before" and NEW means "No, I didn't see it before."

All 28 sentences in their recognition test were related to the ideas in the original sentences. The clever aspect, however, was that only 4 of the 28 sentences had in fact appeared on the original list—just like in Table 7.5, the other 24 are NEW. As you no doubt noticed in Table 7.4, the separate sentences were all derived from four basic "idea groupings," for example, "The ants in the kitchen ate the sweet jelly that was on the table." Each of the complete idea groupings consisted of FOUR separate simple **propositions,** basically idea units. Here are the four "ant" propositions:

(a) the ants were in the kitchen,

(b) the ants ate the jelly,

(c) the jelly was sweet,

(d) the jelly was on the table.

The original sentences (Table 7.4) presented six sentences from each idea grouping. Two per grouping were called ONES, because they presented a single, one-idea proposition like "The jelly was on the table." Another two sentences were TWOS, with two simple

TABLE 7.4

Sample Experiment by Bransford and Franks (1971)

Instructions: Read each sentence in the table individually. As soon as you have read each one, close your eyes and count to five. Then look at and answer the question that follows each sentence. Begin now.

The girl broke the window on the porch.	Broke what?
The tree in the front yard shaded the man who was smoking his pipe.	Where?
The hill was steep.	What was?
The sweet jelly was on the kitchen table.	On what?
The tree was tall.	Was what?
The old car climbed the hill.	What did?
The ants in the kitchen ate the jelly.	Where?
The girl who lives next door broke the window on the porch.	Lives where?
The car pulled the trailer.	Did what?
The ants ate the sweet jelly that was on the table.	What did?
The girl lives next door.	Who does?
The tree shaded the man who was smoking his pipe.	What did?
The sweet jelly was on the table.	Where?
The girl who lives next door broke the large window.	Broke what?
The man was smoking his pipe.	Who was?
The old car climbed the steep hill.	The what?
The large window was on the porch.	Where?
The tall tree was in the front yard.	What was?
The car pulling the trailer climbed the steep hill.	Did what?
The jelly was on the table.	What was?
The tall tree in the front yard shaded the man.	Did what?
The car pulling the trailer climbed the hill.	Which car?
The ants ate the jelly.	Ate what?
The window was large.	What was?

Source: From Jenkins (1974, p. 791).

propositions apiece, as in "The ants in the kitchen ate the jelly." Finally, the last two were THREES, as in "The ants ate the sweet jelly that was on the table."

In Bransford and Franks's (1971) first two experiments, only ONES, TWOS, and THREES were presented on the original list. In the third experiment, a few FOURS also appeared during learning, but this made no difference in the results. In all three experiments, the final recognition test presented ONES, TWOS, THREES, and the overall FOUR for each idea grouping.

So what did they find? Just as you probably discovered, Bransford and Franks's college students overwhelmingly judged THREES and FOURS as OLD. In other words, they

◆ **TABLE 7.5**

Part II of Sample Experiment by Bransford and Franks (1971)

Instructions: Check OLD or NEW for each sentence, then indicate how confident you are on a scale from 1 to 5 (5 is "very high confidence").

		OLD/NEW	*Confidence (–5 to +5)*
1.	The car climbed the hill.	_____	_____
2.	The girl who lives next door broke the window.	_____	_____
3.	The old man who was smoking his pipe climbed the steep hill.	_____	_____
4.	The tree was in the front yard.	_____	_____
5.	The ants ate the sweet jelly that was in the kitchen.	_____	_____
6.	The window was on the porch.	_____	_____
7.	The barking dog jumped on the old car in the front yard.	_____	_____
8.	The tree in the front yard shaded the man.	_____	_____
9.	The ants were in the kitchen.	_____	_____
10.	The old car pulled the trailer.	_____	_____
11.	The tree shaded the man who was smoking his pipe.	_____	_____
12.	The tall tree shaded the man who was smoking his pipe.	_____	_____
13.	The ants ate the jelly on the kitchen table.	_____	_____
14.	The old car, pulling the trailer, climbed the hill.	_____	_____
15.	The girl who lives next door broke the large window on the porch.	_____	_____
16.	The tall tree shaded the man.	_____	_____
17.	The ants in the kitchen ate the jelly.	_____	_____
18.	The car was old.	_____	_____
19.	The girl broke the large window.	_____	_____
20.	The ants ate the sweet jelly that was on the kitchen table.	_____	_____
21.	The ants were on the table in the kitchen.	_____	_____
22.	The old car pulling the trailer climbed the steep hill.	_____	_____
23.	The girl broke the window on the porch.	_____	_____
24.	The scared cat that broke the window on the porch climbed the tree.	_____	_____
25.	The tree shaded the man.	_____	_____
26.	The old car climbed the steep hill.	_____	_____
27.	The girl broke the window.	_____	_____
28.	The man who lives next door broke the large window on the porch.	_____	_____

STOP. Count the number of sentences judged OLD.

Source: From Jenkins (1971, p. 791).

judged that they had seen them on the study list (just as you probably judged question 20, the FOUR, as OLD). Furthermore, they were very confident in their ratings, as shown in ★ Figure 7.4 (p. 214) (taken from experiment 3). That is, people were recognizing the sentences that expressed the overall idea grouping most thoroughly, even when they had not

★ **FIGURE 7.4**

Confidence ratings for subjects' judgments about NEW and OLD sentences. (From Bransford & Franks, 1971).

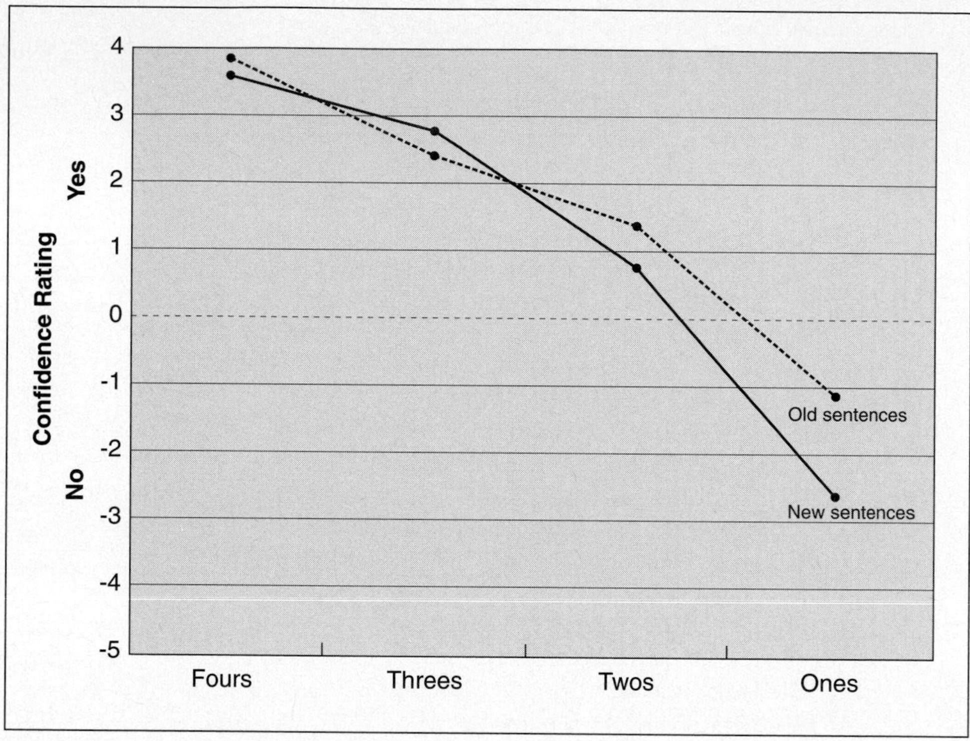

seen exactly those sentences during study. Such responses are called **false alarms** or **false positives,** saying "OLD" when the correct response is "NEW." (In terms we used earlier, recognition sentences that had not been presented originally are called "foils" or sometimes "lures.")

Moreover, subjects weren't especially confident about having seen genuinely OLD sentences, because the OLD sentences didn't express the entire idea in the whole grouping. There were only two kinds of sentences they were sure they hadn't seen: NONCASE sentences (e.g., sentence 3, Table 7.5, p. 213), which combined ideas from *different* groupings (e.g., the old man climbing the hill), and OLD–ONES. Why were they so sure about OLD–ONES, especially since they had seen several of those? Apparently, since the shorter sentences didn't express the whole idea they had stored in memory, subjects believed that they had not seen them before.

THE INTEGRATION INTERPRETATION

What do these results suggest? Bransford and Franks (1971, 1972) concluded that their participants had acquired a more general idea than any of the individual study sentences had expressed, that they "integrated the information communicated by sets of individual sentences to *construct wholistic semantic ideas*" (1971, p. 348, emphasis added). Bransford and Franks's college students were reporting a *composite* memory, one in which related information was stored together in memory. All the related ideas expressed in the individual sentences seem to have been fused together into one semantic representation, one memory record of the whole idea. As such, their performance was entirely reasonable—they were matching the combined ideas in the recognition sentences to their composite memory representations. Rather than finding verbatim memory, Bransford and Franks found "memory for meaning," memory based on the semantic integration of related material (see also Radvansky, Spieler, & Zacks, 1993; Radvansky & Zacks, 1991; Richardson, 1985).

TECHNICAL AND CONTENT ACCURACY

Note two general points here. First, recall or recognition of meaningful material seems quite unlike the recall and recognition we discussed in Chapter 5. That is, whereas episodic memory tasks often show rather good accuracy, we're seeing rather poor accuracy for detail in this chapter, when we test memory for meaningful material. In terms of **technical accuracy,** the recollection of exact, specific information, performance on meaningful material is often rather poor—"abysmally awful" in one researcher's words.

But the second point is, if anything, more important. Maybe technical accuracy is the wrong way to evaluate recollection of meaningful material. Maybe we should instead focus on **content accuracy,** recollection of general ideas, gist, and theme. When scored according to strict, verbatim criteria, technical accuracy ranges from not especially impressive to dramatically inaccurate. But content accuracy for meaningful material can be quite good, as Bransford and Franks's (1971) results showed.

Different circumstances emphasize different criteria. We should not dismiss technical accuracy too casually, Bartlett's (1932) opinion notwithstanding ("literal recall is extraordinarily unimportant"). There are, after all, many situations in the real world in which technically accurate memory is important. It doesn't help me to remember the *concept* of "retrieving a document" if I've forgotten which keystrokes make *my* word processor do that—content accuracy doesn't help when I have to remember my social security number, the classroom I teach in, or my mother's birthday. (Did you ever have a professor who insisted on word-for-word recall of definitions?) On the other hand, there are also countless situations in which technical accuracy is not called for—the question "What did Dr. Wallace lecture on yesterday?" is *not* asking for verbatim recall, but for the gist, the overall theme of the lecture.

Consider Bransford and Franks's (1971) results again, and the kind of memory system that produces false alarms to related sentences that have never been shown. People in Bransford and Franks's study made false alarms to FOURS such as "The ants in the kitchen ate the sweet jelly that was on the table." Their technical accuracy, in other words, was low.

But isn't that the whole point of memory? Isn't this an instance of high—even perfect—content accuracy? In other words, what good would a memory system be to us if it *didn't* combine related information together into a unified, composite idea? Memory would be pretty useless to us if we didn't first notice the semantic relationships among separate ideas, and then store them together. If our memories couldn't do this, then in a sense we could never understand—we could only record isolated fragments in memory, without drawing connections among them. To reduce it to concrete terms, think how useless your memory would be if you didn't realize that the jelly that the ants ate was the *same* jelly that was on the kitchen table!

In a very real sense, then, the advantages of semantic integration represent the *power* of memory that Schacter (1996) described. With memory, and a reasonable comprehension mechanism, not only can we remember huge amounts of material, but we can understand it too, and then use that for further understanding.

Summary

1. Semantic integration refers to the way related information is stored in memory. When meaningful material is comprehended and recorded in memory, it is stored in an interrelated fashion. Details coming from different sentences are stored together in a composite memory representation.
2. Technical accuracy refers to remembering exactly what was presented, whereas content accuracy refers to remembering whole ideas. With meaningful material, technical accuracy is often rather low, but content accuracy can be quite good. This illustrates the power of the human memory and comprehension system.

False Memories, Eyewitness Memory, and "Forgotten Memories"

Preview: false memories in the lab; leading questions and eyewitness memory; distortions and errors in eyewitness memory; the misinformation effect and source memory; forgotten and recovered memories

But Schacter (1996) also spoke of the *fragile* nature of memory, how our memories can fail us in certain situations. Where's the weakness in a memory system that functions according to the principle of semantic relatedness and integration? The answer is—in exactly those situations that call for technical accuracy. The weakness of such a memory system is that there *are* situations when it's important to be able to distinguish between what *really* happened and what our existing knowledge and comprehension processes might have contributed to recollection. We'll discuss two research programs that show incorrect or distorted memory, then tackle the difficult issues raised by these results.

FALSE MEMORIES

A simple yet powerful laboratory demonstration of **false memories**—memory for something that didn't happen—was reported by Roediger and McDermott (1995), based on a demonstration by Deese (1959). Roediger and McDermott's participants studied 12-item lists made up of words like *bed, rest, awake, pillow,* and so forth, words highly associated with the word *sleep*. Importantly, *sleep* was never presented in the list—it was the "critical lure" word. In immediate free recall, 40 percent of the participants recalled *sleep* from the list, and then later recognized it with a high degree of confidence. This is, of course, a false memory.

In a second study, participants studied multiple lists, constructed in the same fashion, either recalling the list of words immediately or performing a distractor task (arithmetic). Everyone then was given a recognition task. During free recall, an even larger percentage of the participants—55 percent—recalled the lure than in experiment 1. The recognition ▲ results, shown in Figure 7.5, were even more dramatic. Of course, a few people "recognized" nonstudied words, words that were unrelated to the real list words. More importantly, correct recognition for studied words increased to well above chance for the Study/Arithmetic lists, and even higher for Study/Recall lists. But false recognition of the critical lure was slightly higher than correct recognition of words actually shown on the list, showing the same pattern of increases across conditions. Indeed, there was an 81 percent false-alarm rate for critical lures when the lists had been studied and recalled. In other words, falsely remembering the lure during recall *strengthened* participants' memories of the lure word, leading them to an even higher false-recognition rate. When questioned further, most of the participants claimed to "remember" the critical lure word, ■ rather than merely "know" it had been on the list. *Prove It*.

▲ **FIGURE 7.5**

Roediger and McDermott's (1995) results. (From Roediger & MacDermott, 1995.)

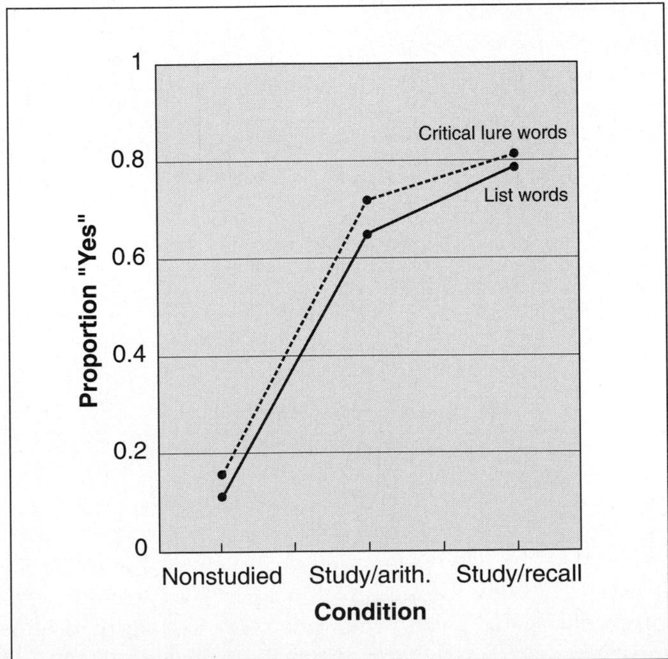

PROVE IT

This is a fairly easy demonstration to perform, if you have several volunteers and about 15 minutes available. It is an adaptation of the Roediger and McDermott (1995) methodology, shorter than the original experiment while demonstrating the same effect. Prepare enough copies of your "distractor task," for example, a page full of simple arithmetic problems, to have one for each volunteer.

1. Tell your volunteers they'll be hearing three lists, and afterward will be asked to recall as many of the words as they can; order of recall is not important.
2. Read the three lists to your volunteers, at an "easy" speaking rate, about one word per two seconds. Pause only briefly between lists.
3. After finishing the third list, have your volunteers do two minutes of arithmetic, finishing as many problems as they can.
4. Ask your volunteers to write down as many words as they can remember from the three lists. Give ample time (approximately three minutes) so they can get as many words as possible.
5. When everyone is done, have them turn over their sheets of paper, and make recognition decisions, one by one, to the 20-word recognition test. For each word, they should say "no" if the word was not on the list, and "yes" if it was on the list. When they say "yes," also have them note whether they remember the word specifically, or whether they just "know" it was on the list.
6. Look especially for recall of the words *sleep, thief, chair,* because these are the nonpresented, "critical lures." On recognition, look for false alarms—saying "yes"—to the critical lures in positions 5, 13, and 16.

Word Lists

1. bed, rest, awake, tired, dream, wake, snooze, blanket, doze, slumber, snore, nap, peace, yawn, drowsy
2. steal, robber, crook, burglar, money, cop, bad, rob, jail, gun, villain, crime, bank, bandit, criminal
3. table, sit, legs, seat, couch, desk, recliner, sofa, wood, cushion, swivel, stool, sitting, rocking, bench

Recognition List

1–dream, 2–fork, 3–weather, 4–bracelet, 5–chair, 6–robber, 7–stool, 8–traffic, 9–snooze, 10–couch, 11–radio, 12–jail, 13–sleep, 14–sand, 15–blanket, 16–thief, 17–bed, 18–boy, 19–skin, 20–cushion

Scoring Key

"Yes" words	"No" words	"Critical Lures"
1, 6, 7, 9	2, 3, 4, 8	5, 13, 16
10, 12, 15	11, 14, 18	
17, 20	19	

In terms of content accuracy, of course, this performance is good, exactly what we'd expect; you see a list of words like *bed, rest, awake, pillow,* and since the list is "about" sleep, you then recall *sleep*. But in terms of technical accuracy, this performance is quite poor, since the *participants* came up with the word *sleep* based on their understanding of the list, and then couldn't distinguish between what had really been on the list and what

had been supplied from memory. Roediger and McDermott's (1995) conclusion about this *memory illusion* summarized the situation aptly:

> *All remembering is constructive in nature. . . . The illusion of remembering events that never happened can occur quite readily. Therefore, as others have also pointed out, the fact that people may say they vividly remember details surrounding an event cannot, by itself, be taken as convincing evidence that the event actually occurred.* (p. 812)

LEADING QUESTIONS AND MEMORY DISTORTION

The second line of research is another simple yet powerful demonstration of how inaccurate our memories can be. This is the now-famous program of research begun by Elizabeth Loftus and her colleagues (e.g., E. F. Loftus & Palmer, 1974) on the topic of **leading questions** and memory distortion. Loftus started by examining the effects of leading questions, that is, questions that tend to suggest to the individual what answer is appropriate. She wondered if there were long-term consequences of leading questions, in terms of what people remember about events they've witnessed.

In an early study, Loftus and Palmer (1974) showed several short traffic safety films to college classes, with films depicting car accidents. The students were asked to describe each accident after seeing the film, and then answer a series of questions about what they had seen.

One of the questions asked for an estimate of the car's speed, something people are notoriously poor at. One group of students responded to the question

About how fast were the cars going when they hit each other?

The other four groups were asked virtually the same question, except that the verb *hit* was replaced with either *smashed, collided, bumped,* or *contacted.* As you might expect, those

who got the stronger verbs like *smashed* in their questions gave higher estimates of speed—the question led them to a biased answer.

Hold it. *Why* would we expect this effect? Why aren't we surprised that people estimated higher speeds when the question said "smashed" instead of "bumped" or "hit"? The answer is straightforward—and you know the answer already. When you're asked a question, you understand the question by retrieving the meanings of the words from semantic memory. Your concept node for SMASH includes semantic information about car speeds and damage from accidents. We understand by accessing our conceptual, semantic knowledge, including whatever scripted knowledge we have about car accidents. So the phrasing of the question *leads* you to respond based on your semantic interpretation of SMASH—a straightforward demonstration of leading questions.

The longer-term importance of this effect, however, gets to the heart of issues about eyewitness testimony and memory distortion. Loftus and Palmer wondered if the question about speed had in some way *altered* the subjects' memory representation of the filmed scene. In other words, if participants are exposed to the implication that the cars had "smashed" together, would they literally remember a more severe accident than they had actually seen? This kind of effect would be referred to as a **memory impairment**—a genuine change or alteration in memory for an experienced event as a function of some later event. (Note that the episodic memory literature also has a name for this kind of effect—*retroactive interference*.)

This is exactly what Loftus and Palmer found in their second experiment. A week after the original film and questions, the participants were given *another* set of questions about the original film (but they didn't see the film again). One of the questions asked

Did you see any broken glass?

Many of the participants in the "smashed" group said *yes*, even though there had been no broken glass in the film—in fact 34 percent of the "smashed" group said *yes*, versus only 14 percent of the group who saw "hit" (and 12 percent of those who had not been asked for a speed estimate). Furthermore, the likelihood of saying *yes* grew stronger and stronger

FIGURE 7.6

Loftus and Palmer's (1974) results. (From Loftus & Palmer, 1974.)

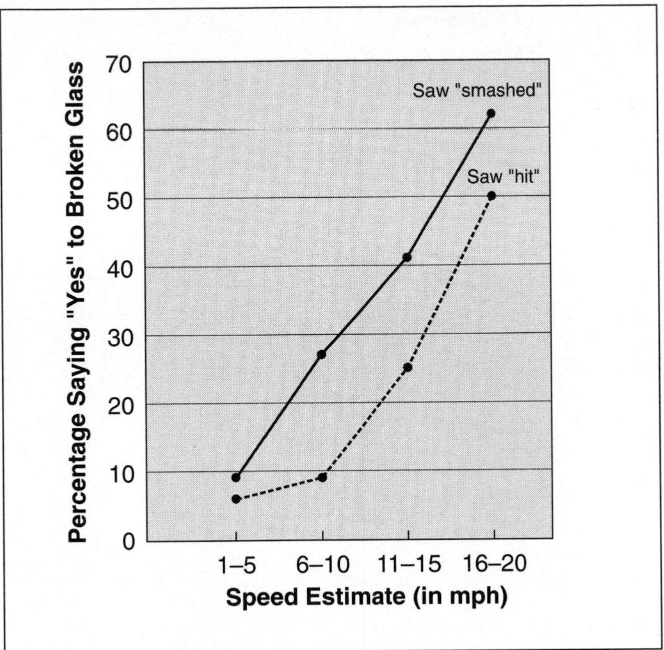

as the estimates of speed went up, as shown in Figure 7.6. At each point in the graph, "remembering" broken glass was more common for the participants who had been "smashed," so to speak.

Think about that again—despite the fact that they had not seen any broken glass in the original film, they *remembered* broken glass, partly as a function of their own speed estimate, and partly as a function of the verb they'd been questioned with a week earlier. It genuinely seemed that what happened *after* the memory was formed altered the nature of that memory. The question about "smashed" was not just a leading question, it was a source of *misleading information*, plausible but not wrong. (I've deceived you ever so slightly since Chapter 6, by the way, in referring to mudlarks as a kind of bird. The term is actually British slang for street urchins, who presumably scrounge for their existence the way a lark might scrounge in the mud for food. The purpose of my deception, of course, was to show how easily we accept information that appears plausible.)

THE MISINFORMATION EFFECT

Investigators have now developed a standard task to test for the effects of misleading information. The typical experiment goes like this:

- The participants see the original event in a film or set of slides—for example, slides depicting a car accident, with one slide showing a stop sign.

★ **FIGURE 7.7**

Loftus, Donders, Hoffman, and Schooler's (1989) results. Mean reaction time to correct and incorrect targets (e.g., stop sign, yield sign) depending on whether the subject had been misled or not. Note that misled subjects were faster on "incorrect" responses, that is, saying "yes" to the yield sign. (From Loftus et al., 1989.)

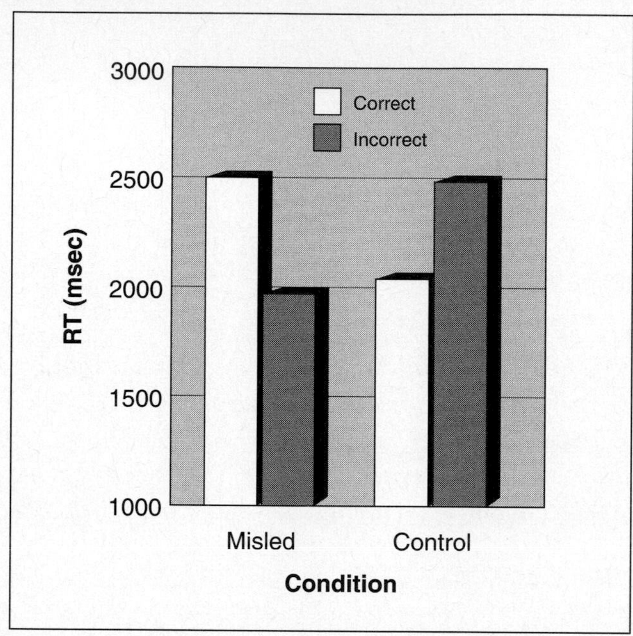

- Later, they are exposed to some additional information, for example, a narrative account of the car accident. Some of the participants receive only neutral information at this stage, whereas others are given a specific bit of misinformation—the narrative mentions "the yield sign," for instance.
- Finally, there is a memory test, often a yes-no recognition task, which asks about the critical piece of information—was there a stop sign or a yield sign? (See also Zaragoza, McCloskey, & Jamis, 1987, who used a recall task.)

The common result is that some individuals will incorrectly claim to remember the yield sign, the standard *misinformation effect*. Belli (1989), for instance, found that misled subjects showed more than a 20 percent reduction in accuracy, compared to control groups who were not exposed to the misinformation. Loftus, Donders, Hoffman, and Schooler (1989) found, furthermore, that misled groups were faster in their incorrect judgments—picking the yield sign—than in their correct decisions, as shown in Figure ★ 7.7. This suggests a rather surprising degree of misplaced confidence on the part of the misled subjects.

While these results implied that memory might truly be impaired or altered by the misinformation, several later studies called into question the original methods of testing, and hence the conclusion of memory impairment. The crux of the debate involves the nature of the recognition test, and the "different ways of arriving at the same memory report" (Loftus & Hoffman, 1989, p. 103). In particular, it's always possible that the subjects did not actually encode the original item (stop sign) when they saw the slides. If so, then the misinformation effect could either reflect guessing or remembering the yield sign from the narrative (McCloskey & Zaragoza, 1985). In either case, the misinformation effect would not signify true memory impairment at all, but instead some other process. In fact, several studies (McCloskey & Zaragoza, 1985; Zaragoza & Koshmider, 1989) used a modified task that corrected for this problem; the results seemed to support the nonimpairment interpretation.

Source Misattribution and Misinformation Acceptance

Several recent reviews and summaries (e.g., Loftus, 1991; Loftus & Hoffman, 1989; Roediger, 1996) have outlined the overall message of this research. As Loftus (1991) noted, genuine alteration of the original memory may be only one part of the full explanation. Based on the accumulated evidence, in fact, there seem to be three important effects: source misattribution, misinformation acceptance, and overconfidence in the accuracy of memory.

Source Misattribution Sometimes people *do* come to believe that they remember something that never happened. This has been called a **source misattribution effect,** when the participant cannot distinguish whether the original event or some later event was the true source of the information. In essence, the source misattribution effect suggests a confusion in memory, in which we cannot clearly remember the true source of a piece of information (e.g., Zaragoza & Lane, 1994). Using the stop sign/yield sign example, the source misattribution effect basically says that we can't correctly distinguish whether memory for the yield sign came from the original film or from some other source, maybe the narrative that was read later, or maybe from existing knowledge and memory.

Misinformation Acceptance According to Loftus (1991), a second, possibly larger component of memory distortion is at least as disturbing as genuine memory impairment. This is called **misinformation acceptance,** in which participants accept additional information as having been part of an earlier experience without actually remembering that information. For example, the individual in a misinformation experiment does not remember seeing a stop sign at all, but is nonetheless quite willing to "accept" that there was a yield sign when the narrative mentions that detail. Later on, the participant reports having seen the yield sign. In short, people seem quite willing to accept information presented after the fact. They then often become quite certain about these "secondhand" memories. These tendencies probably grow stronger as more and more time elapses since the original event, and the original memory becomes less accessible (e.g., Payne, Toglia, & Anastasi, 1994).

Overconfidence in Memory Despite our feeling that we remember events accurately ("I saw it with my own eyes!"), we often misremember what we've experienced, or we form memories on the basis of suggestion from some other source besides the original event.

And as if this weren't bad enough, we often become unjustifiably confident in the accuracy of our own memories—and surprisingly unaware of how unreliable memory can be (a classic illustration is shown in Figure 7.8). As you read a moment ago, Roediger and McDermott's (1995) participants not only (falsely) recalled and recognized the critical lure, the majority of them claimed that they genuinely "remembered" it, for instance had explicit, "vivid memory" of hearing the word in the list. The ultimate reason for this overconfidence—aside from a basic, bedrock belief in ourselves—seems to involve two factors. The first, as implied above, is **source memory,** our memory for the exact source of information. As several investigators have noted (e.g., Schacter, 1996), our source memory

FIGURE 7.8

Which penny is correct? (From Nickerson & Adams, 1979.)

Administer the coin recognition test shown below to several people, to see how heavily we rely on reconstructive long-term memory. Be sure to have your subjects indicate how certain they are about their choice.

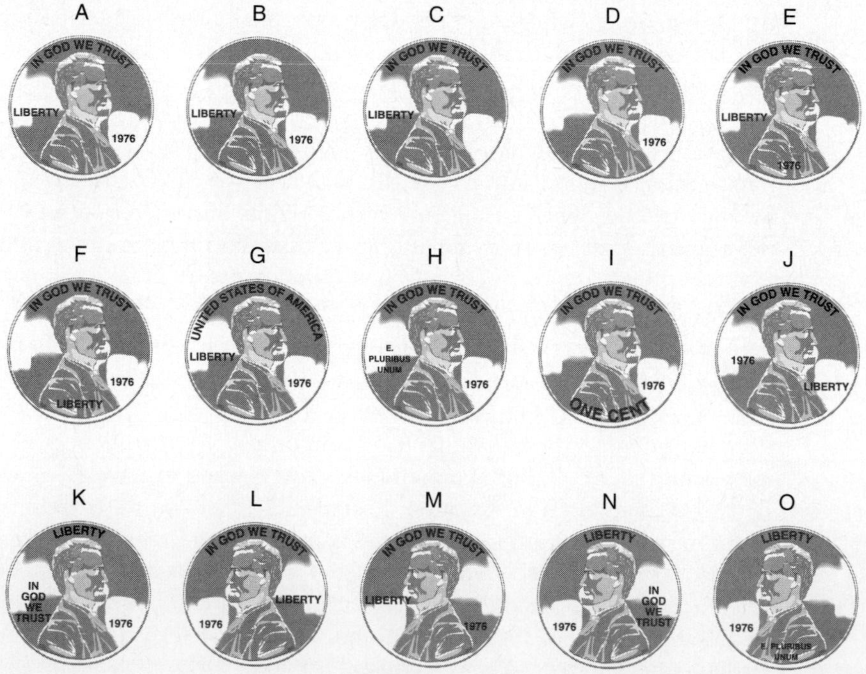

Which is a correct drawing of a U.S. penny?

is often very flawed—we cannot accurately distinguish whether the source of some piece of information was the original event, some later event, or even our own general knowledge of the relevant situation. A second reason may have something to do with *processing fluency*, something like "I *remembered* 'sleep' too easily to have just imagined it was on the list, so it must have been on the list." As Loftus and Hoffman (1989) put it, both memory psychologists and the courts should find it interesting that such memories can arise through the process of suggestion or exposure to misinformation, and then become "as real and as vivid as a memory that arose from . . . actual perception" (p. 103).

Stronger Memory Distortion Effects

But can something as simple as this in the laboratory explain real-world inaccuracies in memory? Probably so. Consider just a sampling of recent experiments on false memories and memory distortions:

- Repeated exposure to misinformation increases memory reports for the misinformation (Mitchell & Zaragoza, 1996). Repeated recall of misinformation strengthens later recall and confidence about the misinformation (Roediger, Jacoby, & McDermott, 1996). And repeated questioning about an event can enhance recall of certain details, and induce forgetting of others, even when no misinformation was present (Shaw, Bjork, & Handal, 1995). Repeated questioning also increases confidence in one's memories, whether they're correct or incorrect (Shaw, 1996).
- Imagining that something happened increases later memory reports that it actually did happen (Garry, Manning, Loftus, & Sherman, 1996; Hyman & Pentland, 1996).
- Misinformation effects are found even when participants are warned that misleading information might be presented (Belli, Lindsay, Gales, & McCarthy, 1994).

It doesn't take much to realize the implications of this work—memory is *suggestible*. People's memory for events can be altered and influenced, both by the knowledge they have when the event happens and also by information they encounter afterward. People report that they remember events that didn't happen. And in many cases, they become quite confident about the accuracy of their memory for those events.

REPRESSED AND RECOVERED MEMORIES

There are broad, seriously disturbing implications of these findings. If we can "remember" things with a high degree of confidence and conviction, even though the remembered things never happened, then how seriously should eyewitness testimony be weighed in court proceedings? Juries are usually heavily influenced by eyewitnesses—is this justified? Should a person be convicted of a crime based solely on someone's memory for a criminal act? The current controversy over recovered memories is an obvious—and truly worrisome—arena in which our understanding of human memory is critical.

Here's a "generic" summary of a **recovered memory** case, when a "forgotten" memory is "remembered" years later. An individual "recovers" a memory, possibly a horrible, childhood memory of abuse; the absence of that memory for many years indicates that the experience was *repressed*, intentionally forgotten. Although the recovery is sometimes spontaneous, it can also be an outcome of psychotherapy, in which the individual and therapist have done "memory work" to bring the memory into awareness. Now that the awful memory is "recovered," the individual sometimes seeks restitution, for instance, by having the remembered perpetrator brought to trial.

It goes without saying that, often as not, there is no objective way to determine if the recovered memory is real or not, no sure way to decide if the remembered event actually happened. As such, these cases often simply become one person's word against another's, both individuals claiming to be telling the truth.

The past few years have seen a huge rise in court cases involving recovered memories, and several individuals have been convicted of crimes based on someone's recovered memory (e.g., Loftus, 1993; Loftus & Ketcham, 1991). Cognitive science has become involved in this controversy for the obvious reason, our understanding of how memory works. As the research has developed, there are certain aspects of the recovered-memory situation that have fallen under greater scrutiny.

Of these, two are especially important. First is the notion of **repression,** intentional forgetting of painful or traumatic experiences (Freud, 1905/1953). From the clinical standpoint, "the evidence for repression is overwhelming and obvious" (Erdelyi & Goldberg, 1979, p. 384). There is little hard, empirical evidence on the nature of this type of forgetting, however, often not even reliable estimates on how frequently it occurs. And some data suggest that the opposite reaction may occur in some cases of trauma, that is, painfully clear and explicit memory for the trauma. Cognitive science is no closer than clinical psychology in determining whether the evidence weighs more heavily for or against the process of repression.

More worrisome is that some of the therapeutic techniques for helping a client recover a memory are disturbingly similar to variables shown to increase false memories, including imagery, suggestive questioning, and—to be sure—repetition. In fact, essentially these techniques were used in a case that documents how a completely false, fabricated memory can be "implanted" in a susceptible individual (Ofshe, 1992). And as several laboratory studies have shown, it isn't necessary to go to extreme lengths to implant a memory (e.g., Loftus & Coan, 1994)—indeed, on a minor scale, all you have to do is present a list of words like *bed, rest, awake, pillow,* and *voilà—sleep*.

No one doubts the fact that child abuse and other personal traumas occur, nor the need for genuine victims to grapple with and—hopefully—overcome such tragedy. But it is equally important that cognitive science provide its expertise on issues that hinge so critically on memory. And the indications, as you've been reading, are that we should be especially mindful that "memories" are—sadly—prone to distortion and error. The very reconstructive processes that bestow power on long-term memory bring with them a degree of fragility.

Summary

1. It is surprisingly easy to demonstrate false memories in the laboratory; when participants study a list like *bed, rest, awake, pillow,* they misremember that *sleep* was on the list, with very high confidence. Several lines of research establish this phenomenon, including the important studies on leading questions and eyewitness testimony by Loftus.

2. When people "remember" an event that was not in the original information, part of the effect is due to source misattribution, confusion as to whether the source of the detail was the original event or some subsequent event. A second part is due to misinformation acceptance, a willingness to accept a detail in the absence of memory for the original event. People tend to be overconfident of a memory regardless of its source.
3. The suggestibility of memory, and factors that influence misremembering, must be taken into account when instances of repressed and recovered memories are considered. A fear is that some portion of such memories are in fact memory illusions.

Autobiographical Memory

Preview: autobiographical memory; prolonged acquisition and personal relevance; flashbulb memories; the irony of memory

Let's conclude this chapter on a somewhat less controversial topic, the study of one's lifetime collection of personal, autobiographical memories. In the past several years, there has been a big increase in the number of studies about genuine **autobiographical memory,** investigations of memory for the more natural experiences and information we encounter in a lifetime. A set of impressive investigations by Bahrick and his colleagues illustrates the nature of real-world memory for personal events.

THE BAHRICK WORK

Bahrick, Bahrick, and Wittlinger (1975) reported a fascinating study entitled "Fifty Years of Memory for Names and Faces." Nearly 400 participants, ranging in age from 17 to 74, were asked to remember the names and faces of their own high school classmates. For the youngest subjects, this represented a retention interval of only two weeks; for the oldest, the retention interval was 57 years. Pictures and names were taken from people's high school yearbooks, and were used in a variety of memory tests. In particular, participants were asked for simple free recall of names, and then were given five other tests: name recognition, picture recognition, picture-to-name matching, name-to-picture matching, and cued recall of names using pictures as cues.

Figure 7.9 shows the average performance on these six tests across the retention intervals, that is, time since graduation. The free-recall curve (notice that the y-axis on the right panel is for free recall) shows an average of just under 50 names accessible for free recall a mere three months after graduation. Since the average size of graduating classes for all participants was 294 (the smallest class size was 90), this level of free recall is actually quite low—it works out to only about 15 percent of classmates' names. This number then dwindles further, so that the oldest group, having graduated an average 48 years earlier, recalled only about 18 names, something like 6 percent recall. Cued recall, with pictures as cues, was largely the same as free recall.

FIGURE 7.9

Results obtained by Bahrick et al. (1975) in their study of memory of faces and names across 50 years. (From Bahrick, Bahrick, & Wittlinger, 1975.)

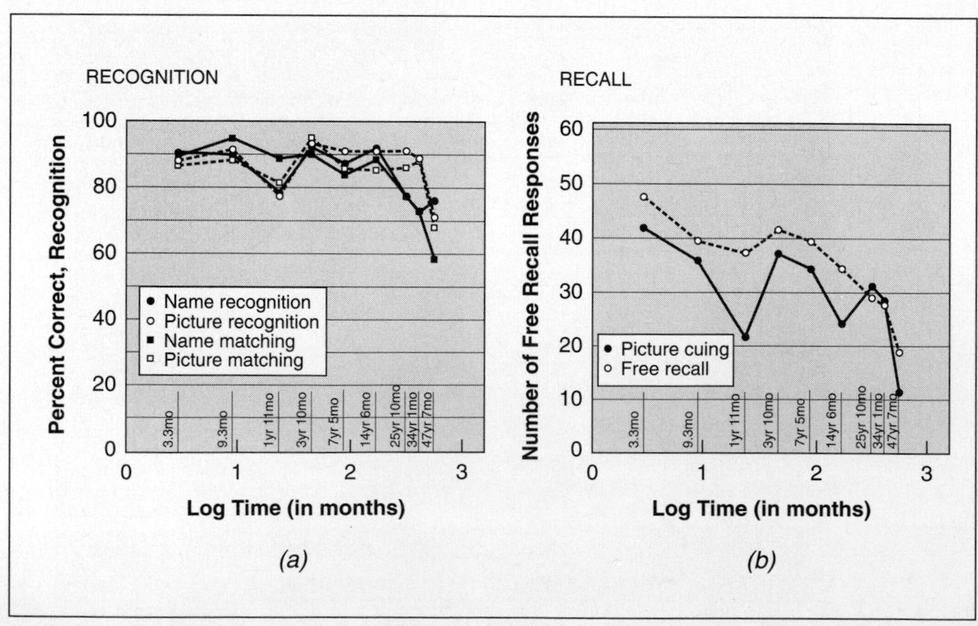

In obvious contrast, however, all four of the recognition tests showed impressive levels of retention. Simple recognition of names and faces was 90 percent at the three-month retention interval. Name recognition did not begin to decline noticeably until about 15 years later, and picture recognition remained in the 80 to 90 percent range until about 35 years later. And, as Bahrick et al. (1975) pointed out, the decline in the very oldest group may have been influenced by factors related to physical aging, possibly introducing a negative bias for the oldest group.

Overlearning and Distributed Practice

What leads to such impressive levels of retention, particularly when we compare them to the relatively lower performance of subjects in laboratory studies of memory? As Bahrick et al. (1975) noted, in the typical situation, individuals have learned the names and faces of their classmates across a four-year (or longer) period. This situation is termed *prolonged acquisition*. According to the authors, this principle has two important components associated with it, *overlearning* and *distributed practice*. First, the information tested in the Bahrick et al. study was overlearned, in fact to a much higher degree than laboratory studies have examined (even Ebbinghaus didn't test the effects of a four-year-long learning phase). The result of such overlearning is much-improved retention. (Will you remember 80 to 90 percent of your cognitive psychology course material 35 years from now?)

Second, prolonged acquisition represents learning that was distributed across a very long period of time, in contrast to typical memory experiments in which learning opportunities are "massed" together over a short period. This neatly confirmed the standard laboratory finding that distributed practice (say, an hour a night for three nights) leads to much better retention than massed practice (three hours in one night, e.g., Underwood, Keppel, & Schulz, 1962).

Bahrick's work, including memory for Spanish (Bahrick, 1984) and math (Bahrick & Hall, 1991) learned in school, and for a city's streets and locations 50 years later (Bahrick, 1983) shows this to be one of the soundest bits of advice that cognitive psychology gives to students. Distribute your practice and learning; don't mass it together (better known as "cramming"). Indeed, the Bahrick results suggest that the laboratory-based effect is not only general to more naturalistic settings, but it is greatly magnified when naturalistic, everyday memories are tested (see also S. M. Smith & Rothkopf, 1984; Hyman & Rubin, 1990).

PSYCHOLOGISTS AS SUBJECTS

Several modern-day Ebbinghauses have reported tests of their own memories in carefully controlled, long-term studies—not for artificial laboratory stimuli, but for naturally occurring events (e.g., Linton, 1975, 1978; Sehulster, 1989; Wagenaar, 1986). For instance, Wagenaar recorded daily events in his own life for over six years, some 2400 separate events, and then tested his recall with combinations of four different cue types: *what* the event was, *who* was involved, and *where* and *when* it happened. Although he found that pleasant events were recalled better than unpleasant ones at shorter retention intervals, his evidence also showed that none of the events could truly be said to have been forgotten. Time-based cues, furthermore, were particularly useful in recalling events.

Interestingly, Wagenaar found that the time since an event had occurred was less important than the salience or importance of the event, and the degree of emotional involvement. Sehulster's (1989) data, on memory for 25 years of performances at the Metropolitan Opera, showed very similar effects, that is, the importance or "intensity" of the performance was a predictor of superior recall. One imagines that such effects are due to naturally occurring rehearsal—we think about, and hence rehearse, salient events more often, so strengthen them in memory.

Personal Relevance and Distinctiveness

Salience and degree of emotional involvement are probably very much the same as personal relevance of the event, a factor which has also been shown to be important (e.g., Conway, Anderson, et al., 1994; Wagenaar, 1986)—the more personally relevant, the better the event is encoded in the first place, hence the better it's remembered. There's also a remarkable resemblance to the effect of distinctiveness (e.g., Schmidt, 1985), that we remember distinctive events better than less colorful, more nondescript ones. All of these sound quite familiar to cognitive psychology—they seem to be the venerable **von Restorff effect,** improved retention for a list item that is made distinct or different from the rest of the list, say, by underlining it in red (e.g., Cooper & Pantle, 1967). They also sound suspiciously like the Tag that becomes attached to a Script Pointer—in an otherwise standard story about going to the movies, you remember the unusual, nonscripted event quite well.

SPECIAL "FLASHBULB" MEMORIES

But is there a special category of autobiographical memories, a category of very vivid, nearly "photographic" quality memories? The term **flashbulb memories** has been used to describe this kind of memory (R. Brown & Kulik, 1977). In a flashbulb memory, we seem

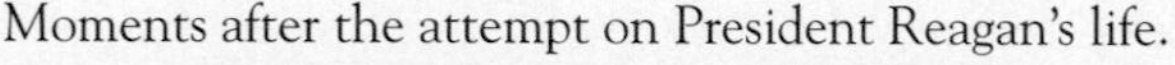

Moments after the attempt on President Reagan's life.

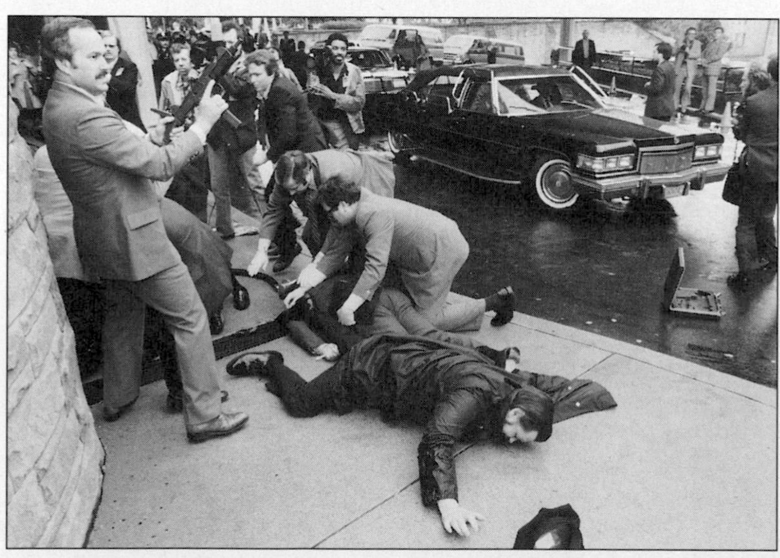

to have—or believe we have—extremely accurate and very detailed memories for particular events, especially when the events were surprising or highly unusual. For example, Winograd and Killinger (1983) examined the "flashbulb memories" (Brown & Kulik, 1977) of college students for a significant event, the assassination of President Kennedy in 1963 (note that subjects are asked to recall their own particular circumstances when news of the event reached them, not whether they remembered the event itself). While the data showed an increase in the amount of recallable information as a function of the subject's age in 1963, the evidence also showed that the surprise or shock *per se* may not be necessary for high levels of retention—participants showed high recall for the Nixon resignation and the moon landing of the U.S. astronauts, neither of which was an unexpected, surprise occurrence.

More recent studies, however, suggest that flashbulb memories may not differ in kind from more ordinary types of memories (e.g., McCloskey, Wible, & Cohen, 1988). For instance, Christianson (1989) tested Swedish subjects' memories for the assassination of their prime minister in 1986, barely six weeks after the assassination and then again a year later. He found that only the general information was recalled with any degree of accuracy. Details that were recalled, in contrast, seemed to be a creative mixture of a few specifics plus more general knowledge—reconstructive memory, in other words.

Interestingly, one factor that *did* seem to differ between flashbulb and regular memories was the overconfidence participants had about the accuracy of their flashbulb memory. In general, we believe that we have accurate and vivid memory, even for details (Weaver, 1993), and are rather confident in those judgments. But despite our intuitions—"I remember *exactly* what happened" (see also Neisser, 1982)—the data indicate no special or extraordinary accuracy for flashbulb memories, but apparently a special degree of confidence that we *have* flashbulb memories. To at least some researchers, this sounds remarkably like the overconfidence people have in other memory settings, including eyewitness situations.

What were you doing when you heard about the *Challenger* explosion?

SO IS MEMORY ACCURATE OR NOT?

We complain about how poor our memories are, how forgetful we are, how hard it is to learn and remember information. Is our memory that bad?

Probably not. First, Anderson and Schooler (1991) note that when we complain about memory failures, we neglect the "huge stockpile" of facts and information that we expect memory both to store and to provide quick acccess to. We underestimate the complexities, not to mention the sheer quantity, of information stored in memory. Second, we fall into the trap of equating remembering with recall. When we say we've forgotten something, we probably mean we are unable to recall it right now. But recall is only one way of testing memory. Recognition is far more "forgiving" in terms of showing that information has indeed been retained in memory.

How much cognitive psychology will you remember in a dozen years? Your honest estimate is (probably) "not much at all." If so, then you've seriously underestimated your memory. A study by Conway, Cohen, and Stanhope (1991) examined *exactly* that, students' memory for the concepts, specific facts, names, and so forth from a cognitive psychology course taken up to 12 years earlier. Figure 7.10 shows their results. While recall of material dwindled quite a bit across the 12 years, from 60 percent to 25 percent for concepts, for example, recognition for the same material dropped only a bit, from 80 percent to around 65 or 70 percent. And recognition scores for all categories of information remained significantly above chance across all 12 years.

FIGURE 7.10

A. Mean percentages of correctly recognized names and concepts across retention intervals. B. Mean percentages of correctly recalled names and concepts across retention intervals. (From Conway, Cohen, & Stanhope, 1991.)

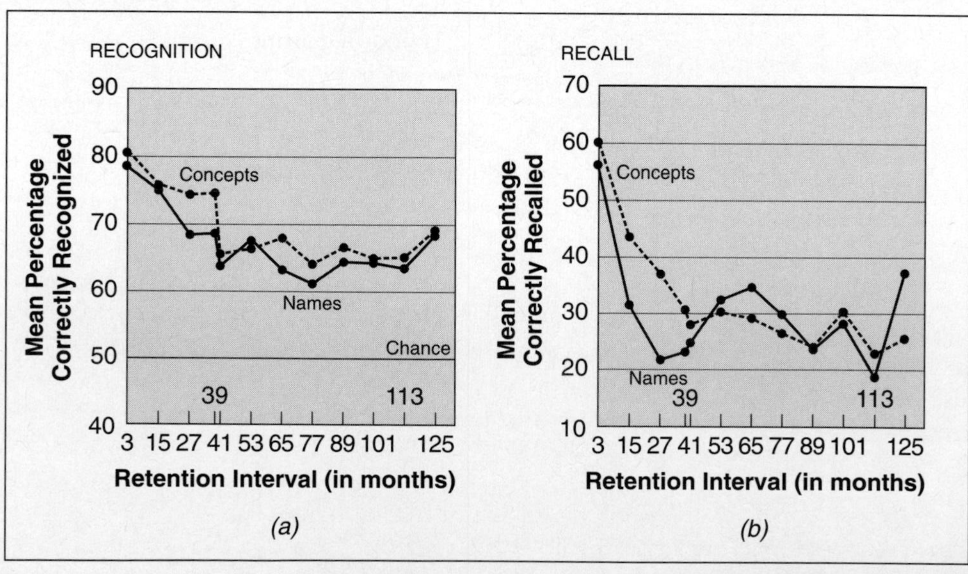

Your honest estimate—your metacognitive awareness of having information in storage—can be quite inaccurate. You can remember a considerable amount of information, without giving yourself credit for it.

Point—and now counterpoint. We fall prey to memory illusions, by "remembering" events that never happened, by accepting misleading information (mudlarks), by failing to remember the source of different bits of information. We "remember" seeing the FOURS in Bransford and Francks's (1972) studies, "remember" *sleep* in Roediger and McDermott's (1995) work, and "remember" yield signs and other implanted memories.

THE IRONY OF MEMORY

So which is it? Is memory accurate or not? Maybe the answer has to do with information you deliberately and intentionally learned, versus real-world information you merely noticed or experienced.

Our underestimates of memory often seem to involve the former, situations that involved intentional learning to begin with. That is, we claim to have "forgotten" information that we once learned deliberately—high school French, a college class in cognitive psychology, the list learned just five minutes ago in an experiment. A (probably) large part of this memory failure is that we are confusing true forgetting with retrieval difficulties. And as you learned in Chapter 5, these are *not* the same. And, as Loftus (1980) once wisely observed, "We must never underestimate one of the most obvious reasons for forgetting, namely, that the information was never stored in memory in the first place" (p. 74).

Our *overestimates,* on the other hand, seem to involve memory for meaningful, real-world experiences—or meaningful lab information that resembles the real world. We don't deliberately *memorize* experiences that happen to us, of course. Instead, we attempt to understand them, as they happen. This is more like *incidental learning,* in which learning and memory are by-products of having experienced something. Maybe merely remembering that some event happened—"I remember seeing the car accident"—tends to mislead us, tends to make us believe that we can also remember specific details about the event. It might also blind us, in a sense, to the possibility that our memory may have been distorted by other experiences or by our own existing knowledge.

In any event, the work on memory illusions points out a notable irony of memory: When we try deliberately to learn and remember, we think we've forgotten when we haven't, and we have low confidence. But when we didn't try intentionally, we later think we *do* remember, often with unreasonably high confidence. Memory's fragile power!

Summary

1. Bahrick's research on memory for high school classmates and other school-related information showed surprisingly high, long-term accuracy in recognition. It appears that a high degree of overlearning, combined with distributed practice, contributes heavily to such performance.
2. In several studies, psychologists have tested their own autobiographical memories, finding that the distinctiveness and personal relevance of events are important predictors of what will be remembered.
3. Some evidence demonstrates that there is a special, vivid "flashbulb" memory for experiences that are personally relevant. Other tests of this idea indicate, however, that

these memories are influenced by reconstructive memory processes too. People do have great confidence in the accuracy of these memories, rightly or not.

4. The irony of long-term memory is that we often feel that deliberately learned information has been forgotten, when in fact it is often retained rather well. We subjectively feel that information acquired through everyday experience is remembered accurately, when in fact it is often distorted and inaccurate.

Important Terms

autobiographical memory
default value
false alarms/false positives
false memories
flashbulb memories
frames/slots
headers
leading questions
memory impairment
misinformation acceptance
propositions
reconstructive memory
recovered memories
repression
schema/schemata
scripts
semantic integration
source memory
source misattribution effect
technical/content accuracy
thematic effect
von Restorff effect

Suggested Readings

There is now an extensive literature—not to mention full bookshelves—on the topic of repressed and recovered memories, false memory syndrome, and the like. For the cognitive science approach, start with the important paper by Loftus (1993), and a set of comments on that paper in the May 1994 issue of the *American Psychologist* (1994, 439–445). The entire April 1996 issue of *Journal of Memory and Language* (1996, 75–334) contains reviews and new empirical work on various aspects of "Illusions of Memory." Book-length treatments of the topic include Loftus and Ketcham's (1991) *Witness for the Defense*. The most common reference work for those who believe strongly in the reality of repressed and recovered memories is *The Courage to Heal* by Bass and Davis (1988). In Loftus's (1993) words, "Readers [of Bass and Davis] without any abuse memories of their own cannot escape the message that there is a strong likelihood that abuse occurred even in the absence of such memories" (p. 525).

Several books present interesting papers on autobiographical memory. The original was Gruneberg, Morris, and Sykes (1978); Neisser (1982) has edited a book entitled *Memory Observed: Remembering in Natural Contexts*, which delves into both autobiographical memory and the topic of ecologically valid memory research. See also sources such as Rubin (1986, 1995a, 1995b) and Cohen (1989). Consult the Banaji and Crowder (1989) paper and the entire "Science Watch" section of the *American Psychologist*, January 1991, for extensive discussion—and occasional "zingers"—in the debate between laboratory and real-world memory advocates.

SECTION

THREE

LANGUAGE AND COMPREHENSION

CHAPTER EIGHT

LANGUAGE

Language is the most common and universal feature of human society. More than any other aspect of human knowledge, language pervades every aspect of our lives, from innermost private thoughts to public behavior. We can imagine societies with no interest in art or music, for example, or even one with no formal system of numbers and arithmetic. But it's inconceivable that a society would have no language, no means of communication among individuals. Every culture, no matter how primitive or isolated, has language, and every individual, unless deprived by nature or accident, develops skill in the use of language.

This chapter presents some of the basics of language, its characteristics, functions, and structure. **Linguistics** is the academic discipline that studies language *per se*, and much of what we understand about language has come to us from that discipline. Indeed, developments in linguistics, especially Chomsky's (1959) rejection of the behaviorist explanation of language, had a profound influence on the development of cognitive psychology. Chomsky's insistence that language was based on mental rules, rather than habits learned through reinforcement, meant that a cognitive approach to language was needed.

That approach is known as **psycholinguistics,** *the study of language as it is used, and learned, by people*. We examine different aspects of people's behavior as they "do" language—for instance the time it takes to comprehend a word in a sentence, the occasional errors we make in speech, the way a child misuses a word. All of these provide a "window" on the mental processes of language. They give us data on the mental mechanisms that enable us to communicate with each other.

This chapter presents a brief survey of the field of psycholinguistics, and serves as an introduction to Chapter 9, where we discuss additional research on comprehension, both written and spoken. Especially in that chapter, we will be concerned with the interrelationships between language and the human cognitive system responsible for its use and acquisition.

Linguistic Universals, Functions, and Levels of Analysis

Preview: language defined; linguistic universals; iconicity and sign language; animal communication systems; three levels of analysis

DEFINING LANGUAGE

Let's begin with a definition of language, to see where we're going here. Psycholinguistics defines the term as

- **Language:** A shared symbolic system for communication.

First, language is symbolic. It consists of units that form words, where the units are either spoken sounds or written characters. These units *symbolize* or stand for the referent of the word—the word "car" *refers* to an object, it *symbolizes* that object. Just as the symbols "$" and "%" refer to concepts, so do language symbols like *car* and *microorganism*.

Second, the symbol system and the rules that form it are *shared* by the speakers of a language culture. That is to say, the speakers (and listeners) of a language have all learned the same set of arbitrary connections between symbols and meaning, and the same rules for combining those symbols into meaningful sentences. You and I both mean the same thing when we use the symbol *bachelor,* for example, which means we'd all agree that there's something wrong with sentence (1*). (According to custom in psycholinguistics, a sentence that violates conventional rules for language is preceded by an asterisk.)

(1*) *The bachelor and his wife went to the movies.*

And our shared system of rules for forming sentences means that we all would judge sentence (2) as a "better," more grammatical English sentence than sentence (3*).

(2) *The speaker showed us a picture of her son.*

(3*) *Us a picture of her son showed the speaker.*

Third, the rule and symbol system we share enables *communication.* A speaker translates a thought into a public message, using the rule system for expressing meaning. The listener then translates that message back into the underlying thought or meaning, by means of the same rule system. To make communication successful, obviously, we all need to be using the same system, the same rules.

UNIVERSALS OF LANGUAGE

Needless to say, if the rule system you know is the English language, you won't be able to communicate successfully with someone who speaks only French or Japanese—different rule systems, different symbols. And yet if we peer beneath the surface differences among languages, there is tremendous underlying similarity in terms of more abstract characteristics. Hockett (1960, 1966) called those characteristics **linguistic universals,** the *characteristics that are universally true of all human languages.* Hockett proposed that only human language, as distinct from various animal communication systems, contains all of the features.

Several of the universals he described are not now considered essential characteristics of language, although they were probably essential to the evolution of language. For example, the Vocal-Auditory Channel universal states that true language is spoken and heard. But this excludes non-spoken forms of language, like writing and sign language, so is not taken that seriously now. Several other features, however, are critically important to our analysis here. Table 8.1 presents all 13 universals on Hockett's list. We'll limit our discussion to five of these, plus two that flesh out some of Hockett's thinking.

Semanticity

The term *semantic* means "meaning," as you know. It is an obvious yet important point that language exhibits semanticity. This is to say that the sounds of human language carry meaning, whereas other sounds that we make, say coughing or clearing our throats, are not part of our language because they do not convey meaning. Of course, coughing *could* convey meaning—for example if all the students in a classroom cough in unison to "comment" on a professor's boastful remark. Here, the coughing sound would be *paralinguistic*, and would function much the way rising vocal pitch indicates anger.

TABLE 8.1

Hockett's (1966) Linguistic Universals

1. **Vocal-auditory channel:** Language is spoken and heard, that is, is transmitted vocally and received auditorily.
2. **Broadcast transmission and directional reception:** Language messages are "broadcast" in all directions from the source, and can be received by any hearer within range.
3. **Transitoriness; rapid fading:** The spoken language message is transitory, lasting only as long as its transmission (compare with written messages).
4. **Interchangeability:** Messages and speakers are interchangeable; any speaker can in principle convey any message (compare with male vs. female birdsong).
5. **Total feedback:** Speakers have total auditory feedback for their messages, simultaneous with listeners.
6. **Specialization:** The sounds of language are specialized to convey meaning.
7. **Semanticity:** Language symbols, and hence utterances, convey meaning (compare with sounds like coughing).
8. **Arbitrariness:** The connection between a symbol and its referent is arbitrary, is not built in (compare with iconic systems).
9. **Discreteness:** Language uses only a small number of discrete ranges, say on vowel duration, to convey meaning, rather than changing meanings continuously across the dimension.
10. **Displacement:** Language messsages are not tied in time or space to the present.
11. **Productivity:** Language is novel and creative, produced by a set of rules, rather than repetitive.
12. **Duality of patterning:** A small set of sounds is combined and recombined into an infinitely large set of sentences. By themselves, the sounds have no meaning, but in combinations they do.
13. **Cultural or traditional transmission:** Language is acquired by exposure to the culture, to the language of surrounding individuals (compare with genetically governed systems in animals).

Arbitrariness

Hockett's feature of arbitrariness derives directly from the point above about language as a system of symbols. **Arbitrariness** means that *there is no inherent connection between the units (sounds, words) employed in a language and the meanings referred to by those units*. There are a very few exceptions to this, for instance the onomatopoeia of *buzz*, *hum*, *zoom*, and the like. But far more commonly, the symbol we use to refer to something has no inherent relationship to the thing itself. The word "dog," in and of itself, is not similar to the creature it names, just as the spoken symbol "silence" does not resemble its referent, true silence. Hockett's clever example makes the same point; "whale" is a small symbol for a very big thing, while "microorganism" is big symbol for an extremely small thing.

The implication of arbitrariness is absolutely key to our purposes here. It is that language users have to *learn* the connections between symbols and their referents, since the connections are not built in. The connections, further, have to be stored in a system that enables rapid retrieval—in other words, human memory, a cognitive system equipped with sufficient abilities and mechanisms that the learned connections can be used efficiently. This is this sense of language being a *shared* system, that we've all learned essentially the same connections, stored them in memory, and have them available for retrieval.

Flexibility and Naming

Two important consequences of arbitrariness deserve special attention, partly because they help to distinguish human language from several animal communication systems, and partly because they tell us about the human language user. Although neither of these was listed by Hockett, they are clearly derived from his point about arbitrariness.

First, we *name* things—things don't *have* names so much as we *give* names to things. We name *everything*, concrete objects, abstract ideas, emotions, and so forth. We invent names for the new things that are invented, and for new distinctions and shadings of

MARK TWAIN ON "NAMING"

Mark Twain captured the essence of naming and arbitrariness in a wonderful story called "Eve's Diary." On Wednesday of the second week after creation, Eve writes:

> *During the last day or two I have taken all the work of naming things off his [Adam's] hands, and this has been a great relief to him, for he has no gift in that line, and is evidently very grateful. He can't think of a rational name to save him, but I do not let him see that I am aware of his defect. Whenever a new creature comes along I name it before he has time to expose himself by an awkward silence. . . . The minute I set eyes on an animal I know what it is. I don't have to reflect a moment; the right name comes out instantly. . . . I seem to know just by the shape of the creature and the way it acts what animal it is. . . . When the dodo came along [Adam] thought it was a wildcat—I saw it in his eye. But I saved him. . . . I just spoke up in a quite natural way of pleased surprise . . . and said, "Well, I do declare, if there isn't the dodo!"*

meaning that we wish to express, borrowing and adapting existing words as we go. For instance, a "computer" used to be a person who performed computations, until a machine was invented to do the work; right now, I am "word processing," an activity unheard of prior to the invention of the machine. We have names for intangibles like emotions and ideas, even though words like *intangible* don't name a physical object. And we "know" that things have names, even if we don't know what the precise name is; most people don't know the name of the plastic "thing" on the end of their shoelaces (it's called a "collar").

Second, we change the meanings of words freely, showing a high degree of *flexibility*. We rearrange the connections between symbols and meanings, substituting one term for another, changing connotations at will. Terms become outmoded (*aeroplane* and *phonograph*), connotations change (*monitor, gay*), and analogies, borrowings, and slang inject change and creativity into language (*mouse, chic, cool*). That's the flexibility of language, that our symbol for a concept or idea can change if the entire language group decides to change it. The implication, of course, is that language users must be able to make those changes in memory.

Displacement

One of the most powerful devices our language gives us is *the ability to talk about something other than the present moment*, a feature Hockett called **displacement.** By conjugating verbs to form past or future tense, we can communicate about objects, events, and ideas that are not in the present time, but are remembered or anticipated. And, when we use constructions such as "If I go to the library tomorrow, then I'll be able to . . ." we demonstrate a particularly powerful aspect of displacement—we can communicate about something that has never happened, and indeed might never happen, while clearly anticipating future consequences of that never-performed action. To illustrate the power and importance of displacement to yourself, try speaking *only* in the present tense for about five minutes. You'll discover how incredibly limiting it is to be "stuck in the present" by language.

Productivity

By most accounts, the principle of productivity (also termed *generativity* by some authors) is the most important of all the linguistic universals, since it gives language its most notable characteristic, *novelty*. Although it is featured in Hockett's list of universals, he was by no means the first to appreciate its importance. Indeed, the novelty of language, and the productivity that novelty implies, formed the basis of Chomsky's (1959) critique of Skinner's book, and the foundation for Chomsky's own influential theory of language (e.g., 1957, 1965).

Putting it simply, **productivity** means that *language is novel, consisting of utterances that have never been uttered or comprehended before*. In other words, speakers literally *invent* sentences as they speak them, and listeners comprehend these new inventions. Aside from trite phrases and greetings, hardly any of our normal language is standardized or repetitive. So language is a *productive* system—knowledge of the rules and the words allows us to *produce* or *generate* language.

What does productivity mean for language? It means that language is a *creative* system as opposed to a repetitive system. We do not recycle sentences, so to speak. Instead, we create them on the spot, in real time. In a very real and important sense then, applying our productive rules of language to the words in our vocabulary permits us to generate an infinite number of utterances. And, similarly, the same rules and vocabulary permit us to understand any of those utterances.

ICONICITY AND SIGN LANGUAGE

Contrast the flexibility of language with the opposite of a symbolic system, which Hockett termed an "iconic" system. In an **iconic** system, *each unit has a physical resemblance to its referent*, just as a map is physically similar to the terrain it depicts. In such a system, there is essentially no flexibility at all, because the connection between the icon and its referent is built in and therefore unchangeable.

In fact, the human language that comes closest to being iconic is sign language. Originally, the "words" in sign language, the sequences of hand movements, were chosen to resemble the thing being referred to. And some proportion of the ASL (American Sign Language) vocabulary remains physically similar to the referent, as shown in Figure 8.1.

But far more commonly now, the signs in ASL have become abstracted and stylized, such that there is often little discernible similarity between the sign and its referent (Frishberg, 1975). ASL words blend, simplify, and combine signs, or rely on rules that violate simple iconic connections. Consider two examples.

First, ASL has fairly iconic signs for the tools screwdriver, hammer, and pliers (Bellugi & Klima, 1979). But to express the concept TOOL, it uses a naming rule—you'd sign SCREWDRIVER–HAMMER–PLIERS, a short list of members of the category to name the category itself.

Second, to intensify meaning, a sign is made more rapidly than usual (Howard, 1983). Thus, to sign the concept of VERY QUICKLY, you would sign QUICKLY in a

FIGURE 8.1

An American Sign Language sign showing a degree of iconicity. A signer creates an American Sign Language depiction of a grand piano. The sign is partially iconic because it resembles the physical object. (From Newport & Bellugi, 1978.)

rapid, tense fashion. But using this rule can literally contradict the iconic relationship, for instance when signing the concept of VERY SLOWLY. For this, you would apply the normal rule for intensifying, making the sign for SLOWLY in a rapid, tense fashion.

ANIMAL COMMUNICATION SYSTEMS

Now contrast the flexible, productive human language system with the various animal communication systems that have been studied, for instance the vervet monkey signaling system (Marler, 1967). In the wild, these monkeys have a system of distress and warning calls, to alert an entire troupe of monkeys about imminent danger. They produce a guttural "*rraup*" sound to warn others in the troupe of an eagle, one of their natural predators; they "*chutter*" to warn of snakes, and "*chirp*" to warn of leopards.

The monkey signaling system does exhibit semanticity, an important characteristic of human language. That is, each signal has a different, specific referent—eagle, snake, and leopard. And furthermore, these seem to be arbitrary connections—"*rraup*" doesn't resemble eagles in any physical way.

But the signaling system is not flexible, in the sense used earlier. As Glass and Holyoak (1986) note, the troupe of monkeys cannot get together and decide to change the meaning of "*rraup*" from eagle to snake—the arbitrary connections to meaning are completely inflexible in these systems. Moreover, this inflexibility is most probably due to at least partial genetic influence. Contrast this with the learned basis of human language wherein any child will learn whichever language the culture teaches (this is Hockett's last universal, *cultural transmission*).

Furthermore, there is a vast difference between naming in human languages and in the animal systems. For instance, there seem to be no words in the monkey signaling system for other obviously important objects and concepts in their environment, "tree" for example (or presumably for their more emotional or abstract concepts, given Harlow's, 1953, famous demonstrations of the security and comfort needs of baby primates). And as for displacement and productivity, consider the following delightful quotation from Glass

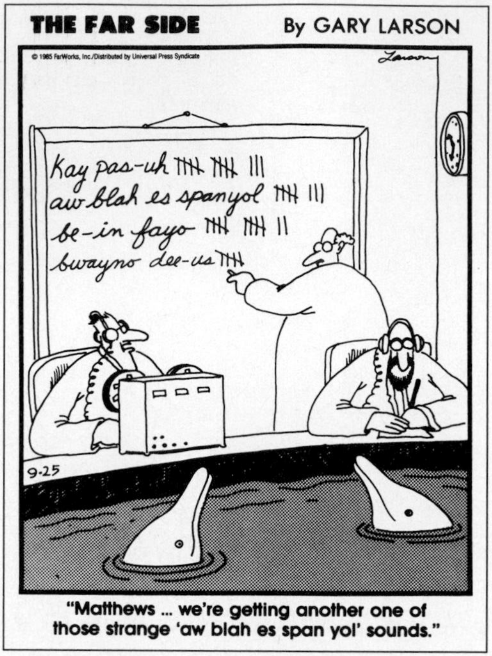
THE FAR SIDE
By GARY LARSON
Kay pas-uh
aw blah es spanyol
be-in fayo
bwayno dee-us
9-25

"Matthews ... we're getting another one of those strange 'aw blah es span yol' sounds."

and Holyoak (1986): "The monkey has no way of saying 'I don't see an eagle,' or 'Thank heavens that wasn't an eagle,' or 'That was some huge eagle I saw yesterday'" (p. 448).

The monkey signaling system is not unique in these respects. In fact, as far as is known, the same kinds of limitations—or more severe ones—apply to all animal communication systems. Thus, beyond the levels of semanticity and arbitrariness, no animal communication system seems to exhibit those characteristics that appear to be universally true of—and vitally important to—human language. In the wild, at any rate, there appear to be no genuine languages. In human cultures, genuine language is the rule, apparently with no exceptions.

Three Levels of Analysis

Linguistics traditionally approaches language as a system to be investigated and understood at three levels of complexity, the three layers of knowledge that (in their view) compose language. First is

- **Phonology:** The study of the production and perception of language sounds.

As you'll learn, the sounds of language are not at all simple—they present daunting problems in terms of speech comprehension, problems so difficult that no modern computer yet has the general capability of understanding spoken language.

Then there's

- **Syntax:** The study of the structure of sentences, and of rules determining the order of words and phrases in those sentences.

LANGUAGE TRAINING PROJECTS

What about the well-known projects in which animals, usually chimpanzees or gorillas, are taught a language? Don't these show that animals *can* achieve true language?

Among the best known of such projects are the ones described by Gardner and Gardner (1969), Patterson and Linden (1981), and Rumbaugh (1977), in which the animals were taught either a form of sign language or another symbolic system. Apes like Washoe, Koko, and Kanzi (Savage-Rumbaugh & Lewin, 1994) have not only learned appreciable vocabularies, they have also demonstrated several other interesting features we normally think of as rooted in language; for instance, inventing new terms (Washoe signed "candy" and "fruit" when he first tasted watermelon), expressing emotions, and even telling lies (Patterson & Linden, 1981). And newer work has shown greater comprehension abilities than we would have thought possible for nonprimates—Herman's (1987) dolphins show remarkable comprehension, not just for symbols but also for how the symbols are sequenced.

Regardless of these accomplishments, there are at least two serious differences between these demonstrations and what we refer to as genuine language. First, the animals' use of the trained language seldom becomes advanced enough to convey complex ideas, especially when "word" order is taken into account. If anything, longer and longer utterances on the part of animals simply become more repetitive. And second, however amazing the demonstrations are, including evidence that a chimp can learn the trained language from another chimp, it remains true that the language does not occur naturally and spontaneously in the natural habitat.

What is it about our language, and our knowledge of it, that tells us to put words into one order but not another? Why is the phrase "big red dump truck" a better, more natural sounding one than "red big dump truck"?

Finally, we'll turn to

- **Semantics:** The study of word meaning.

This is essentially the study of the mental lexicon, a term we used in Chapter 6 to refer specifically to our knowledge of words and their meanings. Earlier you read a sentence about "the bachelor and his wife." It was your semantic system, your mental lexicon, that alerted you to the fact that something was wrong there—that is, that a bachelor is an unmarried man, and "wife" contradicts "unmarried."

A Critical Distinction

In the next chapter, we'll add two more levels of analysis, levels which make it even clearer how *psycho*linguistics differs from more traditional linguistics. For a preview of this difference, consider Chomsky's (1957, 1965) critical distinction between competence and performance.

- **Competence** is the internalized knowledge of language and its rules that fully fluent speakers of a language have.

Competence is idealized knowledge, in a sense, because it represents a person's complete knowledge of how to generate and comprehend language. On the other hand,

- **Performance** is the actual language behavior that a speaker might generate, the string of sounds and words that the speaker utters.

Chomsky argued that competence was a purer basis for understanding language than performance, because performance is flawed, imperfect, and full of errors. When we speak, he argued, we are revealing not only our knowledge of language—our competence—but also various limitations and shortcomings of the human system. Speakers lose their train of thought, pause, repeat themselves, make pronunciation mistakes, and so forth. These irregularities or errors in otherwise fluent speech, called *dysfluencies*, are not part of our

★ **TABLE 8.2**

Speech Errors

Type	*Example*	*Intended to Say*
Shift	she decide to hits it	she decides to hit it
Exchange	slicely thinned	thinly sliced
Anticipation	stowing to the store	going to the store
Perseveration	a silly sistake	a silly mistake
Deletion	to mutter intelligibly	to mutter unintelligibly
Substitution	it's too light	it's too heavy
Blend	to explain clarefully	to explain carefully/clearly

Source: Adapted from Carroll (1994).

basic competence. Instead, they reflect limitations in the *language user*. Not surprisingly, linguistics was not particularly interested in studying the language user—that's psychology's job.

So that's *precisely* the focus of psycholinguistics, the language user's behavior. Our thinking goes like this: Lapses of memory, speech errors, and difficulties in generating fluent speech—indeed all dysfluences—give us strong hints about how the human system *does* language. Just as an example, we understand far better how language is represented mentally, and how our language production system works, when we consider the kinds of ★ errors people often make in overt speech, as shown in Table 8.2. Theories of language, from our perspective, need to accommodate the *data* of language, the things people say, including the mistakes.

Summary

1. Language is defined as a shared symbolic system for communication. The symbols of the language, sounds or written characters, are combined and recombined according to rules that are shared among all members of the language culture. This enables speakers and listeners to communicate.
2. Characteristics true of all human languages are called linguistic universals. Of the full list, the universals of semanticity, arbitrariness, displacement, and productivity, along with the additional characteristics of flexibility and naming, show the true nature of language.
3. Even American Sign Language, which was originally very iconic, is now largely a system based on arbitrary connections between the symbols and their referents.
4. Few if any naturally occurring animal communication systems display linguistic universals beyond semanticity, and none that we know of is a truly productive or generative system.
5. The three traditional levels of analysis in linguistics are phonology, syntax, and semantics. We examine these both in terms of people's competence, their idealized knowledge of the language, and performance, including various errors people make as they speak and comprehend.

Phonology—The Sounds of Language

Preview: phonology; phonemes and the phonological grammar; the variability of speech sounds; coarticulation; the problem of invariance; the role of context

In any language interaction, the task of a speaker is to communicate an idea by translating that idea into spoken sounds. The listener goes in the opposite direction, translating from sound to intended meaning. Although there are many sources of information available in a spoken message, the most obvious and concrete one is the sound of the language itself, the stream of speech signals that must be decoded. This is the study of phonology and the *system of rules*, the phonological **grammar** that enables us to put sounds together into words. (For work on the information available in gestures, see Krauss, Morrel-Samuels, & Colosante, 1991.)

TABLE 8.3

English Consonants, Vowels, and Diphthongs

English Consonants

Manner of Articulation		1 *Bilabial*	2 *Labiodental*	3 *Dental*	4 *Alveolar*	6 *Palatal*	7 *Velar*	9 *Glottal*
Stops	Voiceless	p (*p*at)			t (tack)		k (cat)	
	Voiced	b (*b*at)			d (*d*ig)		g (get)	
Fricatives	Voiceless		f (*f*at)	Θ (*th*in)	s (sat)	š (*f*i*sh*)		h (*h*at)
	Voiced		v (*v*at)	ð (*th*en)	z (*z*ap)	ž (*az*ure)		
Affricatives	Voiceless					č (*ch*urch)		
	Voiced					ǰ (judge)		
Nasals		m (*m*at)			n (*n*at)		ŋ (sing)	
Liquids					l (*l*ate)	r (rate)		
Glides		w (*w*in)				y (*y*et)		

English Vowels

	Front	*Center*	*Back*
	i (beet)		u (boot)
High			ʊ (book)
	ɪ (bit)		
		əɪ (bird)	o (bode)
Middle	e (baby)	ə (sofa)	
	ɛ (bet)		ɔ (bought)
	æ (bat)	ʌ (but)	
Low			
			a (palm)

English Diphthongs

/au/	cow
/oi/	boy
/ai/	mice
/ey/	bait

Source: From Glucksberg and Danks (1975) and Palermo (1978).

SOUNDS IN ISOLATION

The basic sounds that compose a language are called **phonemes.** A survey of human languages would find somewhere around 200 different phonemes present across all known languages. No single language uses even half that many, however. English, for instance, contains about 46 phonemes (Chomsky & Halle, 1968; experts disagree on whether some sounds are separate phonemes or blends of two phonemes), whereas Hawaiian has only about 15 (Palermo, 1978). Notice that there is actually little significance to the total tally of phonemes in a language—no language is superior to another because it has more (or fewer) phonemes (or because of any other difference, for that matter).

Table 8.3 shows the articulation table of English phonemes (Glucksberg & Danks, 1975). Figure 8.2 accompanies the table, showing a diagram of the vocal tract with numbered locations keyed to Table 8.3. For consonants, three variables are relevant:

FIGURE 8.2

The human vocal tract, illustrating places of articulation: 1, bilabial; 2, labiodental; 3, dental; 4, alveolar; 5, palatoalveolar; 6, palatal; 7, velar; 8, uvular; 9, glottal. (From Fromkin & Rodman, 1974.)

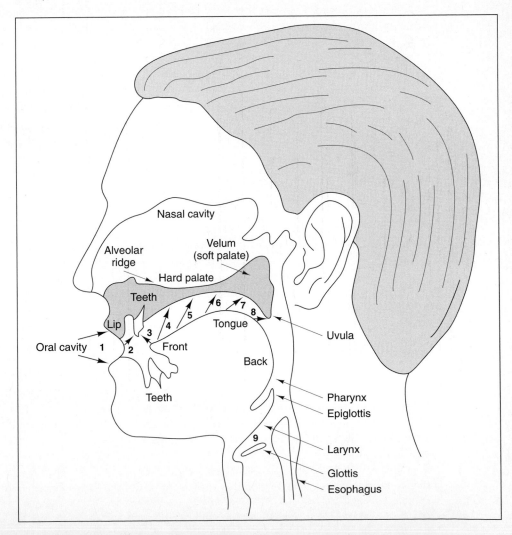

- *place of articulation*, the physical location in the vocal tract where the airflow is disrupted;
- *manner of articulation*, the way the airflow is disrupted; and
- *voicing*, whether the vocal cords begin vibrating immediately with the disruption of the airflow.

A few examples will help you here. Say "Bob" out loud several times, nice and clearly, focusing on the initial /b/ sound. The /b/ phoneme is a *bilabial consonant;* its *place of articulation* is the lips, hence it's a "bilabial." This simply means that the column of air coming up from the lungs is disrupted at the lips for this phoneme, as it is for /p/, /m/, and /w/.

Second, /b/ is a *stop consonant*. This means that the airflow is completely *stopped* during articulation of /b/, and then the momentary blockage is released.

Third, /b/ is a *voiced consonant*. Start to say "Bob" out loud, but hold your lips together rather instead of releasing the air. You can hear and feel the vibrations in your vocal cords—it's *voiced*. Contrast this with the phoneme /p/, which has the same place and manner of articulation, but is not voiced at the same time as the blockage of air. If you'll try saying "Pete" while keeping your lips together, there's no noise, just a buildup of air pressure. There is no vibration of the vocal cords in articulating /p/, so it's *voiceless*.

Vowels, by contrast, involve no disruption of the airflow. Vowels are articulated with an uninterrupted column of air through the vocal tract. They differ on two dimensions; placement in the mouth, whether front, center, or back, and tongue position in the mouth, high, middle, or low. Scan the table, pronouncing the sample words, and try to be consciously aware of the characteristics that you (if you're a native or fluent English speaker) know so thoroughly at an unconscious, automatic level.

VARIABILITY IN SPEECH SOUNDS

What isn't obvious to you in this exercise is the amazing variability in speech sounds that we tolerate as speakers and hearers of the language. Obviously, different speakers articulate sounds somewhat differently, one kind of variability that we tolerate. Another kind is the moment-to-moment differences within any particular speaker—your articulation of /b/ varies somewhat from one time to the next. But there is also variability depending on the *rest* of the word being articulated, because articulation of any phoneme is influenced by the phonemes that surround it. As a simple example, put your hand in front of your mouth and then say the words *pot* and *spot*—even though the /p/ sounds belong to the same phoneme category, we pronounce them differently (one with a puff of air, one without).

◆ Look at Figure 8.3, a stylized depiction of the individual phonemes in the word *bag*. The initial /b/ sound is present more than halfway through the pronunciation of the whole word, as shown by the diagonal lines. Likewise, the /g/ sound, shown in dotted lines, extends its influence back in time, overlapping the /b/ phoneme. And the vowel sound /ae/ influences both consonants, the one that comes before it as well as the one that follows it.

This overlapping of sounds is called **coarticulation,** that *more than one phoneme at a time is affecting articulation*. A more realistic depiction of the same phenomenon is shown

★ in Figure 8.4 (p. 252). The initial phonemes, /b/ on the left side and /d/ on the right, show up in the early part of the word, say the first 200 milliseconds. If you'll look down each column of patterns, you can see how /b/ changes depending on the later sounds in the words, and likewise for the /d/ patterns on the right.

What you haven't articulated yet, the later phonemes in a word, influences what you're saying right now. And the reverse is true too—what you've already articulated continues to have an influence on current pronunciation. A useful analogy here is skilled typ-

◆ **FIGURE 8.3**

Coarticulation in "bag." Coarticulation is illustrated for the three phonemes in the word *bag*; solid diagonals indicate the influence of the /b/ phoneme, dotted diagonals the influence of /g/. (From Liberman, 1970.)

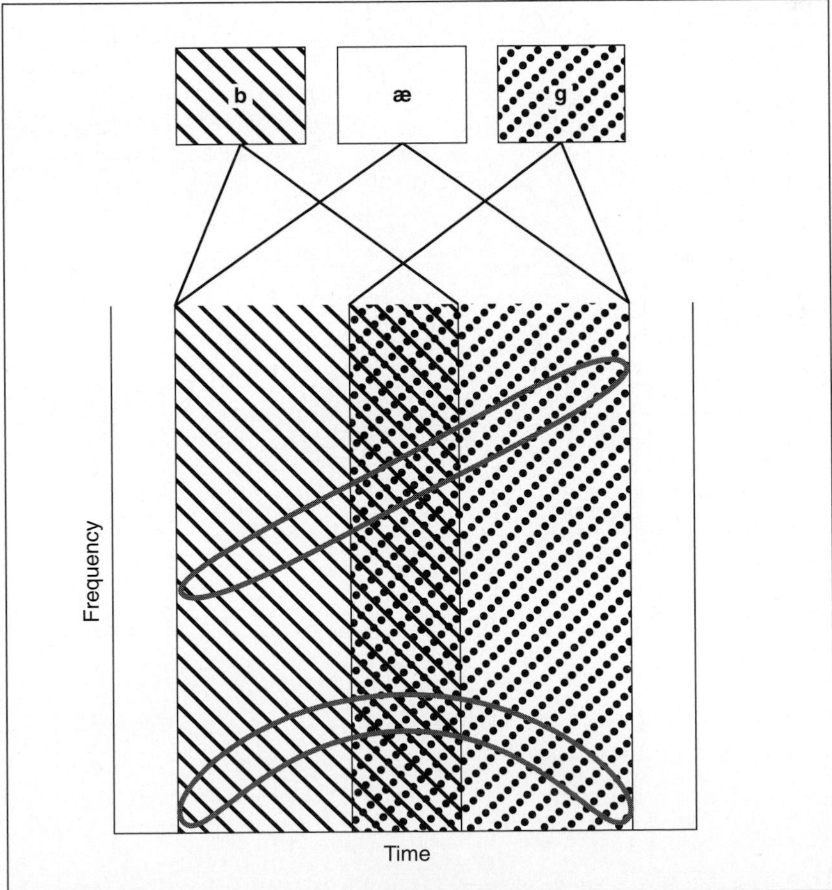

★ **FIGURE 8.4**

Spectrograph patterns for the /b/ and /d/ families. Spectrographic patterns of two families of syllables, showing the changes across time in the physical sound patterns. Depicted is "the problem of invariance" for consonants. There are dramatic changes in the initial portions of the patterns, induced by the following vowel, even though the consonant sounds from top to bottom are all classified as the same phoneme. For instance, the /b/ in *bet* and *bird* are physically different, yet both are perceived as /b/. In contrast, the /b/ and /d/ sounds in *bet* and *debt* are very similar physically but are perceived as different phonemes. (From Jusczyk, Smith, & Murphy, 1981.)

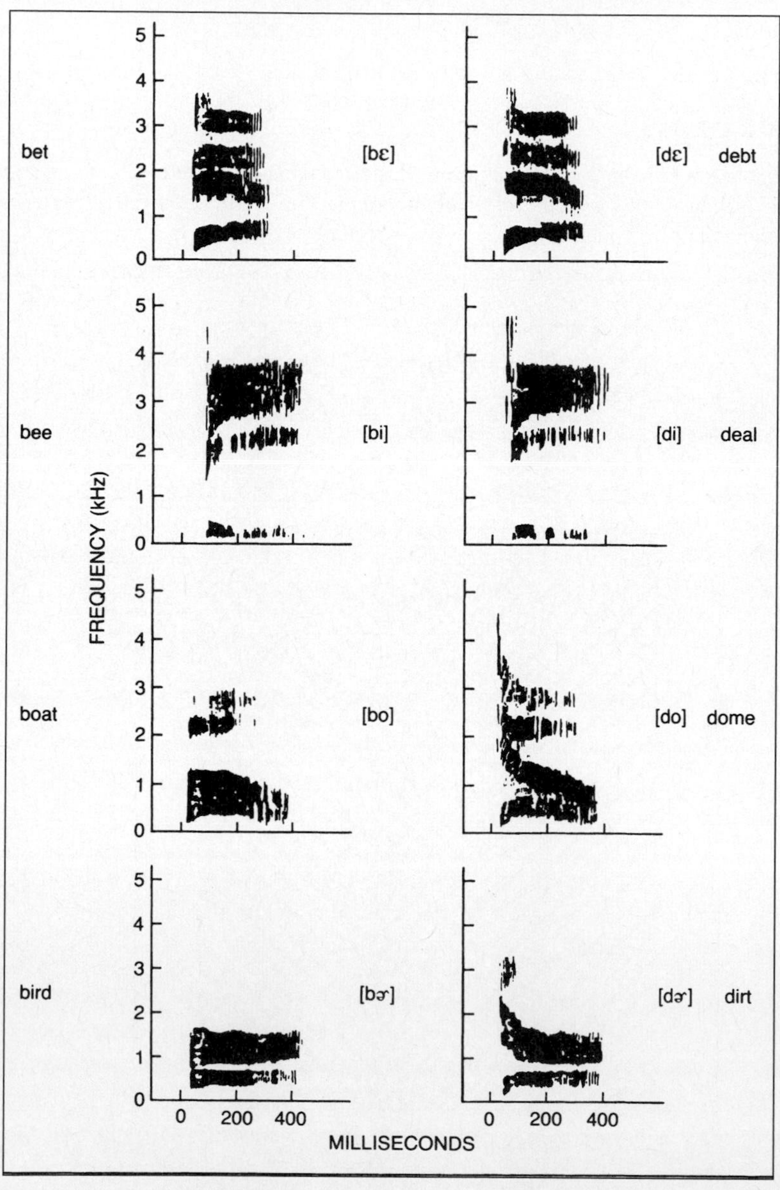

ing, where your right index finger starts moving toward 'h' before your left index finger has struck the 't' in the word "the." In like fashion, your vocal tract begins to move toward the /ae/ in "bag" before you have articulated /b/, and toward /g/ before even finishing the /b/.

This gets us to the true sense of the term *phoneme;* it's a *category of different language sounds treated as the same, regardless of physical differences* (e.g., Liberman, Harris, Hoffman, & Griffith, 1957). As long as a sound falls within the appropriate boundaries, it's classified as a member of that phoneme category.

Phonemic Differences Across Languages

What's interesting about this is a comparison of phonemes across different languages, because the boundaries and categories differ dramatically from one language to another.

Compare the initial consonant sounds of "keep" and "cool." English speakers discern no real difference between these two *hard k* sounds, even though they are physically different (if you alternate between "keep" and "cool," you'll eventually feel a difference in the initial sounds—the "k" feels somewhat higher in your throat than the "c"). In other words, those two different sounds (called *phones*) belong to the same phoneme category in English, so demonstrate **categorical perception**—they are *perceived as belonging to the same category*. Interestingly, exactly these two sounds are different phonemes in Arabic (Glucksberg & Danks, 1975). That language contains two words that differ *only* in those sounds, and yet have entirely different meanings—/kalb/, with the "k" from "keep," means "heart," and /qalb/, with the "c" from "cool," means "dog" (Gleason, 1961).

Here's a second example, an easier one for English speakers to understand. The /s/ and /z/ sounds are different phonemes in English—by changing from one to the other, we get words with different meanings, as in "ice" and "eyes." But these two sounds are the same phoneme in Spanish, making it as difficult for Spanish speakers to hear the difference between "ice" and "eyes" as it is for English speakers to hear the two hard k sounds differently. (Similarly, English differentiates between the liquids /l/ and /r/, whereas Japanese doesn't, making *that* distinction especially difficult for native speakers of Japanese when they master English.)

COMBINING PHONEMES INTO WORDS

From a pool of about 46 phonemes, English generates *all* of its words, however many thousands that might be. This illustrates an aspect of language's *productivity*, the fact that a small number of units can be combined and recombined into an essentially infinite number of words. The *rules* for combining the units are referred to as the **grammar** of the language.

Your knowledge of the phonological grammar of English, your *phonological competence*, tells you which sound combinations are legal in English phonology and which ones aren't. Consider the three phonemes in *bat*. You can rearrange them into *tab*, but **abt*, **bta*, and **tba* are illegal. Why? It's not because those combinations are unpronounceable, although English speakers find them difficult to pronounce. Instead, it's simply that English doesn't use those combinations. English phonology doesn't permit a stop consonant followed by another stop consonant within the same syllable. In fact, English doesn't permit all sorts of sequences that other languages do permit—the 'p' is silent in "pneumonia" in English, but not in French.

The *grammar* of the language, then, specifies the phoneme sequences that are actually found in the language, and calls them *legal sequences*. Thus you know that **bnench* is an illegal sound combination in English, whereas *blench* could be an English word (Glucksberg & Danks, 1975). These judgments are based solely on your phonological competence, your internalized grammar of the language. The fact that you can't verbalize the rules means that your phonological grammar is implicit—you have extensive phonological competence, even though you don't have explicit knowledge of the rules. (Incidentally, "blench" *is* an English word, a verb meaning roughly the same as to "bleach.")

SPEECH PERCEPTION AND CONTEXT

We are now ready to approach the question of how people produce and perceive the speech signal. Do we merely hear a word and segment it into its separate phonemes, or is this even a possibility given the nature of spoken speech? When we speak, do we merely string phonemes together, one after another, like stringing beads on a necklace?

The answer to both questions is "no." The variability in speech that you read about is usually referred to as **the problem of invariance**—a puzzling term because the "problem" is *that speech sounds are not invariant*. We'd never comprehend if we perceived speech by segmenting the signal into individual phonemes, because the individual phones change so much depending on the sounds around them. And likewise, stringing one phoneme after another to pronounce a word, like stringing necklace beads, ignores how the surrounding sounds influence articulation.

Instead, consider a *cognitive* explanation. The answer to the question "how do we produce and perceive speech?" is *context*. Putting it another way, the answer is *conceptually driven processing*. If we had to rely entirely on the spoken signal to figure out what was being said, then we would be processing speech in an entirely data-driven fashion, a bottom-up process. We would have to find some basis for figuring out what every sound in the word was, and then retrieve that word from memory based on the analysis of sound. This is virtually impossible, given the variability of phonemes. Instead, the words, phrases, and ideas already identified—the context—lead us to correct identification of new, incoming sounds.

A clever demonstration of this was performed by Pollack and Pickett (1964). They tape-recorded several spontaneous conversations, spliced out single words from the tapes, then played the spliced words to subjects. When the words were presented one at a time, in isolation, subjects identified them correctly only 47 percent of the time. But performance improved when longer and longer segments of speech were played, because more and more supportive syntactic and semantic context was then available.

In a related study, Miller and Isard (1963) presented three kinds of "word strings" to their participants: fully grammatical sentences such as "Accidents kill motorists on the highways," anomalous strings such as "Accidents carry honey between the house," and completely ungrammatical strings such as "Around accidents country honey the shoot." They also varied the loudness of the background noise, from the difficult –5 ratio, when the noise was louder than speech, to the easy ratio of +15, when the speech was considerably louder than the noise. Participants were asked to shadow the strings they heard, that is, to repeat immediately afterward what the speaker on the tape recording was saying. Correct responses were the percentage of strings they were able to shadow accurately.

The results, shown in Figure 8.5, demonstrated the importance of supportive syntax and meaning. Accuracy improved significantly going from the difficult to easy levels of speech-to-noise ratios, which isn't surprising of course. But the improvement was especially dramatic for the sensible, grammatical sentences. For instance, the figure shows that when the loudness of the speech and white noise were balanced (the point marked 0 ratio), 63 percent of the grammatical sentences were repeated correctly, versus only 3 percent of the nonsense, ungrammatical strings. And even with the easiest signal/noise ratio of +15, fewer than 60 percent of the ungrammatical strings could be repeated correctly. Clearly, the words and ideas we've already comprehended in a spoken message assist us in comprehending the rest of the message.

So the evidence points toward a combination of data-driven and conceptually driven processing in speech recognition. In such a combination, features of the speech signal are analyzed perceptually, and tentative identifications of different sounds are made. At the same time, the listener's *other* linguistic knowledge is being called into play. These higher levels of knowledge and analysis operate in parallel with the phonemic analysis, and provide information to the perceptual mechanism that helps identify the

FIGURE 8.5

Percentage of strings shadowed correctly. (From Miller & Isard, 1963.)

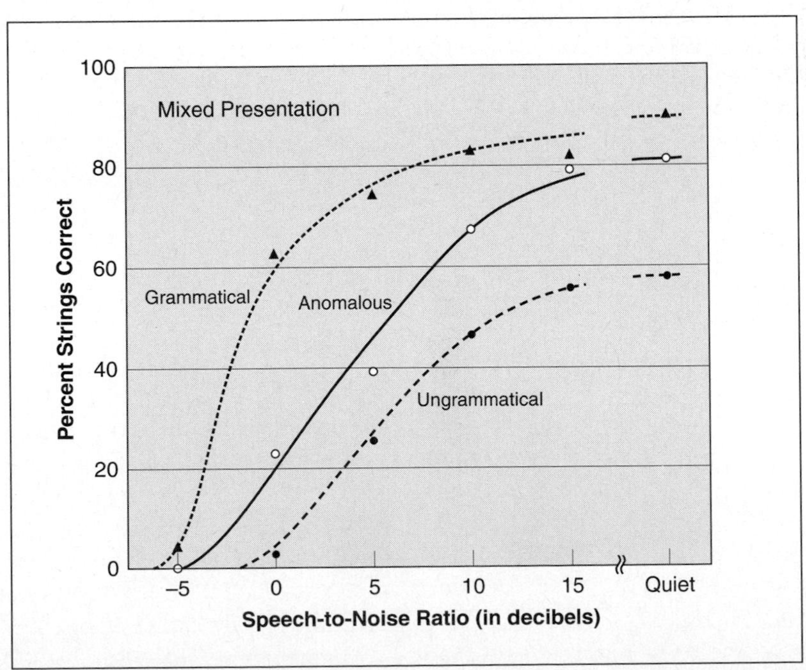

sounds being analyzed. (For further information on the role of context in phoneme detection, see Dell & Newman, 1980, and Pitt & Samuel, 1995.)

A specific connectionist model that does exactly that was proposed by McClelland and Elman (1986). In their TRACE model, information is continually being passed among the several levels of linguistic analysis in a spreading activation fashion. Lexical or semantic knowledge, if activated, can thus alter the ongoing analysis at the phonological level by "telling" it what words are likely to appear next. At the same time, phonemic information is being passed to higher levels, thus altering the patterns of activation there.

Pauses Between Words

As if the preceding sections weren't enough to convince you of the need for conceptually driven processing, consider one final feature of the stream of spoken speech. Despite coarticulation, categorical perception, and the problem of invariance, we naively believe that *words* are somehow separate from each other in the spoken signal, that there is some physical pause or gap between spoken words just as there is a blank space between printed words.

Guess what—it just isn't true. Analysis of the speech signal shows there is virtually no consistent relationship between pauses and the ends of words. Indeed, if anything, the pauses we produce while speaking are longer *within* words than between words, as shown in Figure 8.6.

FIGURE 8.6

A spectrogram from the sentence "John said that the dog snapped at him," taken from fluent spoken speech. Note that the pauses or breaks do not occur regularly at the ends of words; if anything, they occur more frequently *within* the individual words (e.g., between the /s/ and /n/ sounds, between the /p/ and /t/ sounds; compare with the end of *the* and the beginning of *dog*). (From Foss & Hakes, 1978.)

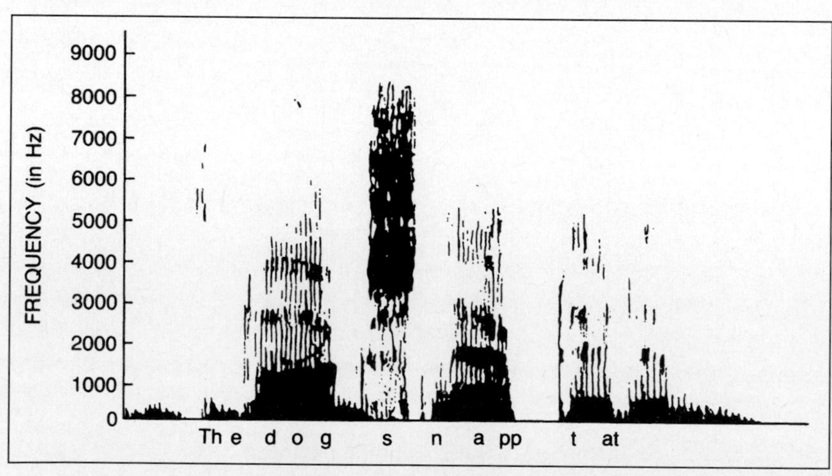

But don't you "hear" those pauses, the breaks between words? What you're "hearing," as it were, is supplied to you by top-down processing, by your knowledge of the language and your understanding of the sentence. Top-down processing enables you to "know" ahead of time what it is you're going to hear, so makes it easier to comprehend it when you finally do hear it. Because of this knowledge, it's no wonder that you "hear" breaks between words in your native language—in a very real sense, hearing the pauses is a perceptual illusion. What language *really* sounds like is the uninterrupted stream of sound you hear when a foreign language is spoken—with no knowledge to assist you in top-down processing, you just hear sounds.

Summary

1. The basic sounds of a language are called phonemes. Each phoneme is actually a category of sounds, including a fairly broad range of sounds that are physically similar but not identical.
2. Articulation of consonants depends on place of articulation, manner of articulation, and voicing. Vowels differ in placement in the mouth and tongue position. Articulation of phonemes is influenced by the surrounding phonemes in the word, a phenomenon called coarticulation.
3. Phonemes differ across languages. This means that a phonemic difference in one language may not be present in another. Likewise, different languages have different rules for combining phonemes into words.
4. Detection of phonemes and recognition of words depend heavily on context. The phonological illusion that there are pauses or breaks between words is also due to conceptually driven processing.

Syntax and Semantics—Word Order and Meaning

Preview: word order and syntactic structure; Chomsky's transformational grammar; the cognitive role of syntax; the semantic/lexical level; case grammar

SYNTAX

At the second level of analysis of language we have **syntax,** *the ordering of words in a sentence to show their relationship to one another; sentence structure*. Notice that this is *not* the normal, everyday connotation of "syntax," which people usually associate with "school grammar." The rules in school grammar—don't say "ain't," for example—are prescriptive, telling you (prescribing) what you should and shouldn't say. This is somewhat irrelevant to psycholinguistics, where the interest instead is in a *descriptive* grammar, one that merely describes how people arrange words and phrases into meaningful sentences. Thus your syntactic grammar tells you what combinations of words are meaningful, and how the words and phrases should be arranged.

With the permission of Bob Thaves.

Word Order

An obvious and important point here is that the meaning of a sentence is far more than the meanings of the individual words in the sentence. In particular, the relationships among the words, as specified by word order, supply meaning too. More than some languages (Latin, for example), English relies heavily on word order to specify meaning. Consider "red fire engine" versus "fire engine red." Despite the fact that all three words can be nouns, our English grammar tells us that the first word in these phrases is to be treated as an adjective that modifies the following noun. Thus, just by varying word order, "red fire engine" is a fire engine of the usual color, and "fire engine red" is a particular shade of red.

Words and Phrases

There's more to it than just word order, however. We also rely on the ordering of larger units such as phrases or clauses to convey meaning. Consider the following sentences:

(4) *Richard told the students that he'd grade their assignments on Monday.*

(5) *Richard told the students on Monday that he'd grade their assignments.*

In these examples, the position of the phrase "on Monday" helps us figure out what meaning was intended—whether the assignments would be graded on Monday, or whether Richard told the students something on Monday. Thus, the sequencing of words and phrases contains clues to meaning—clues that speakers use to express meaning and clues that listeners use to decipher meaning.

English is similar to many languages in its syntactic preference for standard **S-V-O sentences,** *subject-verb-object*. Earlier, you read two versions of a sentence, the S-V-O version (2)—*The speaker showed us a picture of her son*—and the unacceptable version (3*)—*Us a picture of her son showed the speaker*. The unacceptable sentence (3*) is in O-V-S order, an illegal syntactic ordering in English. It's your syntactic competence, your implicit knowledge of word and phrase order rules, that tells you that sentence (3*) is illegal. More generally, these rules are called a *grammar,* or more specifically a *syntactic grammar*. What *is* the grammar of English syntax?

CHOMSKY'S TRANSFORMATIONAL GRAMMAR

The important linguist Noam Chomsky (e.g., 1957, 1965) proposed a highly influential theory of language and syntax called **Transformational Grammar**—TG for short. This theory focused on two separate sets of rules, based on Chomsky's insights about language and the rules we follow in producing grammatical language.

Begin with one of Chomsky's most critical insights: sentences exist on several different levels. Loosely speaking, a sentence exists at the *idea* level, at the level of an abstract *deep structure*, and finally at the level of an overt *surface structure*. Changing the sentence from one level to the next is a matter of applying different sets of rules to the sentence, moving it along toward its eventual spoken form.

Consider the following idea, something like

/OLD TRUCK CLIMB STEEP HILL/

(we have to use words to depict the idea here, of course, even though the "idea" level contains no real words). In Chomsky's scheme, a basic set of grammatical rules called **phrase structure rules** would be applied to this idea, giving it a sort of quasi-sentence structure, like

(OLD TRUCK) (CLIMB STEEP HILL).

The second phrase should also be further subdivided, like

((CLIMB) STEEP HILL)

to indicate that CLIMB is part of one subunit, and STEEP HILL forms another subunit. Thus, Chomsky's phrase structure rules specified the components or subunits of a sentence, and showed how they should be ordered. A typical way of portraying those rules is ◆ shown in Figure 8.7 (p. 260).

Chomsky noted that this kind of simple grammar has at least two major difficulties. One involves paraphrases. Most speakers would consider sentences (6) and (7) to be closely related:

(6) *The minister led the congregation.*

(7) *The congregation was led by the minister.*

But phrase structure grammar focuses so heavily on word and phrase order that it does not capture that close relationship at all. The second difficulty involves ambiguity, situations

FIGURE 8.7

A depiction of a phrase structure grammar: (A) the rewrite rules of the grammar, (B) sentence generation by the rules, (C) a tree diagram or hierarchical representation, and (D) a "bracket equivalent" diagram of the sentence. (From Lachman, Lachman, & Butterfield, 1979.)

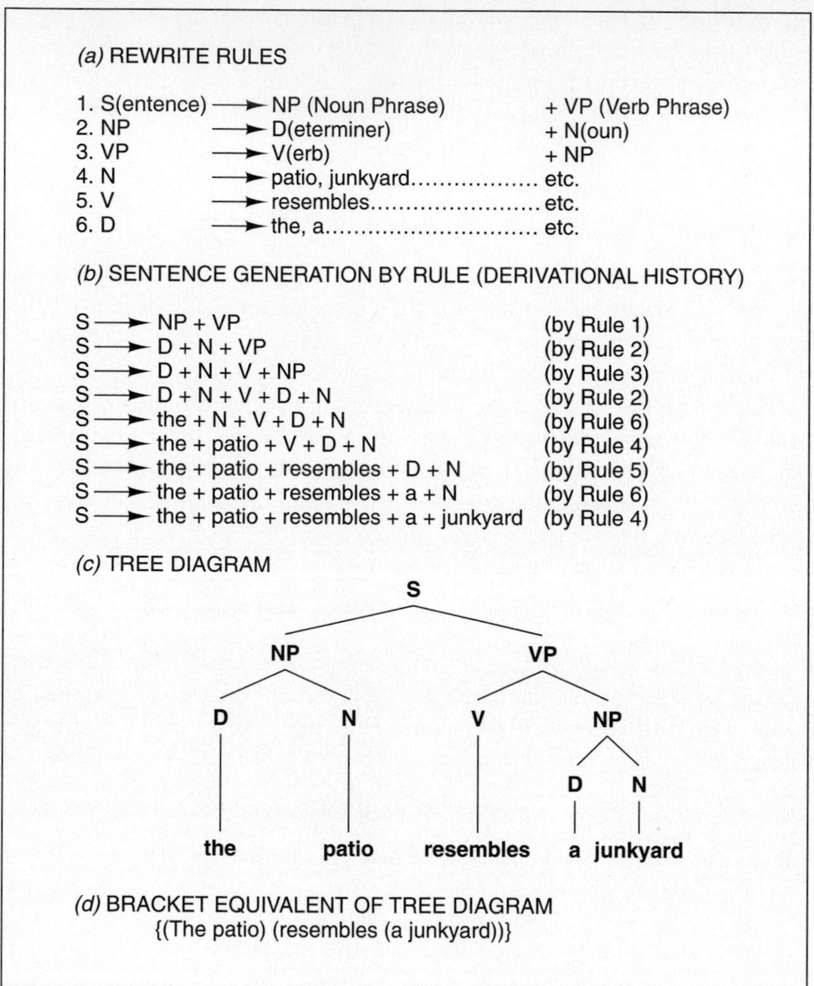

in which the sentence has more than one meaning. Sentences like (8) and (9) are ambiguous even though each has only one phrase structure.

(8) *Visiting relatives can be boring.*

(9) *The shooting of the hunters was terrible.*

In other words, two different ideas—that having your relatives visit can be boring, and that going to visit them can be boring—are turned into the same surface structure by this grammar. This is evidence that the grammar, by itself, is either wrong or incomplete.

★ Chomsky fixed this problem by adding a second set of rules, the transformational grammar. Figure 8.8 gives an overview of the theory, showing where the transformational rules fit in. This grammar contained rules for rearranging words and phrases, inserting and deleting words, and so forth. As a simple example, there are transformational rules for turning an active declarative sentence into a question, for negating the sentence, and for combining the question and negative transformations, as in:

(10a) *Dave sells tickets at the theater.*

(10b) *Does Dave sell tickets at the theater?*

(10c) *Dave does not sell tickets at the theater.*

(10d) *Doesn't Dave sell tickets at the theater?*

The Shortcomings of the TG Approach

Chomsky's theory captured an important aspect of language, its productivity. That is, this kind of grammar is *generative*—by means of the phrase structure and transformational rules, entire families of sentences could be generated by the grammar.

★ **FIGURE 8.8**

A summary of Chomsky's transformational grammar. (Adapted from Lachman et al., 1979, fig. 10.10.)

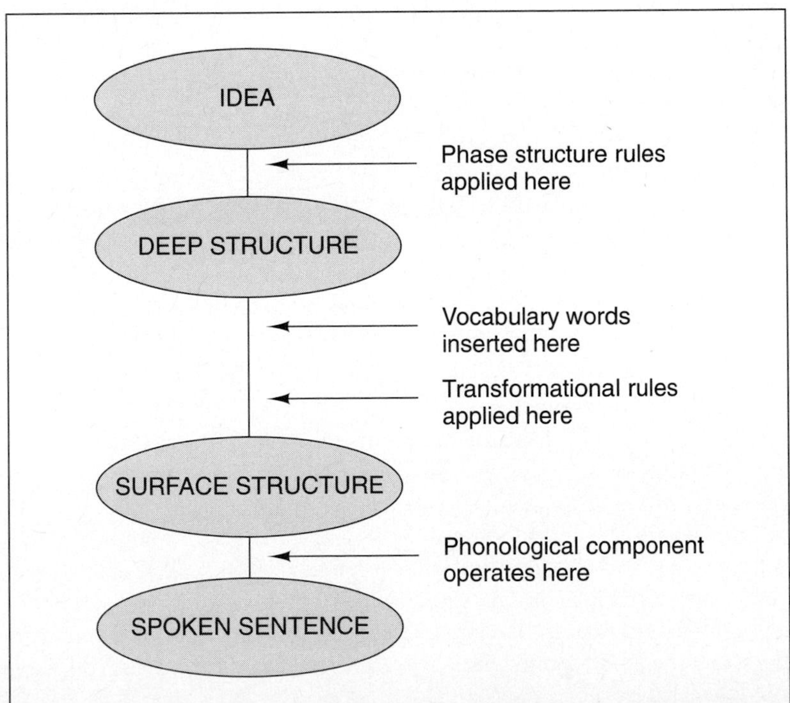

On the other hand, as psychology began using this approach to make predictions about language use, several dissatisfactions arose. Primary among these was the fact that Chomsky's heavy emphasis on syntax tended to shortchange *semantics*, the meanings of words and sentences. Transformational grammar had a set of rules for inserting vocabulary words into the abstract, deep structure, but—even as Chomsky noted—blindly inserting words without concern about overall sentence meaning could lead to some bizarre sentences, such as

(11) *Colorless green ideas sleep furiously.*

Moreover, inserting words into sentence structures in this fashion almost seemed to suggest that *how* you say something takes precedence over *what* you're saying. And, as recent work has shown, people use syntax, and make syntactic adjustments to their speech, in service of semantics—in other words, communicating *meaning* is more important than syntax. (In fairness, Chomsky invented the "Colorless green ideas" sentence to illustrate exactly this point, that a sentence could be syntactically acceptable yet still have no meaning.)

THE COGNITIVE ROLE OF SYNTAX

From a psychological perspective, what is syntax for? Why do our sentences have to follow a set of syntactic rules? The answers are obvious, of course—we need syntax to help the listener figure out meaning, to minimize the processing demands of comprehension as much as possible. Syntax helps listeners determine meaning, and helps speakers convey it.

Bock's (1982) excellent paper on a "cognitive psychology of syntax" places these issues in context for us. To begin with, she notes that the syntactic burden falls somewhat more heavily on the speaker than the listener. That is, the speaker has to produce a sentence with a surface structure that assists listeners in their job of comprehension. In a very real sense, syntax becomes a feature of language that is particularly related to the speaker's mental effort, the information processing involved in producing the sentence (see also Bock, 1995). Two of Bock's points illustrate the current psycholinguistic approach to syntax.

Automaticity

As we know, automatic processes are the product of a high degree of practice or overlearning. Bock notes that several aspects of syntactic structure are consistent with the notion of automaticity. For instance, children rely heavily on regular word order, even if the native language they are learning has relatively irregular word order. The purpose for this is fairly obvious—by relying over and over on the same syntactic frames, those frames can be generated and used more automatically.

Similarly, adults tend to use only a very few syntactic structures with any regularity, especially S-V-O orders, suggesting that these few can be called into service quite rapidly and automatically. Furthermore, those syntactic frames we use can be strongly influenced by a previous sentence. In several studies, participants have been found to produce syntactic structures that were *primed* by a previous sentence (e.g., Bock, 1986; West & Stanovich, 1986).

Planning

Second, the syntax of our sentences often reflects semantic factors. There is a strong tendency to put important words early in the sentence, especially in the subject position, in order to highlight that concept, to focus attention on it (e.g., Ferreira, 1994). Further, we often make on-line adjustments to syntax depending on the accessibility of the words we're using. If a word is easy to retrieve, that is, very accessible, it occurs earlier in a sentence. If a word is rare or difficult to retrieve, however, then the phrase it appears in tends to occur later in the spoken sentence.

These effects tell us something interesting about the mental mechanism that "plans" sentences. Early theories of sentence planning, for instance Fromkin's (1971) theory ▲ shown in Table 8.4, described planning as a sequential process; first you identify the meaning to be conveyed, then you select the syntactic frame, etc. Recent research, however, shows how *interactive* the planning process is. Difficulties in one component, say word retrieval, can return you to an earlier planning stage, in order to rearrange the syntax of the sentence. By selecting an alternate syntax, the speaker "buys" more time for retrieving the intended word (see also Kempen & Hoehkamp, 1987).

In other words, recent data show that we begin our utterances when the first part of the sentence has been planned, but *before* the syntax and semantics of the final portion have been worked out or selected. Hesitations in our spoken speech are excellent clues to the planning process, as are the effects of momentary changes in priming, lexical access, and working memory load (e.g., Bock & Miller, 1991; Lindsley, 1975).

LEXICAL AND SEMANTIC FACTORS—THE MEANING IN LANGUAGE

Now let's consider lexical and semantic factors, the third traditional level of linguistic analysis. This is the level of meaning in language, the level at which word and phrase

▲ **TABLE 8.4**

Stages of Speech Planning

Stage	*Process*
1	Identification of meaning; generate the meaning to be expressed.
2	Selection of syntactic structure; construct a syntactic outline of the sentence, specifying word slots.
3	Generation of intonation contour; assign stress values to different word slots.
4	Insert content words; retrieve appropriate nouns, verbs, adjectives, and so on from the lexicon and insert into word slots.
5	Add function words and affixes; fill out the syntax with function words (articles, prepositions, etc.), prefixes, suffixes.
6	Specify phonetic segments; express the sentence in terms of phonetic segments, according to phonological (pronunciation) rules.

Source: From Fromkin (1971).

meanings are "computed," to use the psycholinguistic jargon; in cognitive psychology, we call this *retrieval from memory*.

Of course, there is more to this level than merely retrieving word meanings—we have to extract the whole meaning of the sentence, relating the words and phrases to one another correctly. You've seen how syntax assists in this process. Now let's consider the lexical/semantic level.

Morphemes

We've been speaking throughout the chapter about "words" and "word meanings." These terms are technically inaccurate if we want to refer to the basic units of meaning in language. The correct term, instead, is **morpheme:** a morpheme is *the smallest unit of language that has meaning*. As a simple example, the word *cars* is actually composed of two morphemes: *car* refers to a semantic concept and a physical object, and the final s is a meaningful suffix denoting "more than one of." To take another example, the word *unhappiness* is composed of three separate morphemes: *happy*, the base concept, the prefix *un-*, meaning "not," and the suffix *-ness*, meaning "state or quality of being."

At our current level, it makes little difference whether we speak of words or morphemes as they occur in sentences (although there is a debate over the issue of whether the meaning of a word such as "unhappiness" is literally stored in memory, or whether it is "computed" from the three individual morphemes; see Carroll, 1994). Later on, when we talk about language acquisition, and especially in Chapter 10 when we consider neurological impairments of language skill, we will need the distinction between words and morphemes, and between *free morphemes* such as *happy*, *car*, *legal*, and *bound morphemes* such as *un-*, *-ness*, *-s*, and so forth.

THE MENTAL LEXICON

It isn't enough, however, to talk just about morphemes, or to pretend that the only thing that matters is the simple meaning or definition of a word. To be sure, your **mental lexicon,** your *mental dictionary of words*, includes simple definitions. But by most accounts it also contains *other* information about words, including phonology and syntax.

Think about the verb "chase," as an example of how concepts might be represented in the mental lexicon. The lexical representation of CHASE specifies the meaning of this morpheme in the lexicon. It must indicate that *chase* is a verb meaning "to run after or pursue, in hopes of catching." As for all semantic memory concepts, CHASE is represented as a node in memory with pathways connecting it to related information, say, RUN, PURSUE, CATCH, and the like.

But you know a great deal more about *chase* than just this. Your mental lexicon also tells how the word can be used, and what other kinds of concepts it can be used with—it's an active verb, requiring an animate subject, and so forth. Your semantic competence tells you that sentence (12) is a perfectly acceptable sentence based on semantic grounds, that (13) is semantically possible although unusual, that (14) violates the literal meaning of *chase*, and that (15*) is simply unacceptable.

(12) *The policeman chased the burglar through the park.*

(13) *The mouse chased the cat through the house.*

Calvin and Hobbes
by Bill Watterson
I LIKE TO VERB WORDS.
WHAT?
I TAKE NOUNS AND ADJECTIVES AND USE THEM AS VERBS. REMEMBER WHEN "ACCESS" WAS A THING? NOW IT'S SOMETHING YOU *DO*. IT GOT VERBED.
VERBING WEIRDS LANGUAGE.
MAYBE WE CAN EVENTUALLY MAKE LANGUAGE A COMPLETE IMPEDIMENT TO UNDERSTANDING.
© 1993 Watterson/Distributed by Universal Press Syndicate

(14) *His insecurities chased him even in his sleep.*

(15*) *The book chased the flower.*

CASE GRAMMAR

The best account of how we use this wealth of linguistic knowledge is the **semantic case grammar** approach, also simply called **case grammar.** A case grammar is a *set of semantic rules for language comprehension and production*. Like any other grammar, it's a set of rules stored in memory. Very much unlike the grammars you've just studied, the rules depend on *semantic* relationships, not syntactic ones.

Fillmore (e.g., 1968) is the one who developed the idea of the case grammar approach. He noted a serious drawback to purely syntactic approaches to grammar, that the syntactic role played by different words in a sentence is often quite irrelevant to the meaning of the sentence. As an example, read the following sentences and ask yourself a question, What role does "key" play in each sentence?

(16) *The janitor opened the door with the key.*

(17) *The key opened the door.*

Obviously, "key" plays completely different syntactic roles in the two sentences. But Fillmore pointed out that such a syntactic analysis completely misses the semantics of the situation, that the "key" *does* the same thing in both sentences. Similarly, we understand sentence (17) to mean that *someone*, probably the unmentioned janitor, used the key in (17), instead of supposing that the key did the opening on its own in that sentence. In other words, our semantic knowledge is far more important in determining sentence meaning than our syntactic knowledge.

Fillmore and several other investigators have proposed that language processing involves a *semantic* parsing, in which we focus on the *semantic roles played by the content words in the sentences*. These semantic roles are called **semantic cases,** or simply, **case roles.** In the above sentences, OPEN is the overall relationship being expressed in the sentences, DOOR is the *recipient* or *patient* case for the action of OPEN, JANITOR is the *agent* case, KEY is the *instrument* that was used, and so forth. Study Table 8.5 for a listing of several common cases and examples of how semantic case roles are assigned.

In short, it is now assumed that the mental lexicon does not merely contain simple word entries. Instead, each word entry includes a listing of the semantic cases (or arguments) that accompany that word, and any restrictions that apply too. Thus, the lexical entry would state the definition of CHASE, and would indicate that CHASE requires an animate agent, and a recipient capable of moving (or being moved) rapidly, and so forth. Accordingly, when we comprehend sentences, the process looks up the concepts in the mental lexicon, accessing word meaning, syntactic, *and* semantic case roles (e.g., Bresnan, 1978; Bresnan & Kaplan, 1982).

Evidence for Case Grammar

The major claims of the case grammar approach are that

- listeners (and readers) begin to analyze sentences *immediately*, as soon as the words begin, and that
- this analysis is a process of assigning each word to a particular semantic case role, with each assignment contributing its part to overall sentence comprehension.

An excellent way of testing these claims is to "fool" the process responsible for determining case roles, and see how the process responds. That is, we can present sentences to readers, and measure their comprehension processes. If we're successful in fooling the comprehension mechanism, there should be some noticeable change in comprehension.

An especially popular method for doing such research involves **eye gaze** (or eye fixation) methodology, simply *recording where and how long the eyes gaze at words during reading* (e.g., Rayner, 1993). If you were being tested with such a methodology, what do you think would happen when you read the following sentences?

(18) *After the musician had played the piano was quickly taken off the stage.*

(19) *After the musician had bowed the piano was quickly taken off the stage.*

TABLE 8.5

Semantic Cases and Examples

Case	*Example (in Italics)*
Agent	*Dave* wrote the paper.
	The accident was investigated by the *policewoman*.
Patient	Dave wrote the *paper*.
	The hippie touched the *debutante* in the park.
Instrument	He hit the ball with the *bat*.
	The janitor opened the door with the *key*.
Location	The hippie touched the debutante in the *park*.
	She came into the *office* with a box.
Time	The hippie touch*ed* the debutante in the park.
	I met my sister *yesterday* for lunch.

Comprehension of sentence (19) proceeds easily and without disruption—it's a fairly straightforward sentence. But for sentence (18), several experiments show significant disruption of comprehension. In particular, readers' eyes generally slow down considerably on the word "was" in sentence (18). Why at that word? Because it's at that point in the sentence that readers realize they've made a mistake earlier in the sentence, that they have incorrectly assigned "piano" to the *patient* case for the verb PLAY. Why the slowdown? Because once readers are aware of the mistake, they need time to *re*interpret the earlier part of the sentence, to go back and figure out where their mistake was.

Sentences like (18) are called *garden-path sentences*—the early part of the sentence "sets you up" so that the later phrases in the sentence don't make sense given the way you assigned case roles in the first part. Figuratively speaking, the sentence leads you "down the garden path"; when you realize your mistake, you have to retrace your steps back up the path in order to *reassign* earlier words to different cases.

Many researchers have studied how people comprehend such garden-path sentences, as a way of evaluating the case grammar approach to sentence comprehension (e.g., Frazier & Rayner, 1982; Mitchell & Holmes, 1985; Singer, 1990). And the typical result, longer eye fixations at the "disambiguating" word, provides support for both predictions from case grammar, first that we begin comprehending the sentence immediately rather than later, and second that comprehension involves assigning words to semantic case roles. (For a similar report using the "makes sense" task, see Boland, Tannenhaus, Garnsey, & Carlson, 1995.)

Semantics Can Overpower Syntax

And, as a closing comment on the importance of semantics, consider Fillenbaum's (1974) evidence that meaning can sometimes overpower the syntax of the sentence. As you read, notice that in many ways this is another demonstration of the power of top-down processing.

Fillenbaum presented "perverse" and disordered sentences to his subjects, sentences that were meaningful but expressed an unusual or atypical meaning (of course, straightforward, "normal" sentences were also presented). For instance, in the conjunctive sentence "John dressed and had a bath," the normal order of events is backward. The sentence "Don't print that or I won't sue you," is a "perverse" threat, the opposite of a customary threat. After reading each of the sentences, the participants had to write a paraphrase. Fillenbaum then scored their paraphrases against the originals.

◆ Virtually no one changed the normal sentences when they paraphrased them; as Figure 8.9 (p. 268) shows, normal sentences were changed only 1 percent of the time. But a striking percentage of the paraphrases "normalized" the perverse and disordered conjunctive sentences, making them conform to the more typical state of affairs. For example, a paraphrase of the perverse threat was "Don't print that, or I'll sue you." Even when the participants reread their paraphrases, they failed to see even a "shred of difference" from the originals.

Apparently, general knowledge was influential enough that it easily overpowered the syntactic and lexical aspects of the sentences (see also Britt, Perfetti, Garrod, & Rayner, 1992; McDonald, Bock, & Kelly, 1993). Sometimes we comprehend *not* what we hear or read, but what we *expect* to hear or read: as Fillenbaum (1974) put it, "people focus not on linguistic messages per se, but on the information they embody or appear to convey, considering and assimilating this information in relation to their preexisting knowledge of

FIGURE 8.9

Fillenbaum's (1974) results. Two kinds of normal sentences were shown, threats and "conjunctives" (labeled "C") like "John got off the bus and went into the store." Threats were then altered to be "perverse," and conjunctives were disordered (e.g., threat C, "John dressed and had a bath"). (From Fillenbaum, 1974.)

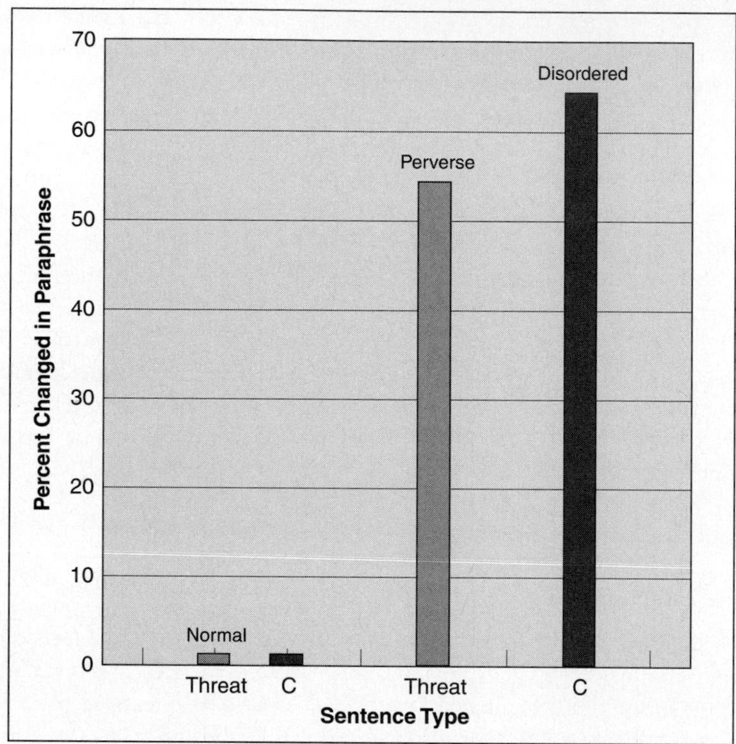

the ways of the world" (p. 578). To demonstrate it yourself, try these on your friends: "Nice we're having weather, isn't it?" and "Ignorance is no excuse for the law."

Summary

1. Syntax concerns the rules that determine word and phrase order. English relies rather heavily on word order to determine meaning, since different orders can convey very different meanings.
2. Chomsky's influential theory of syntax and language was called transformational grammar. In the theory, ideas were given a sentencelike structure by phrase structure rules, and then various transformations were applied to yield the surface structure.
3. Psycholinguistics became dissatisfied with the heavy emphasis on syntax, and developed the semantic case grammar approach to emphasize the importance of meaning. In case grammar, the concepts in sentences play semantic roles like *agent* and *patient*, and comprehension involves assigning concepts to those roles.

4. The evidence indicates that comprehension is well described by semantic case grammar, and that occasionally what we know to be true is more powerful than what is expressed syntactically in the sentence.

Language Acquisition

Preview: early stages of language acquisition; measuring language complexity in children; semantic and syntactic developments; children's language errors

A fascinating question—maybe one of the most fascinating of all ages—is, How does language acquisition happen? How do we become proficient language users, in the face of the variability of the sounds and the difficulty of figuring out the syntactic and semantic rules? What a tremendous feat it is for a child to learn language in the space of about five years—and this with little if any formal "teaching" on the part of adults.

This final section presents the highlights of language acquisition, as a complement to the topics you've studied so far in this chapter. The basic issues to be grappled with are fundamentally the same as in that earlier material—how do children master the phonology, syntax, and semantics of language?

EARLY STAGES OF LANGUAGE ACQUISITION

★ Table 8.6 presents an overall listing of the many different stages of language acquisition, from birth through about age five. Most people think that the first really significant event

★ **TABLE 8.6**

Stages of Language Acquisition with Ages of Onset

I. Prelinguistic stages
1. Reflexive crying: birth
2. Cooing, laughing: 8 to 20 weeks
3. Vocal play: 16 to 30 weeks
4. Reduplicated babbling: 25 to 50 weeks
5. Jargon babbling: 9 to 18 months

II. One-word utterance stage: 10 to 13 months

III. Two-word utterance stage (also called stage I): 18 to 24 months; MLU from 1.0 to 2.0

IV. Three-word utterances and beyond: 18 to 24 months
- Stage II: MLU from 2.0 to 2.5
- Stage III: MLU from 2.5 to 3.0
- Stage IV: MLU from 3.0 to 3.5; relative clauses begin to appear
- Stage V: MLU from 3.5 to 4.0

(Beyond this point, MLU becomes a less useful measure of sentence complexity.)

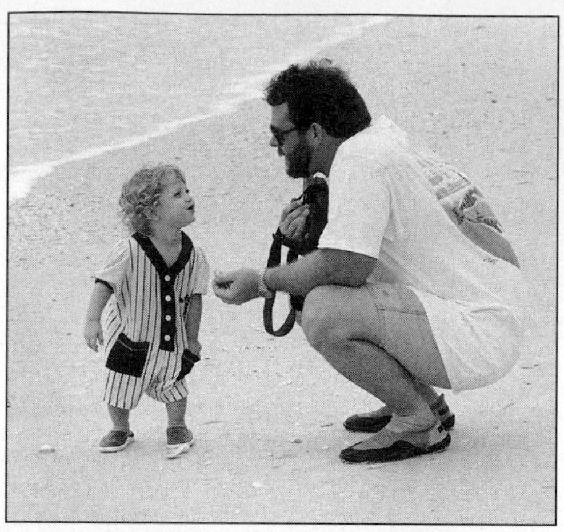

in a child's language development is his or her first spoken word, usually occurring around the first birthday. But as the table shows, there are several important precursors to that first word.

Prelinguistic Stages

Infants' *prelinguistic development*, development of language skill prior to true language, depends heavily on the physical maturation of the vocal apparatus. That is, during the first year, voluntary control over the mouth, tongue, and vocal cords develops. This enables the average six-month-old, for instance, to begin babbling, in particular making the "mum-mum-mum-mum" and "ba-ba-ba-ba" sounds known as *reduplicated babbling*. There's a clear influence here from the maturity of the infant's musculature. That is, first sounds are generally the easiest sounds to pronounce. So, for example, it only takes the gross motor movements of closing and opening the lips to make bilabial consonants like /b/ and /m/, and little or no tension in the mouth and tongue to babble vowel sounds like "ah" and "uh."

With greater voluntary control over the muscles, infants begin **jargon babbling,** producing *syllablelike phoneme combinations*, usually around nine months of age. This babbling is often very sentencelike, both in the variety of phoneme combinations and in the phrasing, intonation, and vocal emphasis the infant uses; For example, "ah DIM wap-ah-di BOOM!" (Ashcraft, 1989, p. 481). Especially with jargon babbling, one gets the impression that this is true vocal *play*, that the infant is experimenting with this vocal apparatus, trying it out, seeing what it will do. It's very likely that such play develops the necessary coordination of muscle movements and breathing necessary for true speech (e.g., Sachs, 1985).

One-Word Utterances

Finally, at about the first birthday, the child utters a word, either in isolation or embedded in a stream of jargon babbling. Again, the easier-to-pronounce phonemes are more prevalent—making it more likely that the child will say "important" words like "ma-ma" and "da-da."

Two features of this one-word utterance stage are particularly important to notice.

- First, one-word sentences usually coexist with jargon babbling—that is, the child will continue to babble even as the vocabulary available for one-word sentences grows larger. It's a mistake, in other words, to think of the successive stages of language acquisition in a strict "one by one" fashion. Instead, the stages overlap a great deal. Just because one-word sentences are the most common utterances at a stage doesn't mean that babbling as well as two-word sentences don't also occur.
- Second, focusing on how many words the child produces in a sentence fails to capture all of the child's language expertise. In general, the child's *receptive* vocabulary, the collection of words that can be comprehended, is always larger than the *expressive* vocabulary, words that are produced spontaneously. For instance, in Benedict's (1979) study, children at age 13 months comprehended about 50 different words, but did not produce 50 words on their own until about 19 months of age.

K. Nelson's work (1973, 1974) tells us a great deal about what children talk about at this one-word stage, and hence about the cognitive processes being used by these children. Overwhelmingly, children's vocabulary reflects semantics, and in particular those things in the child's environment and experience that are important to the child. For instance, in a sample of children whose expressive vocabulary was about 50 words, fully 51 percent of their words consisted of *general nominals*—in other words, *names* of things (doggie, juice). Another 14 percent of the words were *specific nominals*, names of specific people and things (Mommy, Daddy). But syntactic function words like "for" or "on" made up only 4 percent of their vocabulary.

Furthermore, the general nominals consisted largely of names for action-oriented, dynamic things, things the child can interact with—"ball," for a child who has fun rolling a ball during play, but not "sofa" or "floor." Thus, concepts that are important for the child to communicate about—talking about things to play with, things to do, things that are fun—are the concepts that are named.

MULTIWORD UTTERANCES

Beginning somewhere around 18 months of age, children begin combining words, first in two-word utterances, then three- and so forth. The patterns children use for combining words begin to show us the development of syntactic and semantic rules in the child's grammar.

It is sometimes quite difficult to decide whether an utterance should be counted as one, two, or several words; for example is "night night" a one- or two-word sentence? Most researchers therefore adopt a fixed way of counting words, and of describing the complexity of children's sentences. The measurement is called **MLU,** which stands for *mean length of utterance*. According to rules proposed by R. Brown (1973), the most appropriate way to measure complexity is to count the number of morphemes per utterance, not the number of words. Repetitions like "night" are counted as one morpheme, as are units that always occur together, like "allgone" and "gonna." The average of these sentence lengths across a sample of the child's utterances is the child's MLU.

An early theory of two-word utterances by Braine (1963) claimed that a simple, syntactic rule system governed these sentences, a grammar called the *pivot-open grammar*. In it are just two rules governing word order:

1. **S1** → P1 + O2
   (Type 1 Sentence rewritten as Pivot word plus Open word—for example, "Wanna cookie.")
2. **S2** → O1 + P2
   (Type 2 Sentence rewritten as Open plus Pivot—for example, "Daddy bye-bye." In both cases, the arrow → means "rewritten as.")

According to this scheme, there are two categories in the child's vocabulary, the large *open* word group, naming things and people, and the smaller category of *pivot* words, function words or sometimes verbs (e.g., "wanna," "more," and "no"). One rule specifies that the pivot word occurs first, followed by the open word, and the other rule specifies the opposite order.

▲ Table 8.7 portrays a variety of two-word utterances, from Brown's (1973) study of children's language. The most important point about these examples is that they demonstrate *semantic* rather than syntactic features. Indeed, Brown's data indicated that eight types of semantic relations accounted for about 75 to 80 percent of children's two-word sentences. Thus, rather than expressing syntactic rules, as the pivot-open grammar did, children's two-word sentences express *ideas,* semantic relations. And the bulk of these ideas are exactly the kind you learned about in the semantic case grammar approach, for example *agent* + *action* and *action* + *object*.

Beyond Two-Word Sentences

Beyond two-word sentences, that is, beyond an MLU of 2.5, children's sentences become increasingly complex, both syntactically and semantically. They combine more semantic relations together (e.g., *agent* + *action* + *object,* as in "Daddy eat grape"), and begin to add

TABLE 8.7

Brown's (1973) Eight Semantic Relations, Stage I, Two-Word Utterances.

Semantic Relation	*Examples*
agent + action	mommy come; daddy sit
action + object	drive car; eat grape
agent + object	mommy sock; baby book
action + location	go park; sit chair
entity + location	cup table; toy floor
possessor + possession	my teddy; mommy dress
entity + attribute	box shiny; crayon big
demonstrative + entity	dat money; dis telephone

Source: From Brown (1973).

some of the syntax of the language—adding meaningful morphemes like *-ing* ("I running"), plurals, articles like "the" and "a," and so forth. Figure 8.10 portrays this increasing complexity of language in terms of MLU, as a function of age (Miller & Chapman, 1981). Note that by age four or five, when MLU has clearly exceeded 4.0, the child's language has become complex enough, and enough like adult speech, that the task of language acquisition is largely, though not completely, done.

ERRORS IN CHILDREN'S SPEECH

Table 8.8 (p. 274) shows the typical *order* of acquisition of grammatical morphemes, grammatical forms that convey meaning. The basic purpose of showing this table is to demonstrate the kind of syntactic complexity that is added as children acquire the finer points of language. For example, the first form added is the *-ing* suffix, which appears far earlier than the most common word in the language—"the" (8). The last grammatical addition in the table (14) is illustrated with the sentence "I'll do it," a complex form in which the auxiliary verb *will* is turned into a contraction in appropriate settings; note that the uncontractible form appears slightly earlier (12, "I will.").

Past Tense Errors

The second purpose for the table is to show how various tense forms of regular and irregular verbs are added to speech. For example, an early form (5) is the irregular past tense, as in "Jordan hit me." Later on (9), regular past tense forms begin to appear. The fascinating thing about this is that once the regular past tense begins to appear, children then *overreg-*

FIGURE 8.10

Relationship between age and MLU. (From Miller & Chapman, 1981.)

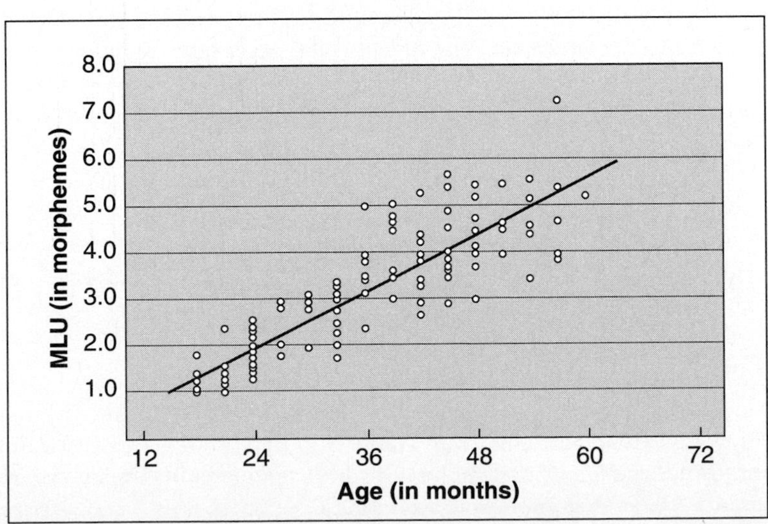

TABLE 8.8

Brown's (1973) 14 Grammatical Morphemes, with Sample Utterances

Morpheme	Sample utterance
1. Present progressive	I running.
2-3. Prepositions (in/on)	Put the water in. Put my sock on.
4. Plural	Want many books.
5. Irregular past tense	Jordan hit me.
6. Possessive	My teddy.
7. Copula, uncontractible	(Who's going night-night?) The dollie is.
8. Articles	Go on the porch.
9. Regular past tense	I walked to Suzie's.
10. Third person present tense, regular verb	Noel walks like this.
11. Third person present tense, irregular verb	Jordan rides a bike.
12. Auxiliary, uncontractible	(Will you drink your milk?) I will.
13. Copula, contractible	I'm happy now.
14. Auxiliary, contractible	I'll do it.

Source: From Brown (1973).

ularize past tense in both regular and irregular verbs—not always, but often enough for this to be a noteworthy feature of their language. A child who had said "Jordan hit me" will probably start saying "Jordan hitted me." It may take a substantial amount of time before correct irregular verb forms reappear.

The import of this concerns the child's grammar, the internalized set of rules, and memory. It seems that at point (9), the child has now learned the rule for forming past tense, add *-ed* to the verb stem. The rule plus the exceptions stored in memory for irregular verbs governs formation of the past tense. Most of the time—96 percent of the time according to Marcus (1996)—preschoolers use the correct irregular form, retrieving it from memory in normal fashion. But occasionally, with retrieval failure, the past tense rule is applied, yielding an error like "I forgetted." It makes little difference that the child has probably *never* heard such constructions as "I forgetted" or "he goed" (and, for that matter, it seems to make little difference that parents correct the errors). When the irregular form is more difficult to retrieve from memory, say, because the verb is relatively infrequent, the rule governs speech (Marcus, 1996).

Overextensions

A second type of error in children's speech concerns semantics directly, in particular, the topic of word meaning for children's words. Children often *overextend* words, using "doggie" not just for the family dog but for *any* furry creature, and "Daddy" for any adult male; Bowerman's (1978) 18-month-old said "milk" upon seeing a snow-covered backyard.

These **overextensions,** in which *a term is used beyond its appropriate level of reference*, are not limited to nouns either—a child will say, for example, "I open the light," that is, turn the light on (Ashcraft, 1989).

What do overextensions (also called *overgeneralizations*) tell us about children's language and cognition? An early explanation (E. V. Clark, 1973) suggested that the child's word meanings may be considerably simpler than adults' meanings. If so, then "doggie" might be overextended simply because the child's lexical entry lists only "four legs and furry" as the definition of "doggie."

A more sophisticated explanation (e.g., Clark, 1983) suggests that overextensions are a *communication strategy* on the part of the child. In essence, the child is confronted with a situation he or she wants to talk about, and has no word for that thing. Therefore, the child selects the most suitable vocabulary word available—"doggie" comes closest to an appropriate name for the zebra at the zoo, so the child calls it "doggie" (see Merriman, 1986, and Huttenlocher & Smiley, 1987, for reviews). The appealing thing about this explanation is that it strengthens our view on the purpose of language; language exists for communication, a purpose that even the youngest of language users appreciate and accept.

Summary

1. Infants proceed through several prelinguistic stages during their first year, gaining mastery over the physical speech mechanism. Babbling, especially jargon babbling, is probably an essential aspect of this mastery.
2. The child's first word usually occurs around the first birthday. Children's one-word utterances are composed largely of either general or specific names, especially names of the dynamic things and people they can interact with.
3. Two-word sentences begin to show effects of grammar, that is, rules governing sentence formation. An early syntactic grammar for two-word sentences gave way to Brown's demonstration that these sentences express semantic relationships, much the way semantic case grammar claims. Errors in children's speech also emphasize the importance of semantics over purely syntactic features, and the communicative purpose of language.

Important Terms

arbitrariness
case grammar/semantic case grammar
categorical perception
coarticulation
competence versus performance
displacement
eye gaze
grammar
iconic
jargon babbling
language
linguistics
linguistic universals
mental lexicon
MLU
morpheme
overextensions

phoneme
phonology
phrase structure rules
problem of invariance
productivity
psycholinguistics
semantics
semantic case/case roles
S-V-O sentence
syntax
transformational grammar

Suggested Readings

A variety of books provide excellent introductions to language and psycholinguistics, for instance, *Psycholinguistics* (Slobin, 1979) and *Language and Speech* (G. A. Miller, 1981). Greene (1972) provides a good review of Chomsky's theory of language (see also Rosenberg, 1993, and Chomsky, 1968).

I used the example sentence "His insecurities chased him even in his sleep" to hint at the topic of figurative language, in which the literal meanings of the words are not intended. Some excellent sources on metaphor, simile, and other figurative language phenomena are Ortony's (1979) book *Metaphor and Thought,* Lakoff and Johnson's (1980) *Metaphors We Live By,* and papers by Gibbs (1992) and Glucksberg and Keysar (1990).

Finally, for good treatments of language acquisition, see Reich (1986), Berko Gleason's (1985) edited book for original contributions, and an anthology edited by Franklin and Barten (1988).

CHAPTER NINE

COMPREHENSION, WRITTEN AND SPOKEN

There's more to language than just the words. (Jean Redpath, on *A Prairie Home Companion,* May 4, 1985)

I really like that quotation. It's so true, for every aspect of language you can think of. I can say, "You did a great job on the midterm," to my class in a straightforward way, and it means just that. Or I can say it with a hesitant tone of voice, and then add, "The class average was seventy-two percent, a low C ," and it means something entirely different. And you do the same thing. If you tell a classmate, "I didn't think the test was that hard," your classmate judges whether you mean it sincerely, whether you're boasting about getting a good grade, or whether that slight smile on your face means you're being sarcastic.

Language is a puzzle. Whether written or spoken, it presents us with a task—comprehend this message using any and all relevant information. Obviously, a big part of that information is contained in the message itself. This was the focus of Chapter 8, where we discussed the three traditional levels of analysis of language, phonology, syntax, and semantic or lexical factors.

But another big part of the information comes from you, from the person doing the comprehending. Miller (1973; incidentally, this is the famous "seven plus or minus two" George Miller) pointed out that there are at least two additional levels of analysis in language that are critical to cognitive psychology. These are the conceptual and the belief levels of analysis.

- At the **conceptual level,** comprehension involves *analysis of the message with respect to general world knowledge, that is, semantic memory.*
- For the **belief level,** comprehension involves *analysis of the message with respect to the speaker's and listener's knowledge of each other, and the context of the utterance.*

Let's consider Miller's example sentence:

(1) *Bill and Mary saw the mountains while they were flying to California.*

If someone said this to you, your phonological analysis would identify the phonemes and combinations that make up the spoken words, your syntactic analysis would parse the sentence into phrases, and your lexical/semantic analysis would identify the meanings of the individual words, assigning the words to their different semantic case roles (e.g., Bill and Mary are the agents in the first clause, California is the "location" case in the second clause, and so forth). Recall that the "semantic" or lexical level in traditional linguistics means word meaning, in the limited, dictionary sense.

But Miller's point was that there is still some cognitive work to be done beyond that, certainly at the conceptual level, and often at the belief level as well. Consider the pronoun "they" in the second clause. What does it refer to? Bill and Mary, of course. But technically speaking, "they" could refer to "mountains" instead. In other words, sentence (1) is ambiguous—it could have been Bill and Mary who were flying to California, or the mountains could have been flying to California. Nothing at the traditional three levels, in particular the lexical/semantic level, can determine this. Paraphrasing Miller, you can look in any dictionary you want, and you're not going to find a definition of "mountains" that says, "They don't fly."

Instead, it's your *conceptual analysis* that tells you that "they" refers not to mountains but to Bill and Mary. It's what you have stored in semantic memory, your encyclopedia of knowledge, that informs you that mountains are *not* the kind of thing that can fly. Similarly, your semantic memory, including your script knowledge, led you to comprehend "flying" in terms of airplanes—you didn't think Bill and Mary were flying like birds, after all.

This is a clear case of *conceptually driven processing,* where your existing knowledge guided your understanding. You probably imagined a scenario in which Bill and Mary

were on an airplane trip, looked out the windows during the flight, and saw the mountains in the distance. In fact, such a scenario is so easy to imagine, you may not have even noticed the ambiguity at all. There's a straightforward but powerful principle at work here. When we comprehend, we do so by accessing our semantic memories, our general knowledge of the world, which tells us what *can* and what *can't* be true.

Now add to this the belief level of analysis. Imagine that someone said sentence (1) to you, and then added the comment "I'm serious—it was the mountains that were flying to California." What would happen to your comprehension now? In Miller's words: "I don't know what you would say, but my response would be 'I don't believe you.' In the final analysis, I would appeal to my system of beliefs in order to evaluate what the speaker was saying" (p. 9). In other words, we comprehend not just the language we encounter, but also the speaker's intent. To prove it to yourself, reflect for a moment on how you comprehend a politician's speech, or the claims you hear in TV advertisements. You evaluate not just the literal message but also the speaker's *reasons* for saying those things, and you decide whether or not to believe the message.

This chapter is about these additional levels of analysis, levels at which our comprehension is guided by the contents of semantic memory, and occasionally our belief system. We'll start with the idea that we comprehend discourse by forming propositions, mental structures that code meaning. We'll then consider the processes of reference and inference—how you decide that "they" refers to Bill and Mary, for example—and how these processes occur as you comprehend. Then we'll discuss two of the most important settings in which comprehension takes place, reading and conversation. And to emphasize the dynamic, "right now" aspects of comprehension, we'll depend heavily on the various *online* performance tasks used to assess comprehension, for example the *eye-gaze* methods you read about in the last chapter.

Propositions

Preview: remembering the meaning of sentences; propositions representing meaning; rules for propositions; empirical support for propositional theories

MEMORY FOR MEANING

★ Let's start with a well-known demonstration, taken from an early study on memory for meaning (Sachs, 1967). Read the paragraph in Table 9.1 (p. 280), then do the multiple-choice question at the end of the paragraph.

Sachs (1967) was testing a very general notion about memory, that people tend to remember meaning rather than superficial, verbatim information in the sentences they hear or read. Participants in her experiment heard passages of connected text like the paragraph you just read. At some point during the passage, participants heard a bell and then a test sentence, at which point they had to decide if the test sentence was identical or not to one they had heard earlier. In one condition, the bell interrupted the tape recording

★ **TABLE 9.1**

Sample Passage from Sachs (1967), Including Multiple-Choice Recognition Test for Critical Sentence

Read the passage below at a comfortable pace, but without looking back. After you have finished reading, your memory for one of the sentences in the paragraph will be tested.

There is an interesting story about the telescope. In Holland, a man named Lippershey was an eye-glass maker. One day his children were playing with some lenses. They discovered that things seemed very close if two lenses were held about a foot apart. Lippershey began experimenting and his "spyglass" attracted much attention. He sent a letter about it to Galileo, the great Italian scientist. Galileo at once realized the importance of the discovery and set about to build an instrument of his own. He used an old organ pipe with one lens curved out and the other in. On the first clear night he pointed the glass toward the sky. He was amazed to find the empty dark spaces filled with brightly gleaming stars! Night after night Galileo climbed to a high tower, sweeping the sky with his telescope. One night he saw Jupiter, and to his great surprise discovered near it three bright stars, two to the east and one to the west. On the next night, however, all were to the west. A few nights later there were four little stars.

Now, without looking back, decide which of the following sentences occurred in the paragraph.

a. He sent Galileo, the great Italian scientist, a letter about it.
b. Galileo, the great Italian scientist, sent him a letter about it.
c. A letter about it was sent to Galileo, the great Italian scientist.
d. He sent a letter about it to Galileo, the great Italian scientist.

Check to see whether your answers were correct by referring back to the paragraph.

Source: From Sachs (1967).

immediately after the critical sentence; in another condition, 80 additional syllables were heard before the bell sounded (about 27 sec after the critical sentence), and in the third, 160 syllables intervened before the bell (about 46 sec after the critical sentence).

The various test sentences she administered were exactly like the four alternatives in the table. One was identical to the critical sentence, word for word. A second type involved a semantic change—in other words, the meaning of the sentence was changed. The other two types of test sentences merely involved changes in surface form—one switched from the active to the passive voice, and one involved a formal change, like moving "the great Italian scientist" to a different place in the sentence. Participants indicated whether the test sentence was identical or changed from the sentence they remembered in the paragraph, and then stated how confident they were about their decision.

▲ Sach's (1967) results are shown in Figure 9.1, for the four types of alternatives and the three delays, 0, 80, or 160 syllables, after the critical sentence. On the left, you'll see that the percentage of correct decisions on the unchanged, identical sentences was very high with a 0 syllable delay. But accuracy declined dramatically at the longer delays—after 80 syllables, only about 55 percent of the identical sentences were correctly judged as

FIGURE 9.1

Percentage of correct decisions for identical and changed sentences. (From Sachs, 1967.)

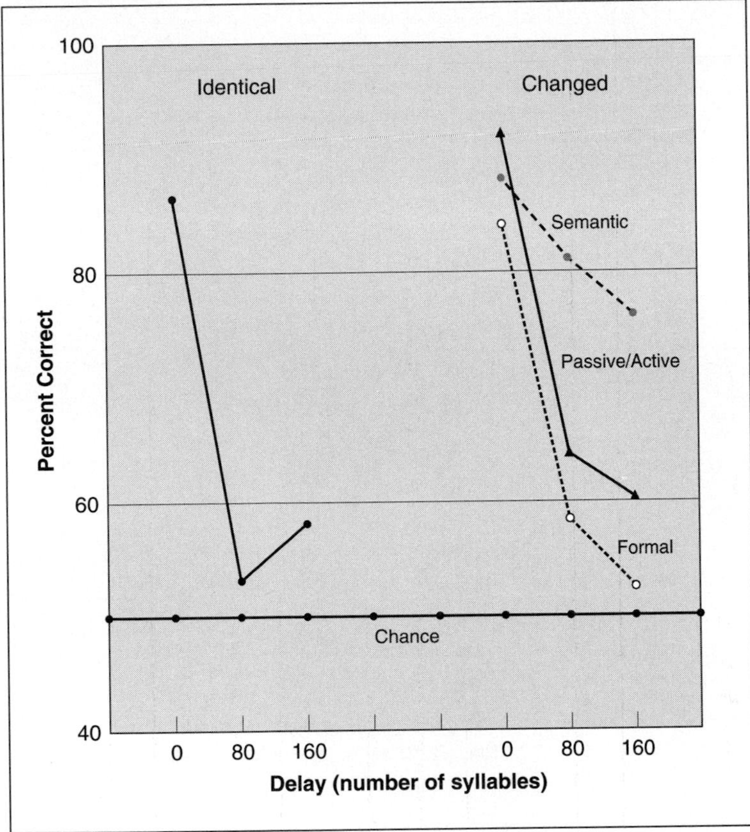

"identical." On the right are the three types of sentences that should have been judged "changed." The two types of paraphrases, passive/active and formal, showed the same decline as the identical sentences—approaching chance after 80 syllables. In fact, the only type of changed sentence that showed a high level of correct decisions was the semantic change type, when the test sentence changed the meaning of the critical sentence.

Sachs's findings were especially clear-cut. When the test sentence changed the meaning, participants noticed the change. But when the test sentence preserved the meaning but changed the wording somewhat, participants did *not* notice the change. The conclusion is very straightforward: normally, we lose information concerning the actual, verbatim string of words that we hear (or read), but we store and retain meaning quite well. Usually we only remember verbatim information when the wording is special in some way—for example, punch lines—or when there is high "interactive content" to the sentence, for example, insults (e.g., Murphy & Shapiro, 1994; see also Bates, Masling, & Kintsch, 1978; Kintsch & Bates, 1977; Masson, 1984).

FIGURE 9.2

Propositional representations for two sample sentences.

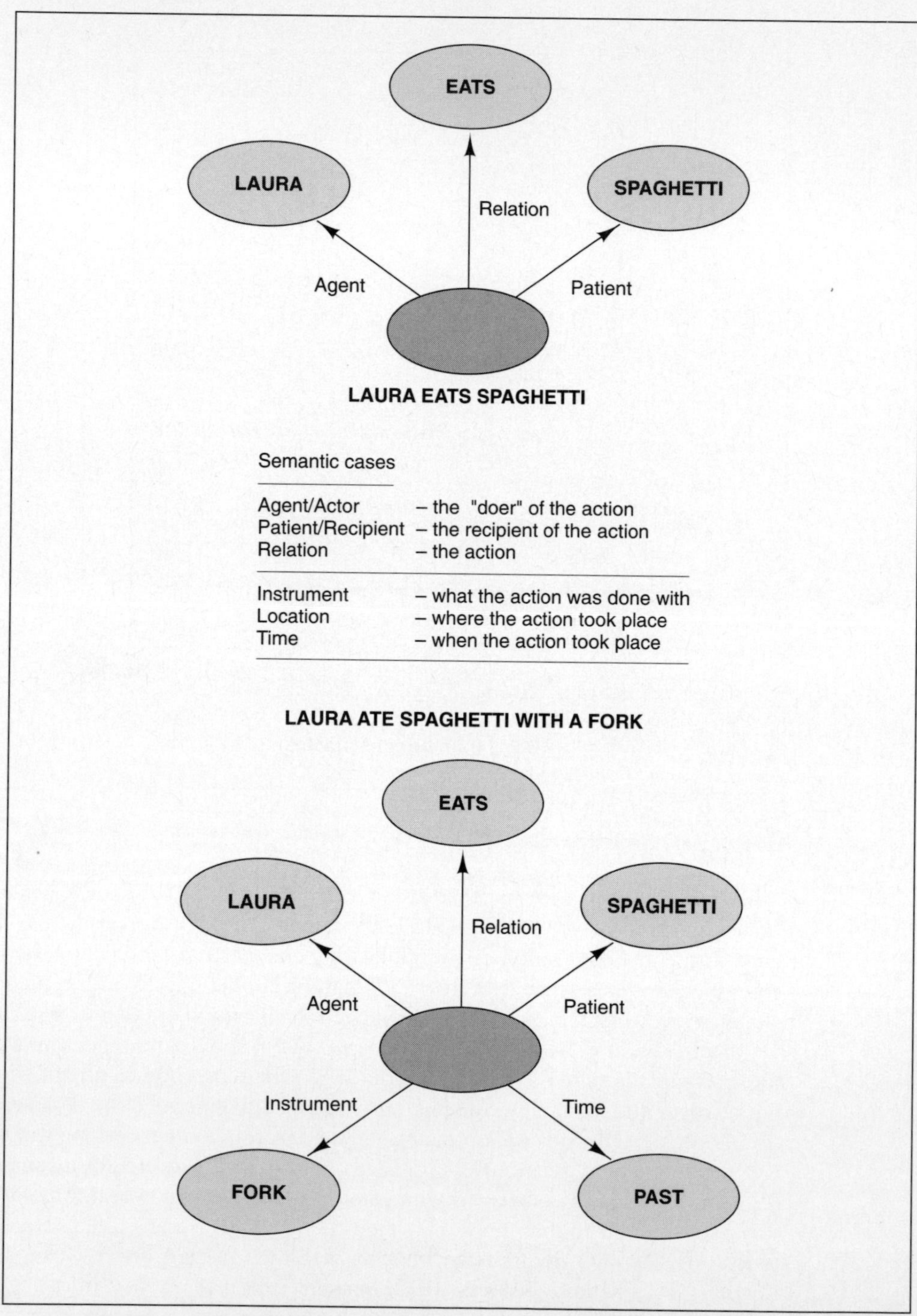

REPRESENTING MEANING AS PROPOSITIONS

What people remember from meaningful material is the idea or gist of the sentence or paragraph. But to talk about remembering ideas and meaning, we need a way of representing those ideas, so we'll know what we *mean* by "meaning." And, in order to do research on comprehension, we need some way of scoring performance to see how well (or poorly) people remember the meaning of a sentence.

By nearly unanimous agreement, cognitive psychology has settled upon a single term to represent such meaning. The semantic unit that codes meaning is called a **proposition.** A proposition is a *set of conceptual nodes connected by labeled pathways, where the entire collection of concepts and relationships expresses the meaning of a sentence*. Thus, what we store in memory and remember later on is in the form of a proposition.

Propositions can easily represent very simple meanings, for instance the basic semantic relationships discussed in Chapter 6. There, we talked about pairs of concepts with a connecting pathway, such as *ROBIN has WINGS*. It's quite easy to represent semantic relationships either in the conventional way or as a simple proposition.

The advantage of propositions, however, is that they can represent the meaning of sentences, all the way from simple to rather complex meanings. Let's take two examples, sentences (2) and (3):

(2) *Laura eats spaghetti.*

(3) *Laura ate spaghetti with a fork.*

The most common way of diagramming the propositions for these sentences is shown in Figure 9.2, based on networklike diagrams with connecting pathways. You'll notice that the format depends heavily on case grammar, the approach you read about in the last chapter. In other words, Chapter 8 claimed that when you hear or read a meaningful sentence, you analyze the words into their *semantic cases*, things like *agent*, *patient*, *location*, and the like. This is *exactly* the approach taken in proposition theories.

Rules for Propositions

Let's illustrate how to construct a proposition by taking a somewhat more complex sentence, such as Anderson's (1980):

(4) *The hungry lion ate Max, who starved it.*

A full set of rules for deriving the propositions in a passage of text has been provided by Anderson (1980, pp. 106–107), and is summarized in Table 9.2 (p. 284). Basically, the rules have you break the original sentence or passage down into separate simple sentences or phrases, each specifying a simple idea or *relation*—STARVE in sentence (7), for example.

(5) *The lion was hungry.*

(6) *The lion ate Max.*

(7) *Max starved the lion.*

The concepts that apply to each idea are added, along with the types of connections that join the concepts—for example MAX is the *agent* in (7), but the *patient* in (6). Finally, the relationships among the simple sentences are added to the structure, making it

TABLE 9.2

Rules for Deriving Propositions

This is a modified list of the rules for deriving propositions, adapted from Anderson (1980, pp. 106–107). The sample sentence is

(4) *The hungry lion ate Max, who starved it.*

(4) THE HUNGRY LION ATE MAX, WHO STARVED IT.

Rule 1. Find all the relational terms in the sentence. These will usually be verbs, but can also be adjectives, relational expressions like *father of*, or prepositions like *above* or *on top of*.

Relations are HUNGRY, EAT, STARVE

Rule 2. Write a simple sentence or phrase for each relation and give each one a number. Each sentence is a separate proposition, and will contain only its relation and its noun arguments.

Simple sentences are
(5) THE LION WAS HUNGRY.
(6) THE LION ATE MAX.
(7) MAX STARVED THE LION.

Rule 3. Draw an oval to represent each proposition, and number it. Write the relation next to its oval, and connect the node to the relation by an arrow labeled *relation*.

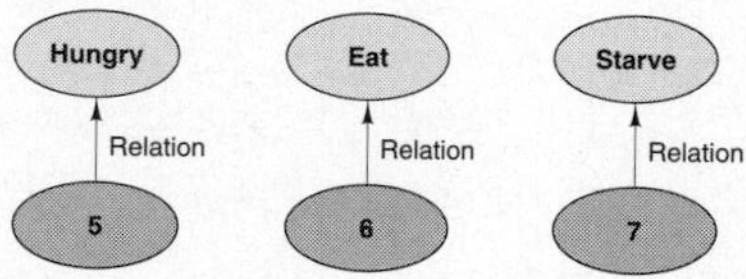

Rule 4. Add a node to each proposition for each *argument*, each noun or "noun-like" word in the proposition (ignore function words like "the"). If a noun refers to a specific person or object, like Max, simply write the noun. If a noun refers only to an instance of a category, like lion, then create a new node and give it an arbitrary name like X. The X will stand for this particular instance of the category. Connect the X to its class noun with an *isa* arrow. Use the same node each time the noun appears; for example, there will only be one *Max* node.

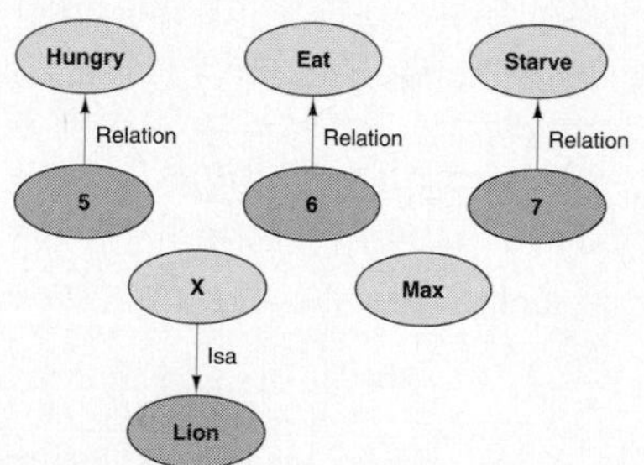

Rule 5. Connect all the arguments to the numbered oval with arrows. Label the arrows with the appropriate semantic case role (e.g., agent, patient, etc.).

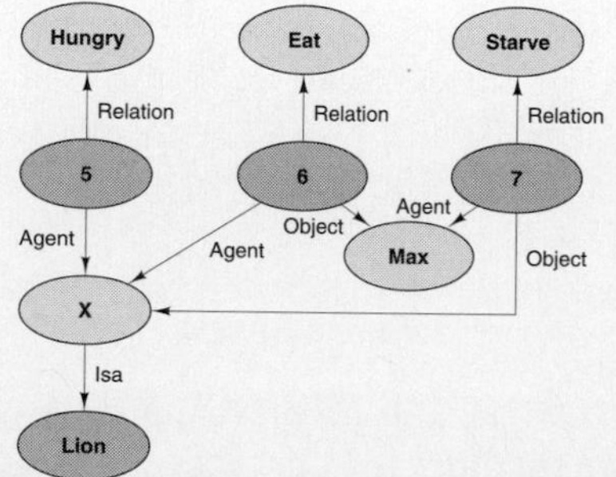

Rule 6. Rearrange the network to make it neat—in other words, meaning is coded by the nodes and their connections, not by the position of the nodes in the diagram.

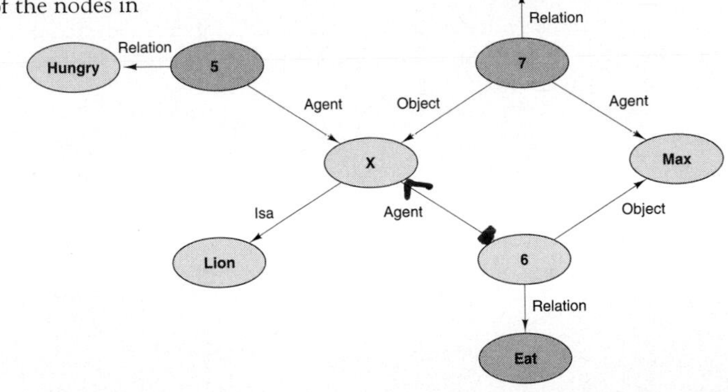

clear for example that the lion that ate Max in (6) is the same one that was hungry in (5), that starving the lion was the reason the lion was hungry, and so forth.

Bear in mind here that what we're doing is simply devising a way of diagramming or representing the *meaning* of a sentence (unlike what you did in seventh-grade English, when you diagrammed the grammatical roles played by the words). The more constituents there are in a sentence, the more concepts and pathways are needed to represent the full meaning. Nonetheless, the entire meaning will still be shown by the proposition or set of propositions that represent the sentence.

Elaborated Propositions

Just as we attempted to account for semantic knowledge in terms of a network structure, propositional theories attempt to account for our mental representations of sentence meaning as networks of interconnected propositions. To illustrate, consider a particularly  memorable sentence and its propositional representation, on the left of Figure 9.3 (p. 286) (sentence from Anderson & Bower, 1973; notational scheme based on Anderson, 1980, and Kintsch, 1974). The sentence

(8) *The hippie touched the debutante in the park*,

is represented here as a set of interrelated concepts, one for each main word in the sentence. The relationships among the words are specified by the type of pathway that connects the nodes. Thus sentence (8) is composed of five relationships or connections of meaning:

- TOUCHing is the **relation** in the sentence, the topic or major event in the sentence.
- HIPPIE is the **agent** for this event, the actor or individual who did the TOUCHing.
- DEBUTANTE is the **patient** (or **recipient**) of the event, the one who received the action of TOUCHing.
- PARK is the *location* of the event, and the
- TOUCHing occurred at some unspecified *time* in the PAST.

★ **FIGURE 9.3**

Propositional representation of "The hippie touched the debutante in the park. So, she slapped him." (Adapted from Anderson, 1980; Anderson & Bower, 1973; Kintsch, 1974.)

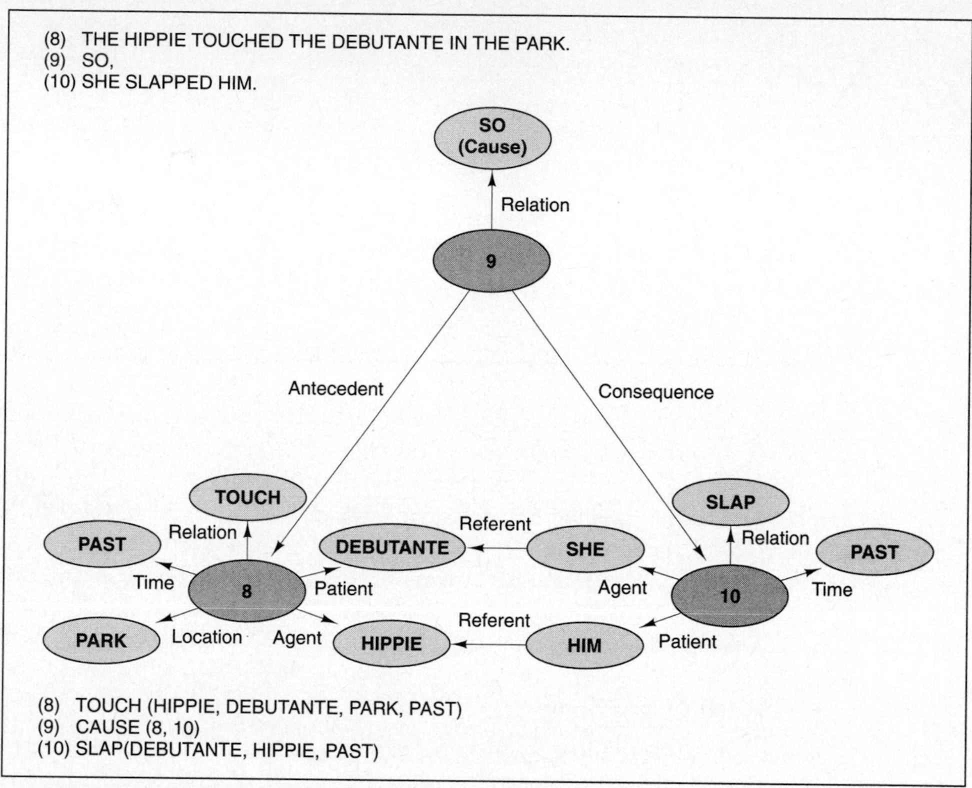

STRENGTHS OF PROPOSITIONAL THEORIES

What are the advantages of a proposition-based theory of long-term memory for meaning? First, note that the proposition accurately reflects the meaning of the sentence, both the original sentence and paraphrases of it. In other words, the propositional representation is relatively *unaffected* by superficial aspects of the sentence, for example the specific wording—the representation does not change for the paraphrase in (8b):

(8b) In the park, it was the debutante who was touched by the hippie.

This is exactly what we would expect, given Sachs's (1967) demonstration that we remember meaning, and not specific wording.

An additional advantage is that propositions enable us to capture the relationships among sentences, to illustrate the meaning of a whole group of related ideas. As an example, let's expand the hippie story just a bit.

(8) *The hippie touched the debutante in the park.*

(9) *So,*

(10) *she slapped him*.

The complete diagram in Figure 9.3 shows all three of these propositions, and connects them with the idea of *causation*, the idea that the TOUCHing in node (8) was the *cause* for the SLAPping in node (10). Thus the full meaning of the expanded story is captured by the propositional representation. (In a moment we'll turn to the process that determines who "she" and "him" refer to; e.g., O'Brien & Albrecht, 1991.)

Evidence for Propositions

Propositional theories make three basic claims:

- first, that we analyze and comprehend a sentence by determining the semantic roles played by the words in the sentence;
- second, that we construct a proposition based on those semantic roles and relationships; and
- third, that we store the results of the analysis in memory in the form of a proposition.

A score of research reports have documented the psychological validity and utility of these hypothesized propositions, as well as the consequences of the three basic claims. We'll discuss only a very few, to give you the flavor of this evidence, and then talk about one specific propositional model of comprehension, Gernsbacher's *Structure Building Framework*.

Kintsch published several early reports on the psychological reality of propositions. In one set of studies (1974), he tested the notion that a sentence with more underlying propositions is a more difficult sentence to comprehend, hence harder to remember. He presented short sentences for simple free recall (five sentences were presented, followed by a two-minute recall interval, followed by another five sentences, etc.). The sentences had between two and four content words each, and from one to three propositions each; for instance, "The crowded passengers squirmed uncomfortably" has three embedded propositions, while "The horse stumbled and broke a leg" has only two (both sentences have four content words).

Kintsch's predictions about propositions were upheld. Whereas people tended to recall about the same overall amount from all sentences, recall for the elements of any single proposition went down as the total number of propositions increased. Thus the more complex a sentence is, as indicated by the number of propositions it contains, the more there is to remember, hence less will be recalled.

Priming

Another set of experiments not only supported these general findings about propositions, but also explored some of the memory consequences implied by propositional theories. In particular, one consequence of storing propositions in memory (the third claim above) resembles the semantic relatedness effect you learned about in Chapter 6. For propositions, this effect is that concepts within the same proposition should be stored together in memory. If so, then retrieving one part of a proposition should activate the other parts—*hippie* should activate *debutante* if they're both stored together in one proposition, for example.

Exactly this kind of prediction was tested in a priming study by Ratcliff and McKoon (1978, experiment 2). These investigators tested this prediction with a priming task. They

TABLE 9.3

Priming Results from Ratcliff and McKoon (1978)

Condition	*RT to Target*	*Priming Effect*
Across sentences	847 msec	None; baseline
Between two propositions in the same sentence	752 msec	95 msec facilitation
Within a single proposition	709 msec	138 msec facilitation
Examples		
Across sentences:	geese–clutch	
Between two propositions in the same sentence:	geese–clouds	
Within a single proposition:	geese–horizon	

Source: From Ratcliff and McKoon (1978).

asked their participants to read sets of sentences, and remember them for a later unspecified memory test. Each test sentence contained two separate propositions, for example:

(11) *Geese crossed the horizon as wind shuffled the clouds.*

(12) *The chauffeur jammed the clutch when he parked the truck.*

After a 20-minute interval, filled with an unrelated task, the participants were shown single words in a recognition task. They responded "yes" if the test word had been in one of the learned sentences and "no" otherwise.

The priming manipulation here involved the sequence of trials in the recognition task. In the baseline condition, the word on one trial was followed on the next trial by a word from a different sentence, for example *geese–clutch* for sentences (11) and (12). The average RT to these target words was 847 milliseconds, as shown in Table 9.3. In a second condition, consecutive words came from the same sentence, but from different propositions—for example, *geese–clouds*. Because they were from the same overall sentence, RT to the targets here averaged 752 milliseconds, a 95-millisecond benefit due to priming within the sentence. But the biggest priming effect was in the third condition, when the words came from the *same* proposition, as in *geese–horizon*. Here, RT to the target was 709 milliseconds, a full 138 milliseconds faster than baseline.

This evidence confirmed several basic predictions from proposition theory, that concepts from the same sentence should be stored together in the proposition, and that words from the same phrase or clause should be even more closely related in those propositions. So even though the words were not related in the strict sense of semantic memory—"horizon" is not a semantic property of "geese" after all—words stored together in a sentence's proposition still prime one another.

GERNSBACHER'S STRUCTURE BUILDING FRAMEWORK

Gernsbacher's (1985, 1990, 1991) recent program of research and her overall theory of sentence comprehension, called the *Structure Building Framework*, provide a concrete way of understanding propositions in language comprehension. Her basic theme is that language comprehension—indeed *any* comprehension of coherent material—is a process of building mental structures, propositions. The three principal components of this **structure building** process are *laying a foundation, mapping information onto the structure*, and *shifting to new structures*.

Laying a Foundation and Mapping Information

According to Gernsbacher, as we read (or hear) sentences we begin to build a mental structure that stores the meaning of the sentence in memory. This structure is in the form of a proposition. The foundation is initiated as the sentence begins, and most commonly is built around the first character or idea in the sentence. This is equivalent to saying that sentence (13) is *about* the character named Dave:

(13) *Dave was studying hard for his statistics midterm.*

More formally, we would say that the **discourse focus** (e.g., Rayner, Garrod, & Perfetti, 1992) of sentence (13) is DAVE, which means that "Dave" will be more memorable in the final representation (e.g., Birch & Garnsey, 1995; McKoon, Ratcliff, Ward, & Sproat, 1993).

Comprehending this sentence, in Gernsbacher's scheme, involves building a new sentence structure, focused on the central character, Dave, then elaborating that structure. As the words "was studying" are read, their meanings are accessed in lexical and semantic memory, and *memory cells* corresponding to those meanings are mapped onto the current "Dave structure"—the term "cells" in Gernsbacher's model means the same thing as "nodes" or "concepts." Mapping here simply means that the additional meanings now become attached to the basic proposition DAVE STUDIES, elaborating the structure by specifying Dave's activities. Further elaboration continues with the prepositional phrase "for his statistics midterm." Because the concept MIDTERM is a coherent idea in the context of studying, these concepts or memory cells are also added to the DAVE structure.

Shifting to a New Structure. We continue to map incoming words to the current structure, on the assumption that those words "belong to" the first idea unit, the structure under construction right now. But at some point, a *different* idea is encountered, an idea that does not fit well in the current structure. As an example, consider sentence (14) as a continuation of the Dave story:

(14) *Because the professor had a reputation for giving difficult exams, the students knew they'd have to be well prepared.*

In Gernsbacher's model, when you read "Because the professor," a *coherence* component detects the change in topic or focus. As you'll read in a moment, one clue to this change in focus is the chain of information you need to retrieve in order to figure out who "the professor" is; midterms are exams given in college classes that are taught by professors; therefore, "the professor" must be the professor who teaches Dave's statistics class. Another clue, of course, is the word "because."

At such moments, you react by closing off the DAVE structure and beginning a new structure about "the professor." While the DAVE structure still retains its prominence in your overall memory of the story, you are now working on a new *current structure*, map-

FIGURE 9.4

Results from Gernsbacher and Hargreaves (1988), showing the advantage of first mention. (From Gernsbacher, 1990; data from Gernsbacher & Hargreaves, 1988.)

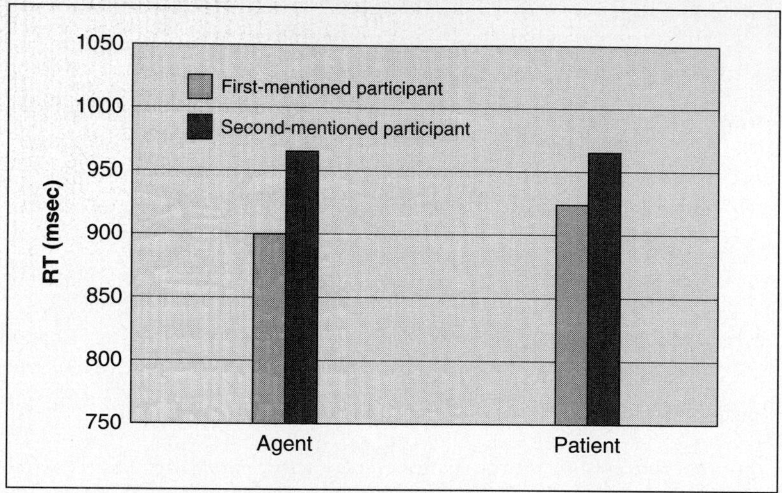

ping the incoming ideas (reputation, difficult exams, etc.) onto that second structure—and then a third structure for "the students," and so forth.

Evidence for Structure Building

Several empirical effects have been reported by Gernsbacher in support of these theoretical claims. Two important ones are the **advantage of first mention,** and the **advantage of clause recency.** In the advantage of first mention, characters and ideas that were mentioned in the very first sentence, at the beginning of the entire episode, retain a special significance. Because DAVE was the first-mentioned participant, and is the focus of the story, you will remember "Dave" better than other participants; DAVE was at the very *foundation* of your propositional structure. Indeed, Gernsbacher and Hargreaves's (1988) data support this explanation. As shown in Figure 9.4, it didn't matter whether a character was the semantic agent or the patient in a sentence. What mattered, in terms of speeding up the decision, was that the character was *mentioned first*.

This effect is also shown in the next graph, Figure 9.5, along with the second major effect, the *advantage of clause recency*. Here, the most recently mentioned character shows an advantage in the Immediate condition—if you have to make a decision *immediately* after hearing the sentence, then there is an advantage for information in the most recent clause. (Yes, it's a recency effect, just like the one found in short-term memory research.) This advantage of clause recency disappears when the decision is delayed even by 150 milliseconds. And beyond that delay, the advantage of first mention prevails (Gernsbacher, Hargreaves, & Beeman, 1989). Thus, for a sentence like "Tina gathered the kindling, and Lisa set up the tent," you would be faster to decide that "Lisa" was in the sentence for only the briefest of intervals. Beyond that 150 milliseconds, "Tina" would show

FIGURE 9.5

Results from Gernsbacher, Hargreaves, and Beeman (1989), showing the advantages of clause recency and first mention. (From Gernsbacher, 1990; data from Gernsbacher et al., 1989.)

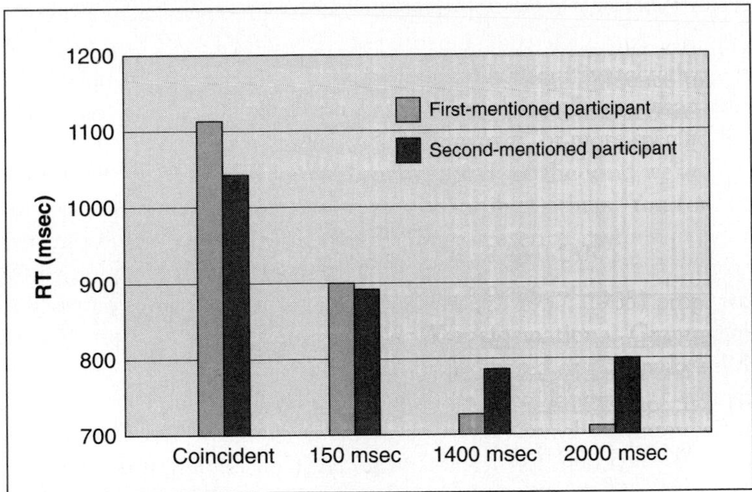

the advantage of first mention. In short, TINA is in the basic foundation of the propositions, part of the *discourse focus*, whereas LISA is represented in a *substructure*, a less important part of the propositional structure stored in memory.

Enhancement and Suppression

Finally, two control mechanisms operate in Gernsbacher's model, both having to do with the momentary changes in sentence focus. Let's repeat the "Dave story," then add one more sentence so we can understand these two mechanisms:

(13) *Dave was studying hard for his statistics midterm.*

(14) *Because the professor had a reputation for giving difficult exams, the students knew they'd have to be well prepared.*

(15) *Dave wanted an A on that test.*

Two prominent ideas in sentence (14) map onto the ideas from sentence (13)—EXAMS refers to the same concept as "midterms," and "the professor" maps onto the statistics course implied by sentence (13). According to Gernsbacher, such mappings reflect the activation of related memory cells. That is, the PROFESSOR memory cell becomes activated. This activation then combines with the activation from "midterm" and STATISTICS COURSE, because of their semantic relatedness. This is the process of **enhancement,** that the many related memory cells are now being boosted or *enhanced* in their level of activation—of course, enhancement is the same thing as *priming* and *spreading activation*. The more frequently the same set of cells is enhanced or primed across the entire story, the more accessible those cells will be.

But enhancement of some memory cells implies that other cells will lose activation. That is, while sentence (14) enhances the activation of memory cells related to PROFESSOR, EXAM, and so forth, there is a simultaneous **suppression** of memory cells that are now out of the main discourse focus. In other words, activated cells that become unrelated to the focus will *decrease in activation* by the process of *suppression*. So, during sentence (14), it's very likely that the activation level for DAVE will go down—DAVE gets suppressed. Although the memory cells related to Dave remain important because they were part of the first structure, they are momentarily out of the discourse focus, so their activation is suppressed. Then, as the story concludes in sentence (15), the memory cells for DAVE regain their enhancement, but the PROFESSOR cells dwindle down.

Many studies have examined how enhancement and suppression influence comprehension. For example, Albrecht and O'Brien (1991) constructed paragraphs that contained concepts that were central, moderately central, or peripheral to the topic. After reading a paragraph, the participants either had to judge a series of words as having been in the paragraph, or had to perform a speeded recall task. Concepts that had been enhanced, because they were central to the topic of the passage, were judged and recalled more rapidly than those only moderately or peripherally related to paragraph topic. Gernsbacher and her co-workers (Gernsbacher & Shroyer, 1989; also Gernsbacher & Jescheniak, 1995) found that the indefinite *this* (e.g., "There was *this* guy in my class last semester") enhances the activation level of the referent ("guy"). This enhancement made it more accessible, more central to the focus of the discourse, and faster to respond to.

Suppression, on the other hand, can occur when a concept is dropped from mention in the discourse, for instance the way the PROFESSOR idea dropped out at the end of the "Dave story." Suppression can also occur when a concept is negated—for instance, if you read "There was *no* bread in the house," the concept BREAD is suppressed (MacDonald & Just, 1989). And in a fascinating extension of her theory to an applied problem, Gernsbacher (1990, 1993) found that poor readers were less adept than good readers at suppressing irrelevant information while they are reading. This would mean that tangential ideas remain activated during reading, reducing comprehension. She also discovered that poor readers shift from building one substructure to another too frequently, making the end product of their comprehension less coherent (e.g., Gernsbacher, 1990, chap. 5; see Gernsbacher & Robertson, 1995, to see how comprehension of puns is related to suppression).

Summary

1. The research shows that we remember meaningful discourse in terms of meaning, rather than verbatim wording of the sentences. This suggests that a structure that codes meaning is stored in memory as a result of comprehension, a structure referred to as a proposition.
2. A proposition represents the meaning of a simple sentence in terms of the overall relation being expressed, along with the concepts that play different semantic roles in sentence meaning. Because entire propositions can be connected to other propositions, the meaning of related sentences can also be represented.
3. A variety of results support the predictions from propositional theory, including tests of priming between concepts within a proposition.

4. Gernsbacher's propositional model explains comprehension as the process of building propositions and storing them in memory, and the moment-by-moment fluctuations in the levels of activation of the concepts in the sentence. Analysis of structure building and concept activation helps explain some of the difficulties poor readers have in comprehension.

Reference, Inference, and Memory

Preview: reference and inference; types of reference; bridging as a comprehension strategy; the role of memory in inferences

Reference is the *linguistic device of alluding to a concept by using another name*, for example by using a synonym or pronoun. **Implication** is *the speaker's (or writer's) intended reference in a sentence or utterance*. It's a connection that is not explicitly mentioned by the speaker, but is intended nonetheless. So *implication* can be said to be "in the mind of the speaker"—the speaker implied something in the sentence.

Inference, on the other hand, is "in the mind of the listener." It is the process of *drawing connections between concepts, determining the referents of words and ideas in the passage, and deriving conclusions from a message*. So *implication* is something that the speaker does, and drawing *inferences* is something that the hearer does. If the speaker's implication was intended, it's referred to as an **authorized** *implication*—and the listener's inference, likewise, as an *authorized inference*. The unintended versions of these are termed **unauthorized**—so for example, if a classmate says "That's a hard course," you might draw the unauthorized inference that it's difficult to get a good grade, when the speaker merely meant that there's a lot of outside reading (see, for instance, McKoon & Ratcliff, 1986).

Why do speakers (and writers) use reference as a linguistic device? Part of the reason is that it allows us to name an object or idea with different words, to avoid boring, repetitive phrasing, as shown in sentences (16a) and (16b):

(16a) *Mike went to the pool to swim some laps. After his workout, he went to his psychology class. The professor asked him to summarize the chapter that he'd assigned the class to read.*

(16b*) *Mike went to the pool to swim some laps. After Mike swam some laps, Mike went to Mike's psychology class. The professor of Mike's psychology class asked Mike to summarize the chapter that Mike's psychology professor had assigned Mike's psychology class to read.*

The more important reason for using reference is that it is impossible to specify everything in a sentence; *no* sentence ever "stands on its own" completely. Sentence (16b*) avoids pronouns by saying *Mike* instead of *he* or *his*, but it's still incomplete in that the full meaning of each term is not specified in the sentence itself. Instead of mentioning everything, we rely on listeners (and readers) to know the meanings of our words, to know about syntactic devices that structure our discourse, and to share our general conceptual knowledge of the world. So, I imply that swimming laps can be "a workout," that professors assign chapters for their students to read, and so forth. I then rely on you to infer those connections when you comprehend. (And as you'll read in the last section of this chapter, if I *do* specify everything exactly, I'm breaking an important conversational rule.)

TABLE 9.4

Types of Reference and Implication

Direct Reference
a. *Identity:* Michelle bought a computer. The computer was on sale.
b. *Synonym:* Michelle bought a computer. The machine was on sale.
c. *Pronoun:* Michelle bought a computer. It has a left-hand mouse.
d. *Set membership:* I talked to two people today. Michelle said she had just bought a computer.
e. *Epithet:* Michelle bought a computer. The stupid thing doesn't work.
Indirect Reference—by Semantic Association
f. *Necessary parts:* Eric bought a used car. The tires were badly worn.
g. *Probable parts:* Eric bought a used car. The radio doesn't work.
h. *Inducible parts:* Eric bought a used car. The salesperson gave him a good price.
Other Indirect References
i. *Reasons:* Derek asked a question in class. He hoped to impress the professor.
j. *Causes:* Derek answered a question in class. The professor had called on him.
k. *Consequences:* Derek asked a question in class. The professor was impressed.
l. *Concurrences:* Derek asked a question in class. Jeff tried to impress the professor too.

Source: Adapted from Clark (1977).

SIMPLE REFERENCE AND INFERENCE

Natural discourse involves several different kinds of reference and inference, ranging from very direct to very indirect. H. H. Clark (1977) listed several types of reference, shown along with examples in Table 9.4.

In the *direct reference* category, the simplest type of reference is *identity reference*, as in

(17) *I saw a convertible yesterday. The convertible was red.*

The reference here, of course, is that *the* convertible mentioned in the second sentence is the same one that was introduced with the indefinite article *a* in the first sentence. The speaker has clearly authorized this implication, by using the definite article "the" in the second sentence. Just as clearly, someone who hears the sentence must *infer* the equivalence in order to comprehend the second sentence in a reasonable fashion. Likewise, *synonym reference* involves substituting a different word in referring to a concept, as the Dave Story did in the previous section with the concepts MIDTERM, EXAM, and TEST.

Pronoun reference involves a pronoun substitution, as in "he" referring back to "Mike" in sentence (16a). Here, the pronoun reference is quite straightforward. *Mike* is called the *antecedent* of *he*, since it comes before the pronoun, and the act of using *he* later on is called *anaphoric reference*.

How do you know that a connection from *Mike* to *he* is intended? Simple—in English the word *he* must refer to an individual, a male, so the only antecedent it can be equated with is *Mike*. Similarly, because you know that a debutante must be female, the pronoun reference in the sentence "she slapped him" was straightforward. Contrast this with a sentence with two possible antecedents, and no gender contrast to disambiguate the reference:

(18) *Jim saw his friend at the basketball game, but he didn't have time to chat.*

BRIDGING

Clark (1977) used the term **bridging** to refer to all of the mental processes involving reference and inference. That is, Clark described all forms of reference and inference as *a process of constructing a connection between concepts*. Metaphorically speaking, the process is one of constructing a *bridge* across which comprehension can pass—I built a direct bridge between "debutante" and "she," and you must build the same bridge in order to comprehend.

The bridge is easy to build for identity and synonym reference, but is somewhat more difficult for pronoun reference. Even more difficult is the *set membership* type of reference, for instance

(19) *I talked to two people yesterday. Michelle said she had caught a cold,*

where the implication is that Michelle was one of the two people. Finally, consider the explicit bridge you need to construct—the inference you need to draw—to understand sentence (20), illustrating *reference by epithet:*

(20) *I saw Bob yesterday. The jerk criticized my tie.*

The reference between Bob and "the jerk" is clearly intended in sentence (20), authorizing your inference that Bob is a jerk. Notice how much harder it is to make this connection if we substitute the word "psychologist" for "jerk"—in fact, with that wording you might even conclude that the second sentence was unrelated to the first.

Complex Bridges

Table 9.4 also lists several forms of *indirect reference*, cases that usually require much more work on the part of the listener in order to comprehend. Consider sentences (21) and (22) as examples of indirect reference by association:

(21) *Marge went into her office. The floor was very dirty.*

(22) *Marge went into her office. The African violet had bloomed.*

In the first, a reference back to *office* is made with the word *floor*. Since an office *necessarily* has a floor, it is clear that the implication in sentence (21) is that it was Marge's office floor that was dirty—this information is easily retrieved from your semantic network. But the implication in sentence (22) has to be *induced by the listener*—an office *may* have a flowering plant in it, but since it's not a *necessary* part of an office, the listener must induce the bridge based on knowledge of what *might* be.

In Clark's view, these "associated" pieces of information must be retrieved or induced from semantic memory. The ease with which that retrieval takes place therefore should predict comprehension time. And indeed, this is exactly what the research has shown. Very typical concepts or properties—"desk" for office, for example—are very predictable, and are read and comprehended more rapidly (e.g., McKoon & Ratcliff, 1989; O'Brien, Plewes, & Albrecht, 1990).

THE ROLE OF SEMANTIC AND SCRIPT MEMORY

We are obviously discussing phenomena that you're already familiar with—scripts, and retrieval of knowledge from semantic memory. Sentences activate relevant knowledge in semantic memory, and *instantiate* relevant scripts. This activated knowledge then guides comprehension, including the ease with which we can infer connections. The Dave

FIGURE 9.6

Lexical decision times to superordinate and subordinate inferences and to unrelated words. (From Long, Golding, & Graesser, 1992.)

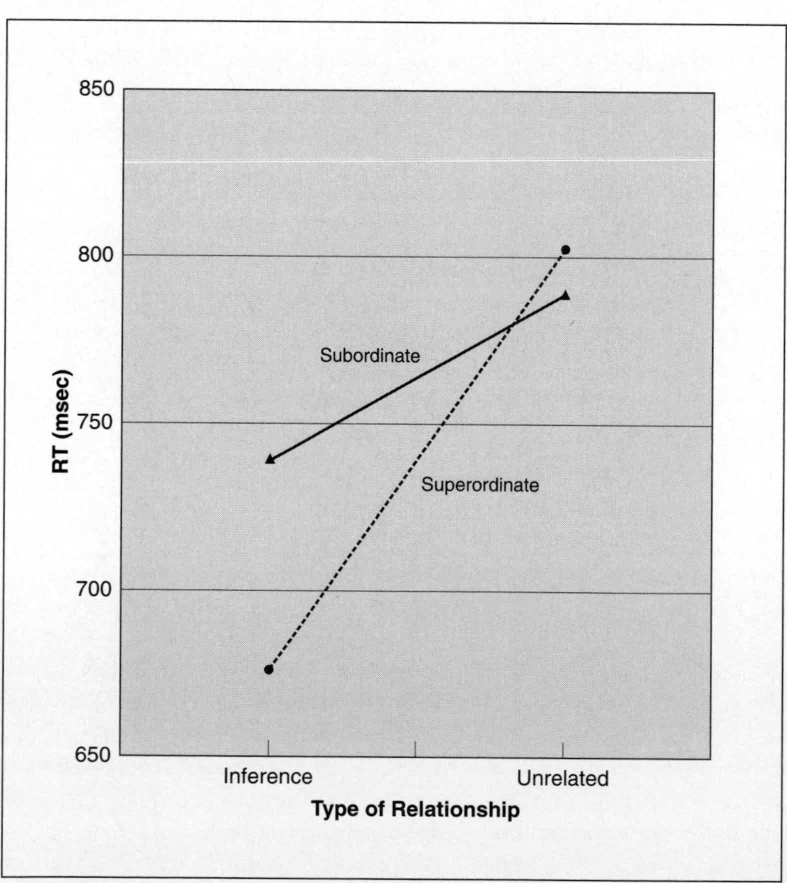

Story instantiated your College Class script when you read it, activating typical, accessible concepts like TEST and PROFESSOR. This then smoothed the way for you to comprehend the story, enabling you to draw inferences and construct bridges among the relevant concepts.

Supporting Evidence

We comprehend based on the message and the knowledge we have stored in memory. Retrieving information like *an office has a floor* and *professors give exams* allows you to understand the various forms of reference that are so common in language. But what research supports all of these claims about reference and inference?

There has been an explosion of research addressing these claims across the past several years. Quite literally, *dozens* of studies have examined bridging and inferences in language comprehension, studying how readers develop a coherent understanding of discourse. The evidence has shown overwhelmingly that we indeed draw inferences from text in an on-line fashion (e.g., Keefe & McDaniel, 1993; Lea, 1995; Myers, O'Brien, Albrecht, & Mason, 1994). This is especially the case if the inference is about a central, focused concept in the passage (e.g., Whitney, Ritchie, & Crane, 1992), and if the inference is necessary for maintaining coherence. Because these inferences are stored in memory as part of the propositional representation of the passage, various memory effects are observed too. For example, after reading and comprehending a passage, we make faster responses to the concepts we inferred from the passage while reading (e.g., Noordman, Vonk, & Kempff, 1992; O'Brien, Shank, Myers, & Rayner, 1988).

As an example, Long, Golding, and Graesser (1992) had their participants read simple children's stories and then perform in a lexical decision task. Some of the words named important inferences likely to have been drawn during reading, called Superordinate Inferences, and some named less important Subordinate inferences. (As an example, in one of their stories, a dragon kidnaps the Czar's three daughters. The Superordinate Inference involved the *why* of the kidnapping, whereas the Subordinate Inference concerned the *how*.) Of course, none of those words had actually been presented in the stories themselves.

In the lexical decision results, words likely to have been inferred from the story were judged considerably more rapidly than words unrelated to the story, as shown in Figure

9.6. More interestingly, words related to the Superordinate inference (the *why*) were judged more rapidly than those related to the Subordinate inference (the *how*).

The relationship between comprehension and memory has also been intensively investigated. Several studies have examined inferences as a function of the limited capacity of working memory (e.g., Fletcher & Bloom, 1988; King & Just, 1991). One such study, by Singer, Andrusiak, Reisdorf, and Black (1992), went one step further than this, explaining individual differences in bridging as a function of working-memory capacity and vocabulary knowledge. The gist of this work is that the greater your working-memory capacity and vocabulary size, the greater the likelihood that information necessary for an inference will still be in working memory, hence can be used for building the bridge between concepts.

Similarly, Kintsch (1994) has discussed the relationship between a reader's long-term memory knowledge of a topic and the coherence of a text. Texts need to be as explicit and coherent as possible, if readers with low background knowledge of the topic are going to learn from the passages they read. Interestingly, readers who already have sufficient background knowledge of the topic actually learn better from texts that have some coherence gaps. That is, when the text leaves out some important inference, readers with good background knowledge engage in a constructive effort to draw the inference on their own.

Summary

1. Reference is the linguistic device of alluding to a concept by a different name, for instance by synonym or pronoun. Speakers and writers imply references, and readers and listeners must infer the intended concepts. These processes are called bridging processes.
2. Some reference is very direct, and some quite indirect; the more indirect the reference, the slower and more difficult it is to comprehend. All inferences, however, depend on retrieving relevant information from semantic memory, and from script knowledge.
3. On-line evidence demonstrates that readers do draw such inferences during reading, and that the inferences are then included in the propositions stored in memory. Additional research has related the process of drawing inferences to the capacity of working memory, and the background knowledge of the reader.

Reading

Preview: on-line reading tasks; two critical assumptions; eye-gaze durations; the Just and Carpenter model of reading

ON-LINE TASKS

Traditionally, reading was studied by giving a passage of text to participants, having them read the passage and then take some sort of test, say a multiple-choice test. While this procedure is not completely uninformative, consider its primary weakness—it reveals almost *none* of the details of mental processing that we want to understand. To learn about those details, cognitive science has developed a variety of **on-line tasks,** which measure reading as it happens. In this methodology, a time-based measure of performance is always collected, for example eye-gaze durations or decision RTs to words related to the passage. These kinds of data give us much more precise information about the mental processes of comprehension than was ever afforded by more traditional methodologies.

An early demonstration of the power of on-line methods was presented by Just (1976), concerning what happens when readers have to resolve a difficult reference. Just used a method whereby a camera photographed the readers' eye movements, and those movements could then be superimposed on the text being read. The filmed results showed the participants' visual fixations as a spot of light that moved across the words in the text.

BASIC EFFECTS IN READING

People are fascinated by the topic of reading, and how the eyes move and obtain information from printed text. Here are a few of the basic facts about these processes (see Just & Carpenter, 1987, and Rayner, 1993, for full reports).

As you recall from Chapter 2, the eyes move in quick, jerky movements called *saccades,* then stop and fixate for a brief moment. Although the average fixation lasts about 250 milliseconds, there is tremendous variability in these durations. Fixations last longer for more difficult text, and for text about which the reader knows relatively little information. The bulk of a skilled reader's fixations are *forward fixations,* from earlier to later words. *Regressive fixations,* in which gaze returns to an earlier word, occur about 10 to 15 percent of the time, and are more common for poor readers than skilled ones.

Virtually all of the information we obtain from a fixation is for the letters projected onto the *fovea,* the central region of the retina where most of the *cones* are located. This region extends approximately 1 degree to the left and right of fixation, a region sufficient for about three or four printed letters in each direction. Similarly, the distance of a normal saccade is about eight to nine letter spaces. While word length determines where to move the eyes for the next fixation, the decision about when to move the eyes depends on cognitive factors related to the difficulty of the fixated word. Most interestingly, we obtain the bulk of the information from a printed word within the first 50 milliseconds of the fixation. Masking the fixated word earlier than that disrupts reading considerably, whereas masking it afterward generally does not.

For the most part, individual-content words are the target of fixations. We do obtain some limited information *parafoveally,* that is in the region adjacent to the fovea, extending out 5 degrees on either side of fixation. Interestingly, most of that information is obtained from the right of fixation, at least for readers of left-to-right languages like English.

Finally, Just and Carpenter (1987, chap. 14) present specific results on tests of speed-reading. Speed-readers in their studies fixated many fewer words in a passage than normal readers, and fixated them for shorter durations. But they did *not* perform some elaborate and successful scanning or fixating on just important words, despite some claims to that effect. And on tests of comprehension, speed-readers only scored well on high-level, "gist" questions, and this only for texts about familiar topics. The conclusion was that speed-readers basically rely more heavily on top-down processing, on drawing inferences from the information that was "fortuitously sampled" in the eye fixations. And, speed reading was reported to be very effortful and stressful, as if "there may be some costs to extended running of the mental engine at high speeds" (p. 449).

The results were amazing. For a passage like

(23) *The tenant complained to his landlord about the leaky roof. The next day, he went to the attic to get his luggage,*

the spot of light remained for a moment on the ambiguous "he," proceeded to "his luggage," and then immediately bounced up to "tenant." When the second sentence was changed, as in

(24) *The next day, he went to the attic to repair the damage,*

the spot of light bounced up to "landlord." When readers were free to move their eyes back to earlier words in the passage, the mental process of finding antecedents and determining pronoun reference was reflected overtly in the readers' eye movements.

The Gaze Duration Task

More typically in current research we use the eye-fixation or **gaze duration** method, in which we record *the amount of time the eyes spend on each word in a passage*. Commonly, participants are asked to read a passage silently as it appears on a computer monitor, and to prepare for some sort of comprehension test after they've finished reading. A computer monitor presents the passages, permitting the investigator to control exactly where and for how long the passage is visible. A camera of some sort is interfaced with the computer to record the person's eye movements as the passage is read. Importantly, the computer-camera device allows the investigator to know exactly what word is being fixated at what time, and to record how long that fixation lasts. Finally, participants are instructed to avoid making regressive eye movements, but instead to spend as much time on each word as they need in order to comprehend fully without actually memorizing the passage. This means that the duration of fixations is actually a sum, reflecting the total time spent fixating each word.

Two Assumptions

Two central assumptions in all on-line research on reading are the immediacy assumption and the eye-mind assumption (Just & Carpenter, 1980, 1987).

- The **immediacy assumption** states that *readers try to interpret each content word of a text as that word is encountered in the passage*.
- The **eye-mind assumption** states that *the eye remains fixated on a word as long as that word is being actively processed during reading*—as long as your *mind* is working on it.

These "assumptions" are now completely accepted, based on countless demonstrations from the gaze duration task. For example, in the last chapter you read about *garden-path sentences*, such as "*After the musician played the piano was quickly taken off the stage*." In such sentences, gaze durations become significantly longer when the error in interpretation becomes obvious, at the word "was" (e.g., Rayner, Carlson, & Frazier, 1983). This effect is shown in Figure 9.7.

Basic On-line Reading Effects

A clear demonstration of the exquisite detail afforded by on-line tasks is shown in Figure 9.8 (p. 302), taken from Just and Carpenter's (1980) theory of reading (see also Just & Carpenter, 1987). In the figure, you see two sentences taken from a scientific passage that

FIGURE 9.7

A depiction of the effect of garden-path sentences on reading time. The curves show eye fixations on phrases before and after D, the point in the sentence where the ambiguity is noticed and disambiguated. The top curve shows the data from garden-path sentences; eye fixation time grows noticeably longer for these curves at D, when the ambiguity is noticed (the D phrase is underlined in the sample sentences). The bottom curve shows data from the control sentences, and no increase in reading time at point D. (Data from Rayner, Carlson, & Frazier, 1983.)

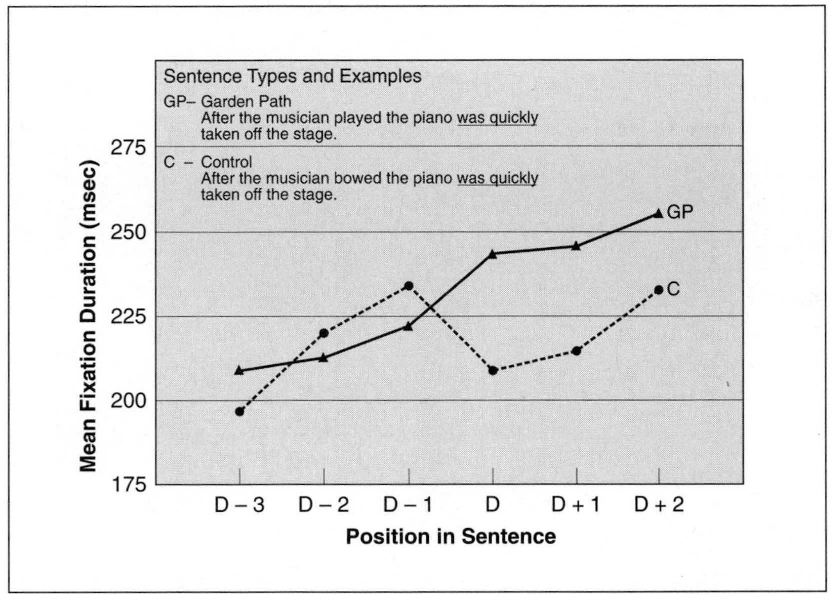

college students in Just and Carpenter's research were asked to read. The top number above the words indicates the order in which the reader fixated or gazed at the elements in the sentence; 1 to 9 in the first sentence, and 1 to 21 in the second. The number below this is the summed *gaze duration*, measured in milliseconds, the precise duration of each eye fixation during reading. So, "Flywheels" in sentence (1) was fixated for 1566 milliseconds, slightly over a second and a half. The next word gazed at, "are," was only fixated 267 milliseconds. The fourth word, "of," wasn't fixated at all by this reader, so neither a gaze number nor time is presented there.

Note that every content word in Figure 9.8 was fixated by the reader, which is the norm for all kinds of texts that have been studied (and for all readers, too). Short function words like *the*, *of*, and *a* tend not to be fixated, however. Also, readers tend to tailor their reading to the type of material they're dealing with, for instance, a newspaper versus a literary story (Zwaan, 1994). Sometimes they skip some content words if the passage is very simple for them (say, a children's story given to an adult), or if they are skimming. The fixations in Figure 9.8 are relatively long, because it's a fairly difficult scientific passage and because readers knew relatively little beforehand about the topic.

★ **FIGURE 9.8**

Duration of eye fixation by a college student reading a scientific passage (the "flywheels" passage). Gazes within each sentence are sequentially numbered above the fixated words with the durations (in msec) indicated below the sequence number. (From Just & Carpenter, 1980.)

1 2 3 4 5 6 7 8 9
1566 267 400 83 267 617 767 450 450
Flywheels are one of the oldest mechanical devices known to man.

1 2 3 4 5 6 7
400 616 517 684 250 317 617
Every internal-combustion engine contains a small

8 9 10 11 12 13
1116 367 467 483 450 383
flywheel that converts the jerky motion of the pistons into the

14 15 16 17 18 19 20 21
284 393 317 283 533 50 366 566
smooth flow of energy that powers the drive shaft.

THE JUST AND CARPENTER MODEL

A real strength of the on-line reading task is that it provides evidence at *two* levels of comprehension. First, the figure shows the durations of rather microscopic, word-level processes. Here, the gaze durations are affected by a series of *local* variables. For instance, durations are longer for long words, for low-frequency words, and for words related to the discourse focus of the passage.

But Just and Carpenter also examined larger, *macroscopic* processes, comprehension time at the level of ideas and propositions, by summing the durations for the words within a proposition. Table 9.5 shows the "Flywheels" passage in this "sector by sector" fashion—roughly speaking, idea by idea. To the left of each line there is a "category" label, naming the sector's role in the overall paragraph structure. To the right are two columns of numbers, observed gaze durations for a group of participants, and durations predicted from Just and Carpenter's READER model. Notice that different kinds of sectors take different amounts of time. For instance, definition sectors tend to have more difficult words in them, and are a bit longer than other sector types, so show longer gaze durations. Even a casual examination of the observed and predicted scores shows that the model does a commendably good job of predicting gaze durations (in fact, for the numbers in Table 9.5, the correlation between observed and expected is +.985).

Model Architecture and Processes

Figure 9.9 (p. 304) illustrates the overall architecture and processes of the Just and Carpenter (1980, 1987) model. Of course, several elements of this model are already familiar

TABLE 9.5

Sectors in the "Flywheels" Passage, Along with Observed and Predicted Gaze Durations

	Gaze Duration (msec)		
Category	*Sector*	*Observed*	*Predicted*
Topic	Flywheels are one of the oldest mechanical devices	1921	1999
Topic	known to man.	478	680
Expansion	Every internal-combustion engine contains a small flywheel	2316	2398
Expansion	that converts the jerky motion of the pistons into the smooth flow of energy	2477	2807
Expansion	that powers the drive shaft.	1056	1264
Cause	The greater the mass of a flywheel and the faster it spins,	2143	2304
Consequence	the more energy can be stored in it.	1270	1536
Subtopic	But its maximum spinning speed is limited by the strength of the material	2440	2553
Subtopic	it is made from.	615	780
Expansion	If it spins too fast for its mass,	1414	1502
Expansion	any flywheel will fly apart.	1200	1304
Definition	One type of flywheel consists of round sandwiches of fiberglass and rubber	2746	3064
Expansion	providing the maximum possible storage of energy	1799	1870
Expansion	when the wheel is confined in a small space	1522	1448
Detail	as in an automobile.	769	718
Definition	Another type, the "superflywheel," consists of a series of rimless spokes.	2938	2830
Expansion	This flywheel stores the maximum energy	1416	1596
Detail	when space is unlimited.	1289	1252

Source: From Just and Carpenter (1980).

to you. For instance, the major "combining" place in the model is working memory, the location at which visual, lexical, syntactic, and other kinds of information are active. Thus working memory plays a central role in the READER model, one largely confirmed by recent evidence (e.g., Just & Carpenter, 1992; Miyake, Just, & Carpenter, 1994). Long-term memory, furthermore, contains a wide variety of knowledge types, conceptual knowledge as well as knowledge of discourse structure and domain knowledge, including script knowledge.

Each of these types of knowledge can "match" the current contents of working memory, and update or alter those contents. In simple terms, what you know combines with what you've already read and understood. These together permit comprehension of what you are reading now.

FIGURE 9.9

The READER model of Just and Carpenter (1980). Solid lines represent the pathways of information flow; the dashed line shows the typical sequence of processing.

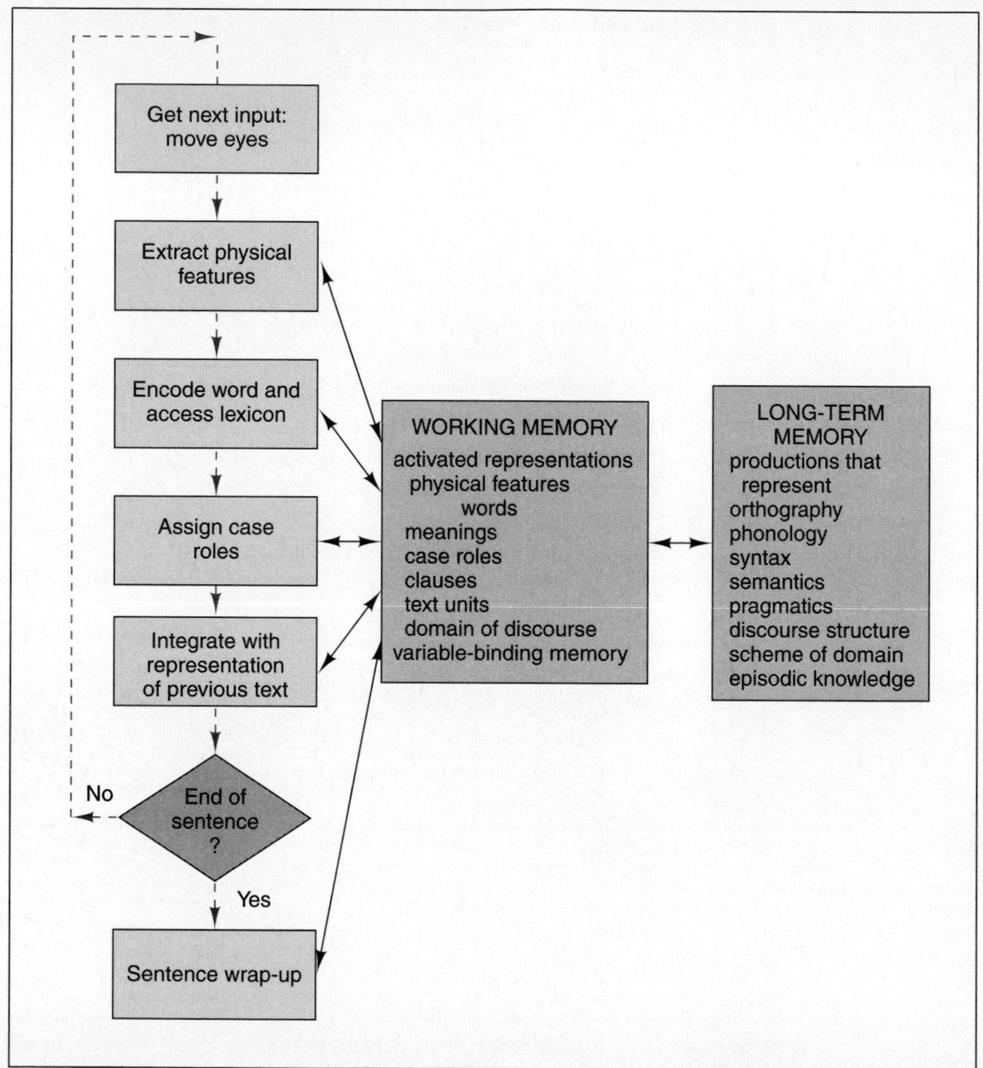

Finally, in more lengthy passages such as the "Flywheels" text, two additional processes are observed. *Sentence wrap-up* refers to an integrative process that occurs at the end of a sentence. During sentence wrap-up, readers tie up any remaining "loose ends"; for instance, any remaining inconsistencies or uncertainties about reference are resolved here, and any final bridging inferences that may be necessary are drawn here. Note that sentence wrap-up occurs at the *end* of sentences. *Interclause integration* seems to be a similar component, but one that operates on the separate clauses *within* a sentence.

INTERACTIVE PROCESSING

As you might expect, such a powerful technology has led to a tremendous upsurge in research on reading comprehension, far too many to cover here (but see the Suggested Readings for some review articles). While the studies differ in some detail, when viewed at arm's length they all converge on the same overall position: Reading and reading comprehension are affected both by linguistic and cognitive effects. The language in the text exerts a strong influence, to be sure (e.g., Just & Carpenter, 1980), even to the extent that tongue twisters disrupt ongoing silent reading (McCutchen & Perfetti, 1982; Zhang & Perfetti, 1993; see Luo, 1996, on phonological effects in reading). But the cognitive influence is strong too—the structure of the mental lexicon, the nature of semantic and scripted knowledge, and the effects of expectations or top-down processes, all of these exert a tremendous *interactive influence* on how we read (e.g., Marslen-Wilson & Tyler, 1980; Marslen-Wilson, Tyler, & Koster, 1993).

The usual effect of such cognitive influences is to smooth and facilitate our reading. Words and ideas are more predictable in one context than in another, and the cognitive system capitalizes on its immense store of knowledge to develop and use an elaborate context. Such context affects eye movements during reading, as when the eyes dwell on a word for a shorter duration because the word was predictable from the sentence context (e.g., Balota, Pollatsek, & Rayner, 1985). Embedding the new information into an existing contextual framework should, of course, lead to better comprehension and a stronger, more durable memory record of the information. Sentences such as these,

(25) *How many animals of each kind did Moses take onto the ark?*

(26) *What is the nationality of Thomas Edison, inventor of the telephone?*

on the other hand, or the garden-path sentences mentioned previously, show the less-than-desirable context and cognitive effects that occasionally crop up. Read these two sentences again, if you didn't notice the so-called "semantic illusion" (Erickson & Mattson, 1981; Reder & Kusbit, 1991; the Moses sentence appeared in Chapter 6, by the way). The reason we fall for the illusion, that we do not immediately notice what is wrong with the sentence, should be clear—it's merely another illustration of the power of conceptually driven processing.

Summary

1. Research on reading has advanced tremendously with the advent of on-line tasks that record the location and duration of eye movements and fixations during reading. The research operates under the assumptions that readers begin comprehending immediately, and that the movements of the eyes reflect underlying mental processing.
2. The duration of time the eye fixates a word in text depends on variables such as word length and frequency. Just as important are macroscopic variables like the focus of the word in the discourse, the reader's knowledge of the concepts and domain, and the role of text units in the overall meaning of the passage.
3. Reading and reading comprehension are governed by complex interactions among text variables and the reader. Even in silent reading there is an effect of phonology; semantic illusions show how what we know can mislead us in certain comprehension situations.

Conversation

> **Preview:** turn taking; social and status relationships; conversational maxims; topic maintenance; on-line theories; indirect requests

We turn now to a brief consideration of spoken language, specifically the comprehension of conversation. By *conversation* we mean normal, everyday language interactions, say, an ordinary talk among friends. But the issues extend to *all* spoken language interactions—how professors lecture, how people converse on the telephone, how an interviewer and a job applicant talk, and so on. An overriding theme here is that we follow *rules* in conversations, rules that determine both the content and the tone of our contributions. A key bit of evidence that we indeed follow such rules is our surprise or puzzlement—or annoyance (or worse)—when someone *breaks* one of the rules.

THE STRUCTURE OF CONVERSATIONS

Taking Turns

Conversations are structured by a variety of cognitive and social variables, and rules governing the *what* and *how* of our contributions. To begin with, we take turns. Typically, there is relatively little overlap between participants' utterances. Generally, two people will speak simultaneously only at the change of turns, when one speaker is finishing and the other is beginning. On the other hand, there tends to be a fair amount of nonverbal interaction during a turn, for example when a listener nods or mutters "um-hmm" to indicate attention or agreement (Duncan, 1972).

The rules we follow for turn taking are rather straightforward (Sacks, Schegloff, & Jefferson, 1974).

- First, the current speaker is in charge of selecting the next speaker. This is often accomplished by directing a comment or question toward another participant—"What do you think about that, Fred?"

CALVIN and HOBBES
WHEN A PERSON PAUSES IN MID-SENTENCE TO CHOOSE A WORD, THAT'S THE BEST TIME TO JUMP IN AND CHANGE THE SUBJECT!
IT'S LIKE AN INTERCEPTION IN FOOTBALL! YOU GRAB THE OTHER GUY'S IDEA AND RUN THE OPPOSITE WAY WITH IT!
THE MORE SENTENCES YOU COMPLETE, THE HIGHER YOUR SCORE! THE IDEA IS TO BLOCK THE OTHER GUY'S THOUGHTS AND EXPRESS YOUR OWN! THAT'S HOW YOU WIN!
CONVERSATIONS AREN'T CONTESTS!
OK, A POINT FOR YOU, BUT I'M STILL AHEAD.

- The second rule is that if the first rule isn't used, then any participant can become the current speaker.
- Third, if no one else takes the turn, the current speaker may continue to speak but is not obliged to.

Speakers use a variety of signals to indicate whether they are finished with their turn. For example, a long pause at the end of a sentence is a *turn-yielding* signal, as is a comment directed at another participant, a drop in the pitch or loudness of the utterance, and establishing direct eye contact with another participant. If the current speaker is not relinquishing the conversational turn, however, these signals are withheld. Other "failure to yield" signals include trailing off in midsentence without completing the grammatical clause or the thought, withholding such endings as "you know," or even looking away from other participants during a pause (Cook, 1977).

Social Roles and Settings

The social roles of conversational partners, along with conversational setting, exert considerable influence on the contributions made by participants (e.g., Kemper & Thissen, 1981). Formal settings among strangers or mere acquaintances lead to more structured, rule-governed conversations than informal settings among friends (e.g., Blom & Gumperz, 1972). Conversations with a "superior"—for instance, your boss, a police officer—are more formal and rule-governed than conversations with peers (e.g., R. Brown & Ford, 1961; Edwards & Potter, 1993; and Holtgraves, 1994, discuss the social and interpersonal aspects of such situations).

Because of the status relationship between participants, a "superior" is given (or takes) more leeway in breaking the turn-taking rules. Gender may also be a factor here. Some reports indicated that men interrupt women far more frequently than the reverse (Zimmerman & West, 1975), although other studies have not found this effect, for instance Beattie's (1983) analysis of interruptions in university tutorial classes. (See Carroll, 1994, for a more complete discussion of these points.)

COGNITIVE CONVERSATIONAL CHARACTERISTICS

Conversations are also structured by cognitive factors. We'll focus on three, the *conversational rules* we follow, the issue of *topic maintenance*, and the *on-line theories of conversational partners*.

Conversational Maxims

Grice (1975; see also Norman & Rumelhart, 1975) suggested a set of four **conversational maxims,** rules that govern our conversational interactions with others, which all derive from the *cooperative principle*. The idea here is that each participant in a conversation implicitly assumes that all speakers are following the rules, and that each contribution to the conversation is a sincere, appropriate contribution—this *is* the **cooperative principle.** As Table 9.6 (p. 308) shows, the four maxims specify in more detail how to follow the cooperative principle. (Two additional rules have been added to the list, for purposes that will become clear in a moment.)

TABLE 9.6

Grice's (1975) Conversational Maxims, with Two Additional Rules

The Cooperative Principle
Be sincere, reasonable, and appropriate.
1. Relevance: Make your utterances relevant to the conversation (e.g., stick to the topic; don't state what others aren't interested in).
2. Quantity: Be as informative as required (e.g., don't overspecify; don't say more or less than you know; don't be too informative).
3. Quality: Say what is true (e.g., don't mislead; don't lie; don't exaggerate).
4. Manner and tone: Be clear (e.g., avoid obscurity and ambiguity; be brief; be polite; don't interrupt).
Two Additional Rules
5. Relations with conversational partner: Infer and respond to partner's knowledge and beliefs (e.g., tailor contributions to partner's level; correct misunderstandings).
6. Rule violations: Signal or mark intentional violations of rules (e.g., use linguistic or pragmatic markers—stress, gestures; use blatant violations; signal the reason for the violation).

Source: From Grice (1975); see also Norman and Rumelhart (1975).

A simple example or two should help you understand the point behind these maxims. When a speaker violates—or seems to violate—one of the maxims, the listener assumes there is a *reason* for the violation. That is, the listener still assumes that the speaker was following the overarching cooperative principle, so must have intended the remark as something else, maybe sarcasm, maybe a nonliteral meaning. As an example, imagine studying in the library, when your friend Steve asks

(27) *Can I borrow a pencil?*

If Steve asked you this, it would be a normal speech act, one you could respond to directly. But if you had already loaned a pencil to Steve, and then he said

(28) *Can I borrow a pencil with lead in it?*

the question means something entirely different. Assuming that Steve was being cooperative, you now have to figure out why he broke the Quantity maxim about overspecifying. Your inference is probably that it was a deliberate violation, where Steve's authorized implication can be expressed something like "The pencil you loaned me doesn't have any lead in it, so would you please loan me one I *can* use?"

Topic Maintenance

We also follow the conversational rules in terms of **topic maintenance,** *making our contributions relevant and to the topic*. Topic maintenance actually depends on two processes, *comprehension* of the speaker's remark, and then *expansion*, contributing something new to the topic.

Comprehension. Schank (1977; see also Litman & Allen, 1987) has provided a provocative analysis of topic maintenance and topic shift, including a consideration of what is and is not *a permissible response*, called simply a *move*, after one speaker's turn is over. The basic idea here is that the listener comprehends the speaker's comment, and represents it in memory as a proposition, exactly the kind of proposition we've been discussing throughout the chapter. Furthermore, the listener must infer what the speaker's main point was, that is, must infer what the discourse focus was in the speaker's remark. If the speaker—call him Ben, to facilitate the discussion—says

(29) *I bought a new car in Baltimore yesterday*

then Ed, his conversational partner, needs to infer Ben's main point, and then *expand* on that in his reply. Thus, sentence (30) would be a *legal move* because it apparently responds to the speaker's authorized implication, whereas sentence (31#) is probably not a legal move (denoted by the # sign).

(30) Ed: *Really? I thought you said you couldn't afford a car.*

(31#) Ed: *I bought a new shirt yesterday.*

Sentence (30) intersects with two main elements in the proposition for sentence (29), BUY and CAR, so is probably an acceptable *expansion* for a conversational turn, according to Schank (1977). Sentence (31#) intersects with BUY, but the other common concept seems to be the *time case role* YESTERDAY, an insufficient basis for most expansions. Thus, in general a participant's responsibility is to infer the speaker's focus, and then expand on that in an appropriate way. That's the *Relevance* maxim—sticking to the topic means you have to infer it correctly. Ed seems to have failed to draw the correct inference.

On the other hand, maybe Ed *did* comprehend Ben's statement correctly. If so, then he has deliberately violated the Relevance maxim. But it's such a blatant violation that it suggests some other motive—Ed may be expressing disinterest in what Ben did, or may be

"I want you to know that I'm not nearly the great human being everyone seems to think me to be."

saying indirectly that he thinks Ben is bragging. And if Ed suspects Ben is telling a lie, then he makes his remark even more blatant, such as

(32) *Yeah, and I had lunch with the Queen of England.*

On-line Theories During Conversation

A final cognitive point involves the theories we develop of our conversational partners. The most obvious one we construct can be called a direct theory. This is the theory or mental model of what the conversational partner knows and is interested in, what the partner is like. We tailor our speech so that we're not being too complex or too simplistic, and so that we're not talking about something of no interest to the listener. Some of the clearest examples of this involve adult-child speech, where a child's lesser vocabulary and knowledge prompt adults to modify and simplify their utterances in a remarkably large number of ways (e.g., DePaulo & Bonvillian, 1978; Snow, 1972; Snow & Ferguson, 1977). But this sensitivity to the partner's knowledge and interests is displayed to some degree in all conversations. I don't talk to a college class the way I would to a group of second graders, nor do I launch into a conversation with a bank teller about my research.

But there is another layer of theories during a conversation, an interpersonal level related to "face management," that is, public image (e.g., Holtgraves, 1994). Let's call this the **second-order theory** during conversation. This second-order theory is *an evaluation of the other participant's direct theory—what you think the other participant believes about you.* Someone says to you,

(33) *Maybe you shouldn't take that class next term—don't you have to be pretty smart to do all that reading?*

Your reaction is something like "*He* thinks I'm not smart enough." In other words, your second-order theory is that *his* direct theory of you is that you're not smart.

EMPIRICAL EFFECTS IN CONVERSATION

Let's conclude with some evidence about the conversational effects we've been discussing. One of the most commonly investigated aspects of conversation involves **indirect requests,** for example when we ask someone to do something (Close the window) by an indirect and presumably more polite statement ("It's cold in here.")

One of the most impressive investigations of such indirect requests was reported by Clark (1979). The study involved telephone calls to some 950 merchants in the San Francisco area, in which the caller asked a question that the merchant would normally be expected to deal with on the phone (e.g., what time do you close, do you take credit cards, how much does something cost). The caller would write down a verbatim record of the call after hanging up. A typical conversational interaction was:

(34) Merchant: "*Hello, Scoma's Restaurant.*"
Caller: "*Hello. Do you accept any credit cards?*"
Merchant: "*Yes we do—we even accept Carte Blanche.*"

Of course, the caller's question here was indirect—"Yes" isn't an acceptable answer, because the authorized implication was "What credit cards do you take?" Merchants' virtually always responded to the authorized implication, rather than merely to the literal question posed by the caller. Furthermore, they tailored their answers so as to be as informative as possible, while not saying more than was necessary; for instance, "We *only* accept Visa and MasterCard," or "We accept *all* major credit cards." Such responses are both informative and brief.

In an interesting extension of such research, Holtgraves (1994) examined comprehension speed for indirect requests as a function of the status of the speaker, whether the speaker was of higher status than the listener (e.g., boss and employee) or whether both were of equal status (two employees). Participants read a short scenario (e.g., getting a conference room ready for a board of directors' meeting), which concluded with one of two kinds of indirect statements. Conventional statements were normal indirect requests, such as "Could you go fill the water glasses?" Negative State remarks were even more indirect, merely stating a negative situation and only indirectly implying that the listener should do something; for example, "The water glasses seem to be empty." The participants pressed a key when they understood what the speaker meant by the original remark, and then saw a paraphrase ("Go fill the water glasses"), which they also had to comprehend. Holtgraves timed participants on both the original indirect statements and the paraphrases.

The results showed a clear effect of the speaker's status on people's comprehension times. When the statement was a Conventional indirect request ("Could you go fill the water glasses?"), comprehension speed was unaffected by the speaker's status, as shown on ★ the left in Figure 9.10 (p. 312); this was true for the paraphrases too, the lower curve on the left. But when the speaker used the very indirect Negative State form ("The water glasses seem to be empty."), status made a substantial difference. Comprehension was considerably slower when a speaker of equal status used that form than when a speaker of higher status used it, both for original statements and also paraphrases. In other words, we aren't surprised when the boss *implies* very indirectly that we should do something—

★ **FIGURE 9.10**

Comprehension times for original Conventional and Negative State remarks and their paraphrases, as a function of speaker status. (From Holtgraves, 1994.)

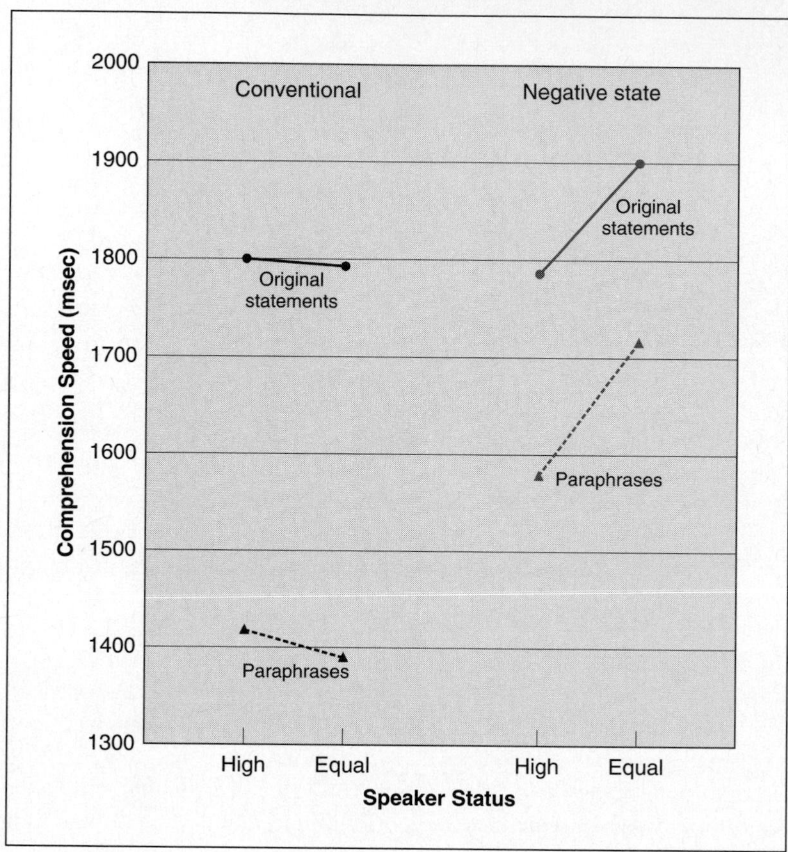

bosses do that, we expect it, and so we comprehend readily. But we are surprised when a peer uses the very indirect form, as shown by the slower comprehension times (my reaction in such a situation is "well, do it yourself").

Summary

1. Conversations are structured by social and cognitive factors. Turn taking, for example, is governed by a set of rules, but some rules can be violated depending on status relationships among speakers.
2. The Cooperative Principle is assumed by conversational partners, with specific details concerning relevance, quantity, quality, and manner of contributions. The rules govern topic maintenance, and listeners' attempts to understand when a speaker violates one of the rules.

3. Evidence on comprehension of indirect requests show both the influence of conversational rules and also status relationships among conversational partners.

Important Terms

advantage of clause recency/first mention
authorized versus unauthorized
belief versus conceptual levels of analysis
bridging
conversational maxims
cooperative principle
direct versus second-order theory
discourse focus
enhancement
eye-mind and immediacy assumptions
gaze duration
implication
indirect request
inference
on-line tasks
propositions
reference
structure building
suppression
topic maintenance

Suggested Readings

Several sources provide up-to-date information on reading research. See especially *The Psychology of Reading and Language Comprehension* by Just and Carpenter (1987), *The Psychology of Reading* by Rayner and Pollatsek (1989), and a collection of symposium papers, introduced by Rayner, that appeared in the September 1993 issue of *Psychological Science*. An interesting focus in reading comprehension research involves the "illusion of knowing," the illusion that you *do* understand a passage, even though testing reveals that you have not understood (e.g., Epstein, Glenberg, & Bradley, 1984). Maki and Berry (1984) have reported an interesting study on metacomprehension of textual material; in the naturalistic setting of the university classroom, they had students predict what would be remembered.

Indirect speech acts such as requests and commands still provide fertile ground for research, for example how we overcome anticipated obstacles in requesting information (Francik & Clark, 1985; Gibbs, 1986b). For work on the pragmatic and nonlinguistic contexts of conversations, see McNeill's (1985) review, entitled "So you think gestures are nonverbal?" and see Giles and Coupland (1991) for a treatment from sociological perspectives. For work on figurative language and metaphors, see Gibbs (1989, 1990), Ortony (1979), and Gibbs (1986a) on sarcasm. And continue to consult Clark (e.g., Clark & Wilkes-Gibbs, 1986; Isaacs & Clark, 1987; Wilkes-Gibbs & Clark, 1992) for work on conversation.

SECTION

FOUR

THE BRAIN

CHAPTER TEN

NEUROCOGNITION

A man known as patient K.C. had a serious motorcycle accident in 1980, at age 30. The brain damage he sustained left him with a profound and unique amnesia—K.C. "cannot remember, in the sense of bringing back to conscious awareness, a single thing that he has ever done or experienced in the past" (Tulving, 1989, p. 362). His perception, attention, language, and intelligence remain intact—casual conversation with him seems not at all unusual. But his episodic memory, his memories of his own personal experiences and history, are gone. Question: Can episodic and semantic memories be one and the same, given that K.C.'s semantic memory is intact but his episodic memory is completely gone? Probably not.

Patient P.S. was a 38-year-old financial analyst when a malformation of blood arteries and vessels in her brain hemorrhaged, causing appreciable damage in the temporal lobe of her left hemisphere. Extensive testing (Sokol, McCloskey, Cohen, & Aliminosa, 1991) revealed a startling disruption in her ability to perform simple mathematics. She made a substantial number of errors to simple multiplication facts—to problems like 7×7 and 9×4, she was 80 percent *inaccurate*. And to *any* single-digit problem with a zero, she was *always* wrong (e.g., she'd say $0 \times 2 = 2$). But she only made two *rule* errors in the 66 long multiplication problems she worked, problems like 193×17. Is our knowledge of arithmetic and math one single, indivisible collection of information? P.S.'s disruption suggests not. Instead, it seems that simple fact retrieval and rule knowledge are rather separate, since one could be damaged while the other was not.

How must the cognitive system be organized for disruptions like these to take place?

Now that you have a foundation of knowledge about normal cognitive processing, we're ready to explore one of the most important and increasingly active branches of cognitive science, the field of **cognitive neuropsychology.** A useful definition of this term is that cognitive neuropsychology—neurocognition for short—is the study of the neurological basis of cognitive processing, as revealed by measures of normal brain functioning and disrupted performance due to brain damage. (Another term, cognitive neuroscience, is also gaining in popularity—it means essentially the same thing.)

To be sure, it's important to understand the consequences of brain damage for medical, humane, and personal reasons. After all, it's not just the individual's brain that is damaged in cases of accident or disease, it's his or her whole life—and any help and understanding we can offer is obviously important.

But we have a different goal in neurocognition. First we study patients, either singly or in groups, to see how their cognition has been disrupted due to disease or brain injury—the case studies of K.C. and P.S., for instance. We then draw inferences about the *normal* cognitive system based on the evidence we've collected (e.g., McCarthy & Warrington, 1990; McCloskey, 1992). For example, if brain damage can selectively affect episodic memory but not semantic memory, it stands to reason that those types of long-term memory can't be identical. If they were the same, then *both* would show a disruption—and likewise for the facts and rules of arithmetic.

We'll begin by covering some of the basics of brain anatomy and organization, and several methods of investigating the brain. Then we'll turn to three major topics, brain-related deficits in perception and attention, in language, and in long-term memory. Consider this chapter as a true introduction, barely scratching the surface of a genuinely complex but fascinating area of cognitive science. And, bear in mind that the cognitive science of the future will be even *more* neurocognitive in its interests and scope.

Basics of Anatomy and Functioning

Preview: basic brain anatomy; two principles of functioning, contralaterality and specialization; left brain–right brain; language on the left

Of fundamental importance, the nervous system is the product of a long evolution. The original functions of some parts have been altered by layer upon layer of modifications. . . . We cannot expect the design of the brain to resemble anything that a human would consider optimal. (Sejnowski & Churchland, 1989, p. 341)

At birth, the human brain weighs approximately 400 grams (about 14 oz), growing to an average of 1450 grams in adults, slightly over 3 pounds. It is roughly the size of a ripe grapefruit or a head of cauliflower. The basic building block of the nervous system, brain included, is the **neuron,** the cell that is specialized for receiving and transmitting a neural impulse. Neurons are the components that form nerve tracts throughout the body as well as all of the structures of the brain.

How many neurons are there in the brain? Although estimates vary rather widely (Squire, 1987), Kolb and Whishaw (1990) suggest a grand total of 180 *billion* cells of all types in the brain, including not only neurons but connective and circulatory tissue as well. An estimated 50 billion of these cells are "directly engaged in information processing" and cognition (Kolb & Whishaw, 1990, p. 4), and possibly up to 100 billion. To put that figure in perspective, consider that the Milky Way galaxy has on the order of 100 billion stars.

★ **FIGURE 10.1**

Anatomy of a neuron.

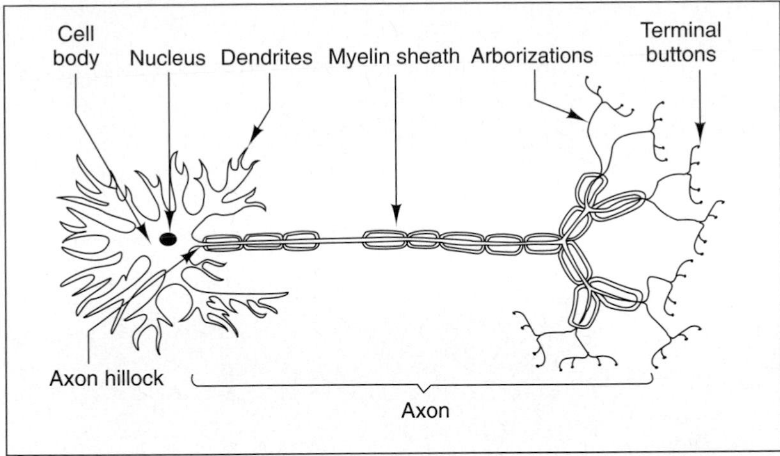

NEURONS AND NEUROTRANSMITTERS

★ Figure 10.1 illustrates an idealized or prototypical neuron. While the details vary, each neuron within the nervous system shows the same basic structure. At one end of the neuron, many small branchlike fingers called *dendrites* serve to "gather" a neural impulse into the neuron—in somewhat more familiar terms, the dendrites are the *input* structures of the neuron. The neural message travels down the *axon,* the long extended tube, reaching the *axon terminals,* the "output" branches that pass the message along to other neurons.

Of particular importance for neurocognition is an understanding of the chemical **neurotransmitters** that are released into the **synapse,** the physical gap between the axon terminals and the dendrites of other neurons. The different neurotransmitters, for instance *acetylcholine, dopamine, norepinephrine,* "fit" into different receptor sites on the adjacent dendrites, much like a particular key will fit into a particular door lock. Some of these neurotransmitters increase the likelihood that the next neuron will fire—this is the process of *excitation.* Other neurotransmitters have an *inhibitory* effect, by making it less likely that the next neuron will fire. (The entire neural process is *tremendously* more complex than this simplified explanation indicates. See sources like Grilly, in press, and Kolb & Whishaw, 1996, for more detailed accounts.)

Some of the secrets of neurocognition are undoubtedly to be found in the neurotransmitters. For example, of the 30 or so different neurotransmitters that have been identified and studied (Iversen, 1979), *acetylcholine* and possibly norepinephrine seem to be especially important for cognition (summarized in Squire, 1987). For example, decreased levels of acetylcholine have been found in the brains of people with Alzheimer's disease. It's tantalizing to suggest this as part of the explanation for the learning and memory deficits observed in these patients, although it could instead be a side effect of the disease (e.g., Riley, 1989). In either case, it seems clear that acetylcholine plays an essential role in normal learning and memory processes (see also Thompson, 1986).

FIGURE 10.2

Cutaway illustration of the brain. Some of the major components of the human brain. The lower components ("old brain") are visible in the figure because the outer layer of the neocortex has been cut away.

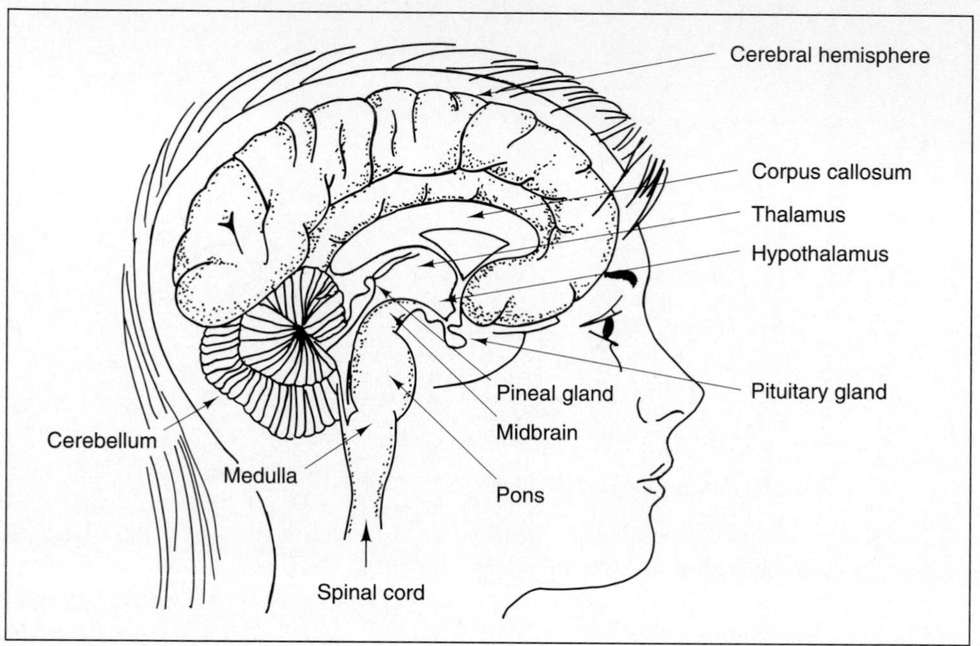

BRAIN ANATOMY

Let's jump now to the level of the entire brain, the awesomely complex "biological computer." Figure 10.2 shows a view of some of the lower, more primitive brain structures referred to collectively as the *old brain* or *brain stem*. This portion of the brain is older in terms of evolution, and governs very basic, primitive functions such as digestion, heartbeat, balance, and the like.

For neurocognition, however, we are largely interested in the *new brain*, the **neocortex** (also **cerebral cortex**), the top layer of the brain, responsible for higher-level mental processes. The neocortex is a wrinkled, convoluted structure that virtually surrounds the old brain. Laid out flat, the two *halves* or **hemispheres** would cover up to 2500 square centimeters (nearly 20 square in.); the thickness varies from about 1 to 3 millimeters (no more than ¼ in.; Kolb & Whishaw, 1990). The wrinkling is "nature's solution to the problem of confining the huge neocortical surface area within a shell that is still small enough to pass through the birth canal" (Kolb & Whishaw, 1990, p. 15). It is the most recent structure to have evolved in the human brain, and is considerably larger in humans than in lower animals. Because it is primarily responsible for higher mental processes such as language and thought, it is not surprising that the human neocortex is so large, relative to the rest of the brain.

FIGURE 10.3

The four lobes of the neocortex.

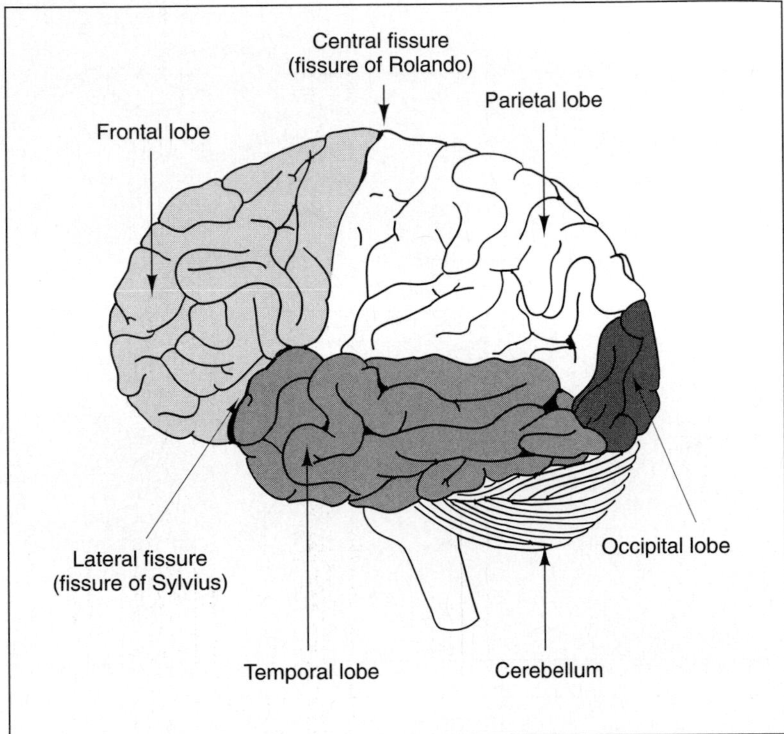

A side view, shown in Figure 10.3, reveals the four general regions or *lobes* of the neocortex. Clockwise from the front, these are the *frontal lobe*, *parietal lobe*, *occipital lobe*, and *temporal lobe*, named after the skull bones on top of them (e.g., the temporal lobes lie beneath your temples). Notice that these lobes are not separate structures. Instead, each hemisphere of the neocortex is a single sheet of neural matter. The lobes are formed by the deeper folds and convolutions of the cortex, with the names used as convenient reference terms for the regions.

Three other subcortical (below the neocortex) structures are important to neurocognition; they are shown in Figure 10.4 (p. 322), as if looking through a transparent neocortex and seeing the interior structures. Deep inside the lower brain structures is the **thalamus,** meaning "inner room" or "chamber." It is often referred to as the gateway to the cortex, since virtually all messages entering the cortex come through the thalamus (a portion of the sense of smell is one of the very few exceptions). In other words, the thalamus is the major relay station from the sensory systems of the body into the neocortex.

Just above the thalamus is a broad band of nerve fibers called the **corpus callosum.** As described later, the corpus callosum ("callous body") is the primary bridge across which messages pass between the left and right halves of the neocortex.

FIGURE 10.4

Lower brain structures.

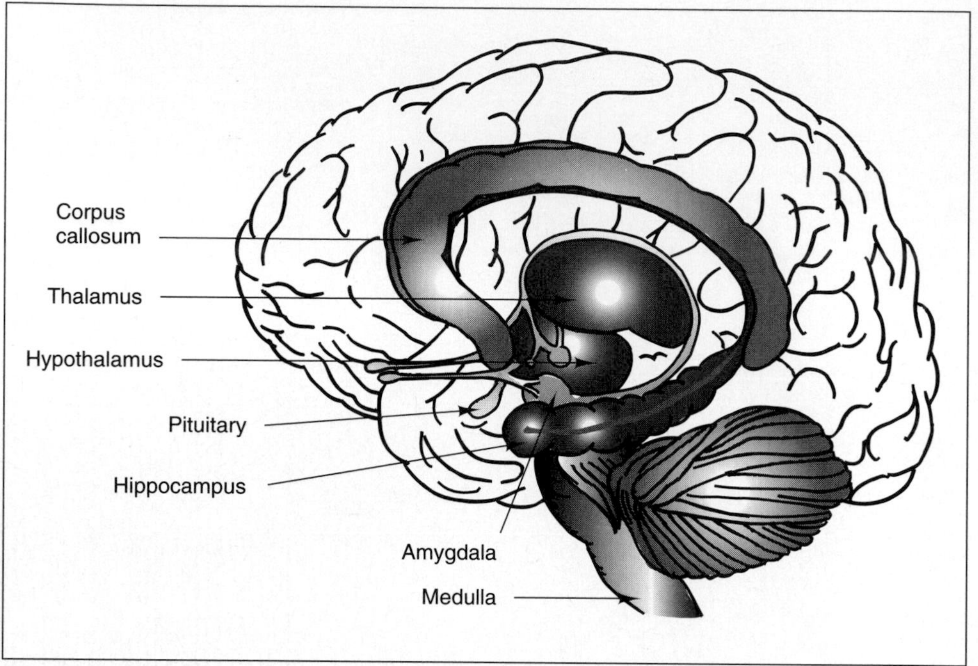

The third structure is the **hippocampus,** from the Latin for "sea horse," referring to its curved shape. The hippocampus lies immediately interior to the temporal lobes, that is, underneath the temporal lobes but in the same horizontal plane. Research on the effects of damage to the hippocampus will be described later, including one of the best-known case histories in neuropsychology, that of patient H.M. For now, just learn one new fact—the hippocampus is *critical* for storing new information into long-term memory.

TWO PRINCIPLES OF FUNCTIONING

Two important principles of functioning in the neocortex are vital for understanding the effects of brain damage on cognitive processes. These principles involve the ideas of **contralaterality** and **hemispheric specialization.**

Contralaterality

When viewed from the top, the neocortex is seen to be divided into two mirror-image halves, the left and right cerebral hemispheres. This of course follows a general law of anatomy, that with the exception of internal organs like the heart, the body is basically bilaterally symmetrical, has symmetrical structure on both sides (*lateral* simply means "to the side").

What is somewhat surprising, however, is that the control centers for one side of the body are in the opposite hemisphere of the brain. This is **contralaterality,** where the prefix *contra* means against or opposite. In other words, for evolutionary reasons that will probably remain obscure forever, the right hemisphere of the brain receives its input from the left side of the body, and also controls the left side. Likewise, the left hemisphere receives input from and controls output to the right side of the body.

Figure 10.5 (p. 324) shows the principle of contralaterality in the context of vision, where the principle is trickier to understand. Contralaterality in vision goes from the visual field to the hemispheres of the brain—whatever you see "out there" on your left is in your *left visual field*. It is sent first to the *right* hemisphere of the brain, in particular the *right occipital lobe*. Likewise any information in your right visual field is first sent to the left occipital lobe. The reason for this is the arrangement of neural connections from the retina—those on the right half (dashed line in the figure) project to the right hemisphere, and those on the left (solid line) to the left hemisphere. Normally, of course, once the visual information is registered in the visual cortex, the visual region of the occipital lobes, it is then transmitted freely to the other hemisphere via the corpus callosum.

Hemispheric Specialization

A second surprise concerning lateralization in the neocortex involves different specializations within the two cerebral hemispheres. Despite their mirror-image appearance, the two hemispheres *do not* mirror one another's abilities. Instead, each hemisphere tends to specialize in different abilities, and tends to process different kinds of information. This is the full principle of **cerebral lateralization and hemispheric specialization,** that different functions or actions within the brain tend to rely more heavily on one hemisphere or the other, or tend to be performed differently in the two hemispheres.

This is not to say that some process or function can *only* happen in one particular hemisphere. And it certainly doesn't mean that there are "left-hemisphere cognitive processes" and "right-hemisphere cognitive processes." It merely says that there is often a tendency, sometimes strong, for one or the other hemisphere to be especially dominant in different processes or functions.

The most obvious evidence of lateralization in humans is the overwhelming incidence of right-handedness, across all cultures and apparently throughout the known history of human evolution (e.g., Corballis, 1989; Fabbro, 1994). Accompanying this tendency toward right-handedness is a particularly strong left-hemispheric specialization in humans for language. That is, for the majority of people, language ability is especially lateralized in the left hemisphere of the neocortex—countless studies have demonstrated this general tendency, as well as the limits to this generalization (see Language on the Left, below).

In contrast, the right cerebral hemisphere seems to be somewhat more specialized for nonverbal, spatial, and more perceptual information processing (e.g., Eslinger, Damasio, Damasio, & Butters, 1993; see Moscovitch, 1979, for a review of the range of such left-right hemisphere characterizations). The evidence suggests, for instance, that face recognition (Ellis, 1983; McCarthy & Warrington, 1990) and mental rotation (Deutsch, Bourbon, Papanicolaou, & Eisenberg, 1988), both requiring spatial and perceptual processing,

are especially dependent on the right cerebral hemisphere. Table 10.1 (p. 325) provides a summary of data on cerebral lateralization.

★ **FIGURE 10.5**

Contralaterality in vision. The figure depicts the binocular pathways of information flow from the eyes into the visual cortex of the brain. The patterns of stimulus-to-brain pathways demonstrate the contralaterality of the visual system. Note that the pine tree is shown entirely in the left visual field, so it is projected onto the visual cortex of the right hemisphere; the house is presented to the right visual field and hence is projected onto the left hemisphere.

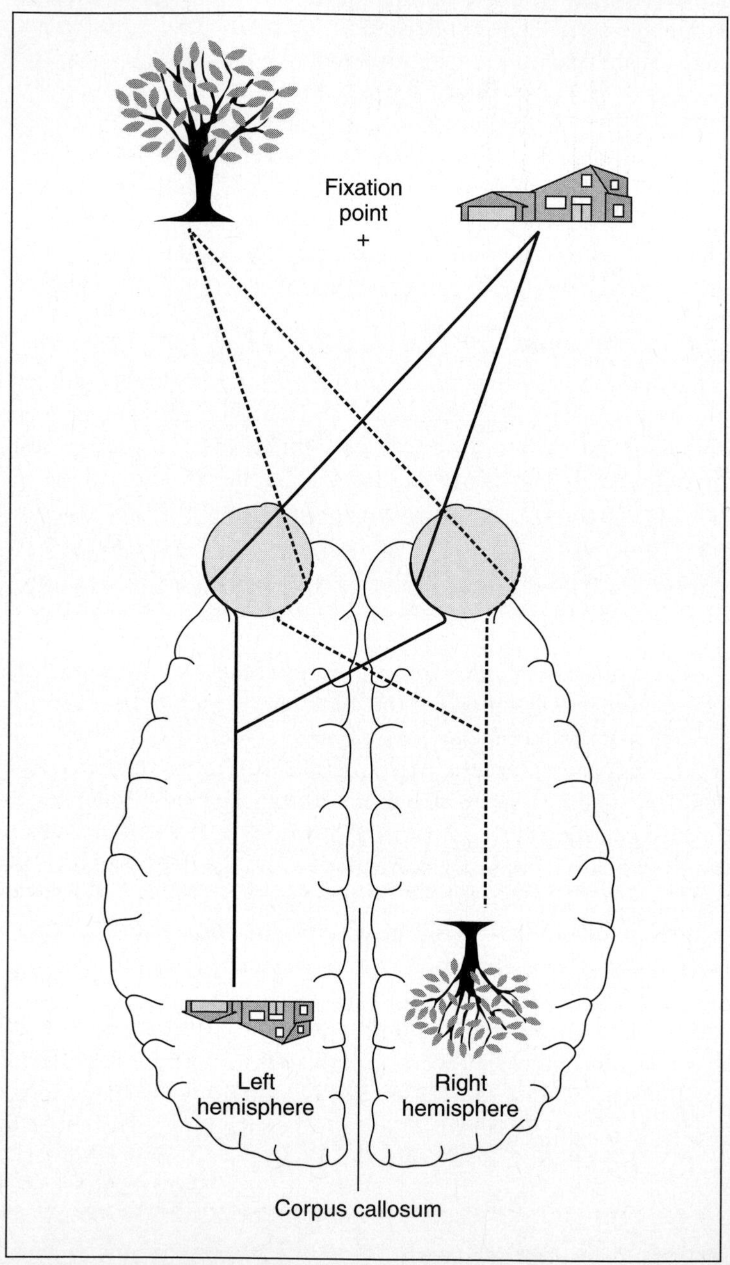

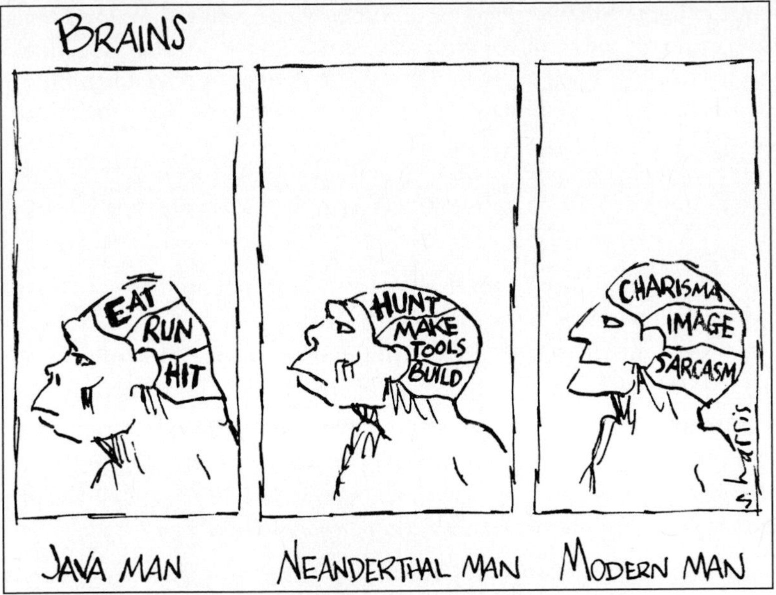

LEFT BRAIN–RIGHT BRAIN

Most people have heard of "left brain–right brain" issues, often from the popular press. Such treatments are notorious for exaggerating and oversimplifying what's known about laterality and specialization—the left hemisphere ends up with the rational, logical, and

TABLE 10.1

Summary of Data on Cerebral Lateralization

Function	*Left Hemisphere*	*Right Hemisphere*
Visual system	Letters, words	Complex geometric patterns, faces
Auditory system	Language-related sounds	Nonlanguage environmental sounds, music
Somatosensory system	?	Tactile recognition of complex patterns, Braille
Movement	Complex voluntary movement	Movements in spatial patterns
Memory	Verbal memory	Nonverbal memory
Language	Speech, reading, writing, arithmetic	Prosody?
Spatial processes		Geometry, sense of direction, mental rotation of shapes

Source: From Kolb and Whishaw (1990).

symbolic abilities—the boring ones, in other words, while the right hemisphere gets the holistic, creative, and intuitive processes—the sexy ones. Instead, think of almost any act of cognition as involving many individual components, each contributing some information, each having to coordinate with other components—and almost certainly, each residing in a different anatomical region.

Take a simple example. Look at the photograph in Figure 10.6 and name it out loud. Now, let's analyze your cognitive processes from the standpoint of activity within the brain.

- The visual input from your eyes went to both hemispheres of the occipital cortex, where vision begins in the brain.
- There was then a projection of the information to a portion of the right parietal lobe, an area especially involved in spatial perception and organization of whole patterns.
- A region in the left hemisphere, probably somewhere near the junction of the occipital and temporal lobes, then attached meaning to this organized pattern.
- Another left-hemisphere area, in the temporal lobe, supplied you with the name of the object. This information was then forwarded to
- a left frontal lobe region, and into the motor part of that hemisphere which governs your speech muscles. Action here sent out the message to the vocal apparatus, causing you to say "barn" (which you then heard through both ears, forwarded to both hemispheres, and so forth).

Disruption of any one of these steps or processes could lead to an inability to name the picture, of course. That is, several different patients, each with rather different localized brain damage, could show an inability to name the picture, but each for a very different reason. The more important point is that "simple" picture naming is anything but simple—it taps mental processes from a variety of brain regions in both hemispheres, and requires complex coordination of those processes all along the way. And of course, the same is true for nearly every cognitive process of interest.

FIGURE 10.6

A simple recognition test.

Language on the Left

Nonetheless, there is rather striking division of labor in the neocortex, in which the left cerebral hemisphere is specialized for language. This is almost always true—it characterizes up to 85 or 90 percent of the population. The percentages are this high, however, *only if* you are a right-handed male, with no family history of left-handedness, and if you write with your hand in a normal rather than inverted position (e.g., Freidman & Polson, 1981). If you are female, if you are left-handed, if you write with an inverted hand position, and so on, then the "left hemisphere/language rule" is not quite as strong. For these groups, the majority will have the customary pattern, but it's a slimmer majority—for example, Kolb and Whishaw (1990, p. 128) allude to the "one-third" of left-handed people with right- or mixed-hemisphere dominance in language. (For simplicity, however, we will rely on the convenient fiction of "language in the left hemisphere" for the rest of the chapter.)

Summary

1. The brain is composed of 50 to 100 billion neurons, individual nerve cells specialized for transmitting messages. All neurons share the same basic structure, with the dendrites, cell body, axon, and axon terminals as the four major regions.
2. The synapse is the space or gap between neurons. Neural messages cross the gap when neurotransmitters are released into the synapse and occupy receptor sites on the adjacent dendrites. Some neurotransmitters excite activity in the adjoining neurons, and some inhibit activity. Acetylcholine in particular has been identified as essential to learning and memory.
3. Each of the two hemispheres of the brain has four major regions, the frontal, parietal, occipital, and temporal lobes. For the majority of people, the left hemisphere is specialized for language processing, and the right for nonverbal, spatial processing. Most cognitive tasks of any interest, however, require the participation and coordination of regions in both hemispheres.

Methods of Investigation

Preview: lesions of the brain; direct stimulation method; split-brain patients; imaging and brain wave techniques; the method of dissociations

The methods for investigating the structure and functioning of the brain fall into three broad categories, those involving physical methods and procedures, those that use imaging techniques to tap into patterns of brain activity, and those based on behavioral assessments.

PHYSICAL METHODS AND TECHNIQUES

Lesions

Long before modern neuroscience and high-tech machines, investigators used the *lesion method* to study brain-to-cognition relationships. Most commonly this was done by careful examination and testing of individuals with brain damage, for instance those who had suffered a stroke, hemorrhage, head injury, or other medical condition. In such circumstances, the accident or disease leaves physical damage to the brain tissue, a **lesion.** The investigation then attempts to relate the behavioral deficit or change to the site or extent of the lesion. You'll read about two classic examples of the lesion technique in a few moments, Broca's study of language disruption due to naturally occurring brain damage, and a patient whose surgical lesions had completely unanticipated cognitive consequences.

Direct Stimulation

Another technique of investigation is the method of direct stimulation, pioneered by the Canadian neurosurgeon Penfield. In his technique, the patient in brain surgery remains conscious during the surgery, having only a local anesthetic in order to prevent pain in the scalp. The surgeon then applies minute electrical charges to the exposed brain, thus

FIGURE 10.7

The exposed cortex of one of Penfield's patients. Numbers indicate the areas of the brain Penfield stimulated with the electric probe. When the area numbered 13 was stimulated, the patient recalled a circus scene. Stimulation of other areas also evoked specific memories. (From Penfield, 1958.)

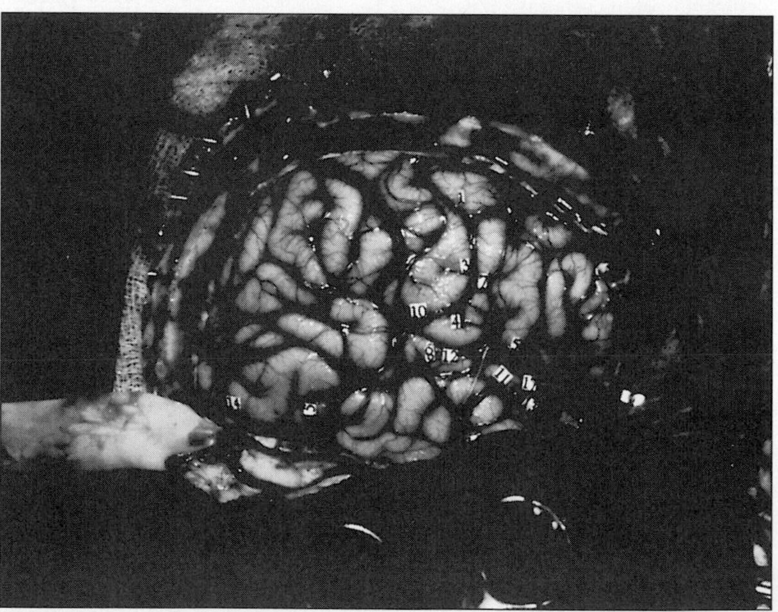

triggering very small regions. The patient is then asked to answer questions or report out loud on the thoughts and memories that enter awareness. By comparing the patient's reports to the different regions that are stimulated, a kind of map of cerebral functioning can be developed. Figure 10.7 shows one such picture, a case in which a particular stimulated region seemed associated with a specific episodic memory.

Though Penfield's patients often reported rather distinct memories during this procedure, it was seldom possible to check on the accuracy of the reports. Furthermore, the reports usually had a dreamlike quality to them, possibly indicating that the memories were heavily influenced by reconstructive processes—in other words, they may not have been genuine, recalled memories (Penfield & Jasper, 1954; Penfield & Milner, 1958). On the other hand, more recent work involves stimulating different regions of the exposed brain, then asking the patient to retrieve certain kinds of information, for example answers to simple multiplication problems. This work shows definite promise of helping to isolate regions of the cortex responsible for different kinds of processing (e.g., Ojemann, 1982; Ojemann & Creutzfeldt, 1987; Whalen, McCloskey, Lesser, & Gordon, in press).

Split-Brain Studies

One physical method that you've probably heard about is the study of the so-called **split brain.** More precisely, we're interested in the study of patients whose corpus callosum has been cut, severing the left and right hemispheres. This operation has been performed on people who had chronic, damaging seizures, usually due to epilepsy. The critical manipulation here involves the function of the corpus callosum—it's the "bridge" between the left and right hemispheres. Thus, when the bridge is severed, the two hemispheres cannot communicate or share information. From the medical standpoint, the surgery minimizes the severity of the patient's seizures, by limiting them to one hemisphere of the brain. But from a neurocognitive standpoint, it enables us to examine abilities and processes that are lateralized to one or the other side of the brain.

The technique, pioneered by Sperry (e.g., Sperry, 1964, who incidentally won the Nobel prize in medicine in 1981 for his work) involves presenting sensory information to one side or the other of the body—for instance, placing a pencil in the patient's right hand (but preventing the patient from seeing it), or presenting a picture of a pencil to the patient's left visual field. Because of the principle of contralaterality, we know that input from the right hand will go to the left hemisphere of the brain. Likewise, the picture presented in the left visual field will go to the right hemisphere. And because of the surgery, these pieces of information cannot then cross over to the other hemisphere.

So what happens in these circumstances? When the pencil was placed in the patient's right hand, the neural message was projected to the left hemisphere. Typically, patients in this setting had no difficulty naming the object—"pencil." But if the picture was shown in the left visual field (or if a pencil was placed in the left hand), patients typically could *not* name it. If asked, patients could usually indicate that they recognized the object nonverbally—for instance, they could make appropriate movements with the hand, as if writing with the pencil. But they couldn't name it. In another case, a patient was shown the word "telephone" in the left visual field—hence the information was sent to the right hemisphere. He was not able to say what he had seen, but with his left hand he drew a picture of a telephone (remember—left hand controlled by right hemisphere).

Why? This pattern of performance is understandable if we assume that most patients' language abilities, including word retrieval, are lateralized in the left hemisphere. In fact, this is precisely what Gazzaniga and others have reported since the early 1960s—split-brain patients' ability to name objects and pictures depends on delivering the input to the left hemisphere (e.g., Gazzaniga, 1985, 1989). If the information is delivered to the right hemisphere instead, recognition of the object or picture is usually limited to nonverbal modes. Baynes and Gazzaniga (1997) have summarized the overall findings as follows: "The LH [left hemisphere] is not only more able than the right to express itself verbally but . . . it plays a dominant role in interpreting behavior and providing a rationale for events in the world. . . . The isolated RH [right hemisphere] usually cannot read, write, or speak, despite displaying a variety of conscious behaviors," especially in visuospatial tasks (pp. 421, 423).

Warning! Notice carefully—the quotation uses terms like "more able" and "usually." We're not saying that *all* knowledge of language is in the left hemisphere and *only* there, just that the left hemisphere is *more* responsible for language-based performance than the right. We're saying that the right hemisphere is *more* associated with visuo-spatial, *usually* more specialized for perceptual and nonverbal abilities (e.g., see Gardner, 1985, for a particularly lucid discussion of such differences and their consequences).

IMAGING TECHNOLOGY

Considerable work is now being done with recent developments in the medical technology of brain imaging. Imaging techniques such as the *CT scan* (computerized tomography), shown in Figure 10.8, and *MRI* (magnetic resonance imaging) can give surprisingly clear pictures of the structure of the brain. More exciting still, from the standpoint of neurocognition, are techniques that yield images of the *functioning* of the brain, for instance *functional MRI* (fMRI) and *PET scan* (positron emission tomography) techniques.

fMRI and PET Scans

The images on the color plate show the results of such scans. In the top pair of images, regions of the visual cortex have been color coded to reflect which parts of the stimulus activated which regions. Notice the correspondence between the visual field and the contralateral hemisphere—the yellow color in the left visual field is projected to the right occipital lobe.

The middle images are five color PET scans, each taken when the patient was engaged in a different cognitive task. The scans show regions of the brain with heightened neural activity, with different colors reflecting high or low levels of blood flow, oxygen uptake, and the like ("hotter" colors show greater activity).

The bottom pair of images, from Tulving's (1989) paper, show PET scan results in two conditions. On the left, the patient was performing a semantic-memory retrieval task, while in the right picture, an episodic-memory task was being performed. You'll note that the pattern of activation during episodic retrieval shows much greater activity in the frontal regions—*anterior* activation. The semantic task, on the other hand, triggered activity only in the *left* frontal lobe, and also a broad bilateral region of the parietal lobes—*posterior* activation. (For further results on episodic/semantic differences in the cortex, see for example Petersen, Fox, Posner, Mintun, & Raichle, 1988, and Tulving, Kapur, Craik, Moscovitch, & Houle, 1994.)

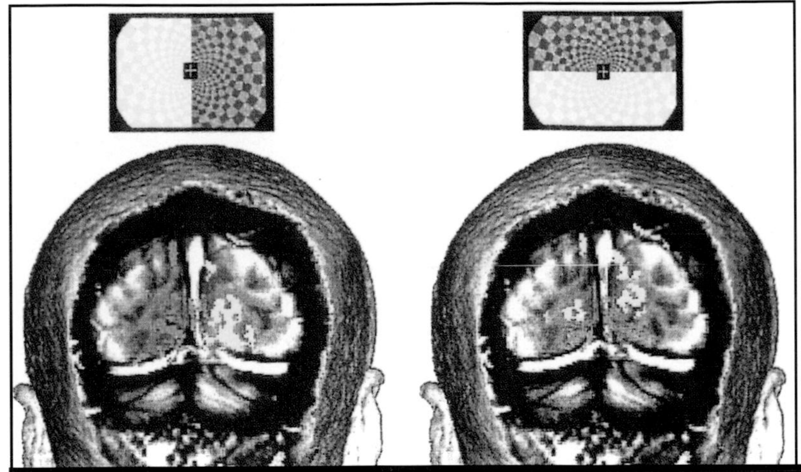

fMRI scan during visual perception. (*From Schneider, Noll, and Cohen, 1993.*)

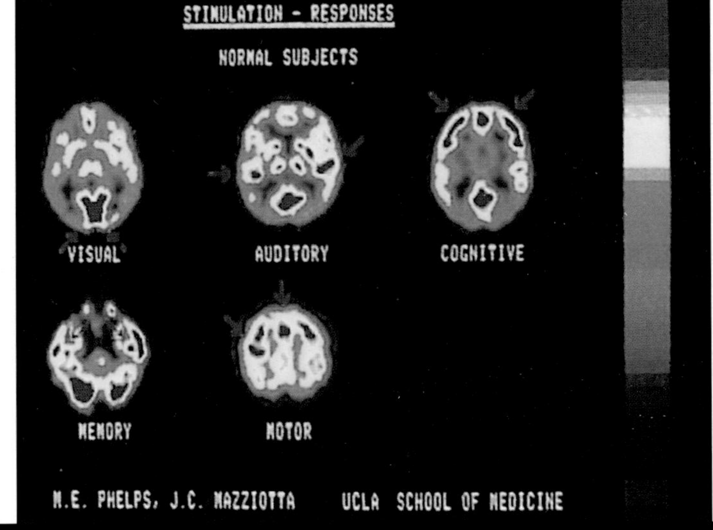

PET scans during different cognitive tasks. (*Courtesy of Drs. Michael E. Phelps and John C. Mazziotta, UCLA School of Medicine.*)

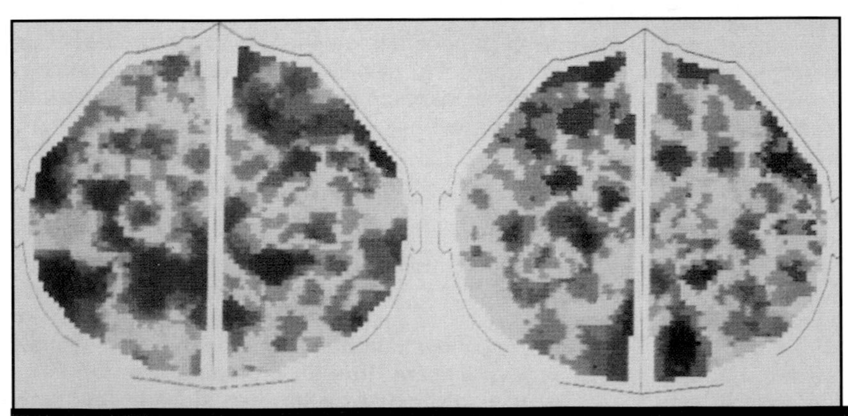

PET scans during semantic (left) and episodic (right) retrieval. (*From Tulving, 1989.*)

★ **FIGURE 10.8**

CT and PET imaging techniques. (a) CT scan procedure, in which low-intensity x-ray beams scan the brain. (b) PET scan procedure, in which radioactive tracers are detected by peripheral sensors. These techniques have been useful in medical diagnosis and in studies of neurocognition.

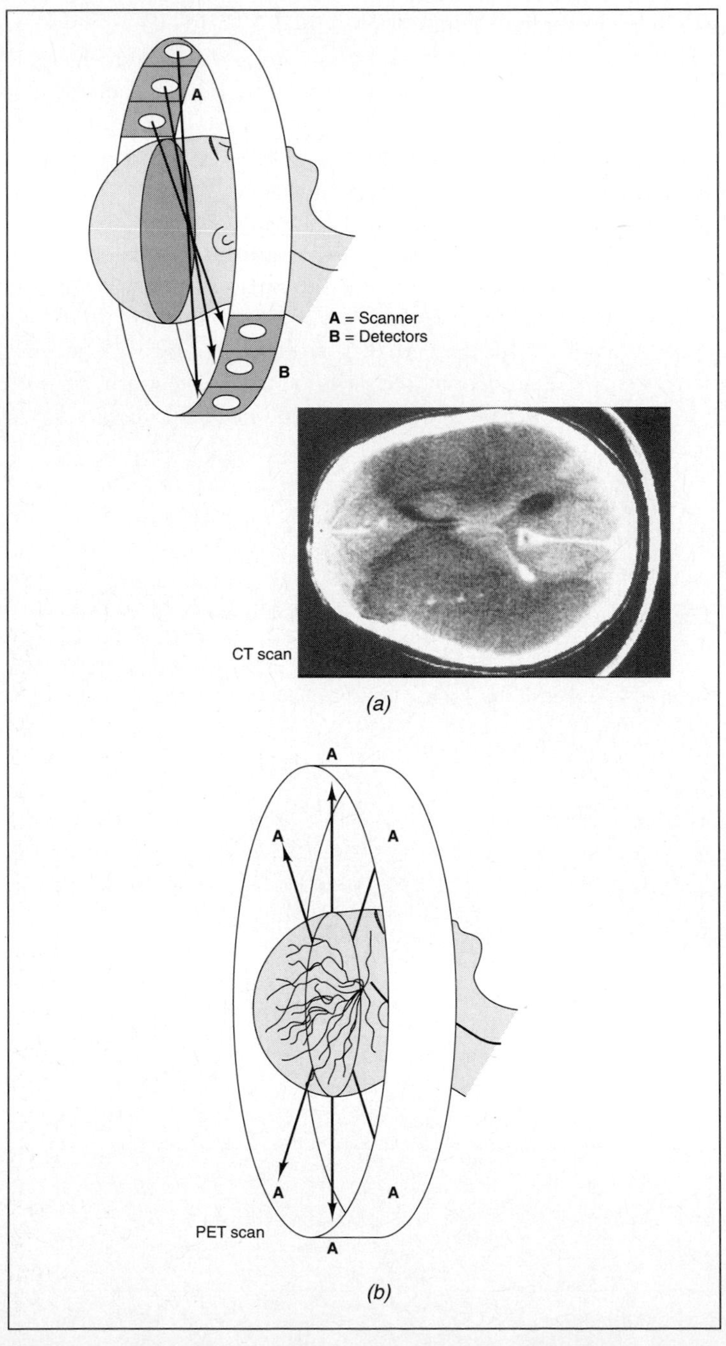

EEGs and ERPs

Traditionally, brain wave patterns were studied rather crudely with EEG recordings, electroencephalograms. In this technique, electrodes are attached to the person's scalp, and the device records the patterns of brain waves. More recently, researchers have focused in particular on event-related potentials, ERPs, the momentary changes in electrical activity of the brain when a particular stimulus is presented (e.g., Donchin, 1981).

▲ Figure 10.9 shows the kind of data obtained in an ERP study. Here, Osterhout and Holcomb (1992) had participants read either syntactically acceptable sentences ("The woman struggled to prepare the meal") or sentences with anomalous syntax ("The woman persuaded to answer the door"), one word at a time. By carefully controlling surrounding conditions, measuring the elapsed time since the stimulus was presented, and averaging over many similar trials, they were able to see changes in the ERP pattern that were attributable to the individual words in the sentences.

In particular, acceptable sentences yielded the pattern shown in the solid line, across the 1100 milliseconds following the critical word "to." But when "to" was anomalous, that is when it didn't "fit" with the earlier part of the sentence ("The woman persuaded to . . ."), then a very different ERP pattern was found. This pattern, shown by the dashed line, began to differ from the solid line at about 450 or 500 milliseconds after the critical

▲ **FIGURE 10.9**

ERP patterns to acceptable and syntactically anomalous sentences. Mean ERPs to syntactically acceptable sentences (solid curve) and syntactically anomalous sentences (dotted curve). The P600 component, illustrated as a downward dip in the dotted curve, shows the effect of detecting the syntactic anomaly. Note that in this figure, positive changes go in the downward direction. (From Osterhout & Holcomb, 1992.)

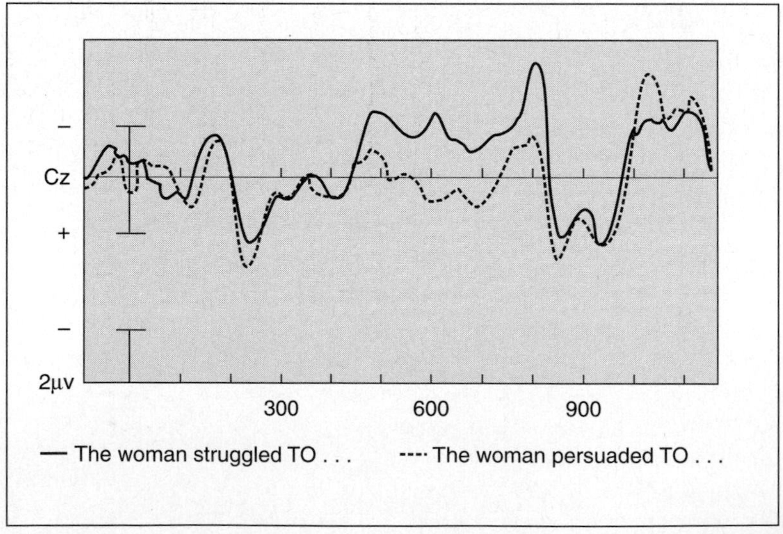

word, and had a midpoint around 600 milliseconds. It's called a P600, 600 because that was roughly how long the average deviation followed the critical word, and P because the dashed line goes in a *positive* direction when it diverges (positive is *below* the baseline in this particular figure).

The stunning thing about the ERP technique is that we can see how electrical activity in the brain changes *moment by moment* at different points in cognitive processing—and connect those moment-to-moment changes to *specific* stimuli and cognitive conditions. For example, distinctive ERP patterns have been found when the subject and verb of a sentence differ in number (*"the cars is") or gender ("The boy next door never loses her temper"; Osterhout & Mobley, 1995), and when participants "recollect" or remember having seen a word previously (Paller, Kutas, & McIsaac, 1995). There's even a distinctive pattern when participants realize they've made an error, say, in a true/false task—call it the "Oh, shoot" (!) response (see Dehaene, Posner, & Tucker, 1994; Gehring, Goss, Coles, Meyer, & Donchin, 1993). A disadvantage of the ERP techique, on the other hand, is that the patterns give only a crude indication of the location of the measured electrical activity in the brain, unlike the rather precise localizing accomplished with fMRI and PET scans.

BEHAVIORAL METHODS OF INVESTIGATION

Two general behavioral methods for investigating brain-cognition effects are in use. In the first, we adapt standard laboratory tasks to search for laterality and specialization of function. Klatzky and Atkinson (1971), for example, presented a visual stimulus to the "wrong" hemisphere, and managed to measure the extra time required for processing, presumably the time it took to transfer the information to the correct hemisphere (see also Koenig, Wetzel, & Caramazza, 1992, for "wrong hemisphere" effects in the lexical decision task).

Sometimes this method involves the dual-task procedure you've read about throughout the book. Here, normal intact participants perform two tasks that either depend on the same or different hemispheres, for instance doing a verbal task while balancing a yardstick in either the left or right hand (e.g., Freidman & Polson, 1981; Kinsbourne & Cook, 1971). Typically, participants (right-handed ones, anyway) can't balance the yardstick as long when doing a simultaneous verbal task (e.g., naming every third letter of the alphabet) as they can in a silent, control condition (Kemble, Filipi, & Gravlin, 1996).

Dissociations

In the second behavioral method, we search for patterns of preserved and damaged functions in the performance of brain-damaged individuals, patterns that tell us about the architecture of mental processes. This is typically called the **method of dissociations.** This is a logical technique in which we search for behavioral evidence for the independence of processes or functions. The terminology deserves a bit of expansion here, since the technique is one of the foundations of neurocognition.

Consider two mental abilities or functions, *a* and *b*. If damage to a particular region of the neocortex disrupts both *a* and *b*, this is evidence that these two abilities rely—at

DISSOCIATIONS AND DOUBLE DISSOCIATIONS

The concept of **dissociation**—the opposite of *association*—is important, so let's spend a little more time on it.

Consider two mental processes that "go together" in some cognitive task, called process *A* and process *B*. By looking at these processes as they may be disrupted in brain damage we can determine how separable the processes are.

Complete separability is a **double dissociation.** Evidence for a double dissociation requires at least two patients, with "opposite" or reciprocal deficits. For example,

- Patient X has a lesion in one region of the brain, which has disrupted process *A*. His performance on tasks that require process *B* is intact, not disrupted at all.
- Patient Y has a lesion that has damaged process *B*, but tasks that use process *A* are normal, not disrupted by the damage.

Think of a double dissociation as illustrated by the following simple Venn diagram—and refer back to it in a few moments, when you read about the double dissociation of language comprehension and production. If these circles depicted actual brain regions, as they do in the language example, then damage to either one of them could easily leave the other one unaffected.

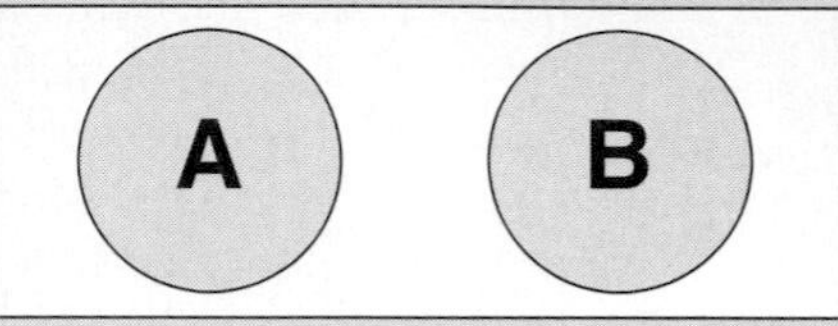

- In a simple dissociation, process *A* could be damaged and process *B* intact, yet no other known patient has the reciprocal pattern. For example, semantic retrieval of a concept could be intact while lexical retrieval, finding the name for the concept, could be disrupted—this is called anomia (which you'll read about in a moment). In this situation, lexical retrieval is dissociated from semantic retrieval, but it's probably impossible to observe the opposite pattern—how could you name a concept if you can't retrieve the concept in the first place?
- In a full or complete *association* (lack of dissociation), disruption of one of the processes *always* accompanies disruption in the other process. This pattern implies that both process *A* and *B* rely on the same region or brain mechanism—for example, recognizing objects and recognizing pictures of those objects.

least in part—on the same damaged region. The abilities are said to be *associated*—that is, nonindependent. Conversely, if *a* and *b* are completely separate, then damage to one of them would *not* alter performance of the other. This pattern is known as a **dissociation.** A common example here is the independence of vision and hearing, where each relies on different regions, and each represents a different ability. In fact, vision and hearing form a **double dissociation,** a pattern in which each ability is independent of the other.

The significance of this is that the double dissociation implies that the two abilities are separate and distinct, both anatomically and psychologically—if they weren't separate, then brain damage affecting one ability would necessarily affect the other one as well. When evidence of a double dissociation exists, particularly when data from normal participants also suggest that the abilities are independent, we have a powerful demonstration of separate components or *modules* of processing (Fodor, 1983).

Summary

1. Physical methods of investigating brain functions have always studied lesions, attempting to determine the relationship between the damaged region and the disrupted cognitive performance. Most lesion studies deal with accidental damage, due to medical conditions like stroke.
2. Direct stimulation of brain tissue is occasionally used to study brain functioning. While classic stimulation studies may have been contaminated by reconstructive processes, this may be less of a problem in current studies, in which the patient is tested on general information.
3. Studies of split-brain patients, whose corpus callosum has been lesioned, have revealed considerable information about the lateralization of language abilities in the left hemisphere, and visuo-spatial and perceptual abilities in the right hemisphere.
4. Several imaging techniques have been developed to study both brain structure and functioning, for instance PET and fMRI scans. The ERP technique is increasingly used to study cognitive processing in normal, intact participants.

Cognitive Disruptions—Attention, Language, and Memory

Preview: perception and attention disorders; language disorders; memory disorders

A particularly large literature exists on brain-related disorders of cognition, based on individuals who because of illness or injury have *acquired deficits* in what were formerly intact mental processes (acquired deficits are contrasted with developmental deficits, which are present from birth or early childhood). Formal studies of such disorders date back to the mid-1800s, although records dating back to 3500 B.C. mention language loss due to brain injury (see Feinberg & Farah, 1997). A brief list of the major disorders and deficits ◆ seen in patients is provided in Table 10.2 (p. 336), along with short explanations of the terms. We'll discuss three general types of deficits here, those of perception and attention, of language, and of memory.

PERCEPTION AND ATTENTION

Damage to the processes of visual perception, recognition, and attention is usually associated with posterior (rearward) portions of the neocortex, in particular the occipital lobe for sensory aspects of vision, and the posterior portions of the parietal lobes for recognition and attentional processes. Damage to the visual cortex itself, not surprisingly, disrupts normal vision; for example, if the left visual cortex is lesioned, patients will have abnormal vision for stimuli in the right visual field, or possibly no vision at all in the right field.

◆ **TABLE 10.2**

List of Cognitive Disruptions due to Brain Damage

Disorder	*Disruption of:*
Language Related	
Broca's aphasia	Speech production, syntactic features
Wernicke's aphasia	Comprehension, semantic features
Conduction aphasia	Repetition of words and sentences
Anomia (anomic aphasia)	Word finding, either lexical or semantic
Pure word deafness	Perceptual or semantic processing of auditory word comprehension
Alexia	Reading, recognition of printed letters or words
Agraphia	Writing
Other Symbolic Related	
Acalculia	Mathematical abilities, retrieval or rule-based procedures
Perception, Movement Related	
Agnosia	Visual object recognition
Prosopagnosia	(Visual) face recognition
Apraxia	Voluntary action or skilled motor movement

Source: Adapted from McCarthy and Warrington (1990).

Visual Neglect

More interestingly, several deficits that seem to be visual can actually be attributed to stages that occur *after* the stimulus is registered in the cortex. In particular, the disorder of **visual neglect** is a disorder in which visual information in the contralateral field is not noticed or attended; notice that simpler sensory or motor disorders are not included in this syndrome. A patient with visual neglect will simply not respond to stimuli on the contralateral side—will not *perceive or pay attention to* what's there.

Look at the top pattern in Figure 10.10. Copy the black pattern onto a sheet of paper—now draw the white part of the figure. Of course, when you're drawing the black part, the jagged edge is in the right field of vision and attention—and it's on the left side when you're drawing the white pattern.

In Marshall and Halligan's (1994) report, a patient with left hemispatial neglect (neglect of the left half of the visual-spatial world) drew the patterns shown at the bottom of the figure. When copying the black pattern, the jagged edge was drawn accurately because it was in the patient's *right* visual field—it was on the right side of the figure being drawn. But when copying the white pattern, the patient did not draw the jagged edge—because in the white pattern, the jagged edge is on the neglected *left* side.

Sacks (1970) reported on a similar patient, Mrs. S, who believed the hospital staff was not bringing her enough to eat on her meal trays. The reason was, simply, that her deficit had caused a left spatial neglect. She literally only *saw* the right half of a piece of meat on her plate—indeed, only saw the right half of the plate! Through experience, she learned to eat what she saw, then turn the plate around so she could see and eat some more. Likewise, to see something she knew was on her left, she learned to turn a three-quarters turn turns to the *right*, thus getting the object into her right visual field.

Visual Neglect and Imagery Visual neglect can even extend to completely *mental* aspects of processing, suggesting that visual imagery relies on the same structures and processes as perception and attention. In one study, patients with visual neglect were asked to imagine themselves in a well-known location, then report on their mental image (the patients were Italian, and asked to imagine standing in the main *piazza* in Milan, either on the cathedral steps looking out, or looking *at* the cathedral from across the way). Regardless of the "mental point of view," they mostly reported landmarks on the right side of the scene, as if their *mental* image lacked the same half of the world that was missing in their visual world (Bisiach & Luzzatti, 1978). As Rafal (1997) explains it, it's as if you were asked to imagine yourself standing at home plate on a baseball field (you're the catcher), and only had a right half to your mental image (the first baseman and right fielder)—*and then* imagining yourself standing in center field, facing home plate, and seeing only the third baseman and the outfield behind him.

Agnosia

Other perceptual-attentional deficits include deficits in object recognition, called **visual agnosia,** and disrupted face recognition, called **prosopagnosia** ("proso" from Greek, meaning face or mask). The disorders are usually associated with damage in the parietal lobes, especially in the right hemisphere.

For instance, Rubens and Benson (1971) described a patient who could not identify objects or demonstrate their use when they were shown to him. When allowed to touch the objects, however, he could identify them immediately. The man in Sacks's (1970) *The Man Who Mistook His Wife for a Hat* showed such disruptions, as you read in Chapter 1—

★ **FIGURE 10.10**

Visual pattern demonstrating visual neglect. Object-based neglect is demonstrated by the copying performance of a patient with left hemispatial neglect. When asked to copy the black object, the patient did well, since the jagged contour is on the right side of the black object. When asked to copy the white object, the patient was unable to copy the jagged contour, since it is on the left side of the object being attended. (From Marshall & Halligan, 1994.)

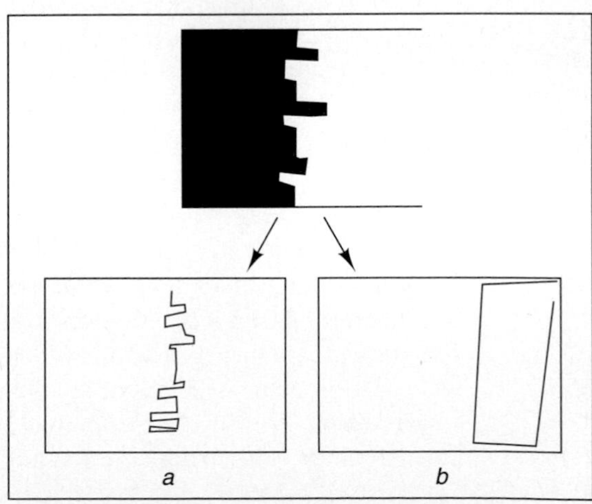

FIGURE 10.11

Language centers in the brain. (Adapted from Geschwind, 1979, and Posner & Raichle, 1994.)

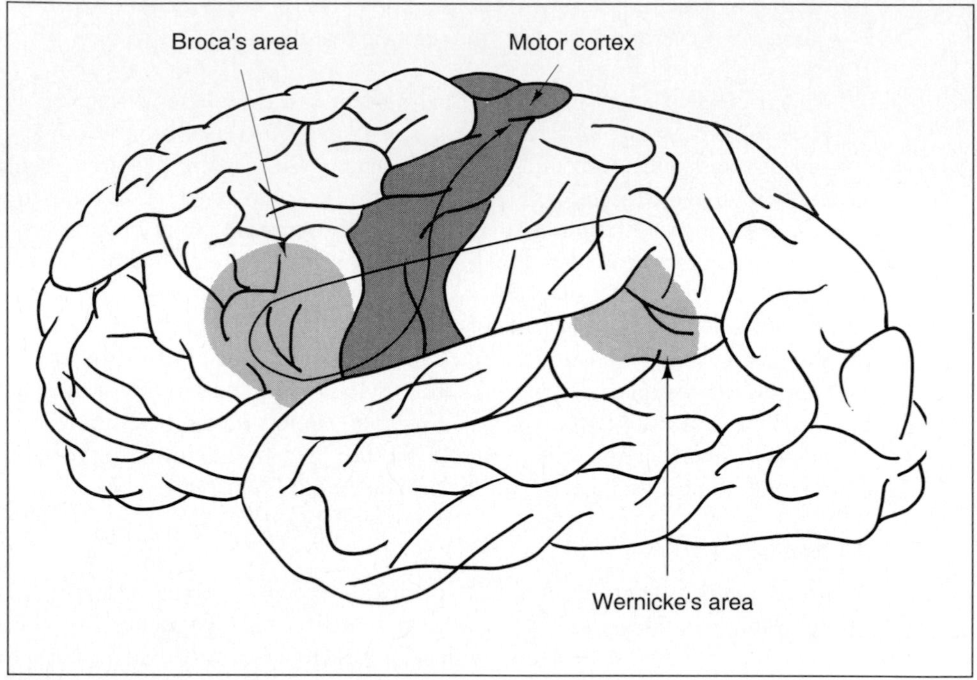

Dr. P. couldn't recognize his wife's face (or other faces or objects), although he could recognize some *features* or components of a visual display. In Sacks's words, "He failed to see the whole, seeing only details" (p. 10). After being unable to identify a rose, Sacks then brought it close—and Dr. P. immediately recognized it by its distinctive fragrance.

LANGUAGE

The disruption of language due to a brain-related disorder is known as an **aphasia.** Aphasia is always the product of some sort of physical injury to the brain, either brain damage sustained in an accident or a blow to the head, or diseases and medical syndromes such as stroke. A major goal in neurology is to understand the aphasic syndromes more completely, so that individuals who suffer aphasia may be helped more effectively. From the standpoint of neurocognition, the disruptions of language that are observed in aphasic patients can also help us understand language and its neurological basis.

There are many different kinds of aphasic disorders, with great variety in their effects, severity, and overlap. We'll focus especially on the two most common forms here, then discuss a few other types of language deficit.

Broca's Aphasia

As described by Kertesz (1982), **Broca's aphasia** is characterized by severe difficulties in producing speech; it is also called *expressive* or *production aphasia*. Patients with Broca's aphasia show speech that is hesitant, effortful, and phonemically distorted. Aside from relatively "automatic" sequences such as "I don't know," such patients generally respond to questions with only one-word answers. If words are strung together, there are few if any grammatical markers. Commonly, such patients typically show less or even no impairment of comprehension, whether for spoken or written language.

This syndrome was first described by the French neurosurgeon Pierre–Paul Broca in the 1860s, who was also able to identify the damaged area responsible for the disorder (see Feinberg & Farah, 1997, for the whole story). The site of the brain damage, an area toward the rear of the left frontal lobe, is therefore called *Broca's area*. As shown in Figure ▲ 10.11, Broca's area lies adjacent to a major motor control center in the brain. This no doubt accounts for the motor difficulties typical of the aphasia, the inability to produce fluent spoken speech.

Wernicke's Aphasia

Loosely speaking, the impairments in **Wernicke's aphasia** are the opposite of those in ■ Broca's aphasia; see Table 10.3 for a listing of the typical impairments in both aphasias, including speech samples. In patients affected by Wernicke's aphasia, comprehension is impaired, although the syntactic aspects of speech are preserved. It is sometimes referred to as *receptive* or *comprehension aphasia*. In this syndrome, the patient generally shows comprehension deficits when listening to speech, and produces "copious unintelligible jargon" (Kertesz, 1982, p. 30) when speaking. The speech of a Wernicke's aphasic is quite distinctive, as shown in Kertesz's description of a female Wernicke's aphasic:

> *She speaks in sentences and uses appropriate pauses and inflectional markers . . . without articulatory errors or hesitations. . . . She does not appear to have any word-finding difficulty, but in an extraordinary fashion, neologisms [invented nonsense words] of variable length and phonemic complexity replace substantive words, mostly nouns and verbs. She talks as if she spoke without mistakes. . . . There is a rather curious cool and calm manner about her speech as if she did not realize her deficit. . . . a very characteristic feature of this disturbance.* (pp. 41–42)

The German neurologist Carl Wernicke identified this disorder in 1874, as well as the left-hemisphere region that is damaged. This region is thus known as *Wernicke's area*, also illustrated in Figure 10.11. Note that the area, toward the rear of the left temporal lobe, is adjacent to the auditory cortex, an area associated with retrieval of words and word meanings.

Dissociation of Speech Production and Comprehension

If you'll think about these two aphasias for a moment, you'll notice that several rough distinctions can be drawn between them in terms of linguistic characteristics you studied in Chapter 8. A Broca's aphasic, with neurological damage near the motor control area,

TABLE 10.3

Classic Impairments in Broca's and Wernicke's Aphasias

Broca's Aphasia	*Wernicke's Aphasia*
Quality of Speech	
Severely impaired; marked by extreme effort to generate speech, hesitant utterances, short (one-word) responses	Little, if any, impairment; fluent speech productions, clear articulation, no hesitations
Nature of Speech	
Agrammatical; marked by loss of syntactic markers and inflections, and use of simple noun and verb categories	Neologistic; marked by "invented" words (neologisms) or semantically inappropriate substitutions; long strings of neologistic jargon
Comprehension	
Relatively unimpaired, compared to speech production. Word-finding difficulty may be due to production difficulties.	Severely impaired; marked by lack of awareness that speech is incomprehensible; comprehension impaired also in nonverbal tasks (e.g., pointing)

Speech Samples

Broca's aphasia: Experimenter asks the patient's address. "Oh dear. Um. Aah. Oh! Oh dear. very-there-were-ave.avedeversher avenyer." (Correct address was Devonshire.)
Wernicke's aphasia: Experimenter asks about the patient's work prior to hospitalization. "I wanna tell you this happened when happened when he rent. His-his kell come down here and is—he got ren something. It happened. In these ropiers were with him for hi-is friend—like was. And he roden all o these arranjen from the pedis on from iss pescid."

Source: Adapted from Kertesz (1982).

demonstrates disorders in the motoric aspects of language—the ability to produce fluent, coordinated speech—but relatively normal semantic comprehension. Syntactic markers are especially absent here, as if *bound or grammatical morphemes* such as *-er* and *-ing* had become unavailable. Indeed, this aphasia is sometimes called *agrammatic aphasia*, referring to the lack of grammatical form that is evidenced. In contrast, *free morphemes*, word stems and content words, seem relatively unaffected.

On the other hand, a Wernicke's aphasic can generate speech fluently and grammatically, but the *semantic* aspects of the speech are severely impaired—invented nonsense words substitute for true words. As a product of brain damage in different locations, in other words, quite opposite aspects or components of linguistic ability seem to be lost and preserved. This is a classic demonstration of double dissociation—one patient shows a deficit in process *a* but no difficulty with process *b*, while a different patient shows the reverse, preserved *a* and damaged *b*.

The very different pattern of behavioral impairments in these two disorders, stemming from damage to different physical regions in the brain, certainly implies that these two regions are responsible for different aspects of linguistic skill. By extension, these aphasias reinforce the notion that syntax and semantics are two separable aspects of normal language (e.g., Osterhout & Holcomb, 1992). The double dissociation indicates that different, independent modules govern comprehension and speech production.

Other Aphasic Disorders

Considerably less common than Broca's or Wernicke's aphasia is *conduction aphasia*, a more narrow disruption of language ability. Both Broca's and Wernicke's areas seem to be intact in conduction aphasia—and indeed, a conduction aphasic can both understand and produce speech quite well. The language impairment, however, is that such individuals are unable to repeat what they have just heard. In intuitive terms, the intact comprehension and production systems seem to have lost their normal connection or linkage. And indeed, the site of the brain lesion in conduction aphasia appears to be the primary pathway between Broca's and Wernicke's areas, called the *arcuate fasciculus* (Geschwind, 1970). Quite literally, the pathway between the comprehension and production areas is no longer able to *conduct* the linguistic message.

As Table 10.2 shows, a variety of highly specific aphasic disruptions have also been isolated. Though most of these are quite rare, they nonetheless give evidence of the separability of several aspects of language performance. For instance, in *alexia* there is a disruption of reading without any necessary disruption of spoken language or aural comprehension. In *agraphia*, conversely, there is disruption of writing, without any necessary disruption in other language abilities. In other words, it's possible for a patient to be able to write a sentence but then be unable to read it, or the other way around (Benson & Geschwind, 1969). In *pure word deafness*, a patient cannot comprehend spoken language, although is still able to read and produce written and spoken language.

Anomia One final type of aphasia deserves brief mention here, because it relates to the separation of the semantic and lexical systems discussed in Chapters 6 and 8. **Anomia** (or sometimes anomic aphasia) is a disruption of word finding, an impairment in the normal ability to retrieve a semantic concept and say its name. In other words, some aspect of the normally automatic semantic or lexical components of retrieval has been damaged in anomia. Although moderate word-finding difficulty can result from damage virtually anywhere in the left hemisphere, full-fledged anomia seems to involve damage to the left temporal lobe (e.g., Coughlan & Warrington, 1978; see McCarthy & Warrington, 1990, for details).

On the surface, anomia resembles the normal tip-of-the-tongue (TOT) phenomenon—anomic patients seem to "know the word" yet be unable to name it. Several researchers (e.g., Geschwind, 1967; Goodglass, Kaplan, Weintraub, & Ackerman, 1976), however, have noted some differences. For example, in a normal TOT state, people usually have partial knowledge of the target word, for instance the sound it begins with, the number of syllables, and so on. Anomics in Goodglass et al.'s (1976) study, however, showed no evidence for this partial knowledge. And more recent work suggests that anomia can involve retrieval blockage *only* for the lexical component of retrieval, without disruption of semantic or conceptual retrieval (e.g., Ashcraft, 1993; Kay & Ellis, 1987)—the patient retrieves the concept successfully, but then cannot find its name.

MEMORY

Amnesia is the loss of memory or memory abilities. Amnesia is one of the most thoroughly investigated mental disruptions due to brain disorders, as well as one of the more common results of brain injury and damage. While some amnesias may be quite temporary, due for example to a strong blow to the head, the amnesias we are interested in here are relatively permanent, due to enduring changes in the brain.

Many different kinds of amnesia have been studied, and we have space only to discuss a few of these. A few bits of terminology will help you understand the disorder, and will alert you to the distinctions in memory that are particularly relevant for neurocognition.

First, the loss of memory in amnesia is always considered in relation to the date of the brain injury or damage.

- If a person suffers loss of memory for the events prior to brain injury, this is called a **retrograde amnesia**—just as in *retro*active interference in Chapter 5, the loss is backward in time.
- The other form of amnesia is **anterograde amnesia,** loss of memory for events occurring after brain injury.

An individual will often show both forms of amnesia, although the extent of the memory loss is usually different for events prior to and after the damage.

Second, both the kind of memory system being tested and the kind of task being administered are critically important, because so many kinds of memory disruptions are possible. There are amnesias that reflect disruption of only short-term memory, amnesias that interfere with declarative long-term memories while leaving procedural long-term memories intact, and several "material-specific amnesias" (McCarthy & Warrington, 1990). And evidence is now accumulating that amnesia interferes with *explicit* memory performance, remembering deliberately learned and normally recallable facts, while often preserving *implicit* memory, information retrieved without conscious intent or awareness.

We'll focus here on a classic, extremely well-known case history of amnesia, that of a patient H.M. In preparation, try to remember what you read early in the chapter about the *hippocampus*. If you remember the one fact you were asked to learn, that the hippocampus is critical for storing new information in long-term memory, you have done *exactly* what H.M. is unable to do, learn.

Patient H.M.

In Kolb and Whishaw's (1990) view, an accidental discovery by the neurosurgeon William Scoville, in the early 1950s, "revolutionized the study of the memory process" (p. 525). Scoville performed radical surgery on a patient known as H.M., sectioning H.M.'s hippocampus in both the left and right hemispheres, in an attempt to gain control over his severe epileptic seizures. To Scoville's surprise, the outcome of this surgery was a pervasive *anterograde amnesia*—H.M. became completely unable to learn and recall anything new. While his memory for events prior to the surgery remained intact, as did his overall IQ (in fact, his IQ is 118, well above average), he completely lost the ability to store new information in long-term memory. As Kolb and Whishaw put it, "Surgery had interfered with the process of storing or retrieving new memories but had not touched stored memories themselves. The case of H.M. . . . shifted the emphasis from a search for the location of memory to an analysis of the process of storing memories" (pp. 525–526; see also Scoville & Milner, 1957).

Across the intervening years, H.M. has been tested on hundreds of tasks, documenting the many facets of his pervasive anterograde amnesia. His memory for events prior to surgery, including his childhood and school days, is quite good, his language comprehension is normal, and his vocabulary is above average. Yet any task that requires him to retain information across a delay shows severe impairment, especially if the delay is filled with an interfering task. For instance, after a two-minute interference task of repeating digits, he was unable to recognize photographs of faces he had been shown. He is unable to learn sequences of digits that go beyond the typical short-term memory span of seven items. The impairments apply equally to nonverbal and verbal materials, a result apparently related to the bilateral (both sides) lesions from his surgery; left-hemisphere lesions in the hippocampus tend to yield amnesia for only verbal memories (Squire, 1992).

But here's the truly fascinating part. The evidence shows that H.M. is completely *normal* when it comes to motor learning. In one study, he was able to learn a rather difficult motor skill, mirrordrawing, illustrated in Figure 10.12 (p. 344). As the graphs of his errors show, his learning curves were completely normal in this task, with very few errors on the third day of practice. But he has no *explicit* memory of the mirror-drawing task—on days 2 and 3, he does not remember ever having done the task before. Likewise, H.M. has also shown systematic learning and improvement on a procedural task, the Tower of Hanoi problem you'll read about in Chapter 12—but again with no conscious recollection of the problem. (For full summaries of patient H.M., see Kolb & Whishaw, 1996, and a 14-year follow-up study by Milner, H.M.'s primary investigator, and her colleagues, Milner, Corkin, & Teuber, 1968).

Implications for Long-term Memory

What do we know about human memory now as a function of H.M.'s disrupted and preserved mental capacities? How much has this person's misfortune told us about memory and cognition?

The most apparent source of H.M.'s amnesia is a disruption in the process of transferring information to long-term memory. That is, H.M.'s retrieval of presurgical information is intact, indicating that his long-term memory *per se*, including retrieval, was unaffected by the surgery. Likewise, his ability to attend to questions and answer them, and to perform other simple short-term memory tasks, indicates that simpler attentional and awareness functions are also intact.

But he has a widespread disability in transferring new information into long-term memory. Importantly, this disability seems to affect his deliberate, *explicit* storage of information, while leaving implicit memory functions unaffected. Thus, it seems that material

Figure 10.12

The mirror-drawing task and patient H.M.'s performance. A. In this test the subject's task is to trace between the two outlines of the star while viewing his or her hand in a mirror. The reversing effect of the mirror makes this a difficult task initially. Crossing a line constitutes an error. B. H.M. shows clear improvement in motor tasks on the star test, which is a procedural memory. (From Blakemore, 1977.)

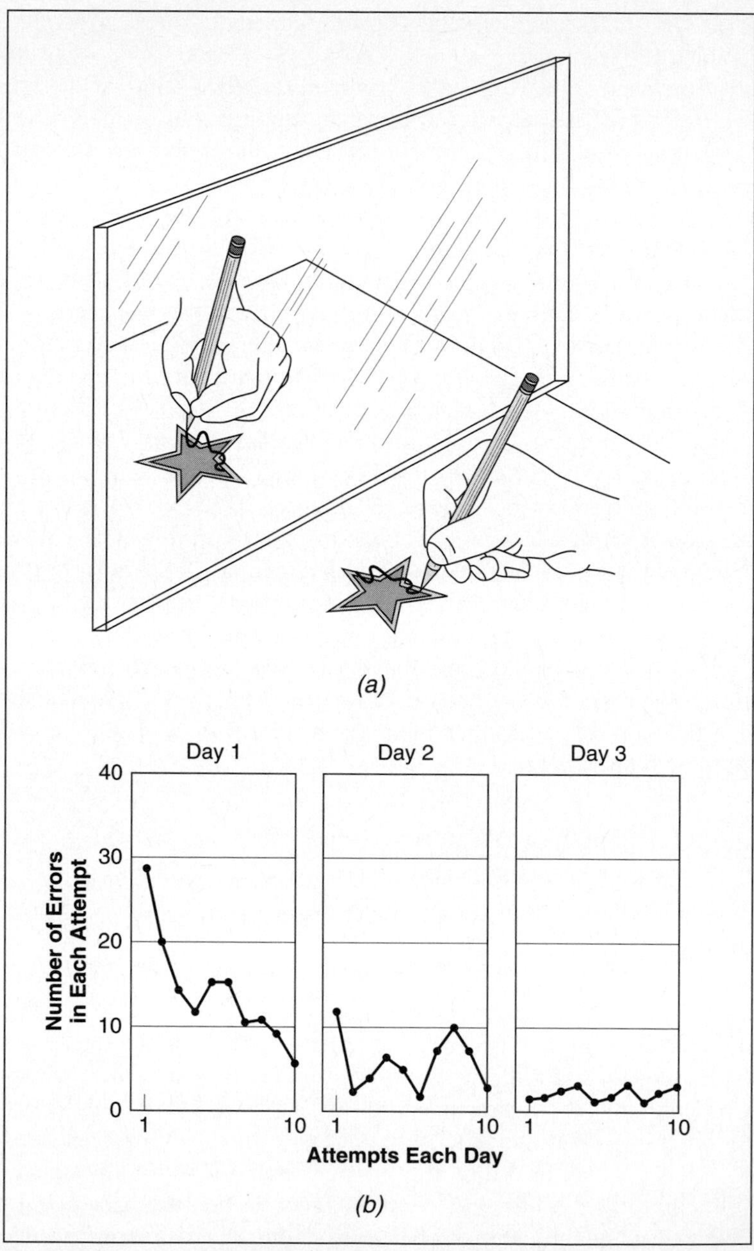

requiring deliberate transfer to long-term memory, including laboratory and real-world episodic information, was disrupted by the lesions to the hippocampus (e.g., Squire, 1987, 1992; Zola-Morgan, Squire, & Amalral, 1986). The hippocampus, previously thought to have something to do with the sense of smell, turns out to be the critical gateway for forming new long-term memories.

Disruption Within Working Memory

There are also cases of individuals whose brain damage has disrupted their short-term or working-memory functioning, for instance impaired short-term memory spans yet unimpaired long-term retention of verbal material (Cermak, 1982; Shallice & Warrington, 1970). Such cases generally involve different anatomical regions of damage, with evidence for the left parietal lobe (McCarthy & Warrington, 1990), and, depending on the task used, the frontal lobes (Kimberg & Farah, 1993).

Schacter (1989) notes two important conclusions from such data. First, they describe a double dissociation between short-term and long-term memory. This of course indicates that separate processes or cognitive systems are used for the two kinds of memory functioning. Even by itself, this is a profoundly important conclusion—the distinction between brief retention of recent information and permanent retention of the past, noted even by James in 1890 (James, 1890/1983), is supported by the finding of a double dissociation.

The second conclusion, in Schacter's (1989) view, is that the results pose a difficulty for traditional information-processing models like Atkinson and Shiffrin's (1968). That is, if an amnesic patient shows seriously impaired short-term memory span, yet is still able to store new information in long-term memory, we are forced to reexamine the notion that previous storage in short-term memory is required for eventual long-term memory formation.

On the other hand, there are several indications that a model like Baddeley's (1986) working-memory system *can* account for such disruptions. Recall that this model postulated that working memory has three separate components, the central executive, the articulatory loop, and the visuo-spatial sketchpad. Within this framework, damage only to the articulatory loop component would cause short-term memory deficits, for example in a memory span task, while damage to the central executive should produce difficulties in storing new long-term memories. Indeed, exactly these patterns have been observed—a patient with seriously disrupted memory span but normal long-term memory (Vallar & Baddeley, 1984), and just the reverse, patients with normal memory span but deficits in long-term memory (e.g., Van der Linden, Coyette, & Seron, 1992). More generally, the neurocognitive research suggests that the components of working memory can be dissociated, that is, that they are isolable, separate components of memory processing.

Implicit and Explicit Memory

As discussed above, amnesia seems to compromise a patient's explicit memory, while leaving implicit memory intact or nearly intact (e.g., Ferraro, Balota, & Connor, 1993). Deliberately stored, verbalizable, explicit memories are damaged in amnesia. Patient H.M. shows that pattern, as does patient K.C.—you read about his *retrograde amnesia,* his total loss of episodic memory, at the beginning of this chapter. But implicit memories, those that do not "demand conscious recollection of a specific previous experience" (Schacter, 1989), seem preserved in amnesia. H.M. learns and "remembers" the mirror-drawing task, albeit in a fashion not accessible to conscious, verbal recollection. Likewise, K.C. remembers how to play chess, though he doesn't remember ever having played it before.

Laboratory demonstrations of this distinction work both with normal and also brain-damaged individuals—normals demonstrate both implicit and explicit memory, amnesics only implicit. For example, normal individuals are likely to complete a word fragment like TAB_____ with TABLET if shown that word earlier in a learning task. Because they don't *have* to remember it consciously in order to fill in the word stem—although they often do, of course—this task taps implicit memory processing, as do priming tasks (McAndrews, Glisky, & Schacter, 1987).

Amnesic patients will complete the word fragments the same way, demonstrating the implicit memory influence of the earlier task. But amnesics do this *without* remembering any of the words on the earlier task—indeed, without remembering the earlier task at all (e.g., Tulving, Schacter, & Stark, 1982; Warrington & Weiskrantz, 1968).

Similar results have been obtained by Graf, Squire, and Mandler (1984). Several amnesic patients were given the word stem completion task with explicit memory instructions ("remember the words you just saw"). They showed impaired performance on the word stems compared to patients who received implicit instructions ("complete the word stem with the first word that comes to mind"; see Schacter, 1989, 1992, for reviews of such studies).

The implications of these studies are fascinating. They imply rather separate long-term memory systems in the brain, one for explicit, deliberately acquired and recalled information, and a separate one for implicit information not open to conscious recollection. Alternatively, the results imply separate routes into (or out of) a common mental representation. The veritable explosion of recent research on this topic, including fascinating attempts to simulate memory disruptions by means of connectionist models (e.g., Farah & McClelland, 1991), attests to the importance of the topic, especially because of its implications for an understanding of normal cognition.

Summary

1. Disorders of perception and attention are especially related to the right hemisphere and the parietal lobes. Visual neglect is a disruption in the visual attention processes, which can even extend to visual images. Visual agnosia is a disruption in object recognition, also associated with damage in the parietal lobes.
2. Aphasia is a disruption of language ability due to brain damage, usually in the left hemisphere. Broca's and Wernicke's aphasias, respectively, show disruptions of syntactic, fluent speech, and disruptions of comprehension. Other, less common aphasias include conduction aphasia, alexia and agraphia, and anomia. The research indicates that many of these language functions are separate components to overall language ability.
3. Amnesia is the loss of memory due to brain damage, either for memories prior to (retrograde) or after (anterograde) the damage. Patients like H.M. display severe impairments in the ability to learn new information, associated with lesions of the hippocampus.

4. Amnesia often, if not always, shows a disruption of explicit or declarative memories, while seeming to leave implicit memory intact. This suggests that explicit and implicit memory processes are quite different in the normal cognitive system too.

Important Terms

agnosia
amnesia
anomia
anterograde and retrograde amnesia
aphasia—Broca's, Wernicke's
cerebral lateralization
cognitive neuropsychology
contralaterality
corpus callosum
dissociations/method of dissociations
double dissociation
hemispheric specialization
hippocampus
implicit versus explicit memory
lesions
neocortex
neurons
neurotransmitters
prosopagnosia
split brain
synapse
thalamus
visual cortex
visual neglect

Suggested Readings

A variety of texts and chapters can be consulted for accounts of neurocognition. If you're new to the area, start with the stunning case histories presented in Sacks's (1970) *The Man Who Mistook His Wife for a Hat* or *Toscanini's Fumble* by Klawans (1988), intriguing, informative, and accessible to the layperson. Ornstein and Thompson's (1984) *The Amazing Brain* is a superb newcomer's introduction to the structure and functioning of the brain. Good treatments at a higher level are Ellis and Young (1988), McCarthy and Warrington (1990), Posner and Raichle (1994), and Shallice (1988). Kolb and Whishaw's (1990; revised in 1996) book is a veritable Bible of neuropsychology, as is the new Feinberg and Farah (1997) volume.

Chapters by Schacter (1989) and by Sejnowski and Churchland (1989) in Posner's *Foundations of Cognitive Science* provide excellent, high-level reviews of memory and cognition from a neurocognitive standpoint. Schacter's (1992) paper focuses on the neurocognition of implicit memory. Antrobus (1991) suggests a neurocognitive explanation of dreaming, and proposes a connectionist model to simulate dreaming. An excellent series of papers on cognitive neuroscience appears in *Science*, 14 March 1997 (Vol. 275, pp. 1579–1610), including articles on working memory, consciousness, language, and mental illness. And finally, Corballis's (1989) review article on the possible evolutionary influences for laterality is fascinating reading, as are Geary's (1992) and Lewontin's (1990) papers on the evolution of cognition.

For recent work on the involvement of the frontal lobes in executive control functions, see especially Case (1992) and Stuss (1992), both in an entire issue of *Brain and Cognition* devoted to the frontal lobes.

SECTION

FIVE

THINKING AND REASONING

CHAPTER ELEVEN

REASONING AND DECISION MAKING

This chapter, and the next one on problem solving, probably comes closer to the layperson's conception of "human thought" than any of the material you've read so far. "Thought," in this view, is whatever mental processes you're aware of, the relatively slow, conscious mental work you do when faced with a difficult decision or a complex problem. But that's not entirely true, is it? After all, you're not consciously aware of how you recognize words on the page or how you comprehend language, but those are *clearly* thought processes, the very stuff of cognitive science.

Nonetheless, it is time now to turn to topics like decision making, reasoning, and problem solving, and explore the slower, more conscious aspects of cognition. Two general threads run through much of research you'll be reading about.

- First, we are often overly influenced by the information we have stored in memory. If the information is correct, then there's no problem, of course. But if it's incorrect or misleading in some way, this can lead to a form of bias due to conceptually driven processing. We'll call this the **top-down bias,** when existing knowledge biases your reasoning.
- The second thread is the well-researched **confirmation bias**—far more than is logical, we tend to search for evidence that confirms our decisions, beliefs, and hypotheses. We are, in short, considerably less logical—and less skeptical—than we ought to be.

We'll start with the seemingly simple decisions and comparisons we make, and then turn to two classic forms of reasoning in logic; this section includes some help for those who are "logically challenged." Then we'll consider the fascinating processes of reasoning and decision making under uncertainty, when we have to make a decision without having all the information we need. You'll get a glimpse of yourself—and your occasional illogic—in the strategies people use to deal with those situations. And, you'll also see a reasonable, cognitive explanation of stereotyping and forms of bias like sexism and racism. Humbling and embarrassing, but true—the research provides convincing examples of the often surprising inaccuracies in our stored knowledge, and the surprising inaccuracies and biases in our reasoning too.

"Oh, just put me down as undecided."

Simple Decisions and Comparisons

Preview: physical comparisons; symbolic comparisons; semantic congruity and symbolic distance

DECISIONS ABOUT PHYSICAL DIFFERENCES

One of the very earliest areas of research in psychology was the area of **psychophysics**—indeed, psychophysics research was being done well before psychology *per se* came into existence (e.g., Fechner, 1860/1966). The topic of interest in psychophysics was the *psychological* experience of physical stimulation, that is, how perceptual experience differs from the physical stimulation that is being perceived.

What the early researchers discovered was that the subjective experience of magnitude—for instance brightness and loudness—was *not* identical to the physical magnitude of the stimulus. Instead, there is a *psychological dimension* of magnitude that forms the basis of our perceptions; our perceptual experience is not a direct and perfect function of the physical stimulus.

Here's a quick example. The perceived brightness of a light depends not only on the light's physical brightness, but also on factors like the brightness of the background or a comparison light, the duration of the stimulus, and so forth. The amount by which brightness must be *changed* in order to perceive that change, likewise, depends on more than just the physical change. If the light is dim, a small change is noticeable, say from a 25-watt lightbulb to a 30. But if it's very bright, a much larger change is necessary—maybe from 150 watts to 175.

We refer to this as a **jnd,** which stands for **just noticeable difference,** the amount of change required in order to detect that change. *Jnds* are small for stimuli of low intensity, but larger at higher levels of intensity (as in Weber's Law; see Haber & Hershenson, 1973, for example). If it's totally silent outside, you can hear one car horn, but if you're in a traffic jam with 25 drivers honking, one more honking horn isn't noticeable. So *jnds* have to do with a **discriminability effect,** also called a **distance effect**—the greater the distance or difference between the two stimuli being compared, the faster the decision that they differ (Moyer & Bayer, 1976; Woodworth & Schlosberg, 1954).

DECISIONS ABOUT SYMBOLIC DIFFERENCES

What's fascinating about the distance effect is that it applies to *symbolic differences* too, not just physical stimuli like lights or noises, but also *concepts*, and the symbols that name them. A straightforward demonstration of this involves number magnitude. For each of the following pairs, pick the smaller number:

1 2   1 4   8 9

As Banks and co-workers (Banks, 1977; Banks, Clark, & Lucy, 1975) and others have shown, picking the smaller number is *faster* for the 1 4 pair than for either of the others. Why?—because 1 and 4 differ more in magnitude than the other two. This of course is a straightforward extension of the psychophysical distance effect to conceptual or symbolic stimuli, which we refer to as the **symbolic distance** effect. Simply, this effect is that the greater the distance between two concepts on some dimension, the faster the decision that they differ.

But that's not the only effect these pairs of numbers show. If you're asked to pick the smaller from the 1 2 pair, and then asked for the smaller of 8 9, you're faster for the 1 2 pair. Despite the fact that the numerical difference is 1 in both cases, you can select the  smaller of 1 2 more rapidly. This effect is shown in Figure 11.1 (p. 354).

How can we explain that? The reason is the **semantic congruity effect** (e.g., Banks, 1977; Banks et al., 1975). The semantic congruity effect refers to the match or agreement ("congruity") between the stimuli, on the one hand, and the dimension being judged on the other. It states that the decision will be faster when the dimension being judged *matches* or is *congruent* with the stimuli being evaluated. I asked you to pick the *smaller* number. Both 1 and 2 are *small,* whereas 8 and 9 are, roughly speaking, *large*. Consequently, you're faster to select the smaller of two small numbers than the smaller of two large numbers. And it works the other way too—if I asked you to pick the *larger* value, you'd be faster for the 8 9 pair than picking the smaller of the two—picking *large* for *large* quantities is faster.

▲ Idealized curves of these two effects are depicted in Figure 11.2 (p. 354), the symbolic distance effect on the left, and the semantic congruity effect on the right. The powerful thing about these two effects is that they apply to all sorts of symbolic comparisons, not just numbers. Let's consider three different kinds of comparisons.

Imagery

Which is larger, a squirrel or a rabbit? Which is smaller, a ram or a cow? Several investigators (e.g., Banks, 1977; Moyer, 1973) have found symbolic distance and semantic congruity effects when people make judgments of this sort. What is fascinating is that the judgments are made on the basis of the *visual image* of the object—that is, people retrieve

★ **FIGURE 11.1**

RT performance on number comparisons. (From Banks, Fujii, & Kayra-Stuart, 1976, figure 1.)

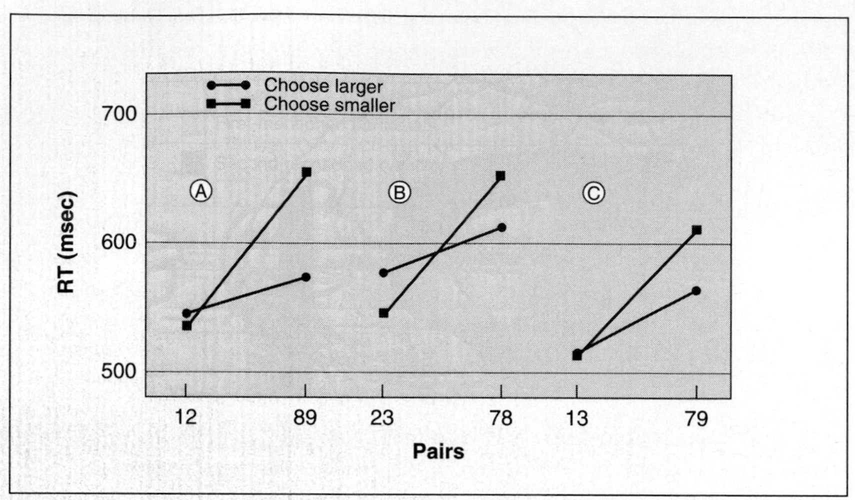

▲ **FIGURE 11.2**

Idealized curves showing (a) the symbolic distance and (b) semantic congruity effects. (From Banks, 1977.)

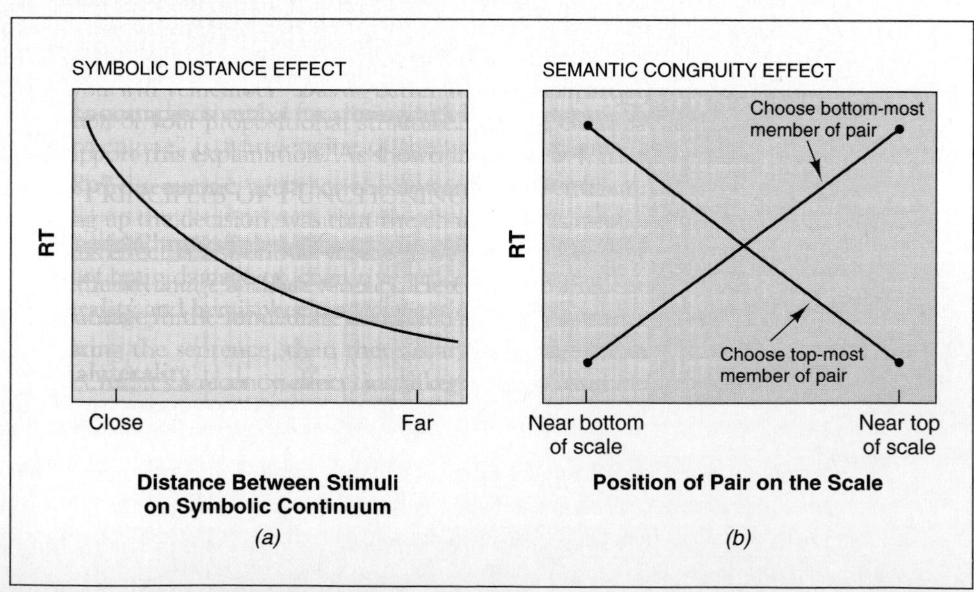

a mental image of the objects, then mentally scan the images to decide which one is larger or smaller.

Moyer had his participants estimate the absolute sizes of animals and then make timed comparisons between different pairs. His results, depicted in Figure 11.3, showed that RT decreased as the differences in size between the animals increased—the symbolic distance effect. Interestingly, the relationship between image size and RT was logarithmic, as shown on the logarithmic scale of the x-axis. In other words, the size differences are compressed at the larger end of the scale relative to the smaller end. This is exactly what Banks (1977) found about the mental number line—psychologically, 8 and 9 are "closer" on the mental number line than 1 and 2 are (see also Kosslyn & Pomerantz, 1977; Marschark & Paivio, 1979; Shoben, Sailor, & Wang, 1989).

Semantic Orderings

Holyoak and Walker (1976) asked participants to make semantic comparisons on dimensions of time, quality, and temperature; for example,

- Which is longer, minute or hour?
- Which is worse, perfect or good?
- Which is hotter, cool or cold?

FIGURE 11.3

RT performance to judge which of two animals is larger as a function of estimated difference in size of animals. Note that the *x*-axis is plotted on a logarithmic scale. (From Moyer, 1973.)

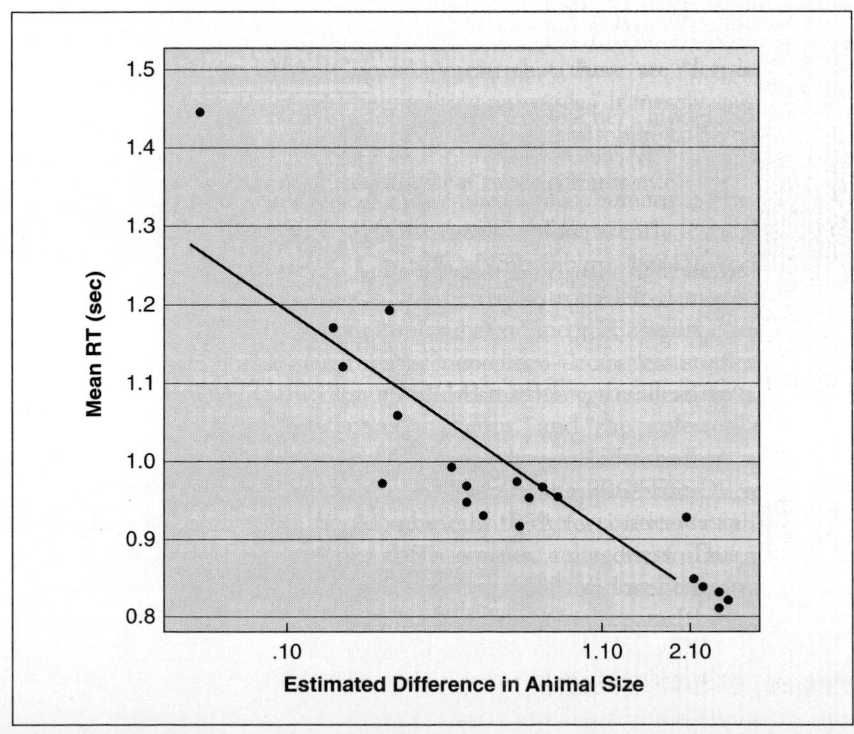

Judgments were faster when the pair of terms differed a great deal (e.g., perfect vs. poor) than when they differed by less (perfect vs. excellent); that's the symbolic distance effect. And judgments were faster if the dimension of judgment was congruent with the stimulus values, the semantic congruity effect. For example, choosing the longer of "century vs. decade," was easier than choosing the shorter of those two (see also Freidman, 1978).

Judgments of Geographical Distance

Even people's judgments of geographical distance seem to follow the same principles (e.g., Baum & Jonides, 1979; Holyoak & Mah, 1982). In one experiment, Holyoak and Mah (1982) asked participants to rate the distances between American cities, on a 1 to 9 scale. When no particular geographical reference point was given—the Neutral condition—participants based their judgments on their own local viewpoint (Ann Arbor, Michigan, since these were University of Michigan students). But in another experiment, participants were asked, "Which city is farther west, Denver or Salt Lake?" Western cities were judged more rapidly than eastern cities with "farther west" questions, especially when the participants took a western perspective (e.g., imagine you're on an island one mile off the California coast). Imagined perspective thus added to the distance and congruity effects—if you're on that western island, Denver and Salt Lake are more discriminable to you than Pittsburgh and Indianapolis (see Radvansky, Carlson-Radvansky, & Irwin, 1995, on the effects of uncertainty in distance estimation).

Summary

1. Psychophysics studied the perception of magnitude, and showed that there is a separate psychological dimension that influences our perceptions. The greater the difference between two stimuli, the easier it is to judge them as different.
2. The symbolic distance effect names the same phenomenon when symbols or concepts are being compared; the more dissimilar two concepts are, the easier it is to judge them as different. Furthermore, when asked to make these comparisons, the congruity between the concepts and the dimension being judged also affects performance, the semantic congruity effect.
3. The symbolic distance and semantic congruity effects have been demonstrated with numbers, with comparisons based on visual imagery, with completely semantic judgments, and even for comparisons and judgments based on geographical location.

Formal Logic and Reasoning

Preview: syllogisms; conditional reasoning; hypothesis testing; the confirmation bias

At some point during high school or college, most students are exposed to the classic forms of reasoning, often in a course on logic. For our purposes, two of these forms, *syllo-*

gisms and *conditional reasoning problems*, are important to understand. A general finding in this research is that people are not particularly good at solving such problems correctly when the problems are presented in an abstract form. Our solutions are often better when the problems are presented in terms of concrete, real-world concepts. If we generate our own examples, however, the accuracy of our solutions depends on how critically or skeptically we generated the examples. In some situations, our general world knowledge almost prevents us from seeing the "pure," that is, logical, answer to logic problems.

SYLLOGISMS

A **syllogism,** or **categorical syllogism,** is a three-statement logical form; the first two parts state the premises, which are taken to be true; the third part states a conclusion based on those premises. The goal of syllogistic reasoning is to understand how different kinds of premises can be combined to yield logically true conclusions, and to understand what combinations of premises lead to invalid or incorrect conclusions.

Often, syllogisms are presented in an abstract form, such as:

(1a) *All A are B.*
All B are C.
Therefore, all A are C.

In this example, the two premises state a certain relation between the elements A, B, and C, basically a class inclusion or subset-superset relation; *All A are B* says that the set A is a subset of the group B. The "therefore" statement is the conclusion. By applying the rules of syllogistic reasoning, it can be determined that the conclusion *All A are C* is true here. That is to say, the conclusion follows logically from the premises. Inserting words into the syllogism will verify the truth of the conclusion: for instance,

(1b) *All poodles are dogs.*
All dogs are animals.
Therefore, all poodles are animals.

One difficulty or confusion that people have, however, is illustrated by the following example:

(1c) *All poodles are animals.*
All animals are wild.
Therefore, all poodles are wild.

The difficulty here is that the conclusion is *logically* valid—because the conclusion follows from the premises, the syllogism is valid. But of course it isn't true in the real world—hardly any poodles are wild, after all (Feldman, 1992). Yet by the rules of syllogistic reasoning, the truth of the premises is *irrelevant* to the validity of the argument. What matters, instead, is whether the conclusion does or does not follow from the premises.

So in example (1c), the conclusion is valid even though the second premise is empirically false. Thus, applying syllogistic reasoning to real-world problems is at least a two-step process.

- First, determine if the syllogism itself is valid, if the conclusion follows from the premises.
- Second, if the syllogism is valid, determine the empirical truth of the premises. In example (1c), the premise "All animals are wild" is false, so the syllogism is false despite being logically valid.

Confirmation Bias

Now consider an example that illustrates *confirmation bias* (the syllogism is starred because it's wrong).

> (2a*) *All A are B.*
> *Some B are C.*
> *Therefore, some A are C.*

(In formal logic, *some* means "at least one, and possibly all.") If you try inserting words into the example to see if the conclusion is correct, you tend to use words that make the conclusion seem true; for example:

> (2b*) *All polar bears are animals.*
> *Some animals are white.*
> *Therefore, some polar bears are white.*

Because it's true that some (or all) polar bears are white, we tend to judge the syllogism as true. But the syllogism is *false*—the two premises do *not* invariably lead to a correct conclusion, as shown by (2c*):

> (2c*) *All polar bears are animals.*
> *Some animals have wings.*
> *Therefore, some polar bears have wings.*

The difficulty involves the qualifier *some*. So the best advice is to try very hard to find concepts that lead to an obviously false conclusion. If you can find them, then the conclusion is false because the syllogism is invalid.

Professors often recommend that you draw a Venn diagram of the premises in order to decide if the syllogism is true. There's a danger here—we tend to draw confirming diagrams, exactly the bias illustrated in (2b*). Look at the second syllogism in Figure 11.4. The first diagram shows why the syllogism is false—and in fact it's pretty easy to find a way of diagramming the problem to show just that. But, it's also temptingly easy to come up with a diagram like the one on the right, where the circles coincide and thus appear to prove the syllogism true. Obviously, the diagram on the right illustrates confirmation bias, the tendency to try to find evidence that confirms or proves (the same goes for the diagrams for the third problem).

In general, people's performance on syllogisms improves when they are shown how to use Venn diagrams or how to generate specific examples (Helsabeck, 1975). This procedure only works if you try to find ways of showing the syllogism to be false, in other words if you try to avoid the confirmation bias. Adopting a skeptical attitude about the conclusion, and trying to diagram the situation to show how the conclusion is false, is the more helpful strategy.

CONDITIONAL REASONING

Conditional reasoning is a second important kind of logical reasoning to understand. Conditional-reasoning problems always contain two major parts, a *conditional clause* or statement that expresses some relationship, followed by some *evidence* pertaining to the conditional clause. **Conditional reasoning** involves a logical determination of whether the evidence supports, refutes, or is irrelevant to the stated relationship.

The first statement in such problems is called the *conditional*, and consists of two parts in *if-then* format. Respectively, the *if* clause and the *then* clause are known as the **antecedent** and the **consequent** of the conditional clause (for clarity, I'll simply refer to the

FIGURE 11.4

Venn diagrams of three sample syllogisms, showing both correct diagrams and two diagrams illustrating the confirmation bias. If a diagram can be constructed that shows the conclusion doesn't hold for all cases, then the conclusion is false. The first diagram in (2*) shows why (2*) is incorrect, since it is not necessarily true that some A are C. The second diagram in (2*) shows that an arrangment can be found that seems to support the argument. Likewise, the first diagram in (3*) shows why (3*) is incorrect, since it is not necessarily true that no A are C. The second diagram in (3*) shows an arrangement that does seem to support the conclusion.

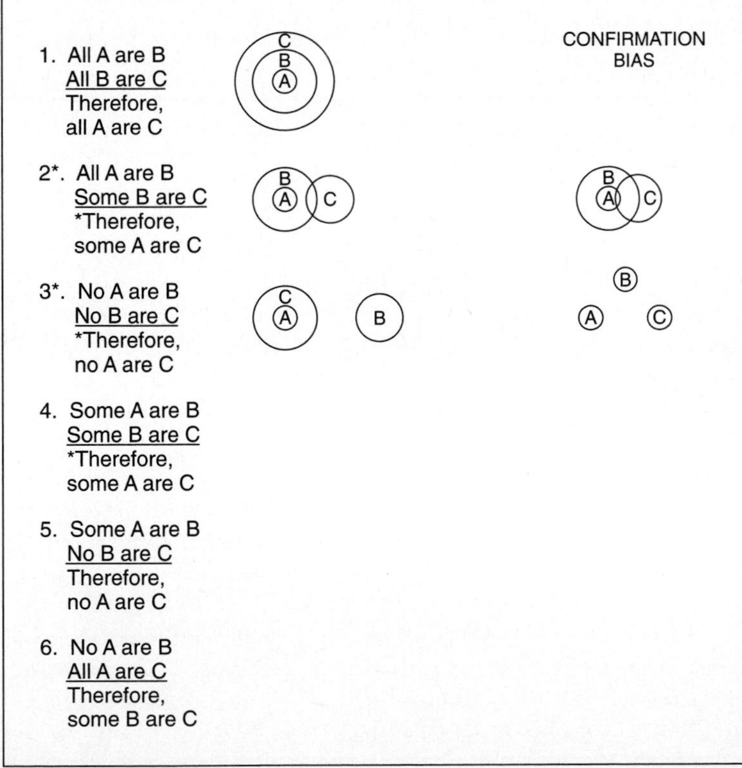

if or antecedent, and the *then* or consequent). The *if* states the possible cause, and the *then* states the *effect* of that possible cause.

After the *if-then*, you are given a second statement, some evidence about the truth or falsity of one of the propositions in the *if-then* relationship. The goal of such reasoning is to take the evidence and decide what follows from the evidence and the *if-then* statement. In other words, you must determine whether the conditional *if-then* statement is true or false given this observed evidence, or if the evidence is irrelevant to the *if-then*.

The most general form of the conditional statement is:

If p, then q.

The conditional statement is then followed by the evidence, any one of the following four possibilities:

A. *p* (that is, *p* is true), *therefore q*

B. *not p* (that is, *p* is not true) no conclusion

C. *q* (that is, *q* is true) no conclusion

D. *not q* (that is, *q* is not true), *therefore not p*

The conditional *if p, then q* means that if some antecedent condition *p* is true, then its consequence (the *consequent*) *q* is true. Now, if the evidence shows that *p* is indeed true (possibility A), it follows logically that *q* must be true. As a simple example of such condi-

★ **TABLE 11.1**

Conditional Reasoning

	Form	*Name*	*Example*
A.	If p, then q Evidence: p Therefore, q	Modus ponens: affirming the antecedent **Valid inference**	If there is fog, the plane will be diverted. Evidence: There is fog. Therefore, the plane will be diverted.
B.	If p, then q Evidence: not p *Therefore, not q	Denying the antecedent **Invalid inference**	If there is fog, the plane will be diverted. Evidence: There is no fog. *Therefore, the plane will not be diverted.
C.	If p, then q Evidence: q *Therefore, p	Affirming the consequent **Invalid inference**	If there is fog, the plane will be diverted. Evidence: The plane will be diverted. *Therefore, there is fog.
D.	If p, then q Evidence: not q Therefore, not p	Modus tollens: denying the consequent **Valid inference**	If there is fog, the plane will be diverted. Evidence: The plane will not be diverted. Therefore, there is no fog.

tional reasoning, consider the following example (adapted from Johnson-Laird, Byrne, & Schaeken, 1992):

If there is fog, then the plane will be diverted.

When given the evidence that *p* is true, then the consequent *q* must be true, *There is fog, so the plane will be diverted;* this is possibility A from above. Likewise, on evidence that *q* is not true, *the plane will not be diverted,* it must therefore be that *p* is not true, *there is no fog;* this is possibility D from above.

★ The forms in conditional reasoning are shown in Table 11.1, along with the formal terminology from logic. You can either *affirm* or *deny* either of the propositions in the *if-then* statement, so there are four possibilities in the table.

Valid Arguments

As the table shows, however, only two of the four are correct, that is, only two lead to a true conclusion. The first and easiest is A, called *affirming the antecedent*—*p* is correct, in other words. People are quite good at reasoning from this that therefore *q* must be true—there *is* fog, so the plane *will* be diverted. In classical logic, this is called the **modus ponens.**

The other correct form, **modus tollens,** is harder for people to adopt. Here, you're *denying the consequent*, finding evidence that *q* is not true; the shorthand here is to simply say *not q*. So, if the evidence is *not q, the plane will not be diverted,* then it follows that *there is no fog, not p*.

Invalid Arguments

What's wrong with the other two possibilities? In B, called *denying the antecedent*, we find evidence that *p* is not true, in other words *not p*. People are tempted to claim that the conclusion *not q* follows from this—because there is no fog, the plane will not be diverted. But that's illogical—planes can be diverted for other reasons, like high winds or excess air traffic. Clearly, the fact that there's no fog is irrelevant to the conclusion in this case. Likewise, the other incorrect argument is C, *affirming the consequent: q, therefore p*. This is wrong for essentially the same reason—the mere fact that the plane was diverted doesn't mean it was because of fog—it could have been one of those other conditions instead.

EVIDENCE ON CONDITIONAL REASONING

Generally, the research shows that people are relatively good at inferring the truth of the consequent given evidence that the antecedent is true (affirming the antecedent, the *modus ponens*). When given the conditional *if p, then q* and the evidence that *p* is true, people usually infer correctly that *q* is true. For instance, Rips and Marcus (1977) found that 100 percent of their sample drew this correct conclusion. Much more difficult, apparently, is denying the consequent (the *modus tollens*), in which the evidence *not q* leads to the valid conclusion *therefore, not p*. Only 57 percent of Rips and Marcus's participants drew this conclusion correctly (in a simpler version of the problem, 77 percent concluded correctly that *p* could never be true given the evidence *not q*). Wason and Johnson-Laird (1972) found similar results in their investigation of conditional reasoning, in which problems were stated in either concrete or relatively abstract form.

Safety

If you are sitting in an exit row and you can not read this card or can not see well enough to follow these instructions, please tell a crew member.

安全
安全
안전

非常口の隣にご着席で、英語がおわ かりにならない方は、
乗務員にお申 し出ください。

您若坐在走道位子並且不懂英文,請告知本機服務員。

출구쪽 줄에 앉으시고 영어를 못읽아드시면
승무원에게 말씀하십시요.

Sicherheit

Wenn sie neben einem ausgang sitzen und sie verstehen kein Englisch, bitte verständigen sie die flugzeugbesatzung.

Sécurité

Si vous êtes assis dans une rangée de sièges à côté d'une sortie, et vous ne comprenez pas la langue anglaise, veuillez le dire à un membre de l'équipage.

Seguridad

Si usted se encuentra sentado/a en una fila de asientos a la par de una salida u usted no entiende el idioma inglés, favor de avisarle a un tripulante.

Errors in Conditional Reasoning

Our errors in conditional reasoning seem to fall into three categories. First, we sometimes draw incorrect conclusions by means of the two invalid forms, denying the antecedent (B) and affirming the consequent (C). A second, more subtle error is often found as well. People have a tendency to reverse the propositions in the *if* and *then*. They then proceed to evaluate the given evidence against the now reversed conditional. This kind of error is termed an *illicit conversion*. As an example, with a conditional of *If p, then q*, and evidence *q*, people tend to switch the conditional to **If q, then p*. They then proceed, incorrectly, to decide that the evidence *q* implies that *p* is true. The major reason this is incorrect is that the order of *p* and *q* in the conditional is meaningful—the *if* often specifies some possible *cause*, and the *then* specifies a possible *effect*. Obviously, we cannot draw correct *cause-effect* conclusions if we reverse the roles of the cause (*p*) for some outcome and the result (*q*) of some cause.

The third kind of error that is found relates to *confirmation bias*. As a demonstration, consider the now classic study of conditional reasoning (reported in Wason & Johnson-Laird, 1972) illustrated in the top part of Figure 11.5, the Wason Card problem. Four cards are visible to you, as shown in the figure. Each has a letter on one side and a number on the other. The task is to pick the card or cards you need to turn over to gather *conclusive* evidence on the following rule:

If a card has a vowel on one side, then it has an even number on the other side.

Give this question some thought before you continue reading.

Of the people that Wason tested on this problem, 33 percent turned over only the E card, a correct choice conforming to the *modus ponens* method of affirming the antecedent. But a more thorough test of the rule requires that another card be turned over (in other words, the rule might be rephrased "Only if a card has a vowel on one side will it have an even number on the other side"). Only 4 percent of the participants turned over the correct combination of cards to check on this possibility, the E card (the *modus ponens*) and the 7 card (the *modus tollens*).

In other words, turning over the 7, which would serve as negative evidence (*not q*), was rarely considered. Instead, participants much preferred turning over the E and the 4 cards—46 percent of them did this, where turning over the 4 is an instance of the invalid process of affirming the consequent. In other words, the rule doesn't say anything about what will be on the other side of a consonant; it could be an odd or an even number.

In short, turning over the E represents a search for positive evidence about the rule, evidence that *p* is true. The general tendency in such situations, however, is to stop the search for evidence there, or to continue searching for additional positive evidence (turning over the 4). Searching for *negative* evidence, that is, evidence that might show *p* to be false, was seldom done. Although people make a variety of errors in such situations, especially as the if-then relationship becomes more complex (Cummins, Lubart, Alksnis, & Rist, 1991), the typical mistake is the confirmation bias, simply searching for positive, confirming evidence (e.g., Klayman & Ha, 1989).

The abstractness or concreteness of the problem can be surprisingly important here. In a study by Johnson-Laird, Legrenzi, and Legrenzi (1972), participants were given a specific, concrete situation, in which they tried to find cheaters on the postal regulations—if unsealed envelopes can be mailed using a less expensive stamp, it's important that envelopes with the cheaper stamp be unsealed. The conditional, in essence, said:

FIGURE 11.5

The Wason Card problem, in abstract (top) and concrete (bottom) forms. Which card or cards would you turn over to obtain conclusive evidence about the following rule: A card with a vowel on it will have an even number on the other side? At the bottom of the illustration are four envelopes. Which envelopes would you turn over to detect postal cheaters, under the rule that "an unsealed envelope can be stamped with the less expensive stamp"? (From Anderson, 1980.)

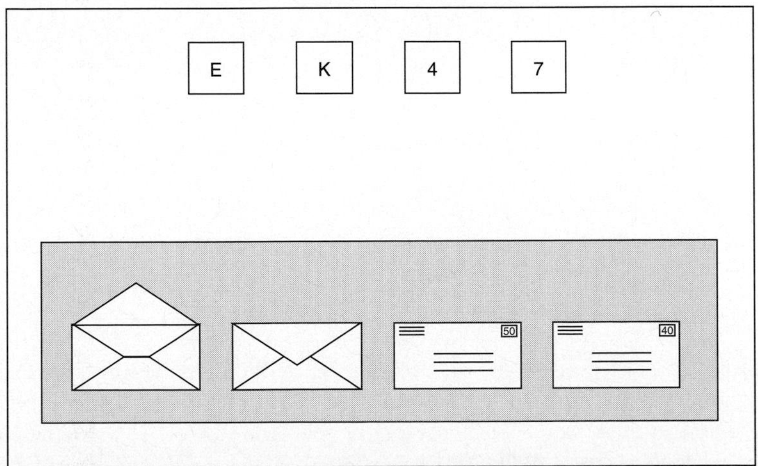

If the envelope is sealed, then it must carry the expensive stamp.

When asked to detect cheaters, 21 of 24 participants made *both* correct choices—they not only turned over the sealed envelope, but also the envelope stamped with the less expensive stamp, that is, the *modus tollens* choice corresponding to the 7 card above. Since the participants were not postal workers, it seems clear that the concreteness of the situation oriented them toward the "skeptical" attitude mentioned earlier. Their skepticism led them to search actively for negative evidence—and in the process, they demonstrated logical conditional reasoning.

HYPOTHESIS TESTING

Conditional reasoning is *exactly* the reason that the inferential statistics we teach you in statistics classes test the null hypothesis. Why? Because the experimental hypothesis is something like this:

If Independent Variable A is important, then data resembling B should be obtained (for instance, the groups will have different means).

When data resembling B are in fact obtained, we would like to conclude that our Independent Variable is important—but that's an invalid argument, by affirming the consequent. And if data not resembling B are obtained (*not q*), that leads to the valid conclusion that Independent Variable A is not important (*not p*)—well, science is going to proceed pretty slowly if the only conclusions we can draw are that independent variables are *not* important.

Instead, we test the null hypothesis:

If Independent Variable A is unimportant, then the groups will perform at approximately the same level.

Now it's easy—if the groups do not perform at the same level, our evidence is *not q*, which allows us to conclude that the antecedent must be wrong, *not p*. In short, we conclude that Independent Variable A *is* important. Hence, the general form of the test is:

*If the null hypothesis is true (*if p*), then there will be no effect of the variable on performance (*then q*).*

If we obtain evidence that there *is* an effect of the variable, i.e., that the consequent is not true, we can then conclude that the antecedent is not true—we reject the null hypothesis.

This is the essence of hypothesis testing, to conclude that the if portion of the null hypothesis is false based on an outcome that denies the consequent of the null hypothesis.

Summary

1. Syllogistic reasoning (e.g., All A are B) is difficult partly because of the abstract statement of premises and conclusions, so is often improved when people use concrete concepts. A danger is that the concepts, and the Venn diagrams used in reasoning, will demonstrate the confirmation bias.

2. Conditional reasoning (if *p*, then *q*) permits conclusions when the antecedent is affirmed (*p*, therefore *q*) and when the consequent is denied (*not q*, therefore *not p*). Errors involve the other two types of evidence (*not p*, *q*) and illicit conversion of the antecedent and consequent, and are more common in abstract problems.
3. Hypothesis testing, as in inferential statistics, is an exact case of conditional reasoning. Given the acceptable kinds of evidence, we test the null hypothesis in research.

Decisions and Reasoning Under Uncertainty

Preview: algorithms and heuristics; the availability heuristic, the representativeness heuristic; the simulation heuristic; misconceptions in physics

Although you may have been unfamiliar with syllogisms and conditional reasoning when you started this chapter, there are clear and definite rules for solving those logic problems, rules that logic students learn in their classes. But there are countless situations that you confront in which you lack the specific information you need, you don't know the rules needed to come up with an answer, or there are no set rules to follow. How do we reason in situations like this? To gain some insight into this, read the questions in Table 11.2 and keep track of your answers.

ALGORITHMS AND HEURISTICS

By far the most influential work done in this area of decision making has been that of Tversky, Kahneman, and their co-workers (Tversky & Kahneman, 1973, 1974, 1980; Kahneman & Tversky, 1972, 1973, 1996; Kahneman, Slovic, & Tversky, 1982; Shafir & Tversky, 1992). Their work has had a tremendous influence not only in cognitive science, but in a variety of other fields too—law, medicine, and business, to name a few (e.g., Libbey, 1981; Parker, Porter, & Finley, 1983). Indeed, any situation involving human reasoning and decision making would probably be an appropriate area to study within the framework these authors have provided.

TABLE 11.2

Sample Questions for Reasoning and Decision Making

1. Estimate the ratio of sales for Chevrolets versus Cadillacs; that is, for every *x* Chevrolets sold, *y* Cadillacs are sold.
2. What percentage of American households have purchased a home personal computer?
3. Why are more graduate students first-born than second-born children?
4. Why do more hotel fires start on the first ten floors than the second ten floors?
5. You've watched a fair coin toss come up heads five times in a row. If you bet $10 on the next toss, would you choose heads or tails?

Source: Adapted from Johnson and Finke (1985).

A basic idea in this work is that there are two different approaches that can be taken in reasoning and decision-making situations; one is called an *algorithmic* approach, and the other is a *heuristic* approach.

- An **algorithm** is a specific rule or solution procedure, often quite detailed and complex, that is guaranteed to furnish the correct answer if it is followed correctly. We are familiar with algorithms especially through our schoolwork in arithmetic and mathematics, for example, the algorithm (the set of rules) for doing multiplication. If the rules are applied correctly, the algorithm provides the correct answer.
- In the other approach, the solution method involves what is known as a **heuristic.** A heuristic is *a "rule of thumb,"* an informal strategy or approach that works under some circumstances, for some of the time, but is not guaranteed to yield the correct answer. (The word *heuristic* comes from the Greek stem meaning "to invent or discover." The same word stem leads to the word *eureka,* the classic exclamation uttered by Archimedes in his bathtub, meaning roughly "Aha, I've found it!" What he had found was a way to solve a difficult problem, measuring the purity of the gold in the King's crown by seeing how much water it displaced.)

As Nisbett and Ross (1980; also McKenzie, 1994) point out, heuristics can be extremely useful in many situations, especially when a precise answer is not called for, and especially when the heuristic uses reliable, unbiased information from memory. When that information is biased or incomplete, however, we tend to rely on heuristics (N. R. Brown & Siegler, 1993) that can and do lead to errors or systematic biases. Let's explore those biases and errors a bit. (Hints and solutions to the questions in Table 11.2 are found in Table 11.3.)

TABLE 11.3

Hints and Solutions for Questions in Table 11.2

1. People tend to make an initial estimate, then revise it upward because of cost factors, an example of the *anchoring and adjusting heuristic* (e.g., Carlson, 1990). Most settle on ratios like 10:1 or 15:1. In reality, the ratio is almost exactly 5:1 for all models of Chevrolets versus all models of Cadillacs.
2. If you own a PC, your estimate tends to be higher than if you don't own a PC. The estimated percentage (Electronic Industries Association, Sept. 1996) is that 40 percent of American households have purchased a home personal computer. In an informal test, one owner estimated 60 percent, and a nonowner estimated 5 percent.
3. *Hint:* How many first-born versus second-born *people* are there?
4. *Hint:* How many hotels even *have* a second ten floors?
5. The Gambler's Fallacy is that the next toss will come up tails, because "it's time for tails to show up." But the five previous tosses have no bearing on the sixth toss, assuming a fair coin. The fallacy is related to the so-called "law of small numbers," explained in the text.

Source: Adapted from Johnson and Finke (1985).

THE AVAILABILITY HEURISTIC

The first of the three major heuristics Tversky and Kahneman studied (e.g., 1973) is called the **availability heuristic.** This refers to making a decision based on the ease of retrieval from memory. (Note that this definition matches what we called *accessibility* in Chapter 5, and is different from the term *availability* as Tulving and others use the term in memory research). When people have to make estimates of likelihood or frequency of events, their estimates are influenced by the ease with which relevant examples or information can be remembered. A simple example of this heuristic involves questions like the following:

> *In the English language, are there more words beginning with the letter* k *or more words with* k *in the third position?*

The algorithmic way of answering the question is to count—go to the dictionary and count the number of entries in the *k*'s, then go through the whole dictionary counting words with *k* as the third letter. Why don't we do that?—obvious, it would take *way* too much time and energy.

Instead, we use a heuristic. We try *thinking of* words beginning with *k*, and words with *k* in the third position. The ease with which words come to mind leads us to an estimate. Since most of us can think of many more words beginning with *k*, we conclude that *k*-initial words must be more common than words with *k* in position 3. In fact, Tversky and

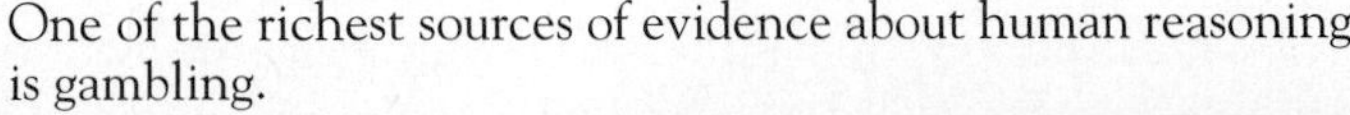

One of the richest sources of evidence about human reasoning is gambling.

Kahneman's (1973) participants estimated that there are about twice as many words beginning with *k* than there are words with *k* in the third position (they also tested *l*, *n*, *r*, and *v*).

It's a great example of a heuristic—it's a quick and dirty method people can use readily. It's also a great example because it illustrates the problem with heuristics in general—heuristics are seriously prone to bias and error. Objective word counts show there are *many more* words with k in the third position than words beginning with k. But because our mental lexicon is organized according to word-initial letters and sounds, it's far easier to retrieve words beginning with k. Thus, ease of retrieval is the source of the error here. The heuristic misleads us because of the *top-down bias*—the way information is stored in memory has a misleading effect on our reasoning.

Because there are many influences on what gets stored in long-term memory, there are many different sources of bias that can affect reasoning via the availability heuristic. Some of the influences are personal and idiosyncratic—your specific preferences, dislikes, interests, and so forth—while others can be more systematic. Let's consider three such sources of bias here.

Frequency

The frequency with which events occur is a kind of information that is coded in memory (e.g., Hasher & Zacks, 1984), perhaps automatically. So, when we attempt to retrieve examples of the events from memory, the way their frequency has been stored can be an important factor. If the retrieval of examples is easy, we infer that the event must be fairly frequent or common. If retrieval is difficult, then we estimate that the event must *not* be frequent.

What's wrong with making judgments based on frequency information in long-term memory? What's wrong with it is that our preferences and interests can easily influence what we store in memory. If I own a Plymouth, and like it, I'm at least somewhat more likely to notice other Plymouths, and therefore store an inflated estimate of their frequency in my memory. Likewise, if I *dislike* Fords, I might be more attuned to noticing Fords on the side of the road with mechanical problems, and to remembering stories told by unhappy Ford owners. My estimates of how common Plymouths are, and how reliable Fords are, will be biased by my likes and dislikes.

This line of influence is startlingly relevant to personal beliefs and attitudes, and topics like prejudice. If a person has a bias or prejudice against members of a particular group, that person is more likely to notice actions and events that match the prejudice or stereotype—and then, of course, the inflated estimate gets stored in memory. As a consequence, any time a judgment is made, it's based on the inflated or biased knowledge in memory.

To continue with the analogy to car preferences, it may not matter how many Fords I see *without* mechanical difficulties. What probably matters more is how I notice, and store in memory, instances in which Fords break down. I end up maintaining and strengthening my prejudice by the frequency with which I notice evidence—and of course by selectively focusing on evidence that confirms my beliefs. Similarly, I may simply ignore Plymouths with mechanical problems, thus accentuating the halo effect in the direction of my preference. In the same fashion, the racist only notices and stores events that conform to the prejudice—that's the confirmation bias. Then, based on the availability heuristic, that biased information is easier to retrieve than neutral or positive information. (Selective focusing on evidence that supports one's beliefs may even include behavioral scientists; see Nisbett, 1995, and R. J. Sternberg, 1995, on commentaries about Herrnstein and Murray's, 1994, *The Bell Curve*.)

Familiarity Biases

Another source, studied directly by Tversky and Kahneman, shows very clearly how the bias in availability is related to ease of recall (**the familiarity bias**). The authors constructed lists of names, 39 names per list, with 19 women's and 20 men's names on each. One group of participants heard the lists, and then had to recall as many names as they could remember. Another group heard the lists, then estimated whether the list contained more names of men or women. In two of the four lists that were tested, the women's names were famous (e.g., Elizabeth Taylor) and the men's names were not; in the other two lists, the men's names were famous (e.g., Richard Nixon), and the women's names were not.

People recalled more of the famous names (12 out of 19) than the less famous names (8 out of 20). More interestingly, the groups that had to estimate the proportion of male versus female names were influenced by fame and familiarity. Participants who heard the "famous female" lists estimated that there had been more women's names, and those who heard the "famous male" lists said there had been more men's names. Thus there was clear evidence that the famous names were indeed more easily recalled and that this greater availability for recall influenced the estimates of frequency.

Salience and Vividness Biases

Especially salient or vivid events leave a strong record on the information stored in long-term memory, which then can also bias our reasoning. Thus, hearing or reading even just one vivid story of an airplane crash can influence your estimate of airline safety far more than dull, dry statistical evidence can. The news accounts of an airline accident are far more vivid, and are given far more attention, than accounts of passenger car accidents. And even though airplane crashes are rare, the number of victims involved is often dramatic enough that the event makes a much stronger impression than is objectively called for.

Thus, when you estimate air versus car safety factors, the vividness of the recalled information tends to bias your judgment. (For those who *do* know intellectually that air travel is safer, we might look for other evidence of the bias—for instance, people are surely more nervous when traveling in an airliner, on the average, than when traveling in a private car.)

In essence, any factor that leads to biased or flawed or incomplete information in memory can introduce bias in our reasoning, since our judgments are based on what can be remembered easily. If reasonably accurate and undistorted information is in memory, then the availability heuristic probably does a reasonable job. But to the extent that our memory contains information that is inaccurate, incomplete, or influenced by nonobjective factors, there may be biases and distortions in our reasoning.

THE REPRESENTATIVENESS HEURISTIC

If you toss a coin six times in a row, which of the following two outcomes is more likely, HHHTTT or HHTHTT? Most of us would agree, and quite rapidly at that, that the second alternative, the one with the alternations between heads and tails, is more likely than the run of three heads followed by three tails. But we're wrong—if you'll stop and think about it for a moment, you'll realize that each of these alternatives is *exactly* as likely as the other. Each is *just one* of the possible ways six coin tosses can occur (the total number of distinct outcomes is 2 to the sixth, i.e., 64 distinct sequences of heads and tails).

What goes wrong when we make such decisions? According to Kahneman and Tversky (1972), we're basing our decision on the *representativeness heuristic*. We're thinking of coin tosses as a random process, and HHTHTT *looks* more random than HHHTTT—HHTHTT *looks* more representative of a random process. But this is incorrect here, since the problem asked about the likelihood of *these two* sequences, not the general class of sequences with alternations.

The **representativeness heuristic** is a judgment strategy in which we make estimates based on how similar an event seems to its population. More specifically, we estimate the probability of an event based on

(a) whether the event seems similar to the process that produced it, or

(b) how similar the event is to the population of events it came from.

Let's consider (a) first. For the coin toss example, the process that produced it is known to be random, so we judge the event on how similar it is to a random process. A particular flaw in reasoning here involves a general *insensitivity to sample size*. That is, people fail to take into account the size of the sample or group on which the event is based. It's a fact of sampling and statistics that a small sample will be less representative of a population than a larger sample will be. A consequence is that small samples are more likely to have noticeably "unusual" characteristics—the "unusual" will be much less noticeable in a larger sample. (See Pollatsek, Konold, Well, & Lima, 1984, for evidence on people's beliefs about random sampling processes.)

Another way of expressing this insensitivity is that people believe in *the "law" of small numbers*. Now, the *law of large numbers*—that a *large* sample will be more representative of its population—is true. But people erroneously believe that the law of small numbers is true as well. People incorrectly assume that a small sample will be just as representative as a large sample will (see also Bar-Hillel, 1980). For a telling example, consider ★ Kahneman and Tversky's (1972) "hospital births" problem in Table 11.4.

Stereotypes

Now let's turn to (b), how similar the event is to the population it came from. Perhaps the most obvious application of this type of judgment involves stereotypes—and it's the most heavily investigated in the research too. Kahneman and Tversky (1973) reported some fascinating evidence on estimates based on personality descriptions. They read various personality descriptions to their participants, then had them estimate the likelihood or probability that the described individual was a member of one versus another profession.

★ **TABLE 11.4**

Hospital Births

In a certain town there are two hospitals, one in which about 45 babies are born each day, the other only about 15 per day. Typically, of course, about 50 percent of all births are baby boys, although this percentage varies somewhat from day to day. Across one year, both hospitals kept track of the number of days on which 60 percent or more of the births were male babies. Which hospital do you think had more such days, the smaller hospital, the larger hospital, or is it about the same for both?

Hint: Reason by analogy from another 50-50 situation, coin tosses. The 60 percent or more criterion would mean 9 or more heads out of 15 tosses (the small sample), and 27 or more heads out of 45 tosses (the large sample).

Solution: Sixty percent or more males is not particularly extreme for the smaller hospital, but is very extreme for the larger hospital. If you said the larger hospital, or decided that it would be the same for both, you've fallen for the "law of small numbers," that the small sample should be as representative as the larger sample.

Source: Adapted from Kahneman and Tversky (1972, p. 443).

To a surprising degree, people's estimations were influenced by the similarity of a description to a widely held stereotype.

Here's a typical situation given to participants in this research. Imagine that 100 people are in a room, 70 of them lawyers, 30 of them engineers. Given this situation, answer the following question:

1. *An individual named Bill was randomly selected from this roomful of 100 people. What is the likelihood that Bill is a lawyer?*

Simple probability tells us that the chances of selecting a lawyer are .70, given the situation described. And people generally reason correctly in such situations, according to Kahneman and Tversky, that is, in a "bare bones" situation. The technical term for these "bare bones," the 70:30 proportion, is *prior odds* or simply, *base rates*. Prior to any other information, the base rate of sampling a lawyer is .70, and .30 for sampling an engineer.

Consider now two slightly different situations. There are still the same 70 lawyers and 30 engineers. But now you are given a description of two randomly selected individuals, and are asked "what is the likelihood that this individual is an engineer?" (adapted from Kahneman & Tversky, 1973, pp. 241–242):

2. *"Dick is a 30-year-old man. He is married with no children. A man of high ability and high motivation, he promises to be quite successful in his field. He is well liked by his colleagues."*
3. *"Jack is a 45-year-old man. He is married and has four children. He is generally conservative, careful, and ambitious. He shows no interest in political and social issues and spends most of his free time on his many hobbies, which include home carpentry, sailing, and mathematical puzzles."*

"This CD player costs less than players selling for twice as much."

Drawing by Weber © 1989, The New Yorker Magazine, Inc.

Kahneman and Tversky's participants did not judge the probabilities for these two descriptions to be the same as the prior odds, that is, .70 for lawyers, .30 for engineers. Instead, they assumed that the personality descriptions contained relevant information, and adjusted their estimates accordingly. In particular, for both descriptions 2 and 3, people responded that the probability was close to .50, that is, about a 50-50 chance that Dick and Jack were engineers.

Description 3 was intended to resemble the stereotype many people have of engineers. It mentions such factors as "careful" and "mathematical puzzles," which presumably are representative of engineers—at least they are representative of our *stereotypes* of engineers. Here, participants essentially ignored the prior odds, and based their judgments on the description itself. Surprisingly, people ignored the base rates with description 2 as well, even though that description was intentionally written to be totally uninformative with regard to Dick's profession. That is, despite the irrelevance of the personality description, people viewed it as evidence for a more accurate prediction (e.g., Fischhoff & Bar-Hillel, 1984). As Kahneman and Tversky put it, "people respond differently when given no specific evidence and when given worthless evidence. When no specific evidence is given, the prior probabilities [base rates] are properly utilized; when worthless specific evidence is given, prior probabilities are ignored" (1973, p. 242).

In both cases 2 and 3, the appropriate strategy is to weight the new evidence, taking into account its predictive accuracy along with the prior odds. Instead, people went with the descriptions, as if stereotypes are highly informative, or as if *any* information is informative (or possibly as if the participants inferred that the information was *intended* to be informative; see the Be Relevant conversational maxim in Chapter 9).

THE SIMULATION HEURISTIC

The final heuristic to be discussed is called the **simulation heuristic.** In this heuristic, we are asked to *make a prediction of some future event, or imagine a different outcome of some event or action*. The use of the term *simulation* here comes from computer simulation, in which certain "starting" values are entered into the program, and the simulation then proceeds to forecast or predict some set of outcomes. In similar fashion, we apply the simulation heuristic by substituting different "starting" values into our own mental model of a situation, to see if that changes the outcome. In almost all cases, the "ease of imagining" these different values ends up determining how we use the heuristic.

Think about the following setting, an example discussed by Kahneman and Tversky (1982):

> *Mr. Crane and Mr. Tees were scheduled to leave the airport on different flights, at the same time. They traveled from town in the same limousine, were caught in a traffic jam, and arrived at the airport 30 minutes after the scheduled departure time of their flights. Mr. Crane is told that his flight left on time. Mr. Tees is told that his flight was delayed, and just left five minutes ago. Who is more upset, Mr. Crane or Mr. Tees?* (p. 203)

As you would expect, almost everyone decides that Mr. Tees is more upset—96 percent of Kahneman and Tversky's participants made this judgment. The unusual aspect of this, as the authors note, is that from an objective standpoint, Mr. Crane and Mr. Tees are in *identical* positions—they both *expected* to miss their planes, because of the traffic jam, and in fact both of them did.

So why is Mr. Tees more upset? Because it was more "possible," in some sense, for him to have caught his flight. That is to say, you can easily imagine ways in which the limousine might have arrived only 15 or 20 minutes late—the traffic jam cleared, the driver found an alternate route, and so forth. All of these scenarios involve the simulation heuristic, in which the initial values (e.g., traffic jam, departure time, etc.) are entered into the person's mental simulation of "getting to the airport as quickly as possible." Because it's easier to imagine an outcome in which the limousine arrives a few minutes earlier than it is to imagine one in which it arrives a half hour earlier, we feel that the traveler who "nearly caught his flight" will be more upset.

The Undoing Heuristic

A more complete example of the simulation heuristic, including the data reported by Kahneman and Tversky (1982), is contained in Table 11.5 (p. 374). This example illustrates a particular version of the simulation heuristic, which involves **undoing** some outcome by changing the events that led up to it. Read the story now, and decide how you would complete the "If only . . ." phrase before continuing.

TABLE 11.5

Stories for the Simulation Heuristic

Route Version

1. Mr. Jones was 47 years old, the father of three, and a successful banking executive. His wife has been ill at home for several months.

2a. On the day of the accident, Mr. Jones left his office at the regular time. He sometimes left early to take care of home chores at his wife's request, but this was not necessary on that day. Mr. Jones did not drive home by his regular route. The day was exceptionally clear and Mr. Jones told his friends at the office that he would drive along the shore to enjoy the view.

3. The accident occurred at a major intersection. The light turned amber as Mr. Jones approached. Witnesses noted that he braked hard to stop at the crossing, although he could easily have gone through. His family recognized this as a common occurrence in Mr. Jones's driving. As he began to cross after the light changed, a light truck charged into the intersection at top speed and rammed Mr. Jones's car from the left. Mr. Jones was killed instantly.

4a. It was later ascertained that the truck was driven by a teenage boy, who was under the influence of drugs.

5. As commonly happens in such situations, the Jones family and their friends often thought and often said, "If only . . . ," during the days that followed the accident. How did they continue this thought? Please write one or more likely completions.

Time Version

Substitute for 2a:

2b. On the day of the accident, Mr. Jones left the office earlier than usual to attend to some household chores at his wife's request. He drove home along his regular route. Mr. Jones occasionally chose to drive along the shore, to enjoy the view on exceptionally clear days, but that day was just average.

"Boy" Focus Version

Substitute for 4a:

4b. It was later ascertained that the truck was driven by a teenage boy named Tom Searler. Tom's father had just found him at home under the influence of drugs. This was a common occurrence, as Tom used drugs heavily. There had been a quarrel, during which Tom grabbed the keys that were lying on the living room table and drove off blindly. He was severely injured in the accident.

Percentage of Participants Responding to the "If Only" Stem in the Five Different Categories of Responses

Response Category	*Story Version*	
"If only" completion focuses on	*Route*	*Time*
Route	51%	13%
Time	3	26
Crossing	21	31
Boy	20	29
Other	5	1

Source: From Kahneman and Tversky (1982).

Kahneman and Tversky found a strong tendency for people to favor one particular type of change in their "if only . . ." completions, one in which an unusual detail in the story is changed to a more normal value, a change that "normalizes" the story. For the Mr. Jones story, participants wrote "if only he had taken his regular route home"; if they read the "Time Version" in the table, they often wrote "if only he hadn't left work early," and so forth. By analogy to cross-country skiing, Kahneman and Tversky called such changes *downhill changes*—it's easier to ski downhill, and it's easier to think of *normal* values like leaving work on time and taking your normal route home in such scenarios.

Skiing *uphill* is very difficult—and *uphill changes* in the scenarios, in which a normal detail is changed to an unusual one, were quite rare, as shown in the "Other" category in the table. For example, an uphill change might be "if only his car had a flat tire when he got to the parking lot." Why did only 5 percent of the participants make such changes? Again, the reason has to do with ease of imagining—unusual or atypical events are almost by definition more difficult to retrieve from memory, so harder to imagine in the scenario. Likewise, *horizontal changes*, in which one detail is substituted for another of comparable likelihood, were "nonexistent," in Kahneman and Tversky's results (an example might be having him arrive at the intersection 2 or 3 seconds earlier).

The biases operating here are clearly related to retrieval from memory—a downhill change normalizes the story by removing an unusual detail and substituting a regular, easily imagined one in its place. There's also the element of plausibility at work here—it's more plausible that Mr. Jones left on time than that he left early but then had a flat tire.

Strangely, people seldom focused on the teenage boy, and seldom altered anything concerning his behavior, even though he was the actual *cause* of the accident. Kahneman and Tversky speculated that this was due to a *focus rule*, that we tend to maintain properties of the main object or focus of the story unless a different focus is provided; this is of course consistent with Gernsbacher's (e.g., 1990) results on the advantage of first mention, which you learned about in Chapter 9. In support of this speculation, different participants read the alternate version of the story shown at the bottom of the table ("Boy Focus"), in which the boy becomes the principal focus. With that change in focus, 68 percent of the participants changed the boy's actions in their "if only" completions, versus only 20 percent of the participants in the original version of the story (and 29 percent in the Time version).

It's also—in case you hadn't noticed—a rather clear case of *blaming the victim*. It's almost as if people judge Mr. Jones to be in some way responsible for his own death *because* he left work early or took a different route than his usual. An astonishing number of situations seem to call forth this kind of illogic (did you ever hear anyone say, "He was in the 'wrong place' at the 'wrong time'"?).

Hindsight

Notice, finally, that the simulation heuristic provides a compelling explanation of the *hindsight effect*, the after-the-fact feeling that some event was very likely to happen or was very predictable, even though it wasn't predicted to happen *beforehand*. Now that the event is over, it's very easy to imagine how the event could have happened—it *just* did! Because the scenario is now easy to imagine, we feel as if the outcome should have been easy to predict ahead of time.

Interestingly, the availability of the actual outcome tends to make *other* possible outcomes less plausible than they were earlier. In other words, the hindsight effect may be nothing more than a bias in which otherwise plausible outcomes are now less easy to imagine than the outcome that actually happened (for recent evidence on hindsight bias, see Hell, Gigerenzer, Gauggel, Mall, & Muller, 1988, and Hoch & Loewenstein, 1989).

Anticipating Outcomes

Related situations involve cases in which you anticipate both positive and negative outcomes of some (future) event, and then decide what to do based on those anticipations. Hoch (1984) found that generating *favorable* outcomes first tends to blind us to possible negative outcomes, and also makes us more "certain" that a favorable outcome will actually happen. On the other hand, if people generate reasons for why some outcome might *not* happen, their confidence in their predictions tends to be much more realistic (Hoch, 1985).

The warning should be clear—overly optimistic predictions at the outset will then bias our ability to imagine negative outcomes, and will inflate our view of the likelihood of a positive outcome. ("Aw, come on, what could go wrong if I wait until next week to start my term paper?")

Mental Models of the Physical World

It's easy to think that the simulation heuristic only applies in very hypothetical, "if only" situations like those we've been discussing. But this isn't so—*any* reasoning and predicting based on our understanding of a situation involve a similar "what if" process. Some of the most fascinating—and entertaining—evidence on this comes from research on mental models, in particular our models of the physical world and mechanical devices.

Let's define the term **mental model** as simply your *knowledge of a domain*, whether a simple device like a water faucet or something complex like a computer, and see what kind of reasoning difficulties people have because of incorrect or incomplete domain knowledge. (People's awareness that they *do not know* something is actually quite interesting itself; see Gentner & Collins, 1981, and Glucksberg & McCloskey, 1981.)

"Naive Physics"

■ Look at the diagrams in Figure 11.6 and answer the questions. These problems are taken from research by McCloskey and his colleagues, tapping into people's understanding of the motion in the physical world. By asking students to complete such diagrams, and then explain their answers, McCloskey (e.g., 1983) has provided a very convincing example of the misconceptions or faulty mental models that people often have—in physics, the misconceptions are called **naive physics.**

For instance, in one of his studies (McCloskey, Caramazza, & Green, 1980), 51 percent of the participants believed that a marble would follow a curved path after leaving the tube; often they added that the path would eventually straighten out. More dramatically, 60 percent of McCloskey's participants gave incorrect answers to the airplane-bomb problem. In the similar cliff problem, 22 percent drew paths that showed the ball moving in an arc for some time but thereafter falling straight down.

FIGURE 11.6

Stimuli used by McCloskey. (From McCloskey, 1983.)

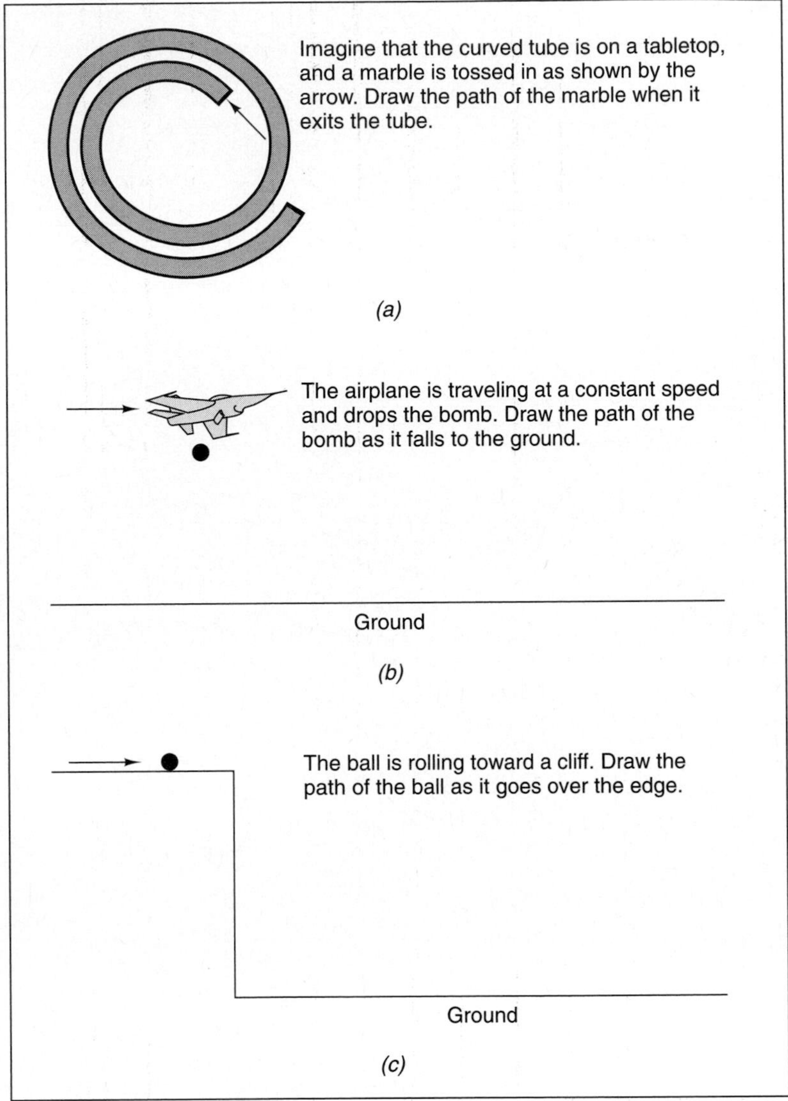

Imagine that the curved tube is on a tabletop, and a marble is tossed in as shown by the arrow. Draw the path of the marble when it exits the tube.
(a)
The airplane is traveling at a constant speed and drops the bomb. Draw the path of the bomb as it falls to the ground.
Ground
(b)
The ball is rolling toward a cliff. Draw the path of the ball as it goes over the edge.
Ground
(c)

The correct answers to all three diagrams are shown on the left in Figure 11.7 (p. 378), along with the percentages of participants who gave the correct answers. The right side of the figure shows some of the most common incorrect answers, along with the relevant percentages. For the airplane-bomb problem, two other errors are also shown, the forward diagonal path that comes closest to correct, and the "to the rear" pathway that was almost as common as the forward diagonal.

FIGURE 11.7

Correct and incorrect pathways, along with the percentages of participants making each response. (From McCloskey, 1983.)

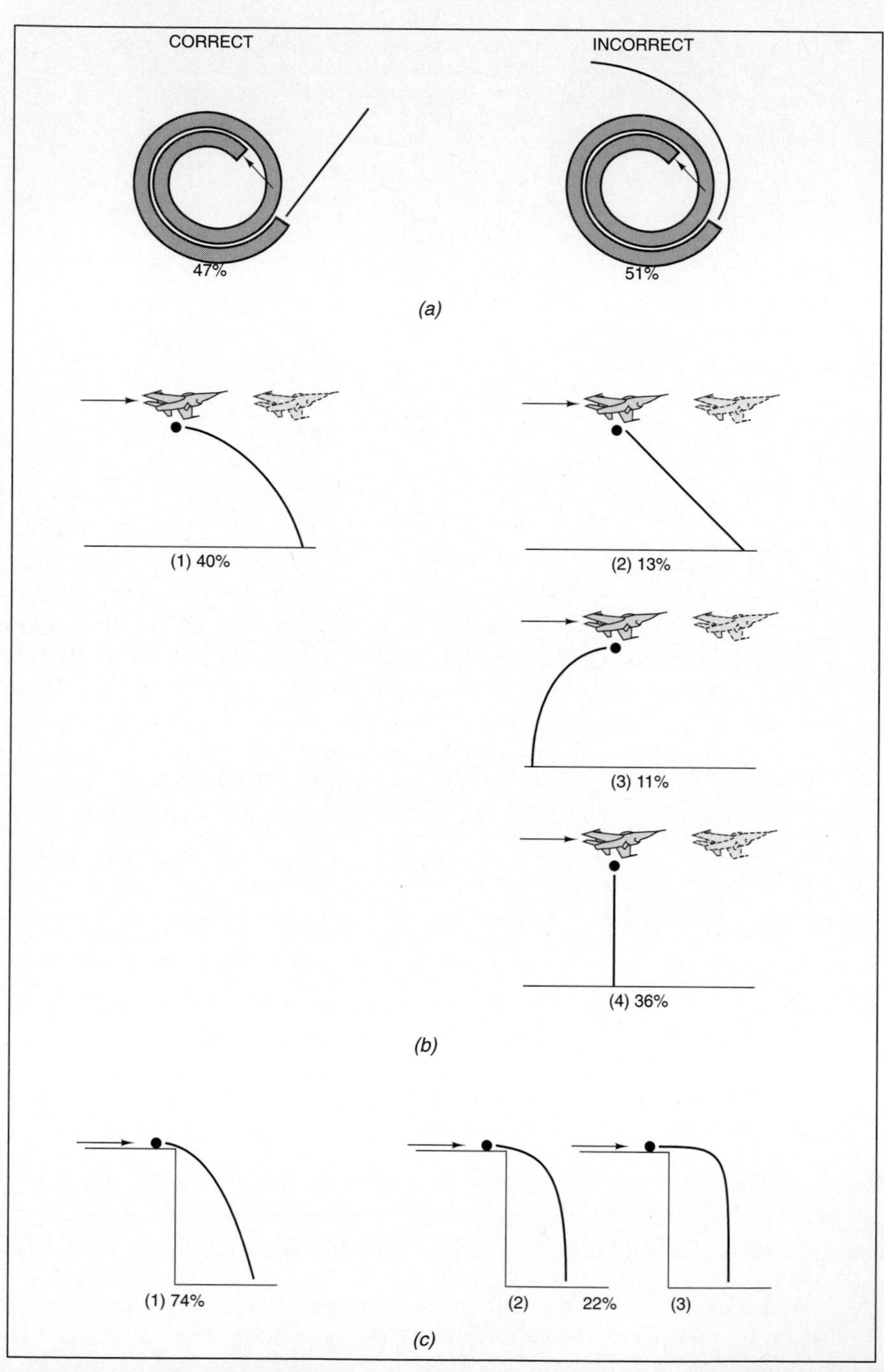

Correcting Misconceptions

★ The misconceptions people often have of these problems are listed in Table 11.6, along with an explanation of the principles leading to correct decisions. If you made any of these mistakes on the motion problems, why haven't you noticed before, in everyday experience, that your mental model is wrong? When you want your house to warm up, say to 70 degrees, do you turn the furnace thermostat up to 80 to make it heat up more rapidly, as if the thermostat works like a water faucet? Do you push the elevator button even if it's already been pushed, the way you'd ring a doorbell repeatedly?

Some sources of difficulty in reasoning are known, especially when the problems are difficult or the principles underlying them are complex (e.g., Medin & Edelson, 1988; Proffitt, Kaiser, & Whelan, 1990). And we do know that relevant instruction and training can improve our reasoning, in physics (e.g., Donley & Ashcraft, 1992), and in probability and statistics (e.g., Agnoli & Krantz, 1989; Fong & Nisbett, 1991).

On the other hand, misconceptions and faulty reasoning can persist even when the individual is aware of the inconsistencies—Shafir and Tversky (1992), for example, found evidence of "quasi-magical" thinking (1992), in which we do something even though we

★ **TABLE 11.6**

Misconceptions and Principles of Physics

1. Curved tube and marble
   Misconception: That the marble will acquire a "circular impetus" as it travels in a curved direction through the tube, so then carries that impetus with it when it exits the tube. Sometimes the path is said to straighten out as the circular impetus "dissipates."
   Principles of physics: There is no such thing as circular impetus being imparted into the marble. Newton's first law of motion applies here; a body persists in its state of rest or of uniform motion in a straight line unless a force is applied to it. Specifically, the path of the marble is a straight line, tangent to the side of the tube at the exit point.

2. Airplane and bomb
   Misconception: That the bomb will fall straight down, because it was being carried passively by the airplane (i.e., that being carried passively negates the forward force applied by the airplane).
   Principles of physics: Being carried passively is irrelevant—the bomb was moving in a forward direction, to which the force of gravity is added when it's released from the airplane. The two forces combine, yielding a parabolic pathway. This is Newton's second law of motion, in which all the forces applied to a body are summed together.

3. Cliff and ball
   Misconception: That the active movement of the ball means there will be a different pathway from that in the airplane-bomb question. A surprisingly frequent error is a "straight out, then straight down" pathway, sometimes referred to as the "Road Runner Effect," from the cartoon.
   Principles of physics: As in the airplane and bomb question, the forward motion sums with the force due to gravity, producing a parabolic curve.

know it does not cause an event to happen (push the elevator button again? knock on wood?). In other cases, however, it's simply unclear why misconceptions develop, or why they are held so strongly despite evidence from the environment, even in the face of expertise (Hecht & Proffitt, 1995). Maybe it's a genuine metacognitive paradox—we often have useful insights into our own mental processing, and just as often have no insight at all.

Summary

1. Algorithms are systematic rules and procedures that generate correct answers to problems, whereas heuristics are quick rules of thumb that are often useful, but are not guaranteed to yield the correct solution. Often because we don't know the correct algorithm, or because it's too difficult or impractical to use, we rely on heuristic processing.
2. In the availability heuristic, people judge the likelihood of events by how easily they can remember examples or instances. These judgments can therefore be biased by any factor, such as frequency, familiarity, or salience and vividness, that affects the information stored in memory. In combination with the confirmation bias, this kind of heuristic may explain how people hold and strengthen prejudiced beliefs.
3. In the representativeness heuristic, we judge the likelihood of outcomes based on how representative they seem, for example if a sequence of heads and tails looks like a random sequence, or if an individual matches a stereotype.
4. In the simulation heuristic, people forecast or predict how some outcome could have been different. These forecasts are influenced by how easily the alternative outcomes can be imagined, and by factors such as the focus of a story or setting. These forecasts are based on informal mental models, as are situations like predicting the path of a moving object. Incompleteness or misconceptions in the mental model lead to errors in reasoning.

Important Terms

algorithm
availability heuristic
conditional reasoning—antecedent, consequent
confirmation bias
distance effect
familiarity bias
heuristic
jnd
mental models
modus ponens
modus tollens
naive physics
psychophysics
representativeness heuristic
salience and vividness
semantic congruity effect
simulation heuristic
syllogisms/categorical syllogisms
symbolic distance
top-down bias
undoing

Suggested Readings

For treatments of reasoning by analogy, a topic not covered here, see Bassok (1996), Holyoak (1985), and R. J. Sternberg (1977); Casey (1993) discusses this in the context of working memory overload, and Schunn and Dunbar (1996) examine the priming of analogical relationships. Contrast this with situations in which correct solutions and reasoning strategies in other domains did not generalize to unfamiliar, abstract problems (e.g., Catrambone, Jones, Jonides, & Seifert, 1995).

Additional readings on naive physics beliefs include papers by Cooke and Breedin (1994), Freyd and Jones (1994), and Ranney (1994). McCloskey and Kohl (1983) discuss curvilinear impetus, and McCloskey, Washburn, and Felch (1983) discuss the straight-down belief.

Kahneman et al. (1982) is an excellent collection of relevant papers on decision making and reasoning, and Kahneman and Tversky (1996) is a recent restatement and elaboration of the entire research program. For research on medical decision making, see such papers as Norman, Brooks, Coblentz, and Babcock (1992), and Patel and Groen (1986). Keren and Wagenaar (1985) have discussed decisions and heuristic strategies in blackjack. Recent work on the training of statistical and deductive-reasoning processes is presented in Fong, Krantz, and Nisbett (1986), and Cheng, Holyoak, Nisbett, and Oliver (1986). See Nisbett, Krantz, Jepson, and Kunda (1983) on statistical heuristics people use in everyday reasoning.

CHAPTER TWELVE

PROBLEM SOLVING

We're now ready to wrap up our exploration of cognition, by turning to the slow and deliberate cognitive processing called problem solving. Just as in the area of decision making and reasoning, problem solving studies an individual who is confronted with a difficult, time-consuming task—a problem has been presented, the solution to the problem is not immediately obvious, and the individual is often uncertain what to do next.

In Newell and Simon's (1972) thumbnail description, "A person is confronted with a *problem* when he wants something and does not know immediately what series of actions he can perform to get it" (p. 72). The "something" is of course the **goal,** the desired end point or solution of the problem-solving activity. Problem solving thus consists of goal-directed activity, going from an *initial state* to a final *goal state*, often by moving through a series of intermediate steps. The difficulty, of course, is in determining *which* intermediate ★ steps are on the correct pathway, and in figuring out how to get to those intermediate steps.

Let's start with a simple recreational problem (Anderson, 1993). It will only take you a minute or two to solve the problem, even if you're one of those people who loses patience with "brain teasers" very quickly; for instance, the nine-year-old tested by VanLehn (1989) seemed to understand it completely in about 20 seconds, and solved it out loud in about two minutes. (In other words, resist the temptation to look at the end of the chapter for the answer—just go ahead and solve the problem, like the nine-year-old did.)

> ***Three Men and a Rowboat.*** *Three men want to cross a river. They find a boat, but it is a very small boat. It will only hold 200 pounds. The men are named Large, Medium, and Small. Large weighs 200 pounds, Medium weighs 120 pounds, and Small weighs 80 pounds. How can they all get across? They might have to make several trips in the boat.* (p. 532)

My favorite example of "problem solving in action" is the following true story. As a graduate student, I attended a departmental colloquium at which a candidate for a faculty position was to present his research. As he started his talk, he realized that his first slide was projected too low on the screen. A flurry of activity around the projector ensued, one professor asking out loud, "Does anyone have a book or something?" Someone volunteered a book, the professor tried it, but it was too thick—the slide image was now too high. "No, this one's too big. Anyone got a thinner one?" he continued. After several more seconds of hurried searching for something thinner, another professor finally exclaimed, "Well, for Pete's sake, I don't believe this!" He marched over to the projector, grabbed the book, opened it halfway, and then put it under the projector. He looked around the lecture hall and shook his head, saying, "I can't believe it. A roomful of Ph.D.s, and no one knows how to *open a book!*"

Why are we interested in such recreational problems? The answer is very straightforward. As is typical of *all* scientific disciplines, cognitive science studies the simple before the complex, identifying principles there that will generalize to more difficult settings. This strategy maintains that we can often see large-scale issues and important processes more clearly when they are embedded in simple situations (this is *science's* problem-solving heuristic).

You'll notice as you read this chapter that problem-solving research is rather different from the cognitive research you've been studying throughout this book. Newell and Simon (1972), two genuine pioneers in this area, pointed out that studies of problem solving must—almost by definition—adopt different methodologies and techniques of investigation. That is, to study problem solving we must examine a lengthy sample of behavior, sometimes up to 20 or 30 minutes' worth of activity. This often makes the typical measures of performance like RT and accuracy rather irrelevant or useless. Instead, the most common form of data in problem solving is the **verbal protocol** (sometimes just called **verbal report**), a transcription and analysis of the participants' verbalizations as they solve the problem.

But wait—there's an issue here that you need to understand. While almost all problem-solving research relies on verbal reports, not all cognitive scientists agree that verbal reports are completely trustworthy. In other words, the status of verbal protocols as scientific *data* is still a topic of some debate; see Ericsson and Simon (1980; 1993) and Russo, Johnson, and Stephens (1989) for contrasting views. For example, there is sometimes a concern that requiring participants to verbalize their thoughts may in fact change the nature of their problem-solving activity—you may solve a problem differently if you have to talk out loud about how you are solving it (for supportive data, see Schooler, Ohlsson, & Brooks, 1993). If so, then heavy reliance on verbal protocols may be misguided, may lead to ungeneralizable results. On the other hand, it's probably also true that the only way to discover the processes that really go into problem solving is by having people actually solve problems, then analyzing what they say.

Good Advice: Possibly more than in any material you've read so far, it's important for you to work the examples and problems in this chapter. Hints usually accompany the problems, and the solutions to all problems are presented either in the text or at the end of the chapter. You'll discover many of the insights of the problem-solving literature on your own as you work through the sample problems, and in the process you'll understand the material better. An added benefit is that you'll probably improve your own problem-solving skills—to paraphrase Bruner (1973), no one ever gets better at problem solving without solving problems.

Classic Problem-solving Research

Preview: *gestalt* defined; early *Gestalt* research; functional fixedness; negative set

Let's begin with a description of the earliest problem-solving research, done by the Gestalt psychologists during the period 1920–1950. Although this work was rather ignored during the behaviorist era in the United States, it was rediscovered with the advent of cognitive psychology, and has become an important influence on current work.

GESTALT PSYCHOLOGY AND PROBLEM SOLVING

Gestalt is a German word that translates *very* poorly into English—the one-word translations of "whole" or "field" fail miserably at indicating what the term actually means. Roughly speaking, a **gestalt** refers to a *whole pattern or a configuration*. It is a cohesive grouping, a perspective from which the entire "field" can be seen. A variety of translations have been used at one point or another (*holism* is probably the best of them; note, however, that holistic psychology, whatever that is, is certainly *not* the same as Gestalt psychology). No single translation of the word ever caught on, however, so we simply use the German term *gestalt* itself. The basic principles of the Gestalt approach are

- first, that humans perceive *wholes* or patterns, rather than pieces or parts, and
- second, the familiar notion that the whole is different from, or greater than, the sum of its individual parts.

(Think *way* back, to Chapter 2, where you read about Biederman's work on the perception of objects. His approach claimed that wholes are made up of *geons*, and that we rely on those geons to recognize whole patterns. It's rather opposite to the Gestalt ideas, isn't it?)

Early Gestalt Research

The connection between the term *gestalt* and problem solving is best explained by anecdote (see Boring, 1950, pp. 595–597). In 1913, Wolfgang Kohler, a German psychologist, went to the Spanish island of Teneriffe to study the behavior of apes. Stranded there by the outbreak of World War I, Kohler decided to study visual discrimination among several animal species, and began to apply Gestalt principles to animal perception. His ultimate conclusion, in essence, was that animals do not perceive individual elements in a stimulus, but that they perceive *relations* among stimuli. Furthermore, "Kohler also observed that the perception of relations is a mark of intelligence, and he called the sudden perception of useful or proper relations *insight*" (Boring, 1950, p. 596).

Kohler pursued "insight learning" by presenting problems to his subjects, and searching for evidence of genuine problem solving in their behavior. The best-known subject was a chimpanzee named Sultan (Kohler, 1927). In a simple demonstration, Sultan was able to use a long pole to reach through the bars of his cage and get a bunch of bananas. When given two short poles, neither of which was long enough to reach the bananas, Sultan (as the story goes) suddenly went over to the poles and put one inside the end of the other, thus creating *one* pole that was long enough to reach the bananas. Sultan also discovered how to stand on a box to reach a banana that was otherwise too high to reach, and to stack two boxes to reach even higher. All of these solutions seemed to illustrate Sultan's perception of *relations*, and the importance of insight in problem solving.

DIFFICULTIES IN PROBLEM SOLVING

Other Gestalt psychologists, most notably Duncker and Luchins, pursued the research tradition with human participants. Two major contributions of this later work are gener-

Grande builds a three-box structure to reach the bananas, while Sultan watches from the ground. *Insight*, sometimes referred to as an "Ah-ha" experience, was the term Kohler used for the sudden perception of useful relations among objects during problem solving.

ally acknowledged, essentially the two sides of the problem-solving coin. One involved *negative* effects related to rigidity or difficulty in problem solving. The other investigated *positive* effects like insight and creativity during problem solving.

Functional Fixedness

One particular difficulty in problem solving is called **functional fixedness,** a tendency to use objects and concepts in the problem environment in only their customary and usual way. Maier (1931), for instance, had human subjects work on the Two String problem.

> *Two strings are suspended from the ceiling, and the goal is to tie them together. The problem is that the strings are too far apart for a person merely to hold one, reach the other, then tie them together. Available to the subject are several other objects, including a chair, some paper, and a pair of pliers. Even standing on the chair does not get the subject close enough to the two strings.*

Only 39 percent of Maier's participants came up with the correct solution during a ten-minute period. The solution (if you haven't tried solving the problem, do so now) involves using an object in the room in a *novel* fashion—tie the pliers to one string, swing it like a pendulum, then catch it while holding the other string. Thus, the functional fixedness in this situation was failing to conceive of the pliers in any but their customary function—people were *fixed* on the normal use for pliers, and failed to appreciate how they could be used as a weight for a pendulum. A similar demonstration is illustrated in Figure 12.1, the Candle problem from Duncker (1945).

FIGURE 12.1

The Candle problem. Using only the pictured objects, figure out how to mount the candle to the wall or door.

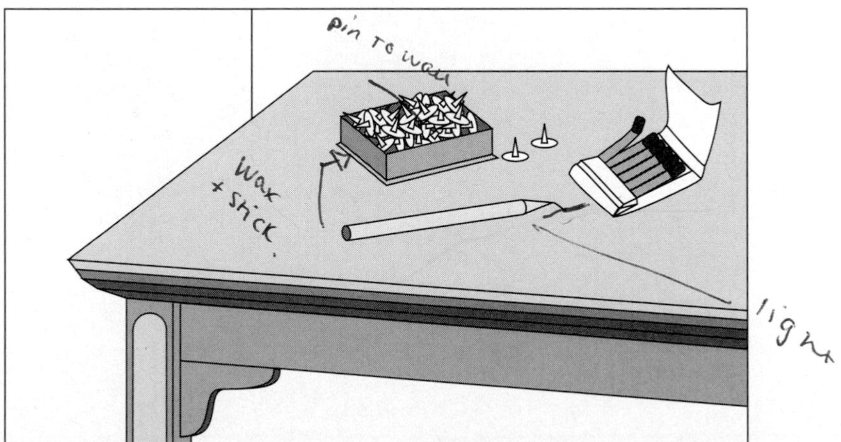

(*Hint:* Can you think of another use for a box besides using it as a container? *Solution:* Empty the box, thumbtack it to the wall, and mount the candle in the box.) (From Duncker, 1945.)

In brief, the notion of functional fixedness is that we generally think of only the customary uses for objects, whereas successful problem solving often involves finding *novel* uses for objects. What leads us into functional fixedness is our general knowledge. When you find PLIERS in semantic memory, the most accessible properties for retrieval involve the normal uses for pliers, not properties like their weight or shape; and likewise, the roomful of Ph.D.s didn't think about the thickness of an opened book (see Greenspan, 1986, for evidence on retrieval of central vs. peripheral properties). Simply from the standpoint of retrieval from memory, we can understand why people often experience functional fixedness.

Negative Set

A related difficulty in problem solving is termed **negative set** (or simply set effects). This refers to a bias or tendency to solve problems in one particular way, using a single approach, even when a different approach might be more productive. The term set is a rough translation of the original German term *Einstellung*, which means something like "approach" or "orientation"; the (awful) word "mind-set" is probably the closest expression we have in English.

TABLE 12.1

Luchins's (1942) Water Jug Problems

Sample Problems	*Capacity of Jug A*	*Capacity of Jug B*	*Capacity of Jug C*	*Desired Quantity*
1	5 cups	40 cups	18 cups	28 cups
2	21 cups	127 cups	3 cups	100 cups

Luchins's Water Jug Problems

Problems	*Capacity of Jug A*	*Capacity of Jug B*	*Capacity of Jug C*	*Desired Quantity*
1	21	127	3	100
2	14	163	25	99
3	18	43	10	5
4	9	42	6	21
5	20	59	4	31
6	23	49	3	20
7	15	39	3	18
8	28	76	3	25
9	18	48	4	22
10	14	36	8	6

Note: All volumes are in cups.

Source: From Luchins (1942).

Table 12.1 shows the classic Water Jug problems studied by Luchins (1942). In these problems, you are given three jugs, each of a different capacity, and are asked to measure out a desired quantity of water using just the three jugs. Work the two sample problems at the top of the table. The first illustrates a simple *addition solution*—you need to measure out 28 cups of water, so fill A twice then C once for 5 + 5 + 18 = 28. The second sample problem is a *subtraction solution* problem—fill B (127), subtract jug C from it twice (–3, –3), then subtract jug A (–21), yielding 100.

Luchins's (1942) demonstration of negative set involved sequencing the problems so that participants developed a particular set or approach for measuring out the quantities. The second group of problems in Table 12.1 illustrates such a sequence. Go ahead and work the problems now before you read any further.

If you were like most people, your experience on problems 1 through 7 led you to develop a particular approach or set, specifically *B* – *2C* – *A* (subtracting A can be done before subtracting 2C, of course). Participants with such a set or *Einstellung* generally failed to notice the far simpler solution possible for problems 6 and 10, simply A – C. That is, about 80 percent of the participants who saw all ten problems used the lengthy *B* – *2C* – *A* method for these problems, versus only 1 percent of the "control" participants who saw only problems 6 through 10. Clearly, the control group had not developed a set for using the lengthy method, so they were much more able to find the simpler solution.

Consider problem 8 now. Only 5 percent of the individuals in Luchins's control group failed to solve problem 8. This was a remarkable result since 64 percent of the "negative set" group, people who saw all ten problems, failed to solve it correctly. These people were so wedded to the method they had already developed that they were surprisingly unable to generate a different method for solving problem 8. In Greeno's (1978) terms, the participants learned an *integrated algorithm*, a single formula, which then prevented them from seeing the simple solution, *28* – *3* = *25* (and they missed *14* – 8 = 6 on problem 10, too).

Additional problems that often yield such negative-set effects are presented in Table 12.2 (p. 390); hints to help overcome negative set, if you experience it, are at the bottom of the table. Although these problems lack the precision of Luchins's demonstration, they resemble real-world problems much more closely than the rather arbitrary water jugs do, and they tend to show the same effect of negative set.

Summary

1. Gestalt psychology conducted the early research on problem solving, beginning in the 1920s. The tenets of Gestalt psychology were that people perceive whole patterns rather than individual parts, and that the whole is greater than or different from the sum of its parts.
2. Two specific difficulties in problem solving were documented in this early research. Functional fixedness is the tendency to use objects or concepts in ordinary ways during problem solving, rather than use them in creative or insightful ways. Negative set is the tendency to attempt new problems with old strategies, rather than to adapt strategies to the new situation.

◆ **TABLE 12.2**

Sample Negative-Set Problems

Buddhist Monk

One morning, exactly at sunrise, a Buddhist monk began to climb a tall mountain. The narrow path, no more than a foot or two wide, spiraled around the mountain to a glittering temple at the summit. The monk ascended the path at varying rates of speed, stopping many times along the way to rest and to eat the dried fruit he carried with him. He reached the temple shortly before sunset. After several days of fasting and meditation, he began his journey back along the same path, starting at sunrise and again walking at variable speeds with many pauses along the way. His average descending speed was, of course, greater than his average climbing speed.

Show that there is a spot along the path that the monk will occupy on both trips at precisely the same time of day.

Drinking Glasses

Six drinking glasses are lined up in a row. The first three are full of water, the last three are empty. By handling and moving only one glass, change the arrangement so that no full glass is next to another full one, and no empty glass is next to another empty one.

Six Pennies

Show how to move only two pennies in the left diagram to yield the pattern at the right.

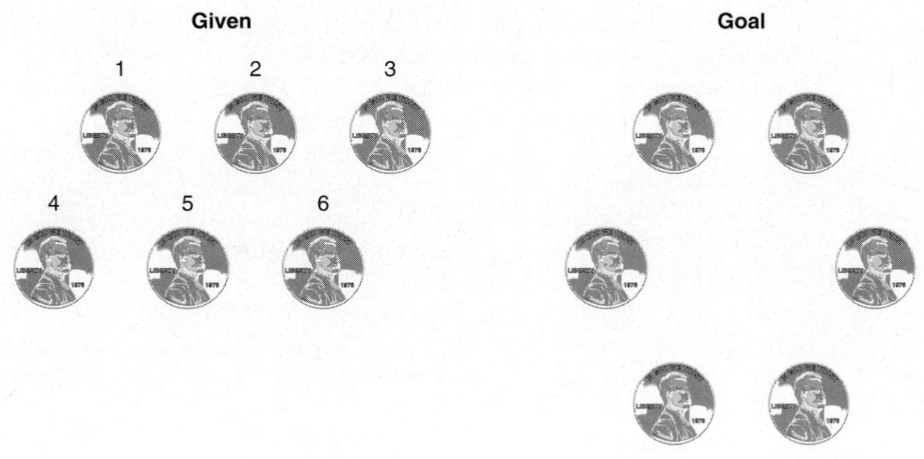

Hints:

Buddhist Monk. Although the problem seems to ask for a quantitative solution, think of a way of representing the problem using visual imagery.

Drinking Glasses. How else can you handle a glass of water besides moving it to another location?

Six Pennies. From a different perspective, some of the pennies might already be in position.

Insight and Analogy

Preview: insight in problem solving; reasoning and problem solving by analogy; the multiconstraint theory of analogical thinking

INSIGHT

On the more positive side of problem solving are the topics of insight and problem solving by analogy. **Insight** is usually thought of as a deep, useful understanding of the nature of something, especially a difficult problem. We often include in this idea that the insight occurs *suddenly*, possibly because a novel approach to the problem has been taken, or a novel interpretation of the problem has been made (R. J. Sternberg, 1996). Puzzle over

the insight problems in Table 12.3 for a moment, to see if you have a sudden "Aha" experience when you realize how to solve the problems.

★ **TABLE 12.3**

Insight Problems

Chain Links
A woman has four pieces of chain. Each piece is made up of three links. She wants to join the pieces into a single closed ring of chain. To open a link costs 2 cents and to close a link costs 3 cents. She has only 15 cents. How does she do it?

Four Trees
A landscape gardener is given instructions to plant four special trees so that each one is exactly the same distance from each of the others. How would you arrange the trees?

Prisoner's Escape
A prisoner was attempting to escape from a tower. He found in his cell a rope which was half long enough to permit him to reach the ground safely. He divided the rope in half and tied the two parts together and escaped. How could he have done this?

Bronze Coin
A stranger approached a museum curator and offered him an ancient bronze coin. The coin had an authentic appearance and was marked with the date 544 B.C. The curator had happily made acquisitions from suspicious sources before, but this time he promptly called the police and had the stranger arrested. Why?

Nine Dots
Connect the nine dots with four connected straight lines without lifting your pencil from the page as you draw.

(continued)

Table 12.3 *(continued)*

Bowling Pins
The ten bowling pins below are pointing toward the top of the page. Move any three of them to make the arrangement point down toward the bottom of the page.

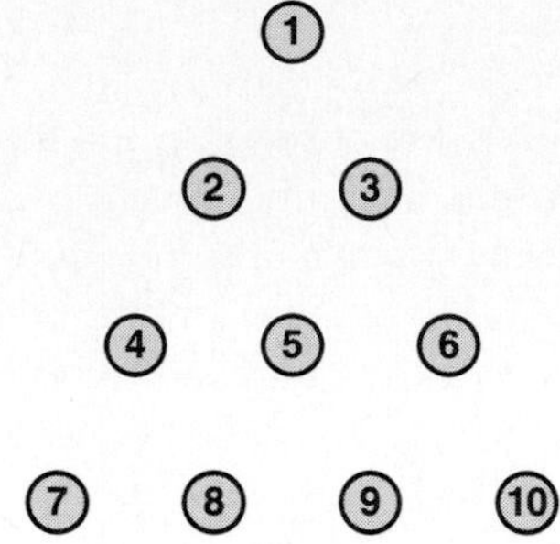

Hints:
Chain Links. You don't have to open a link on each piece of chain.
Four Trees. We don't always plant trees on flat lawns.
Prisoner's Escape. Is there only one way to divide a rope in half?
Bronze Coin. Imagine that you lived in 544 B.C. What did it say on your coins?
Nine Dots. How long a line does the problem permit you to draw?
Bowling Pins. Pins 1, 2, 3, and 5 form a diamond at the top of the drawing. Consider where the diamond might be for the arrangement that points down.

Source: From or adapted from Metcalfe (1986); Metcalfe and Wiebe (1987).

Metcalfe and Wiebe (1987; see also Metcalfe, 1986) studied how people solved such problems, and compared that to how they solved algebra and other routine problems. They found two especially interesting results.

- First, people were rather accurate in predicting whether they'd be successful or not in solving routine problems, but not accurate at all in predicting success with the insight problems.
- Second, solutions to the insight problems seemed to come "all of a sudden," almost without warning.

That is, as they worked through the problems, the participants were interrupted and asked to indicate how "warm" they were, that is, how close they felt to finding the solution. For routine problems, the "warmth" ratings grew steadily as the participants worked through the problems—in essence, they were saying, "I'm getting warmer." But there was little or no such increase for the insight problems until just before the correct solution was found. ▲ The suddenness of this feeling, roughly the same as insight, is shown in Figure 12.2.

While these results lend a degree of support to the notion that insight arrives suddenly, there are still many who remain unconvinced that true insight really exists, or that

Figure 12.2

Modal (most frequent) "warmth" rating in the four time periods leading up to problem solution (Data from Metcalfe & Wiebe, 1987.)

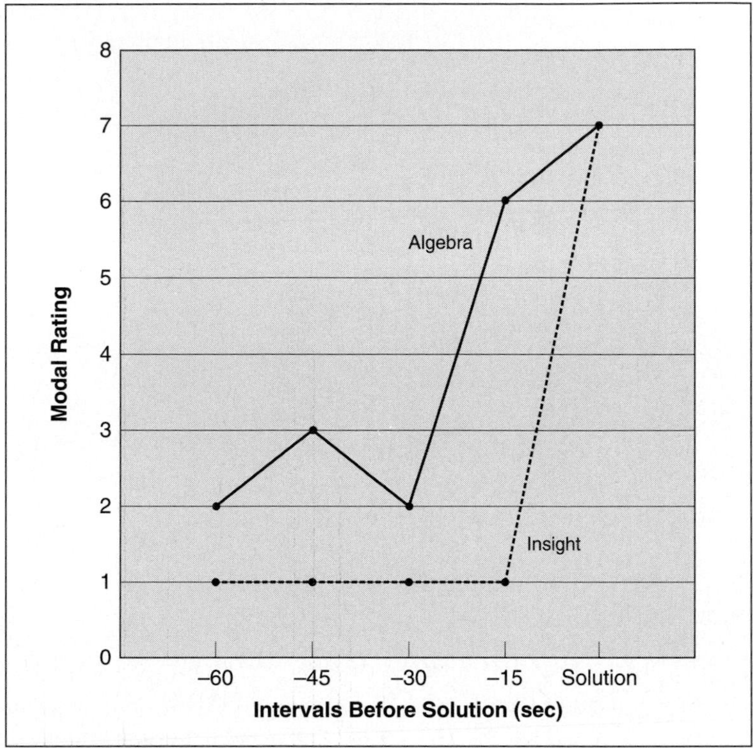

it is critical to problem solving. For example, Weisberg (1995) reports that some people solve so-called insight problems like those in the table *without* any of the sudden restructuring or understanding that supposedly accompanies insight. Conversely, people sometimes report sudden restructuring even on rather routine problems.

It may be just as valid to think of insight in simpler terms, say overcoming functional fixedness or negative set (as in Prisoner's Escape and Nine Dots), taking a different perspective (Bronze Coin), and the like (e.g., S. M. Smith, 1995). As Wickelgren (1974) noted, sometimes "insight" simply means that we've drawn a critical inference that leads to a solution—for example, there's more than one way to divide a rope in half.

Analogy

In general, an **analogy** is a relationship between two similar situations, problems, or concepts. Understanding an analogy means putting the two situations into some kind of alignment or relationship so that the similarities and differences can be seen. Take a simple example, an analogy like MERCHANT : SELL :: CUSTOMER : ________. Here, you must figure out or induce the structure (Greeno, 1978) for the first pair of terms, and then

"I heard von Schleflin yell 'Eureka,' and then kerblam!"

project or **map** that structure onto the second part of the analogy. Because SELL is the critical activity of MERCHANTs, the "critical activity" relationship is then mapped onto CUSTOMERs, and retrieval from memory yields BUY.

Several authors argue strongly that analogies provide excellent, widely applicable methods for solving problems. That is, if you're confronted with a difficult problem, a useful heuristic is to find a similar or related situation, and build an analogy from it to the current problem. According to these authors, such reasoning and problem solving may help us understand a huge variety of situations, for example, how students should be taught in school, how people adopt professional role models, how we empathize with others, and so forth (e.g., Holyoak & Thagard, 1997; Kolodner, 1997). And it's long been held that important scientific ideas, breakthroughs, and explanations have often depended on finding analogies—for instance, that neurotransmitters fit into the receptor sites of a neuron much the way a key fits into a lock (see Gentner & Markman's, 1997, compelling description of reasoning by analogy in Kepler's discovery of the laws of planetary motion).

Analogy Problems

To gain some feeling for analogies, read the Parade story at the top of Table 12.4 (p. 396), a story used by Gick and Holyoak (1980) in an important study of problem solving. Try to solve the problem now, before reading the solution in Table 12.5 (p. 397).

Gick and Holyoak had their participants read either the Parade problem, a somewhat different army fortress story, or no story at all. They then asked them to read and solve a second problem, the classic Duncker (1945) Radiation problem, shown at the bottom of Table 12.4 (which you should read and try to solve now).

The Radiation problem is interesting to study for a variety of reasons, including the fact that it is rather ill defined, and thus comparable to many problems in the real world. Duncker's participants produced two general approaches that led to dead ends—trying to avoid contact between the ray and nearby tissue, and trying to change the sensitivity of surrounding tissue to the effects of the ray. But the third approach, reducing the intensity of the rays, was more productive, especially if an analogy from some other, better understood situation was available.

Gick and Holyoak (1980) used this problem to study problem solving by analogy. In fact, we've just simulated one of their experiments here, by having you read the Parade story first and then the Radiation problem. In case you didn't notice, there are strong similarities between the problems, suggesting that the Parade story can be used to develop an analogy for the Radiation problem.

Gick and Holyoak found that only 49 percent of the participants who first solved the Parade problem realized it could be used as an analogy for the Radiation problem. A different initial story, in which armies are attacking a fortress, provided a stronger hint about the Radiation problem. Fully 76 percent of these participants used the attack analogy in solving the Radiation problem. In contrast, only 8 percent of the control group, which merely attempted to solve the Radiation problem, came up with the so-called "dispersion" solution (i.e., multiple pathways) described at the bottom of Table 12.5.

When Gick and Holyoak provided a strong hint to their subjects, telling them that the "attack" solution might be helpful as they worked on the Radiation problem, 92 percent of them used the analogy to solve the Radiation problem, and most found it "very helpful." In dramatic contrast, only 20 percent of the people in the "no hint" group pro-

EUREKA

The standard historical example of insight is the story of Archimedes, the Greek scientist who had to determine if the king's crown was solid gold, or if some silver had been mixed with the gold. Archimedes knew the weights of both gold and silver per unit of volume, but could not imagine how to measure the volume of the crown. But as he stepped into his bath one day, he noticed how the water level rose as he sank into the water. He then realized the solution to his problem. The volume of the crown could be determined by immersing it in water and measuring how much water it displaced. As the story goes, he was so excited by his insight that he jumped from the bath and ran naked through the streets, shouting, "Eureka! I have found it!" As mentioned in the last chapter, *eureka* comes from the same word base as *heuristic*.

◆ **TABLE 12.4**

The Parade Story and the Radiation Problem

Parade Story
A small country was controlled by a dictator. The dictator ruled the country from a strong fortress. The fortress was situated in the middle of the country, surrounded by farms and villages. Many roads radiated outward from the fortress like spokes on a wheel. To celebrate the anniversary of his rise to power, the dictator ordered his general to conduct a full-scale military parade. On the morning of the anniversary, the general's troops were gathered at the head of one of the roads leading to the fortress, ready to march. However, a lieutenant brought the general a disturbing report. The dictator was demanding that this parade had to be more impressive than any previous parade. He wanted his army to be seen and heard at the same time in every region of the country. Furthermore, the dictator was threatening that if the parade was not sufficiently impressive he was going to strip the general of his medals and reduce him to the rank of private. But it seemed impossible to have a parade that could be seen throughout the whole country.

Radiation Problem
Suppose you are a doctor faced with a patient who has a malignant tumor in his stomach. It is impossible to operate on the patient, but unless the tumor is destroyed the patient will die. There is a kind of ray that can be used to destroy the tumor. If the rays reach the tumor all at once at a sufficiently high intensity, the tumor will be destroyed. Unfortunately, at this intensity the healthy tissue that the rays pass through on the way to the tumor will also be destroyed. At lower intensities the rays are harmless to healthy tissue, but they will not affect the tumor either. What type of procedure might be used to destroy the tumor with the rays, and at the same time avoid destroying the healthy tissue?

Source: From Gick and Holyoak (1980) and Duncker (1945).

duced the dispersion solution, even though they too had read the Attack-Dispersion story. In short, only 20 percent *spontaneously* noticed and used the analogous relationship between the problems. Table 12.6 (p. 398) summarizes the results obtained by Gick and Holyoak.

Multiconstraint Theory

Holyoak and Thagard (1997) have recently proposed an overall theory of analogical reasoning and problem solving, based on such results. The theory, called the multiconstraint theory, predicts how people use analogies in problem solving, and what factors govern the analogies people construct. In particular, the theory says that people are constrained by three factors when they try to use or develop analogies:

- problem *similarity*,
- problem *structure*, and
- *purpose* of the analogy.

Problem Similarity There must be a reasonable degree of similarity between the already-understood situation, the *source* domain, and the current problem being solved, the

★ **TABLE 12.5**

Attack-Dispersion Story and Solution, with Solutions to Previous Problems

Attack-Dispersion Story

A small country was controlled by a dictator. The dictator ruled the country from a strong fortress. The fortress was situated in the middle of the country, surrounded by farms and villages. Many roads radiated outward from the fortress like spokes on a wheel. A general arose who raised a large army and vowed to capture the fortress and free the country of the dictator. The general knew that if his entire army could attack the fortress at once it could be captured. The general's troops were gathered at the head of one of the roads leading to the fortress, ready to attack. However, a spy brought the general a disturbing report. The ruthless dictator had planted mines on each of the roads. The mines were set so that small bodies of men could pass over them safely, since the dictator needed to be able to move troops and workers to and from the fortress. However, any large force would detonate the mines. Not only would this blow up the road and render it impassable, but the dictator would then destroy many villages in retaliation. It therefore seemed impossible to mount a full-scale direct attack on the fortress.

Solutions

Parade Story

The general, however, knew just what to do. He divided his army up into small groups and dispatched each group to the head of a different road. When all was ready he gave the signal, and each group marched down a different road. Each group continued down its road to the fortress, so that the entire army finally arrived together at the fortress at the same time. In this way, the general was able to have the parade seen and heard through the entire country at once, and thus please the dictator.

Radiation Problem

The ray may be divided into several low-intensity rays, no one of which will destroy the healthy tissue. By positioning these several rays at different locations around the body, and focusing them all on the tumor, their effect will combine, thus being strong enough to destroy the tumor.

Attack-Dispersion Story

The general, however, knew just what to do. He divided his army up into small groups and dispatched each group to the head of a different road. When all was ready he gave the signal, and each group marched down a different road. Each group continued down its road to the fortress, so that the entire army finally arrived together at the fortress at the same time. In this way, the general was able to capture the fortress, and thus overthrow the dictator.

Source: From Gick and Holyoak (1980) and Duncker (1945).

target domain. In the Parade story, for example, the fortress and troops can be seen as similar to the tumor and the rays. Similarity between source and target has been shown to be important in several other studies. For instance, Novick (1988) found that novices focus especially on similarities, even when they are only superficial and thus end up interfering with performance.

TABLE 12.6

Summary of Gick and Holyoak's (1980) Results

	Study 1	
Participants given a general hint that their solution to an earlier story might be useful in solving the Radiation problem		
Group	*Order of Stories*	*Percentage Who Used the Analogy*
A	Parade, Radiation	49%
B	Attack, Radiation	76
C	No story, Radiation	8
	Study 2	
A (strong hint)	Attack, Radiation	92
B (no hint)	Attack, Radiation	20

Source: From Gick and Holyoak (1980, table 10).

Problem Structure People must establish a parallel structure between the source and target problems, so they can map elements from the source to comparable elements in the target. Figuring out these one-to-one correspondences or mappings is especially important, in Holyoak and Thagard's view, since it corresponds to working out the exact relationships that the analogy depends on. In the Attack Radiation analogy, you have to map *troops* onto *rays*, so that the important relationship of *different converging roads* can serve as the basis for the solution. The most prominent mappings from Attack to Radiation are shown in Figure 12.3. In a clever investigation of this, Spellman and Holyoak (1992) analyzed analogical mapping in people's reasoning about the 1991 Persian Gulf War (i.e., "If Saddam is Hitler then who is George Bush?").

Purpose of the Analogy The problem solver's goals, and the goal stated in the problem, are an important constraint in solving by analogy. This is deeper than merely the general purpose of trying to solve the problem, of course. Notice that the goals in the Attack and Radiation stories above match, whereas the goals do not match for Parade and Radiation—a parade to show off the troops is very different from the rays of radiation, and being seen widely throughout the region in the Parade story doesn't map well onto the goal of avoiding damage to healthy tissue. These mismatches may have been responsible for the low use of Parade as a source for the analogy to Radiation.

Likewise, Spellman and Holyoak (1996) reported a clever study in which college students had to draw analogies between two soap-opera plots. The participants were told to pretend they were successful soap opera writers whose plot lines had been plagiarized by another team of writers. To prove the plagiarism, they had to predict what the characters in the second story would do, based on the plot of their own story. When different purposes or goals were given in the instructions, that is, when one or another subtheme in

FIGURE 12.3

Prominent mappings between the Attack and Radiation problems

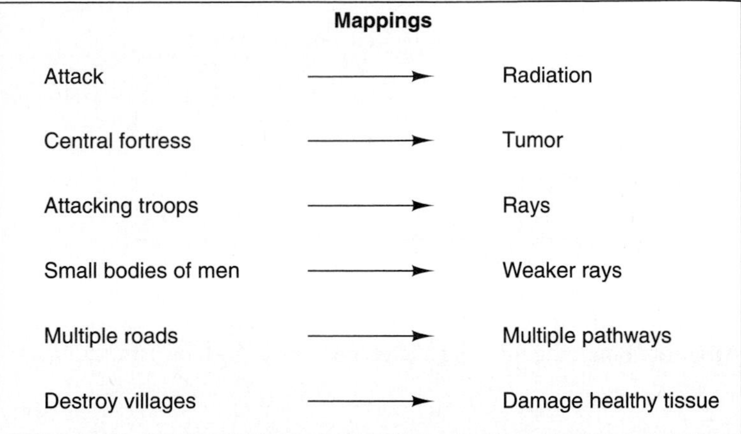

the plot was of interest, the students developed different analogies. Their problem solving by analogy was sensitive to the characters' purposes and overall goals.

Summary

1. Insight refers to a deep understanding of a situation or problem, often thought to occur suddenly and without warning. Although some evidence supports the sudden onset of insight, many researchers question whether insight is actually involved, as opposed to simpler, better-understood processes.
2. Reasoning by analogy is a complex kind of problem solving in which relationships in one situation are mapped onto another in order to solve a problem. People are better at developing analogies if given a useful source problem and an explicit hint that the problem might be used in solving a target problem.
3. Holyoak and Thagard's multiconstraint theory of analogical problem solving claims that we work under three constraints as we develop analogies, constraints related to the similarity of the source and target domains, the structure of the problem, and our purposes or goals in developing the analogies.

BASICS OF PROBLEM SOLVING

Preview: characteristics of problem solving; goals and subgoals; means-end analysis; General Problem Solver; ACT*

Although Gestalt psychology started the systematic investigation of problem solving, there were some difficulties with that approach, as several authors have noted (e.g., Newell & Simon, 1972). Thus modern cognitive psychology had to develop more analytic and focused methods of investigation for understanding problem solving, methods like those used in the study of analogy you just read about. Let's turn to the general approach now, by considering the characteristics of problem solving, and some of the important terminology.

CHARACTERISTICS OF PROBLEM SOLVING

Genuine instances of problem solving share at least four general characteristics (Anderson, 1980, 1985).

1. Goal Directedness

The overall behavior or activity we're examining is directed toward achieving some goal or purpose. This would exclude daydreaming, for instance—it's mental, but it's not goal directed. By contrast, if you've locked your keys in your car, there is considerable physical as well as mental activity going on. The goal-directed nature of those activities, your repeated attempts at getting into the locked car, make this an instance of true problem solving.

2. Sequence of Steps

An activity must involve a sequence of steps or stages in order to qualify as problem solving. In other words, simple retrieval of a fact from memory is not problem solving, since it does not require a discernible sequence of separate operations or stages. Doing a long division problem or solving the "locked car" problem, on the other hand, definitely involves a sequence of mental operations, so these are instances of problem solving.

3. Cognitive Operations

Solving the problem involves the application of various cognitive operations, performed within certain constraints or limitations. Various *operators* can be applied to different problems, where each operator is a distinct cognitive act in the sequence, a permissible step or move in the problem space. For long division, retrieving an answer would be an operator, as would be subtracting or multiplying two numbers at some other stage in problem solution. Often, the cognitive operations will have some behavioral counterpart, some physical act that completes the mental operation, such as writing down a number during long division.

4. Subgoal Decomposition

As implied by the third characteristic, each step in the sequence of operations is a **subgoal,** an intermediate goal along the route to eventual solution of the problem. Subgoals represent the decomposition or breaking apart of the overall goal into its components. In many instances, of course, the subgoals themselves must be further decomposed into even smaller subgoals. Thus, there is often a hierarchical or "nested" structure to the problem-solving attempt.

Terminology

A few terms in these four characteristics deserve further scrutiny and definition. First, **problem space** is a global term, referring to the various states or conditions that are possible in the problem. More concretely, the problem space includes the initial, intermediate, and goal states of the problem, as well as the problem solver's knowledge at each step.

This includes knowledge that is currently being applied as well as knowledge that *could be* retrieved from memory and applied. Any external devices, objects, or resources that are available can also be included in the description of the problem space, for example, the pencil and paper used in solving a difficult arithmetic problem.

In some problem contexts, we speak of problem solving as a *search of the problem space*, or metaphorically, a *search of the solution tree*, in which each branch and twig represents a possible pathway from the initial state of the problem. While some problems have many possibilities, all of which need to be checked, others may permit us to *restrict* the search space, to reduce the relevant search space to a manageable size. Metaphorically, this is called *pruning the search tree*.

A classic example of this is a cryptarithmetic problem, where you must substitute digits for letters to arrive at a correct addition problem. The hint allows you to prune the search tree considerably.

```
  DONALD        Hint: D = 5
+ GERALD
  ROBERT
```

The term **operators** refers to the set of legal operations or "moves" that can be performed during problem solution. The term *legal* means permissible in the rules of the problem—for instance, having Small row the boat back to the start side in Three Men and a Rowboat, moving unknowns to the left side of an equation in algebra, and so forth. Conversely, an *illegal* operator breaks a rule or violates a restriction—in Six Pennies in Table 12.2, for instance, moving *more* than two pennies. In Three Men and a Rowboat, an illegal operator would be having the men swim across the river, or loading the boat with too heavy a load.

The *goal*, of course, is the ultimate destination or solution to the problem. For recreational problems in particular, the goal is nearly always stated explicitly in the problem. Thus, any problem that presents an explicit and complete specification of the initial and goal states can be described as **well defined.** Solutions to such problems involve progressing through the legal intermediate states, by means of known operators, until the goal is reached—DONALD + GERALD is an excellent example of a well-defined problem.

In contrast, in **ill-defined** problems, the states, operators, or both may be only vaguely specified. For instance, the Buddhist Monk problem in Table 12.2 stated a rather vague goal, "Show that there is a spot . . ." Likewise, real-world problems are often distressingly vague in their specification of the goal: Write a term paper that will earn you an A, write a computer program that does X in as economical and elegant a fashion as possible, and so forth.

MEANS-END ANALYSIS: A FUNDAMENTAL HEURISTIC

Several heuristics for problem solving have been discovered and investigated in problem-solving research. You've already read about the analogy approach, and the final section of the chapter describes and illustrates several others. But in terms of overall significance, as well as importance to the field of research, no other heuristic comes even close to the heuristic known as *means-end analysis*. This heuristic formed the basis for Newell and Simon's groundbreaking work (e.g., 1972), including their very first presentation of the

Professor Herbert A. Simon

information processing framework at a conference in 1956 (see Gardner, 1985). Because it shaped the entire area, and the theories devised to account for problem solving, it deserves our special, focused attention here.

The Basics of Means-End Analysis

Means-end analysis is the best known of the heuristics of problem solving. In this approach, the problem is solved by repeatedly determining the difference between the current state and the goal or subgoal state, then finding and applying an operator that reduces this difference. Means-end analysis nearly always implies the use of subgoals, since achieving the goal state usually involves the intermediate steps of achieving several subgoals along the way.

TABLE 12.7

The Missionaries-Cannibals Problem

Three missionaries and three cannibals are on one side of a river and need to cross to the other side. The only means of crossing is a boat, and the boat can only hold two people at a time. Devise a set of moves that will transport all six people across the river, bearing in mind the following constraint: the number of cannibals can never exceed the number of missionaries in any location, for the obvious reason. Remember that someone will have to row the boat back across each time.

Hint: At one point in your solution, you'll have to send the same number of people back to the start side as you just sent to the destination side.

Solution: The solution is depicted in Figure 12.7.

The basic notions of a means-end analysis can be summarized in a sequence of five steps:

1. Set up a goal or subgoal.
2. Look for a difference between the current state and the goal/subgoal state.
3. Look for an operator that will reduce or eliminate this difference. One such operator is the setting of a new subgoal.
4. Apply the operator.
5. Apply steps 2 to 4 repeatedly until all subgoals and the final goal are achieved.

At an intuitive level, means-end analysis and subgoals are very familiar to us, and represent "normal" problem solving. If you have to write a term paper for class, the overall goal is then broken down into a series of subgoals—select a topic, find relevant material, read and understand the material, and so forth. Each of these may contain its own subgoals too, of course—if you can't type or word process the paper yourself, an added subgoal is to arrange for someone to do this, arrange to deliver the paper, then pick up the final copy.

Means-End Analysis and the Tower of Hanoi

The most thoroughly investigated recreational problems are the Missionaries-Cannibals problem in Table 12.7 (it's also known as the Hobbits-Orcs problem) and the Tower of Hanoi problem in Figure 12.4. These famous problems show very clearly both the strengths and the limitations of the means-end approach. (We'll return to the Missionaries-Cannibals problem in a few pages, but you should spend some time on it now, in preparation for that discussion.)

Work on the Tower of Hanoi problem very carefully, using the three-disk version in the figure. Try to keep track of your solution, so you'll understand how it demonstrates the usefulness of a means-end analysis. So that you'll be familiar with the problem, and be able to reflect on your solution, work it several times again after you've solved it. See if you can't become very skilled at solving the three-disk problem by remembering your solution and being able to generate it repeatedly.

FIGURE 12.4

The Tower of Hanoi problem

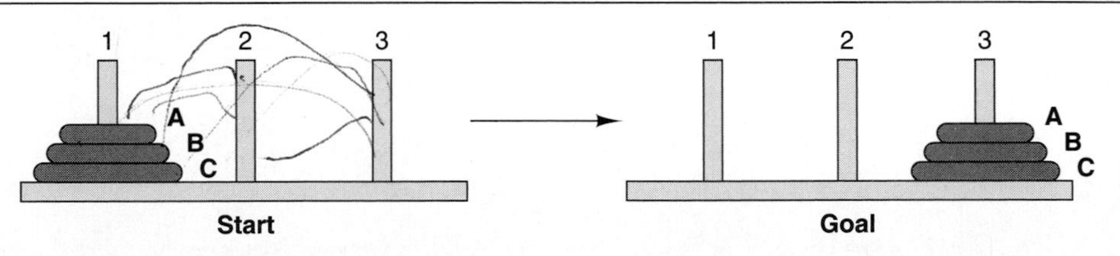

The goal of the problem is to move all three disks from peg 1 to peg 3, so that C is on the bottom, B is in the middle, and A is on top. The restrictions are: you may move only one disk at a time, and only to another peg; you may not place a larger disk on top of a smaller one.

Having done that, now consider your solution in terms of subgoals and means-end analysis. Your goal, as stated in the problem, is to move the ABC stack of disks from peg 1 to peg 3. Applying the means-end analysis, your first step sets up this goal. The second step in the analysis reveals a difficulty—there is a difference between your current state and the goal, simply the difference between the starting and ending configurations. You then look for a method or operator that will reduce this difference, and then apply that operator. As you no doubt learned from your solution, your first major subgoal is "Clear off disk C." This entails getting B off of C, which itself entails another subgoal, getting A off of B.

FIGURE 12.5

The seven-step solution for the Tower of Hanoi problem. Note that the pegs have been renamed as "Source," "Stack," and "Destination." Moving the three disks requires seven moves. Consider these seven moves as one unit, called "moving a pyramid of three disks."

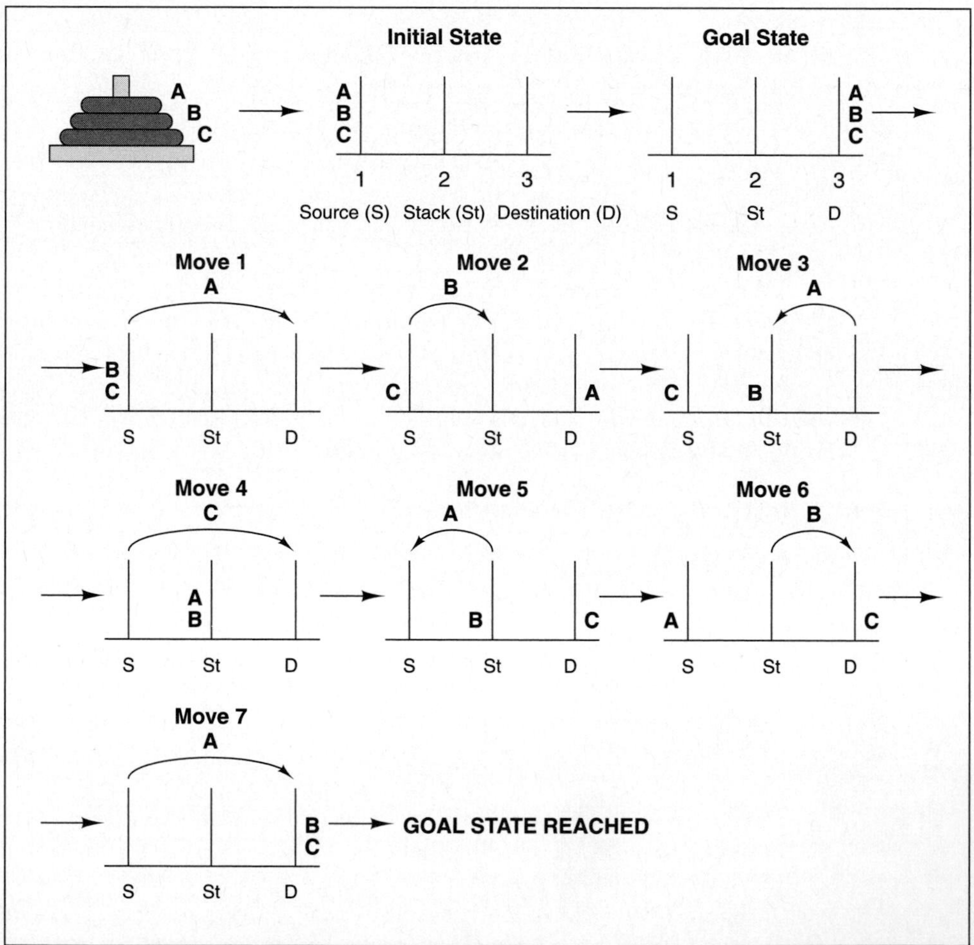

The next step involves a simple operator that satisfies the most immediate subgoal, "Move A to 3," which permits satisfying the *next* subgoal, "getting B off of C." So, the next operator is "move B to 2"—it can't go on top of A (rule violation) and it can't stay on top of C since that prevents achieving a subgoal. Now peg 3 can be cleared, by moving A to 2. This of course allows the major subgoal to be accomplished, putting C on 3.

From here, it's easy to see the final route to solution—"unpack" A from 2, putting it temporarily on 1, move B to 3, then move A to 3. The seven moves that solve the problem are shown in Figure 12.5.

The Four-Disk Version

After you've worked the problem several times, solving it again becomes rather easy. You come to see how each disk needs to move in order to get C on 3, then B, and finally A. Spend some time now on the same problem, but use four disks instead of three. Don't work on this larger version blindly, however. Think of it, instead, as a *variation* on the three-disk problem, where parts of the new solution are "old." As a hint, try renaming the pegs as the *source* peg, the *stack* peg, and the *destination* peg. Further, think of the seven moves not as seven discrete steps but as a single chunk, "moving a pyramid of 3 disks," which according to Simon (1975) should help you see the relationships between the problems more clearly. According to Catrambone (1996), almost any label attached to a sequence of moves will probably help you remember the sequence better.

What did you discover as you solved the four-disk problem? Most people eventually come to the realization that the four-disk problem has *two* distinct three-disk problems embedded in it, separated by the bridging move of D to 3. That is, to free D so it can move to peg 3 requires that you first move the top three disks out of the way, "moving a pyramid of 3 disks," getting D to peg 3 on the eighth move. Then the ABC pyramid has to move again to get *them* on top of D—another seven moves. Moving the disks requires the same order of moves as in the simpler problem, although the pegs take on different functions—for the four-disk problem, peg 2 serves as the destination for the first half of the solution, then as the source for the last half. The entire scheme of 15 moves is illustrated in Figure 12.6 (p. 406).

GPS—GENERAL PROBLEM SOLVER

Means-end analysis was an early focus of modern research on problem solving, largely because of early work by Newell, Shaw, and Simon (1958; see also Ernst & Newell, 1969; Newell & Simon, 1972). Their computer simulation was called **General Problem Solver**—known as **GPS.** This program was the first genuine computer simulation of problem-solving behavior. It was a general-purpose, problem-solving program, not limited to just one kind of problem, but widely applicable to a large class of problems in which means-end analysis was appropriate. Newell and Simon ran their simulation on various logical proofs, on the Missionaries-Cannibals problem, on the Tower of Hanoi, and on many other problems, to demonstrate its generality. (Notice the critical analogy here. Newell and Simon drew an analogy between the way computer programs solve problems and the way humans do—human mental processes are of a symbolic nature, so the computer's manipulation of symbols is a fruitful analogy to those processes. This was a stunningly provocative and useful analogy for the science of cognition.)

FIGURE 12.6

The four-disk Tower of Hanoi problems, with solution. The variation from the three-disk version is that the pegs must switch roles. In the beginning, the subgoal is to "move a pyramid of three disks" so that D can move to peg 3. After that, the subgoal is again to "move a three-disk pyramid." In both the first and second halves, the pegs must switch roles in order for the problem to be solved.

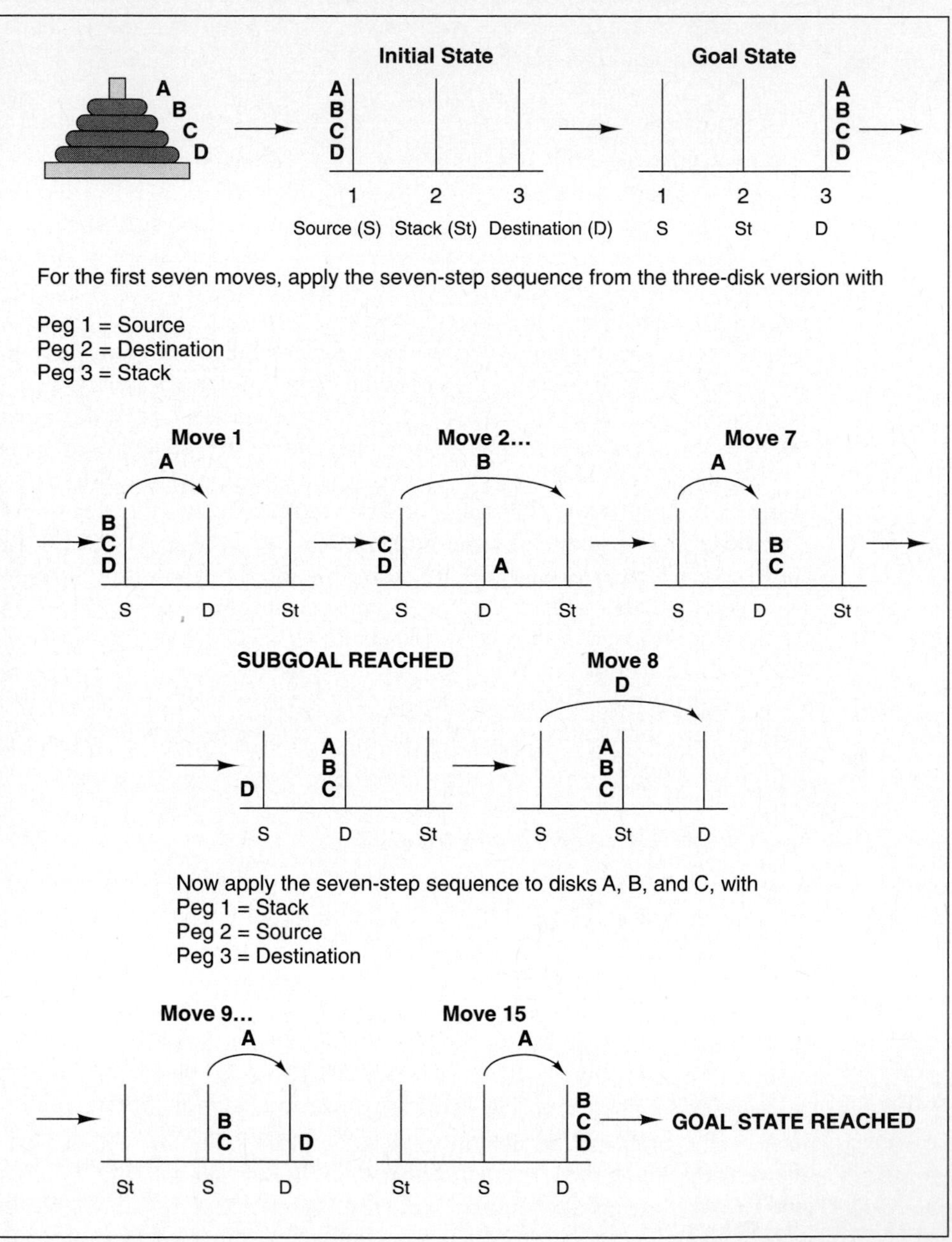

Production Systems

An important characteristic of GPS was its formulation as a *production system* model, essentially the first such model proposed in psychology. A **production** is a pair of statements, called either a *condition-action* pair or an *IF-THEN* pair. In such a scheme, if the production's conditions are satisfied, the action part of the pair takes place. In the GPS application to the Tower of Hanoi, three sample productions might be:

(a) *IF the destination peg is clear* and *the largest disk is free, THEN move the largest disk to the destination peg.*

(b) *IF the largest disk is not free, THEN set up a subgoal to free it.*

(c) *IF a subgoal to free the largest disk is set up* and *a smaller disk is on it, THEN move the smaller disk to the stack peg.*

Such an analysis suggests a very "planful" solution on the part of GPS—setting up a goal and then subgoals that will achieve the goal sounds exactly like what we would call planning. And indeed, such planning characterizes both people's *and* GPS's solutions to problems, not just the Tower of Hanoi, but all kinds of transformation problems. GPS had what amounted to a "planning mechanism," a mechanism that abstracted the essential features of situations and goals, then devised a plan that would produce a problem-solving sequence of moves. Provided with such a mechanism, and the particular representational system necessary to encode the problem and the legal operators, GPS yielded an output that resembles the solution pathways taken by human problem solvers.

Limitations of GPS

Later investigators working with the general principles of GPS found some instances when the model did not do a particularly good job of characterizing or simulating human problem solving. Consider now the Missionaries-Cannibals problem that you (should) ◆ have already worked; the solution pathway is presented in Figure 12.7 (p. 408). The problem is especially difficult, at step 6 most people find, where the *only* legal move is to return one missionary and one cannibal back to the original side of the river. Having just brought two missionaries over, this return trip seems to be moving *away* from the overall goal. That is, the return of one missionary and one cannibal seems to be incorrect because it appears to *increase* the distance to the goal—it's the only return trip that moves *two* characters back to the original side. Despite the fact that this is the only available move (other than returning the same two missionaries who just came over), people have difficulty in selecting this move (Thomas, 1974).

To put it bluntly, GPS did *not* have this difficulty, because sending one missionary and one cannibal back was consistent with its immediate subgoal. On the other hand, at step 10, GPS is trying to fulfill its subgoal of getting the last cannibal to the destination side, and seemingly can't "let go" of this subgoal. People, however, realize that this subgoal should be abandoned—*anyone* can row back over to bring that last cannibal across, and in the process finish the problem (Greeno, 1974). GPS was simply too rigid in its application of the means-end heuristic, however—it tried to bring the last cannibal across and then send the boat back *again*.

◆ **FIGURE 12.7**

The solution to the Missionaries-Cannibals problem.

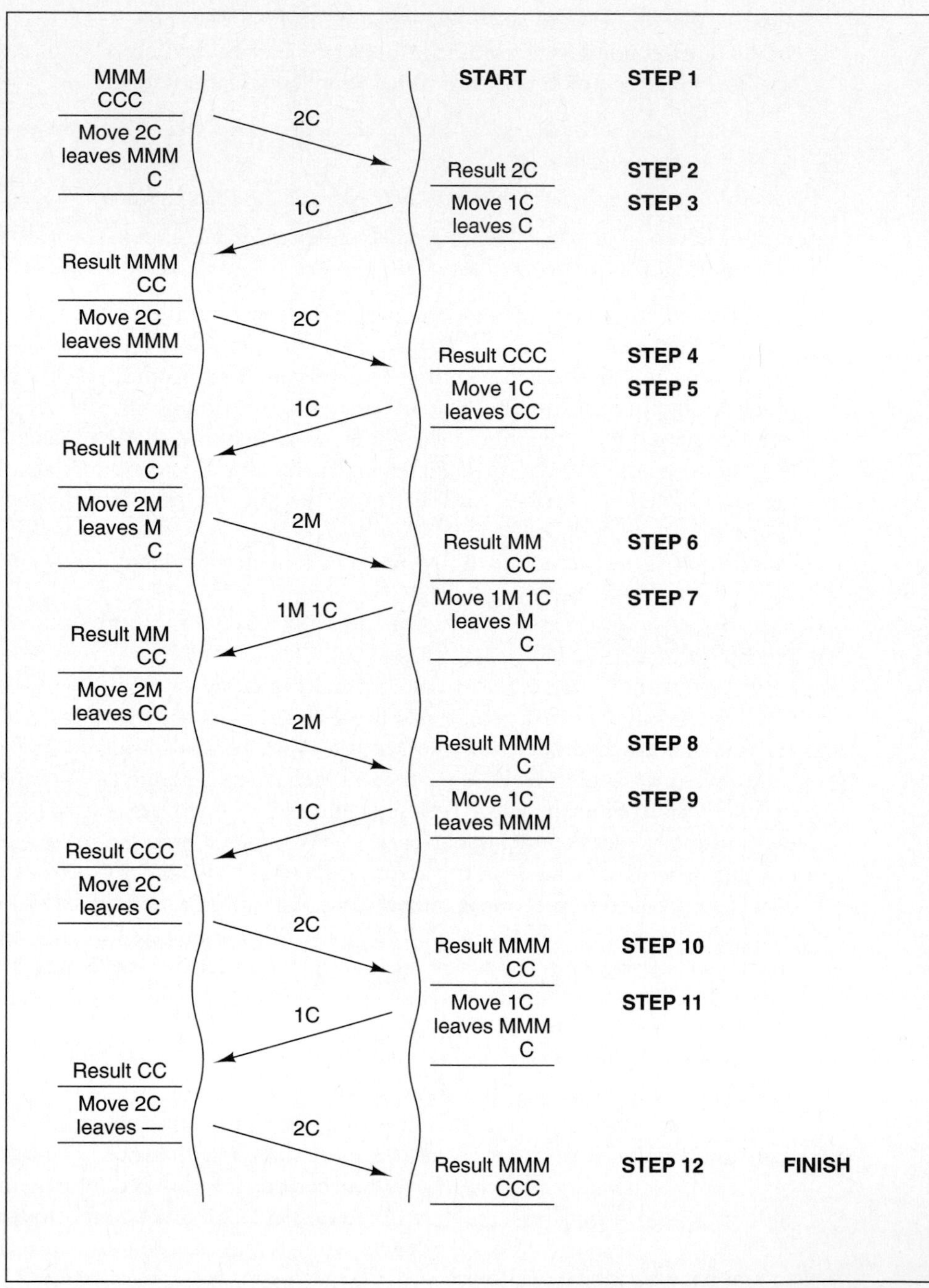

Beyond GPS

Newell and Simon's GPS model, and models based on it, often provided a very good description of human problem-solving performance (e.g., Atwood & Polson, 1976), and provided a precise set of predictions against which new experimental results could be compared (e.g., Greeno, 1974). Despite some limitations (e.g., Hayes & Simon, 1974), the model demonstrated the importance of means-end analysis for an understanding of human problem solving.

ACT*

More recently, Anderson (1983, 1990) has proposed a general model called **ACT*** (pronounced "ACT-star"); ACT stands for *adaptive control of thought*. Although the model covers the entire array of cognitive processes we've been discussing throughout this book, we'll limit our consideration to just the domain of problem solving.

The Structure of ACT*

★ As shown in Figure 12.8, ACT* has three major components, declarative memory, production memory, and working memory.

Declarative memory is essentially what you studied in Chapters 5 and 6—long-term memory, whether episodic or semantic. In Anderson's scheme, declarative memory con-

★ **FIGURE 12.8**

Anderson's (1983) ACT* model. (From Anderson, 1983.)

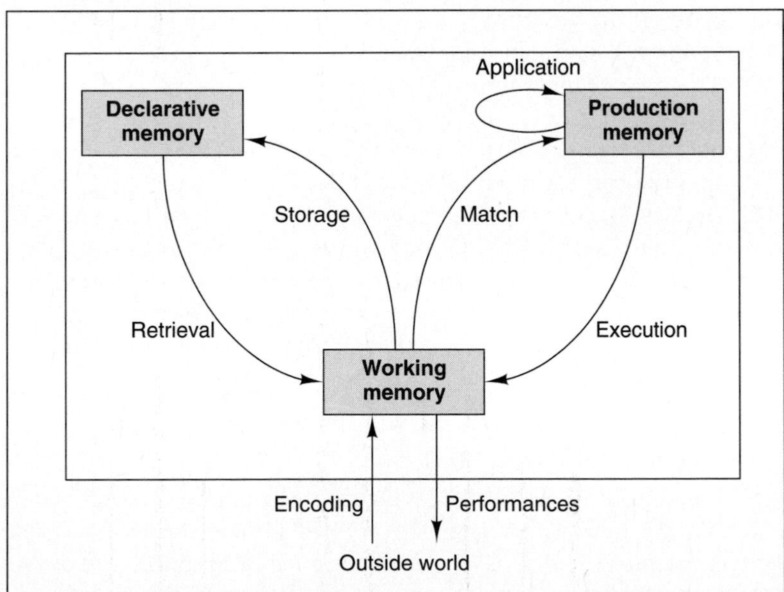

sists of interrelated nodes representing information, a memory network accessed by means of spreading activation. This is essentially what you learned about the structure and processes in semantic long-term memory, of course.

Production memory in this model is the stored collection of IF-THEN pairs that "run" the system, that accomplish all the various cognitive acts involved in problem solving (and everything else). For instance, for simple addition there is an IF-THEN production in production memory that states;

> *IF the goal is to add two numbers, THEN retrieve their sum from declarative memory.*

When a goal is set that matches the IF, the THEN part of the pair—the *action* part—is executed, causing a retrieval from declarative memory.

Notice, finally, that this matching process occurs in *working memory*. That is, when a goal is set, it is registered in working memory, as is the outcome of an IF-THEN pair when it's executed. Thus, working memory is the "keeping track" mechanism in ACT*. It is also, as shown in the figure, the cognitive component that receives information from the outside world, and governs the output of responses or "performances."

How does the system know what to do next? Essentially, there is a scan through working memory, to see what the current state or condition of the system is, for example A, B, and C. This scan is then compared to the IFs stored in production memory. If one of those productions matches the current contents of working memory (IF A *and* B *and* C, THEN do X), that production acts. This satisfies the IF-THEN condition (X happens), updates the contents of working memory, and moves the system one step closer to solving the problem.

Of the three components, production memory is the least familiar to you already, but the most important component of the ACT* architecture. In many ways, production memory is related to **procedural knowledge** (Anderson, 1976, 1982), which means knowledge of how to do things—for example, knowledge of how to ride a bicycle, how to drive a car, how to add and subtract. Thus, production memory is the long-term memory store for procedures, for procedural knowledge, for "knowing how."

An important distinction between procedural and declarative knowledge involves verbalization. You can easily verbalize your declarative knowledge, but usually cannot verbalize the contents of production memory, the procedures you know. Thus, you can verbalize the meanings of words you know (declarative), but usually cannot state the rules you follow for forming sentences (production/ procedural). In this sense, of course, procedural knowledge is very similar to implicit memory (as it was in Chapter 10, where you read that patient H.M. displayed procedural knowledge—implicit memory—for the mirror-drawing task, despite his amnesia).

Empirical Support for ACT*

The empirical tests of ACT* principles have, for the most part, been quite supportive of the model and the general approach. This is especially the case for the domain of problem solving. As Anderson (1993) notes, ACT* assumes a means-end approach to problem solving. By adopting this approach, presumably a great deal of human problem-solving performance—including the errors people make—can be understood.

In fact, this is exactly the approach being taken in the development of computer-based tutors. For example, Anderson (1992; see also Anderson, Boyle, Corbett, & Lewis, 1990) reports on tutoring programs, derived from the ACT* framework, that are now being used to help students in high school mathematics. As the student interacts with the tutor, the tutor tries to interpret the student's problem-solving attempt by consulting its stored productions. In a sense, the computerized tutor asks itself, "Which rules of mathematics does this student still not understand?" Based on this analysis of rules yet to be mastered, the tutor then selects new problems for the student to work on.

By tailoring the questions it asks in this fashion, the program literally tutors the student who is learning mathematics. Early results of this work are impressive: "Typical evaluations have students performing approximately one standard deviation better than control classrooms (if given [the] same amount of time on task) or taking one half to one third the time to reach the same achievement levels as control students" (Anderson, 1993, p. 42). Impressive evidence indeed.

Summary

1. Genuine problem solving involves factors of goal directedness, a sequence of steps being performed, cognitive operations, and decomposition of goals into subgoals. The entire setting of the problem, including your knowledge and any devices you use, is called the problem space.
2. The best-known heuristic for problem solving is means-end analysis, in which the problem solver cycles between determining the difference between the current and goal states, and applying legal operators to reduce that difference. The importance of subgoals is revealed most clearly in problems like the Tower of Hanoi.
3. Newell and Simon's General Problem Solver (GPS) was the earliest cognitive theory of problem solving, implemented as a computer simulation. Studying GPS, and comparing its performance to human problem solving, showed the importance of means-end analysis to human problem solving.
4. A more recent theory of problem solving, ACT*, embeds problem solving within a cognitive system that includes working memory, long-term memory, and production memory. Several applications of ACT* to topics in classroom education have yielded impressive evidence in support of the model and the production system approach it's based on.

Improving Your Problem Solving

Preview: ten ways to improve your problem solving

Sprinkled liberally throughout this chapter have been hints and suggestions about how to improve your problem solving. Some of these were based on empirical research, and some on intuitions that various people have had about the problem-solving process. Let's close this chapter by pulling these hints and suggestions together, and offering a few  new ones too. Table 12.8 (p. 412) provides a convenient list of these suggestions.

TABLE 12.8

Suggestions for Improving Problem Solving

1.	Increase your domain knowledge.
2.	Automate some components of the problem-solving solution.
3.	Follow a systematic plan.
4.	Draw inferences.
5.	Develop subgoals.
6.	Work backward.
7.	Search for contradictions.
8.	Search for relations among problems.
9.	Find a different problem representation.
10.	If all else fails, try practice.

1. Increase Your Domain Knowledge

In thinking about "what makes problems difficult?" Simon has suggested that the likeliest factor is the person's **domain knowledge,** what you know about the topic. Not surprisingly, a person who has only limited knowledge or familiarity with a topic is far less able to solve problems efficiently in that domain.

Much of the research supporting this generalization comes from Simon's work on the game of chess (e.g., Chase & Simon, 1973; see also Reeves & Weisberg, 1993). In several studies of chess masters, an important, although not surprising, result was obtained—chess masters need only a glimpse of the arrangement of chess pieces in order to remember or reconstruct the arrangement, far beyond what novices or individuals of moderate skill can do. This advantage only holds, however, when the pieces are in legal locations, that is, sensible within the context of a real game of chess. When the locations of the pieces are random, then there is no advantage for the skilled players.

2. Automate Some Components of the Problem-Solving Solution

A second connection also exists between the question "What makes problems difficult?" and the topics you've already studied. Kotovsky, Hayes, and Simon (1985) tested adult subjects on various forms of the Tower of Hanoi problem, and also on problem *isomorphs*, problems with the *same form* although different details. Their results showed that a heavy working-memory load was a serious impediment to successful problem solving—if the person had to hold three or four nested subgoals in working memory all at once, performance deteriorated.

Thus, a solution to this memory load problem, they suggested, was to automate the rules that govern moves in the problems—just as you were supposed to master and automate the seven-step sequence in the Tower of Hanoi. Doing this frees working memory to be used for higher-level subgoals (e.g., Carlson, Khoo, Yaure, & Schneider, 1990). This is, of course, the same reasoning you encountered early in the book, where automatic processing uses few if any of the limited conscious resources of working memory.

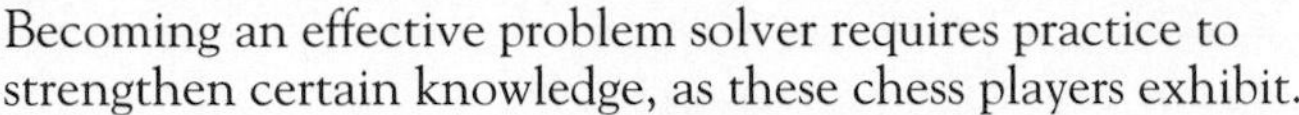
Becoming an effective problem solver requires practice to strengthen certain knowledge, as these chess players exhibit.

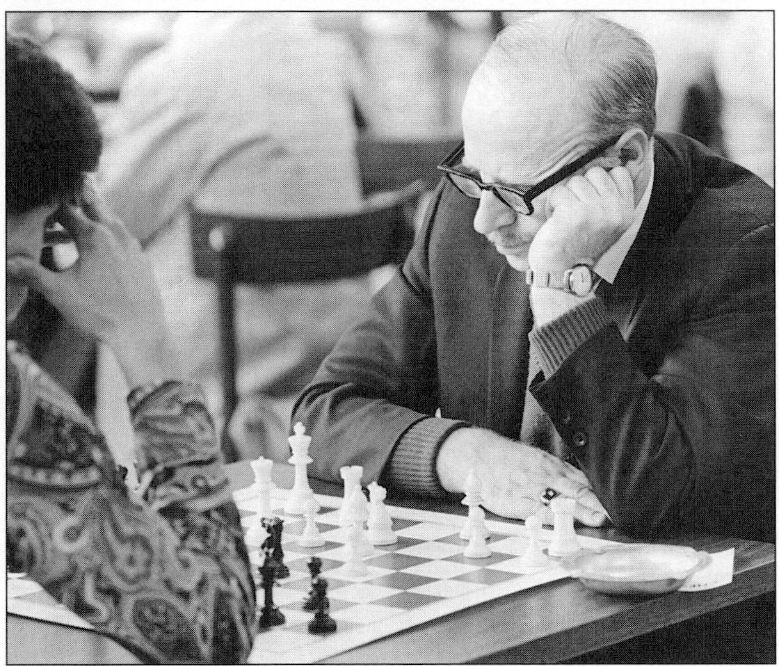

3. Follow a Systematic Plan

Especially in long, multistep problems, it's important to *follow a systematic plan* (e.g., Bransford & Stein, 1993; Polya, 1957). The plan will help you keep track of what you've done or tried, and also keep you focused on the overall goal or subgoals you're working on. For example, on DONALD + GERALD, you need to devise a way of keeping track of which digits you've used, which letters remain, and what you know about them. If nothing else, developing and following a systematic plan will help you avoid redoing what you've already done.

4. Draw Inferences

Wickelgren's (1974) advice is to draw inferences from the givens, the terms, and the expressions in a problem *before* working on the problem itself. If you do this appropriately, it can often save you from wasting time on blind alleys, as in the Two Trains problem in Table 12.9 (p. 414). It can also help you abandon a misleading representation of the problem, and find one that's more suitable to solving the problem (Simon, 1995). Here's a hint: Don't think about how far the bird is flying, think of how far the trains will travel, and how long that will take.

Beware of *unwarranted inferences*, however, the kinds of restrictions we place on ourselves that may lead to dead ends. For instance, for the Nine Dots problem in Table 12.3, an unwarranted inference is that you must stay within the boundaries of the nine dots.

TABLE 12.9

Two Trains and Fifteen Pennies Problems

Two Trains

Two train stations are 50 miles apart. At 2 P.M. one Saturday afternoon, the trains start toward each other, one from each station. Just as the trains pull out of the stations, a bird springs into the air in front of the first train and flies ahead to the front of the second train. When the bird reaches the second train it turns back and flies toward the first train. The bird continues to do this until the trains meet.

If both trains travel at the rate of 25 miles per hour and the bird flies at 100 miles per hour, how many miles will the bird have flown before the trains meet?

Fifteen Pennies

Fifteen pennies are placed on a table in front of two players. Players must remove at least one, but not more than five pennies on their turns. The players alternate turns of removing pennies, until the last penny is removed. The player who removes the last penny from the table is the winner. Is there a method of play that will guarantee victory?

Hints:

Fifteen Pennies. What do you want to force your opponent to do in order to leave you with the winning move? What will the table look like when your opponent makes that move?

Source: Two Trains problem from Posner (1973, pp. 150–151).

5. Develop Subgoals

Wickelgren also recommended a *subgoal heuristic* for problem solving, that is, breaking a large problem into separate subgoals. This, of course, is the heart of the means-end approach, which we discussed extensively. There is a slightly different slant to the subgoal approach, however, that bears mention here. Sometimes in our real-world problem solving, there is only a vaguely specified goal, and as often as not, even more vaguely specified subgoals. How do you know when you've achieved a subgoal, say when the subgoal is "find enough articles on a particular topic to write a term paper that will earn an A"?

Simon's (1979) term **satisficing** is important to bear in mind here—satisficing is a heuristic for finding a solution to a goal or subgoal that is satisfactory, although not necessarily the best possible solution. At least for some problems, the term-paper problem included, an initial *satisfactory* solution to subgoals may provide you with additional insight for further refinement of your solution. For instance, as you begin to write your rough draft, you realize there are gaps in your information. Your originally satisfactory solution to the subgoal of finding references turned out to be insufficient, so you can recycle back to that subgoal to improve your solution. You might only discover this deficiency, notice, by going ahead and working on that next subgoal, the rough draft.

6. Work Backward

Another heuristic that Wickelgren discussed was *working backward,* in which a well-specified goal may permit a tracing of the solution pathway in reverse order, thus working back to the givens. The Fifteen Pennies problem in Table 12.9 is an illustration, a problem that in fact can *only* be solved by working backward. Many math and algebra proofs can also be worked backward, or in a combination of forward and backward methods.

7. Search for Contradictions

In problems that ask, "Is it possible to?" or "Is there a way that?" you should *search for contradictions* in the givens or goal state. Wickelgren uses the following illustration: Is there an integer x that satisfies the equation $x^2 + 1 = 0$? A simple algebraic operation, subtracting 1 from both sides, yields $x^2 = -1$, which contradicts the known property that any squared number will be positive. This heuristic can also be helpful in multiple-choice exams. That is, maybe some of the alternatives contradict some idea or fact in the question, or some fact you learned in the course. Either will enable you to rule out those choices immediately.

8. Search for Relations Among Problems

In searching for relations among problems, you actively consider how the current problem may resemble one you've already solved, or one you already know about. The four- and more-disk Tower of Hanoi problems are clear examples of this, as are situations in which you search for an analogy (Bassok & Holyoak, 1989; Ross, 1987). Don't become impatient, by the way. Bowden (1985) found that people often found and used information from related problems, but only if sufficient time was allowed for them to do so. Try it on the problem in Figure 12.9.

9. Find a Different Problem Representation

Another heuristic involves the more general issue of the problem representation, how you choose to represent and think about the problem you're working on. Often, when you get

FIGURE 12.9

The Sixteen Dots problem.

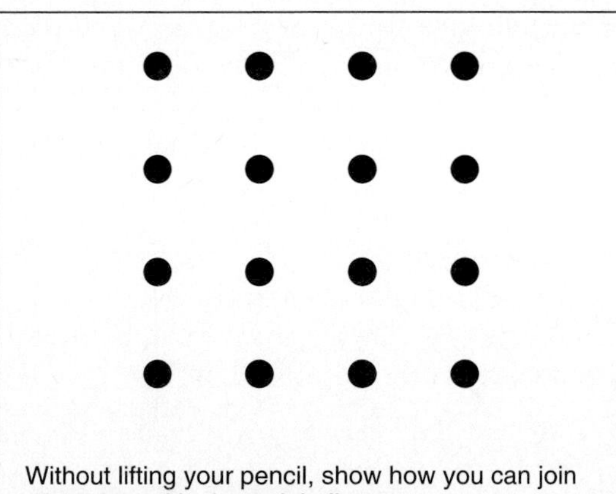
Without lifting your pencil, show how you can join
all 16 dots with six straight lines.

stuck on a problem, it will be useful to go back to the beginning and reformulate or reconceptualize the problem in some way. For instance, as you discovered in the Buddhist Monk problem, a quantitative representation of the situation is unproductive. Return to the beginning and try to think of *other* ways of conceptualizing the situation, for instance a visual-imagery approach, especially a "mental movie" that includes action. In the Buddhist Monk problem, "superimposing" two such mental movies will permit you to see him walking up and down at the same time, thus yielding the solution.

For other kinds of problems, try a numerical representation, including working the problem out with some examples, or a physical representation, using objects, scratch paper, and so forth; for example, to help in the early stages of the Tower of Hanoi, get three coins of different sizes, and move them around on the three pegs you've drawn on a sheet of paper. Simon (1995) makes a compelling point that one representation of a problem may highlight a particular feature of a problem while masking or obscuring a different, possibly important feature. According to Ahlum-Heath and DiVesta (1986), merely verbalizing your thinking also helps in the initial stages of problem solving (but see Schooler et al., 1993).

10. If All Else Fails, Try Practice

Finally, for problems we encounter in classroom settings, from algebra or physics problems up through such vague problems as writing a term paper and studying effectively for an exam, there is a final heuristic that should help your problem solving. It's a well-known effect in psychology—even Ebbinghaus recommended it. If you want to be good at problem solving, *practice* problem solving. Practice within a particular knowledge domain will strengthen that knowledge, push the problem-solving components closer to an automatic basis, and furnish you with a deeper understanding of the domain. While it isn't flashy, practice is without a doubt a *major* component of skilled problem solving, and of gaining expertise in any area (e.g., Ericsson & Charness, 1994).

Summary

1. The set of ten recommendations for improving your problem solving includes increasing your knowledge of the domain, automaticity of components in problem solving, and developing and following a plan. Several special-purpose heuristics are also listed, including the mundane yet important advice about practice.

Important Terms

ACT*
analogy
domain knowledge
functional fixedness
gestalt
goal and subgoal
GPS
insight
mapping
means-end analysis
negative set
operator

problem space
procedural knowledge
production
satisficing
verbal protocol/verbal report
well-defined versus ill-defined problems

Suggested Readings

Four books on how to solve problems (Bransford & Stein, 1993; Hayes, 1989; Levine, 1988; Wickelgren, 1974) provide extensive practice in the different heuristics and approaches. See Mayer (1992) as well, particularly for his discussion of creativity, and the contrasting view on creativity in Weisberg (1993). And fascinating work on expertise and expert performance—for world-class expertise among musicians, chess masters, and so forth—is reported in Ericsson and Charness (1994; see also Ericsson, Krampe, & Tesch-Romer, 1993). In a nutshell—it takes ten years to develop such expertise, and the main ingredient is *practice*.

Three back-to-back papers (Crutcher, Payne, and Wilson, all 1994) review the Ericsson and Simon (1993) book *Protocol Analysis: Verbal Reports as Data,* and discuss the advantages and pitfalls of relying on this kind of data. Spellman and Holyoak's (1992) work on analogies between the Persian Gulf War and World War II inadvertently demonstrated the importance of domain knowledge for reasoning. Very few of their college students knew enough World War II history to draw the analogies, so follow-up studies had to begin by teaching them history.

Problem Solutions

Three Men and a Rowboat Medium and Small row across, and one of them brings the boat back. Large rows across, and the one who stayed after the first move rows back for the other one, then both of the lighter men row to the destination.

Two Strings Tie the pliers to one string, swing it like a pendulum while holding on to the other string, catch the swinging pendulum, and tie the strings together.

Buddhist Monk Superimpose a mental movie of the monk walking up and down on the same day, or imagine two different monks. Because there's only one pathway, the ascending and descending monks must meet at some point. Time and speed are irrelevant.

Drinking Glasses Numbering the glasses from left to right, pour the contents of glass 2 into glass 5.

Six Pennies Align coins 3 and 4 under coins 1 and 2 to form the bottom row.

Chain Links Open all three links on one chain, for 6 cents. Put one opened link at the end of each other piece, then join the pieces by looping a closed link into an opened one. Close the three links, for 9 cents; total is 15 cents.

Four Trees Plant three trees equidistant at the bottom of a hill, and the fourth one on top of the hill, forming an equilateral, three-sided pyramid.

Prisoner's Escape Divide the rope in half by cutting *with* the length, rather than across the length, similar to unbraiding the rope. Tie the two thinner pieces together and lower yourself to the ground.

Bronze Coin In 544 B.C., no one knew what might happen 544 years later, so coins could not have had B.C. stamped on them. The dealer is a crook.

Nine Dots

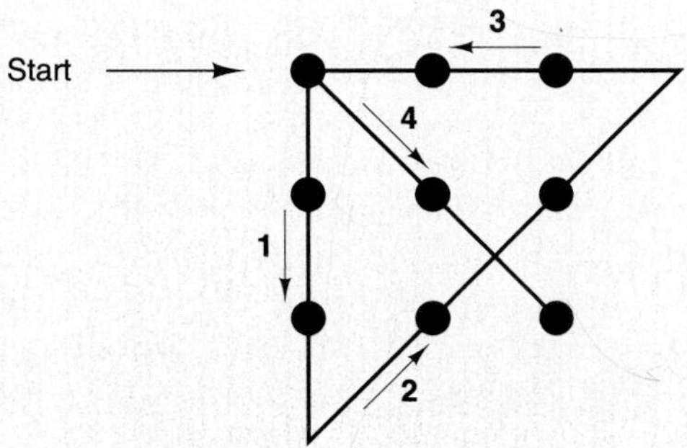

Bowling Pins

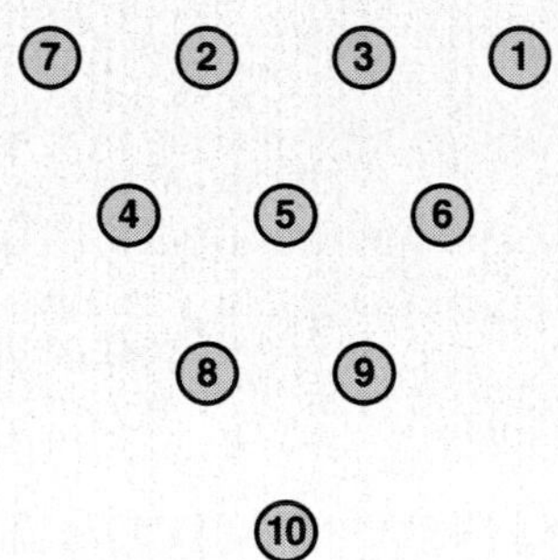

Donald Plus Gerald

DONALD	526485
+ GERALD	+ 197485
ROBERT	723970

Two Trains The trains are 50 miles apart, and travel at 25 miles per hour. The trains will meet halfway between the cities in exactly one hour. The bird flies at 100 miles per hour, so will fly 100 miles.

Fifteen Pennies On your last move you must remove the final penny or pennies. There must be from one to five pennies on the table for you to be the winner. By working backward from this goal, on your next-to-last turn, you must force your opponent to leave you at least one penny on the table. So leave your opponent *six* pennies when you finish your next-to-last turn. To guarantee victory, make sure that your opponent leaves you from one to five pennies, so remove only as many pennies as you must in order to leave your opponent with six pennies on the table.

Sixteen Dots

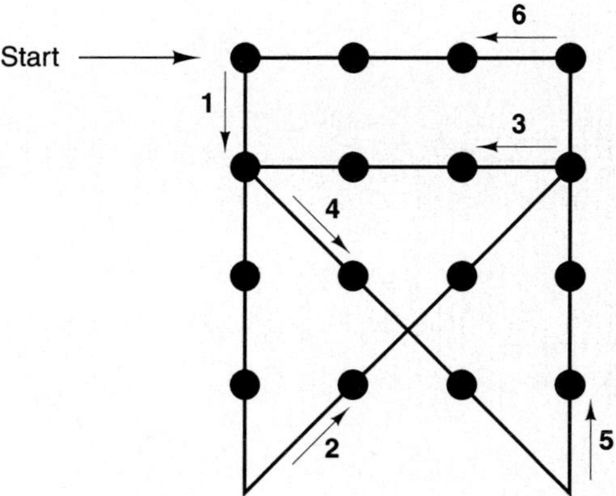

GLOSSARY

Accessibility: The retrievability of information stored in memory. (Ch. 5)

Acoustic-articulatory code: The mental code or format based on sound (acoustic) or pronunciation (articulatory) characteristics of the stimulus. (Ch. 4)

ACT*: Anderson's Adaptive Control of Thought model. (Ch. 12)

Advantage of clause recency: The brief advantage in comprehension for the most recently mentioned character or concept in a sentence. (Ch. 9)

Advantage of first mention: The advantage of a first-mentioned character or concept in sentence comprehension and memory. (Ch. 9)

Agent: In case grammar, the "doer" of the action in a sentence. (Ch. 8, 9)

Agnosia: Disrupted object recognition, due to brain damage. (Ch. 10)

Algorithm: A specific rule or solution procedure that is guaranteed to furnish the correct answer if followed correctly. (Ch. 11)

Ambiguous; ambiguity: A word or sentence has more than one meaning. (Ch. 6, 8)

Amnesia: Disruption in memory, due to brain damage; see also **retrograde amnesia** and **anterograde amnesia.** (Ch. 10)

Analogy: A relationship between two similar situations, problems, or concepts. (Ch. 12)

Anomia: Disruption in word finding, due to brain damage. (Ch. 10)

Antecedent: See **conditional reasoning.**

Anterograde amnesia: Disruption of memory for information and events after brain damage, including learning. (Ch. 10)

Aphasia: Disrupted language abilities or processes due to brain damage. (Ch. 10)

Arbitrariness: The linguistic universal noting that there is no inherent, built-in connection between a unit in language (e.g., a word) and the concept it names. (Ch. 8)

Arousal: Alertness; available attentional capacity. (Ch. 3)

Articulatory rehearsal loop: The component in Baddeley's model of working memory responsible for temporary storage and manipulation of sound- or articulation-based information. (Ch. 4)

Association: The linking together of two events, objects, or ideas because they tend to occur together in experience. (Ch. 1)

Attention: The mental process of concentrating effort on a stimulus or mental event; the limited mental energy or resource that "powers" the mental system. (Ch. 1, 3)

Attenuation: An alternative explanation to filtering in attention, in which competing messages are reduced in strength (loudness, informational value) relative to the primary message. (Ch. 3)

Audition: The sense of hearing. (Ch. 2)

Auditory sensory memory: The component of sensory memory that holds auditory information for a brief interval; also called *echoic memory*. (Ch. 2, 3)

Authorized versus unauthorized: Intended versus unintended. An inference is said to be authorized if it was the inference intended by the speaker. (Ch. 9)

Autobiographical memory: Memory for ordinary, natural experiences and information that we encounter in a lifetime. (Ch. 7)

Automatic versus conscious processing: The distinction between mental processes that happen with little or no awareness and those that consume attentional resources. (Ch. 1, 3)

Automaticity: See **automatic versus conscious processing.**

Availability: The presence of some piece of information in memory. (Ch. 5)

Availability heuristic: A decision strategy based on how easily relevant examples or information can be retrieved from memory. (Ch. 11)

Backward masking: A situation in which a later visual stimulus interferes backward in time with the perception of the first. (Ch. 2)

Belief level of analysis: In language, analysis of the message with respect to the speaker's and listener's knowledge of each other, and the context of the utterance. (Ch. 9)

Benefits: See **facilitation.**

Bottom-up processing: See **data-driven versus conceptually driven processing.**

Bridging: The process of constructing a connection between concepts during comprehension. (Ch. 9)

Broca's aphasia: Disruption in the grammatical and/or fluent articulation of language, but not comprehension, due to brain damage. (Ch. 10)

Brown-Peterson task: A task in which a triad of items, held in short-term memory while performing a distractor task, must then be recalled. (Ch. 4)

Case grammar: A set of semantic rules for language comprehension and production; also called *semantic case grammar*. (Ch. 8)

Case roles: See **semantic case.**

Categorical perception: In language, perceiving slightly different sounds as being the same phoneme. (Ch. 8)

Categorical syllogism: See **syllogism.**

Cerebral cortex: See **neocortex.**

Cerebral lateralization: That different functions are controlled by different sides ("lateral-") of the brain; that different functions tend to rely more heavily on one hemisphere or the other, or are performed differently in the two hemispheres. (Ch. 10)

Characteristic feature: A common or frequent semantic feature of a concept, but not essential or necessary to its meaning (e.g., *perches in trees* for ROBIN). (Ch. 6)

Chunk: Especially in short-term memory, the grouping of information or the enriched item of information. (Ch. 4)

Coarticulation: The phenomenon in which more than one phoneme at a time is affecting articulation. (Ch. 8)

Cognition: The collection of mental processes and activities used in perceiving, learning, remembering, thinking, and understanding, and the act of using those processes; thought. (Ch. 1)

Cognitive economy: The hypothesis that only nonredundant information is stored in semantic memory, thus making storage economical. (Ch. 6)

Cognitive neuropsychology: The study of cognitive processing as revealed by special methods of investigation (FMRI, ERPs) and by disrupted performance due to brain damage. (Ch. 10)

Cognitive science: The hybrid discipline that studies the mind and its processes, including cognitive psychology, artificial intelligence, the neurosciences, and a few other related fields. (Ch. 1)

Competence versus performance: The internalized knowledge of language and its rules that fully fluent speakers of a language possess, versus the actual language behavior that a speaker might generate; distinction advanced by Chomsky. (Ch. 8)

Computer analogy: The similarity between the unseen electrical events in a computer and the unseen mental events in the mind; a guiding analogy in early cognitive science. (Ch. 1)

Conceptual level of analysis: In language, analysis of the message with respect to general world knowledge. (Ch. 9)

Conceptually driven processing: See **data-driven versus conceptually driven processing.**

Conditional reasoning: If-then reasoning, in which we make a logical determination of whether the evidence supports, refutes, or is irrelevant to the stated if-then relationship. The IF is the *antecedent*, and the THEN is the *consequent*. (Ch. 11)

Confirmation bias: A situation in which one searches for evidence consistent with one's decisions, beliefs, or hypotheses. (Ch. 11)

Connectionism: A computer-based approach to modeling cognition, based on the ideas of simple units or nodes interconnected with weighted pathways or links; also called *neural net modeling* and *parallel distributed processing (PDP) modeling*. (Ch. 2, 6)

Connectionist model: A modern, computer-based model of cognitive processing and the human mind; see also **connectionism.** (Ch. 2)

Consequent: See **conditional reasoning.**

Conscious: See **automatic versus conscious processing.**

Content accuracy: The recollection of general ideas, gist, and theme, rather than exact wording, and so on. (Ch. 7)

Context: The accumulated or activated information, say in a sentence, that assists comprehension or guides memory retrieval. (Ch. 2, 6, 7, 8, 9)

Contralaterality: The principle that one side of the body is controlled by the opposite (contra-) side of the brain. (Ch. 10)

Conversational maxims: The rules that govern our conversational interactions with others. (Ch. 9)

Cooperative principle: The rule in conversation that each participant assumes that all speakers are following the conversational rules, and that each contribution to the conversation is sincere and appropriate. (Ch. 9)

Corpus callosum: The neural fiber structure connecting the left and right hemispheres of the neocortex. (Ch. 10)

Costs: See **inhibition.**

Cued recall: A recall task in which cues are provided to assist retrieval. (Ch. 5, 7)

Data-driven versus conceptually driven processing: The distinction between mental processes that rely very heavily or exclusively on incoming information, and those that rely on information already stored in memory; also called *bottom-up versus top-down processing*. (Ch. 1, 2, 3)

Decay: A general explanation for forgetting, in which information is lost because of the passage of time. (Ch. 2, 4, 5)

Default value: In script theory, the common or typical value of a frame; the value that is assumed to be true unless it's changed by a detail in the story; (e.g., the menu in a restaurant script). (Ch. 7)

Defining feature: A necessary semantic feature for a concept to be categorized as belonging to a certain category (e.g., *animate* for BIRD). (Ch. 6)

Depth of processing: The framework in which memory is conceived as a continuum, from a very shallow, sensory level to a deep, semantic level; also called *levels of processing*. (Ch. 5)

Direct theory: In conversation, the speaker's theory of the listener, the mental model of what the conversational partner knows, is interested in, and is like. (Ch. 9)

Discourse focus: The primary or intended topic of a sentence or passage of text. (Ch. 9)

Discriminability effect: See **distance effect.**

Displacement: The characteristic of language that enables us to talk about a time other than the immediate present. (Ch. 8)

Dissociations; method of dissociations: Behavioral evidence for the independence of mental processes or functions, especially from brain-damaged individuals. (Ch. 10)

Distance effect: The greater the distance or difference between two stimuli being compared, the faster the decision that they differ. (Ch. 11)

Domain knowledge: Expertise; knowledge about some particular topic. (Ch. 12)

Double dissociation: The *mutual* independence of mental processes or functions, based on evidence from brain-damaged individuals. (Ch. 10)

Dual-coding hypothesis: Paivio's hypothesis that words denoting concrete, as opposed to abstract, concepts can be encoded in memory twice, once as a word and once as an image, and thus are recalled better. (Ch. 5)

Dual task/dual message: A testing procedure in which two tasks are performed concurrently, or two messages are presented concurrently, such that both tasks/messages together exceed the individual's attentional capacity. (Ch. 3, 4)

Echoic memory: See **auditory sensory memory.**

Ecological validity: The position that the research setting and task should resemble situations in the real world in order for the research to be meaningful or generalizable. (Ch. 2)

Elaborative rehearsal: Rehearsal based on meaning and other elaborative information intended to store the information at deeper levels in memory; also called *type II rehearsal*. (Ch. 5)

Empiricism versus rationalism: The objective scientific approach based on observation versus the more philosophical, deductive approach to knowledge. (Ch. 1)

Encoding: Bringing external information from the environment into the mental system and registering it there. (Ch. 1)

Encoding specificity: The principle that additional information that is present during encoding is stored in memory along with the target information itself. (Ch. 5)

Enhancement: Facilitation of a concept, especially in reading and comprehension; see also **facilitation.** (Ch. 9)

Episodic memory: That portion of long-term memory in which personally experienced events and episodes are stored—one's autobiography. (Ch. 5)

Erasure: In sensory memory, when a later stimulus interferes with memory of an earlier stimulus. (Ch. 2)

Explicit memory: See **implicit versus explicit memory.**

Eye gaze: See **gaze duration.**

Eye-mind assumption: In reading research, the assumption that the mind's activity in comprehension is reflected in the movements of the eye. (Ch. 9)

Facilitation: The positive influence on mental processing of a prime, usually a speedup of processing or an increase in accuracy; also called *benefits*. (Ch. 6)

False alarm/false positive: Saying "yes" to a distractor item; identifying an item as having been presented when it was not. (Ch. 7)

False memories: Memory for information that was never presented, or for events that never happened. (Ch. 7)

Familiarity bias: A bias in reasoning in which one's familiarity with the information misleads reasoning about the information. (Ch. 11)

Feature list: See **pattern recognition and semantic features.**

Feature: A simple, elementary pattern or fragment that appears in combinations with other features. (Ch. 2)

Feature detection: The theoretical approach that explains pattern recognition by the detection of features. (Ch. 2)

Filtering: See **selective attention.**

Fixation: A pause in eye movements, during which the eye focuses on a visual stimulus and encodes it into the visual system. (Ch. 2)

Flashbulb memory: A hypothesized special kind of vivid, nearly "photographic" memory for an event, usually of some highly significant occurrence. (Ch. 7)

Focal attention: See **visual attention.**

Forgetting: Formally, the genuine loss of information from memory; colloquially, the term also refers to difficulties of retrieval. (Ch. 5, 7)

Fovea: Central region of the retina specialized for acute, focused, color vision. (Ch. 2)

Frames: In script theory, details about specific events within a script, or slots to be filled with those details. (Ch. 7)

Free recall: Recalling information in any order. (Ch. 4, 5)

Functional fixedness: A tendency in problem solving to use objects and concepts in the problem environment only in their customary and usual way. (Ch. 12)

Gaze duration: Experimental methodology in which we record where and how long the eyes gaze at words during reading; also called *eye fixation*. (Ch. 8, 9)

General problem solver (GPS): The early computer simulation by Newell, Shaw, and Simon, that solved problems by means-end analysis. (Ch. 12)

Generation effect: Enhanced memory performance for items or information generated by the participant rather than provided by the experimenter. (Ch. 5)

Geons: In Biederman's recognition by components model, the simple components (*geometrical ions*) of physical objects that the recognition system detects and identifies. (Ch. 2)

Gestalt: In Gestalt psychology, a whole pattern or configuration. (Ch. 12)

Goal: The desired end point or solution of the problem-solving activity. (Ch. 12)

GPS: See **general problem solver.**

Grammar: A system of rules for generating language. (Ch. 8)

Headers: In script theory, early words and concepts in a story that help identify the correct script. (Ch. 7)

Hemispheres: The left and right halves of the neocortex.

Hemispheric specialization: The principle that the two hemispheres have different specializations. (Ch. 10)

Heuristic: An informal "rule of thumb" strategy or approach that works under some circumstances but is not guaranteed to yield the correct answer. (Ch. 11)

Hippocampus: The curved structure interior to the temoporal lobe critical for storing new long-term memory information. (Ch. 10)

Iconic: The characteristic in which a language unit has a physical resemblance to its referent (e.g., the word *buzz*). (Ch. 8)

Icon: A term referring to the very brief record of visual information held in visual sensory memory. (Ch. 2)

Iconic memory: See **visual sensory memory.**

Ill-defined problems: Problems in which the information given in a problem, the desired goal, or both are poorly or incompletely specified. (Ch. 12)

Immediacy assumption: The assumption that we begin comprehending and interpreting immediately as we read. (Ch. 9)

Implication: The speaker's or writer's intended reference or intended meaning in a sentence. (Ch. 9)

Implicit versus explicit memory: Memory or memory processes that occur without any necessary involvement of consciousness versus those that occur with conscious awareness. (Chs. 1, 6, 10)

Indirect request: A polite form of request directed toward others in which we do not literally state the actual request, but only indirectly ask for something (e.g., "Excuse me, but do you have the correct time?"). (Ch. 9)

Inference: The connection drawn by a listener or reader that determines the meaning of a message. (Ch. 1, 9)

Inhibition: The negative influence on mental processing of a prime, usually a slowing down of processing or a decrease in accuracy; also called *costs*. (Ch. 6)

Insight: A deep, useful understanding of the nature of something, especially a difficult problem in a problem-solving situation, often thought to occur suddenly. (Ch. 12)

Interference: A general explanation for forgetting, in which other information competes with or disrupts memory for certain target information. (Ch. 2, 4, 5)

Intersection: That place in the semantic network where two separate patterns of spreading activation meet. (Ch. 6)

Introspection: The method of having trained participants "look inward" (introspect) and report their inner sensations and experiences. (Ch. 1)

Jargon babbling: An early phase in language acquisition when infants babble syllable- and wordlike sounds in sentencelike combinations. (Ch. 8)

Just noticeable difference (jnd): The amount by which a stimulus must be changed in order for the change to be detected. (Ch. 11)

Lag: In a priming task, the number of intervening stimuli between a prime and a target. (Ch. 6)

Language: A shared symbolic system for communication. (Ch. 8)

Leading question: A question that suggests the desired answer. (Ch. 7)

Lesions: Physical damage to brain tissue. (Ch. 10)

Levels of processing: See **depth of processing.**

Lexical decision task: The experimental task in which a string of letters is presented and the participant is timed in deciding whether the string is a word. (Ch. 6)

Limited capacity: The relatively small capacity or quantity of mental resources or attention that can be devoted to a task. (Ch. 3, 4)

Linguistic universals: The characteristics that are universally true of all human languages. (Ch. 8)

Linguistics: The academic discipline that studies language *per se*. (Ch. 8)

Location: The semantic case that specifies *where* some action or event happened. (Ch. 9)

Maintenance rehearsal: Rehearsal intended only to keep or maintain information at a particular level; also called *type I rehearsal*. (Ch. 5)

Mapping: In problem solving, the one-to-one correspondences between elements of problems, as in analogies. (Ch. 12)

Mean length of utterance (MLU): Standard measure of the complexity of children's speech, computed as the number of morphemes or words in the child's "average" sentence. (Ch. 8)

Means-end analysis: A problem-solving heuristic in which the problem solver repeatedly finds the difference between the current state and the goal state, then finds and applies an operator that reduces that difference. (Ch. 12)

Memory: The mental processes of acquiring and retaining information for later retrieval, and the mental storage system in which these processes operate. (Ch. 1)

Memory impairment: A genuine change or alteration in memory for an experienced event because of the effect of some later event. (Ch. 7)

Memory search: In short-term memory, how the contents of STM are searched, especially in the Sternberg task (e.g., parallel, serial self-terminating, and serial-exhaustive search). (Ch. 4)

Memory set: The set of items to be held in memory, usually in short-term or working memory research. (Ch. 4)

Memory span: The number of individual items recallable after any short display; also called *span of attention*, *span of immediate memory*, and *span of apprehension*. (Ch. 2, 4)

Mental lexicon: A mental dictionary of words; a hypothesized component of semantic memory containing word knowledge. (Ch. 6, 8, 9)

Mental model: One's knowledge of a domain and how the domain works. (Ch. 11)

Metacognition: Knowledge about one's own cognitive processes and mental system. (Ch. 1)

Metamemory: Knowledge about one's own memory system, how it works and how it fails to work. (Ch. 5)

Method of loci: A mnemonic device based on previously learned physical locations and visual imagery. (Ch. 5)

Misinformation acceptance: Accepting additional information as having been part of some earlier experience without actually remembering that information. (Ch. 7)

MLU: See **mean length of utterance.**

Mnemonic device: An active, strategic kind of learning device or recall method, a rehearsal strategy. (Ch. 5)

Modus ponens: In the conditional-reasoning problem "If *p* then *q*," collecting evidence *p*, thus supporting the conclusion "Therefore, *q*." (Ch. 11)

Modus tollens: In the conditional-reasoning problem "If *p* then *q*," collecting evidence *not q*, thus supporting the conclusion "Therefore, *not p*." (Ch. 11)

Morpheme: The smallest unit of language that has meaning. (Ch. 8)

Naive physics: People's misconceptions about how objects move or behave in the real world. (Ch. 11)

Negative set: In problem solving, a bias or tendency to solve problems in one particular way, using only a single approach even when a different approach might be more productive. (Ch. 12)

Neocortex: The top layer of the brain, responsible for higher-level mental processes; also called *cerebral cortex*. (Ch. 10)

Network: The collection of interrelated concepts and their pathways in semantic memory. (Ch. 6)

Neural net modeling: See **connectionism.**

Neurocognition: See **cognitive neuropsychology.**

Neuron: The cell specialized for receiving and transmitting a neural impulse; nerve cell. (Ch. 10)

Neurotransmitter: The chemical released into the synapse from the axon terminals, either helping to excite or inhibit the postsynaptic neuron. (Ch. 10)

Node: A point or location in the semantic space, roughly corresponding to a concept or a simple fact about a concept. (Ch. 6)

Occipital lobe: The rearmost lobe of the brain, where visual stimuli are first projected in the cortex. (Ch. 2, 10)

On-line; on-line task: Occurring now; used to describe research tasks that measure a process as it happens. (Chs. 1, 9)

Operators: The set of legal operations or "moves" in solving a problem. (Ch. 12)

Organization: The structuring or restructuring of information as it is stored in memory (e.g., clustering or grouping, semantic hierarchies, subjective organization, etc.). (Ch. 5, 6)

Overextension: In language acquisition, use of a term beyond its appropriate level of reference (e.g., "Daddy" for any adult male). (Ch. 8)

Parallel distributed processing (PDP): See **connectionism.**

Partial report: See **whole-report/partial-report condition.**

Pathway: A labeled, directional association or link between concepts, especially in semantic memory. (Ch. 6)

Patient: In case grammar, the recipient of the action in a sentence; also called *recipient*. (Ch. 8, 9)

Pattern recognition: The classification and identification of a pattern. (Ch. 2)

PDP: See **connectionism.**

Peg-word mnemonic: A mnemonic device based on previously learned rhyming pegs (e.g., one is a bun, two is a shoe, etc.). (Ch. 5)

Perception: The process of interpreting and recognizing sensory information. (Ch. 2)

Performance (in linguistics): See **competence versus performance.**

Persistence: See **visual persistence.**

Pertinence: Importance, especially in Norman's theory of selective attention. (Ch. 3)

Phonemes: The basic individual speech sounds that compose a language (e.g., the /b/ sound in *beg*). (Ch. 2, 8)

Phonology: The study of the production and perception of language sounds; the sounds of language. (Ch. 8)

Phrase structure rules: The grammatical rules that group words into phrases, specifying some of the structure of the sentence; a theory of language relying on phrase structure rules. (Ch. 8)

PI: See **proactive interference.**

Primacy effect: Elevated accuracy for items presented early in a list. (Ch. 4, 5)

Prime and target: In a priming task, the prime is the first-presented stimulus, and the target is the stimulus that follows the prime. (Ch. 6)

Priming: The activation of information in memory, making it more accessible for subsequent use. (Ch. 3, 6, 9)

Proactive interference (PI): When older information interferes forward in time with your recollection of the current, or newer, information. (Ch. 4, 5)

Problem space: The initial, intermediate, and goal states of a problem, and the problem solver's knowledge at each step; the overall setting within which a problem is solved. (Ch. 12)

Problem of invariance: The sounds of speech (phonemes) are not invariant from one time to the next. (Ch. 2, 8)

Procedural knowledge: Knowledge of how to do things; the long-term memory store for procedures. (Ch. 12)

Production: An If-Then (condition-action) pair of statements, especially in a model of problem solving. (Ch. 12)

Productivity: The principle that language is novel, consisting of utterances that have never been uttered or comprehended before; also called *generativity*. (Ch. 8)

Propositions: Simple idea units in text or discourse; a set of conceptual nodes connected by labeled pathways, the entire collection of which expresses sentence meaning. (Ch. 7, 8, 9)

Prosopagnosia: Disrupted face recognition, due to brain damage. (Ch. 10)

Psycholinguistics: The study of language as it is learned and used by people. (Ch. 8)

Psychophysics: The study of how perceptual experience differs from the physical stimulation that is being perceived. (Ch. 11)

Rationalism: See **empiricism versus rationalism.**

Reaction time: The time it takes to respond to a stimulus, usually measured in milliseconds (msec), thousandths of a second. (Ch. 1)

Recency effect: Elevated accuracy for the final items in a list, usually in a free-recall task. (Ch. 4, 5)

Recoding: The grouping of items together so that the newly formed group can be remembered (short-term memory); changing the mental format or representation of information. (Ch. 4)

Recognition by components model: Biederman's model of object recognition, in which we identify objects by breaking them down into their simple components, called *geons*. (Ch. 2)

Recognition task: Yes/no task in which the participant decides if the stimulus has been seen or studied before; contrast with recall and relearning tasks. (Ch. 5, 6, 7)

Reconstructive memory: The process in which we construct a memory by combining elements from the original event or material with knowledge we already possess; as distinct from *reproductive memory*, which refers to accurate retrieval of exactly what was stored about the event or material. (Ch. 7)

Recovered memories: Memories that are "remembered" after a long period during which they were "forgotten," especially due to repression; see also **false memories.** (Ch. 7)

Reference: The linguistic device of alluding to a concept by using another name (a *synonym*). (Ch. 9)

Rehearsal: Deliberate mental repetition, recycling, or practicing of to-be-learned material. (Ch. 4, 5)

Relation: In case grammar, the topic, action, or major event in a sentence. (Ch. 8, 9)

Relearning task: The task, invented by Ebbinghaus, in which information is learned, set aside for a period of time, then relearned to the same criterion of accuracy. (Ch. 5)

Release from PI: When proactive interference is reduced or eliminated due to a change in the stimuli. (Ch. 4, 5)

Representation: A general term referring to the way information is stored in memory (e.g., storing information in an auditory or visual representation). (Ch. 1)

Representativeness heuristic: A decision strategy in which an outcome is judged by how representative it is of the process or population that generated it (e.g., judging coin tosses by how random they look). (Ch. 11)

Repression: Intentional forgetting of painful or traumatic experiences, from Freudian theory; see also **recovered memories.** (Ch. 7)

Retina: The three basic layers of neurons in the eye, including the layer that contains the rods and cones that start the process of vision. (Ch. 2)

Retrieval: The process of finding or accessing information in memory. (Ch. 1)

Retrieval failure: Loss of access to information still stored in memory. (Ch. 5)

Retroactive interference: When newer information interferes backward in time with your recollection of older information. (Ch. 4, 5)

Retrograde amnesia: Disruption of memory for information acquired prior to brain damage. (Ch. 10)

S-V-O sentence: A sentence in subject-verb-object order. (Ch. 8)

Saccade: A voluntary, rapid movement of the eyes. (Ch. 2)

Satisficing: The heuristic in which one finds a solution that is satisfactory, although not necessarily the best possible solution. (Ch. 12)

Savings score: In a relearning task, the amount (number of trials) saved during relearning compared to original learning. (Ch. 5)

Schema, schemata: A stored framework or body of knowledge about some topic; see also **reconstructive memory.** (Ch. 7)

Scripts: Large-scale semantic and episodic knowledge structures that accumulate in memory and guide interpretation and comprehension; see especially **schema** and **reconstructive memory.** (Ch. 7)

Second-order theory: In conversation, the speaker's evaluation of the other participant's direct theory—what you think the other participant believes about you. (Ch. 9)

Selecting; selective attention: The mental process of selecting one message or stimulus for further processing and attention while filtering out or not attending to other stimuli. (Ch. 3)

Semantic: Having to do with meaning; see also **semantics** and **linguistics.** (Ch. 6, 7, 8, 9)

Semanticity: The linguistic universal that asserts that language symbols and units convey meaning. (Ch. 8)

Semantic case: The particular semantic role played by a concept in the meaning of a sentence (e.g., agent, patient, instrument). (Ch. 8, 9)

Semantic case grammar: See **case grammar.**

Semantic congruity effect: Judgments are speeded when the things being compared are congruent with the instructions (e.g., instructions to "choose the larger" of two large things). (Ch. 11)

Semantic features: Simple, one-element characteristics or properties of semantic concepts; in the Smith Feature Overlap Model, stored as a *feature list*. (Ch. 6)

Semantic integration: The tendency to store together in memory related pieces of information, even if they did not occur together in experience. (Ch. 7)

Semantic memory: That portion of long-term memory in which general world (conceptual) knowledge is stored, including language; loosely speaking, the mental encyclopedia and dictionary. (Ch. 5, 6)

Semantic relatedness: The principle that related concepts are stored closely together in semantic memory, with strong connecting pathways between them. (Ch. 6)

Semantics: The study of word meaning. (Ch. 8)

Sensation: Receiving or registering physical stimulation and encoding it into the nervous system. (Ch. 2)

Sensory memory: A very brief memory system for sensory events. (Ch. 1)

Sentence verification task: An experimental task in which simple sentences are presented to participants for their timed yes/no decisions. (Ch. 6)

Serial-position curve: A graph showing recall accuracy as a function of an item's original position in a list. (Ch. 4, 5)

Serial recall: Recalling information in its order of presentation. (Ch. 4, 5)

Shadowing: A task in which the participant repeats out loud the message heard in one ear but ignores the message in the other ear. (Ch. 2, 3)

Short-term memory: The limited-capacity memory component for temporary information storage and manipulation; a memory system for information currently being attended or rehearsed; see also **working memory.** (Ch. 1, 4)

Simulation heuristic: A decision strategy in which we forecast or predict an outcome of some future or imagined event. (Ch. 11)

Slots: See **frames.**

SOA: See **stimulus onset asynchrony.**

Source memory: Memory for the exact source of information. (Ch. 7)

Source misattribution effect: The inability to distinguish whether some original event or a later event was the true source of information. (Ch. 7)

Span of apprehension: See **memory span.**

Split brain: Term referring to research performed on patients whose corpus callosum has been cut, thus preventing the two hemispheres from transmitting information to each other internally. (Ch. 10)

Spreading activation: The mental activity of accessing and retrieving information from the semantic network. (Ch. 6)

Sternberg task: The task in which a probe item is mentally compared to the several items being held in short-term memory, to determine if the probe matches one of the items. (Ch. 4)

Stimulus onset asynchrony (SOA): In a priming task, the interval of time between the onset of the prime and the onset of the target. (Ch. 6)

Structure building: The general notion of building a mental representation of sentence meaning; see especially Gernsbacher's Structure Building Framework. (Ch. 9)

Subgoal: An intermediate goal along the route to eventual solution of a problem. (Ch. 12)

Subjective organization: An idiosyncratic organizational scheme imposed by the subject during learning and recall, often on lists of unrelated words. (Ch. 5)

Suppression: Inhibition of a concept, especially in reading and comprehension; see also **inhibition.** (Ch. 9)

Syllogism: A three-statement logical form in which the first two state the premises, and the third states the conclusion (e.g., "All A are B. All B are C. Therefore all A are C."). Also called *categorical syllogism*. (Ch. 11)

Symbolic distance effect: The distance effect in situations in which two symbols are being compared, rather than two perceptual events (e.g., comparing the numbers 2 and 3, or the concepts *warm* and *hot*). (Ch. 11)

Synapse: The gap between the axon terminals of one neuron and the dendrites of another, into which a neurotransmitter is released during neural transmission. (Ch. 10)

Syntax: The study of rules determining the order of words and phrases, and grammatical features of the language (e.g., suffixes like *-ing*); the ordering of words in a sentence to show their relationship to one another; sentence structure. (Ch. 8)

T-scope: See **tachistoscope.**

Tabula rasa: "Blank slate" or "blank wax tablet"; refers to the idea that experience, rather than innate factors, accounts for behavior; a tenet of behaviorism. (Ch. 1)

Tachistoscope: A specialized instrument for presenting visual stimuli for controlled durations; referred to as a T-scope. (Ch. 2)

Target: See **prime and target.**

Technical accuracy: The recollection of exact, specific information, or the scoring of recall based on the exact stimulus material. (Ch. 7)

Template matching: The theory of recognition that exact patterns (templates) are stored in memory and are then matched to a stimulus in order to recognize it. (Ch. 2)

Thalamus: Structure in the "old brain" which serves as a relay station into the cortex for incoming sensory information. (Ch. 10)

Thematic effect: Recalling based on the theme or suggested meaning of a passage, rather than recalling the exact passage; see also **reconstructive memory.** (Ch. 7)

Tip-of-the-tongue (TOT) state: Momentary inability to recall information from long-term memory. (Ch. 5, 10)

Top-down bias: A situation in which existing knowledge biases one's reasoning. (Ch. 11)

Top-down processing: See **data-driven versus conceptually driven processing.**

Topic maintenance: Making contributions to a conversation relevant and to the topic; the processes of selecting then continuing with a topic in conversation. (Ch. 9)

TOT state: See **tip-of-the-tongue state.**

Transformational grammar: Chomsky's theory of language and syntax; that part of Chomsky's theory containing rules for generating active versus passive, affirmative versus negative, and like sentences. (Ch. 8)

Typicality effect: The result that typical members of a category are judged more rapidly than atypical, uncommon members. (Ch. 6)

Undoing: Part of the simulation heuristic, in which minor changes in a situation "undo" or prevent some outcome. (Ch. 11)

Verbal learning: The tradition of research started by Ebbinghaus, in which the learning of verbal materials was studied. (Ch. 1, 5)

Verbal protocol: A transcription and analysis of a participant's verbalizations during problem solving. (Ch. 12)

Verbal reports: Statements made by people about their thoughts, ideas, and strategies during cognitive processing. (Ch. 1, 12)

Visual agnosia: See **agnosia.**

Visual attention: The mental process of directing mental attention to a portion of the information that was perceived visually, usually after the visual stimulus is no longer present; also called *focal attention*. (Ch. 2)

Visual cortex: The region of the occipital lobe specialized for early stages of visual processing. (Ch. 10)

Visual imagery: The mental picturing of a stimulus that then affects later recall or recognition; the mental activity of using a visual representation. (Ch. 5)

Visual neglect: A disorder in which the brain-damaged individual ignores or fails to attend to one half of the visual field (usually the left). (Ch. 10)

Visual persistence: The apparent persistence of a visual stimulus beyond its physical duration. (Ch. 2)

Visual sensory memory: The memory system that receives visual input from the eyes and holds it for a brief amount of time; also called *iconic memory*. (Ch. 2)

Visuo-spatial sketchpad: The component in Baddeley's model of working memory responsible for temporary storage and manipulation of visual and spatial information. (Ch. 4)

Von Restorff effect: Elevated recall of information that was highlighted in some way during original acquisition; improved retention for a list item made distinct or different from the rest of the list. (Ch. 7)

Well-defined problems: Problems in which the initial state, operators, and goal state are well specified. Contrast with **ill-defined problems.** (Ch. 12)

Wernicke's aphasia: Disruption in the comprehension of language, but not grammar or articulation, due to brain damage. (Ch. 10)

Whole-report/partial-report condition: Testing conditions in which participants recall the entire display or are cued to recall only part of the display; used especially in visual sensory memory research. (Ch. 2)

Working memory: (1) Similar to *short-term memory*, but focusing more on the effort involved in mental activities; the mental workbench. (2) Baddeley's model of working memory, containing the *central executive*, the *articulatory rehearsal loop*, and the *visuo-spatial sketchpad*. (Ch. 1, 4)

References

Abbot, V., Black, J. B., & Smith, E. E. (1985). The representation of scripts in memory. *Journal of Memory and Language, 24*, 179–199.

Abelson, R. P. (1981). Psychological status of the script concept. *American Psychologist, 36*, 715–729.

Agnoli, F., & Krantz, D. H. (1989). Suppressing natural heuristics by formal instruction: The case of the conjunction fallacy. *Cognitive Psychology, 21*, 515–550.

Ahlum-Heath, M. E., & DiVesta, F. J. (1986). The effect of conscious controlled verbalization of a cognitive strategy on transfer in problem solving. *Memory & Cognition, 14*, 281–285.

Albrecht, J. E., & O'Brien, E. J. (1991). Effects of centrality on retrieval of text-based concepts. *Journal of Experimental Psychology: Learning, Memory, and Cognition, 17*, 932–939.

Allport, A. (1989). Visual attention. In M. I. Posner (Ed.), *Foundations of cognitive science* (pp. 631–682). Cambridge, MA: Bradford.

Allport, D. A. (1980). Attention and performance. In G. Claxton (Ed.), *Cognitive psychology: New directions* (pp. 26–64). London: Routledge & Kegan Paul.

Anderson, J. R. (1976). *Language, memory, and thought*. Hillsdale, NJ: Erlbaum.

Anderson, J. R. (1980). *Cognitive psychology and its implications*. San Francisco: Freeman.

Anderson, J. R. (1982). Acquisition of cognitive skill. *Psychological Review, 89*, 369–406.

Anderson, J. R. (1983). *The architecture of cognition*. Cambridge, MA: Harvard University Press.

Anderson, J. R. (1985). *Cognitive psychology and its implications* (2nd ed.). New York: Freeman.

Anderson, J. R. (1990). *The adaptive character of thought*. Hillsdale, NJ: Erlbaum.

Anderson, J. R. (1992). Intelligent tutoring and high school mathematics. In *Proceedings of the Second International Conference on Intelligent Tutoring Systems* (pp. 1–10). Montreal, Quebec: Springer-Verlag.

Anderson, J. R. (1993). Problem solving and learning. *American Psychologist, 48*, 35–44.

Anderson, J. R., & Bower, G. H. (1973). *Human associative memory*. Washington, DC: Winston & Sons.

Anderson, J. R., Boyle, C. F., Corbett, A., & Lewis, M. W. (1990). Cognitive modelling and intelligent tutoring. *Artificial Intelligence, 42*, 7–49.

Anderson, J. R., Reder, L. M., & Lebiere, C. (1996). Working memory: Activation limitations on retrieval. *Cognitive Psychology, 30*, 221–256.

Anderson, J. R., & Schooler, L. J. (1991). Reflections of the environment in memory. *Psychological Science, 2*, 396–408.

Antrobus, J. (1991). Dreaming: Cognitive processes during cortical activation and high afferent thresholds. *Psychological Review, 98*, 96–121.

Ashcraft, M. H. (1976). Priming and property dominance effects in semantic memory. *Memory & Cognition, 4*, 490–500.

Ashcraft, M. H. (1978). Property norms for typical and atypical items from 17 categories: A description and discussion. *Memory & Cognition, 6*, 227–232.

Ashcraft, M. H. (1989). *Human memory and cognition*. Glenview, IL: Scott Foresman.

Ashcraft, M. H. (1993). A personal case history of transient anomia. *Brain and Language, 44*, 47–57.

Ashcraft, M. H. (1994). *Human memory and cognition* (2nd ed.). New York: Harper-Collins.

Ashcraft, M. H. (1995). Cognitive psychology and simple arithmetic: A review and summary of new directions. *Mathematical Cognition, 1*, 3–34.

Ashcraft, M. H., & Christy, K. S. (1995). The frequency of arithmetic facts in elementary texts: Addition and multiplication in grades 1–6. *Journal for Research in Mathematics Education, 26*, 396–421.

Atkinson, R. C., & Shiffrin, R. M. (1968). Human memory: A proposed system and its control processes. In W. K. Spence & J. T. Spence (Eds.), *The psychology of learning and motivation: Advances in research and theory* (Vol. 2, pp. 89–195). New York: Academic Press.

Atkinson, R. C., & Shiffrin, R. M. (1971). The control of short-term memory. *Scientific American, 225*, 82–90.

Atwood, M. E., & Polson, P. (1976). A process model for water jug problems. *Cognitive Psychology, 8*, 191–216.

Averbach, E., & Coriell, A. S. (1973). Short-term memory in vision. In Coltheart, M. (Ed.), *Readings in cognitive psychology* (pp. 9–26). Toronto: Holt, Rinehart & Winston of Canada. (Reprinted from *Bell System Technical Journal*, 1961 *40*, 309–328).

Averbach, E., & Sperling, G. (1961). Short-term storage of information in vision. In C. Cherry (Ed.), *Information theory* (pp. 196–211). London: Butterworth.

Baars, B. J. (1986). *The cognitive revolution in psychology*. New York: Guilford.

Baddeley, A. D. (1976). *The psychology of memory*. New York: Basic Books.

Baddeley, A. D. (1978). The trouble with levels: A reexamination of Craik and Lockhart's framework for memory research. *Psychological Review, 85*, 139–152.

Baddeley, A. D. (1986). *Working memory*. Oxford: Clarendon Press.

Baddeley, A. D. (1992a). Is working memory working? The Fifteenth Bartlett Lecture. *Quarterly Journal of Experimental Psychology, 44A*, 1–31.

Baddeley, A. D. (1992b). Working memory. *Science, 255*, 556–559.

Baddeley, A. D., & Hitch, G. (1974). Working memory. In G. H. Bower (Ed.), *The psychology of learning and motivation* (Vol. 8, pp. 47–89). New York: Academic Press.

Baddeley, A. D., & Lieberman, K. (1980). Spatial working memory. In R. Nickerson (Ed.), *Attention and performance VIII*. Hillsdale, NJ: Erlbaum.

Baddeley, A. D., Thomson, N., & Buchanan, M. (1975). Word length and the structure of short-term memory. *Journal of Verbal Learning and Verbal Behavior, 14*, 575–589.

Bahrick, H. P. (1983). The cognitive map of a city—50 years of learning and memory. In G. H. Bower (Ed.), *The psychology of learning and motivation: Advances in research and theory* (Vol. 17, pp. 125–163). New York: Academic Press.

Bahrick, H. P. (1984). Semantic memory content in permastore: Fifty years of memory for Spanish learned in school. *Journal of Experimental Psychology: General, 113*, 1–29.

Bahrick, H. P., Bahrick, P. C., & Wittlinger, R. P. (1975). Fifty years of memories for names and faces: A cross-sectional approach. *Journal of Experimental Psychology: General, 104*, 54–75.

Bahrick, H. P., & Hall, L. K. (1991). Lifetime maintenance of high school mathematics content. *Journal of Experimental Psychology: General, 120*, 20–33.

Balota, D. A., & Paul, S. T. (1996). Summation of activation: Evidence from multiple primes that converge and diverge within semantic memory. *Journal of Experimental Psychology: Learning, Memory, and Cognition, 22*, 827–845.

Balota, D. A., Pollatsek, A., & Rayner, K. (1985). The interaction of contextual constraints and parafoveal visual information in reading. *Cognitive Psychology, 17*, 364–390.

Banaji, M. R., & Crowder, R. G. (1989). The bankruptcy of everyday memory. *American Psychologist, 44*, 1185–1193.

Banks, W. P. (1977). Encoding and processing of symbolic information in comparative judgments. In G. H. Bower (Ed.), *The psychology of learning and motivation* (Vol. 11, pp. 101–159). New York: Academic Press.

Banks, W. P., Clark, H. H., & Lucy, P. (1975). The locus of the semantic congruity effect in comparative judgments. *Journal of Experimental Psychology: Human Perception and Performance, 1*, 35–47.

Banks, W. P., Fujii, M., & Kayra-Stuart, F. (1976). Semantic congruity effects in comparative judgments of magnitude of digits. *Journal of Experimental Psychology: Human Perception and Performance, 2*, 435–447.

Bar-Hillel, M. (1980). What features make samples seem representative? *Journal of Experimental Psychology: Human Perception and Performance, 6*, 578–589.

Barshi, I., & Healy, A. F. (1993). Checklist procedures and the cost of automaticity. *Memory & Cognition, 21*, 496–505.

Bartlett, F. C. (1932). *Remembering: A study in experimental and social psychology*. London: Cambridge University Press.

Bass, E., & Davis, L. (1988). *The courage to heal*. New York: Harper & Row.

Bassok, M., (1996). Using content to interpret structure: Effects on analogical transfer. *Current Directions in Psychological Science, 5*, 54–57.

Bassok, M., & Holyoak, K. H. (1989). Interdomain transfer between isomorphic topics in algebra and physics. *Journal of Experimental Psychology: Learning, Memory, and Cognition, 15*, 153–166.

Bates, E., Masling, M., & Kintsch, W. (1978). Recognition memory for aspects of dialogue. *Journal of Experimental Psychology: Human Learning and Memory, 4*, 187–197.

Baum, D. R., & Jonides, J. (1979). Cognitive maps: Analysis of comparative judgments of distance. *Memory & Cognition, 7*, 462–468.

Baynes, K., & Gazzaniga, M. S. (1997). Callosal disconnection. In T. E. Feinberg & M. J. Farah (Eds.), *Behavioral neurology and neuropsychology* (pp. 419–426). New York: McGraw-Hill.

Beattie, G. (1983). *Talk: An analysis of speech and non-verbal behaviour in conversation*. Milton Keynes, England: Open University Press.

Belli, R. F. (1989). Influences of misleading postevent information: Misinformation interference and acceptance. *Journal of Experimental Psychology: General, 118*, 72–85.

Belli, R. F., Lindsay, D. S., Gales, M. S., & McCarthy, T. T. (1994). Memory impairment and source misattribution in postevent misinformation experiments with short retention intervals. *Memory & Cognition, 22*, 40–54.

Bellugi, U., & Klima, E. (1979). *The signs of language*. Cambridge, MA: Harvard University Press.

Benedict, H. (1979). Early lexical development: Comprehension and production. *Journal of Child Language, 6*, 183–200.

Benjamin, L. T., Jr. (1992, February). The history of American psychology [Special issue]. *American Psychologist, 47* (2).

Benson, D. J., & Geschwind, N. (1969). The alexias. In P. Vincken & G.W. Bruyn (Eds.), *Handbook of clinical neurology* (Vol. 4, pp. 112–140). Amsterdam: North Holland.

Berko Gleason, J. (Ed.). (1985). *The development of language*. Columbus, OH: Merrill Publishing.

Biederman, I. (1987). Recognition-by-components: A theory of human image understanding. *Psychological Review, 94*, 115–147.

Biederman, I. (1990). Higher-level vision. In E. N. Osherson, S. M. Kosslyn, & J. M. Hollerbach (Eds.), *An invitation to cognitive science* (Vol. 2, pp. 41–72). Cambridge, MA: MIT Press.

Biederman, I., & Blickle, T. (1985). *The perception of objects with deleted contours*. Unpublished manuscript, State University of New York, Buffalo.

Birch, S. L., & Garnsey, S. M. (1995). The effect of focus on memory for words in sentences. *Journal of Memory and Language, 34*, 232–267.

Bisiach, E., & Luzzatti, C. (1978). Unilateral neglect of representational space. *Cortex, 14*, 129–133.

Blakemore, C. (1977). *Mechanics of the mind*. Cambridge: Cambridge University Press.

Blom, J. P., & Gumperz, J. J. (1972). Social meaning in linguistic structure: Code-switching in Norway. In J. J. Gumperz & D. Hymes (Eds.), *Directions in sociolinguistics: The ethnography of communication* (pp. 407–434). New York: Holt.

Bock, K. (1982). Toward a cognitive psychology of syntax: Information processing contributions to sentence formulation. *Psychological Review, 89*, 1–47.

Bock, K. (1986). Meaning, sound, and syntax: Lexical priming in sentence production. *Journal of Experimental Psychology: Learning, Memory, and Cognition, 12*, 575–586.

Bock, K. (1995). Producing agreement. *Current Directions in Psychological Science, 4*, 56–60.

Bock, K., & Miller, C. A. (1991). Broken agreement. *Cognitive Psychology, 23*, 45–93.

Boland, J. E., Tannenhaus, M. K., Garnsey, S. M., & Carlson, G. N. (1995). Verb argument structure in parsing and interpretation: Evidence from wh-Questions. *Journal of Memory and Language, 34*, 774–806.

Boring, E. G. (1950). *A history of experimental psychology* (2nd ed.). New York: Appleton-Century-Crofts.

Bousfield, W. A. (1953). The occurrence of clustering in the recall of randomly arranged associates. *Journal of General Psychology, 49*, 229–240.

Bowden, E. M. (1985). Accessing relevant information during problem solving: Time constraints on search in the problem space. *Memory & Cognition, 13*, 280–286.

Bower, G. H. (1970). Analysis of a mnemonic device. *American Scientist, 58*, 496–510.

Bower, G. H., Black, J. B., & Turner, T. J. (1979). Scripts in memory for text. *Cognitive Psychology, 11*, 177–220.

Bower, G. H., Clark, M. C., Lesgold, A. M., & Winzenz, D. (1969). Hierarchical retrieval schemes in recall of categorical word lists. *Journal of Verbal Learning and Verbal Behavior, 8*, 323–343.

Bowerman, M. (1978). The acquisition of word meaning: An investigation of some current conflicts. In N. Waterson & C. Snow (Eds.), *Development of communication: Social and pragmatic factors in language acquisition* (pp. 263–287). New York: Wiley.

Braine, M. D. (1963). The ontogeny of English phrase structure: The first phase. *Language, 39*, 1–13.

Brandimonte, M. A., Hitch, G. J., & Bishop, D. V. M. (1992). Verbal recoding of visual stimuli impairs mental image transformations. *Memory & Cognition, 20*, 449–455.

Bransford, J. D. (1979). *Human cognition: Learning, understanding, and remembering*. Belmont, CA: Wadsworth.

Bransford, J. D., & Franks, J. J. (1971). The abstraction of linguistic ideas. *Cognitive Psychology, 2*, 331–350.

Bransford, J. D., & Franks, J. J. (1972). The abstraction of linguistic ideas: A review. *Cognition: International Journal of Cognitive Psychology, 1*, 211–249.

Bransford, J. D., & Johnson, M. K. (1972). Contextual prerequisites for understanding: Some investigations of comprehension and recall. *Journal of Verbal Learning and Verbal Behavior, 11*, 717–726.

Bransford, J. D., & Stein, B. S. (1984). *The ideal problem solver*. New York: Freeman.

Bransford, J. D., & Stein, B.S. (1993). *The ideal problem solver* (2nd ed.). New York: Freeman.

Bresnan, J. (1978). A realistic transformational grammar. In J. Bresnan, M. Halle, & G. Miller (Eds.), *Linguistic theory and psychological reality* (pp. 1–59). Cambridge, MA: MIT Press.

Bresnan, J., & Kaplan, R. M. (1982). Introduction: Grammars as mental representations of language. In J. Bresnan (Ed.), *The mental representation of grammatical relations* (pp. xvii–lii). Cambridge, MA: MIT Press.

Bridgeman, B. (1988). *The biology of behavior and mind*. New York: Wiley.

Britt, M. A., Perfetti, C. A., Garrod, S., & Rayner, K. (1992). Parsing in discourse: Context effects and their limits. *Journal of Memory and Language, 31*, 293–314.

Broadbent, D. E. (1958). *Perception and communication*. London: Pergamon Press.

Broadbent, D. E. (1992). Listening to one of two synchronous messages. *Journal of Experimental Psychology: General, 121*, 125–127. (Reprinted from *Journal of Experimental Psychology*, 1952, *44*, 51–55.)

Brooks, J. O., III, & Watkins, M. J. (1990). Further evidence of the intricacy of memory span. *Journal of Experimental Psychology: Learning, Memory, and Cognition, 16*, 1134–1141.

Brooks, L. R. (1968). Spatial and verbal components of the act of recall. *Canadian Journal of Experimental Psychology, 22*, 349–368.

Brown, A. L. (1975). The development of memory: Knowing, knowing about knowing, and knowing how to know. In H. W. Reese (Ed.), *Advances in child development and behavior* (Vol. 10, pp. 104–152). New York: Academic Press.

Brown, J. A. (1958). Some tests of the decay theory of immediate memory. *Quarterly Journal of Experimental Psychology, 10*, 12–21.

Brown, N. R., & Siegler, R. S. (1993). Metrics and mappings: A framework for understanding real-world quantitative estimation. *Psychological Review, 100*, 511–534.

Brown, R. (1973). *A first language: The early stages*. Cambridge, MA: Harvard University Press.

Brown, R., & Ford, M. (1961). Address in American English. *Journal of Abnormal and Social Psychology, 62*, 375–385.

Brown, R., & Kulik, J. (1977). Flashbulb memories. *Cognition, 5*, 73–99.

Brown, R., & McNeill, D. (1966). The "tip-of-the-tongue" phenomenon. *Journal of Verbal Learning and Verbal Behavior, 5*, 325–337.

Bruner, J. (1990). *Acts of meaning*. Cambridge, MA: Harvard University Press.

Bruner, J. S. (1973). In J. Anglin (Ed.), *Beyond the information given: Studies in the psychology of knowing*. New York: Norton.

Budd, D., Whitney, P., & Turley, K. J. (1995). Individual differences in working memory strategies for reading expository text. *Memory & Cognition, 23*, 735–748.

Burke, D. M., MacKay, D. G., Worthley, J. S., & Wade, E. (1991). On the tip of the tongue: What causes word finding failures in young and older adults? *Journal of Memory and Language, 30*, 542–579.

Burns, D. J. (1996). The bizarre imagery effect and intention to learn. *Psychonomic Bulletin & Review, 2*, 254–257.

Campbell, J. I. D. (1987). Network interference and mental multiplication. *Journal of Experimental Psychology: Learning, Memory, and Cognition, 13*, 109–123.

Campbell, J. I. D., & Graham, D. J. (1985). Mental multiplication skill: Structure, process, and acquisition. *Canadian Journal of Psychology, 39*, 338–366.

Carlson, B. W. (1990). Anchoring and adjustment in judgments under risk. *Journal of Experimental Psychology: Learning, Memory, and Cognition, 16*, 665–676.

Carlson, R. A., Khoo, B. H., Yaure, R. G., & Schneider, W. (1990). Acquisition of a problem-solving skill: Levels of organization and use of working memory. *Journal of Experimental Psychology: General, 119*, 193–214.

Carr, T. H., & Dagenbach, D. (1986). Now you see it, now you don't: Relations between semantic activation and awareness. *The Brain and Brain Sciences, 9*, 26–27.

Carr, T. H., McCauley, C., Sperber, R. D., & Parmalee, C. M. (1982). Words, pictures, and priming: On semantic activation, conscious identification, and the automaticity of information processing. *Journal of Experimental Psychology: Human Perception and Performance, 8*, 757–777.

Carroll, D. W. (1994). *Psychology of language* (2nd ed.). Pacific Grove, CA: Brooks/Cole.

Case, R. (1992). The role of the frontal lobes in the regulation of cognitive development. *Brain and Cognition, 20*, 51–73.

Casey, P. J. (1992). A reexamination of the roles of typicality and category dominance in verifying category membership. *Journal of Experimental Psychology: Learning, Memory, and Cognition, 18*, 823–834.

Casey, P. J. (1993). "That man's father is my father's son": The roles of structure, strategy, and working memory in solving convoluted verbal problems. *Memory & Cognition, 21*, 506–518.

Catrambone, R. (1996). Generalizing solution procedures learned from examples. *Journal of Experimental Psychology: Learning, Memory, and Cognition, 22*, 1020–1031.

Catrambone, R., Jones, C. M., Jonides, J., & Seifert, C. (1995). Reasoning about curvilinear motion: Using principles or analogy. *Memory & Cognition, 23*, 368–373.

Cermak, L. S. (1975). *Improving your memory*. New York: Norton.

Cermak, L. S. (1982). *Human memory and amnesia*. Hillsdale, NJ: Erlbaum.

Chang, T. M. (1986). Semantic memory: Facts and models. *Psychological Bulletin, 99*, 199–220.

Chase, W. G., & Ericsson, K. A. (1982). Skill and working memory. In G. H. Bower (Ed.), *The psychology of learning and motivation* (Vol. 16, pp. 1–58). New York: Academic Press.

Chase, W. G., & Simon, H. A. (1973). Perception in chess. *Cognitive Psychology, 4*, 55–81.

Cheng, P. W., Holyoak, K. J., Nisbett, R. E., & Oliver, L. M. (1986). Pragmatic versus syntactic approaches to training deductive reasoning. *Cognitive Psychology, 18*, 293–328.

Cherry, E. C. (1953). Some experiments on the recognition of speech, with one and with two ears. *Journal of the Acoustical Society of America, 25*, 975–979.

Cherry, E. C., & Taylor, W. K. (1954). Some further experiments on the recognition of speech with one and two ears. *Journal of the Acoustical Society of America, 26*, 554–559.

Chomsky, N. (1957). *Syntactic structures*. The Hague: Mouton Publishers.

Chomsky, N. (1959). A review of Skinner's *Verbal behavior*. *Language, 35*, 26–58.

Chomsky, N. (1965). *Aspects of a theory of syntax*. Cambridge, MA: Harvard University Press.

Chomsky, N. (1968). *Language and mind*. New York: Harcourt Brace Jovanovich.

Chomsky, N., & Halle, M. (1968). *The sound pattern of English*. New York: Harper & Row.

Christianson, S. (1989). Flashbulb memories: Special, but not so special. *Memory & Cognition, 17*, 435–443.

Clapp, F. L. (1924). *The number combinations: Their relative difficulty and frequency of their appearance in textbooks* (Research Bulletin No. 1). Madison, WI: University of Wisconsin, Bureau of Educational Research.

Clark, E. V. (1973). What's in a word? On the child's acquisition of semantics in his first language. In T. E. Moore (Ed.), *Cognitive development and the acquisition of language* (pp. 65–110). New York: Academic Press.

Clark, E. V. (1983). Meanings and concepts. In P. H. Mussen (Ed.), *Carmichael's manual of child psychology: Vol 3. Cognitive development*. New York: Wiley.

Clark, H. H. (1977). Bridging. In P. N. Johnson-Laird & P. C. Wason (Eds.), *Thinking: Readings in cognitive science* (pp. 411–420). Cambridge: Cambridge University Press.

Clark, H. H. (1979). Responding to indirect speech acts. *Cognitive Psychology, 11,* 430–477.

Clark, H. H., & Wilkes-Gibbs, D. (1986). Referring as a collaborative process. *Cognition, 22,* 1–39.

Cognitive Neuroscience (1997, March 14). *Science, 275,* 1579–1610.

Cohen, G. (1989). *Memory in the real world.* London: Erlbaum.

Collins, A. M., & Loftus, E. F. (1975). A spreading-activation theory of semantic processing. *Psychological Review, 82,* 407–428.

Collins, A. M., & Quillian, M. R. (1969). Retrieval time from semantic memory. *Journal of Verbal Learning and Verbal Behavior, 8,* 240–247.

Collins, A. M., & Quillian, M. R. (1972). How to make a language user. In E. Tulving & W. Donaldson (Eds.), *Organization of memory* (pp. 309–351). New York: Academic Press.

Coltheart, M. (1973). *Readings in cognitive psychology.* Toronto: Holt, Rinehart & Winston of Canada.

Coltheart, M. (1983). Ecological necessity of iconic memory. *The Behavioral and Brain Sciences, 6,* 17–18.

Comments. (1994, May). *American Psychologist, 49* (5), 439–445.

Conrad, C. (1972). Cognitive economy in semantic memory. *Journal of Experimental Psychology, 92,* 149–154.

Conrad, R. (1964). Acoustic confusions in immediate memory. *British Journal of Psychology, 55,* 75–84.

Conway, M. A., Anderson, S. J., Larsen, S. F., Donnelly, C. M., McDaniel, M. A., McClelland, A. G. R., Rawles, R. E., & Logie, R. H. (1994). The formation of flashbulb memories. *Memory & Cognition, 22,* 326–343.

Conway, M. A., Cohen, G., & Stanhope, N. (1991). On the very long-term retention of knowledge acquired through formal education: Twelve years of cognitive psychology. *Journal of Experimental Psychology: General, 120,* 395–409.

Cook, M. (1977). Gaze and mutual gaze in social encounters. *American Scientist, 65,* 328–333.

Cooke, N. J., & Breedin, S. D. (1994). Constructing naive theories of motion on the fly. *Memory & Cognition, 22,* 474–493.

Cooper, E. H., & Pantle, A. J. (1967). The total-time hypothesis in verbal learning. *Psychological Bulletin, 68,* 221–234.

Cooper, L. A., & Shepard, R. N. (1973). Chronometric studies of the rotation of mental images. In W. G. Chase (Ed.), *Visual information processing* (pp. 75–176). New York: Academic Press.

Corballis, M. C. (1989). Laterality and human evolution. *Psychological Review, 96,* 492–505.

Coren, S., & Ward, L. M. (1989) *Sensation and perception* (3rd ed.). Ft. Worth, TX: Harcourt.

Coughlan, A. K., & Warrington, E. K. (1978). Word comprehension and word retrieval in patients with localised cerebral lesions. *Brain, 101,* 163–185.

Cowan, N. (1995). *Attention and memory: An integrated framework*. New York: Oxford University Press.

Craik, F. I. M., & Lockhart, R. S. (1972). Levels of processing: A framework for memory research. *Journal of Verbal Learning and Verbal Behavior, 11*, 671–684.

Craik, F. I. M., & Tulving, E. (1975). Depth of processing and the retention of words in episodic memory. *Journal of Experimental Psychology: General, 104*, 268–294.

Craik, F. I. M., & Watkins, M. J. (1973). The role of rehearsal in short-term memory. *Journal of Verbal Learning and Verbal Behavior, 12*, 599–607.

Crutcher, R. J. (1994). Telling what we know: The use of verbal report methodologies in psychological research. *Psychological Science, 5*, 241–244.

Cull, W. L., & Zechmeister, E. B. (1994). The learning ability paradox in adult metamemory research: What are the metamemory differences between good and poor learners? *Memory & Cognition, 22*, 249–257.

Cummins, D. D., Lubart, T., Alksnis, O., & Rist, R. (1991). Conditional reasoning and causation. *Memory & Cognition, 19*, 274–282.

Dahlgren, K. (1985). The cognitive structure of social categories. *Cognitive Science, 9*, 379–398.

Daneman, M., & Carpenter, P. A. (1980). Individual differences in working memory and reading. *Journal of Verbal Learning and Verbal Behavior, 19*, 450–466.

Darwin, C. (1959). *The origin of species*. New York: Mentor. (Original work published 1859)

Darwin, C. J., Turvey, M. T., & Crowder, R. G. (1972). An auditory analogue of the Sperling partial report procedure: Evidence for brief auditory storage. *Cognitive Psychology, 3*, 255–267.

Davidson, D. (1994). Recognition and recall of irrelevant and interruptive atypical actions in script-based stories. *Journal of Memory and Language, 33*, 757–775.

Deese, J. (1959). On the prediction of occurrence of particular verbal intrusions in immediate recall. *Journal of Experimental Psychology, 58*, 17–22.

Dehaene, S. (1993). Temporal oscillations in human perception. *Psychological Science, 4*, 264–270.

Dehaene, S., & Mehler, J. (1992). Cross-linguistic regularities in the frequency of number words. *Cognition, 43*, 1–29.

Dehaene, S., Posner, M. I., & Tucker, D. M. (1994). Localization of a neural system for error detection and compensation. *Psychological Science, 5*, 303–305.

Dell, G. S., & Newman, J. E. (1980). Detecting phonemes in fluent speech. *Journal of Verbal Learning and Verbal Behavior, 20*, 611–629.

Dempster, F. N. (1985). Proactive interference in sentence recall: Topic-similarity effects and individual differences. *Memory & Cognition, 13*, 81–89.

DePaulo, B. M., & Bonvillian, J. D. (1978). The effect on language development of the special characteristics of speech addressed to children. *Journal of Psycholinguistic Research, 7*, 189–211.

Descartes, R. (1972). *Treatise on man* (T. S. Hall, Trans.). Cambridge, MA: Harvard University Press. (Original work published 1637)

Deutsch, G., Bourbon, T., Papanicolaou, A. C., & Eisenberg, H. M. (1988). Visuospatial tasks compared via activation of regional cerebral blood flow. *Neuropsychologia, 26*, 445–452.

Deutsch, J. A., & Deutsch, D. (1963). Attention: Some theoretical considerations. *Psychological Review, 70*, 80–90.

Dillon, R. F., & Reid, L. S. (1969). Short-term memory as a function of information processing during the retention interval. *Journal of Experimental Psychology, 81*, 261–269.

Donchin, E. (1981). Surprise! . . . Surprise? *Psychophysiology, 18*, 493–513.

Donders, F. C. (1969). On the speed of psychological processes. In W. G. Koster (Ed.), *Attention and Performance II. Acta Psychologica, 30*, 412–431. (Original work published 1868)

Donley, R. D., & Ashcraft, M. H. (1992). The methodology of testing naive beliefs in the physics classroom. *Memory & Cognition, 20*, 381–391.

Dooling, D. J., & Christiaansen, R. E. (1977). Episodic and semantic aspects of memory for prose. *Journal of Experimental Psychology: Human Learning and Memory, 3*, 428–436.

Dooling, D., & Lachman, R. (1971). Effects of comprehension on retention of prose. *Journal of Experimental Psychology, 88*, 216–222.

Dunbar, K., & MacLeod, C. M. (1984). A horse race of a different color: Stroop interference patterns with transformed words. *Journal of Experimental Psychology: Human Perception and Performance, 10*, 622–639.

Duncan, J., & Humphreys, G. W. (1989). Visual search and stimulus similarity. *Psychological Review, 96*, 433–458.

Duncan, S. (1972). Some signals and rules for taking speaking turns in conversations. *Journal of Personality and Social Psychology, 23*, 283–292.

Duncker, K. (1945). On problem solving. *Psychological Monographs, 58* (270).

Ebbinghaus, H. (1964). *Memory: A contribution to experimental psychology* (H. A. Ruger & C. E. Bussenius, Trans.). New York: Dover. (Original, German work published 1885; English translation published 1913)

Edridge-Green, F. W. (1900). *Memory and its cultivation*. New York: Appleton & Co.

Edwards, D., & Potter, J. (1993). Language and causation: A discursive action model of description and attribution. *Psychological Review, 100*, 23–41.

Egan, P., Carterette, E. C., & Thwing, E. J. (1954). Some factors affecting multi-channel listening. *Journal of the Acoustical Society of America, 26*, 774–782.

Egeth, H. E. (1992). Dichotic listening: Long-lived echoes of Broadbent's early studies. *Journal of Experimental Psychology: General, 121*, 124.

Eimas, P. D. (1975). Speech perception in early infancy. In L. B. Cohen & P. Salapatek (Eds.), *Infant perception: From sensation to cognition: Vol. II. Perception of space, speech, and sound* (pp. 193–231). New York: Academic Press.

Ellis, A. W., & Young, A. W. (1988). *Human cognitive neuropsychology*. Hove, London: Erlbaum.

Ellis, H. D. (1983). The role of the right hemisphere in face perception. In A.W. Young (Ed.), *Functions of the right cerebral hemisphere* (pp. 33–64). New York: Academic Press.

Engle, R. W., Cantor, J., & Carullo, J. J. (1992). Individual differences in working memory and comprehension: A test of four hypotheses. *Journal of Experimental Psychology: Learning, Memory, and Cognition, 18*, 972–992.

Epstein, W., Glenberg, A. M., & Bradley, M. M. (1984). Coactivation and comprehension: Contribution of text variables to the illusion of knowing. *Memory & Cognition, 12*, 355–360.

Erdelyi, M. H., & Goldberg, B. (1979). Let's not sweep repression under the rug: Toward a cognitive psychology of repression. In J. F. Kihlstrom & F. J. Evans (Eds.), *Functional disorders of memory* (pp. 355–402). Hillsdale, NJ: Erlbaum.

Erickson, T. D., & Mattson, M. E. (1981). From words to meanings: A semantic illusion. *Journal of Verbal Learning and Verbal Behavior, 20*, 540–551.

Ericsson, K. A., & Charness, N. (1994). Expert performance: Its structure and acquisition. *American Psychologist, 49*, 725–747.

Ericsson, K. A., Krampe, R. T., & Tesch-Romer, C. (1993). The role of deliberate practice in the acquisition of expert performance. *Psychological Review, 100*, 363–406.

Ericsson, K. A., & Polson, P. G. (1988). An experimental analysis of the mechanisms of a memory skill. *Journal of Experimental Psychology: Learning, Memory, and Cognition, 14*, 305–316.

Ericsson, K. A., & Simon, H. A. (1980). Verbal reports as data. *Psychological Review, 87*, 215–251.

Ericsson, K. A., & Simon, H. A. (1993). *Protocol analysis: Verbal reports as data* (rev. ed.). Cambridge, MA: MIT Press.

Eriksen, C. W., & Johnson, H. J. (1964). Storage and decay characteristics of non-attended auditory stimuli. *Journal of Experimental Psychology, 68*, 28–36.

Ernst, G. W., & Newell. A. (1969). *GPS: A case study in generality and problem solving*. New York: Academic Press.

Eslinger, P. J., Damasio, H., Damasio, A. R., & Butters, N. (1993). Nonverbal amnesia and asymmetric cerebral lesions following encephalitis. *Brain and Cognition, 21*, 140–152.

Eysenck, M. W. (1982). *Attention and arousal: Cognition and performance*. Heidelberg: Springer-Verlag.

Eysenck, M. W. (1992). *Anxiety: The cognitive perspective*. Hove, England: Erlbaum.

Fabbro, F. (1994). Left and right in the Bible from a neuropsychological perspective. *Brain and Cognition, 24*, 161–183.

Farah, M. J., & McClelland, J. L. (1991). A computational model of semantic memory impairment: Modality specificity and emergent category specificity. *Journal of Experimental Psychology: General, 120*, 339–357.

Fechner, G. (1966). *Elements of psychophysics* (Vol. 1, H. E. Adler, Trans., D. H. Howes & E. G. Boring, Eds.). New York: Holt, Rinehart & Winston. (Original work published 1860)

Feinberg, T. E., & Farah, M. J. (Eds.). (1997). *Behavioral neurology and neuropsychology*. New York: McGraw-Hill.

Feldman, D. (1992). *When did wild poodles roam the earth? An Imponderables™ book*. New York: HarperCollins.

Ferraro, F. R., Balota, D. A., & Connor, L. T. (1993). Implicit memory and the formation of new associations in nondemented Parkinson's disease individuals and individuals with senile dementia of the Alzheimer type: A serial reaction time (SRT) investigation. *Brain and Cognition, 21*, 163–180.

Ferreira, F. (1994). Choice of passive voice is affected by verb type and animacy. *Journal of Memory and Language, 33*, 715–736.

Fillenbaum, S. (1974). Pragmatic normalization: Further results for some conjunctive and disjunctive sentences. *Journal of Experimental Psychology, 102*, 574–578.

Fillmore, C. J. (1968). Toward a modern theory of case. In D. A. Reibel & S. A. Schane (Eds.), *Modern studies in English* (pp. 361–375). Englewood Cliffs, NJ: Prentice-Hall.

Finke, R. A., & Freyd, J. J. (1985). Transformations of visual memory induced by implied motions of pattern elements. *Journal of Experimental Psychology: Learning, Memory, and Cognition, 11*, 780–794.

Fischhoff, B., & Bar-Hillel, M. (1984). Diagnosticity and the base-rate effect. *Memory & Cognition, 12*, 402–410.

Fletcher, C. R., & Bloom, C. P. (1988). Causal reasoning in the comprehension of simple narrative texts. *Journal of Memory and Language, 27*, 235–244.

Fodor, J. A. (1983). *The modularity of mind*. Cambridge, MA: MIT Press.

Fong, G. T., Krantz, D. H., & Nisbett, R. E. (1986). The effects of statistical training on thinking about everyday problems. *Cognitive Psychology, 18*, 253–292.

Fong, G. T., & Nisbett, R. E. (1991). Immediate and delayed transfer of training effects in statistical reasoning. *Journal of Experimental Psychology: General, 120*, 34–45.

Forgus, R. H., & Melamed, L. E. (1976). *Perception: A cognitive-stage approach*. New York: McGraw-Hill.

Foss, D. J., & Hakes, D. T. (1978). *Psycholinguistics: An introduction to the psychology of language*. Englewood Cliffs, NJ: Prentice-Hall.

Francik, E. P., & Clark, H. H. (1985). How to make requests that overcome obstacles to compliance. *Journal of Memory and Language, 24*, 560–568.

Franklin, M. B., & Barten, S. S. (1988). *Child language: A reader*. New York: Oxford University Press.

Frazier, L., & Rayner, K. (1982). Making and correcting errors during sentence comprehension: Eye movements in the analysis of structurally ambiguous sentences. *Cognitive Psychology, 14*, 178–210.

Frederiksen, C. H. (1975). Acquisition of semantic information from discourse: Effects of repeated exposures. *Journal of Verbal Learning and Verbal Behavior, 14*, 158–169.

Freedman, J. L., & Loftus, E. F. (1971). Retrieval of words from long-term memory. *Journal of Verbal Learning and Verbal Behavior, 10*, 107–115.

Freud, S. (1953). Three essays on the theory of sexuality. In J. Strachey (Ed.), *The standard edition of the complete psychological works of Sigmund Freud* (Vol. 7, pp. 135–243). London: Hogarth Press. (Original work published 1905)

Freyd, J. J., & Jones, K. T. (1994). Representational momentum for a spiral path. *Journal of Experimental Psychology: Learning, Memory, and Cognition, 20*, 968–976.

Friedman, A. (1978). Memorial comparisons without the "mind's eye." *Journal of Verbal Learning and Verbal Behavior, 10*, 107–115.

Friedman, A., & Polson, M. C. (1981). Hemispheres as independent resource systems: Limited-capacity processing and cerebral specialization. *Journal of Experimental Psychology: Human Perception and Performance, 7*, 1031–1058.

Friedrich, F. J., Henik, A., & Tzelgov, J. (1991). Automatic processes in lexical access and spreading activation. *Journal of Experimental Psychology: Human Perception and Performance, 17*, 792–806.

Frishberg, N. (1975). Arbitrariness and iconicity: Historical change in American Sign Language. *Language, 51*, 696–719.

Fromkin, V. A. (1971). The non-anomalous nature of anomalous utterances. *Language, 47*, 27–52.

Fromkin, V. A., & Rodman, R. (1974). *An introduction to language*. New York: Holt, Rinehart & Winston.

Galanter, E. (1962). Contemporary psychophysics. In R. Brown, E. Galanter, E. H. Hess, & G. Mandler (Eds.), *New directions in psychology* (Vol. 1, pp. 87–156). New York: Holt, Rinehart & Winston.

Gardiner, J. M., Gawlik, B., & Richardson-Klavehn, A. (1994). Maintenance rehearsal affects knowing, not remembering; elaborative rehearsal affects remembering, not knowing. *Psychonomic Bulletin & Review, 1*, 107–110.

Gardner, H. (1985). *The mind's new science: A history of the cognitive revolution*. New York: Basic Books.

Gardner, R. A., & Gardner, B. T. (1969). Teaching sign language to a chimpanzee. *Science, 165*, 664–672.

Garry, M., Manning, C. G., Loftus, E. F., & Sherman, S. J. (1996). Imagination inflation: Imagining a childhood event inflates confidence that it occurred. *Psychonomic Bulletin & Review, 3*, 208–214.

Gazzaniga, M. S. (1985). *The social brain*. New York: Basic Books.

Gazzaniga, M. S. (1989). Organization of the human brain. *Science, 245*, 947–952.

Geary, D. C. (1992). Evolution of human cognition: Potential relationship to the ontogenetic development of behavior and cognition. *Evolution and Cognition, 1*, 93–100.

Gehring, W. J., Goss, B., Coles, M. G. H., Meyer, D. E., & Donchin, E. (1993). A neural system for error detection and compensation. *Psychological Science, 4*, 385–390.

Gentner, D., & Collins, A. (1981). Studies of inference from lack of knowledge. *Memory & Cognition, 9*, 434–443.

Gentner, D., & Markman, A. B. (1997). Structure mapping in analogy and similarity. *American Psychologist, 52*, 45–56.

Gernsbacher, M. A. (1985). Surface information loss in comprehension. *Cognitive Psychology, 17*, 324–363.

Gernsbacher, M. A. (1990). *Language comprehension as structure building*. Hillsdale, NJ: Erlbaum.

Gernsbacher, M. A. (1991). Cognitive processes and mechanisms in language comprehension: The structure building framework. In G. H. Bower (Ed.), *The psychology of learning and motivation* (Vol. 27, pp. 217–263). New York: Academic Press.

Gernsbacher, M. A. (1993). Less skilled readers have less efficient suppression mechanisms. *Psychological Science, 4*, 294–298.

Gernsbacher, M. A., & Hargreaves, D. (1988). Accessing sentence participants: The advantage of first mention. *Journal of Memory and Language, 27*, 699–717.

Gernsbacher, M. A., Hargreaves, D., & Beeman, M. (1989). Building and accessing clausal representations: The advantage of first mention versus the advantage of clause recency. *Journal of Memory and Language, 28*, 735–755.

Gernsbacher, M. A., & Jescheniak, J. D. (1995). Cataphoric devices in spoken discourse. *Cognitive Psychology, 29*, 24–58.

Gernsbacher, M. A., & Robertson, R. R. W. (1995). Reading skill and suppression revisited. *Psychological Science, 6*, 165–169.

Gernsbacher, M. A., & Shroyer, S. (1989). The cataphoric use of the indefinite *this* in spoken narratives. *Memory & Cognition, 17*, 536–540.

Geschwind, N. (1967). The varieties of naming errors. *Cortex, 3*, 97–112.

Geschwind, N. (1970). The organisation of language and the brain. *Science, 170,* 940–944.

Geschwind, N. I. (1979). Specializations of the human brain. *Scientific American, 241,* 158–168.

Gibbs, R. W., Jr. (1986a). On the psycholinguistics of sarcasm. *Journal of Experimental Psychology: General, 115,* 3–15.

Gibbs, R. W., Jr. (1986b). What makes some indirect speech acts conventional? *Journal of Memory and Language, 25,* 181–196.

Gibbs, R. W., Jr. (1989). Understanding and literal meaning. *Cognitive Science, 14,* 243–251.

Gibbs, R. W., Jr. (1990). Comprehending figurative referential descriptions. *Journal of Experimental Psychology: Learning, Memory, and Cognition, 16,* 56–66.

Gibbs, R. W., Jr. (1992). Categorization and metaphor understanding. *Psychological Review, 99,* 572–577.

Gibson, E. (1969). *Principles of perceptual learning and development.* New York: Appleton.

Gick, M. L., & Holyoak, K. J. (1980). Analogical problem solving. *Cognitive Psychology, 12,* 306–355.

Giles, H., & Coupland, N. (1991). *Language: Contexts and consequences.* Pacific Grove, CA: Brooks/Cole.

Glanzer, M., & Cunitz, A. R. (1966). Two storage mechanisms in free recall. *Journal of Verbal Learning and Verbal Behavior, 5,* 351–360.

Glass, A. L., & Holyoak, K. J. (1975). Alternative conceptions of semantic memory. *Cognition, 3,* 313–339.

Glass, A. L., & Holyoak, K. J. (1986). *Cognition* (2nd ed.). New York: Random House.

Gleason, H. A. (1961). *An introduction to descriptive linguistics* (rev. ed.). New York: Holt, Rinehart & Winston.

Glenberg, A., Smith, S. M., & Green, C. (1977). Type I rehearsal: Maintenance and more. *Journal of Verbal Learning and Verbal Behavior, 11,* 403–416.

Glucksberg, S., & Danks, J. H. (1975). *Experimental psycholinguistics: An introduction.* Hillsdale, NJ: Erlbaum.

Glucksberg, S., & Keysar, B. (1990). Understanding metaphorical comparisons: Beyond similarity. *Psychological Review, 97,* 3–18.

Glucksberg, S., & McCloskey, M. (1981). Decisions about ignorance: Knowing that you don't know. *Journal of Experimental Psychology: Human Learning and Memory, 7,* 311–325.

Goodglass, H., Kaplan, E., Weintraub, S., & Ackerman, N. (1976). The "tip-of-the-tongue" phenomenon in aphasia. *Cortex, 12,* 145–153.

Gorfein, D. S., & Hoffman, R. R. (Eds.). (1987). *Memory and learning: The Ebbinghaus Centennial Conference.* Hillsdale, NJ: Erlbaum.

Graesser, A. C. (1981). *Prose comprehension beyond the word.* New York: Springer-Verlag.

Graf, P., Squire, L. R., & Mandler, G. (1984). The information that amnesic patients do not forget. *Journal of Experimental Psychology: Learning, Memory, and Cognition, 10,* 164–178.

Greene, J. M. (1972). *Psycholinguistics: Chomsky and psychology.* Harmondsworth, England: Penguin.

Greeno, J. G. (1974). Hobbits and Orcs: Acquisition of a sequential concept. *Cognitive Psychology*, *6*, 270–292.

Greeno, J. G. (1978). Natures of problem-solving abilities. In W. K. Estes (Ed.), *Handbook of learning and cognitive processes: Vol. 5. Human information processing* (pp. 239–270). Hillsdale, NJ: Erlbaum.

Greenspan, S. L. (1986). Semantic flexibility and referential specificity of concrete nouns. *Journal of Memory and Language*, *25*, 539–557.

Grice, H. P. (1975). Logic and conversation. In P. Cole & J. L. Morgan (Eds.), *Syntax and semantics: Vol. 3. Speech acts* (pp. 41–58). New York: Seminar Press.

Grilly, D. M. (in press). *Drugs and human behavior* (3rd ed.). Boston: Allyn & Bacon.

Gruneberg, M. M., Morris, P. E., & Sykes, R. N. (Eds.). (1978). *Practical aspects of memory*. London: Academic Press.

Haber, R. N. (1983). The impending demise of the icon: A critique of the concept of iconic storage in visual information processing. *The Behavioral and Brain Sciences*, *6*, 1–54. (Includes commentaries)

Haber, R. N., & Hershenson, M. (1973). *The psychology of visual perception*. New York: Holt, Rinehart & Winston.

Hampton, J. A. (1984). The verification of category and property statements. *Memory & Cognition*, *12*, 345–354.

Harlow, H. F. (1953). Mice, monkeys, men, and motives. *Psychological Review*, *60*, 23–60.

Hasher, L., Stoltzfus, E. R., Zacks, R. T., & Rypma, B. A. (1991). Age and inhibition. *Journal of Experimental Psychology: Learning, Memory, and Cognition*, *17*, 163–169.

Hasher, L., & Zacks, R. T. (1984). Automatic processing of fundamental information: The case of frequency of occurrence. *American Psychologist*, *39*, 1372–1388.

Hayes, J. R. (1989). *The complete problem solver* (2nd ed.). Hillsdale, NJ: Erlbaum.

Hayes, J. R., & Simon, H. A. (1974). Understanding written problem instructions. In L. W. Gregg (Ed.), *Knowledge and cognition* (pp. 167–200). Hillsdale, NJ: Erlbaum.

Hecht, H., & Proffitt, D. R. (1995). The price of expertise: Effects of experience on the water-level task. *Psychological Science*, *6*, 90–95.

Hell, W., Gigerenzer, G., Gauggel, S., Mall, M., & Muller, M. (1988). Hindsight bias: An interaction of automatic and motivational factors? *Memory & Cognition*, *16*, 533–538.

Hellyer, S. (1962). Frequency of stimulus presentation and short-term decrement in recall. *Journal of Experimental Psychology*, *64*, 650.

Helsabeck, F., Jr. (1975). Syllogistic reasoning: Generation of counterexamples. *Journal of Educational Psychology*, *67*, 102–108.

Herman, L. M. (1987). Receptive competencies of language-trained animals. In J. S. Rosenblatt, C. Beer, M. C. Busnel, & P. J. B. Slater (Eds.), *Advances in the study of behavior* (Vol. 17). Petaluma, CA: Academic Press.

Herrnstein, R. J., & Murray, C. (1994). *The bell curve*. New York: Free Press.

Hilgard, E. R. (1964). Introduction. In H. Ebbinghaus, *Memory: A contribution to experimental psychology* (pp. vii–x). New York: Dover.

Hirshman, E., & Durante, R. (1992). Prime identification and semantic priming. *Journal of Experimental Psychology: Learning, Memory, and Cognition*, *18*, 255–265.

Hirshman, E., Whelley, M. M., & Palij, M. (1989). An investigation of paradoxical memory effects. *Journal of Memory and Language*, *28*, 594–609.

Hirst, W., & Kalmar, D. (1987). Characterizing attentional resources. *Journal of Experimental Psychology: General, 116*, 68–81.

Hirst, W., Spelke, E. S., Reaves, C. C., Caharack, G., & Neisser, U. (1980). Dividing attention without alternation or automaticity. *Journal of Experimental Psychology: General, 109*, 98–117.

Hoch, S. J. (1984). Availability and interference in predictive judgment. *Journal of Experimental Psychology: Learning, Memory, and Cognition, 10*, 649–662.

Hoch, S. J. (1985). Counterfactual reasoning and accuracy in predicting personal events. *Journal of Experimental Psychology: Learning, Memory, and Cognition, 11*, 719–731.

Hoch, S. J., & Loewenstein, G. F. (1989). Outcome feedback: Hindsight *and* information. *Journal of Experimental Psychology: Learning, Memory, and Cognition, 15*, 605–619.

Hockett, C. F. (1960). The origin of speech. *Scientific American, 203*, 89–96.

Hockett, C. F. (1966). The problem of universals in language. In J. H. Greenberg (Ed.), *Universals of language* (2nd ed., pp. 1–29). Cambridge, MA: MIT Press.

Holtgraves, T. (1994). Communication in context: Effects of speaker status on the comprehension of indirect requests. *Journal of Experimental Psychology: Learning, Memory, and Cognition, 20*, 1205–1218.

Holyoak, K. J. (1985). The pragmatics of analogical transfer. In G. H. Bower (Ed.), *The psychology of learning and motivation* (Vol. 19, pp. 59–87). Orlando: Academic Press.

Holyoak, K. J., & Mah, W. A. (1982). Cognitive reference points in judgments of symbolic magnitude. *Cognitive Psychology, 14*, 328–352.

Holyoak, K. J., & Thagard, P. (1997). The analogical mind. *American Psychologist, 52*, 35–44.

Holyoak, K. J., & Walker, J. H. (1976). Subjective magnitude information in semantic orderings. *Journal of Verbal Learning and Verbal Behavior, 15*, 287–299.

Hothersall, D. (1985). *Psychology*. Columbus, OH: Charles Merrill.

Hothersall, D. (1990). *History of psychology* (2nd ed.). New York: McGraw-Hill.

Howard, D. V. (1983). *Cognitive psychology: Memory, language, and thought*. New York: Macmillan.

Hubel, D. H., & Wiesel, T. N. (1962). Receptive fields, binocular interaction, and functional architecture in the cat's visual cortex. *Journal of Physiology, 160*, 106–154.

Hull, C. L. (1943). *Principles of behavior*. New York: Appleton-Century-Crofts.

Hulse, S. H. (1993). The present status of animal cognition: An introduction. *Psychological Science, 4*, 154–155.

Huttenlocher, J., & Smiley, P. (1987). Early word meanings: The case of object names. *Cognitive Psychology, 19*, 63–89.

Hyman, I. E., Jr., & Pentland, J. (1996). The role of mental imagery in the creation of false childhood memories. *Journal of Memory and Language, 35*, 101–117.

Hyman, I. E., Jr., & Rubin, D. C. (1990). Memorabeatlia: A naturalistic study of long-term memory. *Memory & Cognition, 18*, 205-214.

Irwin, D. E. (1991). Information integration across saccadic eye movements. *Cognitive Psychology, 23*, 420–456.

Irwin, D. E. (1992). Memory for position and identity across eye movements. *Journal of Experimental Psychology: Learning, Memory, and Cognition, 18*, 307–317.

Irwin, D. E., & Carlson-Radvansky, L. A. (1996). Cognitive suppression during saccadic eye movements. *Psychological Science, 7*, 83–88.

Isaacs, E. A., & Clark, H. H. (1987). References in conversation between experts and novices. *Journal of Experimental Psychology: General, 116*, 26–37.

Iversen, L. L. (1979). The chemistry of the brain. In *The brain: A Scientific American book* (pp. 70–83). San Francisco: Freeman.

James, W. (1983). *The principles of psychology*. Cambridge, MA: Harvard University Press. (Original work published 1890)

Jenkins, J. J. (1974). Remember that old theory of memory? Well forget it! *American Psychologist, 29*, 785–795.

Johnson, J. T., & Finke, R. A. (1985). The base-rate fallacy in the context of sequential categories. *Memory & Cognition, 13*, 63–73.

Johnson-Laird, P. N., Byrne, R. M. J., & Schaeken, W. (1992). Propositional reasoning by model. *Psychological Review, 99*, 418–439.

Johnson-Laird, P. N., Legrenzi, P., & Legrenzi, M. A. (1972). Reasoning and a sense of reality. *British Journal of Psychology, 63*, 395–400.

Johnston, W. A., & Heinz, S. P. (1978). Flexibility and capacity demands of attention. *Journal of Experimental Psychology: General, 107*, 420–435.

Jones, G. V. (1989). Back to Woodworth: Role of interlopers in the tip-of-the-tongue phenomenon. *Memory & Cognition, 17*, 69–76.

Jusczyk, P. W., Smith, L. B., & Murphy, C. (1981). The perceptual classification of speech. *Perception and Psychophysics, 1*, 10–23.

Just, M. A. (1976, May). *Research strategies in prose comprehension*. Paper presented at the meeting of the Midwestern Psychological Association, Chicago.

Just, M. A., & Carpenter, P. A. (1980). A theory of reading: From eye fixations to comprehension. *Psychological Review, 87*, 329–354.

Just, M. A., & Carpenter, P. A. (1987). *The psychology of reading and language comprehension*. Boston: Allyn & Bacon.

Just, M. A., & Carpenter, P. A. (1992). A capacity theory of comprehension. *Psychological Review, 99*, 122–149.

Kahneman, D. (1968). Method, findings, and theory in studies of visual masking. *Psychological Bulletin, 70*, 404–426.

Kahneman, D. (1973). *Attention and effort*. Englewood Cliffs, NJ: Prentice-Hall.

Kahneman, D., Slovic, P., & Tversky, A. (Eds.). (1982). *Judgment under uncertainty: Heuristics and biases*. Cambridge: Cambridge University Press.

Kahneman, D., & Tversky, A. (1972). Subjective probability: A judgment of representativeness. *Cognitive Psychology, 3*, 430–454.

Kahneman, D., & Tversky, A. (1973). On the psychology of prediction. *Psychological Review, 80*, 237–251.

Kahneman, D., & Tversky, A. (1982). The simulation heuristic. In D. Kahneman, P. Slovic, & A. Tversky (Eds.), *Judgment under uncertainty: Heuristics and biases* (pp. 201–208). Cambridge: Cambridge University Press.

Kahneman, D., & Tversky, A. (1996). On the reality of cognitive illusions. *Psychological Review, 103*, 582–591.

Kay, J., & Ellis, A. (1987). A cognitive neuropsychological case study of anomia: Implications for psychological models of word retrieval. *Brain, 110*, 613–629.

Keefe, D. E., & McDaniel, M. A. (1993). The time course and durability of predictive inferences. *Journal of Memory and Language, 32*, 446–463.

Kellas, G., McCauley, C., & McFarland, C. E., Jr. (1975). Reexamination of externalized rehearsal. *Journal of Experimental Psychology: Human Learning and Memory, 104,* 84–90.

Kemble, E. D., Filipi, T., & Gravlin, L. (1996). Some simple classroom experiments on cerebral lateralization. In M. E. Ware & D. E. Johnson (Eds.), *Handbook of demonstrations and activities in the teaching of psychology* (Vol. 2, pp. 29–32). Mahwah, NJ: Erlbaum.

Kempen, G., & Hoehkamp, E. (1987). An incremental procedural grammar for sentence formulation. *Cognitive Science, 11,* 201–258.

Kemper, S., & Thissen, D. (1981). Memory for the dimensions of requests. *Journal of Verbal Learning and Verbal Behavior, 20,* 552–563.

Keppel, G., & Underwood, B. J. (1962). Proactive inhibition in short-term retention of single items. *Journal of Verbal Learning and Verbal Behavior, 1,* 153–161.

Keren, G., & Wagenaar, W. A. (1985). On the psychology of playing blackjack: Normative and descriptive considerations with implications for decision theory. *Journal of Experimental Psychology: General, 114,* 133–158.

Kertesz, A. (1982). Two case studies: Broca's and Wernicke's aphasia. In M. A. Arbib, D. Caplan, & J. C. Marshall (Eds.), *Neural models of language processes* (pp. 25–44). New York: Academic Press.

Kimberg, D. Y., & Farah, M. J. (1993). A unified account of cognitive impairments following frontal lobe damage: The role of working memory in complex, organized behavior. *Journal of Experimental Psychology: General, 122,* 411–428.

Kimble, G. A., & Garmezy, N. (1963). *Principles of general psychology* (2nd ed.). New York: Ronald Press.

King, J., & Just, M. A. (1991). Individual differences in syntactic processing: The role of working memory. *Journal of Memory and Language, 30,* 580–602.

Kinsbourne, M., & Cook, J. (1971). Generalized and lateralized effects of concurrent verbalization on a unimanual skill. *Quarterly Journal of Experimental Psychology, 23,* 341–345.

Kintsch, W. (1974). *The representation of meaning in memory.* Hillsdale, NJ: Erlbaum.

Kintsch, W. (1977). *Memory and cognition* (2nd ed.). New York: Wiley.

Kintsch, W. (1985). Reflections on Ebbinghaus. *Journal of Experimental Psychology: Learning, Memory, and Cognition, 11,* 461–463.

Kintsch, W. (1994). Text comprehension, memory, and learning. *American Psychologist, 49,* 294–303.

Kintsch, W., & Bates, E. (1977). Recognition memory for statements from a classroom lecture. *Journal of Experimental Psychology: Human Learning and Memory, 3,* 150–159.

Klatzky, R. L. (1980). *Human memory: Structures and processes* (2nd ed.). San Francisco: Freeman.

Klatzky, R. L., & Atkinson, R. C. (1971). Specialization of the cerebral hemispheres in scanning for information in short-term memory. *Perception & Psychophysics, 10,* 335–338.

Klawans, H. L. (1988). *Toscanini's fumble.* Chicago: Contemporary Books.

Klayman, J., & Ha, Y.-W. (1989). Hypothesis testing in rule discovery: Strategy, structure, and content. *Journal of Experimental Psychology: Learning, Memory, and Cognition, 15,* 596–604.

Koenig, O., Wetzel, C., & Caramazza, A. (1992). Evidence for different types of lexical representations in the cerebral hemispheres. *Cognitive Neuropsychology*, 9, 33–45.

Kohler, W. (1927). *The mentality of apes*. New York: Harcourt, Brace.

Kolb, B., & Whishaw, I. Q. (1990). *Fundamentals of human neuropsychology* (3rd ed.). New York: Freeman.

Kolb, B., & Whishaw, I. Q. (1996). *Fundamentals of human neuropsychology* (4th ed.). New York: Freeman.

Kolodner, J. L. (1997). Educational implications of analogy: A view from case-based reasoning. *American Psychologist, 52*, 57–66.

Kosslyn, S. M., & Koenig, O. (1992). *Wet mind: The new cognitive neuroscience*. New York: Free Press.

Kosslyn, S. M., & Pomerantz, J. P. (1977). Imagery, propositions, and the form of internal representations. *Cognitive Psychology*, 9, 52–76.

Kotovsky, K., Hayes, J. R., & Simon, H. A. (1985). Why are some problems hard? Evidence from Tower of Hanoi. *Cognitive Psychology, 17*, 248–294.

Kounios, J., Osman, A. M., & Meyer, D. E. (1987). Structure and process in semantic memory: New evidence based on speed-accuracy decomposition. *Journal of Experimental Psychology: General, 116*, 3–25.

Krauss, R. M., Morrel-Samuels, P., & Colosante, C. (1991). Do conversational hand gestures communicate? *Journal of Personality and Social Psychology, 61*, 743–754.

Kroll, N. E. A., Schepeler, E. M., & Angin, K. T. (1986). Bizarre imagery: The misremembered mnemonic. *Journal of Experimental Psychology: Learning, Memory, and Cognition, 12*, 42–53.

Kruley, P., Sciama, S. C., & Glenberg, A. M. (1994). On-line processing of textual illustrations in the visuospatial sketchpad: Evidence from dual-task studies. *Memory & Cognition, 22*, 261–272.

Kuhn, T. S. (1962). *The structure of scientific revolutions*. Chicago: University of Chicago Press.

Lachman, R., Lachman, J. L., & Butterfield, E. C. (1979). *Cognitive psychology and information processing: An introduction*. Hillsdale, NJ: Erlbaum.

Lakoff, G., & Johnson, M. (1980). *Metaphors we live by*. Chicago: University of Chicago Press.

Larochelle, S., & Pineau, H. (1994). Determinants of response times in the semantic verification task. *Journal of Memory and Language, 33*, 796–823.

Lea, R. B. (1995). On-line evidence for elaborative logical inferences in text. *Journal of Experimental Psychology: Learning, Memory, and Cognition, 21*, 1469–1482.

Leahey, T. H. (1992a). *A history of psychology: Main currents in psychological thought* (3rd ed.). Englewood Cliffs, NJ: Prentice-Hall.

Leahey, T. H. (1992b). The mythical revolutions of American psychology. *American Psychologist, 47*, 308–318.

LeFevre, J., Bisanz, J., Daley, K. E., Buffone, L., Greenham, S. L., & Sadesky, G. S. (1996). Multiple routes to solution of single-digit multiplication problems. *Journal of Experimental Psychology: General, 125*, 284–306.

Levine, M. (1988). *Effective problem solving*. Englewood Cliffs, NJ: Prentice-Hall.

Levine, M. W., & Schefner, J. M. (1981). *Fundamentals of sensation and perception*. London: Addison-Wesley.

Lewis, J. L. (1970). Semantic processing of unattended messages using dichotic listening. *Journal of Experimental Psychology, 85*, 225–228.

Lewontin, R. C. (1990). The evolution of cognition. In D. N. Osherson & E. E. Smith (Eds.), *Thinking: An invitation to cognitive science* (Vol. 3, pp. 229–246). Cambridge, MA: MIT Press.

Libbey, R. (1981). *Accounting and human information processing: Theory and application*. Englewood Cliffs, NJ: Prentice-Hall.

Liberman, A. M. (1970). The grammars of speech and language. *Cognitive Psychology, 1*, 301–323.

Liberman, A. M., Harris, K. S., Hoffman, H. S., & Griffith, B. C. (1957). The discrimination of speech sounds within and across phoneme boundaries. *Journal of Experimental Psychology, 54*, 358–368.

Lindsay, P. H., & Norman, D. A. (1977). *Human information processing: An introduction to psychology*. New York: Academic Press.

Lindsley, J. R. (1975). Producing simple utterances: How far ahead do we plan? *Cognitive Psychology, 7*, 1–19.

Linton, M. (1975). Memory for real-world events. In D. A. Norman & D. E. Rumelhart (Eds.), *Explorations in cognition* (pp. 376–404). San Francisco: Freeman.

Linton, M. (1978). Real world memory after six years: An in vivo study of very long term memory. In M. M. Gruneberg, P. E. Morris, & R. N. Sykes (Eds.), *Practical aspects of memory* (pp. 69–76). Orlando: Academic Press.

Litman, D. J., & Allen, J. F. (1987). A plan recognition model for subdialogues in conversation. *Cognitive Science, 11*, 163–200.

Loftus, E. F. (1979). *Eyewitness testimony*. Cambridge, MA: Harvard University Press.

Loftus, E. F. (1980). *Memory*. Reading, MA: Addison-Wesley.

Loftus, E. F. (1983). Silence is not golden. *American Psychologist, 38*, 564–572.

Loftus, E. F. (1991). Made in memory: Distortions in recollection after misleading information. In G. H. Bower (Ed.), *The psychology of learning and motivation* (Vol. 27, pp. 187–215). New York: Academic Press.

Loftus, E. F. (1993). The reality of repressed memories. *American Psychologist, 48*, 518–537.

Loftus, E. F., & Coan, D. (1994). The construction of childhood memories. In D. Peters (Ed.), *The child witness in context: Cognitive, social, and legal perspectives* New York: Kluwer.

Loftus, E. F., Donders, K., Hoffman, H. G., & Schooler, J. W. (1989). Creating new memories that are quickly accessed and confidently held. *Memory & Cognition, 17*, 607–616.

Loftus, E. F., & Hoffman, H. G. (1989). Misinformation and memory: The creation of new memories. *Journal of Experimental Psychology: General, 118*, 100–104.

Loftus, E. F., & Ketcham, K. (1991). *Witness for the defense*. New York: St. Martin's Press.

Loftus, E. F., & Palmer, J. C. (1974). Reconstruction of automobile destruction: An example of the interaction between language and memory. *Journal of Verbal Learning and Verbal Behavior, 13*, 585–589.

Loftus, G. R. (1983). The continuing persistence of the icon. *The Behavioral and Brain Sciences, 6*, 28.

Loftus, G. R., & Hanna, A. M. (1989). The phenomenology of spatial integration: Data and models. *Cognitive Psychology, 21*, 363–397.

Loftus, G. R., & Loftus, E. F. (1974). The influence of one memory retrieval on a subsequent memory retrieval. *Memory & Cognition, 2*, 467–471.

Logan, G. D., & Etherton, J. L. (1994). What is learned during automatization? The role of attention in constructing an instance. *Journal of Experimental Psychology: Learning, Memory, and Cognition, 20*, 1022–1050.

Logan, G. D., & Klapp, S. T. (1991). Automatizing alphabet arithmetic: I. Is extended practice necessary to produce automaticity? *Journal of Experimental Psychology: Learning, Memory, and Cognition, 17*, 179–195.

Logie, R. H., Zucco, G., & Baddeley, A. D. (1990). Interference with visual short-term memory. *Acta Psychologica, 75*, 55–74.

Long, D. L., Golding, J. M., & Graesser, A. C. (1992). A test of the on-line status of goal-related inferences. *Journal of Memory and Language, 31*, 634–647.

Long, D. L., Golding, J., Graesser, A. C., & Clark, L. F. (1990). Inference generation during story comprehension: A comparison of goals, events, and states. In A. C. Graesser & G. H. Bower (Eds.), *The psychology of learning and motivation* (Vol. 25, pp. 89–102). New York: Academic Press.

Lorayne, H., & Lucas, J. (1974). *The memory book*. New York: Ballantine Books.

Luchins, A. S. (1942). Mechanization in problem solving. *Psychological Monographs, 54* (Whole No. 248).

Luo, C. R. (1996). How is word meaning accessed in reading? Evidence from the phonologically mediated interference effect. *Journal of Experimental Psychology: Learning, Memory, and Cognition, 22*, 883–895.

Luria, A. R. (1968). *The mind of a mnemonist*. New York: Basic Books.

MacDonald, M. C., & Just, M. A. (1989). Changes in activation levels with negation. *Journal of Experimental Psychology: Learning, Memory, and Cognition, 15*, 633–642.

MacLeod, C. M. (1991). Half a century of research on the Stroop effect: An integrative review. *Psychological Bulletin, 109*, 163–203.

Maier, N. R. F. (1931). Reasoning in humans: II. The solution of a problem and its appearance in consciousness. *Journal of Comparative Psychology, 12*, 181–194.

Maki, R. H., & Berry, S. L. (1984). Metacomprehension of text material. *Journal of Experimental Psychology: Learning, Memory, and Cognition, 10*, 663–679.

Malt, B. C. (1990). Features and beliefs in the mental representation of categories. *Journal of Memory and Language, 29*, 289–315.

Mandler, G. (1967). Organization and memory. In K. W. Spence & J. T. Spence (Eds.), *The psychology of learning and motivation* (Vol. 1, pp. 327–372). New York: Academic Press.

Mandler, G. (1985). From association to structure. *Journal of Experimental Psychology: Learning, Memory, and Cognition, 11*, 464–468.

Marcel, A. J. (1980). Conscious and preconscious recognition of polysemous words: Locating the selective effects of prior verbal context. In R. S. Nickerson (Ed.), *Attention and performance VIII* (pp. 435–457). Hillsdale, NJ: Erlbaum.

Marcel, A. J. (1983). Conscious and unconscious perception: Experiments on visual masking and word recognition. *Cognitive Psychology, 15*, 197–237.

Marcus, G. F. (1996). Why do children say "breaked"? *Current Issues in Psychological Science*, *5*, 81–85.

Marler, P. (1967). Animal communication signals. *Science*, *35*, 63–78.

Marschark, M., & Paivio, A. (1979). Semantic congruity and lexical marking in symbolic comparisons: An expectancy hypothesis. *Memory & Cognition*, *7*, 175–184.

Marshall, J. C., & Halligan, P. W. (1994). Left in the dark: The neglect of theory. *Neuropsychological Rehabilitation*, *4*, 161–167.

Marslen-Wilson, W. D., & Tyler, L. K. (1980). The temporal structure of spoken language understanding. *Cognition*, *8*, 1–71.

Marslen-Wilson, W. D., Tyler, L. K., & Koster, C. (1993). Integrative processes in utterance resolution. *Journal of Memory and Language*, *32*, 647–666.

Martin, E., & Noreen, D. L. (1974). Serial learning: Identification of subjective sequences. *Cognitive Psychology*, *6*, 421–435.

Martindale, C. (1991). *Cognitive psychology: A neural-network approach*. Pacific Grove, CA: Brooks/Cole.

Masson, M. E. J. (1984). Memory for the surface structure of sentences: Remembering with and without awareness. *Journal of Verbal Learning and Verbal Behavior, 23*, 579–592.

Masson, M. E. J. (1995). A distributed memory model of semantic priming. *Journal of Experimental Psychology: Learning, Memory, and Cognition*, *21*, 3–23.

Mayer, R. E. (1992). *Thinking, problem solving, cognition* (2nd ed.). New York: Freeman.

McAndrews, M. P., Glisky, E. L., & Schacter, D. L. (1987). When priming persists: Long-lasting implicit memory for a single episode in amnesic patients. *Neuropsychologia*, *25*, 497–506.

McCarthy, R. A., & Warrington, E. K. (1990). *Cognitive neuropsychology: A clinical introduction*. San Diego: Academic Press.

McClelland, J. L. (1979). On the time relations of mental processes: An examination of systems of processes in cascade. *Psychological Review, 86*, 287–330.

McClelland, J. L., & Elman, J. L. (1986). The TRACE model of speech perception. *Cognitive Psychology, 18*, 1–86.

McClelland, J. L., & Rumelhart, D. E. (1981). An interactive activation model of context effects in letter perception: Part 1. An account of basic findings. *Psychological Review, 88*, 375–407.

McCloskey, M. (1983). Naive theories of motion. In D. Gentner & A. L. Stevens (Eds.), *Mental models* (pp. 299–324). Hillsdale, NJ: Erlbaum.

McCloskey, M. (1991). Networks and theories: The place of connectionism in cognitive science. *Psychological Science*, *2*, 387–395.

McCloskey, M. (1992). Cognitive mechanisms in numerical processing: Evidence from acquired dyscalculia. *Cognition*, *44*, 107–157.

McCloskey, M., Caramazza, A., & Green, B. (1980). Curvilinear motion in the absence of external forces: Naive beliefs about the motion of objects. *Science, 210*, 1139–1141.

McCloskey, M., & Kohl, D. (1983). Naive physics: The curvilinear impetus principle and its role in interactions with moving objects. *Journal of Experimental Psychology: Learning, Memory, and Cognition*, *9*, 146–156.

McCloskey, M., Washburn, A., & Felch, L. (1983). Intuitive physics: The straight-down belief and its origin. *Journal of Experimental Psychology: Learning, Memory, and Cognition*, *9*, 636–649.

McCloskey, M., Wible, C. G., & Cohen, N. J. (1988). Is there a special flashbulb-memory mechanism? *Journal of Experimental Psychology: General*, *117*, 171–181.

McCloskey, M., & Zaragoza, M. (1985). Misleading postevent information and memory for events: Arguments and evidence against memory impairment hypotheses. *Journal of Experimental Psychology: General*, *114*, 1–16.

McCutchen, D., & Perfetti, C. A. (1982). The visual tongue-twister effect: Phonological activation in silent reading. *Journal of Verbal Learning and Verbal Behavior*, *21*, 672–687.

McDaniel, M. A., & Einstein, G. O. (1986). Bizarre imagery as an effective memory aid: The importance of distinctiveness. *Journal of Experimental Psychology: Learning, Memory, and Cognition*, *12*, 54–65.

McDonald, J. L., Bock, K., & Kelly, M. H. (1993). Word and world order: Semantic, phonological, and metrical determinants of serial position. *Cognitive Psychology*, *25*, 188–230.

McGeoch, J. A. (1932). Forgetting and the law of disuse. *Psychological Review*, *39*, 352–370.

McKenzie, C. R. M. (1994). The accuracy of intuitive judgment strategies: Covariation assessment and Bayesian inference. *Cognitive Psychology*, *26*, 209–239.

McKoon, G., & Ratcliff, R. (1986). Inferences about predictable events. *Journal of Experimental Psychology: Learning, Memory, and Cognition*, *12*, 82–91.

McKoon, G., & Ratcliff, R. (1989). Inferences about contextually defined categories. *Journal of Experimental Psychology: Learning, Memory, and Cognition*, *15*, 1134–1146.

McKoon, G., Ratcliff, R., Ward, G., & Sproat, R. (1993). Syntactic prominence effects on discourse processes. *Journal of Memory and Language*, *32*, 593–607.

McNamara, D. S., & Healy, A. F. (1995). A generation advantage for multiplication skill and nonword vocabulary acquisition. In A. F. Healy & L. E. Bourne, Jr. (Eds.), *Learning and memory of knowledge and skills: Durability and specificity* (pp. 132–169). Thousand Oaks, CA: Sage.

McNamara, T. P. (1992). Priming and constraints it places on theories of memory and retrieval. *Psychological Review*, *99*, 650–662.

McNeill, D. (1985). So you think gestures are nonverbal? *Psychological Review*, *92*, 350–371.

Medin, D. L., & Edelson, S. M. (1988). Problem structure and the use of base-rate information from experience. *Journal of Experimental Psychology: General*, *117*, 68–85.

Merikle, P. M. (1982). Unconscious perception revisited. *Perception & Psychophysics*, *31*, 298–301.

Merriman, W. (1986). How children learn the reference of concrete nouns: A critique of current hypotheses. In S. A. Kuczaj & M. D. Barrett (Eds.), *The acquisition of word meaning* (pp. 1–38). New York: Springer.

Metcalfe, J. (1986). Feeling of knowing in memory and problem solving. *Journal of Experimental Psychology: Learning, Memory, and Cognition*, *12*, 288–294.

Metcalfe, J., & Wiebe, D. (1987). Intuition in insight and noninsight problem solving. *Memory & Cognition*, *15*, 238–246.

Meyer, A. S., & Bock, K. (1992). The tip-of-the-tongue phenomenon: Blocking or partial activation? *Memory & Cognition, 20*, 715–726.

Meyer, D. E., & Schvaneveldt, R. W. (1971). Facilitation in recognizing pairs of words: Evidence of a dependence between retrieval operations. *Journal of Experimental Psychology, 90*, 227–234.

Meyer, D. E., Schvaneveldt, R. W., & Ruddy, M. G. (1975). Loci of contextual effects on visual word-recognition. In P. M. A. Rabbit & S. Dornic (Eds.), *Attention and performance V* (pp. 98–118). London: Academic Press.

Micco, A., & Masson, M. E. J. (1991). Implicit memory for new associations: An interactive process approach. *Journal of Experimental Psychology: Learning, Memory, and Cognition, 17*, 1105–1123.

Miller, G. A. (1956). The magical number seven, plus or minus two: Some limits on our capacity for processing information. *Psychological Review, 63*, 81–97.

Miller, G. A. (1973). Psychology and communication. In G. A. Miller (Ed.), *Communication, language, and meaning: Psychological perspectives* (pp. 3–12). New York: Basic Books.

Miller, G. A. (1981). *Language and speech*. San Francisco: Freeman.

Miller, G. A., Galanter, E., & Pribram, K. H. (1960). *Plans and the structure of behavior*. New York: Henry Holt.

Miller, G. A., & Isard, S. (1963). Some perceptual consequences of linguistic rules. *Journal of Verbal Learning and Verbal Behavior, 2*, 217–228.

Miller, J. F., & Chapman, R. S. (1981). The relationship between age and Mean Length of Utterance in morphemes. *Journal of Speech and Hearing Research, 24*, 154–161.

Milner, B., Corkin, S., & Teuber, H. L. (1968). Further analysis of the hippocampal amnesic syndrome: 14-year follow up study of H.M. *Neuropsychologia, 6*, 215–234.

Mitchell, D. C., & Holmes, V. M. (1985). The role of specific information about the verb in parsing sentences with local structural ambiguity. *Journal of Memory and Language, 24*, 542–559.

Mitchell, K. J., & Zaragoza, M. S. (1996). Repeated exposure to suggestion and false memory: The role of contextual variability. *Journal of Memory and Language, 35*, 246–260.

Miyake, A., Just, M. A., & Carpenter, P. A. (1994). Working memory constraints on the resolution of lexical ambiguity: Maintaining multiple interpretations in neutral contexts. *Journal of Memory and Language, 33*, 175–202.

Moray, N. (1959). Attention in dichotic listening: Affective cues and the influence of instructions. *Quarterly Journal of Experimental Psychology, 11*, 56–60.

Moray, N., Bates, A., & Barnett, T. (1965). Experiments on the four-eared man. *Journal of the Acoustical Society of America, 38*, 196–201.

Moscovitch, M. (1979). Information processing and the cerebral hemispheres. In M. S. Gazzaniga (Ed.), *Handbook of behavioral neurobiology: Vol 2. Neuropsychology* (pp. 379–446). New York: Plenum Press.

Moyer, R. S. (1973). Comparing objects in memory: Evidence suggesting an internal psychophysics. *Perception & Psychophysics, 13*, 180–184.

Moyer, R. S., & Bayer, R. H. (1976). Mental comparison and the symbolic distance effect. *Cognitive Psychology, 8*, 228–246.

Mulligan, N. W., & Hartman, M. (1996). Divided attention and indirect memory tests. *Memory & Cognition, 24*, 453–465.

Murdock, B. B., Jr. (1962). The serial position effect of free recall. *Journal of Experimental Psychology, 64*, 482–488.

Murphy, G. L., & Shapiro, A. M. (1994). Forgetting of verbatim information in discourse. *Memory & Cognition, 22*, 85–94.

Myers, J. L., O'Brien, E. J., Albrecht, J. E., & Mason, R. A. (1994). Maintaining global coherence during reading. *Journal of Experimental Psychology: Learning, Memory, and Cognition, 20*, 876–886.

Nairne, J. S. (1983). Associative processing during rote rehearsal. *Journal of Experimental Psychology: Learning, Memory, and Cognition, 9*, 3–20.

Navon, D. (1984). Resources—A theoretical soup stone? *Psychological Review, 91*, 216–234.

Neely, J. H. (1976). Semantic priming and retrieval from lexical memory: Evidence for facilitatory and inhibitory processes. *Memory & Cognition, 4*, 648–654.

Neely, J. H. (1977). Semantic priming and retrieval from lexical memory: Roles of inhibitionless spreading activation and limited-capacity attention. *Journal of Experimental Psychology: General, 106*, 226–254.

Neely, J. H., Keefe, D. E., & Ross, K. L. (1989). Semantic priming in the lexical decision task: Roles of prospective prime-generated expectancies and retrospective semantic matching. *Journal of Experimental Psychology: Learning, Memory, and Cognition, 15*, 1003–1019.

Neisser, U. (1964). Visual search. *Scientific American, 210*, 94–102.

Neisser, U. (1967). *Cognitive psychology*. New York: Appleton-Century-Crofts.

Neisser, U. (1976). *Cognition and reality*. San Francisco: Freeman.

Neisser, U. (1978). Memory: What are the important questions? In M. M. Gruneberg, P. E. Morris, & R. N. Sykes (Eds.), *Practical aspects of memory* (pp. 3–24). London: Academic Press.

Neisser, U. (1982). *Memory observed: Remembering in natural contexts*. San Francisco: Freeman.

Nelson, D. L., & Roediger, H. L., III (1996). Illusions of memory [Special Issue]. *Journal of Memory and Language, 35* (2).

Nelson, D. L., & Schreiber, T. A. (1992). Word concreteness and word structure as independent determinants of recall. *Journal of Memory and Language, 31*, 237–260.

Nelson, K. (1973). Some evidence for the cognitive primacy of categorization and its functional basis. *Merrill-Palmer Quarterly, 19*, 21–39.

Nelson, K. (1974). Concept, word, and sentence: Interrelations in acquisition and development. *Psychological Review, 81*, 267–285.

Nelson, T. O. (1985). Ebbinghaus's contribution to the measurement of retention: Savings during relearning. *Journal of Experimental Psychology: Learning, Memory, and Cognition, 11*, 472–479.

Nelson, T. O., & Leonesio, R. J. (1988). Allocation of self-paced study time and the "labor-in-vain effect." *Journal of Experimental Psychology: Learning, Memory, and Cognition, 14*, 676–686.

New World Dictionary of the American Language. (1980). Cleveland: William Collins Publishers.

Newell, A., Shaw, J. C., & Simon, H. A. (1958). Elements of a theory of human problem solving. *Psychological Review, 65*, 151–166.

Newell, A., & Simon, H. A. (1972). *Human problem solving*. Englewood Cliffs, NJ: Prentice-Hall.

Newport, E. L., & Bellugi, U. (1978). Linguistic expression of category levels in a visual-gestural language: A flower is a flower is a flower. In E. Rosch & B. B. Lloyd (Eds.), *Cognition and categorization* (pp. 49–71). Hillsdale, NJ: Erlbaum.

Nickerson, R. S., & Adams, M. J. (1979). Long-term memory for a common object. *Cognitive Psychology, 11*, 287–307.

Nisbett, R. (1995). Race, IQ, and scientism. In S. Fraser (Ed.), *The bell curve wars: Race, intelligence, and the future of America* (pp. 36–57). New York: Basic Books.

Nisbett, R., Krantz, D. H., Jepson, C., & Kunda, Z. (1983). The use of statistical heuristics in everyday inductive reasoning. *Psychological Review, 90*, 339–-363.

Nisbett, R., & Ross, L. (1980). *Human inference: Strategies and shortcomings of social judgment*. Englewood Cliffs, NJ: Prentice-Hall.

Noordman, L. G. M., Vonk, W., & Kempff, H. J. (1992). Causal inferences during the reading of expository texts. *Journal of Memory and Language, 31*, 573–590.

Norman, D. A. (1968). Toward a theory of memory and attention. *Psychological Review, 75*, 522–536.

Norman, D. A. (1976). *Memory and attention: An introduction to human information processing* (2nd ed.). New York: Wiley.

Norman, D. A. (1986). Reflections on cognition and parallel distributed processing. In J. L. McClelland & D. E. Rumelhart (Eds.), *Parallel distributed processing* (Vol. 2, pp. 531–546). Cambridge, MA: Bradford.

Norman, D. A., & Rumelhart, D. E. (1975). Reference and comprehension. In D. A. Norman & D. E. Rumelhart (Eds.), *Explorations in cognition* (pp. 65–87). San Francisco: Freeman.

Norman, G. R., Brooks, L. R., Coblentz, C. L., & Babcook, C. J. (1992). The correlation of feature identification and category judgments in diagnostic radiology. *Memory & Cognition, 20*, 344–355.

Novick, L. R. (1988). Analogical transfer, problem similarity, and expertise. *Journal of Experimental Psychology: Learning, Memory, and Cognition, 14*, 510–520.

Oberly, H. S. (1928). A comparison of the spans of "attention" and memory. *American Journal of Psychology, 40*, 295–302.

O'Brien, E. J., & Albrecht, J. E. (1991). The role of context in accessing antecedents in text. *Journal of Experimental Psychology: Learning, Memory, and Cognition, 17*, 94–102.

O'Brien, E. J., Plewes, P. S., & Albrecht, J. E. (1990). Antecedent retrieval processes. *Journal of Experimental Psychology: Learning, Memory, and Cognition, 16*, 241–249.

O'Brien, E. J., Shank, D. M., Myers, J. L., & Rayner, K. (1988). Elaborative inferences during reading: Do they occur on-line? *Journal of Experimental Psychology: Learning, Memory, and Cognition, 14*, 410–420.

Ofshe, R. J. (1992). Inadvertent hypnosis during interrogation: False confession due to dissociative state, misidentified multiple personality, and the satanic cult hypothesis. *International Journal of Clinical and Experimental Hypnosis, 40*, 125–156.

Ojemann, G. A. (1982). Models of the brain organization for higher integrative functions derived with electrical stimulation techniques. *Human Neurobiology, 1*, 243–250.

Ojemann, G. A., & Creutzfeldt, O. D. (1987). Language in humans and animals: Contribution of brain stimulation and recording. In J. M. Brookhart & V. B. Mountcastle (Eds.), *Handbook of physiology: The nervous system* (Vol. 5). Bethesda: American Physiological Society.

Ornstein, R., & Thompson, R. F. (1984). *The amazing brain*. Los Altos, CA: ISHK Book Service.

Ortony, A. (1979). *Metaphor and thought*. New York: Cambridge University Press.

Osterhout, L., & Holcomb, P. J. (1992). Event-related brain potentials elicited by syntactic anomaly. *Journal of Memory and Language, 31*, 785–806.

Osterhout, L., & Mobley, L. A. (1995). Event-related brain potentials elicited by failure to agree. *Journal of Memory and Language, 34*, 739–773.

Paivio, A. (1971). *Imagery and verbal processes*. New York: Holt.

Palermo, D. S. (1978). *Psychology of language*. Glenview, IL: Scott, Foresman.

Paller, K. A., Kutas, M., & McIsaac, H. K. (1995). Monitoring conscious recollection via the electrical activity of the brain. *Psychological Science*, 6, 107–111.

Parker, L. M., Porter, M., & Finley, D. (1983, August). Halo effects and heuristics in the examination of audit evidence. *Paper presented at the meeting of the American Accounting Association*. New Orleans, LA.

Pashler, H. (1992). Attentional limitations in doing two tasks at the same time. *Current Directions in Psychological Science, 1*, 44–48.

Pashler, H. (1994). Dual-task interference in simple tasks: Data and theory. *Psychological Bulletin, 116*, 220–244.

Patel, V. L., & Groen, G. J. (1986). Knowledge based solution strategies in medical reasoning. *Cognitive Science, 10*, 91–116.

Patterson, F., & Linden, E. (1981). *The education of Koko*. New York: Holt, Rinehart & Winston.

Paul, S. T., Kellas, G., Martin, M., & Clark, M. B. (1992). Influence of contextual features on the activation of ambiguous word meanings. *Journal of Experimental Psychology: Learning, Memory, and Cognition, 18*, 703–717.

Payne, D. G., Toglia, M. P., & Anastasi, J. S. (1994). Recognition performance level and the magnitude of the misinformation effect in eyewitness memory. *Psychonomic Bulletin & Review, 1*, 376–382.

Payne, J. W. (1994). Thinking aloud: Insights into information processing. *Psychological Science, 5*, 241, 245–248.

Penfield, W. (1958). *The excitable cortex in conscious man*. Liverpool, England: Liverpool University Press.

Penfield, W., & Jasper, H. H. (1954). *Epilepsy and the functional anatomy of the human brain*. Boston: Little, Brown.

Penfield, W., & Milner, B. (1958). Memory deficit produced by bilateral lesions in the hippocampal zone. *Archives of Neurology and Psychiatry, 79*, 475–497.

Petersen, S. E., Fox, P. T., Posner, M. I., Mintun, M., & Raichle, M. E. (1988). Positron emission tomographic studies of the processing of single words. *Journal of Cognitive Neuroscience, 1*, 153–170.

Peterson, L. R., & Peterson, M. J. (1959). Short-term retention of individual items. *Journal of Experimental Psychology, 58*, 193–198.

Peterson, L. R., Peterson, M. J., & Miller, A. (1961). Short-term retention and meaningfulness. *Canadian Journal of Psychology, 15*, 143–147.

Pitt, M. A., & Samuel, A. G. (1995). Lexical and sublexical feedback in auditory word recognition. *Cognitive Psychology, 29*, 149–188.

Pollack, I., & Pickett, J. M. (1964). Intelligibility of excerpts from fluent speech: Auditory vs. structural context. *Journal of Verbal Learning and Verbal Behavior, 3*, 79–84.

Pollatsek, A., Konold, C. E., Well, A. D., & Lima, S. D. (1984). Beliefs underlying random sampling. *Memory & Cognition, 12*, 395–401.

Polya, G. (1957). *How to solve it*. Garden City, NJ: Doubleday/Anchor.

Posner, M. I. (1973). *Cognition: An introduction*. Glenview, IL: Scott, Foresman.

Posner, M. I. (1992). Attention as a cognitive and neural system. *Current Directions in Psychological Science, 1*, 11–14.

Posner, M. I., & Raichle, M. E. (1994). *Images of mind*. New York: Scientific American Library.

Posner, M. I., & Snyder, C. R. R. (1975). Facilitation and inhibition in the processing of signals. In P. M. A. Rabbitt & S. Dornic (Eds.), *Attention and performance V* (pp. 669–682). New York: Academic Press.

Postman, L., & Underwood, B. J. (1973). Critical issues in interference theory. *Memory & Cognition, 1*, 19–40.

Price, R. H. (1987). *Principles of psychology*. Glenview, IL: Scott, Foresman.

Proffitt, D. R., Kaiser, M. K., & Whelan, S. M. (1990). Understanding wheel dynamics. *Cognitive Psychology, 22*, 342–373.

Quillian, M. R. (1966). *Semantic memory*. Unpublished doctoral dissertation, Carnegie Institute of Technology, Pittsburgh.

Quillian, M. R. (1968). Semantic memory. In M. Minsky (Ed.), *Semantic information processing* (pp. 216–270). Cambridge, MA: MIT Press.

Radvansky, G. A., Carlson-Radvansky, L. A., & Irwin, D. E. (1995). Uncertainty in estimating distances from memory. *Memory & Cognition, 23*, 596–606.

Radvansky, G. A., Spieler, D. H., & Zacks, R. T. (1993). Mental model organization. *Journal of Experimental Psychology: Learning, Memory, and Cognition, 19*, 95–114.

Radvansky, G. A., & Zacks, R. T. (1991). Mental models and the fan effect. *Journal of Experimental Psychology: Learning, Memory, and Cognition, 17*, 940–953.

Rafal, R. D. (1997). Hemispatial neglect: Cognitive neuropsychological aspects. In T. E. Feinberg & M. J. Farah (Eds.), *Behavioral neurology and neuropsychology* (pp. 319–336). New York: McGraw-Hill.

Ranney, M. (1994). Relative consistency and subjects' "theories" in domains such as naive physics: Common research difficulties illustrated by Cooke and Breedin. *Memory & Cognition, 22*, 494–502.

Ratcliff, R., & McKoon, G. (1978). Priming in item recognition: Evidence for the propositional structure of sentences. *Journal of Verbal Learning and Verbal Behavior, 17*, 403–418.

Ratcliff, R., & McKoon, G. (1988). A retrieval theory of priming in memory. *Psychological Review, 95*, 385–408.

Rayner, K. (1993). Eye movements in reading: Recent developments. *Current Directions in Psychological Science*, *2*, 81–85.

Rayner, K. (Ed.). (1993). Reading symposium. *Psychological Science*, *4*, (5).

Rayner, K., Carlson, M., & Frazier, L. (1983). The interaction of syntax and semantics during sentence processing: Eye movements in the analysis of semantically biased sentences. *Journal of Verbal Learning and Verbal Behavior, 22*, 358–374.

Rayner, K., Garrod, S., & Perfetti, C. A. (1992). Discourse influences during parsing are delayed. *Cognition*, *45*, 109–139.

Rayner, K., Inhoff, A. W., Morrison, P. E., Slowiaczek, M. L., & Bertera, J. H. (1981). Masking of foveal and parafoveal vision during eye fixations in reading. *Journal of Experimental Psychology: Human Perception and Performance*, *7*, 167–179.

Rayner, K., & Pollatsek, A. (1989). *The psychology of reading*. Englewood Cliffs, NJ: Prentice-Hall.

Reder, L. M., & Kusbit, G. W. (1991). Locus of the Moses illusion: Imperfect encoding, retrieval, or match? *Journal of Memory and Language*, *30*, 385–406.

Reed, S. K. (1996). *Cognition: Theory and applications* (4th ed.). Pacific Grove, CA: Brooks/Cole.

Reeves, L. M., & Weisberg, R. W. (1993). Abstract versus concrete information as the basis for transfer in problem solving: Comment on Fong and Nisbett (1991). *Journal of Experimental Psychology: General, 122*, 125–128.

Reich, P. A. (1986). *Language development*. Englewood Cliffs, NJ: Prentice-Hall.

Reiser, B. J., Black, J. B., & Abelson, R. P. (1985). Knowledge structures in the organization and retrieval of autobiographical memories. *Cognitive Psychology, 17*, 89–137.

Richardson, J. T. E. (1985). Integration versus decomposition in the retention of complex ideas. *Memory & Cognition*, *13*, 112–127.

Rifkin, A. (1985). Evidence for a basic level in event taxonomies. *Memory & Cognition*, *13*, 538–556.

Riley, K. P. (1989). Psychological interventions in Alzheimer's disease. In G. C. Gilmore, P. J. Whitehouse, & M. R. Wykle (Eds.), *Memory, aging, and dementia*. New York: Springer.

Rips, L. J., & Marcus, S. L. (1977). Supposition and the analysis of conditional sentences. In M. A. Just & P. A. Carpenter (Eds.), *Cognitive processes in comprehension* (pp. 185–220). Hillsdale, NJ: Erlbaum.

Roediger, H. L., III. (1996). Memory illusions. *Journal of Memory and Language*, *35*, 76–100.

Roediger, H. L., III, Jacoby, D., & McDermott, K. B. (1996). Misinformation effects in recall: Creating false memories through repeated retrieval. *Journal of Memory and Language*, *35*, 300–318.

Roediger, H. L., III, & McDermott, K. B. (1995). Creating false memories: Remembering words not presented in lists. *Journal of Experimental Psychology: Learning, Memory, and Cognition*, *21*, 803–814.

Rosch, E. H. (1975). Cognitive representations of semantic categories. *Journal of Experimental Psychology: General*, *104*, 192–233.

Rosenberg, S. (1993). Chomsky's theory of language: Some recent observations. *Psychological Science*, *4*, 15–19.

Ross, B. H. (1987). This is like that: The use of earlier problems and the separation of similarity effects. *Journal of Experimental Psychology: Learning, Memory, and Cognition, 13*, 629–640.

Ross, J., & Lawrence, K. A. (1968). Some observations on memory artifice. *Psychonomic Science, 13*, 107–108.

Rubens, A. B., & Benson, D. F. (1971). Associative visual agnosia. *Archives of Neurology (Chicago), 24*, 305–316.

Rubin, D. C. (Ed.). (1986). *Autobiographical memory.* New Rochelle, NY: Cambridge University Press.

Rubin, D. C. (Ed.). (1995a). *Memory in oral traditions.* New York: Oxford University Press.

Rubin, D. C. (Ed.). (1995b). *Remembering our past: Studies in autobiographical memory.* New York: Cambridge University Press.

Rumbaugh, D. M. (1977). *Language learning by a chimpanzee: The Lana project.* New York: Academic Press.

Rumelhart, D. E., Lindsay, P. H., & Norman, D. A. (1972). A process model for long-term memory. In E. Tulving & W. Donaldson (Eds.), *Organization of memory* (pp. 197–246). New York: Academic Press.

Rumelhart, D. E., & McClelland, J. L. (1986). *Parallel distributed processing: Explorations in the microstructure of cognition: Vol. 1. Foundations.* Cambridge, MA: Bradford.

Rundus, D. (1971). Analysis of rehearsal processes in free recall. *Journal of Experimental Psychology, 89*, 63–77.

Rundus, D., & Atkinson, R. C. (1970). Rehearsal processes in free recall: A procedure for direct observation. *Journal of Verbal Learning and Verbal Behavior, 9*, 99–105.

Russo, J. E., Johnson, E. J., & Stephens, D. L. (1989). The validity of verbal protocols. *Memory & Cognition, 17*, 759–769.

Sachs, J. (1985). Prelinguistic development. In J. Berko Gleason (Ed.), *The development of language* (pp. 37–60). Columbus, OH: Merrill Publishing.

Sachs, J. S. (1967). Recognition memory for syntactic and semantic aspects of connected discourse. *Perception & Psychophysics, 2*, 437–442.

Sacks, H., Schegloff, E. A., & Jefferson, G. (1974). A simplest systematics for the organization of turn-taking for conversation. *Language, 50*, 696–735.

Sacks, O. (1970). *The man who mistook his wife for a hat, and other clinical tales.* New York: HarperPerennial.

Salthouse, T. A. (1984). Effects of age and skill in typing. *Journal of Experimental Psychology: General, 113*, 345–371.

Salthouse, T. A. (1992). Working-memory mediation of adult age differences in integrative reasoning. *Memory & Cognition, 20*, 413–423.

Savage-Rumbaugh, S., & Lewin, R. (1994). *Kanzi: The ape at the brink of the human mind.* New York: Wiley.

Scarr, S. (1993). Biological and cultural diversity: The legacy of Darwin for development. *Child Development, 64*, 1333–1353.

Schacter, D. (1989). Memory. In M. I. Posner (Ed.), *Foundations of cognitive science* (pp. 683–725). Cambridge, MA: MIT Press.

Schacter, D. L. (1992). Understanding implicit memory: A cognitive neuroscience approach. *American Psychologist, 47*, 559–569.

Schacter, D. L. (1996). *Searching for memory*. New York: Basic Books.

Schank, R. C. (1977). Rules and topics in conversation. *Cognitive Science, 1*, 421–441.

Schank, R. C., & Abelson, R. P. (1977). *Scripts, plans, goals, and understanding*. Hillsdale, NJ: Erlbaum.

Schmidt, S. R. (1985). Encoding and retrieval processes in the memory for conceptually distinctive events. *Journal of Experimental Psychology: Learning, Memory, and Cognition, 11*, 565–578.

Schneider, W., Noll, D. C., & Cohen, J. D. (1993). Functional topographic mapping of human visual cortex using conventional MRI. *Nature, 365*, 150–152.

Schneider, W., & Shiffrin, R. M. (1977). Controlled and automatic human information processing: I. Detection, search, and attention. *Psychological Review, 84*, 1–66.

Schonpflug, W. (1994). The road not taken: A false start for cognitive psychology. *Psychological Review, 101*, 237–242.

Schooler, J. W., Ohlsson, S., & Brooks, K. (1993). Thoughts beyond words: When language overshadows insight. *Journal of Experimental Psychology: General, 122*, 166–183.

Schunn, C. D., & Dunbar, K. (1996). Priming, analogy, and awareness in complex reasoning. *Memory & Cognition, 24*, 271–284.

Science Watch. (1991, January). *American Psychologist, 46* (1).

Scoville, W. B., & Milner, B. (1957). Loss of recent memory after bilateral hippocampal lesions. *Journal of Neurology, Neurosurgery, and Psychiatry, 20*, 11–21.

Segal, S. J., & Fusella, V. (1970). Influence of imaged pictures and sounds on detection of visual and auditory signals. *Journal of Experimental Psychology, 83*, 458–464.

Sehulster, J. R. (1989). Content and temporal structure of autobiographical knowledge: Remembering twenty-five seasons at the Metropolitan Opera. *Memory & Cognition, 17*, 590–606.

Seidenberg, M. S. (1993). Connectionist models and cognitive theory. *Psychological Science, 4*, 228–235.

Seidenberg, M. S., & McClelland, J. L. (1989). A distributed, developmental model of word recognition and naming. *Psychological Review, 96*, 523–568.

Seifert, C. M., Robertson, S. P., & Black, J. B. (1985). Types of inferences generated during reading. *Journal of Memory and Language, 24*, 405–422.

Sejnowski, T. J., & Churchland, P. S. (1989). Brain and cognition. In M. I. Posner (Ed.), *Foundations of cognitive science* (pp. 301–356). Cambridge, MA: MIT Press.

Selfridge, O. G. (1959). Pandemonium: A paradigm for learning. In *The mechanisation of thought processes*. London: H. M. Stationery Office.

Shafir, E., & Tversky, A. (1992). Thinking through uncertainty: Nonconsequential reasoning and choice. *Cognitive Psychology, 24*, 449–474.

Shallice, T. (1988). *From neuropsychology to mental structure*. New York: Cambridge University Press.

Shallice, T., & Warrington, E. K. (1970). Independent functioning of the verbal memory stores: A neuropsychological study. *Quarterly Journal of Experimental Psychology, 22*, 261–273.

Shand, M. A. (1982). Sign-based short-term coding of American Sign Language signs and printed English words by congenitally deaf signers. *Cognitive Psychology, 14*, 1–12.

Shaw, J. S., III. (1996). Increases in eyewitness confidence resulting from postevent questioning. *Journal of Experimental Psychology: Applied, 2*, 126–146.

Shaw, J. S., III, Bjork, R. A., & Handal, A. (1995). Retrieval-induced forgetting in an eyewitness-memory paradigm. *Psychonomic Bulletin & Review, 2*, 249–253.

Shepard, R. N., & Metzler, J. (1971). Mental rotation of three-dimensional objects. *Science, 153*, 652–654.

Shiffrin, R. M., & Schneider, W. (1977). Controlled and automatic human information processing: II. Perceptual learning, automatic attending, and a general theory. *Psychological Review, 84*, 127–190.

Shoben, E. J., Sailor, K. M., & Wang, M.-Y. (1989). The role of expectancy in comparative judgments. *Memory & Cognition, 17*, 18–26.

Siegler, R. S., & Jenkins, E. A. (1989). *How children discover new strategies*. Hillsdale, NJ: Erlbaum.

Simon, H. A. (1975). The functional equivalence of problem solving skills. *Cognitive Psychology, 7*, 268–288.

Simon, H. A. (1979). *Models of thought*. New Haven: Yale University Press.

Simon, H. A. (1995, May). *Thinking in words, pictures, equations, numbers: How do we do it and what does it matter?* Invited address presented at the meeting of the Midwestern Psychological Association, Chicago.

Simpson, G. B. (1981). Meaning dominance and semantic context in the processing of lexical ambiguity. *Journal of Verbal Learning and Verbal Behavior, 20*, 120–136.

Simpson, G. B. (1984). Lexical ambiguity and its role in models of word recognition. *Psychological Bulletin, 96*, 316–340.

Singer, M. (1990). *Psychology of language: An introduction to sentence and discourse processes*. Hillsdale, NJ: Erlbaum.

Singer, M., Andrusiak, P., Reisdorf, P., & Black, N. L. (1992). Individual differences in bridging inference processes. *Memory & Cognition, 20*, 539–548.

Skinner, B. F. (1938). *The behavior of organisms*. New York: Appleton-Century-Crofts.

Skinner, B. F. (1957). *Verbal behavior*. New York: Appleton-Century-Crofts.

Skinner, B. F. (1984). The shame of American education. *American Psychologist, 39*, 947–954.

Skinner, B. F. (1990). Can psychology be a science of mind? *American Psychologist, 45*, 1206–1210.

Slamecka, N. J. (1985a). Ebbinghaus: Some associations. *Journal of Experimental Psychology: Learning, Memory, and Cognition, 11*, 414–435.

Slamecka, N. J. (1985b). Ebbinghaus: Some rejoinders. *Journal of Experimental Psychology: Learning, Memory, and Cognition, 11*, 496–500.

Slamecka, N. J., & Graf, P. (1978). The generation effect: Delineation of a phenomenon. *Journal of Experimental Psychology: Human Learning and Memory, 4*, 592–604.

Slobin, D. I. (1979). *Psycholinguistics* (2nd ed.). Glenview, IL: Scott, Foresman.

Smith, D. A., & Graesser, A. C. (1981). Memory for actions in scripted activities as a function of typicality, retention interval, and retrieval task. *Memory & Cognition, 9*, 550–559.

Smith, E. E. (1978). Theories of semantic memory. In W. K. Estes (Ed.), *Handbook of learning and cognitive processes* (Vol. 6, pp. 1–56). Hillsdale, NJ: Erlbaum.

Smith, E. E., Rips, L. J., & Shoben, E. J. (1974). Semantic memory and psychological semantics. In G. H. Bower (Ed.), *The psychology of learning and motivation* (Vol. 8, pp. 1–45). New York: Academic Press.

Smith, L. C. (1984). Semantic satiation affects category membership decision time but not lexical priming. *Memory & Cognition, 12*, 483–488.

Smith, M. C., Besner, D., & Miyoshi, H. (1994). New limits to automaticity: Context modulates semantic priming. *Journal of Experimental Psychology: Learning, Memory, & Cognition, 20*, 104–115.

Smith, S. M. (1995). Getting into and out of mental ruts: A theory of fixation, incubation, and insight. In R. J. Sternberg & J. E. Davidson (Eds.), *The nature of insight* (pp. 229–251). Cambridge, MA: MIT Press.

Smith, S. M., & Rothkopf, E. Z. (1984). Contextual enrichment and distribution of practice in the classroom. *Cognition and Instruction, 1*, 341–358.

Snow, C. (1972). Mother's speech to children learning language. *Child Development, 43*, 549–565.

Snow, C., & Ferguson, C. (Eds.). (1977). *Talking to children: Language input and acquisition*. Cambridge, England: Cambridge University Press.

Sokol, S. M., McCloskey, M., Cohen, N. J., & Aliminosa, D. (1991). Cognitive representations and processes in arithmetic: Inferences from the performance of brain-damaged subjects. *Journal of Experimental Psychology: Learning, Memory, and Cognition, 17*, 355–376.

Solso, R. L. (1991). *Cognitive Psychology* (3rd ed.). Boston: Allyn & Bacon.

Solso, R. L. (1996). *Cognitive Psychology* (4th ed.). Boston: Allyn & Bacon.

Spelke, E., Hirst, W., & Neisser, U. (1976). Skills of divided attention. *Cognition, 4*, 215–230.

Spellman, B. A., & Holyoak, K. J. (1992). If Saddam is Hitler then who is George Bush? Analogical mapping between systems of social roles. *Journal of Personality and Social Psychology, 62*, 913–933.

Spellman, B. A., & Holyoak, K. J. (1996). Pragmatics in analogical mapping. *Cognitive Psychology, 31*, 307–346.

Sperling, G. (1960). The information available in brief visual presentations. *Psychological Monographs, 74*(48)

Sperling, G. (1963). A model for visual memory task. *Human Factors, 5*, 19–31.

Sperry, R. W. (1964). The great cerebral commissure. *Scientific American, 210*, 42–52.

Sperry, R. W. (1993). The impact and promise of the cognitive revolution. *American Psychologist, 48*, 878–885.

Spieth, W., Curtis, J. F., & Webster, J. C. (1954). Responding to one of two simultaneous messages. *Journal of the Acoustical Society of America, 26*, 391–396.

Squire, L. R. (1987). *Memory and brain*. New York: Oxford University Press.

Squire, L. R. (1992). Memory and the hippocampus: A synthesis from findings with rats, monkeys, and humans. *Psychological Review, 99*, 195–231.

Sternberg, R. J. (1977). *Intelligence, information processing, and analogical reasoning*. Hillsdale, NJ: Erlbaum.

Sternberg, R. J. (1995). For whom the bell curve tolls: A review of *The bell curve*. *Psychological Science, 6*, 257–261.

Sternberg, R. J. (1996). *Cognitive psychology*. Fort Worth, TX: Harcourt Brace.

Sternberg, S. (1966). High-speed scanning in human memory. *Science, 153*, 652–654.

Sternberg, S. (1969). The discovery of processing stages: Extensions of Donder's method. In W. G. Koster (Ed.), Attention and performance II. *Acta Psychologica, 30*, 276–315.

Sternberg, S. (1975). Memory scanning: New findings and current controversies. *Quarterly Journal of Experimental Psychology, 27*, 1–32.

Stroop, J. R. (1935). Studies of interference in serial verbal reactions. *Journal of Experimental Psychology, 18*, 643–662.

Stuss, D. T. (1992). Biological and psychological development of executive functions. *Brain and Cognition, 20*, 8–23.

Sulin, R. A., & Dooling, D. J. (1974). Intrusion of a thematic idea in retention of prose. *Journal of Experimental Psychology, 103*, 255–262.

Talland, G. A. (1967). Short-term memory with interpolated activity. *Journal of Verbal Learning and Verbal Behavior, 6*, 144–150.

Teasdale, J. D., Dritschel, B. H., Taylor, M. J., Proctor, L., Lloyd, C. A., Nimmo-Smith, I., & Baddeley, A. D. (1995). Stimulus-independent thought depends on central executive resources. *Memory & Cognition, 23*, 551–559.

Thapar, A., & Greene, R. L. (1994). Effects of level of processing on implicit and explicit tasks. *Journal of Experimental Psychology: Learning, Memory, and Cognition, 20*, 671–679.

Thomas, J. C., Jr. (1974). An analysis of behavior in the Hobbits-Orcs problem. *Cognitive Psychology, 6*, 257–269.

Thompson, R. F. (1986). The neurobiology of learning and memory. *Science, 233*, 941–947.

Thompson, R. F. (1994). Behaviorism and neuroscience. *Psychological Review, 101*, 259–265.

Thomson, D. M., & Tulving, E. (1970). Associative encoding and retrieval: Weak and strong cues. *Journal of Experimental Psychology, 86*, 255–262.

Thorndike, E. L. (1914). *The psychology of learning*. New York: Teachers College.

Treisman, A. M. (1960). Contextual cues in selective listening. *Quarterly Journal of Experimental Psychology, 12*, 242–248.

Treisman, A. M. (1964a). Monitoring and storage of irrelevant messages in selective attention. *Journal of Verbal Learning and Verbal Behavior, 3*, 449–459.

Treisman, A. M. (1964b). Selective attention in man. *British Medical Bulletin, 20*, 12–16.

Treisman, A. (1988). Features and objects: The Fourteenth Bartlett Memorial Lecture. *Quarterly Journal of Experimental Psychology, 40A*, 201–237.

Treisman, A., & Gelade, G. (1980). A feature integration theory of attention. *Cognitive Psychology, 12*, 97–136.

Treisman, A. M., Russell, R., & Green, J. (1975). Brief visual storage of shape and movement. In P. M. A. Rabbitt & S. Dornic (Eds.), *Attention and performance* (Vol. 5, pp. 699–721). New York: Academic Press.

Trigg, G. L., & Lerner, R. J. (Eds.). (1981). *Encyclopedia of physics*. Reading, MA: Addison-Wesley.

Tucker, D. M., & Williamson, P. A. (1984). Asymmetric neural control systems in human self-regulation. *Psychological Review, 91*, 185–215.

Tulving, E. (1962). Subjective organization in free recall of "unrelated" words. *Psychological Review, 69*, 344–354.

Tulving, E. (1972). Episodic and semantic memory. In E. Tulving & W. Donaldson (Eds.), *Organization of memory* (pp. 381–403). New York: Academic Press.

Tulving, E. (1983). *Elements of episodic memory*. Oxford: Clarendon Press.

Tulving, E. (1989). Remembering and knowing the past. *American Scientist, 77*, 361–367.

Tulving, E. (1993). What is episodic memory? *Current Directions in Psychological Science, 2*, 67–70.

Tulving, E., Kapur, S., Craik, F. I. M., Moscovitch, M., & Houle, S. (1994). Hemispheric encoding/retrieval asymmetry in episodic memory: Positron emission tomography findings. *Proceedings of the National Academy of Sciences, 91*, 2016–2020.

Tulving, E., & Pearlstone, Z. (1966). Availability versus accessibility of information in memory for words. *Journal of Verbal Learning and Verbal Behavior, 5*, 381–391.

Tulving, E., Schacter, D., & Stark, H. (1982). Priming effects in word-fragment completion are independent of recognition memory. *Journal of Experimental Psychology, 8*, 336–342.

Tulving, E., & Thomson, D. M. (1973). Encoding specificity and retrieval processes in episodic memory. *Psychological Review, 80*, 352–373.

Tversky, A., & Kahneman, D. (1973). Availability: A heuristic for judging frequency and probability. *Cognitive Psychology, 5*, 207–232.

Tversky, A., & Kahneman, D. (1974). Judgment under uncertainty: Heuristics and biases. *Science, 185*, 1124–1131.

Tversky, A., & Kahneman, D. (1980). Causal schemas in judgments under uncertainty. In M. Fishbein (Ed.), *Progress in social psychology* (Vol. 1, pp. 49–72). Hillsdale, NJ: Erlbaum.

Uhr, L. (1963). "Pattern recognition" computers as models for form perception. *Psychological Bulletin, 60*, 40–73.

Underwood, B. J. (1957). Interference and forgetting. *Psychological Review, 64*, 49–60.

Underwood, B. J., Keppel, G., & Schulz, R. W. (1962). Studies of distributed practice: XXII. Some conditions which enhance retention. *Journal of Experimental Psychology, 64*, 112–129.

Vallar, G., & Baddeley, A. D. (1984). Fractionation of working memory: Neuropsychological evidence for a phonological short-term store. *Journal of Verbal Learning and Verbal Behavior, 23*, 151–161.

Van der Linden, M., Coyette, F., & Seron, X. (1992). Selective impairment of the "central executive" component of working memory: A single case study. *Cognitive Neuropsychology, 9*, 301–326.

VanLehn, K. (1989). Problem solving and cognitive skill acquisition. In M. I. Posner (Ed.), *Foundations of cognitive science* (pp. 527–579). Cambridge, MA: Bradford.

Wagenaar, W. A. (1986). My memory: A study of autobiographical memory over six years. *Cognitive Psychology, 18*, 225–252.

Warren, R. M., & Warren, R. P. (1970). Auditory illusions and confusions. *Scientific American, 223*, 30–36.

Warrington, E. K., & Shallice, T. (1969). The selective impairment of auditory verbal short-term memory. *Brain, 92*, 885–896.

Warrington, E. K., & Weiskrantz, L. (1968). New method of testing long-term retention with special reference to amnesic patients. *Nature, 277*, 972–974.

Warrington, E. K., & Weiskrantz, L. (1970). The amnesic syndrome: Consolidation or retrieval? *Nature, 228*, 628–630.

Wason, P. C., & Johnson-Laird, P. N. (1972). *Psychology of reasoning: Structure and content*. Cambridge, MA: Harvard University Press.

Watkins, M. H., Peynircioglu, Z. F., & Brems, D. J. (1984). Pictorial rehearsal. *Memory & Cognition, 12*, 553–557.

Watkins, M. J., & Tulving, E. (1975). Episodic memory: When recognition fails. *Journal of Experimental Psychology: General, 104*, 5–29.

Watkins, O. C., & Watkins, M. J. (1980). The modality effect and echoic persistence. *Journal of Experimental Psychology: General, 109*, 251–278.

Watson, J. B. (1903). *Animal education*. Chicago: University of Chicago Press.

Watson, J. B. (1994). Psychology as the behaviorist sees it. *Psychological Review, 101*, 248–253. (Partially reprinted from *Psychological Review*, 1913, *20*, 158–177).

Watson, R. I. (1968). *The great psychologists from Aristotle to Freud* (2nd ed.). Philadelphia: Lippincott.

Waugh, N. C., & Norman, D. A. (1965). Primary memory. *Psychological Review, 72*, 89–104.

Weaver, C. A., III. (1993). Do you need a "flash" to form a flashbulb memory? *Journal of Experimental Psychology: General, 122*, 39–46.

Wegner, D. M. (1994). Ironic processes of mental control. *Psychological Review, 101*, 34–52.

Weisberg, R. (1993). *Creativity: Beyond the myth of genius* (2nd ed.). New York: Freeman.

Weisberg, R. (1995). Prolegomena to theories of insight in problem solving: A taxonomy of problems. In R. J. Sternberg & J. E. Davidson (Eds.), *The nature of insight* (pp. 157–196). Cambridge, MA: MIT Press.

Werner, H. (1935). Studies on contour. *American Journal of Psychology, 47*, 40–64.

West, R. F., & Stanovich, K. E. (1986). Robust effects of syntactic structure on visual word processing. *Memory & Cognition, 14*, 104–112.

Whalen, J., McCloskey, M., Lesser, R., & Gordon, B. (in press). Transient arithmetic impairment during cortical stimulation. *Journal of Cognitive Neuroscience*.

Wheeler, M. A., & Roediger, H. L., III. (1992). Disparate effects of repeated testing: Reconciling Ballard's (1913) and Bartlett's (1932) results. *Psychological Science, 3*, 240–245.

Whitney, P., Ritchie, B. G., & Crane, R. S. (1992). The effect of foregrounding on readers' use of predictive inferences. *Memory & Cognition, 20*, 424–432.

Wickelgren, W. A. (1965). Acoustic similarity and retroactive interference in short-term memory. *Journal of Verbal Learning and Verbal Behavior, 4*, 53–61.

Wickelgren, W. A. (1974). *How to solve problems*. San Francisco: Freeman.

Wickens, D. D. (1972). Characteristics of word encoding. In A. W. Melton & E. Martin (Eds.), *Coding processes in human memory* (pp. 191–215). New York: Winston.

Wickens, D. D., Born, D. G., & Allen, C. K. (1963). Proactive inhibition and item similarity in short-term memory. *Journal of Verbal Learning and Verbal Behavior, 2*, 440–445.

Wilkes-Gibbs, D., & Clark, H. H. (1992). Coordinating beliefs in conversation. *Journal of Memory and Language, 31*, 183–194.

Wilson, T. D. (1994). The proper protocol: Validity and completeness of verbal reports. *Psychological Science, 5*, 249–252.

Winograd, E., & Killinger, W. A., Jr. (1983). Relating age at encoding in early childhood to adult recall: Development of flashbulb memories. *Journal of Experimental Psychology: General, 112*, 413–422.

Wixted, J. T. (1991). Conditions and consequences of maintenance rehearsal. *Journal of Experimental Psychology: Learning, Memory, and Cognition, 17*, 969–973.

Wixted, J. T., & Ebbesen, E. B. (1991). On the form of forgetting. *Psychological Science, 2*, 409–415.

Wood, N. L., & Cowan, N. (1995a). The cocktail party phenomenon revisited: Attention and memory in the classic selective listening procedure of Cherry (1953). *Journal of Experimental Psychology: General, 124*, 243–262.

Wood, N. L., & Cowan, N. (1995b). The cocktail party phenomenon revisited: How frequent are attention shifts to one's name in an irrelevant auditory channel? *Journal of Experimental Psychology: Learning, Memory, and Cognition, 21*, 255–260.

Woodworth, R. S., & Schlosberg, H. (1954). *Experimental psychology* (rev. ed.). New York: Holt, Rinehart & Winston.

Yarbus, A. L. (1967). *Eye movements and vision* (B. Haigh, Trans.). New York: Plenum. Cited in Solso (1991).

Yates, F. A. (1966). *The art of memory*. Chicago: University of Chicago Press.

Yuille, J. C., & Paivio, A. (1967). Latency of imaginal and verbal mediators as a function of stimulus and response concreteness-imagery. *Journal of Experimental Psychology, 75*, 540–544.

Zaragoza, M. S., & Koshmider, J. W., III. (1989). Misled subjects may know more than their performance implies. *Journal of Experimental Psychology: Learning, Memory, and Cognition, 15*, 246–255.

Zaragoza, M. S., & Lane, S. M. (1994). Source misattributions and the suggestibility of eyewitness memory. *Journal of Experimental Psychology: Learning, Memory, and Cognition, 20*, 934–945.

Zaragoza, M. S., McCloskey, M., & Jamis, M. (1987). Misleading postevent information and recall of the original event: Further evidence against the memory impairment hypothesis. *Journal of Experimental Psychology: Learning, Memory, and Cognition, 13*, 36–44.

Zbrodoff, N. J., & Logan, G. D. (1986). On the autonomy of mental processes: A case study of arithmetic. *Journal of Experimental Psychology: General, 115*, 118–130.

Zhang, S., & Perfetti, C. A. (1993). The tongue-twister effect in reading Chinese. *Journal of Experimental Psychology: Learning, Memory, and Cognition, 19*, 1082–1093.

Zimmerman, D. H., & West, C. (1975). Sex roles, interruptions, and silences in conversation. In B. Thorne & N. Henley (Eds.), *Language and sex: Differences and dominance* (pp. 105–129). Rowley, MA: Newbury House.

Zola-Morgan, S., Squire, L., & Amalral, D. G. (1986). Human amnesia and the medial temporal region: Enduring memory impairment following a bilateral lesion limited to field CA1 of the hippocampus. *The Journal of Neuroscience, 6*, 2950–2967.

Zwaan, R. A. (1994). Effect of genre expectations on text comprehension. *Journal of Experimental Psychology: Learning, Memory, and Cognition, 20*, 920–933.

CREDITS

FIGURES

Page 8: From Mental multiplication skill: Structure, process, and acquisition, by J. I. D. Campbell and D. J. Graham. *Canadian Journal of Psychology, 39*, 338–366. Copyright © 1985 by the Canadian Psychological Association. Reprinted by permission. / p. 39: From Short term storage of information in vision, by E. Averbach and G. Sperling. Copyright © 1960. Reprinted by permission. / p. 40: From Short term memory in vision, by Averbach and Coriell. *Bell System Technical Journal.* Copyright © 1961. Reprinted by permission. / pp. 44, 47 and 48: From Higher-level vision, by I. Biederman. In E. N. Osherson, S. M. Kosslyn, and J. M. Hollerbach (eds.), *An invitation to cognitive science, 2*, 41–72. Copyright © 1990 by MIT Press, Cambridge, MA. Reprinted with permission. / pp. 49 and 50: From The perception of objects with deleted contours, by I. Biederman. *Psychological Review, 94*, 115–147. Copyright © 1987 by the American Psychological Association. Reprinted by permission. / p. 52: From Pandemonium: A paradigm for learning, by O. G. Selfridge. *Teddington Symposium, Mechanization of thought processes*, p. 517. Copyright © 1959 National Physical Laboratory, Teddington, England. / p. 53: From *Sensation and perception*, 3rd ed., by Coren and Ward. Copyright © 1989 by Harcourt Brace. / p. 54: From Visual search, by Ulric Neisser. Copyright © 1964 by Scientific American, Inc. All rights reserved. / p. 57: From The appeal of parallel distributed processing, by J. L. McClelland and D. Rumelhart. *Parallel distributed processing, Vol. 1*, p. 23. Copyright © 1986 by MIT Press. Reproduced by permission. / p. 59: From *Principles of psychology*, by R. H. Price. Copyright © 1987 by Scott Foresman and Company. Reprinted by permission. / p. 61: From An auditory analogue of the Sperling partial report procedure: Evidence for brief auditory storage, by C. J. Darwin et al. *Cognitive Psychology*, 3, 259. Copyright © 1972 by Academic Press. Reprinted by permission. / p. 62: From Monitoring and storage of irrelevant messages in selective attention, by A. M. Treisman. *Journal of Verbal Learning and Verbal Behavior*, 3, 449–459. Copyright © 1964 by Academic Press. Reprinted by permission. / p. 73: From Selective attention in man, by A. M. Treisman. *British Medical Bulletin*, 1964, Vol. 20, pp. 12–16. Reprinted by permission. / p. 74: Adapted from figure in *Human information processing: An introduction to psychology*, 2nd ed., by Peter H. Lindsay and Donald A. Norman. Copyright © 1977 by Harcourt Brace & Company. Reprinted by permission of the publisher. / p. 76: From Toward a theory of memory and attention, by D. A. Norman, *Psychological Review, 75*, 522–536. Copyright © 1968 by the American Psychological Association. Reprinted by permission / p. 77: From Flexibility and capacity demands of attention, by W. A. Johnston and S. P. Heinz. *Journal of Experimental Psychology, 107*, 69–76. Copyright © 1978 by the American Psychological Association. Reprinted by permission. / p. 78: From Flexibility and capacity demands of attention, by W. A. Johnston and S. P. Heinz. *Journal of Experimental Psychology, 107*, 69–76. Copyright © 1978 by the American Psychological Association. Reprinted by permission. / p. 85: Adapted with the permission of Macmillan Publishing Company from *Cognitive psychology: Memory, language and thought*, 2nd ed., by Darlene F. Howard. Copyright © 1993 by Macmillan Publishing Company. / p. 87: From *Controlled and automatic human information processing* by W. Schneider. Copyright © 1977 by the American Psychological Association. Reprinted by permission. / p. 88: From *Controlled and automatic human information processing*, by W. Schneider. Copyright © 1977 by the American Psychological Association. Reprinted by permission. / p. 92: From Checklist procedures and the cost of automaticity, by I. Barshi and A. F. Healy, *Memory & Cognition, 21*, 496–505. Copyright © 1993. Reprinted by permission of the Psychonomic Society. / p. 100: From Primary memory, by N. C. Waugh and D. A. Norman. *Psychological Review, 72*, 89–104. Copyright © 1965 by the American Psychological Association. Adapted by permission. / p. 104: From Short-term retention of individual items, by L. R. Peterson and M. J. Peterson. *Journal of Experimental Psychology.* Copyright © 1959 by the American Psychological Association. Reprinted by permission. / p. 106: From Primary memory, by N. C. Waugh and D. A. Norman. *Psychological Review, 72*, 91. Copyright © 1965 by the American Psychological Association. Adapted by permission. / p. 108: Reprinted by permission of Hemisphere Psychological Association. / p. 110: Panel (a): From The serial position effect in free recall, by B. J. Murdock. *Journal of Experimental Psychology, 64*, 486. Copyright © 1962 by the American Psychological Association. Adapted by permission. Panels (b) and (c): From Two storage mechanisms in free recall, by M. Glanzwer and A. R. Cunitz. *Journal of Behavioral Learn-*

ing and Verbal Behavior, 5, 354, 358. Copyright © 1996 by Academic Press. Reprinted by permission. / p. 112: From The control of short-term memory, by R. C. Atkinson and R. M. Shiffrin. *Scientific American, 225*, 82–90. Copyright © 1971 by Scientific American Inc. All rights reserved. / p. 115: Adapted by permission of *American Scientist, Journal of Sigma Xi*, the Scientific Research Society. / p. 121: From Mental rotation of three-dimensional objects, by R. N. Shepard. *Science, 171*, 702. Copyright © 1971 by the AAAS. Reprinted by permission. / p. 126: From Working memory, by A. D. Baddeley and G. Hitch. *The Psychology of Learning and Motivation, Vol. 8*, 56. Copyright © 1974 by Academic Press. Adapted by permission. / p. 145: From Frequency of stimulus presentation and short-term decrement in recall, by S. Hellyer. *Journal of Experimental Psychology*, 64, 650. Copyright © 1962 by the American Psychological Association. Reprinted by permission. / p. 146: From Analysis of rehearsal processes in free recall, by D. Rundus. *Journal of Experimental Psychology*, 89, 66. Copyright © 1971 by the American Psychological Association. Reprinted by permission. / p. 152: From Hierarchical retrieval schemes in recall of categorized word lists, by G. H. Bower et al. *Journal of Verbal Learning and Verbal Behavior*, 8, 324. Copyright © 1969 by Academic Press. Reprinted by permission. / p. 155: From Pictorial rehearsal, by M. H. Watkins, Z. F. Peynirioglu, and D. J. Brems. *Memory & Cognition,12*, 553–557. Copyright © 1984 by the Psychonomic Society. Reprinted by permission. / p. 166: From Mental multiplication skill: Structure, process and acquisition, by J. I. D. Campbell and D. J. Graham. *Canadian Journal of Psychology, 39*, 338–366. Copyright © 1985 by the Canadian Psychological Association. Reprinted by permission. / p. 172: From Retrieval time from semantic memory, by A. Collins and M.R. Quillian. *Journal of Verbal Learning and Verbal Behavior*, 8, 240–247. Copyright © 1969 by Academic Press. / p. 173: Adapted from Theories of semantic memory, by E. E. Smith. In W. K. Estes (Ed.), *Handbook of learning and cognitive process, Vol.6*. Copyright © 1978 by Lawrence Erlbaum Associates, Inc. Reprinted by permission. / p. 174: From Theories of semantic memory, by E. E. Smith. In W. K. Estes (Ed.), *Handbook of learning and cognitive process, Vol.6*. Copyright © 1978 by Lawrence Erlbaum Associates, Inc. Reprinted by permission. / p. 176: From Structure and process in semantic memory, by E. E. Smith et. al. *Psychological Review, 81*, 235. Copyright © 1974 by the American Psychological Association. Adapted by permission. / p. 184: From *Memory & Cognition*, 2, 467–471. Reprinted by permission of the Psychonomic Society, Inc. / p. 187: From *Memory & Cognition*, 4, 648–654. Reprinted by permission of the Psychonomic Society, Inc. / p. 189: From Semantic priming and retrieval from lexical memory: Evidence for facilitatory and inhibitory processes, by J. H. Neely. *Memory & Cognition, 4*, 648–654. Copyright © 1977 by the Psychonomic Society. Reprinted by permission. / p. 194: From *Cognitive psychology: A neural-network approach*, by Colin Martindale. Copyright © 1991 by Wadworth, Inc. Reprinted by permission of Brooks/Cole Publishing Company, Pacific Grove, California 93950. / p. 205: From Intrusion of a thematic idea in retention of prose, by R. A. Sulin and D. J. Dooling. *Journal of Experimental Psychology, 103*, 255–262. Copyright © 1974 by the American Psychological Association. Reprinted by permission. / p. 207: Adapted from *Scripts, plans, goals and understanding*, by R. C. Schank and R. P. Abelson. Copyright © 1977 by Lawrence Erlbaum Associates, Inc. Adapted by permission. / p. 210: From Recognition and recall of irrelevant and interruptive atypical actions in script-based stories, by D. Davidson. *Journal of Memory and Language, 33*, 757–775. Copyright © 1994 by Academic Press. / p. 214: From The abstraction of linguistic ideas, by J. D. Bransford and J. J. Franks. *Cognitive Psychology, 2*, 346. Copyright © 1971 by Academic Press. Reprinted by permission. / p. 217: From Creating false memories: Remembering words not presented in lists, by H. L. Roediger III and K. B. McDermott. *Journal of Experimental Psychology: Learning, Memory, and Cognition, 21*, 803–814. Copyright © 1995 by the American Psychological Association. Reprinted by permission. / p. 221: From Reconstruction of automobile destruction: An example of the interaction between language and memory, by E. F. Loftus and J. C. Palmer. *Journal of Verbal Learning and Verbal Behavior, 13*, 585–589. Copyright © 1974 by Academic Press. Reprinted by permission. / p. 222: From Creating new memories that are quickly accessed and confidently held, by Loftus et al. *Memory & Cognition, 17*, 607–616, 1989. Reprinted by permission of the Psychonomic Society, Inc. / p. 224: From Long-term memory for a common object, by R. S. Nickerson and M. J. Adams. *Cognitive Psychology, 11*, 297. Copyright © 1979 by Academic Press. Reprinted by permission. / p. 228: From Fifty years of memory for names and places, by H. P. Bahrick et al. *Journal of Experimental Psychology, 104*, 66. Copyright © 1975 by the American Psychological Association. Reprinted by permission. / p. 232: From On the very long-term retention of knowledge acquired through formal education: Twelve years of cognitive psychology, by M. A. Conway et al. *Journal of Experimental Psychology, 104*, 666. Copyright © 1975 by the American Psychological Association. Reprinted by permission. / p. 242: From Linguistic expression of category levels, by E. L. Newport and U. Bellugi. In E. Rosch and B. B. Lloyd (Eds.), *Cognition and categorization*. Copyright © 1978 by Lawrence Erlbaum Associates, Inc. Redrawn by permission. / p. 249: Figure adapted from *An introduction to language*, by Victoria A. Fromkin and Robert Rodman. Copyright © 1974 by Holt, Rinehart and Winston, Inc. Reprinted by permission of the publisher. / p. 251: From The grammars of speech and language, by A. M. Liberman. *Cognitive Psychology, 1*, 301–323. Copyright © 1957. Reprinted by permission. / p. 252: From *Perception and Psychophysics, 30*, 10–23. Reprinted by permission of the Psychonomic Society, Inc. / p. 255: From Some perceptual consequences of linguistic rules, by G. A. Miller and S. Isard. *Journal of Verbal Learning and Verbal Behavior, 2*, 217–228. Copyright © 1963 by Academic Press. Reprinted by permission. / p. 256: From *Psycholinguistics: An introduction to the psychology of language*, by Donald J. Foss and David T. Hakes, p. 77. Copyright © 1978. Reprinted by permission of Prentice Hall, Englewood Cliffs, New Jersey. / p. 260: From *Cognitive psychology and information processing: An introduction*, by R. Lachman et al. Copyright © 1979 by Lawrence Erlbaum Associates, Inc. Reprinted by permission. / p. 261: From *Cognitive psychology and information processing: An introduction*, by R. Lachman et al. Copyright © 1979 by Lawrence Erlbaum Associates, Inc. Adapted by permission. / p. 268: From Pragmatic normalization: Further results for some conjunctive and disjunctive sentences, by S. Fillenbaum. *Journal of Experimental Psychology, 33*, 715–736. Copyright © 1974 by the American Psychological Association. Reprinted by permission. / p. 273: From The relationship between age and mean length of utterance in morphemes, by J. F. Miller and R. S. Chapman. *Journal of Speech and Hearing Research, 24*, 154–161. Copyright © 1981. Reprinted by permission. / p. 281: From Recognition memory for syntactic and semantic aspects of connected discourse, by J. S. Sachs. *Perception and Psychophysics, 2*, 437–442. Copyright © 1967. Reprinted by permission. / p. 286: From *Human associative memory*, by J. R. Anderson and G. H. Bower. Copyright © 1973 by Lawrence Erlbaum Associates, Inc. Adapted by permission. Also from *Representation of meaning in memory*, by W. Kintsch. Copyright © 1974 by Lawrence Erlbaum Associates, Inc. Adapted by permission. / p. 290: From Accessing sentence participants: The advantage of first mention versus the advantage of causal regency, by M. A. Gernsbacher et al. *Journal of Memory and Language, 28*, 742. Copyright © 1989 by Academic Press. Reprinted by permission. / p. 291: From Building and accessing causal representations: The advantage of first mention versus the advantage of causal regency, by M. A. Gernsbacher et al. *Journal of Memory and Language, 28*, 742. Copyright © 1989 by Academic Press. Reprinted by permission. / p. 296: From A test of the on-line status of goal-related inferences, by D. L. Long, J. M. Golding, and A. C. Graesser. *Journal of Memory and Language, 31*, 634–647. Copyright © 1992 by Academic Press. Reprinted by permission. / p. 301: From Making and correcting errors during sentence comprehension: Eye movements in the analysis of structurally ambiguous sentences, by L. Frazier and K. Rayner. *Cognitive Psychology, 14*, 193. Copyright © 1982 by Academic Press. Adapted by permission. / p. 302: From A theory of reading: From eye fixations to comprehension, by M. A. Just and P. A. Carpenter. *Psychological Review, 87*, 330, 331. Copyright © 1980 by the American Psychological Association. Reprinted by permission. / p. 304: From A theory of reading: From eye fixations to comprehension, by M. A. Just and P. A. Carpenter. *Psychological Review, 87*, 330, 331. Copyright © 1980 by the American Psychological Association. Reprinted by permission. / p. 312: From Communication in context: Effects of speaker status on the comprehension of indirect requests, by T. Holtgraves. *Journal of Experimental Psychology: Learning, Memory and Cognition, 20*, 1205–1218. Copyright © 1994 by the Academic Press. Reprinted by permission. / p. 328: From *The excitable cortex in conscious man*, by Wilder Penfield. Liverpool University Press, 1958. Reprinted by permission. / p. 332: From Event-related brain potentials elicited by syntactic anomaly, by L. Osterhout and P. J. Holcomb. *Journal of Memory and Language, 31*, 790. Copyright © 1992 by Academic Press. Reprinted by permission. / p. 337: From Left in the dark: The neglect of theory, by J. C. Marshall and P. W. Halligan. *Neuropsychological Rehabilitation, 4*, 161–167. Copyright © 1994. Reprinted by permission. / p. 338: From Specializations of the human brain, by N. I. Geschwind. *Scientific American, 241*, 158–168. Copyright © 1979 by Scientific American, Inc. All rights reserved. / p. 344: From *Mechanics of the mind*, by C. Blakemore. Copyright © 1977 by Cambridge University Press. Reprinted by permission. / p. 354: From Semantic congruity effects in comparative judgments of magnitude digits, by W. P. Banks, H. H. Clark, and P. Lucy. *Journal of Experimental Psychology: Human Perception and Performance, 2*, 435–447. Copyright © 1976 by the American Psychological Association. Reprinted by permission. / p. 354: From Encoding and processing of symbolic information in comparative judgments, by W. P. Banks. *Psychology of Learning and Motivation, 11*, 106. Copyright © 1977 by Academic Press. Reprinted by permission. / p. 355: From *Perception and Psychophysics, 13*, 180–184. Reprinted by permission of the Psychonomic Society, Inc. / p. 363: From *Cognitive psychology and its implications*, by John R. Anderson. Copyright © 1980 by W.H. Freeman and Company. Reprinted with permission. / p. 377: From Naive theories of motion, by M. McCloskey. In D. Gentner and A. L. Stevens (Eds.), *Mental models*. Copyright © 1983 by Lawrence Erlbaum Associates, Inc. Redrawn/reprinted by permission. / p. 378: From Naive theories of motion, by M. McCloskey. In D. Gentner and A. L. Stevens (Eds.), *Mental models*. Copyright © 1983 by Lawrence Erlbaum Associates, Inc. Redrawn/reprinted by permission. / p. 409: Reprinted by permission of the publishers of *Architecture of cognition*, by J. R. Anderson. Cambridge, MA: Harvard University Press. Copyright © 1983 by the President and Fellows of Harvard College.

TABLES

Page 64: From Auditory illusions and confusions, by R. M. Warren and R. P. Warren. *Scientific American, 223*, 32. Copyright © 1970. / p. 161: From *The ideal problem solver*, by Bransford and Stein. Copyright © 1984 by W.H. Freeman and Company. Reprinted with permission. / p. 162: From *The ideal problem solver*, by Bransford and Stein. Copyright © 1984 by W.H. Freeman and Company. Reprinted with permission. / p. 186: From Facilitation in recognizing pairs of words: Evidence of a dependence between retrieval operations, by D. E. Meyer and R. W. Schvaneveldt. *Journal of Experimental Psychology, 90*, 229. Copyright © 1971 by the American Psychological Association. Adapted by permission. / p. 188: From Semantic priming and retrieval from lexical memory: Roles of inhibitionless spreading activation and limited-capacity attention, by J. H. Neely. *Journal of Experimental Psychology: General, 106*, 226–254. Copyright © 1977 by the American Psychological Association. Reprinted by permission. / p. 192: From *Human cognition: Learning, understanding and remembering*, by J. D. Bransford. Copyright © 1971 by Wadsworth, Inc. Reprinted by permission of Brooks/Cole Publishing Company, Pacific Grove, California 93950. / p. 201: From *Remembering: A study in experimental and social psychology*, by F. C. Bartlett. Copyright © 1967 by Cambridge University Press. Reprinted by permission. / p. 209: From Recognition and recall of irrelevant and interruptive atypical actions in script-based stories, by D. Davidson. *Journal of Memory and Language, 33*, 772–773. Copyright © 1994 by Academic Press. Reprinted by permission. / p. 212: From Remember that old theory of memory? Well, Forget it! by J. J. Jenkins. *American Psychologist, 29*, 791. Copyright © 1974 by the American Psychological Association. Adapted by permission. / p. 213: From Remember that old theory of memory? Well, Forget it! by J. J. Jenkins. *American Psychologist, 29*, 791. Copyright © 1974 by the American Psychological Association. Adapted by permission. / p. 239: Copyright © 1960 by the American Institute of Biological Sciences. Reprinted by permission. / p. 246: From *Psychology of language*, 2nd ed., by D. W. Carroll. Copyright © 1994 by Wadsworth, Inc. Reprinted by permission of Brooks/Cole Publishing Company, Pacific Grove, California 93950. / p. 248: From *Experimental psycholinguistics: An introduction*, by S. Glucksberg and H. Danks. Copyright © 1975 by Lawrence Erlbaum Associates, Inc. Reprinted by permission. / p. 263: From The non-anomalous nature of anomalous utterances, by V. A. Fromkin. *Language, 47*, 27–52. Copyright © 1971 by Academic Press. Reprinted by permission. / p. 272: From *A first language: The early stages*, by

R. Brown. Copyright © 1973 by The President and Fellows of Harvard University. Reprinted by permission. / p. 274: From *A first language: The early stages*, by R. Brown. Copyright © 1973 by Harvard University Press, Cambridge, MA. Reprinted by permission / p. 280: From Recognition memory for syntactic and semantic aspects of connected discourse, by J. S. Sachs. *Perception and Psychophysics*, 437–442. Reprinted by permission of the Psychonomic Society, Inc. / p. 284: From *Cognitive psychology and its implications*, by John R. Anderson. Copyright © 1980 by W.H. Freeman and Company. Reprinted with permission. / p. 288: From Priming in item recognition: Evidence for the prepositional structure of sentences, by R. Ratcliff and G. McKoon. *Journal of Verbal Learning and Verbal Behavior, 17*, 414. Copyright © 1978 by Academic Press. Reprinted by permission. / p. 303: From A theory of reading: From eye fixations to comprehension, by M. A. Just and P. A. Carpenter. *Psychological Review*, 87, 348. Copyright © 1980 by the American Psychological Association. Reprinted by permission. / p. 308: From Reflections on cognition and parallel distributed processing. In J. L. McClelland and D. E. Rumelhard (Eds.), Parallel distributed processing. *Psychological Review, Vol. 2* (pp. 531–546). Copyright © 1975 by the American Psychological Association. Reprinted by permission. / p. 325: From *Fundamentals of human neuropsychology*, by Bryan Kolb and Iam Q. Whishaw. Copyright © 1990 by W.H. Freeman and Company. Reprinted with permission. / p. 336: Adapted from *Cognitive neuropsychology: A clinical introduction*, by R. A. McCarthy and E. K. Warrington. Copyright © 1990 by Academic Press. Adapted by permission. / p. 340: From Neural models of language processes, by Kertesz. In M. A. Arbib et al. (Eds.), *Neural models of language processes* (pp. 25–44). Copyright © 1982 by Academic Press. Adapted by permission. / p. 365: Adapted from The base-rate fallacy in the context of sequential categories, by J. T. Johnson and R. A. Finke. *Memory & Cognition, 13*, 63–73. Copyright © 1985 by the Psychonomic Society. Reprinted by permission. / p. 366: From The base-rate fallacy in the context of sequential categories, by J. T. Johnson and R. A. Finke, *Memory & Cognition, 13*, 63–73. Copyright © 1985 by the Psychonomic Society. Reprinted by permission. / p. 374: From The simulation heuristic. In D. Kahneman, P. Slovic, and A. Tversky (Eds.), *Judgment under uncertainty: Heuristics and biases* (p. 201–208). Copyright © 1982 by Cambridge University Press. Reprinted by permission. / p. 388: Adapted from Mechanization in problem solving, by A. Luchins. *Psychological Monographs*, 1942, 1. Reproduced by permission. / p. 391: From Intuition in insight and noninsight problem solving, by J. Metcalfe and D. Wiebe. *Memory & Cognition, 15*, 238–246. Copyright © 1987 by the Psychonomic Society. Reprinted by permission. Also from Feeling of knowing in memory and problem solving, by J. Metcalfe. *Journal of Experimental Psychology: Learning, Memory and Cognition, 12*, 294. Copyright © 1986 by the American Psychological Association. Reprinted with permission. / p. 396: From Analogical problem solving, by M. L. Gick and K. J. Holyoak. *Cognitive Psychology, 12*, 311, 335, 352. Copyright © 1980 by Academic Press. Reprinted by permission. / p. 397: From Analogical problem solving, by M. L. Gick and K. J. Holyoak. *Cognitive Psychology, 12*, 311, 335, 352. Copyright © 1980 by Academic Press. Reprinted by permission. / p. 398: From Analogical problem solving, by M. L. Gick and K. J. Holyoak, *Cognitive Psychology, 12*, 311, 335, 352. Copyright © 1980 by Academic Press. Reprinted by permission.

PHOTOGRAPHS AND CARTOONS

Color insert: Top: From Schneider et al., 1993. Center: Drs. Michael E. Phelps and John C. Mazziotta, UCLA School of Medicine. Bottom: From Tulving, 1989.

Text: Page 5: Fine Arts Museums of San Francisco, Achenbach Foundation for Graphic Arts, Bruno and Sadie Adriani Collection, 1971.28.103.7 / p. 16: Bettmann Archive/Corbis-Bettmann / p. 18: Corbis-Bettmann / p. 19: THE FAR SIDE copyright 1985, 1986 & 1991 FARWORKS, INC. Distributed by UNIVERSAL PRESS SYNDICATE. Reprinted with permission. All rights reserved / p. 20: © Fritz/Monkmeyer / p. 33: Sovfoto / p. 34: Spencer Grant/Stock Boston / p. 35: Tom Ives / p. 36: Estate of Sybil Shelton/Peter Arnold / p. 46: Courtesy of IBM / p. 55: © 1997 Paul Silverman/Fundamental Photographs / p. 56: © 1997 Paul Silverman/Fundamental Photographs / p. 69: Photofest / p. 70: Scott, Foresman and Company / p. 77: ZIGGY copyright ZIGGY AND FRIENDS, INC. Distributed by UNIVERSAL PRESS SYNDICATE. Reprinted with permission. All rights reserved / p. 81: © Bill Bachmann/Photo Researchers / p. 83: UPI/Corbis-Bettmann / p. 93: Mark Antman/The Image Works / p. 102: Spencer Grant/Monkmeyer / p. 125: Akos Szilvasi/Stock Boston / p. 134: Alinari/Art Resource / p. 137: Drawing by W. Miller; © 1973 The New Yorker Magazine, Inc. / p. 139: Bettmann Archive/Corbis-Bettmann / p. 143: Kagan/Monkmeyer / p. 158: © Walt Disney Productions Inc., Photofest / p. 160: Photofest / p. 163: Alan Carey/The Image Works / p. 166: George Holton/Photo Researchers / p. 175: AP/Wide World / p. 219: Shostal / p. 220: © 1993 Barbara Rios/Photo Researchers / p. 227: Spencer Grant/The Picture Cube / p. 230: Michael Evans/The White House / p. 231: NASA / p. 243: Michael Newman/PhotoEdit / p. 244: THE FAR SIDE copyright 1985, 1986 & 1991 FARWORKS, INC. Distributed by UNIVERSAL PRESS SYNDICATE. Reprinted with permission. All rights reserved. / p. 245: © 1997 L. Herman/KBMML / p. 258: With permission of Bob Thaves / p. 265: CALVIN & HOBBES copyright Watterson. Distributed by UNIVERSAL PRESS SYNDICATE. Reprinted with permission. All rights reserved. / p. 270: © Harry Cutting/Monkmeyer / p. 278: With permission of Bob Thaves / p. 306: CALVIN & HOBBES copyright Watterson. Distributed by UNIVERSAL PRESS SYNDICATE. Reprinted with permission. All rights reserved. / p. 309: Drawing by Mulligan; © 1972 The New Yorker Magazine, Inc. / p. 311: © 1989 Ulrike Welsch / p. 325: © Sidney Harris / p. 326: Pace/Monkmeyer / p. 331: R. Roseman/Custom Medical Stock / p. 352: Drawing by Weber; © 1972 The New Yorker Magazine, Inc. / p. 362: Scott, Foresman and Company / p. 367: John Neubauer/PhotoEdit / p. 372: Drawing by Weber; © 1989 The New Yorker Magazine, Inc. / p. 394: Drawing by Stevenson; © 1974 The New Yorker Magazine, Inc. / p. 402: UPI/Corbis-Bettmann / p. 413: Joel Gordon.

Name Index

Subject Index